# THE FIRST CASUALTY

## THE WAR CORRESPONDENT AS HERO, PROPAGANDIST AND MYTH-MAKER FROM THE CRIMEA TO IRAQ

### PHILLIP KNIGHTLEY

with an introduction by

JOHN PILGER

André Deutsch

First published in Great Britain in 1975 by André Deutsch Ltd
Revised paperback edition published 2000 by Prion Books
This updated edition published 2003 by
André Deutsch
an imprint of the
Carlton Publishing Group
20 Mortimer Street
London W1T 3JW

ISBN 0-233-00055-0

A catalogue record for this book is available from the
British Library.

The Siegfried Sassoon poem "The General" is reprinted by the
kind permission of George Sassoon. The lines by Roy Fuller are from
his *Winter in England, A Lost Season*, which appears in his *Collected
Poems*, published by André Deutsch Ltd., London, in 1962. The
excerpts from Alexander Werth's *Russia at War: 1941-1945*, copyright
© 1964 by Alexander Werth, are reprinted by permission of the publishers, E. P. Dutton & Co., Inc., New York, and Barrie and Rockliffe,
London. Herbert L. Matthews kindly gave permission to quote from
his *The Education of a Correspondent*.

Printed in Great Britain
by Mackays

# TO YVONNE

*The first casualty when war comes, is truth.*

—Senator Hiram Johnson, 1917

# Contents

# ACKNOWLEDGEMENTS

I would like to thank the following people: Caroline Gathorne Hardy, Nelson Mews, Jeremy Wilson, and Harry Roberts (in Britain); Kathlee McLaughlin, Margaret McGaughey, Susan E. Bidel, William Shawcross, and Maria Pilar Santocchia (in the United States); Julie Weston (in Canada); Antony Terry (in Germany); Desmond O'Grady (in Italy); Adam Hopkins (for help on chapter 9); and James Bellini (chapter 15).

I have received valuable advice from John Swettenham, of the Canadian War Museum; Dr. G. St. J. Barclay, of the University of Queensland, Australia; Professor W. Prange, of the University of Maryland; and Dr. Peter Gifford, of Murdoch University, Australia. (My conclusions are, of course, my own.)

The late Frederick Brazier, chief librarian of the *Sunday Times*, and his staff gave me access to their collection of some 2 million newspaper clippings. Gordon Phillips, archivist of *The Times*, helped me with his historical records. The London Library provided many books that were elsewhere unobtainable.

Anne Hunt, Sue Dakin, and Lavender da Costa Fernandes typed the manuscript. Ed Barber, Sonny Mehta, and Bruce Page gave me encouragement and help. Richard Hughes steered me in rewarding directions. Hugh Atkinson set me on the road. My publishers in the United States and Britain were remarkably patient. Finally, my deepest thanks go to Ronald Whiting, for the idea, and to Tony Godwin, who took a manuscript and turned it into a book.

# Introduction by
# JOHN PILGER

When I read the first edition of this remarkable book twenty-five years ago, I was struck by the following quotations. During the First World War, Prime Minister David Lloyd George told C. P Scott, editor of the *Manchester Guardian*: "If people really knew [the truth] the war would be stopped tomorrow. But of course they don't know and can't know." The truth *was* reported, insisted *The Times* correspondent, Sir Philip Gibbs, (knighted for his services), "apart from the naked realism of horrors and losses, and criticism of the facts."

Robert C. Miller, a United Press correspondent covering the Korean War in 1952, was less subtle. "There are certain facts and stories from Korea," he said, "that editors and publishers have printed which were pure fabrication ... Many of us who sent the stories knew they were false, but we had to write them because they were official releases from responsible military headquarters and were released for publication even though the people responsible knew they were untrue."

Almost every word of these testimonies could apply to the wars of our time, especially the Gulf War of 1991 and the Nato bombing of Yugoslavia in 1999. Chapters covering these have been added to this new edition, making Knightley's work the most comprehensive *j'accuse* of journalism as propaganda in the English language. It is the author's lament that, for all the dazzling advances in media technology, the media has little or no memory, as the same bogus "truth" is served up again and again. Reading the new material, I wondered when journalism's modern breeding grounds, the media studies courses, would begin to address the most important issue raised in this book: the virulence of an unrecognised censorship, often concealed behind false principles of objectivity, whose effect is to minimise and deny the culpability of Western power in acts of great violence and terrorism, such as the Gulf and Kosovo.

Thus *The Independent* could praise the "miraculously few casualties" in the Gulf War (meaning the few British and American casualties, most of them the result of American "friendly fire"), while the horror of up to a quarter of a million Iraqis slaughtered by the US-led forces was consigned to oblivion. Had this been the headline news, rather than the dubious technological triumph of the West, the public "would have really known the truth", as Lloyd George said in 1917, and the pattern might not have been repeated in the Balkans. At the very least, journalists might have raised the questions that distinguish their duty to keep the record straight.

Instead, and with honourable exceptions, they were "managed" more efficiently than ever before. Editors were called to the Ministry of Defence and handed their guidelines. The BBC and ITV told their correspondents to fall into line. It was right, said *The Economist*, "to suspend the normal play of democratic argument. The truth about the Gulf War must await the end of the fighting." Reporters were pressured to wear uniforms and corralled in a "pool" system. When the great maverick reporter, Robert Fisk, tried to slip the leash, he was told by another correspondent: "Get out of here, you arsehole. You'll prevent the rest of us from working." When American bombs incinerated hundreds of women and children in a bomb shelter in a residential part of Baghdad, and several British correspondents reported that there were no strategic or military targets nearby, their patriotism was called into question and their reporting was pilloried in the tabloid press as "truly disgusting" and "a disgrace to their country."

At the time of writing this, there is virtually no news of Kosovo, scene of Nato's "humanitarian war" and Tony Blair's "moral crusade." The expulsion and terrorising of 240,000 Serbs and Roma Gypsies from the province, now ruled by Nato, is of little interest. Who cares about Gypsies, let alone demonised Serbs? Like the Iraqis, they are the media's unpeople. The most important non-news is the unravelling of Nato's justification for killing and maiming several thousand civilians, both Serbs and Kosovars, and for devastating the environment and economic life of the region. This epic destruction, according to British Defence Secretary George Robertson last March, was to stop "a regime which is bent on genocide." President Clinton referred to "deliberate, systematic efforts at...genocide."

The British press took its cue and the Nazis, World War Two and the holocaust were invoked. The U.S. Defence Secretary, William Cohen, said: "we've now seen about 100,000 military-aged men missing...They may have been murdered." Since Nato took over Kosovo, no place on earth has been as scrutinised by forensic investigators, not to mention 2,700 media people, yet the head of the Spanish forensic team attached to the International Criminal Tribunal, Emilio Perez Pujol, has complained angrily that his colleagues have become part of "a semantic pirouette by the war propaganda machines, because we did not find one—not one—mass grave." Several thousand bodies have been found across the province: a gruesome toll, but a far cry from "the second European holocaust." To my knowledge, the forbidden question has been asked just once. "Could it turn out to be," wrote Andrew Alexander in the *Daily Mail*, "that we killed more innocent people than the Serbs did?" To that I would add: Did Nato's bombs fall on innocent people partly in response to the drum beat of journalists?

One of my prized possessions is a first edition of the diaries of William Howard Russell, who was sent by *The Times* to cover the war in the Crimea nearly 150 years ago, a war described by Queen Victoria as "popular beyond belief'. In fact, as Phillip Knightley describes, it was like all wars: a catalogue of blunders, needless killing and official lies. So independent-minded was Russell that his life on the battlefield was made a misery. No satellite phone for that reporter, no e-mail, no fax. His despatches took a week to get to London by horse and steamer. "Am I to tell these things?" Russell wrote to his editor, "or am I to hold my tongue?" To which Delane replied, "Continue to tell as much truth as you can." Both of them were accused of treason, until the truth of Russell's courageous reporting forced the government to resign.

Like Russell's, the best journalism is the first draft of history: for that we are indebted to Phillip Knightley, whose clear-sighted and principled book throws down a challenge to journalists to examine their role in the promotion of war, in propaganda and its myths, and the subliminal pressures applied by organisations like the BBC, whose news is often selected on the basis of a spurious establishment "credibility". The following pages ought to be read by every young reporter and by those who retain pride in our craft of truth-telling, no matter how unpopular and unpalatable the truth. The rest is not journalism.

JOHN PILGER
*December* 1999

## Chapter One

# "The Miserable Parent of a Luckless Tribe" 1854–1856

At ten minutes past eleven our Light Cavalry Brigade advanced
...They swept proudly past, glittering in the morning sun in all
the pride and splendour of war... At the distance of 1,200 yards
the whole line of the enemy belched forth, from thirty iron
mouths, a flood of smoke and flame. The flight was marked by
instant gaps in our ranks, by dead men and horses, by steeds flying wounded or riderless across the plain. In diminished ranks,
with a halo of steel above their heads, and with a cheer which was
many a noble fellow's death cry, they flew into the smoke of the
batteries; but ere they were lost from view the plain was strewn
with their bodies. Through the clouds of smoke we could see their
sabres flashing as they rode between the guns, cutting down the
gunners as they stood. We saw them riding through, returning,
after breaking through a column of Russians and scattering them
like chaff, when the flank fire of the batteries on the hill swept
them down. Wounded men and dismounted troopers flying
towards us told the sad tale...at thirty-five minutes past eleven
not a British soldier, except the dead and the dying, was left in
front of the Muscovite guns.

—The charge of the Light Brigade, as reported in
*The Times* of London, November 14, 1854

———

This account of the charge of the Light Brigade was written by
William Howard Russell, according to his epitaph in St. Paul's

Cathedral "the first and greatest" war correspondent. The greatest is open to dispute, and he was not the first—that title probably belongs to the *Morning Post*'s man, G. L. Gruneisen. But Russell's coverage of the Crimean War marked the beginning of an organised effort to report a war to the civilian population at home using the services of a civilian reporter. This was an immense leap in the history of journalism, so it is appropriate to begin with Russell, because, whether or not "the first and greatest," he was certainly, as he put it himself, "the miserable parent of a luckless tribe."

Before the Crimea, British editors either stole war news from foreign newspapers or employed junior officers to send letters from the battlefront, a most unsatisfactory arrangement. For not only were these soldier-correspondents highly selective in what they wrote, regarding themselves first as soldiers and then as correspondents; they also understood little of the workings of newspapers or even of what constituted "news." *The Times* engaged one such military privateer, Lieutenant Charles Nasmyth of the East India Company's Bombay Artillery, soon after war broke out with Russia in 1854. He did not last long. "I wish you would impress upon Nasmyth with all your eloquence the absolute necessity of writing as often as he can and sending his letters without delay," *The Times*' manager, Mowbray Morris, wrote to its Constantinople correspondent, Thomas Chenery. "The idea of a newspaper correspondent keeping the journal of a siege till after the affair is over has driven me wild."[1]

Morris and *The Times*' editor, John Delane, realised that traditional methods were not going to work in the Crimea. Britain's declaration of war had resulted in an upsurge of enthusiasm that had surprised everyone. "The war," Queen Victoria wrote, "is popular beyond belief." The workers, who genuinely hated Czarist absolutism, took to the streets shouting slogans and singing patriotic songs. Britain felt that Russia, ambitious to expand her empire, had to be stopped from establishing herself in Europe, and, since the British army was "the finest, most powerful army in the modern world," then it was up to her to undertake the task. Such a popular war created an unprecedented demand for news. "The excitement, the painful excitement for information, beggars all description," wrote one minister. *The Times*, whose circulation was greater than that of all its rivals put together, must meet this demand. "The public expects that we shall have our own agents," Morris wrote. "And as it has long been accustomed to look to *The Times*…for the

1.Source notes are on pages 529 to 545

truth in all things, we disappoint a reasonable expectation when we offer nothing better than reports from other journals, however authentic."[2]

Various trials of locally hired correspondents (such as Nasmyth) having failed, Delane decided, in February 1854, to send Russell from London, at first only to accompany the Guards, who were being sent as a precautionary measure to Malta. Later, when this arrangement worked well, he sent him to the front. Russell, a stocky Irishman, who, in the best tradition of journalists, had forced his way onto the paper by a mixture of cunning, persistence, and solid reporting, turned out a fortunate choice. For, once Delane had found that Russell had a flair for war reporting, he kept him to it, increasing both the paper's prestige and its correspondent's. Russell covered the war between Schleswig-Holstein and Denmark, the Crimean War, the Indian Mutiny, the American Civil War, the Austro-Prussian War, the Franco-Prussian War, the Paris Commune, and the Zulu War of 1879. He helped to topple the British government, was indirectly responsible for the employment of the first war photographer, and helped keep Britain from intervening in the American Civil War. He was appointed a Knight of the Iron Cross, an Officer of the Legion of Honour, and a Chevalier of the Order of Franz Josef of Austria. He was also awarded the Turkish War Medal, the Indian War Medal, and the South African War Medal. He started a newspaper, the *Army and Navy Gazette*, became a friend and honorary private secretary of the Prince of Wales, wrote books, stood for Parliament, and married a countess. He also filled his flat in London with war trophies—a lot of them loot—saw surmounting its horrors the glory of war, and, despite his battles with the establishment, remained basically an establishment figure, fascinated by all things military. One has the feeling that if he had not been a war correspondent, he would have been a soldier, no doubt a general. Like many of the "luckless tribe" he sired, Russell was deeply insecure; Delane could keep him working only by an almost constant flow of praise for his style, his initiative, his perception. But his war reporting was considerably closer to the truth than anything the public had previously been permitted to learn, and his influence on the conduct of the Crimean campaign was immense.

Russell was born in Lilyvale, County Dublin, on March 28, 1820 or 1821. Early attracted by military life, he used to get up at dawn to watch the soldiers drilling at a nearby barracks, and he tried several times to enlist, until his grandfather stopped him. So, instead, he went in for street battles with undergraduates from Trinity College, who were mostly Orangemen, against the Roman Catholic community, particularly the coal porters: "There were glorious doings, particularly during election times. We frequently parted with broken heads but sometimes we had it all our own way and made the most of it."[3]

Russell briefly thought of becoming a doctor, but was shaken by the sight of bodies—an aversion he later overcame on the battle-field—and was still considering a career when, in 1841, his cousin, sent by *The Times* to cover the Irish elections, hired Russell to help him. Russell quickly showed the journalistic initiative that later greatly helped his career. The other reporters, Russell decided, would station themselves at the various meetings and, since they could not cover them all, would miss the broad picture. With his knowledge of political tactics gained from his street-fighting days, Russell reasoned that the one place through which most of the participants in an Irish election would eventually pass was the local hospital. So he stationed himself in the casualty ward and interviewed the candidates and their opponents as they were carried in. He wrote a good, impassioned account of the violence, which *The Times* published, and which it followed a few days later with a leading article, or editorial. Russell was in. He was subsequently invited to London to meet the editor, Delane, and a loose freelance arrangement was worked out.

In August 1844 Delane sent Russell back to Ireland to cover the trial of Daniel O'Connell, the Irish leader who had been charged with seditious conspiracy. The story of how Russell got his scoop illustrates the physical stamina required in the days before the telegraph and shows the sort of competition correspondents faced even in that leisurely period. "Both *The Times* and [its rival] the *Morning Herald* had chartered special steamers to carry the news and the results of the government prosecution to London," Russell wrote later. "It was very late on a Saturday night when the jury retired and the other newspaper's correspondents left to get refreshments. I was sitting outside the court wondering whether I should go to bed when my boy rushed up to me. 'Jury just coming in,' he said. They brought in a verdict of guilty. The moment I heard it I flew from the court, jumped into a carriage and drove to the station where I had ordered a special train to be in readiness. Got to Kingstown, hailed the Iron Duke [the steamer chartered by *The Times*], got up steam within half an hour, and left with consolation

4

that the *Morning Herald* steamer was lying peacefully in harbour. Arrived at Holyhead, sped away on a special train to London, tried to sleep, tight boots, couldn't, so took them off. Reached Euston, *Times* man waiting with cab, struggled with boots, only managed left foot, ran into *Times* office with one boot under my arm. As I entered Printing House Square [*The Times*' office] man in shirt sleeves I took to be *Times* printer came up and said, 'So glad to see you safe over, sir. So they've found him guilty.' 'Yes, guilty my friend,' I replied. Unfortunately he turned out to be a man posted outside *The Times* by the *Morning Herald* and it came out next day with the news as well."[4]

In February 1854, Delane called Russell to his office and asked him to accompany a British force to Malta. Russell was not enthusiastic. He said he did not want to be away from his wife and two children, but Delane persuaded him by assuring him he would be back for Easter. It was two years before he saw London again.

Russell remained at Malta until March 30 and then sailed with the British force to Gallipoli. From there he began sending the dispatches—in the form of letters to Delane—that were to make him famous. Russell was quick to realise that all was not well with the British army. It had not fought, or even engaged in large-scale foreign manoeuvres, since Wellington had beaten Napoleon at Waterloo almost forty years earlier. There was no single War Office, and the command was dominated by noble blood. The expedition's leader was Lord Raglan, a very British hero, who had been military secretary to the Duke of Wellington. Raglan was brave—when a surgeon at Waterloo cut off his arm without anaesthetic, Raglan said only, "Bring my arm back. There's a ring my wife gave me on the finger." He was also a highly competent staff officer, but he was sixty-five and had never commanded so much as a battalion in the field. He was hampered by perhaps the worst collection of subordinate officers ever concentrated in one army, including the Earl of Cardigan, the hard-drinking commander of the Light Brigade. The British officers brought a French chef, Kaffir servants, their favourite horses and wine, their shotguns, dogs, and, in some cases, their wives. A party of "travelling gentlemen" later turned up— wealthy young Englishmen who had come out to watch the war, much as they might have attended a cricket match at Lord's. The French, who had declared war on Russia a day before Britain, could not believe that the British were serious, and neither could Russell.

"The management is infamous," he wrote to Delane, "and the

contrast offered by our proceedings to the conduct of the French most painful. Could you believe it—the sick have not a bed to lie upon? They are landed and thrown into a ricketty house without a chair or a table in it. The French with their ambulances, excellent commissariat staff and boulangerie etc, in every respect are immeasurably our superiors. While these things go on, Sir George Brown only seems anxious about the men being clean-shaved, their necks well stiffened and waist belts tight. He insists on officers and men being in full rig; no loose coats, jackets etc."[5]

Later Russell passed to Delane the problem that has faced many a war correspondent: "Am I to tell these things, or hold my tongue?" Delane told him to go ahead, and those letters of Russell's that he did not use in *The Times*, no doubt from apprehension that *The Times* would be accused of being unpatriotic, he circulated among Cabinet ministers, beginning a process that was eventually to topple the government.

But Russell was not the only correspondent to notice these deficiencies. The year before he arrived in the Crimea, the *London Daily News* had appointed Edwin Lawrence Godkin, another Irishman, "to go to Turkey for the hostilities."* Godkin, who was only twenty-two, had one considerable advantage—an honest assessment of his capabilities. He had written, in an article for the *News* advocating the claims of the Greeks to Constantinople: "I knew nothing about either Greece, or the Greeks, or Constantinople, but I was possessed of that common illusion of young men, that facility in composition indicates the existence of thought."[6] Godkin wandered around the army watching the preparations for battle and was alarmed at what he saw. From Varna, on the Black Sea, he predicted the breakdown of the British supply lines.

> I do not know whether the British Commissariat officers know exactly what difficulties they will have to contend with, but certainly from what I heard and saw at Scutari, I rather think not... I am supported in my conclusions on this point by a piece of folly committed the other day in sending an officer to travel Romania and Bulgaria with a view to ascertaining what facilities there existed in them for supplying the English cavalry with horses...The ignorance which dictated this step is scarcely conceivable. A single interrogatory addressed to the consul here at Varna, for example, would have elicited the fact that there are not 500 horses in all European Turkey fit to mount an English dragoon. When mistakes

* The Irish remain substantially represented in the ranks of correspondents to this day.

such as these are made regarding matters in which information lies within the reach of the most careless observer, one is naturally led to fear that many blunders and oversights may be at first committed in departments where knowledge is more difficult of access.[7]

"Folly…ignorance…mistakes…blunders…oversights"—this was strong stuff. *The Times* was supporting Russell's strictures in its editorial columns, and, with two newspapers openly attacking it, the army found itself on the defensive, its worst fears about the nature of the press fully confirmed. Godkin later recalled what happened when the British consul at Varna introduced an elderly and distinguished *Times* correspondent to General Sir George Brown: "A shudder seemed to pass through his frame at the mention of *The Times*. He maintained a dead silence while the correspondent remained in the room, as if the slightest utterance in his presence might endanger the monarchy."[8]

Lord Raglan decided not to recognise the correspondents, not to give them rations or assistance, and to look the other way at any efforts by junior officers to discourage them. This took the form, with Russell, of cutting down his tent when he pitched it within the lines, forcing him out with the camp followers. But Russell clung on and was with the army when it moved to the Crimea in September 1854. Cholera broke out as the British were preparing to march, but they continued their advance and on September 20 crossed the Alma River, putting a superior Russian force to flight. This was Russell's initiation into some of the problems of his trade. He had decided that he should wear some sort of uniform and had got together a gold-banded commissariat officer's cap, a rifleman's patrol jacket, cord breeches, butchers' boots with huge spurs, and a large sword.* He had bought a horse, "a fiddle-headed, ewe-necked beast, with great bone and not much else." But from where should he watch the battle? "I never was in a more unpleasant position. Everyone else on the field had some *raison d'être*. I had none. They were on recognised business. It could scarcely be recognised or legitimate business for any man to ride in front of the army in order that he might be able to write an account of a battle for a newspaper,"[9] a view he was soon to change.

Russell rode up and down behind the action, making several attempts to attach himself to the entourage of divisional commanders, all of whom sent him packing. He saw little of the action—and what he did see unnerved him—so he resorted to the tactics that

---

* War correspondents today—particularly in Vietnam—have been known to wear equally unlikely outfits.

had first brought him to the notice of *The Times* during the Irish elections and that have been the basis of a war correspondent's *modus operandi* since: he stopped every officer and soldier he could find and asked them to describe what had happened. At first the jumble of impressions Russell recorded only confused him further. "How was I to describe what I had not seen? Where to learn the facts for which they were waiting at home? My eyes swam as I tried to make notes of what I had heard. I was worn out with excitement, fatigue and lack of food. I had been more than ten hours in the saddle; my wretched horse, bleeding badly from a cut in the leg, was unable to carry me. My head throbbed, my heart beat as though it would burst. I suppose I was unnerved by want of food and rest, but I was so much overcome by what I saw that I could not remain where the fight had been closest and deadliest. I longed to get away from it—from the exultation of others in which thought for the dead was forgotten or unexpressed. It was now that the weight of the task I had accepted fell on my soul like lead."[10]

Russell was too confused and depressed to write his account that night, so he slept and began his task the next morning, sitting on the parapet of a Russian redoubt, writing with an inkpot and quill pen in the yellow pages of a dead Russian's account book. An officer of engineers eased his discomfort by making a writing table for him from a plank laid across two casks. Russell wrote a version of the battle, but was dissatisfied with it, so he requisitioned many officers and clarified the situation slightly. (He found what most war correspondents soon discover: eyewitness accounts are frequently contradictory.) Then he rewrote his story of the battle. It was peppered with what were to become the clichés of war: there was a "rain of death" and grapeshot "tore through the enemy ranks" as the British troops "poured in a steady fire from point blank distance." The Russians were the "terrible enemy" and all the British troops were "gallant."

Even in these early days of war correspondents, two distinct techniques were emerging. Russell was basically a battlefield correspondent trying to report the over-all scene, to give a contemporary observer's account of how a battle was lost or won. Godkin, although he had a hatred of war, was interested in its effects on the individual, including himself. Here is Russell describing an attack.

> At five minutes before twelve o'clock the French, like a swarm of bees, issued forth from their trenches close to the doomed Malakoff, scrambled up its faces and were through the embrasures

in the twinkling of an eye. They crossed the seven metres of ground which separated them from the enemy in a few bounds, and in a minute or two after the head of their column issued from the ditch, the Tricolour was floating over the Korniloff Bastion.[11]

Compare this with Godkin, describing what happened to a young French conscript, "beardless, slender, hardly able to trot under his musket, fitter to be by his mother's side than amidst the horrors of a heady fight," who is stopped in panic-stricken retreat by a general.

> The general rushed towards him, tore one of his cotton epaulettes off his shoulder and shouted in his ear, "Comment? Vous n'êtes pas Français, donc!" The reproach stung the poor boy to the quick; all his fiery, chivalrous French blood rose up to him to repel it; his face flushed up, and constantly repeating, "Je ne suis pas Français," he ran back, mounted the top parapet, whirled his musket about his head in a fury of excitement, and at last fell into the ditch, riddled with balls.[12]

Both types of report were eagerly read in Britain, but *The Times* carried more weight, having by now become, in its own words, "not only chief recorder of events of the war [but] counted among the protagonists."[13] Under pressure from *The Times,* Russell's lot improved. He followed the invasion force across the Alma and on to Balaclava, where it camped. By the time the guns had been unloaded the Russians had strengthened their fortifications, and the first assault against them, on October 17, failed. A week later the Russians counter-attacked. This time there were none of the difficulties Russell had encountered at the Alma. He joined the British command on a plateau overlooking Balaclava, from where he could see the disaster that followed "as the stage and those upon it are seen from the box of a theatre."

Before him was the green valley, framed with mountain ridges on all sides and with the harbour shining on the right. Below, the wheeling squadrons of cavalry appeared to be executing parade drill for the benefit of the spectators. But they were not drilling. They were plainly retiring before a superior enemy. Lord Raglan and his staff shared the view; everything was clear to them, and in this, Russell decided later, lay the seeds of the tragedy. "I am persuaded," he said, "that whatever there was of disaster and misfortune on 25th October 1854 was due, first, to the distance of Lord Raglan from the field and secondly, to his failure to understand...that he saw more than his generals below could see; therefore...he did not take pains in wording his orders to make it so plain to them that explanation of his meaning was not needed."[14]

Lord Cardigan was ordered to "advance rapidly" with the Light Brigade and prevent the enemy "carrying away the guns." In front of the Light Brigade were the Russian guns; the British guns, which were being carried away, were on the right. Cardigan could not see them. He charged with his brigade directly into the Russian artillery, muttering, so it is said, "Here goes the last of the Brudenells!"* Of the 673 men who charged down the mile-long valley, fewer than 200 returned. The officers on the hilltop sat stunned as the remains of the Light Brigade trotted back. Russell wrote in his diary: "I looked at the group of officers representing the military mind of England close at hand in this crisis and I was not much impressed with confidence by what I saw." But his account for *The Times* concentrated on the glory of the event—"the pride and splendour of war."[15] The British public reacted with shocked pride. A cartoon in *Punch* showed a mother and her children sitting with excited and tearful faces while the head of the household, brandishing a poker over his head, reads to them from *The Times* Russell's account of the Light Brigade's suicidal charge.

This set-back to the campaign was followed by the bloody but inconclusive Battle of Inkerman on November 5, 1854. Russell was appalled by the casualties and wrote privately to Delane saying that he felt Raglan to be incompetent: "He is a good brave soldier, I am sure, and a polished gentleman, but he is no more fit than I am to cope with any leader of strategic skill."[16] And Godkin, in an outburst against the leadership in general, noted in his diary: "Oh, this slutten aristocracy." Delane circulated Russell's letters to his friends in the Cabinet, but conditions were to grow even worse.

As the Russian winter set in, Russell grew caustic in his criticism of the suffering the soldiers had to endure. His dispatches dwelt on the pitiful condition of the troops and the command's lack of concern. As *The Times* continued to attack Raglan for his leadership, the army began to retaliate. Russell, who had been living in a tiny room in a squalid house that he shared with some Turkish soldiers, their horses and cattle, and the decomposing body of a Tartar in the only well, was asked to move out to make way for some more soldiers and had to seek shelter in the tents of those of his friends who were still on speaking terms with him. A letter to Delane on January 17, 1855, tells of his despair: "This army has melted away almost to a drop of

* Brudenell was his family name.

miserable, washed-out, worn-out spiritless wretches, who muster out of 55,000 just 11,000 now fit to shoulder a musket, but certainly not fit to do duty against the enemy. Let no one at home attempt to throw dirt in your eyes. This army is to all intents and purposes, with the exception of a very few regiments, used up, destroyed and ruined... My occupation is gone; there is nothing to record more of the British Expedition except its weakness and its misery—misery in every form and shape except that of defeat; and from that we are solely spared by the goodness of Heaven, which erects barriers of mud and snow between us and our enemies."[17]

On Delane's advice ("Continue as you have done, to tell the truth, and as much of it as you can, and leave such comment as may be dangerous to us, who are out of danger"), Russell continued to catalogue the army's misfortunes and to supply private information for Delane's leading articles. The government continued publicly to deny the accusations while privately bombarding Raglan with panic-stricken queries: What had gone wrong? What could be done to save both the army and the reputation of the government? One simple way—tried many a time since the Crimea—seemed to be to get rid of the war correspondent causing all the trouble. At one time or another, most of the senior British officers—except Raglan, who never acknowledged his existence—came up to Russell and said, "If I were you I should go away! I would indeed!"

Raglan's tactics were more dangerous. He got the deputy judge-advocate to claim that Russell's dispatches had involved serious breaches of security and had afforded assistance to the enemy. That they were breaches of security was undoubtedly true. In one article alone, published in *The Times* on October 23, 1854, Russell revealed the number of pieces of artillery that had been moved to the front, the position and amount of gunpowder needed to supply them, the exact positions and names of two regiments, and the fact that there was a dearth of round shot. Since this was no doubt telegraphed to Russia the day it appeared in London, even Delane agreed that Russell should be curbed, and he told the government he would "confine all [his] correspondents exclusively to the version of past events." It is doubtful, however, that Russell's dispatches afforded much assistance to the enemy. After the war, the Russian commander at Sevastopol was emphatic in saying that he never learned anything from *The Times* that he had not already been told by his spies.

Once the public had been fully aroused to the state of the army in the Crimea, reaction was rapid. The government, at first worried only in case recruiting might be affected, soon had to face an angry *Times* demanding that the army's medical services be reformed, a move that eventually took Florence Nightingale, a nurse of professional skill, to the war.

Russell is usually credited with being responsible for her place in history,[18] but the facts are different. Godkin was the first to foresee the strain the medical services would be under. As early as January 1854 he had written: "One would imagine that thousands of young surgeons who are starving in England and France would flock here to fill up the vacancies which exist in every regiment"; but nothing was done. It was true that Russell wrote movingly about the sufferings of soldiers in the field, but it was actually Thomas Chenery, the Constantinople correspondent of *The Times*, and its future editor, with his descriptions of conditions at the base hospital in Scutari, on the opposite side of the Bosporus from Constantinople, who created the biggest impact in England.

In a dispatch published October 12, Chenery wrote:

> ... it is with feelings of surprise and anger that the public will learn that no sufficient medical preparations have been made for the proper care of the wounded. Not only are there not sufficient surgeons—that, it might be urged, was unavoidable—not only are there no dressers and nurses—that might be a defect of system for which no one is to blame—but what will be said when it is known that there is not even linen to make bandages for the wounded? The greatest commiseration prevails for the suffering of the unhappy inmates of Scutari, and every family is giving sheets and old garments to supply their want. But, why could not this clearly foreseen event have been supplied?...It rests with the Government to make enquiries into the conduct of those who must have so greatly neglected their duty...

*The Times* supported Chenery's article with an editorial appeal for private charity to come to the rescue. The following day *The Times* carried in response a number of letters offering money, including one from Sir Robert Peel, son of the former Prime Minister, who set out a scheme for supplying comforts to the sick and wounded and promised £200 for such a cause. In the news columns of the same issue—October 13—*The Times* ran a further dispatch from Chenery. This and the earlier dispatch have since been wrongly attributed to Russell, a mistake that was probably the origin of the legend that it was one of Russell's dispatches which moved Miss Nightingale to offer her services. Chenery wrote:

The worn-out pensioners who were brought out as an ambulance corps are totally useless, and not only are surgeons not to be had, but there are no dressers or nurses to carry out the surgeon's directions and to attend on the sick during intervals between his visits. Here the French are greatly our superiors. Their medical arrangements are extremely good, their surgeons more numerous, and they have also the help of the Sisters of Charity, who have accompanied the expedition in incredible numbers. These devoted women are excellent nurses.

The next day *The Times* carried a letter signed "A Sufferer by the Present War," who asked, "Why have we no sisters of charity?" and added, "There are numbers of able-bodied and tender-hearted English women who would joyfully and with alacrity go out to devote themselves to nursing the sick and wounded." Later the same day Miss Nightingale wrote to her friend Mrs. Sidney Herbert, wife of the Secretary for War, saying, "I do not mean to say I believe *The Times* accounts but I do believe that we may be of use to the wounded wretches," and setting out a scheme for recruiting a private nursing corps.[19] Her letter crossed with one from Herbert himself asking her to go out to the war as the accredited head of a government nursing service, which she promptly agreed to do. No doubt Russell's reports had helped in general to contribute to this, but long overdue credit must go to Chenery for his dispatches from Scutari.

As money and crates of clothing for the Crimean army poured into the *Times* office, the paper switched its criticisms of the government to the high command in the field and began to demand the recall of Lord Raglan and his staff. At the end of January 1855 the government succumbed, railing to the last at *The Times* and Russell.*

If Russell felt any sense of triumph, there is little evidence of it. He was preoccupied with the erection of a prefabricated iron hut *The Times* had sent him from London and—probably in preparation for the battle that he knew would eventually come with *The Times'* accountants—in cataloguing the cost of living: "£5 for a ham; 15s for a small tin of meat; 5s for a little pot of marmalade; £6 for a pair of seamen's boots, and £5 for a Turkey."[20]

At this stage, someone in the establishment, possibly Prince Albert, realised that to restore public confidence in the conduct of the war some form of counter-propaganda was necessary, and what

---

*When the new Secretary for War, the Duke of Newcastle, came to the Crimea later in the year, he told Russell "It was you who turned out the Government."

better form could there be than the newly discovered medium that never lied—the camera? Accordingly, Roger Fenton, an unsuccessful painter and one of the founders of the Royal Photographic Society, who frequently photographed the royal family, was encouraged to go out to the Crimea to record what was happening.

With letters of introduction from Prince Albert, Fenton arrived at Balaclava on March 8, 1855, and set about establishing an axiom that still stands good: although in most cases the camera does not lie directly, it can lie brilliantly by omission. Fenton's photographs, technically excellent though they are, portray a war where everything looks ship-shape and everyone happy. They show well-dressed officers and men eating, drinking, or smoking; ships in Balaclava Harbour; a convivial party between French and English troops; Lord Raglan, looking rather drawn; a group of happy Zouaves and Turks; quiet scenes at a mortar battery; and the interiors of captured forts after the bodies had been removed. Yet in the valley where the charge of the Light Brigade had taken place Fenton noticed, and described in a letter, this macabre reminder of what the war was really like: "We came upon many skeletons half buried. One was lying as if he had raised himself upon his elbow, the bare skull sticking up with still enough flesh left in the muscles to prevent it falling from the shoulders. Another man's feet and hands were out of the ground, and shoes on the feet and the flesh gone."[21] Fenton did not bother to unpack his camera. He knew the sort of photograph he should take, and this was not one of them. Fenton and Russell never worked together, and Fenton, having finished his assignment, returned to England to collect the royal praise he felt he deserved.*

In mid-June the allies launched a major attack on Sevastopol, which failed. Russell blamed Raglan for having allowed his plans to be influenced by the French. The disaster found Raglan at the end of his strength. He sickened and ten days later died. Florence Nightingale wrote to her parents that he died "without sufficient physical reason...he was so depressed. He was not a very great general but he was a very good man." There was a shift of sentiment in Britain. Queen Victoria let it be known that she was displeased with *The Times* and its attacks on Raglan. Prince Albert called Russell "that miserable scribbler." Sidney Herbert, the former Secretary for War, wrote, "I trust the Army will lynch *The Times* correspon-

---

* To be fair, the two other photographers in the Crimean War, James Robertson and the Frenchman Charles Langlois, did little better.

dent," and there were suggestions that the behaviour of *The Times* and Russell was little short of treason.

This helped the new commander-in-chief, Sir William Codrington, to acquire support for some form of restraint on the press. After a consultation with Lord Panmure, Secretary for War, whose only suggestion for handling war correspondents was to "put it to their patriotism and honour whether they would endanger the success of the army by premature and improper publication of its number, conditions etc.," Codrington issued a general order, on February 25, 1856, that must rank as the origin of military censorship. It forbade the publication of details of value to the enemy, authorised the ejection of a correspondent who, it was alleged, had published such details, and threatened future offenders with the same punishment.[22] This historic step was taken too late—by the time news of it reached Britain, hostilities had ceased—and its importance was overlooked. But a precedent had been established. When Britain next became involved in a major war—against the Boers—censorship was accepted as necessary and just, and it became the dominating feature of the reporting of the First World War, crushing correspondents into virtual silence.

Russell returned to London and fame. *The Times* made the gesture every war correspondent dreams of: it put aside his IOUs for advance expenses and told him he could start again "with what tradesmen call a clean slate." He was placed on the list of *Times* foreign correspondents at £600 a year, providing "you will render monthly accounts of your expenditure showing a clean balance so that we may both know how we stand."[23] He had breakfast with the Prime Minister, Lord Palmerston, who, mistakenly believing that Russell's criticisms of the conduct of the war must have been inspired by his having evolved constructive alternatives, disconcerted Russell by asking him what he would do if he were commander-in-chief of the army. After the war Russell's dispatches were published in book form, and while awaiting new battles to cover he went on a lecture tour.

Clearly, it would have been hard for Russell not to have made a name for himself in the Crimea. This was the first time that a British army in the field had been subjected to any form of independent scrutiny, and it would have been difficult to miss its shortcomings. Russell certainly chronicled them, but he failed to understand and expose the causes. He concentrated his attacks on Raglan rather than on the system, not knowing that Raglan, a humane and sensitive man,* had done his best to overcome the results of years of government neglect. Throughout the campaign, Raglan had made repeated requests for all manner of equipment and supplies to overcome deficiencies in the commissariat and the medical departments, but most of his requests had been ignored. When public clamour led to a demand for a scapegoat, Russell's dispatches helped make Raglan a convenient choice.

Although Russell criticised the lot of the ordinary soldier in the Crimea, he was careful not to hammer too hard at a comparison with that of the officers, to whose social class he himself belonged. He did not write, as he could quite accurately have done: "While the troops, ill-clad to weather a Russian winter, try to ease their hunger with a watery stew made of doubtful horseflesh, tonight in the officers' mess the menu consists of soup, fresh fish, liver and bacon, a shoulder of mutton, pancakes with quince preserve, cheese, stout, sherry and cigars." Above all, Russell made the mistake, common to many a war correspondent, of considering himself part of the military establishment. The one thing he never doubted or criticised was the institution of war itself. He realised he had hit the right note in criticising the conduct of the war and that his dispatches suited *The Times*' politics of the moment. (Russell tended to toe his paper's editorial line despite his professional assessments.)

Perhaps the best summary of Russell's importance in the Crimea is by his colleague Godkin, of the *Daily News*. Nearly fifty years after the war, Godkin, who had a distinguished career, wrote:

> If I were asked now what I thought the most important result of the Crimea War, I should say the creation and development of the "special correspondents" of the newspapers…The real beginning of newspaper correspondence was the arrival of "Billy" Russell with the English Army in the Crimea. He was then a man of mature age, had had a long newspaper experience, and possessed just the social qualities that were needed for the place. In his hands correspondence from the field really became a power before which generals began to quail…I cannot help thinking that the appearance of the special correspondent in the Crimea…led to a real awakening of the official mind. It brought home to the War Office the fact that the public had something to say about the conduct of wars and that they are not the concern exclusively of sovereigns and statesmen.[24]

* He went himself in a snow-storm to take clothing and food to a corporal's wife who had given birth in a hole in the ground.

16

It is clear that before the war ended the army realised that it had made a mistake in tolerating Russell and his colleagues, but by then it was too late. The war correspondent had arrived, and when the American Civil War broke out, five years later, 500 of them turned out to report the conflict on the Northern side alone.

## Chapter Two

# The First Challenge
# 1861–1865

I have made arrangements for the correspondents to take the field
...and I have suggested to them that they should wear a white uniform to indicate the purity of their character.

—Union general Irvin McDowell, quoted by
William Howard Russell in *My Diary North and South*

---

The Civil War remains the greatest single event in American history, and it was therefore vital that it be properly reported by
correspondents of ability and integrity. The opportunities for good
reporting were clearly present. The war created a tremendous
demand for news, and as newspaper circulations soared and
incomes increased, proprietors ploughed back much of their new
riches into sending more correspondents to provide a wider coverage of the conflict. Some 500 went off to report the war for the
North alone. The *New York Herald* put sixty-three men into the
field and spent nearly $1 million in covering the war. The *New York
Tribune* and the *New York Times* each had at least twenty correspondents, and smaller papers, in such places as Cincinnati and
Boston, all had their own men at the front.* European war correspondents, such as William Howard Russell of *The Times* of London and Georges Clemenceau of *Le Temps*, were there, and many
European newspapers devoted almost as much space to the war as
did the American press.

---

* The South, for reasons to be discussed later, was less well served.

Only on the visual side did technology fail to meet demand. The photographer Mathew Brady followed the Northern armies into battle and produced a comprehensive pictorial account of the war, but, unfortunately, no newspaper was able to use his or any other photographs because they all lacked the equipment and technique for making half-tone blocks. Instead, the war artist flourished, and although some became caught up in the production of faked or exaggerated reporting that afflicted many correspondents, others produced detailed and accurate records of the battles they witnessed. Illustrated weeklies, such as *Harper's* and *Frank Leslie's Illustrated Weekly*, flourished, the latter alone employing some eighty artists and publishing in four years more than 3,000 sketches and drawings of "battles, sieges, bombardments, stormings, and other scenes incidental to war."

The telegraph was available for large-scale use for the first time. Almost 50,000 miles of telegraph line were in use in the eastern states, and although the rates were high and the companies often demanded cash in advance before they would begin transmission, the by-line "By Telegraph" became more frequent as the war progressed. Newspapers that had never carried more than an occasional column of telegraphed news now carried two and three pages, at least one of which had been kept open until the last minute so as to include the latest news. As a result, the reporting of the Civil War was not only more extensive than in any previous war, but also more immediate. For the first time in American history, it was possible for the public to read what had happened yesterday, rather than someone's opinion on what had happened last week.

Everything was ready, then, for the sweeping change in journalistic practice that was to make America a nation of newspaper readers. "It was during the Civil War," the *New York Times* noted in 1901, "that the New York newspapers gained their first realising sense of two fundamental principles that have made them what they are today—first, the surpassing value of individual, competitive, triumphant enterprise in getting early and exclusive news, and second, the possibility of building up large circulations by striving increasingly to meet a popular demand for prompt and adequate reports of the day-to-day doings of mankind the world over."[1]

Yet despite the opportunities that this great watershed in history offered correspondents, the conclusion must be that they measured up poorly to the task. Like many other aspects of the Civil War, its war correspondents have been romanticised into legend. "The science of military correspondence was brought to its highest development and maximum effectiveness during the Civil War," wrote Havilah Babcock in 1929,[2] by which time the story of "the Bohemian Brigade" braving shot and shell to bring an eager public a true account of the great struggle was firmly established. The incidents concern men like Henry Wing of the *New York Tribune* being kissed by Lincoln for bringing a message from Grant; William Croffut, also of the *Tribune*, reading Byron to Union soldiers around the fire; Joseph Howard of the *New York Times* telegraphing the genealogy of Jesus to prevent his rivals from using the wire; and Edmund Stedman of the *New York World* sitting with his colleagues and writing dispatches by the light of a candle on top of a keg of gunpowder.

The legend conveniently overlooks the fact that the majority of the Northern correspondents were ignorant, dishonest, and unethical; that the dispatches they wrote were frequently inaccurate, often invented, partisan, and inflammatory. Edwin Godkin wrote of his American colleagues: "Their communications are what you might expect from men of this stamp—a series of wild ravings about the roaring of the guns and the whizzing of the shells and the superhuman valour of the men, interspersed with fulsome puffs of some captain or colonel with whom they happened to pass the night."[3] Henry Villard, one of the better American correspondents, said, "Men turned up in the army as correspondents more fit to drive cattle than to write for newspapers,"[4] and Professor J. Cutler Andrews, in his mammoth work *The North Reports the Civil War*, wrote, "Sensationalism and exaggeration, outright lies, puffery, slander, faked eye-witness accounts, and conjectures built on pure imagination cheapened much that passed in the North for news."[5] Given that it was an age of declamatory journalism and that objectivity was a rare quality, it is still a little disconcerting to find that one correspondent saw his job in these terms: "It is not within the province of your correspondent to criticize what has been done by the army or navy; nor will he state occurrences which it may be unpleasant to read."[6] Like him, most correspondents on both sides saw as an integral part of their task the sustaining of both civilian and army morale. A skirmish became "a glorious overwhelming victory," a rout was transformed into "a strategic withdrawal before a vastly superior enemy," a dead Confederate soldier had been not merely killed in battle but "sacrificed to the devilish ambitions of his implacable masters, Davis and Lee"; Confederate women had necklaces made from Yankee eyes, while the "unholy Northerners" used heads of Confederate dead for footballs. In this sort of reporting, accuracy mattered little, and the Northerner Henry Adams wrote from London to complain that "people have become so accustomed to the idea of disbelieving everything that is stated in the American papers that all confidence in us is destroyed."[7]

The correspondents fared little better in recognising the historic incident, in realising that they were privileged to be present at moments millions would later want to study as part of their nation's development. No correspondent attending the dedication of a national cemetery at Gettysburg took any notice of President Lincoln beginning, "Four score and seven years ago..." At the best, they reported, as did the *Cincinnati Commercial*, "The President rises slowly, draws from his pocket a paper, and when the commotion subsides, in a sharp, unmusical treble voice, reads the brief and pithy remarks," and, at the worst, ended their accounts of the event with the single sentence "The President also spoke."[8]

One would have expected that the war correspondents from Europe, more experienced, more mature, and less involved than their American colleagues, performed more ably in the Civil War. Unfortunately, the majority were as bad, if not worse. More subtle in their bias, more devious in their propaganda, and better assisted by the political intrigues of their editors, they completely misled their readers on what was really occurring in America. *The Times* of London was particularly bad.

"There never was a war which afforded such materials for special correspondence of the best kind as this one," wrote Edwin Godkin.[9] Yet, faced with this great opportunity, most Civil War correspondents failed miserably. The reasons are not hard to find. The main one was that no American correspondent had had any previous experience to fit him for such a task. The Associated Press, the only organisation that had the resources to attempt a comprehensive coverage of the war, was in its infancy. Most of its correspondents had been chosen primarily because of their ability to use a telegraph key, and the techniques of military reporting had to be learnt by trial and error. Correspondents sent to the front by Northern newspapers were young—most of them were in their late twenties; six were only nineteen or younger—inexperienced penny-a-liners, who were more at home covering the police courts. The pay and conditions were not calculated to attract men of ability. Salaries ranged from $10 to $25 a week, including expenses, and it was not until late in the war, when individual correspondents had made names for themselves, that editors were prepared to pay more generously. The work was physically and emotionally exhausting.

Stories had to be written on the same day as the battle, and so correspondents would work all night, gallop off at daybreak to the nearest rail or telegraph head, lodge their copy, and then gallop back to witness that day's activities. Small wonder that few—estimates range from one to ten—of the 500 Northern reporters were able to last the whole war.

In spite of this, editors were unreasonably demanding. As the public's hunger for war news mounted, so did circulations; a large New York newspaper could sell *five times* its normal circulation when it ran details of a big battle, while the *Philadelphia Inquirer*, nearer the front, frequently sold 25,000 copies of a single issue to the troops alone. This meant "serious money," and when no news was available editors chafed at the loss of income and pressed their correspondents harder. Wilbur F. Storey of the *Chicago Times* sent an order to one of his men: "Telegraph fully all news you can get and when there is no news send rumours."[10] Soon initiative and resource in getting a scoop came to count for more than accuracy and balance, and the commercial pressures were such that a correspondent was far more likely to be sacked for sending no news at all than if he sent an interesting but completely fabricated story.

All this did nothing for correspondents' morale or ethics. They were constantly short of money and had difficulty getting themselves reimbursed even for justified expenses.* Soon many correspondents came to see nothing wrong in making a little money on the side. Some accepted cash from officers in return for a favourable mention in their dispatches and thought nothing of it. "If ever a man needed $50 it is I," Edmund Stedman of the *New York World* wrote to his wife after General Charles T. James, a Northern artillery officer, had pressed it on him. "Of course he expects me to keep a lookout for his guns hereafter, and I believe I can do so with a clear conscience.[11] Others became involved in stock-exchange manipulations, using their knowledge of forthcoming legislation or the sway of a battle to tip off influential financiers. "Allow me to assure you that I...will make you a pile," wrote one New York financier to a correspondent in Washington, "if you can get the news in advance when the market is not excited by the same news."[12]

Pressure for a scoop forced many correspondents into positions that compromised any ethics they might have started with. Tom Cook of the *New York Herald* wanted a boat to enable him to cover

* When Villard of the *New York Tribune* presented one expense account, his editor knocked him to the floor.

naval engagements. Realising his newspaper would be unlikely to provide him with one, he made his own arrangements and then wrote to his editor: "I think the Navy Department could be induced to procure for us an outside vessel which we might call our own were [we] to promise that the Navy Department would be exempt from attacks in the columns of the Herald—this hint is, of course, *sub rosa*."[13] Other correspondents took paid or unpaid jobs with the administration or the army. Horace White of the *Chicago Tribune* was clerk of the Senate Committee on Military Affairs; L. A. Whitely of the *New York Herald* worked also as a clerk in the Treasury Department; Sam Wilkeson of the *New York Tribune* had a second job preparing Northern propaganda for distribution in Europe; William Shanks of the *New York Herald* was a volunteer aide to General Lovell H. Rousseau; DeB. R. Keim of the *Herald*, a volunteer aide to General Sherman; Tom Cook, a volunteer aide to General Daniel Sickles.

The fault was not always with the correspondents; poor communications hampered better reporting. The Union Army's inefficient mail service frequently lost letters; the *New York Tribune* estimated that half its mail dispatches from correspondents in the field never reached New York; and in the South a letter could take a month to reach its destination. This tended to confine correspondents to those areas where they were assured of telegraphic contact with their offices or, if the lines were down or occupied, were within striking distance by horse or train of New York, Washington, or any large rail junction, a handicap that, as will be seen, coloured the entire Northern reporting of the war. Censorship, imposed to prevent the publication of information of value to the enemy, was expanded to stifle criticism of the conduct of the war. When all these factors combined to harry the already hard-pressed correspondent, his reporting of the war grew worse instead of better, and the few competent men gave up in disgust and withdrew.

In the South, the outbreak of war found a partisan, political press that was thirty years behind the times. Most newspapers were weeklies with small circulations, and even a daily like the *New Orleans Picayune* sold less than 6,000 copies. The presses, most of the newsprint, and many an editor came from the Northern states. There was little attempt to separate news from editorial opinion, news columns were filled with political propaganda, and fair and objective reporting was almost unknown. Without sufficient general appeal to produce a larger income, the Southern press found

24

itself with neither the resources nor the men to attempt a coverage of the war on anything approaching the scale of the North.

Although it managed to put about a hundred war correspondents into the field, many of these were serving officers who had volunteered to send a telegram or a letter when circumstances permitted and do not qualify as genuine correspondents. Newspapers had to rely heavily on the Press Association of Confederate States, formed to replace the loss of the Associated Press service from New York, and on a small corps of civilian correspondents—including one or two women—many of whom worked for more than one newspaper.*

The South's initial handicap became even greater as the war progressed. When the Northern forces moved into the Confederacy, many newspapers suffered curtailment or total and peremptory dissolution at the hands of the Union Army. A few, such as the *Memphis Appeal* and the *Chattanooga Rebel*, managed to survive by retreating with the Southern forces and printing in other towns, always one move ahead of the Northern armies. For all of them, there was the constant struggle to get the paper out with staffs depleted by the call to arms. "There was no paper issued from the *Confederate* office on Saturday morning," its editor, in Macon, Georgia, wrote the next day. "Every man in the establishment was in the field on Saturday. We hope our subscribers will consider this a sufficient excuse."[14] As newsprint and ink supplies dried up, the Southern papers grew smaller, until, for example, the *Charleston Courier* was down to a single sheet. Others took to printing on wrapping paper, writing paper, paper bags, and even on the blank side of wallpaper—the Alexander, North Carolina, *Pictorial Democrat* and the Thibodaux, Louisiana, *Stars and Stripes* were but two that were forced to such lengths.

It would have been difficult enough to produce a record of the war's progress under these circumstances; the attitude of most of the Confederate war correspondents made it impossible. They believed that loyalty to the cause of the South came before any professional requirements of truth and objectivity. Accordingly, they maintained an attitude of optimism in their reporting even when, in the later stages of the war, the Confederacy was collapsing around them. They exaggerated Northern casualties, minimised Southern ones, reported the capture of Northern towns that had not even been attacked, and refused to admit that the Confederate Army ever retreated. A series of backward movements, "improperly

* Using various pseudonyms, George W. Bagby contributed to twenty-three!

called a retreat by those who do not comprehend them," was in reality "retrograde manoeuvres." A dispatch reporting a Southern victory was likely to begin "Glory to God in the highest." The North was "the cursed, cowardly nation of swindlers and thieves," the "abolition, infidel foe"; Northern soldiers went into battle "primed with whisky" or "drunken with wine, blood and fury."

Cowed by censorship, determined to maintain morale, and poorly served by the majority of its correspondents, the Confederate press lent itself to the government's propaganda line much more readily than did the Northern press. Evidence for this is the fact that at least twenty newspapers were suppressed in the North, compared with only one in the South. The rest swung behind the Confederate war effort, keeping their criticism within well-defined limits, avoiding a "despondent fault-finding tone," and trying, as one editor instructed his correspondent at the front, "to give the dear weakly public as much as possible of the bright side of things."

The North, on the other hand, was witnessing the first attempt at saturation coverage. As a mass of correspondents jostled for positions, the very strength of their numbers began to militate against good reporting. Comradeship and compassion vanished in the race for exclusive news. One correspondent begged a wounded officer not to die before he had finished interviewing him and, as an inducement, promised him that his last words would appear in "the widely-circulated and highly influential journal I represent."[15] J. A. Daugherty of the *Louisville Journal* and William Furay of the *Cincinnati Gazette*, returning from a battle, were in a train crash. They surprised each other groping about in the dark, each looking for the other man's body to steal his notes on the battle. The *Gazette*, scooped on a Northern retreat, said that there should be an investigation and that, if the story proved exaggerated, then the correspondent who had written it "should be hung [*sic*] by the neck until dead."

Accuracy became a minor consideration. Casualties were grossly underestimated; generals listed as killed lived on to die of old age; battles were reported on days when there was no action at all; at times the whole Southern army was reported to be marching on Washington; Atlanta was reported captured a week before the battle for the town took place. It was but a small step from ignoring accuracy to faking whole reports. Junius Browne of the *New York Tribune* collected from officers details of the Battle of Pea Ridge (March 1862) and wrote a brilliant, but entirely imaginary, *eye-witness* report. To the chagrin of the two correspondents who had actually seen the battle, Browne's dispatch was acclaimed by *The Times* of London as "the ablest and best battle account which has been written during the American war."[16] The Battle of Shiloh (April 1862) caught correspondents by surprise, so they dashed off dispatches about desperate hand-to-hand fighting that had never occurred, a mass effort of faking reports that led to a cynical acceptance of the practice. Even war artists were not above faking their sketches. When Southern cavalry set fire to some Northern army trains near Chattanooga in October 1863, *Harper's Weekly* carried sketches of the scene from its artist "on the spot," whereas in fact the artist had been twenty miles away at the time.[17]

Censorship had been applied in a loose and haphazard manner since Bull Run, the first clash of the war. There, early indications of Northern superiority had sent the Northern war correspondents hurrying to Washington to write accounts of a great victory. Back on the battlefield, the Southern troops turned the Union Army and a rout followed. Although the Associated Press in Washington managed to get news of this momentous defeat to the telegraph office, to be sent to New York, it went no farther. The general-in-chief of the Northern forces, Winfield Scott, had stopped its transmission, and so the result of the first major act of censorship in the war was chaos, with all the New York newspapers carrying stories of a glorious victory that was, in fact, a scandalous defeat. Later, censorship suffered from confusion over who was to enforce it—at different times during the war it was administered by the State, Treasury, and War Departments—and, inevitably, the intention to suppress only information of value to the enemy became also the desire to suppress material damaging to the Northern side.

The Secretary of War, Edwin M. Stanton, began to dicker with casualty figures. He altered an account of Grant's failure at Petersburg, reducing the losses to about a third of their actual number. His department withheld news of the surrender of Harper's Ferry for twenty-four hours and changed "10,000 Union troops surrendered" first to "6,000" and in later dispatches to "4,000."[18] The actual figure was 11,200. Stanton took to suspending newspapers that had broken his censorship rules, arresting editors, threatening proprietors with court-martial, and banning correspondents from the front, and he actually issued orders for Henry Wing of the *New York Tribune* to be shot for refusing to hand over a dispatch he had written for his newspaper. Still censorship did not work. So, early in 1864, Stanton began issuing his own dispatches, in the form of a war diary addressed ostensibly to the chief military authority in

New York but put out through the Associated Press—a scheme that Southern newspapers failed to persuade the Confederate government to follow. These daily war bulletins, the beginning of a practice adopted in later wars in most countries of the world, set forth briefly the situation in each command and represented the administration's attempt to counter the lies, rumours, and alarmist reports some war correspondents were writing.

Stanton's feud with the correspondents had a mixed reception in the army. Some of the more politically minded generals had come to enjoy the publicity that dispatches from the front had brought them—one senior officer even wrote a report of one of his actions and gave it to the Associated Press for distribution. Others had formed close relationships with correspondents they trusted. Grant allowed Sylvanus Cadwallader of the *New York Herald* to travel in his entourage and used him to carry messages to Lincoln. But in general the army hated the correspondents and did its best to get rid of them. General George Meade objected to the way he was treated in a dispatch filed by Edward Crapsey of the *Philadelphia Inquirer* and ordered Crapsey to be expelled by the army. The unfortunate correspondent was placed backwards on an old horse, a placard marked "Libeler of the Press" was tied to his chest, and he was paraded through the army to the tune of "Rogue's March." Meade later relented and said he had realised, on reflection, that the punishment was unnecessarily severe, but by that time it was too late. Crapsey's colleagues had got together and decided that Meade's name would never be mentioned in a dispatch again, a boycott so effective that some claim it was a major factor in the failure of the politically ambitious Meade to become president of the United States. But no one hated war correspondents more than General Sherman did: "Now to every army and almost every general a newspaper reporter goes along, filling up our transports, swelling our trains, reporting our progress, guessing at places, picking up dropped expressions, inciting jealousy and discontent, and doing infinite mischief."[19] Sherman said he would willingly agree to give half his pay to have his name kept out of the newspapers, and he took all the steps he could to try to prevent correspondents from travelling with him, including the threat to treat them as spies.*

* General Joseph Hooker introduced a simpler stratagem. With Stanton's support, he issued orders that all dispatches had to be published under the correspondent's name. Robbed of the anonymity that had protected their speculation, inaccuracy, and comment, the correspondents with Hooker became much more discreet.

Sherman's attitude, combined with the communication difficulties that the reporting of his battles involved, frightened away all but the most determined correspondents. Thus the weight of reporting in the North was about Grant, while Sherman's campaigns in the west and south were poorly reported. Yet they were the campaigns that won the war, and for sheer richness of material went unrivalled. When Sherman captured Atlanta and then set out to march through Georgia to the sea, thus splitting the Confederacy and destroying its resources, only eight correspondents went along with him—a handful, compared with the contingents of correspondents on other fronts—and many major papers, including the *New York Times*, were not represented. Their reporting was accurate and fair, but they lacked the imagination to comprehend what they were witnessing. They saw Sherman's sixty-mile-wide scorched-earth sweep as an army living off the country, "Sherman's bummers" reducing the collection of supplies to a science, and if the Southerners along the line of march suffered, then "it has been the fortune of a war they voted for." None of them realised they were seeing an important concept—total war—in the making. Sherman himself did. In a dispatch that shows a talent the correspondents might well have envied, Sherman set out for Lincoln exactly what he had done to the Confederacy.

> We have consumed the corn and fodder in the region of country thirty miles on either side of a line from Atlanta to Savannah, as also the sweet potatoes, cattle, hogs, sheep and poultry, and have carried away more than 10,000 horses and mules as well as countless numbers of slaves. I estimate the damage done to the State of Georgia and its military resources at $100,000,000; at least $20,000,000 of which has ensured to our advantage and the remainder is simple waste and destruction.[20]

And, instead of a war correspondent, it was left to one of Sherman's staff officers, Major George Nichols, to write the best account of this march of "waste and destruction." It appeared in the *New York Evening Post* and was later expanded into a book (*The Story of the Great March—From the Diary of a Staff Officer*), one of the most successful of the early post-war period.

What other stories did correspondents miss, fail to get passed by the censors, underplay, or refrain from writing? One of the cruel facts of the war was that the North, although it considered itself to be fighting for the survival of democracy, could not raise enough volunteers willing to risk their lives for this cause. The South claimed that Northern men of military age were so unwilling to join the army that the majority of the Union troops were foreigners. This seems unlikely, but, even taking the Northern official figures, one soldier in three was foreign, most of them being German or Irish. Some eastern states had to introduce a bounty system to fill their regiments, a practice that led to men being shanghaied into service, and when conscription was introduced, in 1863, New York was hit by the worst riots in the nation's history. From the thirteenth to the sixteenth of July, the city went completely out of control as the riots took on anti-Negro as well as anti-draft overtones. Finally a state of insurrection was proclaimed, and troops were brought by forced marches from victorious Gettysburg to crush the rioters. The draft in New York was suspended, but the riots continued intermittently and remained front-page news until October.* [21] The New York newspapers reported the insurrection fully—"The reign of the Rabble," the *New York Times* called it— but the Southern newspapers had a field day. Many posed the question the North was reluctant to ask: if the cause of the Union was such a noble one, why was there such violent opposition to the idea of fighting for it?

The reluctance to serve in the Union Army should be placed in context. Conditions were poor, many army surgeons were incompetent, and contractors made fortunes by selling uniform cloth made from factory clippings and sweepings.** The quartermaster's and commissary departments in both armies were staffed by thieves; defective cartridges were not unusual; and punishment for minor offences in both North and South was barbarous. The penalty for desertion or bounty-jumping was death, and sometimes a mass shooting took place in front of an entire regiment, with an enclosure for war correspondents and artists from *Harper's* or *Frank Leslie's Illustrated Weekly*, and a band to play a dirge before the shooting and the popular hit tune "The Girl I Left Behind Me" afterwards. [22] Capture meant imprisonment under vile conditions. Both sides cared little for the health of prisoners-of-war, and exposure, inadequate medical care, ignorance of ordinary sanitation, and malnutrition in the midst of plenty caused the deaths of thousands

* The final death roll amounted to nearly 1,000, many more were injured, and property damage ran to several million dollars.
** The South was little better. Some Confederate shoes were made of wood, glue, and stained paper, and fell to pieces so rapidly that not only were thousands of ordinary Confederate soldiers forced to march and fight without shoes, but even officers, including at least one of the rank of lieutenant-colonel, went barefooted.

of prisoners. There was friction between eastern and western regiments in the Northern army, and enmity between regular officers and volunteers.* In the North there was a powerful prejudice against accepting Negro troops, which was overcome only by the failure to get enough white volunteers, and although many Negro units fought well, they were never really accepted. The South organised a few regiments of slaves only when the war was nearly over—"negroes will do to fight negroes," one Confederate war correspondent wrote—and bitterly resented the North's use of black troops against white men. So when the Southern general Bedford Forrest stormed Fort Pillow, in April 1864, and found a Union force that included 262 Negroes, he massacred them (according to a Congressional investigation) "after resistance had ceased."[23]

How many of these sensitive yet important facts were reported? The difficulties the Union Army had in filling its ranks were ignored where possible—the New York draft riots could not, for example, be overlooked. In its turn, the South suppressed reports of the Richmond bread riots of April 1863 and failed to report that many plantation owners flatly refused to lend their slaves to be used as labourers on military projects. The brutality of army discipline was not reported except when it was thought, as in the case of the mass shootings, that publicity would have a deterrent effect. Friction in the army was generally not reported unless it involved high-ranking officers, and, in fact, Northern correspondents were known to write about fraternal fellowship between eastern and western troops when in reality only ill feeling existed: "They are fighting side by side for the Union and the blood they are shedding together will add another bond of eternal friendship between East and West."[24] Racism in the Union Army was overlooked, and, in any event, stories about it would certainly not have been passed by the censor, because of the difficulty the army was having in getting the troops to accept Negro recruits and to agree, as a popular Union song expressed it, that there existed "Sambo's Right to Be Kilt." Neither side made capital out of conditions in the other's prisons, in case this led to too close a look at its own.

In the North there was some mild reporting of graft, and Franc Wilkie of the *New York Times* exposed some medical mismanagement, but, as the foundation of many a present-day fortune testifies, none of the major scandals in either the quartermaster's corps

---

* In the South, the friction was between troops from Virginia and North Carolina.

or the army contracting system were uncovered. The South fared better in this field. Frauds in the commissary and quartermaster's departments, which had deprived the troops of blankets and food, were exposed in Confederate newspapers. Peter Alexander wrote movingly, in the *Mobile Daily Advertiser and Register*, on the inhuman treatment of the wounded in grossly inadequate army hospitals: "A planter who would take as little care of the health of his slaves as the Government does of its soldiers...would be driven out of the community by his indignant neighbours."[25] Pay scandals—some troops were not paid for a year—and misconduct by officers and public officials were the subjects of bitter attack by one or two of the better Southern correspondents. But the real extent of sickness, low morale, wartime profiteering, and desertion from the Southern armies was never revealed. Confederate correspondents, when they mentioned desertion at all, tried carefully to avoid the actual word and preferred to use "absentees" or "stragglers."

There were few good correspondents. A handful in the North and one or two in the South worked hard to keep the public informed on what was going on. In the North, H. Whitelaw Reid of the *Cincinnati Gazette*, one of the foremost correspondents in the war, and later an author of note, wrote the facts as he saw them "without fear or favour," but he was a racist and believed that between whites and Negroes "a separation should be made as soon as practicable." Charles Coffin of the *Boston Journal* was a good, straight battle reporter, describing only what he saw or knew on good authority to be true. George Smalley of the *New York Tribune* wrote what was generally acclaimed as the best report of the Battle of Antietam, and perhaps of the whole war.

Henry Villard of the *Tribune* was an outspoken correspondent, not afraid of telling even Lincoln what he felt was wrong with his army, and Sylvanus Cadwallader of the *New York Herald* had an eye for the historic moment. He was present when Lee surrendered to Grant at Appomattox on April 9, 1865, and while his colleague Henry Wing, of the Tribune, rushed off to try for a scoop, Cadwallader was able to note the shameful scramble for souvenirs from the room where the surrender had been signed. It began quietly, with General George Custer paying the owner, Wilmer McLean, $25 for one of the tables used during the signing. Then officers began forcing money into McLean's hands, but now McLean threw it back. Suddenly there was a rush, and the furniture was gone. Cadwallader wrote:

Cane-bottomed chairs were ruthlessly cut to pieces, the cane splits broken into pieces a few inches long, and parcelled out among those who swarmed around. Haircloth upholstery was cut from chairs, and sofas were also cut into strips and patches and carried away.[26]

Isolated pieces of reporting showed that some correspondents, unlike the majority, saw the futile, bloody side of war and were disgusted by it. Ned Spencer of the *Cincinnati Times* made no great name for himself, but he did write this disturbing paragraph about the aftermath of the Battle of Shiloh:

As I sit tonight writing this epistle, the dead and wounded are all around me. The knife of the surgeon is busy at work, and amputated legs and arms lie scattered in every direction. The cries of the suffering victim, and the groans of those who patiently await for medical attendance, are most distressing to anyone who had any sympathy for his fellow man. All day long they have been coming in, and they are placed upon the decks and within the cabins of the steamers, and wherever else they can find a resting place. I hope my eyes may never again look upon such sights.[27]

Samuel Wilkeson of the *New York Times* wrote what was probably the most poignant piece of the war. Sent to help cover the battle at Gettysburg, he learned that his son had been wounded in the leg and, abandoned by the doctors, had died. Wilkeson sat down just the same and wrote his story.

Headquarters, Army of the Potomac, Saturday Night, July 4:

Who can write the history of a battle whose eyes are immovably fastened upon a central figure of transcendingly important interest—the dead body of an eldest born, crushed by a shell in a position where a battery should never have been sent, and abandoned to death in a building where surgeons dared not to stay? The battle of Gettysburgh! I am told that it commenced on the first of July, a mile north of the town, between the weak brigade of infantry and some doomed artillery and the whole force of the rebel army. Among other costs of fatal error was the death of Reynolds. Its value was priceless, however, though priceless was the young and the old blood with which it was bought... For such details as I have the heart for, the battle commenced at daylight, on the side of the horseshoe position, exactly opposite to that which Ewell had sworn to crush through...

The story closed with these words:

My pen is heavy. . . . O, you dead, who died at Gettysburgh

have baptized with your blood the second birth of Freedom in America, how you are to be envied! I rise from a grave whose wet clay I have passionately kissed, and I look up to see Christ spanning this battlefield. [28]

In the South, the only outstanding correspondent was Peter Alexander, a lawyer from Georgia, who had opposed disruption of the Union but remained loyal to the South when the break occurred. Alexander was reliable, accurate, and honest, and the suffering of the ordinary soldier distressed him. He campaigned for shoes for barefooted troops, better medical attention, and action against drunken officers and army surgeons, whom he had seen "so stupefied by liquor that they could not distinguish between a man's arm and the spoke of a wagon wheel and who would just as soon have sawed off one as the other."[29]

With these exceptions, the coverage of the Civil War by American correspondents left, then, a lot to be desired. But it was immeasurably better than the corrupt and distorted picture of the war presented by the British press, particularly by its leading newspaper, *The Times*.

The American Civil War held considerable importance for Britain. In 1861 it was estimated that one-fifth of the entire British population was dependent directly or indirectly on the prosperity of the cotton-manufacturing areas, which in turn depended on the American South for 80 per cent of their supplies. This clear commercial relationship made for sympathy with the South, but after Lincoln's Emancipation Proclamation it also became an embarrassment, because then the commercial interest had to be reconciled with Britain's long-preached sentiments of humanity. A country so experienced in moral accommodation would no doubt have had little difficulty in bringing about this reconciliation, but the issue was further complicated by a major political factor. The ruling class in Britain had nurtured a barely concealed hatred of America and her democratic institutions, and now clearly desired their downfall. If the American experiment in democracy could be shown to have failed, demands for greater democracy in Britain could be kept from becoming an issue. Britain's interests in the war were, then, very strong, and at one stage it appeared highly likely that she would actually intervene—the American general Winfield Scott, in Paris on a propaganda mission for Lincoln, had to return to New York to prepare for its defence against a British invasion.

Lincoln had realised from the beginning that "the favour or dis-favour of foreign nations," particularly English favour, could have considerable influence on the outcome of the war. The South, at first without the means of making a single gun, realised it would have to rely on Britain for arms and also considered, correctly, that there was a good chance of bringing Britain into the war on the Confederate side. So both North and South mounted propaganda campaigns in Britain aimed at influencing opinion. The North began by dispatching abroad, in October 1861, "some gentlemen of intelligence and experience, possessing a good knowledge of all the circumstances preceding and accompanying the rebellion...to dis-abuse the public mind, especially in England and France, where numerous and active agents of secession and rebellion have been at work."[30] In Washington, war correspondents were engaged to prepare a stream of propaganda material. Lincoln himself wrote a letter to the working-men of Manchester on January 19, 1863, and another, on February 2, to London working-men. Speakers toured Britain putting the Northern case; the *New York Herald* corre-spondent, George Train, made twenty-three speeches in two months. Northern propagandists wrote secretly for the British press.[31]

The South's approach was more venal. A war correspondent called Henry Hotze, a Swiss immigrant who had worked for the *Register* of Mobile, Alabama, was sent to Britain with a fund of Confederate secret-service money to be used for suborning British journalists. He was apparently very successful. In his reports, he notes that he was able to find seven London journalists willing to place news items and even editorials favourable to the Southern cause in return for payments either in the form of "Boxes of cigars ...Whiskey and other articles" or in cash.[32] Hotze was also behind a weekly newspaper called the *Index*, which was started in Britain on May 1, 1862, nominally as a purely British publication but secretly as a straight propaganda medium for the South.

So with Britain's direct interest in the outcome of the Civil War, and with both sides operating secret propaganda complexes there, it was vital that public opinion be accurately informed about what was really happening in America. *The Times*, of course, was the major newspaper of the day. "I think I never felt so much as in this matter the enormous power which *The Times* has," wrote Goldwin Smith, the historian, in 1863. "Not from the quality of its writing ...but from its exclusive command of publicity and its exclusive access to a vast number of minds."[33]

35

But *The Times* began with a heavy disadvantage. Its chief proprietor, its editor, and its foreign manager were all singularly ill-equipped to handle the news from America during this important period of history. The chief proprietor, John Walter III, was openly anti-Unionist. The editor, John Delane, was ignorant of American affairs and had little feeling for American institutions. The foreign manager, Mowbray Morris, had been born in the West Indies and was in sympathy with the South and slavery.[34] Since these were the men who not only engaged the correspondents to cover the war but also presented the news the correspondents sent, it is not surprising that *The Times*' coverage of the Civil War caused such a cleavage between the two nations that it required a generation to heal it.

*The Times* prepared for the war by sending William Howard Russell to America. Russell's reputation had grown greatly since the Crimean War. He had covered the Indian Mutiny in 1857-58 and had shown a much sharper perception of the issues than that of his colleagues or his newspaper.* His name was well known in America, and when he arrived he dined with Lincoln and met other Northern leaders, who put the Union case to him. He then went off on a tour of the South, where a first-hand study of the slave market disgusted him. The outbreak of war thus found him deeply attached to the Union cause and with a high opinion of Lincoln's motives.

But, as a seasoned war reporter, he had to report the first engagement at Bull Run the way he saw it. The untried federal troops, watched by members of Congress and their ladies, who had arrived from Washington with picnic baskets and luggage ticketed south to Richmond, broke before the Southern attack and fled in panic. Early reports had been of a Northern advance, and the New York newspapers carried their stories of a great victory.

To have to accept that this "victory" was actually a resounding defeat was bad enough. But when Russell's report appeared in *The Times* and was relayed back to New York, and American readers learned from it that their troops had fled in a disgraceful rout, the nation, shocked, went into a period of gloom and apprehension, during which the easiest target for blame was Russell. Fury against

---

* While *The Times* was counselling bloody revenge against the Sepoys and their leaders, Russell had clearly seen that Britain's days in India were numbered: "The Anglo-Saxons must either abate their strong natural feeling against the coloured race...or look forward to the day ...when the indulgence of their passions will render the government of India too costly a luxury for the English people."

him became so great that he was advised to seek protection within the walls of the British Embassy. This had convinced *The Times* that its low opinion of the North was justified. When the *Trent* affair flared up, Delane prepared for war.* "The whole Army, Navy, and Volunteers are of one mind and all mad for service in America," he wrote to Russell. "If we are foiled by a surrender of the prisoners, there will be a universal feeling of disappointment. We expect, however, that they will show fight—and hope for it, for we trust that we will give them such a dusting this time…"[35] Russell wrote urging restraint, and the crisis passed with the release of the envoys on January I, 1862.

There is reason for believing that *The Times* was not by now entirely happy with Russell and his still pro-Northern sentiments, and that Russell himself was having an unhappy time. A telegram he had sent to an American business friend when he had learnt, through British diplomatic contacts, that the Trent affair was about to be settled leaked to the *New York Herald*, which accused him of financial speculation. Russell was unable to explain the situation satisfactorily (nor have his biographers been able to), and his reputation suffered. As well, he was having difficulty in getting permission to accompany any Northern army, so he left for Canada for a few weeks' break. The foreign manager, Morris, was furious. *"You must either go to the front or come home…* up to the beginning of this year you did well, but since then you seem to have lost heart and to have thrown us overboard."[36]

Russell made one more attempt to obtain a pass to the front, and when this failed, without telling *The Times* he packed up and sailed for Britain. There he was awarded a pension, but he contributed no more to *The Times* on American affairs. "As I from the first maintained the North must win, I was tabooed from dealing with American questions in *The Times* even after my return to England, but *en revanche* I have had my say in the *Army and Navy Gazette*, which I have bought."[37]

Russell's sudden departure left *The Times* without a war correspondent in the North, and hurried arrangements were made to find one. The man chosen was Charles Mackay, a journalist and poet of some reputation, who on a tour of America in 1857 had contributed to the *Illustrated London News*. It is clear that Mackay was

---

* On November 8, 1861, a Union warship intercepted the British steamer *Trent*, and a boarding party arrested two Southern diplomatic envoys on their way to Europe.

selected because he could be relied upon to send anti-Northern dispatches. "I had apparently been successful in my application because my sympathies in the struggle were in accordance with those of [*The Times*]," he wrote.[38] Although Morris let Mackay know what sort of article he wanted— "The Northern Government and its policy are an abomination to me and I greatly enjoy to hear them abused"—he soon felt that Mackay had gone too far. "I ask myself whether any Government or set of men can be so wholly bad that not a single good word can be said for them by an impartial observer…If any such there be, let them be made known, if only to …redeem your correspondence from the charge of systematic vituperation."[39] Mackay was not moved, and the South became delighted with him. It missed him badly when he returned to Britain for a holiday, and there is evidence suggesting that it became so anxious to get him back to New York that it even paid his steamship passage. James Spence, a Liverpool merchant, who acted as the Confederate financial adviser in Britain, reported: "I have … taken a berth for Mackay by Saturday's boat, so he will soon be out again and he is dead for our side."[40]

*The Times*' war correspondent in the South was Francis Lawley, formerly on the staff of the British minister in Washington. He managed to get dispatches through at irregular intervals, usually sending them via the French diplomatic bag to Paris, from where the *Times* office then sent them to London. Lawley was a poor choice, strongly pro-South—"I am at a loss to convey to you the contemptuous tone in which the tried and war-torn soldiers of General Lee talk of the huddled rabble of black, white, and copper-coloured victims…who are at times goaded up to the Southern lines."[41] What was worse, he lacked the most elementary qualification of a good reporter: the ability to recognise what is news. His first dispatch, filed from Richmond after he had made his way through the blockade, set the tone for the rest of his term. It ran to two and a half columns and, as if to justify his expenses, Lawley carried on at length about the cost of living. Most of the rest of the dispatch was an outburst against the North and a reminder of the South's fine pedigree.

> And these men, many of them bearing some of England's most honoured names and descended from England's most honoured families, are in the field, and have been so for nineteen months, fighting against mercenaries who have repudiated England as though she were governed by a Nero, and have escaped from

German penury and conscriptions. Whatever may have been the truth last winter, it is not pretended now that Northern armies are not mainly composed of men of foreign birth![42]

The engagement of war correspondents like Mackay and Lawley and the adoption of a pro-South attitude in its leading articles were bad enough, but *The Times* went even further to promote the Southern cause. When New Orleans fell it carried black mourning borders; it suppressed the fact that a Liverpool shipyard was building a warship, the famous *Alabama*, for the South and recorded her sailing to begin a career as a commerce raider in only five words in its "Ship News" column. And it commissioned Spence, the Confederate agent in Liverpool, to write a series of pro-South articles for *The Times*, under the signature "S," for which it made him a gift of a specially bound edition of the *Encyclopaedia Britannica*.[45] The combination of poor and subjective war correspondents and the attitude at *The Times*' office towards America produced a disastrous coverage of the war.

In July 1863, misled by Mackay (who was to be made to pay for it later), *The Times* confidently predicted that the Southern general Lee was about to capture Washington. In 1864 it reported Sherman's march to the sea as a folly from which he would find it difficult to extricate himself. When Sherman reached Savannah, Delane was made physically ill by the set-back, but recovered rapidly and was able to write that *The Times* was doing its best "to attenuate the mischief." This took the form of a piece in which Sherman was given credit for "one of the ablest, certainly one of the most singular military achievements of the war," but which then went on to say that the South had little use for Savannah as a port anyway. * [44]

At the beginning of the war *The Times* referred to Lincoln as an uneducated rail-splitter. Half-way through the war he was "a sort of moral American Pope" or "Lincoln the Last." When he was assassinated, he was suddenly recognised as having been "one of England's best friends." Naturally, this recognition that it had been wildly astray in its military and political estimates of the war was not accomplished by *The Times* without some unpleasant recrimi-

---

*Russell, too, had to alter his views radically as a result of Sherman's campaign. In the *Army and Navy Gazette* Russell had said that Sherman was "wriggling about like a snake in the presence of an ichneumon." Sherman took Atlanta on the very day this article appeared, but Russell had a skin even thicker than *The Times*'. In his next issue he wrote implying that he had foreseen Sherman's success all along : "General Sherman has fully justified his reputation as an able and daring soldier."

nations and extensive scapegoat-hunting. Although it was clear that at least some responsibility lay with the executives, who had allowed their prejudices to interfere with their selection of war correspondents and with the manner in which they were briefed, blame had to be placed farther down the editorial ladder. So Mackay was peremptorily sacked. Morris broke the news to him. "This has been brought about by your blind and unreasonable condemnation of all public men and measures on the Federal side," he wrote. "You have presented the English public with a distorted view of the Federal cause...Every statement was one-sided and every remark spiteful."[45]

One cannot but feel a certain sympathy for Mackay. The shattering condemnation contrasts strongly with what *The Times* had thought of him only two years before. "I assure you that [your correspondence] deserves, in my opinion, the most unqualified praise," the very same Morris had written then.[46] The crux of the matter was, of course, that Mackay had been in high favour with *The Times* "as long as Fortune seemed to smile on the cause of the Southern Confederacy." When the South lost the war, Mackay lost his job.

There was not a single British war correspondent who saw the great forces at work in the American Civil War and who tried to convey them to his readers. The *Daily Telegraph* had George Augustus Sala with the Army of the Potomac. Sala had a low opinion of American reporting—"hydra-headed, Argus-eyed, Dionysius-eared, multi-tongued, New York press"[47]—but wrote nothing remarkable on the war himself. M. B. Hewson, an English civil engineer, sent reports to the *Herald*, but was known for his markedly pro-Southern sympathies. The *Daily News* sent an artist, Frank Vizetelly, one of a family of famous journalists, to cover the Northern side, but Vizetelly could not get accredited and so he crossed to the South by a secret route. There he visited Lee and sent sketches and portraits to the *News*, but, since they went by sea, many were intercepted by Northern ships as booty of war and appeared, instead, in the Northern *Harper's Illustrated Weekly*. The *News* did its best to balance the pro-Southern stance of *The Times* by devoting long leading articles to the North, written by Harriet Martineau (probably the first woman in Britain to become a regular journalist), who had visited America from 1834 to 1836.

Edwin Godkin saw the issues clearly and would have made an excellent correspondent, but, unfortunately, he was ill during the early part of the war and spent most of his time in Europe recuperating. When he returned to America—a country he had adopted

—he wrote for the *Daily News*, setting out the military and political situation with remarkable prescience. But his health prevented his undergoing the rigours of a long campaign in the field, and so he devoted most of his writing to dispelling the English prejudice about America. There was no one, therefore, who could overcome the influence of *The Times*, with its seeming impartiality. Due in no small way to this newspaper and its correspondents, the British public received a biased, inaccurate impression of the war, and the anger that this created in the American government caused long-lasting mistrust between the two nations. Since the American newspaper reader was only a little better informed than his British counterpart, the Civil War, despite the sweeping changes it brought in journalistic techniques, was one of the poorer periods in the progress of the war correspondent.

The war did, however, have the effect of making war correspondence a separate section in the practice of journalism. It established a new breed of reporter, and also of reader, to justify his expensive existence. All that was needed now were bigger and better wars. So, until the changed circumstances of the First World War killed the correspondents off, there was hardly a corner of the globe that did not see one of them searching for a skirmish, a clash, a battle, a campaign. It was an inglorious fifty-year free-for-all that one cynic termed the profession's "Golden Age."

# Chapter Three

# The Golden Age
# 1865–1914

A large number of the Tommies had never been under fire before
…and there was a curious look of suppressed excitement in some
of the faces…Now and then I caught in a man's eye the curious
gleam which comes from the joy of shedding blood—that mysterious impulse which, despite all the veneer of civilisation, still holds
its own in a man's nature, whether he is killing rats with a terrier,
rejoicing in a prize fight, playing a salmon or potting Dervishes. It
was a fine day and we were out to kill something. Call it what you
like, the experience is a big factor in the joy of living.

—Ernest Bennett in the
*Westminster Gazette*, 1898

T he period between the American Civil War and the First
World War was a "Golden Age" for the war correspondent,
because of the rise of the popular press, the increasing use of the
telegraph, and the tardy introduction of organised censorship. The
newspaper expansion in the two major newspaper-reading countries was explosive. In Britain, due mainly to the Education Acts of
1870, which had made it compulsory for every child to be taught to
read, the number of newspapers doubled between 1880 and 1900.
During the Franco-Prussian War the *Daily News* trebled its circulation. In the United States, growing circulations meant that an
increasingly affluent press could afford to use the telegraph to

report distant events, in spite of the enormous cost: to send a report from Europe to the United States cost $5 a word.

Despite what had happened in the Crimea, the military establishment was slow to realise the power of this newly awakened section of public opinion and allowed correspondents to write virtually what they liked. So for the first time it was both physically and financially possible for a newspaper to carry its own correspondent's report of a battle within days, instead of weeks or months, of its conclusion. Also, it was clear to the editors and proprietors of the popular press that public demand for these reports was immense—providing they were written mainly as narratives of adventure, without too much political comment or moralising to interrupt the narrative.*

There was the added attraction that the outcome of most wars in this period did not directly concern the future of the two countries where the major newspaper-reading public resided, Britain and the United States. Thrilling accounts of battles, slaughter, and bravery could be reported from both sides with no danger of the reader's identifying himself with anyone except the intrepid war correspondent, who, as a result, rapidly became the hero of his own story. The by-line "From our own correspondent" vanished from the popular press, and personal names took its place.** An elite corps of journalists was born, prepared to endure the punishing demands of war reporting for the delight of its rewards.

Russell was still the father of the profession, but his reputation was already fading under the challenge of changed conditions and the thrusting tactics of a younger, more ambitious breed. His dispatches were still eloquent and comprehensive, but they were no longer always the first. He had difficulty keeping up with the troops and was scooped so often that he complained of a conspiracy of younger men to outdo him and *The Times*. He had to be reminded that things had changed since the Crimea—"I beg you," wrote his foreign editor, "to use the telegraph freely"[1]—and eventually he suffered the humiliation of being instructed to try to employ for *The Times* his arch-rival, Archibald Forbes.

---

\* It is significant that two of the big-name correspondents of this period, the *London Daily News*' representative, Archibald Forbes, and Stephen Crane of the *New York Journal*, got their jobs because their editors had been impressed by their fictional descriptions of battles.

\*\* Newsboys in Milan sold *Corriere della Sera* not by shouting the headlines but by yelling "Article by Barzini!"

Forbes and his colleagues were tough and resourceful. No major events involving violence occurred anywhere in the world, however remote, during this period without at least one of them being there to report it. They travelled by horse, donkey, camel, sled, steamer, and train. They carried letters of credit, gold pieces, *laissez-passers*, and often a brace of pistols. There was one—an Associated Press correspondent called Mark Kellogg—with Custer at Little Big Horn. There were dozens in the Franco-Prussian War. They were inside Paris during the siege and during the Commune. They reported the Turkish massacre of the Bulgarians. One—Frank le Poer Power of *The Times*—was with Gordon in Khartoum. Five died in the Turko-Serbian War, five in the Sudan. One—Richard Harding Davis of the *New York Journal* and *Harper's New Monthly Magazine*—helped to start the Spanish-American War. They watched the suppression of the Boxer Rebellion and were themselves crushed by censorship in the Russo-Japanese War. The British, especially *The Times*' correspondents, were not averse to a little intelligence work for the Foreign Office on the side, and one of the Americans, H. M. Stanley, was not above starting his own small wars in Africa and then reporting them. They were the bane of the military authorities—"these newly-invented curses to armies"—who were not very impressed with the class of person attracted to the job: "I have seldom met a rougher or more disreputable set." Whisky and claret ran like a *leitmotiv* through their lives, they tended to go to bed with their boots and spurs still on, and they had little time for the social graces. Many had been set on a military life, and when, for various reasons, this proved impossible, they took up reporting wars as the next-best career. Whatever their background, their main motivation was a thirst for battle and adventure, or, as Ernest Vizetelly, who covered the Franco-Prussian War at the age of seventeen, wrote, "a search for real romance in the midst of the workaday nineteenth century."[2]

No one denied their physical bravery, and no one suggested that they were non-combatants. A Dervish bullet, almost spent, hit Bennett Burleigh of the *Daily Telegraph* in the neck. "Pick it out," he told Melton Prior, the *Illustrated London News* artist, and went on firing. James Creelman of the *New York Journal* led a bayonet charge in Cuba during the Spanish-American War. Forbes rode through Zulu lines to reach a telegraph office with news of the Battle of Ulundi. But it is hard to escape the impression that they were all slightly mad. H. H. Munro (the author "Saki"), the *Westminster*

*Gazette's* correspondent in the Balkans, kept cool by playing a syphon of soda water on his shoulder blades. Frederick Villiers went to war with a bicycle. Burleigh turned up at official receptions dressed in a seedy frock-coat and posing as an American senator. Maurice Baring sent to the *Morning Post* dispatches on the Russo-Japanese War so lengthy and so scholarly that the editor recalled him to London and appointed him as drama critic.[3] Luigi Barzini was so terrified of being accused of being corrupt that he would accept no foreign decorations, and Edmond O'Donovan of the *London Daily News* danced drunk and naked around what the Muslims believed to be Eve's tomb, shouting, "To the devil with the Mahdi!"

They were, everyone agrees, a colourful crew. But they did not measure up to their job. They showed little humanity and no historical perspective. With one or two exceptions, they pandered to the bloodthirsty tastes of the age, chronicling the deaths of thousands of men with little concern beyond whether the event they were witnessing would make a good report. I have been able to find only one, Moncure D. Conway of the *New York World*, who was so sickened by what he saw that he gave up being a war correspondent altogether. The rest devoted themselves to the battle of getting news back to their newspapers before their rivals did.* War, for most of them, was a highly profitable game, and they became thrill purveyors, serving, as the author-correspondent Vincent Sheean put it, "as professional observers at the peep show of misery." Since the misery they were observing was usually that of natives or foreigners, it did not really matter, as witness Ernest Bennett's reference at the beginning of this chapter to "potting Dervishes," or this report by Winwood Reade of *The Times*: "I went out after breakfast and found an Ashantee skirmisher...I stalked the man until I got near enough to see him. I missed him twice, the third time I silenced his fire, and I think I silenced him—at all events, I afterwards found a body lying close to the spot."[4]

Only two or three, like the Americans Januarius MacGahan and James Creelman and the Italian Luigi Barrini, felt sufficiently concerned over what they witnessed to write in protest against the conduct of war, to be partisans for truth and compassion rather than adventure and glory. Even fewer had "the hearing ear and the seeing eye" that enabled them to discern the deeper implications in the

---

* "I have known an Arab servant to be followed for yards and beaten most cruelly with a heavy stick," wrote Ernest Bennett, "because owing to a breakdown of the telegraph he was unable to forward a message sent by his master."

chance events they witnessed. In general, the war correspondent during the Golden Age regarded war much as Bennett has described it: "a big factor in the joy of living." Their needs were accurately assessed by General Sir Hector MacDonald, who greeted their arrival, as his troops got ready to receive a Dervish charge, with these words: "Gentlemen, I am delighted to welcome you. I think I can give you good sport."

It was the Franco-Prussian War that marked the decline of William Russell and the rise of Archibald Forbes, the leader of the new guard. Forbes, moved by a lecture given by Russell, had enlisted in the Royal Dragoons, where he had learnt something of military matters. After five years his health had broken down, and he left the service to start a newspaper, called the *London Scotsman*. He also wrote a novel about the Indian Mutiny. The battle scenes in this (based on the recollections of a veteran) attracted the attention of the *Morning Advertiser*, which offered him a commission to cover the Franco-Prussian War on a "pay-if-used" basis, with £10 for outfitting and £20 for expenses. Forbes, who spoke German, was convinced that the Germans would win, and so, against most advice, he chose the German side. This turned out to be a wise move.

France had made no plans for war, and its high command was corrupt and inefficient.* It is understandable, therefore, that France decided she would allow no war correspondents to operate at all. On the other hand, the German Chancellor, Bismarck, realised the propaganda value of a friendly press: "Nothing will be more favourable for our political standing in England and America than the appearance, in the two most influential newspapers of these countries...of very detailed accounts of our army in the field."[5]

In England and in America there was a great deal of interest in the war, although both countries were determinedly neutral, Britain so much so that at first the government ruled that if there were to be no reporting of the French side, because of the French government's attitude, then the only neutral thing to do would be to refuse to allow any British war correspondents to cover the German side. A spirited protest by *The Times'* editor, Delane, helped to

---

*At the Battle of Sedan, the Army of Châlons had three commanders-in-chief in almost as many hours, and various officers were not above telegraphing news of non-existent victories to rig the stock markets.

reverse this decision, and Forbes and his colleagues set out for the front.

The first decisive engagement of the war, a battle at Gravelotte-Saint-Privat in August 1870, saw the French put to flight, and also saw two major events in the history of war reporting. Forbes, who was soon to dominate the profession, wrote his first major war report and realised his own ability. Bismarck and the King of Prussia are awaiting the battle's outcome. Forbes is observing them.

> The old King sat, with his back against a wall, on a ladder, one end of which rested on a broken gun-carriage, the other on a dead horse. Bismarck, with an elaborate assumption of coolness which his restlessness belied, made pretence to be reading letters. The roll of the close battle swelled and deepened till the very ground trembled beneath us. The hoofs of a galloping horse rattled on the causeway. A moment later Moltke, his face for once quivering with emotion, sprang from the saddle, and running to the King, cried out, "It is good for us; we have carried the position, and the victory is with your Majesty!" The King started to his feet with a fervent "God be thanked!" and then burst into tears. Bismarck, with a great sigh of relief, crushed his letters in the hollow of his hand..."[6]

The second major event, a landmark, was the organised use of the telegraph, arranged by the seasoned American Civil War reporter George W. Smalley, of the *New York Tribune*. Smalley first set up a "pool" arrangement between the *Tribune* and the *London Daily News*: each would have a right to use the dispatches of the other's correspondents. Then he carefully briefed each correspondent on what was required of him.

> My instructions were very simple, but I believe at that time were novel in England. Each was to find his way to the front, or wherever a battle was most likely to be fought...If he had the good luck to witness an important battle, he was not to telegraph, but, unless for some very peremptory reason, he was to start at once for London, writing accounts by the way or after his arrival. If he could telegraph a summary first, so much the better. But there must be no delay. The essential thing was to arrive in London at the earliest moment. Only when in London was a correspondent master of the situation.[7]

The plan worked well. The Battle of Gravelotte was described by one of the *Tribune* team in a telegram costing $5,000, and his report appeared in the United States only two days after the event, "the first attempt in the Old World to describe a battle over the telegraph wires." A full account of the battle reached London, almost as if Smalley had arranged it, when Moncure D. Conway of the *New York World* walked into the *Daily News* office and said he had telegraphed to his own paper an outline of the battle, but wanted to describe what he had witnessed during his train journey back through France. He had travelled on the roof of a hospital train and had seen the ghastly plight of the wounded: "At times I was sick and faint. The earth yawned into one vast grave, the blue sky was a pall, the sun had turned to blood."[8] Smalley snapped up Conway's account, and it was telegraphed all over Europe. Conway could have gone on to a brilliant future, but for weeks his dreams were plagued by what he had seen. He decided he was not cut out to be a war correspondent and abandoned the career.

The war continued badly for the French. At the Battle of Sedan they were surrounded and forced to surrender, and Napoleon III was taken prisoner. Paris was soon under siege. Forbes had done extremely well. He and a Dutch correspondent had been the only civilians to witness Napoleon surrendering himself to Bismarck at an isolated weaver's cottage. But the *Morning Advertiser* had a correspondent in Paris who would cover the siege, so Forbes was ordered to return to London. There he offered his services to the *Daily News*, was engaged at the then princely sum of £20 a week; and began a partnership with the paper that was to make them both famous.

Meanwhile, William Russell was having a difficult time. *The Times* had sent him to accompany the Germans, and he was received by them as an honoured guest. But he soon found that his dispatches were arriving in Britain days after the *Daily News* had printed the highlights of the battle. The problem for Russell was not simply how to reorganise his communications system, but to recognise that he needed a new approach to his writing. While correspondents were still sending their dispatches by mail or by courier, they could afford a leisurely literary approach to their stories. Sending a summary of a battle by telegraph meant adopting a new style: crisp, concise, and packed with facts—the beginning of the who-how-where-when-why dictum that remains basically unchanged in popular news reporting today. Russell, firmly set in his ways, and some twenty years older than Forbes and his colleagues, could not cope. "No paper has been so badly served as *The Times* during this great war by all its correspondents, old and new," wrote *The Times*' manager. And, in a letter to Russell begging him to use the telegraph freely, he added, "*The Daily News* has beaten us hollow and continues to do so."

Forbes' success was largely due to careful planning, the free use of money, and his native ingenuity. He went to great trouble to work out a communications route before setting out for the battlefield. When Paris was under siege, he had an arrangement whereby he could post a letter at any German military post-office in the environs of the city; it was collected by the field-post wagon, placed on the post-train to Saarbrücken, and there delivered to the station telegraph master, who transmitted it to London. So efficient was the German postal system and so carefully briefed was the telegraph master that, no matter at what point around Paris Forbes found himself, a dispatch sent in this manner reached London within twenty-four hours—an amazing feat.

Given a little latitude, even more remarkable scoops were possible. Forbes acquired in advance details of the projected German bombardment of the Paris quarter of Saint-Denis. These he sent to London, where they were set in type by the *Daily News* and held in readiness. As the first gun was fired, Forbes, standing in the doorway of a telegraph office at the German headquarters, bellowed to the operator the two words "Go ahead," and on receipt of this message in London the prepared account was rushed to press, where it made the noon edition that same day, easily beating all rival newspapers.

While Forbes was taxing his ingenuity with the besieging Prussian forces, an even more colourful figure, Henry Labouchere, an English newspaper owner, was delighting *Daily News* readers with his provocative and entertaining accounts of life within the besieged city. Labouchere, the witty and talented son of a banker, had been something of a dilettante. As an undergraduate at Cambridge he had run up gambling debts of £6,000, and his career in the diplomatic service had been cut short by his refusal to accept a posting as second secretary in the British Embassy at Buenos Aires unless he was allowed to operate from Baden-Baden. He had become a shareholder in the *Daily News*, and when the siege caught him in Paris he persuaded the resident correspondent, a married man with children, to take the last train out of the city. Labouchere then began sending, by balloon, a series of dispatches, which the *News* published under the by-line "Besieged Resident" so as to protect Labouchere from reprisals by the French.

Labouchere scorned the bravado expected of war correspondents. "I confess I am not one of those persons who snuff up the battle from afar and feel an irresistible desire to rush into the middle of it. To be knocked on the head by a shell merely to gratify one's curiosity appears to me to be the utmost height of absurdity..." So Labouchere ignored the daily shelling, by which some ten or twelve people were killed, and concentrated on chronicling the Parisians' determination to survive as food supplies rapidly ran out and they began to eat animals from the zoo and then to cook substances no one had before considered as food. *The Daily News'* circulation soared steadily, despite its readers' horror at what Labouchere had sampled for his latest dinner. Cat he found "something between rabbit and squirrel, with a flavour all of its own. It is delicious. Kittens either smothered in onions or in a ragout are excellent." Donkey was like mutton, and a "salami of rats" tasted something between frog and rabbit. Being an Englishman, eating dogs worried him. "I have a guilty feeling when I eat dog, the friend of man. I had a slice of spaniel the other day; it was by no means bad, something like lamb, but I felt like a cannibal."[9]

Paris surrendered at the end of January 1871, and in the early hours of the armistice Labouchere was astonished to meet Archibald Forbes. Forbes was very welcome, since he had thought to bring with him seven pounds of ham, although Labouchere was not certain he would be able to get used to the strange taste. Forbes had got into Paris during the preliminary armistice by a typical mixture of initiative and luck. Fifty correspondents were waiting on the Versailles side to enter the city. None of them succeeded. Forbes got in on the north, and rode with deliberate blindness past the gendarmes examining papers. He stayed for eighteen hours, gathering material for a long dispatch with which, once again, the *Daily News* scooped the world's press.

The Germans entered Paris on March 1. *The Times*, determined to regain some of the reputation it had lost to the *Daily News*, engaged a special train for Russell to travel in as far as Calais, then chartered a steamer to Dover and another special train to London. In spite of these expensive arrangements, Russell's descriptive story was out only an hour ahead of that of Forbes, who had used the ordinary means of transport. Russell finally realised that his career was in decline. He was persuaded to accompany Sir Garnet Wolseley to South Africa in 1879, but an accident with his horse made him lame, and he never covered another war. He came to believe, by the time of his death in 1907, that the war correspondent's best days were over and that increasing military censorship had killed the craft he had helped pioneer.

Forbes went on to more successes covering the Paris Commune

and its brutal end. The stark cruelties of the class war that broke out in March impelled him, against his normal sympathies, to take the side of the underdog. His dispatches, sent back to England with his usual ingenuity—one he carried himself, dressed as a diplomatic courier and clutching a big envelope addressed to "Her Majesty, the Queen of England"—attracted considerable attention. During the Bloody Week of May 21 to 28 he reported the troops at Versailles "enjoying the fine game of Communist hunting."

> The Parisians of civil life are caitiffs to the last drop of their thin, sour, white blood. But yesterday they had cried, "Vive la Commune". Today they rubbed their hands with livid, currish joy to have it in their power to denounce a Communist and reveal his hiding place. Very eager at this work are the dear creatures of women…They have found him, the miserable!…A tall, pale hatless man with something not ignoble in his carriage. His lower lip is trembling but his brow is firm, and the eye of him has some pride and defiance in it. They yell—the crowd—"shoot him; shoot him!" An arm goes into the air, and there is a stick in the fist. The stick falls on the head of the man in black. Ha, the infection has caught; men club their rifles, and bring them down on that head, or clash them into splinters in their lust for murder. A certain British impulse, stronger than consideration for self, prompts me to run forward. But it is useless. They are firing into the flaccid carcass now, thronging about it like blowflies on a piece of meat. His brains spurt on my foot and splash into the gutter, whither the carrion is bodily chucked, presently to be trodden on and rolled on by the feet of multitudes and wheels of gun carriages.[10]

The "Eastern Question" became the next crisis. The Prime Minister, Disraeli, sympathised with Turkey, for the Russians who threatened her had persecuted Jews. Gladstone, on the other hand, supported the rebellious Balkan peoples. At this point, it fell to a war correspondent to write what still stands as one of the major exposure stories of history, one that became directly responsible for a war and eventually led to the independence of Bulgaria.

The correspondent concerned was Januarius Aloysius MacGahan, an American of Irish extraction, who had a passionate hatred of injustice and oppression. He was already a journalist of distinction, who had astonished the newspaper world by a remarkable ride across the Central Asian steppe in order to catch up with a Russian military expedition on its way to Turkestan. After this, he had sailed on the barque *Pandora* in search of the Northwest Passage and had written successful books about both expeditions.

In 1876, reports began to reach Constantinople of terrible atrocities by Turkish forces in southern Bulgaria against the Christian population. The *London Daily News* commissioned MacGahan to go to southern Bulgaria and try to find out the truth. Between July 28 and August 16, a series of his letters was published in the *Daily News*, afterwards being reprinted world-wide and later republished as a booklet.* It is difficult to overestimate the influence of MacGahan's report, the accuracy of which was confirmed by investigation years later, when passions had cooled. Over 12,000 men, women, and children had been killed by the Kurds and *bashibazouks* let loose by the Turkish rulers to crush the Bulgarian revolt. MacGahan interviewed hundreds of survivors and clearly was deeply moved by what he heard and saw.

> I think I came in a fair and impartial frame of mind...I fear I am no longer impartial, and I am certainly no longer cool...There are things too horrible to allow anything like calm inquiry; things the vileness of which the eye refuses to look upon, and which the mind refuses to contemplate.
>
> We came to an object that filled us with pity and horror. It was the skeleton of a young girl not more than fifteen...It was still clothed in a chemise; the ankles were enclosed in footless stockings; but the little feet, from which the shoes had been taken, were naked, and owing to the fact that the flesh had dried instead of decomposing, were nearly perfect...The procedure seems to have been as follows: They would seize a woman, strip her carefully to her chemise, laying aside...any ornaments and jewels she might have about her. Then as many of them as cared would violate her, and the last man would kill her or not as the humour took him...
>
> We were told there were three thousand people lying in this little churchyard alone...It was a fearful sight—a sight to haunt one through life. There were little curly heads there in that festering mass, crushed down by heavy stones; little feet not as long as your finger on which the flesh was dried hard;...little baby hands stretched out as if for help; babes that had died wondering at the bright gleam of sabres and the red hands of the fierce-eyed men who wielded them; children who had died shrinking with fright and terror;...mothers who died trying to shield their little ones with their own weak bodies, all lying there together festering in one horrid mass.[11]

---

*The Times* was furious because it had to wait several days for its own correspondent to confirm MacGahan's story, a humiliating delay that forced its manager to admit, "These Yankees are undoubtedly pushing fellows with a great gift for routing out facts."

MacGahan's stories caused world-wide indignation against the Turks. Russia decided that his disclosures justified a war and on April 29, 1877, began hostilities against Turkey. Eighty correspondents turned up to cover the Russian side. The Russians gave them a virtual carte-blanche. There was to be no field censorship, and correspondents were put on their honour not to reveal details of impending manoeuvres. Despite this auspicious start, by the end of the war, which lasted barely a year, only four of the original correspondents were still in action. Sickness, wounds, and exhaustion had eliminated the rest. MacGahan, Forbes, and the correspondent-artist Villiers were among the survivors.

The depth of MacGahan's personal commitment to the cause he was reporting can be gauged by the fact that he went to the war with one foot in a plaster cast, the result of an injury from a fall. He ignored this disability completely, and even after two further accidents had crippled him seriously he carried on, watching the fighting from a gun-carriage. The strain of the campaign took its toll, and a few months after he reached Constantinople, following the Turkish surrender, MacGahan fell ill with typhus. Within a week he was dead. He was buried in a little Greek cemetery at Pera, his funeral being attended by generals and correspondents alike, and in St. Petersburg masses were said for his soul. Five years later his body was brought by an American warship to New York, where it lay in state in City Hall, before being buried in the Ohio village where MacGahan was born. The Bulgarians, who considered he had played a crucial role in the birth of their state, commemorated his death for years afterwards with an annual Requiem Mass at Tirnova.

Forbes, too, emerged from the Russo-Turkish War with distinction. It was he, in August 1877, who carried the first news of the Russian victory at Shipka not only to the world, but to the Czar himself. The Czar was so pleased that he decorated Forbes with the Order of St. Stanislaus with the Crossed Swords, awarded only for personal bravery, and ordered a carriage to help him to get the story out. Forbes crossed the Danube at Rustchuk and then rode on to Bucharest, where he arrived at 8:00 P.M. He had been three days and nights either in the saddle or under fire in the trenches at Shipka, without sleep, often without food. "I was dead tired. Not a word of my dispatch was written, and I had news for which I knew the world was waiting—news on which the fate of an Empire and the fortunes of half Europe depended. And it was as much as I could do to keep my eyes open, or sit up in the chair into which I had dropped. I told the waiter to bring me a pint of dry champagne, unopened. I took the cork out, put the neck of the bottle into my mouth, drank it with all the fizz, sat up and wrote the four columns you read next morning in the *Daily News*."[12]

Forbes' next major campaign was the Zulu War in 1879. At the Battle of Ulundi he watched from inside a British square as thousands of Zulu warriors pitted their spears against artillery and rifle fire. When the Zulus eventually fled, Forbes learned that no messenger was to be sent with the news of the victory until the following morning. He left immediately, taking his own dispatch and a sketch hurriedly prepared by Melton Prior of the *Illustrated London News*, and rode through ten miles of Zulu country swarming with remnants of the defeated Zulu army. Using the British forts situated at fifteen-mile intervals as staging posts, he made Landsmann's Drift, 120 miles from Ulundi, in twenty hours. Here he telegraphed his dispatch, which was read in both houses of Parliament. "A proud moment," *The Times* said, "for the confraternity of special correspondents."

But despite the fame that these achievements brought him, and although he lived for another twenty years, Forbes did little more active reporting, and after the Zulu campaign he went into virtual retirement. A clue to his motives for this decision lies in his description of the scene at Isandhlwana, where a British column had been wiped out. The newcomer to such a scene of horror might blunder inarticulately in passionate identification and emotional involvement. Forbes does not; he orders his material cold-bloodedly, moving at a steady pace to the climax of the transfixed skull, then cushioning the reader with a touch of homely sentiment in a perfectly judged anticlimax.

A thousand corpses had been lying there in rain and sun for four long months. The dead lay as they had fallen, for... the vultures of Zululand, that will reduce a dead ox to a skeleton in a few hours, had apparently never touched the corpses of our ill-fated countrymen. All the way up the slope I traced, by the ghastly token of dead men, the fitful line of flight. It was like a long string with knots in it, the string formed of single corpses, the knots of clusters of dead where, as it seemed, little groups must have gathered to make a hopeless, gallant stand, and so die.

Still following the trail of dead bodies through long rank grass and among stones, I approached the crest. Here the slaughtered dead lay very thick, so that the string became a broad belt. A strange dead calm reigned on this solitude of nature. Grain had grown luxuriantly round and under the waggons, sprouting from the seed that had dropped from the loads, fallen on soil fertilised by the lifeblood of gallant men...

As one strayed aimlessly about, one stumbled in the grass over skeletons that rattled to the touch. Here lay a corpse with a bayonet jammed into the mouth up to the socket, transfixing the head and mouth a foot into the ground. There lay a form that seemed cosily curled in calm sleep, turned almost on its face; but seven assegai stabs had pierced the back. It was the miserablest work wandering about the desolate camp, amid the sour odour of stale death, and gathering sad relics, letters from home, photographs, and bloodstained books.[13]

A clever piece of reporting; yet it has the cold touch of a professional who has been too long familiar with scenes that would arouse in most men a lifetime's horror. Did Forbes realise this? Whether he did so or not, it was the last war piece he wrote. He died in London in 1900, raving in his final delirium about the battlefield: "Those guns, man, those guns, don't you hear those guns?"

It was in Africa that the British army made a stand against the incursions war correspondents had been making into a field it regarded as its own. Senior officers felt that by the actions of men like Forbes they were being robbed of the glory of reporting their victories.

So Sir Herbert (later Lord) Kitchener, sirdar of the Egyptian army, advancing against the Dervishes in the Sudan to avenge the death of General Gordon, did his utmost to hamper correspondents in every way he could. He particularly disliked Winston Churchill, who had pulled every string available to him to see action in the Sudan and thus advance his army career. Churchill eventually managed to get there by persuading the War Office to allow him to go out as a supernumerary lieutenant at his own expense. Kitchener was much annoyed, and it is hard to believe that, as Churchill tells it, when Kitchener learned that Churchill proposed to finance his campaign by writing for the *Morning Post* "he simply shrugged his shoulders and passed on to what were after all matters of greater concern." Kitchener's tactics were to make the twenty-six correspondents with him run exactly the same risks as his soldiers, to limit their telegraphic facilities to 200 words a day, and to give them no help, no briefings, no guidance, and little courtesy. It was not surprising that they hated him, and his disdain for them was behind what was to happen over war news at the outbreak of the First World War.

The correspondent who attracted the most attention during this campaign was George Warrington Steevens of the *Daily Mail*, whose career was to be cut short by his death of enteric fever at Ladysmith in 1900. Steevens, a Balliol man, joined the *Daily Mail* after a brilliant career at Oxford, where he took a first in classics, and he introduced into the urgent world of war writing an elegance of style and a much-admired standard of accuracy: "I vowed to state nothing on any authority unless I saw it myself or heard it from a European who had seen it."

Steevens appears to have felt more than most the difficulty in reconciling the glories of battle with its horrors, and, although he wrote the usual jingoistic clichés, he at least made an effort to point out the gruesome side of war as well. Here he describes Kitchener's advance at Atbara to cut the Dervish army to pieces.

> It was not so difficult to go on—the pipes picked you up and carried you on—but it was difficult not to hurry: yet whether they aimed or advanced, they did it orderly, gravely, without speaking. The bullets had whispered to raw youngsters in one breath the secret of all the glories of the British Army...Three men went down without a cry at the very foot of the Union Jack, and only one got to his feet again: the flag shook itself and still blazed splendidly. Beyond is a low stockade and trenches, but what of that? Over and in! Hurrah, hurrah, hurrah!
>
> Now fall in, and back to the desert outside. And unless you are congenitally amorous of horrors, don't look too much about you. Black spindle-legs curled up to meet red-gimleted black faces, donkeys headless and legless or sieves of shrapnel, camels with necks writhed back on to their humps, rotting already in pools of blood and bile-yellow, heads without faces and faces without anything below, cobwebbed arms and legs, and black skins grilled to crackling on smouldering palm-leaf—don't look at it. Here is the Sirdar's white star and crescent on red; here is the Sirdar, who created this battle, this clean-jointed, well-oiled, smooth-running clockwork-perfect masterpiece of a battle. Not a flaw, not a check, not a jolt; and not a fleck on its shining success. Once more, hurrah, hurrah, hurrah.[14]

The development in war reporting in Europe and Africa had by now left America somewhat behind, and so the outbreak of the Spanish-American War in 1898 was seized upon by the newspapers in the United States—particularly the so-called "yellow press"—as a chance to catch up. American correspondents, such as the flamboyant Richard Harding Davis, had been reporting the Cuban insurgents' struggles for independence from Spain for almost two years. Davis and his newspaper's proprietor, William Randolph Hearst, believed that the United States should intervene to help the rebels, and they did their best to inflame public opinion with articles like Davis' famous "The Death of Rodriguez."

Rodriguez, a rebel captured in a skirmish, was publicly executed by firing squad. Davis watched and then filed a long description of the event, ending it with: "As...I looked back, the figure of the young Cuban, who was no longer a part of the world of Santa Clara, was asleep in the wet grass, with his motionless arms still tightly bound behind him, with the scapular twisted awry across his face, and the blood from his breast sinking into the soil he had tried to free."[15]

Hearst was delighted with the success of Davis' story. His newspaper, the *New York Journal*, was in the middle of a battle with Joseph Pulitzer's *World*, and war was good circulation-building material. If, of course, America could be involved in the war, then circulation prospects would be even better. Hearst did all he could to bring this about. He sent Karl Decker to rescue Evangelina Cisneros, daughter of a Cuban insurgent leader, from jail. He sent an artist, Frederic Remington, to convey visually what Davis had done with words. Remington was not keen on the assignment and found things quiet when he arrived. There is a story about an exchange of telegrams that followed which, even if it is apocryphal, illustrates Hearst's determination to get America into the war. Remington telegraphed to Hearst:

> EVERYTHING IS QUIET. THERE IS NO TROUBLE HERE.
> THERE WILL BE NO WAR. I WISH TO RETURN.

Hearst replied:

> PLEASE REMAIN. YOU FURNISH PICTURES. I WILL FURNISH WAR.[16]

When the American battleship *Maine* blew up in Havana Harbour, the Spaniards insisted it was an accident and suggested a court of enquiry. Hearst, without a particle of proof, attributed it to "an enemy's secret infernal machine," and in the wave of patriotic fervour that swept the United States ("Remember the *Maine!*") he was finally able to furnish his correspondents with a war.

From a correspondent's point of view, it was an ideal campaign. Two hundred turned up to cover it, including twenty-five from Hearst's group alone. Expenses were no object. Cable charges for a single story ran to $8,000. The Associated Press chartered a flotilla of boats, which, throughout the naval engagements, cruised at will through the battle lines, ignoring fire from both sides and scurrying back and forth to the nearest cable station. The circulations of Hearst's newspapers climbed dizzily as his success forced other owners to compete. Larger and larger headline type was used to attract the readers' attention, until letters four inches high, often in red, occupied almost all the front-page space. Correspondents' copy had to match the headlines and some took to such gross exaggeration that a *New York Herald* man insisted that there was "a factory out there for faking war news."

One way of drawing readers was by employing as a war correspondent someone with a famous name, which was how Stephen Crane, author of the widely read Civil War book *The Red Badge of Courage*, entered the business. Crane had written the battle scenes in his book out of his imagination and had never seen action, but this had not deterred Hearst from employing him as a correspondent for the *Journal*. After failing to get through to the Cuban rebels, Crane had gone to Greece to write about the Greco-Turkish campaign. There he had not been very popular with his colleagues, who resented his engagement as a war correspondent on his reputation as a novelist. One reported: "Crane came up and wrote a 1,300 word story. He was never near the front, but don't say I said so."[17] They particularly disliked his digs at the conventional descriptions of battle, like this one: "The roll of musketry was tremendous...It was more impressive than the roar of Niagara and finer than thunder or avalanche...It was the most beautiful sound of my experience, barring no symphony...This is one point of view. Another might be taken from the men who died there."[18]

Crane switched to the *New York World* for the Spanish-American War and covered the famous charge up San Juan Hill by the Rough Riders—volunteers who had learnt their horsemanship playing polo and who were led by the remarkable Theodore Roosevelt, noted for his jingoistic view of life: "We must play a great part in the world, and especially perform those deeds of blood and valour which above everything else bring national renown." But, after the American naval victory at Santiago, the closing stages of the war slipped into comedy, and finally only nine correspondents remained. When the Americans invaded Puerto Rico, the inhabitants welcomed them with bottles and bouquets, which encouraged Crane to try to capture a town himself. Richard Harding Davis was to accompany him, but Crane double-crossed him, did not awaken him as arranged and went alone. Crane got his scoop, but it is Davis' delightful description of what happened that is remembered.

> While I slumbered, Crane crept forward between our advance posts and fell upon the doomed garrison. He approached Juana Diaz in a hollow square, smoking a cigarette. His khaki suit, slouched hat and leggings were all that was needed to drive the first man he saw, or rather the man who first saw him, back upon the town in disorderly retreat. The man aroused the village and ten minutes later the Alcalde...surrendered to him the keys of the cartel. Crane told me that no general in the moment of victory had ever acted in a more generous manner. He shot no one against a wall, looted no churches, levied no forced loans. Instead, he lined up the male members of the community in the plaza, and organised a joint celebration of conquerors and conquered. He separated the men into two classes, roughly divided between "good fellows" and "suspects." Anyone of whose appearance Crane did not approve, anyone whose necktie even did not suit his fancy, was listed as a "suspect." The "good fellows" he graciously permitted to act as his host and bodyguard. The others he ordered to their homes. From the barred windows they looked out with envy on the feast of brotherly love that overflowed from the Plaza into the by-streets and lashed itself into a frenzied carnival of rejoicing. It was a long night and it will be long remembered in Juana Diaz.

The following morning a colonel and 800 American troops crept cautiously up to take Juana Diaz by surprise. "The Colonel's astonishment at the sight of Crane was sincere. His pleasure was no less great. He knew that it did not fall to the lot of every colonel to have his victories immortalised by the genius who had written *The Red Badge of Courage*. 'I am glad to see you,' he cried eagerly. 'Have you been marching with my men?' Crane shook his head. 'I am sorry,' said the Colonel, 'I should like you to have seen us take this town.' 'This town!' said Crane in polite embarrassment. 'I'm really very sorry, Colonel, but I took this town myself before breakfast yesterday morning.' "[19]

The other correspondent best remembered from the Spanish-American War is James Creelman, who not only wrote news but often made it as well. Creelman, a Canadian by birth, had reported the Japanese invasion of Manchuria and the capture of Port Arthur, perhaps his most famous piece. It is a textbook sample of vivid, concise reporting, forced on Creelman by communication difficulties. He was later able to elaborate his short cable, but the first account, on December 11, 1894, stands on its own.

> The Japanese troops entered Port Arthur on November 21 and massacred practically the entire population in cold blood. The defenseless and unarmed inhabitants were butchered in their houses and their bodies were unspeakably mutilated. There was an unrestrained reign of murder which continued for three days. The whole town was plundered with appalling atrocities. It was the first stain upon Japanese civilisation. The Japanese in this instance relapsed into barbarism. All pretense that circumstances justified the atrocities are false. The civilized world will be horrified by the details. The foreign correspondents, horrified by the spectacle, left the army in a body. [20]

The Japanese had offered Creelman a bribe to tone down his story, but he refused it. American public opinion, until then friendly to Japan, changed overnight. With this reputation, Creelman was in heavy demand to go to Cuba, and he finally agreed to do so for Hearst's *Journal*. He was with General Adna Chaffee in an attack on the Spanish blockhouse at El Casey, on the outskirts of Santiago. Pinned down under heavy fire, Creelman seems to have forgotten that he was a correspondent and offered to lead a bayonet charge on the blockhouse. The charge was a success, and Creelman had a front-page story. But before he could begin to write it a bullet smashed his left arm. He was found by William Randolph Hearst himself, playing war correspondent and gripped by fever for yet another scoop. Someone knelt in the grass beside me and put his hand on my fevered head. Opening my eyes I saw Mr Hearst...a revolver at his belt, and a pencil and notebook in his hand. The man who had provoked the war had come to see the result with his own eyes, and, finding one of his correspondents prostrate, was doing the work himself. Slowly he took down my story of the fight...That battle had to be reported somehow. 'I'm sorry you're hurt, but'— and his face was radiant with enthusiasm—'wasn't it a splendid fight! We must beat every paper in the world.' " [21]

Hearst's enthusiasm for American victories became even more marked in the American campaign to suppress the revolt in the Philippines that raged from 1899 to 1902. Wholesale and indiscriminate killing by American troops had depopulated large sections of the country. There were complaints that the troops had on one occasion been ordered to "kill everything over ten years old" and that the Twentieth Kansas had swept through a town of 17,000 inhabitants leaving not one native alive. In a defence that foreshadowed the attitude of many Americans to Vietnam more than sixty years later, Hearst's *New York Journal* said. "The weak must go to the wall and stay there…We'll rule in Asia as we rule at home. We shall establish in Asia a branch agent of the true American movement towards liberty."[22]

While the Spanish-American War was in progress, there were rumblings in the Far East. In 1898 a Chinese secret society called the Righteous Harmony Fists—or Boxers by Europeans—had begun persecuting Christians in north-eastern China. This was symptomatic of the social unrest and anti-foreign feeling that followed China's humiliating defeat by Japan in 1895, but the European powers still proceeded with plans for partitioning the country.

Eventually, in 1900, bands of Boxers, who believed they had divine immunity from foreign bullets, fell upon all foreigners they could find and killed them. An international force set out to suppress the uprising and punish the Boxers. It was a little-covered campaign, because the eyes of Britain and America were on South Africa, where a ridiculously small force of Boers was tackling the might of the British army. But a shy, nervous Italian war correspondent, Luigi Barzini, was in China, beginning to make a reputation for himself that was to carry him through eight wars and make him one of the best-known journalists in Europe. Barzini was a rare correspondent. He saw no glory, no heroics in war, only slaughter. He had "the hearing ear and the seeing eye" to perceive repercussions beyond the battle he was witnessing, and the courage to write what he believed. He never learned to administer his talents or to exploit his reputation. He considered it undignified to ask for more money from his newspaper, and his family lived in penury. He refused foreign decorations, for fear they might be considered as payment, and the editorship of a rival paper "because it seemed to me like a desertion." In his later years, he grew bitter as men with less talent made more successful careers, but he is remembered as a fine correspondent.

It was in the Far East, beginning with the Boxer Rebellion, that he flourished. He described the brutality of the suppression, foresaw that it would lead only to a more violent rejection of Western influence, denounced the poor equipment of the Italian section of the international force, and caught the tragi-comic aspects of the campaign. Italian journalism had never known such immediacy and veracity. Here he is describing the blood lust of a hundred Cossacks as they put to flight 2,000 Boxers.

> We were about 300 yards from them. Their heads, swathed in red, recalled a regiment of French soldiers marching; their red waistbands flamed in the sun. Above was a whirl of swords, a dance of lances with red tassels. All of a sudden, those in front, then others, then all, threw themselves on their knees to pray...Then they began to advance. That mad courage was fantastic. What was happening before my eyes absorbed me completely...At that moment I did not consider that I was armed and that perhaps I should think of defending myself. All my life was concentrated in my eyes.

The Boxers were halted by a volley from the Cossack infantrymen, but thirty of them left the main body and advanced. The last of these thirty to be killed "flourished two sabres, one in each hand, like a juggler."

> A shot and he fell flat on his face; but he immediately raised himself on his knees waving his sabre. Another shot flattened him again, but he raised himself on his elbow, brandishing the weapon again, until the last shot threw him in the dust for ever. At this point, all the Boxers turned and fled.
>
> Then it seemed that a hurricane had swept out from the corn stalks. The Cossacks had charged. Bent over their horses, with their sabres in the air, shouting: "Ah! Yah!" they galloped like a pack of hounds behind the fox. An immense cloud of dust rose to hide everything: one could barely see their white jackets swaying as they galloped. A great cry arose. They had reached the Boxers...One Boxer fled, holding his lance horizontally on his head with his arms raised. A Cossack followed close on his heels. From the road the Chinese had crossed a field and were about to enter the corn stalks when the scimitar, which was raised above him, fell. The lance was broken like a twig and the sabre blade entered the Chinaman's head. The blows which landed on heads made horrible wounds. One Boxer, an old man with a grey beard, killed in the middle of the road, had his literally split in two.
>
> After some minutes the ground was covered with dead, plastered with dust which, over their wounds, became bloody mud. Meanwhile the hunters had gone further away; their shouts could barely be heard every so often. A trumpet sounded in a vain attempt

to make them return. Every now and again a Cossack emerged on the road and crossed it at a gallop. The officers would shout at him to stop, but he would continue his pursuit. It was like trying to recall hounds chasing stags.

Captain Makofkine returned alone, trotting through the dead, smiling. Slapping his sabre, he shouted to me: "I killed two, only two, but what do you expect? That rabble ran like a pack of hares! What did you do?" "Nothing; now I've taken some photographs for my paper." "Good. But tell the truth; you enjoyed yourself, didn't you?"[23]

Barzini returned to the Far East for the Russo-Japanese War in 1904, the first modern war in which a Western nation was beaten by an Asian power. The Japanese imposed a stifling censorship and kept the band of international correspondents cooling their heels in Tokyo's best hotels. Few of them saw anything of the decisive battles. Jack London, the novelist, representing the Hearst group, lost his patience, struck a Japanese, and was rescued only by the intervention of Richard Harding Davis. The others were loud in their complaints. Frederick Palmer of *Collier's* complained that all the Japanese censor would allow him to write was that "everything is going to plan." John Fox reported, in *Scribner's Magazine*: "In simple kindness the Japs might have said, 'Over here we do not recognise the ancient, Occidental, God-given right of the newspapers to divulge the private purposes of anybody.'"[24] The Japanese were easier on their own correspondents. *Asahi*, *Mainichi*, and *Jiji* all had men at the front, and a *Mainichi* reporter wrote an eye-witness account of the Battle of Nanshan after accompanying the Japanese Eleventh Division into action as a munitions carrier.

The attitude of the Japanese to foreign correspondents can be partly explained by their feeling that some of the correspondents were spies. This was understandable in view of the activities of some of the journalists with whom the Japanese had previously come in contact, especially those representing *The Times* of London. *The Times* had not considered it unwise to allow some of its correspondents also to work for various government departments. Thus we find Frank le Poer Power, when he was with Gordon in Khartoum, acting as British consul and sending daily telegrams to the British agent in Egypt for forwarding to the Foreign Office. George Ernest ("Chinese") Morrison, the Australian who became Far Eastern correspondent of *The Times*, had gone off on a special mission for the Foreign Office through Burma, China, and Siam, pretending he had nothing to do with either the newspaper or the British government but was simply "a private individual." And when Lionel James, also of *The Times*, turned up to cover the naval side of the Russo-Japanese War in a chartered steamer fitted up as a mobile radio station, the Japanese agreed to allow him to operate providing he carried with him an intelligence officer of the Japanese navy. In other words, in return for permission to report naval engagements the *Times* ship also acted as a spy for the Japanese.

Eventually most of the correspondents packed up and returned home, defeated by censorship, until finally only Barzini and two news agency men remained. But while the agency men had to stay at Japanese headquarters, Barzini was free to roam the forty-mile front during the Battle of Mukden, a ghastly month-long battle of attrition, won by the Japanese at a cost of 71,000 casualties to the Russians' 85,000. Barzini worked in terrible conditions, the cold often freezing the ink in his pen. But he sensed he was witnessing a major moment in history, and he filled 700 pages of notes, drew dozens of maps, took hundreds of photographs. (The book he wrote is still studied in Japanese staff schools.) Militarily, Barzini was right. The war saw significant tactical changes resulting from increased fire-power, the growth of artillery, and even the use—by the Japanese—of a crude form of poison gas. Politically, the war had tremendous impact. Asia stirred from one end to another—an unknown and non-European race had scattered a European colonial power; the old-time glory and greatness of Asia seemed destined to return. Alone among the correspondents, Barzini understood the historical importance of what he had seen.

The Russo-Japanese War marked the eclipse of the Golden Age. It had been a bloody period of history. Life had counted for little when measured against empire, glory, and mass circulations. If most correspondents had shown little perception or historical insight, at least their news reporting had been accurate, and so one would like to believe that their graphic description of man's inhumanity to man, reaching as it did a larger audience than ever before, influenced public feeling against war. But, apart from MacGahan's reports on the Turkish atrocities in Bulgaria and Creelman's dispatch on the Japanese behaviour in Port Arthur, there is no evidence that it did. On the contrary, it could be argued that the war correspondent in this period was only providing what the public wanted to read. Far from his arousing pacifist sentiment, the opposite could occur, as witness Hearst's whipping up of American sentiment in favour of the United States' intervention in Cuba and his justification of American military atrocities in the Philippines.

To readers in London or New York, distant battles in strange places must have seemed unreal, and the Golden Age style of war reporting—where guns flash, cannons thunder, the struggle rages, the general is brave, the soldiers are gallant, and their bayonets make short work of the enemy—only added to the illusion that it was all a thrilling adventure story. Certainly when their own country was involved, as Britain was in South Africa, the attitude of the war correspondent and his readers was markedly different. Then the first trials of internal propaganda, which was to become such a powerful weapon in the First World War, and the patriotic hysteria that swept Britain had a strong influence on war reporting.

# Chapter Four

# Quite Another Game
# 1899–1902

It was only Smith-Dorrien's Brigade marching into Bloemfontein, but if it could have been passed, just as it was, down Piccadilly and the Strand it would have driven London crazy…Here are a clump of Highlanders, their workmanlike aprons in front, their keen faces burned black with months of the veldt. It is an honoured name that they bear on their shoulder-straps. "Good old Gordons!" I cried as they passed me. The sergeant glanced at the dirty enthusiast in the undershirt. "What cheer, matey!" he cried, and his men squared their shoulders and put a touch of ginger into their stride…What splendid fellows there are among them! Here is one who hails me; the last time I saw him we put on seventy runs together when they were rather badly needed, and here we are, partners in quite another game.

—Dr. A. Conan Doyle in *The Friend*,
Bloemfontein, April 4, 1900

The Boer War came to Britain at the high noon of her imperialism. The Victorian Englishman, excited by the lyricism of Rudyard Kipling, who captured, H. G. Wells said, "the very odours of Empire," was the most patriotic citizen in the world. With honesty and impartiality he ruled the greatest empire the world had known. Only when his right to govern was questioned did he call in the army, and then, from the mountain passes of the North-West Frontier to the upper reaches of the Nile, the natives trembled at England's might.

At home, few questioned force as an arm of policy, and there was none of that searching of conscience on the morality of killing for king and country that was to follow the First World War. In Victorian Britain war was a marvellous game, the greatest game of all, "the clash of sword and hollow reverberating clang of brazen buckler, the storm and wild joy of battle." Winston Churchill, in South Africa as a soldier-correspondent, wrote of troops moving up to the lines, a "ceaseless living stream...and before them a guiding star, the red gleam of war."[1]

Editors were quick to arouse public demand for news of the fight against the rebellious Boers, and they spent freely to get the best possible coverage.* All the stars of the craft headed south to write about a war that was expected to last only weeks. They included Dr. Conan Doyle, who combined the organising of field hospitals with a spot of patriotic descriptive writing not up to his Sherlock Holmes level; Bennett Burleigh of the *Daily Telegraph*, interested not in the issues but in getting yet another scoop; Angus Hamilton of *The Times*, a conscientious journalist who gave up the frustrating business of trying to tell the truth; Richard Harding Davis, who criticised the cavalier attitude of the British to the killing of Boers and as a result was expelled from his London club; George Warrington Steevens, who had made his name in the Sudan; Julian Ralph of *Collier's* and the *Daily Mail*, an uncritical Anglophile; A. B. ("Banjo") Patterson, an Australian poet who wrote poor jingoist verse modelled on Kipling's; and Kipling himself, worried at the early successes of the wily Boers and their leader Kruger, "cruel in the shadow, crafty in the sun."

They had much to report. This was the first time since the Crimean War that the British army was fighting other white men, and, crude farmers though the Boers might be, certain standards had to be maintained. No native troops were to be used,** and under all circumstances a high level of behaviour was expected. Soon correspondents were able to send back reports of the pluck, grit, and fighting qualities of the troops, of the chivalry shown on the battlefield, and, above all, of the absolutely splendid way the British officers were dying.

There was General Penn Symons, who had ignored warnings of the danger of standing on a hill to get a better view at the Battle of

---

* *The Times* had twenty correspondents at one stage, and carried excerpts from official dispatches as well.
** Not since Agincourt had Britain sent abroad an entirely white army.

Talana. Symons suddenly turned to his aide-de-camp and said, with the utmost calm, "I am severely, mortally, wounded in the stomach"—a perfectly accurate statement—and he died soon afterwards.[2] And there was Colonel G. E. Benson, who developed a successful system of surprise attack that involved forced night marches. With 178 of his men, Benson was overrun in a fight at Bakenlaagte and lost 161 dead or wounded. He refused medical attention for himself until his men had been treated, and then died murmuring to his second in command, "We shall do no more night marching. It is all day now. Good bye—God bless you."[3]

Stories like these sent a thrill through the Empire, and the *Morning Post*'s correspondent, F. D. Baillie, was able to write, apparently with no trace of embarrassment: "It is a good thing to be an Englishman. These foreigners start too quick and finish quicker."[4]

Another *Morning Post* correspondent in South Africa, Winston Churchill, then twenty-five years old, held similar views. Although Churchill had gone to South Africa as a war correspondent, he was a most unusual one, in that his main aim was not to report the war but to push on with the campaign of "self-advertisement" about which he had been so blatant in the Sudan.* Using an offer from the *Daily Mail* as a bargaining point, he dictated terms to his friend Oliver Borthwick of the *Morning Post* and settled on £1,000 for four months, plus £200 a month for any longer period, all expenses, and the option to retain copyright of his dispatches—remarkably generous terms. But from the beginning Churchill was unable to make up his mind whether he was primarily a soldier or a reporter.

Offered the chance of going on a British armoured train, he ignored a fellow correspondent's advice that he was being paid to report the war, not fight it, and went, because "I have a feeling, a sort of intuition, that if I go something will come of it." When the train was ambushed, he took an active part in directing the action against the Boers. He had, as he later freely admitted in his own account of the action, "taken with me, correspondent-status notwithstanding, my Mauser pistol," and he would have fired on the Boer who captured him had he not left the pistol on the side of the engine—"I thought that I could kill this man and after the treatment I had received I earnestly desired to do so. I put my hand

*He had offered the Reuters correspondent his story of the charge of the lancers at Omdurman on the condition that Reuters mentioned his name.

to my belt, the pistol was not there."[5]

Now, it was not unusual for war correspondents of this period to go armed, but in doing so in South Africa Churchill was risking both his life (the Boers would, on his own evidence, have been justified in shooting him out of hand) and the non-combatant status of the other correspondents. Churchill lied to the Boers, claiming that he had taken no part in the armoured-train action, so they eventually decided to treat him as a non-combatant, but—the most devastating irony of the affair—he escaped the day before news of this decision reached his gaolers. He made his way to Lourenço Marques, from where, on December 21, 1899, he sent to the *Morning Post* his famous dispatch: "I am very weak but I am free. I have lost many pounds but I am lighter in heart. I shall also avail myself of every opportunity from this moment to urge with earnestness an unflinching and uncompromising prosecution of the war."[6]

Now he persuaded General Sir Redvers Buller to give him a lieutenant's commission in the South African Light Horse, and, in contravention of a War Office ruling that no man should be both correspondent and soldier, he also persuaded the General to allow him to carry out both jobs. So in spite of criticism in the *Westminster Gazette*—"Mr Churchill's non-combatancy is indeed a mystery but one thing is clear: that he cannot have the best of both worlds"—that was just what Churchill succeeded in doing, to the anger and disgust of other correspondents.

As a soldier he rode with his irregulars and showed his mother, Lady Randolph Churchill, around the front. As a correspondent he followed the troops (using a wagon with a raised floor, underneath which rested a two-foot layer of the best tinned provisions and alcoholic stimulants London could provide) and wrote some not very accurate dispatches. All the while he was "searching in the carelessness of youth for every scrap of adventure, experience or copy." He compiled a book, *London to Ladysmith via Pretoria*, from his reports and successfully demanded an advance of £2,000. On his return to Britain he went on a lecture tour, receiving £100 a night. He later extended the tour to the United States and Canada, so that when it all ended he calculated that he had made from his South African adventure no less than £10,000.

How does Churchill finally emerge? There is little doubt that much of the criticism of him at the time was motivated by envy. He wrote statements about the war that few wanted to hear—"It is foolish not to recognise that we are fighting a formidable and terrible adversary...The individual Boer mounted in suitable country, is worth from three to five regular soldiers." Although he was usually indifferent to Boer casualties—"We had a good bag today, ten killed, seventeen wounded"—he did, on one occasion, recognise the futility of it all. He had seen a dead Boer, a grey-haired officer, clutching a letter from his wife, lying next to a seventeen-year-old boy shot through the heart. "Ah, horrible war," he wrote, "amazing medley of the glorious and the squalid, the pitiful and the sublime, if modern men of light and leading saw your face closer, simple folk would see it hardly ever."[7]

His main shortcomings were his lust for publicity and his dual role as soldier-correspondent. His attitude to the war-correspondent side of this split profession is best summed up in a statement he made during a House of Commons debate in 1944. Churchill, then Prime Minister, admitted that he had ordered stricter censorship of correspondents' reports from Italy and added, "Such words as 'desperate' ought not to be used about a position in a battle when they are false. Still less should they have been used if they were true." An MP asked whether Churchill, as a former war correspondent, would not have fiercely resented a policy by which his reports were dictated by generals in the field. Churchill replied, "I should not have been allowed in South Africa where I was a war correspondent for some time to say, for instance, that the position in Ladysmith was desperate."[8] Given these strictures, with which he obviously agreed, Churchill's reputation as a war correspondent in South Africa clicks into place. He saw South Africa through a soldier's eyes, and this inhibited him from all but general criticisms about the prosecution of the war.

There was a lot to criticise. Years of cheap victories over natives had ill prepared the British army for an action against the intelligent and highly motivated enemy it found in South Africa. If the British army staff had been of a higher calibre, it might have recognised earlier that the Boers could not be easily defeated by conventional methods. But the generals were at the best bumbling, and at the worst approaching lunacy.

What are we to make of Kitchener, brought up in Ireland to sleep under newspapers because his father considered blankets unhealthy, the man who had looted the Mahdi's tomb and carried off the head in an old paraffin can as a trophy, a tactician with no idea of the nature of the Boers—"savages with a thin white veneer"—a general who collapsed and took to bed with his nerves "all gone to pieces" when told of a defeat? What are we to decide about General Lord Frederick Roberts, the commander-in-chief in 1900, who packed up and went home saying the war was won and over—only to see it go on for another year and a half?

And, above all, what are we to make of Colonel Robert Baden-Powell, the hero of the siege of Mafeking? It is worth pausing at Baden-Powell and his siege, because the legend that grew up around him represents one of the most serious failures on the part of the war correspondents in South Africa. Baden-Powell, when ordered to raise two regiments in Bechuanaland and Rhodesia to harass the enemy's rear and flank, marched his force, instead, into Mafeking, a small, dusty, tin-roofed town, only eight miles from the Transvaal border, and allowed the Boers to surround him, afterwards saying he was prepared to "sit tight." Communications, including the post and the telegraph, remained open during the 217-day siege, and Baden-Powell began sending out a series of plucky messages that caused shivers of admiration all over the Empire. Even now, no one can accuse Baden-Powell of having lied in these dispatches. On the contrary, he stuck strictly to the truth— "One or two small field guns shelling the town. Nobody cares"; or "All well. Four hours bombardment. One dog killed." But a news-hungry public, desperate for reassurance after the war's early set-backs, took these literal truths as typical British stiff-upper-lip understatements, and the more casual, gay, and off-hand Baden-Powell's dispatches became, the more the world believed that Mafeking must be suffering dreadfully.

There were five war correspondents in Mafeking throughout most of the siege—Angus Hamilton of *The Times*, Emerson Neilly of the *Pall Mall Gazette*, F. D. Baillie of the *Morning Post*, Vere Stent of Reuters, and E.G. Parslow of the *Daily Chronicle*. They could have told the truth about Mafeking in the earlier stages—Hamilton tried; his office ignored him—but once Baden-Powell's version had caught the public imagination, they decided that the myth was a better story than the facts and went wholeheartedly along with it.

Yet what a story they could have written if they had had the courage. Baden-Powell came from one of those upper-middle-class English backgrounds where it is difficult to draw the line between eccentricity and psychosis. At school at Charterhouse he was known as "Old Bathing Towel." During service in India with the Thirteenth Hussars he specialised in pig-sticking, polo, musketry, drawing caricatures with his right or left hand, singing comic songs, and playing practical jokes. When the siege at Mafeking was under way, he utilised these talents to maintain morale. He organised cricket on Sundays, which scandalised the devout Boers, ran sports carnivals, was judge at a baby show, captained a polo team, acted in sketches, recited and sang, ran a billiards tournament, dressed up as a circus ring-master in white-tie and tails, wielded a whip nearly thirty feet long. He carried this make-belief world over into his military operations. Through a megaphone he shouted orders to non-existent troops about non-existent attacks on the enemy lines, and squads of men were made to walk around the perimeter of the town pretending to get through imaginary wire fences. He marked out non-existent mine fields and ordered his men to parade with home-made lances carried against the skyline to make the Boers think reinforcements had arrived. He sent out fake signals for the Boers to capture and constantly invited them to surrender. He was an obsessive whistler and kept up his own morale by warbling operatic airs and music-hall ditties from morning to night. Only the incompetence of the besieging force prevented the town from being overrun and Baden-Powell's theatricals from being ended for ever. The Boers' shells were either duds or ineffective, and when they themselves attacked they never pressed home their advantage. Like Baden-Powell, they, too, decided to "sit it out."

There is evidence that Baden-Powell realised this. Early on, he called all the war correspondents together and told them he would not permit criticism of the conduct of the siege or of the officers, "because the correspondents could not be conversant with all the facts on which to base their opinions."[9] From then on he censored their dispatches personally. Hamilton was able to get out a message, which *The Times* published on October 25, 1899, insisting on the smallness of the operation, but, compared with Baden-Powell's crisp reports listing animal casualties and the state of Mafeking's morale, it was poor reader material and the public ignored it.

Yet while the correspondents dined each night "with no small degree of luxury" and the officers sat down on Christmas Day to an eight-course meal that included oysters and sucking-pig, the natives in Mafeking were starving. Baden-Powell had initiated a system of rationing for them, which involved their paying three-pence for a pint bowl of horsemeat soup. Few had enough money, and by the later stages of the siege many were dying of hunger. Hamilton accused Baden-Powell of adopting a policy of starvation to drive the natives out of the town, but he found *The Times* reluctant to use the story. When it was suggested that the natives have a share of the white man's still-plentiful rations, Baden-Powell issued an order that anyone hearing the idea repeated should "apply the toe of the boot." Emerson Neilly of the *Pall Mall Gazette* was so horrified at the conditions of the natives that he wrote a vivid descriptive piece—unfortunately, not for his newspaper, but for a book, published when it was too late to be effective.

> I saw them fall down on the veldt and lie where they had fallen, too weak to go on their way…words could not portray the scene of misery; five or six hundred human frameworks of both sexes and all ages, from tender infant upwards…standing in lines, awaiting turn to crawl painfully up to the soup kitchen where the food was distributed. Having obtained the horse soup, fancy them tottering off a few yards and sitting down to wolf up the life-fastening mass…They fed like outcast curs. They went farther than the mongrel…Day after day I heard outside my door continuous thumping sounds. They were caused by the living skeletons who, having eaten all that was outside the bones smashed them up with stones and devoured what marrow they could find. They looked for bones on the dust heaps, on the roads, everywhere.[10]

But the evidence is that a correspondent determined enough could have got a dispatch like that through the enemy lines and back to his editor. A Reuters correspondent, J. E. Pearson, rode from Capetown into Mafeking, had a look around, and then rode out again.* Hellawell, the correspondent of the *Daily Mail*, rode in and out of "besieged" Mafeking for two months, getting his cables away regularly, until finally the Boers captured him. Churchill's aunt Lady Sarah Wilson, "the heroine of heroic Mafeking," "the good genius of the siege," who won Baden-Powell's admiration for her "splendid pluck," became the *Daily Mail*'s correspondent in Mafeking and succeeded in getting her stories out without much trouble. She even managed to receive a letter from Cecil Rhodes, besieged in Kimberley, which does not say much for the Boer "ring of steel" around both towns.

When it became clear that the war was not going to be over quickly, the division of opinion in Britain became deeper. Ranged against the war were a Stop-the-War Committee, W. T. Stead with his famous pamphlet *Shall I Slay My Brother Boer?*, the Liberal

---

*His plan to do this regularly went astray. On his way back to Capetown, he sent off a message to Baden-Powell by pigeon, which, instead of flying to Mafeking, landed in a Boer camp, where it was shot and Pearson's incriminating message captured.

leader Lloyd George—"the war is an outrage perpetrated in the name of human freedom"—and the *Manchester Guardian*, the *Morning Leader*, and the *Star*. The fact that the nation was not wholeheartedly behind them caused some bitterness among the troops, and so the government did everything it could to mobilise public opinion for queen and country. This involved encouraging racialism and jingoism, in their most virulent forms, and creating animosity against the enemy with the timeless ploy of the atrocity story. In both these fields, the newspapers, the church, and the war correspondents played their part.

*The Times* wrote leaders peppered with phrases like "the common man of Empire," "the fundamental grit of the breed," "the unanalysable qualities that have made the Empire." This was to be expected. *The Times* had lost any claim to be able to view the issues objectively after the involvement of some of its senior staff in the Jameson Raid—the plot to overthrow Kruger. Only very suspect testimony before a Parliamentary Select Committee saved the paper from being totally compromised. L. S. Amery, its chief correspondent in South Africa, was not unsympathetic to the Boers— he spoke Afrikaans and was even an authorised correspondent with the Boer forces until General Petrus Joubert, their commander, threw him out—but he was deeply concerned with the war's effect on Britain and warned that what was occurring was "the greatest political event in the history of the British Empire since the conclusion of the Napoleonic Wars."

Kipling, in South Africa working on *The Friend*, an army newspaper run by four war correspondents in Bloemfontein, wrote his "Song of the White Men," a stronger version of "The White Man's Burden," with its demand for "freedom or war." The church in Britain contributed a poem of dreadful rhyme and jingoist sentiment about a fourteen-year-old bugler who had lost his bugle at Tugela, and the Dean of St. Paul's spoke of "the breed of Englishmen with its...traditional tenacity, its stubborn pluck."

When things were at their worst, the Queen said, "I will have no depression in my house."[11] The editor of the *Daily Chronicle* was dismissed for failing to reflect the patriotic sentiment of his readers. Punch showed a drawing of a baby saying his first word—"Bang!"— and Thos. Cook and Sons advertised a tour of the battlefields. The jingoists had their finest day when Mafeking was relieved. Reuters flashed the news to London at 9:17 P.M. on May 18, 1900, and Britain went mad. The celebrations lasted for five nights, and surpassed the victory celebrations of the First and Second World

Wars in size, intensity, and enthusiasm. Baden-Powell became the most popular English hero since Nelson, and a household name not only in Britain but also throughout the United States.*

In the field, the war correspondents could not help but sense the mood of the home front. This was obviously no time for debunking heroes, exposing incompetence, or describing the horrors of war. They wrote of a dog following its master into battle and staying by his body when he fell, of lucky escapes, of gallant charges and heroic retreats.

"Our indomitable soldiers walked erect and straight onward," wrote Burleigh. "Not Rome in her palmiest days ever possessed more devoted sons. As the gladiators marched proud and beaming to meet death, so the British soldiers doomed to die saluted, and then, and with alacrity, stepped forward to do their duty—glory or the grave."[12]

The grave it frequently was. The British trenches at Spion Kop were piled with British dead three deep and more—"an acre of massacre," J. B. Atkins, Russell's biographer, wrote later. But photographs showing the slaughter, caused by a staff blunder, were not published in Britain, because the newspapers considered them "revolting Boer propaganda," and correspondents played down the extent of British casualties.

The Boers, in their turn, were also slaughtered. In a raid, British troops overran a Boer trench, bayoneting the defenders or decapitating them with the sword. Only one war correspondent, Emerson Neilly of the *Pall Mall Gazette*, wrote about the most important element of the affair, and he excused it: "The work was largely held by boys who, of course, had to take their chance with the men in the massacre. It is not too much to the taste of your soldier to bayonet a lad of thirteen or fourteen; but if any shame attaches to the killing of the youngsters it must rest on the shoulders of those fathers who brought them there."[13]

No war correspondent reported at the time that some 300 Australian troops had mutinied because a British officer had told them that they were "a lot of wasters and white-livered curs," and the story did not come out until the Australian government intervened to get the mutineers pardoned, instead of hanged. No one exposed that many of the troops coming out from Britain could neither ride

* He went on to become a major-general, founder of the Boy Scout movement, and in the pre-First World War period a spy. Sent to Dalmatia, he "scouted" and sketched a fort disguised as an eccentric English butterfly collector. He died in Kenya in 1941.

nor shoot. And the scandal of military hospitals that had no bandages, no cots, no sheets, no pillows, no measuring glasses, and no thermometers was revealed not by British war correspondents, but by a British MP, William Burdett-Coutts, and an Australian correspondent, A. G. Hales.* Hales wrote of "criminal neglect of the most simple laws of sanitation" and described camps where no latrines were dug and no supervision exercised over the men's health. "The so-called medical staff looked on," Hales wrote, "and puffed their cigarettes and talked under their eyeglasses."[14]

Burdett-Coutts had had experience in military-hospital administration in the Russo-Turkish War, as a special commissioner for the Turkish Compassionate Fund. Hearing rumours of the poor conditions in South Africa, he went out there, in January 1900, to see for himself how British sick and wounded were being cared for. He was so shocked that he wrote for *The Times* a series of highly critical articles, including one on June 27 in which he said that the men were "dying like flies for want of adequate attention." On his return, he took up the matter in Parliament and was successful in having a Royal Commission appointed. The commissioners reported that Burdett-Coutts' strictures were justified and that the army medical corps was "wholly insufficient in staff and equipment for such a war."

As a result of poor sanitation and primitive hospital facilities, of the 22,000 men the British lost in the war 14,000 died of sickness, rather than from enemy action—a shocking indictment of the medical corps and of the correspondents who failed to expose its inadequacies.

True, the correspondents worked under harsh and repressive censorship. One censor used to throw correspondents' dispatches straight into the wastepaper bin without bothering to read them, and the chief censor told one of them, "There is only one thing I will allow you to write today—a description of the new Union Jack which has just been run up over headquarters."[15] Burleigh wrote bitter stories about censorship, only to see them cut to pieces and the criticism struck out. The point about censorship is that while it can prevent a correspondent from sending a story the military does not want published, it cannot force him to send a false or exaggerated one.

---

* Kipling was so angry about the state of military hospitals that he loaded a handcart with bandages and delivered them to a hospital in Capetown, only to be told that army regulations prohibited the acceptance of supplies from an individual. Kipling dumped the bandages on the hospital doorstep.

Yet throughout the latter stages of the war the British press carried a stream of reports from its correspondents of Boers murdering wounded men, massacring pro-British civilians, flogging natives, and executing Boers who wanted to surrender. Since, in most cases, the stories contained little evidence to support the charges, an artist would be employed to render a highly realistic version of the atrocity. There was virtually no limit to such invention. An early newsreel film shown to British audiences depicts a Red Cross tent under fire from the Boers while brave British doctors, nurses, and orderlies try to treat a wounded soldier. The film was a fake shot with actors on Hampstead Heath, a suburb of London.[16]

Some correspondents went too far. Edgar Wallace, who had gone out to South Africa as a medical orderly and had then succeeded Julian Ralph as the *Daily Mail*'s correspondent, wrote such vivid atrocity stories on such flimsy evidence that the British government told him to tone down his reporting. The *Mail* could have argued that Wallace was merely keeping pace with those atrocity stories appearing in European newspapers like the *Tribunal de Genève*, which claimed that Kipling, on an assignment with Burleigh, had taken part in the murder of a civilian near Karee Siding, or the Vienna *Neue Freie Presse*, which regularly carried anti-British stories.

The anti-Boer atrocity story should be set against *The Times*' history of the war, published in 1906, when passions had cooled a little. It said: "In the moment of their triumph the Boers behaved with the same unaffected kindheartedness...which they displayed after most of their victories. Although exultant they were not insulting. They fetched water and blankets for the wounded and treated prisoners with every consideration."[17]

British concentration camps were a different matter. Kitchener's policy of burning the farms of Boers who had broken their parole not to fight again, or who had supplied or harboured fighting men, left him with the problem of accommodating the homeless women and children. He decided to intern them, along with the women and children of all Boers who were on commando. It is likely that he would have caused less trouble for himself if he had left them all where they were, to fend for themselves as best they could. Instead, he packed them into tents in camps, apparently not realising the difficulties he was creating. The crowded tents, foul water, shortage of clothes, lack of proper sanitary facilities in the heat, and an outbreak of measles sent the death rate soaring. At Bloemfontein, the figure was 383 per thousand adults and 500 per thousand children. It now became safer to be in the Boer army than to be a civilian. This was one story any war correspondent worth his passage should have written. Instead, it was left to Emily Hobhouse, a Quaker, who was leader of the South African Conciliation Committee. In a report to members of Parliament, she described conditions in a camp she had visited: "…a six month old baby [is] gasping its life out on its mother's knee. Next [tent]: a child recovering from measles sent back from hospital before it could walk, stretched on the ground white and wan. Next a girl of twenty one lay dying on a stretcher. The father…kneeling beside her, while his wife was watching a child of six also dying and one of about five drooping. Already this couple had lost three children."[18]

The leader of the Opposition, Sir Henry Campbell-Bannerman, raised the matter in the House of Commons and spoke of Britain's "methods of barbarism." German newspapers snapped up the story, referring with relish to the British "*Hunnen in Sud Afrika*." But many British newspapers were quick to justify Kitchener's actions. The *St. James's Gazette* wrote: "Women and children are frequently employed to carry messages. Of course they must be included in military measures and transported or despatched…. We have undertaken to conquer the Transvaal and if nothing will make sure except the removal of the Dutch inhabitants, they must be removed, men, women, and children."[19] Kitchener defended himself with "the inmates are far better looked after in every way than they are in their own homes." In spite of all this, the government had to appoint a Commission of Enquiry and eventually carry out reforms.

The Boers were less interested in capitalising on the exposure of British concentration camps (they rather liked the idea that their enemy had to expend rations and supplies in this manner) than in the possibility that the British might arm the natives against them—"an enormous act, the wickedness of which no man can foresee." British policy in this respect was in line with the Boers'. Having only recently clashed with armed Zulus, they, too, saw the danger to their position in Africa if the natives, instead of remaining spectators at battles fought on their territory, decided to take part.

With few exceptions, correspondents ignored these wider issues. One exception was Richard Harding Davis, who felt that imperialism's days were numbered and that the Boers, fighting against odds for their independence, deserved to have their case and their struggle reported. He loved England and, despite his views, might well have remained with the British troops, but trouble with the censor convinced him that he should join the Boers. From Pretoria he wrote: "As I see it, it has been a Holy War, this Burgher Crusade, and their motives are as fine as any that called a 'minute man' from his farm, or sent a Knight of the Cross to die for it in Palestine."[20] This caused much offence in Britain, and cost Davis membership in his London club as well as many friends.

George Warrington Steevens wrote a good description of the aftermath of battle: "In the rain-blurred light of the lantern…the doctor, the one doctor, toiled buoyantly on. Cutting up their clothes with scissors, feeling with light firm fingers over torn chest or thigh, cunningly slipping round the bandage, tenderly covering up the crimson ruin of strong men—hour by hour, man by man, he toiled on."[21]

Burleigh, though sometimes flowery, was frank when he could avoid the censor. When the British army streamed into Ladysmith, he rushed to the telegraph and persuaded the operator to send for him a message beginning: "We are beaten and it means investment. We shall all be locked up."[22] Unlike the other correspondents, Burleigh could see no sense in remaining in Ladysmith for the siege, and while the others were keeping diaries, which they later published to a world soon bored by volume after volume of recollections, Burleigh joined Lord Roberts on the western campaign and managed to get a scoop on the peace talks.

The rest of the correspondents either were crushed by censorship, joined the atrocities campaign, or were incompetent and wrote nonsense; the *Daily Mail* said at one stage that the Boers were determined to have Kruger crowned at Westminster. They contradicted each other. The reader could believe either that "the Boers are running short of ammunition" or "the Boers are stated on good authority to have ammunition and stores for at least five years."[23] And when they had to explain why the war they had said would be over quickly was dragging bloodily on, they blamed the easiest target: the wily Boer, with his unsporting guerrilla tactics. The honest, straightforward, upright-in-battle Englishman had been foiled by the cunning Colonial. "Everywhere the slimy, slippery ranchers and tavern keepers and merchants welcomed us with the heartiest of speech and always we were fooled by it," Julian Ralph wrote. "Half the people or more in all that great region were 'out on commando'. No man except a pro-Boer or a born Boer could have been where we found these double-faced people with their Judas-like pretence of friendship…It was self-evident that they must have been siding with our enemies…We were fooled! Fooled! Fooled!"[24]

Britain was fooled, but it was her own fault. She never had a full and accurate picture of what was happening in South Africa. The correspondents blamed the military for this, claiming that censorship kept the public ignorant. The military blamed the correspondents and the public: "The interest of the general public in a narrative of a campaign is unfortunately in inverse ratio to their historical value."[25] There is little doubt that the Boer War offered correspondents a remarkable opportunity. They could have seen that the imposition of imperial rule requires an ever-increasing amount of force, and that when this force is faced with a determined nationalist sentiment the point must eventually be reached at which the expending of it is no longer worth the return. They could have recorded the success of an unorthodox military strategy—guerrilla warfare. The Boer, neither completely civilian nor completely a soldier, alternating between tending his farm and fighting the British, lightly armed with an accurate repeating rifle, mobile, able to live for long periods on strips of dried meat and a little water, drawing on the hidden support of his countrymen, unafraid to flee when the battle was not in his favour, choosing his ground and his time for attack, was more than a match for any regular army, no matter what its strength. Kitchener's policy of retaliation, with its farm-burning, concentration camps, and collective punishment, was as ineffective as a similar policy employed in Vietnam sixty-five years later.

The political importance of the war was underestimated; only now are its errors and tragedies reaching full realisation. And despite the swarms of war correspondents—and military observers from nearly every major power in the world—the main military lessons of the war went unnoticed. The British soldier learned the value of accurate rifle fire, but the only conclusions drawn from the Boers' use of trenches proved to be false ones. James Barnes, an American war correspondent, saw the truth: that trenches too long to be outflanked would lead to stalemate. But he thought this too obvious a point to drive home, and he wrote with certainty that trench warfare was "a thing of the past except in wooded country or where all preliminary movements are concealed." Events were soon to prove how wrong he was.

# Chapter Five

# The Last War
# 1914–1918

This, the greatest of all wars, is not just another war—it is the last war!

—H. G. Wells in *The War That Will End War*

The last war, during the years of 1915, 1916, 1917 was the most colossal, murderous, mismanaged butchery that has ever taken place on earth. Any writer who said otherwise lied. So the writers either wrote propaganda, shut up, or fought.

—Ernest Hemingway in *Men at War*

———

T he First World War was like no other war before or since. It began with the promise of splendour, honour, and glory. It ended as a genocidal conflict on an unparalleled scale, a meaningless act of slaughter that continued until a state of exhaustion set in because no one knew how to stop it.

At first, the sacrifices, which all wars demand, were offered only too willingly. "My only regret is that the opportunity has been denied me to repay you for the lavish kindness and devotedness which you have always shown me," Lieutenant Glyn Morgan wrote to his father two days before he was killed in action. "Now, however, it may be that I have done so in the struggle between Life and Death, between England and Germany, Liberty and Slavery. In any case, I shall have done my duty in my little way…goodbye dearest of fathers." Walter Limmer, a student from Leipzig, later to die of wounds, wrote to his mother: "This hour is one such as seldom strikes in the life of a nation and it is so marvellous and moving as to be in itself sufficient compensation for many sufferings and sacrifices."[1]

But when the generals, commanding larger armies than the world had ever seen before, could find no way of using them except as fodder for the machine guns, a mood of disillusion with the pointlessness of it all set in. Siegfried Sassoon, in his poem "The General," expressed it perhaps best of all.

> *"Good morning; Good morning!" the General said*
> *When we met him last week on our way to the line.*
> *Now the soldiers he smiled at are most of 'em dead,*
> *And we're cursing his staff for incompetent swine.*
> *"He's a cheery old card," grunted Harry to Jack*
> *As they slogged up to Arras with rifle and pack.*
>
> . . . . . . . . . . . . . . . . . .
>
> *But he did for them both by his plan of attack.*[2]

To enable the war to go on, the people had to be steeled for further sacrifices, and this could not be done if the full story of what was happening on the Western Front was known. And so began a great conspiracy. More deliberate lies were told than in any other period of history, and the whole apparatus of the state went into action to suppress the truth.

In Britain, under the Defence of the Realm Act, a system of censorship was created so severe that its legacy lingers today.* The willingness of newspaper proprietors to accept this control and their co-operation in disseminating propaganda brought them the rewards of social rank and political power. But it also undermined public faith in the press.

A large share of the blame for this must rest with the British war correspondents. They were in a position to know more than most men of the nature of the war of attrition on the Western Front, yet they identified themselves absolutely with the armies in the field; they protected the high command from criticism, wrote jauntily

---

* The government can examine incoming and outgoing cables and can censor newspapers.

about life in the trenches, kept an inspired silence about the slaughter, and allowed themselves to be absorbed by the propaganda machine. Some of them had sufficient decency to feel shame at the way they were discrediting their craft, and when the post-war revulsion set in, one of them, Sir Philip Gibbs (who had been knighted for his services), was able to look back and attempt an explanation. "Nobody believed us. Though some of us wrote the truth from the first to the last—*apart from the naked realism of horrors and losses, and criticism of the facts*, which did not come within the liberty of our pen [emphasis added]."[3]

Perhaps the war correspondents of the First World War were to be pitied. Propaganda dates back 2,400 years, to Sun-tzu's *The Art of War*, but the First World War saw its first use in an organised, scientific manner. War correspondents were among its first victims.

For several weeks before the outbreak of war in August 1914, Britain's attention had been fixed on the Irish troubles. To the ordinary Englishman, apathetic to the Continent for two generations, the rumblings across the Channel passed almost unnoticed. Even among the men of power, aware of what was happening, there was a strong section of opinion bitterly against Britain's being dragged into a European conflict. The financier Lord Rothschild told *The Times*' city editor that he was "hounding the country into war." The Free Churches passed an anti-war resolution. The professors and Fellows of Cambridge signed a petition in favour of neutrality. The *Manchester Guardian* carried a full-page advertisement announcing the formation of a league to stop war, and there was a huge anti-war demonstration in Trafalgar Square. Bishops, mayors, and businessmen signed manifestoes urging Britain to keep out. The *Manchester Guardian*, the *Labour Leader*, the *Daily News*, and citizens of the stature of Ramsay MacDonald, Keir Hardie, Thomas Hardy, and Gilbert Murray all protested against Britain's being involved in a European war. When the Cabinet had its way and war was declared on August 4, liberal and nonconformist England demanded a moral reason for fighting. The government suddenly had to face the fact that it lacked that most essential element for successfully waging war: the wholehearted support of the nation. What could be done about it?

The professional army posed no difficulty—apart from switching the minds of the service chiefs to thinking of Germany as the enemy instead of France! But the civilians, who would have to supply recruits for the front and for the war industries, who would have to bear the sacrifices of war without complaints that might spread dissension and discouragement—how could they be united behind the war effort? From a faltering start, with a series of appeals to purely nationalistic interests, a propaganda machine developed that became the envy of the world. Beginning with a Parliamentary War Aims Committee and a small department at Wellington House in the office of the Insurance Commissioners—financed from revenue for "HM Foreign and Other Secret Services"—Britain by the end of the war had created a propaganda organisation that became the model on which Goebbels based that of the Germans some twenty years later.

The Germans never recovered from their initial set-back, were never able to efface the impression that they were the aggressors, were never able to popularise so striking an epithet as "Hun" or "Boche," and throughout the war referred bitterly to the Allies as "the All-Lies," to Reuters as "the fabricator of War Lies," and to Lord Northcliffe, proprietor of *The Times* and the *Daily Mail* and the director of propaganda in enemy countries, as "the Minister of Lying." The Germans were particularly inept at handling "human interest" cases, like that of Edith Cavell, a matron at a hospital in Brussels. When they executed her on October 12, 1915, they handed the Allies a ready-made atrocity story—"cold-blooded murder...poor English girl shot for housing refugees...the greatest crime in history"[4]—which was sent all over the world. Yet the Germans could have quite justifiably presented Miss Cavell as an enemy citizen who had freely confessed to helping Allied servicemen to escape under cover of her mission as a nurse, an act she knew to be punishable by death. The French had *already* shot one woman for exactly the same offence and were to shoot another eight for other capital offences before the end of the war. Given German bungling of this degree, there was more than enough material for the campaign to mobilise the animosity of Englishmen against Germany and thus to weld the nation into a fighting whole.

The war was made to appear one of defence against a menacing aggressor. The Kaiser was painted as a beast in human form. (In a single report on September 22, 1914, the *Daily Mail* succeeded in referring to him as a "lunatic," a "barbarian," a "madman," a "monster," a "modern judas," and a "criminal monarch.") The Germans were portrayed as only slightly better than the hordes of Genghis Khan, rapers of nuns, mutilators of children, and destroyers of civilisation. Once the commitment to war had been made, an overwhelming majority of the nation's political and intellectual leaders joined this propaganda campaign. Prime Minister Asquith, using the technique of atrocity confirmation by sweeping generalisation, told the House of Commons, on April 27, 1915, "We shall not forget this horrible record of calculated cruelty and crime." Bonar Law, the Colonial Secretary, referring to British patriotism, told an American correspondent, "It is as well to have it properly stirred by German frightfulness." Northcliffe told his editors, "The Allies must never be tired of insisting that they were the victims of a deliberate aggression." Even liberals swung behind the war. H. G. Wells decided that war was inevitable because of the wickedness of Germany, but that out of war would spring a lasting peace. This led him to coin the phrase "the war that will end war," which was to haunt him for the rest of his life.*

In their sweep through Belgium, the Germans caused the deaths of some 5,000 civilians.** The Allies set out to turn this into a deliberate campaign of terror, torture, sacrilege, and barbarism. The Bureau de la Presse, which controlled war news in France, and which had been financed at the outbreak of war with 25 million gold francs from secret-service funds, disseminated atrocity stories at such a rate that the French press ceased to put individual headings on them and, simply ran them week after week under the same headline: LES ATROCITÉS ALLEMANDES.

British newspapers lent their prestige to the campaign. The *Financial News*, in what now seems an unbelievable editorial, said on June 10, 1915, that the Kaiser had ordered German airmen to make special efforts to kill King Albert's children, that double rewards were paid to German submarine crews for sinking ships carrying women and children, and that the Kaiser had personally ordered the torturing of three-year-old children, specifying the tortures to be inflicted.***

A committee of lawyers and historians under the chairmanship of Lord Bryce, a former ambassador to the United States, produced a report, which was translated into thirty languages, in which it was

---

* A few maintained an anti-war stance, at considerable cost. Bertrand Russell was dismissed from his post as a lecturer in mathematics at Cambridge, was deprived of his passport and prevented from addressing public meetings, and spent six months in gaol for writing a seditious article.

** They were shot as guerrilla fighters, as hostages, or simply because they got in the way of a victorious advancing army in which not every soldier was a saint.

*** Hardly more believable was the *Norddeutsche Allgemeine Zeitung* of December 1, 1914, which said that Gurkha and Sikh troops liked to sneak across the lines at night to slit German throats and drink the blood.

stated that the Germans had systematically murdered, outraged, and violated innocent men, women, and children in Belgium. "Murder, lust, and pillage," the report said, "prevailed over many parts of Belgium on a scale unparalleled in any war between civilised nations during the last three centuries." The report gave titillating details of how German officers and men had publicly raped twenty Belgian girls in the market place at Liège, how eight German soldiers had bayoneted a two-year-old child, and how another had sliced off a peasant girl's breasts in Malines. Bryce's signature added considerable weight to the report, and it was not until after the war that several unsatisfactory aspects of the Bryce committee's activities emerged. The committee had not personally interviewed a single witness. The report was based on 1,200 depositions, mostly from Belgian refugees, taken by twenty-two barristers in Britain. None of the witnesses were placed on oath, their names were omitted (to prevent reprisals against their relatives), and hearsay evidence was accepted at full value. Most disturbing of all was the fact that, although the depositions should have been filed at the Home Office, they had mysteriously disappeared, and no trace of them has been found to this day.[5] Finally, a Belgian commission of enquiry in 1922, when passions had cooled, failed markedly to corroborate a single major allegation in the Bryce report. By then, of course, the report had served its purpose. Its success in arousing hatred and condemnation of Germany makes it one of the most successful propaganda pieces of the war.

By now, even the churches, bound by Christian teaching to condemn war in general, were able to approve this particular war, because "civilisation is at issue." The fact that the Kaiser had told his people to "go to church and kneel before God and pray for his help for our gallant army" caused no concern. Clearly, God would be able to discern the essential difference between Christian Englishmen and Christian Germans.

Under the influence of a nation-wide campaign to rally the forces of good against the forces of evil ("there are only two divisions in the world today," Kipling wrote, "human beings and Germans"),[6] the nation swung behind the war effort. The call went out to Empire—"our common history, our common language, our one King and Emperor." The war, from being a European affair of no concern to Britain, had become a splendid crusade, a duty imposed on every man of honour.

As the war progressed, as mechanised slaughter reached a scale never before envisaged (nearly 10 million killed in the fighting or as a direct result of it, 21 million wounded), and as a rotting corpse on barbed wire became a symbol of a world gone mad, so the propaganda machine that had made possible the transition from peace to war multiplied like a tumour on the brain of Europe. In Britain, the Parliamentary War Aims Committee and an improvised Press Bureau expanded into a Department of Information and finally a Ministry of Information (headed by Lord Beaverbrook) with so many sections, often bitter rivals of each other, that it is difficult to sort them all out even today.* The government had realised at an early stage that the ideal recruiting ground for propagandists was from among the most powerful newspaper proprietors and editors (although some historians and a few literary men also excelled). The editors of *The Times*, the *Express*, the *Daily Mail*, the *Evening Post*, and the *Chronicle* and the managing director of Reuters all did their bit. (Reuters placed its entire resources at the disposal of the Allied cause.)[7] Their skill lay in knowing how to get the war over to the man in the street, how to exploit his vocabulary, prejudices, and enthusiasms. They were not hampered by what Dr. Johnson termed "needless scrupulosity," they had a feeling for words and moods, and they knew that the public was not convinced by logic but seduced by stories. The German ambassador to the United States wrote to the Foreign Office in Berlin begging it to stop sending him arguments and send him some news.

At first the war correspondent did not fit into the propaganda effort. The newspaper proprietors were most anxious to cover the war, not only because of any connection a proprietor may have had with propaganda work, but also because war was good business for newspapers. "War not only creates a supply of news, but a demand for it," wrote an anonymous Northcliffe editor. "So deep-rooted is the fascination in war and all things pertaining to it…that a paper has only to be able to put up on its placard, A GREAT BATTLE for sales to mount up."[8] But when newspapers made a move to accredit correspondents to the British army in France they ran into an unexpected obstacle—Lord Kitchener.

Kitchener had hated war correspondents since the Sudan ("Out of my way, you drunken swabs") and was determined not to have them in France at any price. The Regular Army officers tended to agree with him. Northcliffe thought that the right approach might

---

* The task is not made easier by the fact that all propaganda files and records were deliberately destroyed after the war.

be to appoint a sporting man. Someone who could ride and knew horses might appeal to the cavalry officers who made up most of the general staff. Accordingly, he ordered the sporting editor of the *Daily Mail* to buy a horse and report at the War Office. The War Office told the editor that there were no immediate plans to accredit war correspondents and sent him off to exercise his horse in Hyde Park, where he met five or six other prospective correspondents doing the same thing.

*The Times* had exchanged one or two letters with the War Office, but nothing had been decided, and, like the other newspapers, it found itself at the outbreak of war without any coverage in Europe other than that provided by its regular correspondents. In Paris, their only source of information was the daily communiqués issued by the army. These were crisp, beautifully written, and punctually presented, but, unfortunately, they were closer to fiction than to fact, and while Germany's best armies were crashing through Belgium these communiqués continued to report French army advances on the Alsace-Lorraine frontier as if it would be only a matter of weeks before the Allies were in Berlin.

The Russians had a few correspondents—M. Lebeder of the Moscow daily *Russkoye Slovo* and M. Sukhovich of *Kievskaya Muysel*—but they were not allowed near the front while fighting was in progress. The Germans imposed military censorship at the start of the war. No German war correspondents were allowed near the front, and all news for home consumption was issued at a twice-weekly press conference between one GHQ staff officer and journalists. The items for this conference might theoretically have been vetted by six different censors and fifteen other bureaux, and the officer in charge followed standing instructions that included this stricture: "It is not so much the accuracy of news as its effect that matters." Germany did, however, rapidly evolve its own agency to report army operations for consumption abroad and had the admirable cheek to offer the reports on a subscriber basis to *The Times*. (This was before they began to be broadcast daily.) All these activities came under the Kriegpresseamt, the war press office, which in turn was under the direct control of the general staff. This office prepared and distributed periodicals, sponsored the production of pamphlets and books, co-ordinated censorship, and expanded the network of OKBs, or officer correspondents, who provided flesh for the basic military communiqués. So the only source of information for the German public was official. No criticism of the conduct of the war was permitted, and editors were told not only what facts could be printed, but also what views could be expressed on them.[9]

In Britain, it soon became clear that the British general staff had similar ideas on the role of the press. Censorship had been imposed on August 2, 1914, and Kitchener's only concession to informing the public about the military situation was to appoint an officer, Colonel Sir Ernest Swinton, to the staff of the commander-in-chief to write reports on the progress of the war. These, after being vetted by several generals and Kitchener himself, were released to the press under the by-line "Eyewitness." One editor is reported to have remarked, after reading Swinton's first, heavily censored dispatch, "Eye-wash would have been a better pseudonym."*

Swinton, a Royal Engineer, who had written two books before the war under the pseudonym "Ole Luk-Oie," did his best, but the aims he had set himself were, in order of importance: avoid helping the enemy; mislead him where possible; and tell the public only as much of the truth as is compatible with safety. How inadequate the resulting reports were is best demonstrated by quoting briefly from one of them, dated September 18, 1914. It describes the beginning of trench warfare on the Aisne.

> ...It may be said that along the greater part of our front the Germans have been driven back from the forward slopes on the north of the river. Their infantry are holding strong lines of trenches amongst and along the edges of the numerous woods which crown these slopes. These trenches are elaborately constructed ...Where our men are holding the forward edges of the high ground on the north side they are now strongly entrenched. They are well fed and in spite of the wet weather of the past week are cheerful and confident.

This was hardly the stuff to satisfy editors, and so they began to try influence, approaching powerful members of the government for help. Churchill, a former war correspondent and now First Lord of the Admiralty, seemed a natural choice, but he turned out to be as immovable as Kitchener: "A warship in action has no room for a journalist," Churchill ruled. Could he influence the army? "The war is going to be fought in a fog. The best place for correspondence about this war will be in London." Hungry for news,

---

* The French had a similar system. Each army had attached to it an *officier informateur*, whose job it was to collect all the dramatic episodes after a battle and then write a suitably discreet story for the government to send all over the world.

and yet faced with accepting the situation or organising an unofficial coverage of the front on their own initiative and risking the consequences, most newspapers decided to take the chance. There was no lack of volunteers to be correspondents. As Philip Gibbs wrote:

> There was a procession of literary adventurers up the steps of the buildings in the Street of Adventure—all those men who get lost somewhere between one war and another and come out with claims of ancient service on the battlefields of Europe when the smell of blood is scented from afar; and scores of new men of sporting instincts and jaunty confidence, eager to be 'in the middle of things', willing to go out on any terms so long as they could see a 'bit of fun', ready to take all risks.[10]

They were rather upset, these literary adventurers, that one of the first scoops of the war, the German invasion of Belgium, had been achieved not by an English correspondent, but by an American free-lance called Granville Fortescue. Fortescue, a soldier of fortune, had been a White House aide in Washington, a military observer in the Russo-Japanese War, an explorer in Venezuela, and a war correspondent in the Riff wars in Morocco for the British newspaper the *Standard*. He was in Belgium, living at Knocke, near Ostend, when war threatened, so he packed his family off to London and sent a telegram to the *Daily Telegraph* offering his services. He got no reply, but decided to go to Brussels to see if he could learn what was happening from the American Embassy. While waiting in the reception room, Fortescue overheard an excited conversation in Flemish between the embassy doorman and his brother. The brother, it appeared, had travelled all night to bring news that German motorcycle troops were already around his farm near Visé, in the eastern province of Liège. Fortescue got to a telephone, called the *Daily Telegraph* in London, identified himself, and filed a story about German scouting units inside Belgian territory. In its issue of August 3, 1914, the *Telegraph* splashed the story under the headline COUNTRY INVADED BY GERMAN TROOPS and by-lined it "From our own correspondent, Brussels, Monday." Within hours the *Daily Telegraph* was on to Fortescue at his Brussels hotel with furious reproaches: no other newspaper had the story, and the Foreign Office had denounced it as untrue. Fortescue insisted he was right, but felt that the *Telegraph* did not believe him. Twenty-four hours later the *Telegraph* telephoned Fortescue again, with fulsome apologies, and offered him a contract as a roving war correspondent. Britain had just declared war on Germany for violation of

Belgian neutrality. Fortescue's story had given the *Telegraph* a twenty-four-hour world scoop, and the other British papers were rushing men to Europe to try to catch up.

The difficulties were immense. Kitchener had ordered that any correspondent found in the field should be arrested, have his passport taken, and be expelled. The correspondents tried to get around this. *The Times*' man in Paris organised a group of "keen young men" to travel behind the Allied lines. They were well briefed: "Be as inconspicuous as possible…go over the ground by train to a certain point, then by bicycle or on foot…the principal thing is to keep rigidly away from the English, who take a fiendish delight in arresting war correspondents."[11] They got their material, such as it was, back to London by couriers, who ran a car shuttle service between Paris and Boulogne and, on the other side of the Channel, between Folkstone and London.

Philip Gibbs of the *Daily Chronicle* had been in France since August 2. Gibbs, a small, emotional man, had started his career on the *Daily Graphic*, travelling the war front in Serbia making quick sketches, which were then "worked up" by an artist back in the office. He had, he cheerfully admitted, "an immeasurable ignorance of the meaning of warfare. I knew nothing about its methods and machinery, the immensity and range of its destruction. I thought it would be like the South African affair: remote, picturesque and romantic." He was excited at the chance of becoming a war correspondent, because it seemed at first "the crown of journalistic ambition, the heart of its adventure and romance."[12] He was soon to be disillusioned. Gibbs, who spoke good French, had an authorisation from the French army permitting him to receive in Paris the daily war communiqués. By flashing this and using his charm, he managed to make his way to northern France and across the Belgian border.

Others, usually with less success, were trying to do the same thing. As the Germans stormed across Belgium, their uhlans only an hour or two behind the stampeding population, six other correspondents fought their way onto trains or pushed up roads filled with panic-stricken people. William Beach Thomas, a tall, military-looking man, who was representing the *Daily Mail*, had early success with a *laissez-passer* that he had made himself. It consisted of a mauve-and-gilt invitation card signed by the Mayor of Epernay, the wine magnate Pol Roger. It worked until he reached Hazebrouck, a railway centre in northern France. There his companion, a *Times* correspondent, insisted that they present their credentials to a

British lieutenant standing in the town square. The officer became annoyed when the *Times* man, replying to the question "Who are you?," answered, "Chiefly a man of letters, but for the moment a war correspondent," and he rushed them both into gaol, where the *Times* man complained bitterly about the standard of the cuisine.

Geoffrey Pyke, who had been a Reuters correspondent in Copenhagen, persuaded the *Daily Chronicle* to let him try to smuggle himself into Germany. Using a false American passport and posing as a printing-machinery salesman, Pyke travelled via Denmark to Berlin and then spent six days eavesdropping in cafés. Then the police arrested him, threatened to shoot him as a spy, and finally put him in gaol, where he stayed for six months and was then sent to Ruhleben, a civilian internment camp. He managed to escape and walked to Holland, where he cabled his story to London. The *Chronicle* ran it on July 26, 1915—DAILY CHRONICLE CORRESPONDENT ESCAPES FROM RUHLEBEN—but the newspaper and Pyke parted company when Pyke said he could not follow this story, as the editor requested him to do, with one on the low state of morale and poor food standards in Germany. That, said Pyke, was simply not true, and he resigned. The full story of his adventures, *To Ruhleben and Back*, was one of the First World War's best sellers.

While the war correspondents were in and out of prison; while "Eyewitness" was reporting on the weather ("fine with less wind, although the nights are now much colder"), the conditions of the troops ("several have received their baptism of fire during the week"), no man's land ("bodies of German infantry are still lying in heaps where they have fallen at different times"), and espionage ("secret agents have been found at rail-heads observing entrainments and detrainments"); and while French newspapers were filled with pages of heroic sentiment but not an item of news, this is what was really happening.

One million French soldiers had advanced in the wrong place to meet one and a half million Germans. While the bulk of the French army had gone to the eastern end of the frontier, Germany's best and largest army had smashed its way through on the west, storming across Belgium and Luxembourg, sweeping all before it.

Four hundred thousand civilians were in flight from Antwerp towards neutral Holland. A quarter of a million were crossing the Scheldt in anything that would float. The roads, railways, and waterways were choked with Belgians running from the dreaded uhlans. One war correspondent managed to capture the terror the nation felt.

After the Russo-Japanese War, Luigi Barzini had covered two Balkan flare-ups and then the Mexican Revolution before *Corriere della Sera* commissioned him to go to France. He arrived in Paris on August 20 and found that the Paris–Brussels express was still running. At Hal, ten miles from Brussels, his journey ended.

> I was looking for the war and it came to meet me…all of a sudden the train stopped, and a cry was heard, "The Uhlans! The Uhlans!" Massed against a level crossing barrier, a small obscure crowd, which waited for it to open so that they could resume their flight, threw this news to the passengers in the train…In the whirring reflection of an electric lamp we glimpsed anxious and pallid faces, hands nervously gripping the gates. "Where are the Uhlans?" a hundred voices ask. "Three kilometres away. They've shot two cyclists. Open, in the name of God!" The train slowly entered Hal station, but rather than continue towards Brussels, it changed track and headed for the French frontier, crowded with refugees. One old woman cries and howls, "Le Pape est mort." Who knows what connection her simple pious soul finds between the Pope and her country's disaster? She must see a fearful presage in the death of the head of Christianity…one thinks with profound anguish of the myriad lives that end at this hour in bloodied Europe, of the nations in agony….The Uhlans enter Hal as we leave….On the main road a procession of fleeing inhabitants silently passes, confused, swift and black, afraid of even being heard. It is the twilight of a world.[13]

Britain was also in trouble, with the retreat from Mons, centre of a mining area in Belgium. Compared with later events in the war, the Mons affair was a skirmish. But the fact remains that the British army was defeated in its first encounter with the Germans, and the Press Bureau's attempts to hide this made the shock doubly great when the news eventually came out. According to the Press Bureau, "the British forces were engaged all day Sunday and after dark with the enemy in the neighbourhood of Mons and held their ground…" It described the retreat in these words: "The British forces have reached their new position. Fighting has gone on more or less continuously, but the enemy has not effectively harassed our operations…The casualties cannot be estimated exactly but are not heavy."

Two correspondents were close enough to the retreat to form a better idea of what had happened: Arthur Moore of *The Times* and

Hamilton Fyfe of the other Northcliffe paper, the *Daily Mail*. Both were stunned by what they considered a major British defeat, and because of an unusual set of circumstances they succeeded in telling part of the story to the British public, thus marking the first breakthrough in the reporting of the war.

The story begins on the afternoon of Saturday, August 29. A courier arrived at *The Times*' foreign desk with a dispatch from Moore written earlier that day at Amiens. The foreign editor, Wickham Steed, read it with the acting editor, George Freeman. Both were shocked by Moore's report. "I read this afternoon in Amiens this morning's Paris papers," Moore wrote. "To me, knowing some portion of the truth, it seemed incredible that a great people should be so kept in ignorance of the situation which it had to face....It is important that the nation should know and realise certain things. Bitter truths, but we can face them. We have to cut our losses, to take stock of the situation, to set our teeth." Moore went on to describe the rapidity of the German advance, the relentless pursuit, the broken British regiments, the men weak with hunger and exhaustion, the "great losses" the British Expeditionary Force had sustained. It was strong, emotional stuff and, since Moore was an experienced man, appeared likely to be true, but Steed and Freeman considered that it had no chance of passing the censor in its original form. So, despite a plea in the text of Moore's copy that the censor pass his dispatch in the national interest, they set about giving the message a preliminary censoring themselves. Then they sent it around by hand to the chief of the Press Bureau, F. E. Smith, already famous as a King's Counsel and later, as Lord Birkenhead, to become Lord Chancellor. Two hours passed before the dispatch came back, with a covering note signed by Smith: "I am sorry to have censored this most able and interesting message so freely, but the reasons are obvious. Forgive my clumsy journalistic suggestions, but I beg you to use the parts of this article which I have passed to enforce the lesson—reinforcements and reinforcements at once."

Steed and Freeman turned anxiously to Moore's dispatch and found, to their amazement, that not only had many of their deletions been restored by the printer's mark "stet" and the initials F. E. S., but that Smith had written in some phrases of his own actually strengthening Moore's conclusions. "[The BEF] has suffered terrible losses and requires immediate and immense reinforcement," wrote Smith, censor-turned-war-correspondent. "[It] has won indeed imperishable glory, but it needs men, men, and yet more men…We want reinforcements and we want them now."

Steed and Freeman considered Smith's note tantamount to an order to publish, and so Moore's message duly appeared next morning, in the special Sunday edition of *The Times*, under the headline BROKEN BRITISH REGIMENTS BATTLING AGAINST ODDS. Beside it appeared another dispatch, reprinted from that day's *Weekly Dispatch*, Northcliffe's Sunday paper. This was headlined GERMAN TIDAL WAVE—OUR SOLDIERS OVERWHELMED BY NUMBERS and was written by Moore's colleague Hamilton Fyfe. It, too, bore the touch of F. E. Smith: "England should realise and realise at once that she must send reinforcements and still send them…We want men and we want them now."

Here was a clear case of a politician using his powers as censor to push his own views. As far as the two correspondents and their papers were concerned, this could have been overlooked in their satisfaction of at least getting their message printed, if it had not been for Smith's next move.

On Monday the storm broke. There was considerable public alarm. *The Times* and the *Dispatch* were denounced in Parliament and in other newspapers for "catch-penny" tactics. Smith could have set the whole matter straight, but to *The Times*' amazement he said little about his additions and nothing about his note. He merely hinted that he had been too busy to give proper time to considering the articles. The government had decided that the defeat at Mons, despite its possible appeal in a recruiting drive, was not the sort of news the British public should read, and Smith was busy back-pedalling to get into line. In the national interest *The Times* let him off lightly, publishing on Tuesday morning a short statement to the effect that Moore's dispatch had been printed not merely with the consent but at the request of the head of the Press Bureau. Within a few weeks Smith resigned from the bureau, and the whole sorry matter was forgotten in the tide of further disasters.[14]

While Moore and Hamilton Fyfe succeeded in revealing the Mons defeat, no one had any such luck with the Battle of the Frontiers. Between August 14 and 25, 1914, a German Victory that wiped out about 300,000 French soldiers, or nearly 25 per cent of the combatants—a rate of wastage never equalled in the rest of the fighting on any front—remained *completely unreported in Britain until after the war was over*. Yet there was a war correspondent with the French army at the time, Gerald Fitzgerald Campbell, representing *The Times*. Campbell must have known of the disaster, but not a single word about it appeared in his dispatches to his newspaper or even in his private letters to his editor. He ignored it completely, and in his book *Verdun to the Vosges*, published in 1916, he glossed over it. Even more surprisingly, *The Times* approved: "Such silence was prudent…had it been known in England that France had lost more than a quarter of a million men from her regular army in the first month of fighting, British determination must have been gravely weakened."[15]

The French felt the same. After the report that the French army had captured Mulhouse, in Alsace, on August 9, 1914, *nothing* further was published in French newspapers about the state of the war for nine crucial days. Rumours were optimistic: there were anti-war strikes and riots in Berlin; the Prussians were driving soldiers to fight at pistol point; soldiers from the German army were deserting in droves; one French soldier had frightened fifty Germans into surrendering. Then, on August 20, as the Germans pushed towards Paris, a stunned capital read in *Le Matin* the frightening headline ARE THEY AT BRUSSELS? By August 30, when, as *The Times'* Paris correspondent noted, "great preparations being made around Paris do not altogether reassure people here," the truth could no longer be concealed. The government prevented a collapse of civilian morale only by covering up the army's failure with stories of a dastardly German surprise attack.

Equally, nothing appeared in British or French newspapers about the annihilation of three Russian army corps at the Battle of Tannenberg, between August 26 and 31, 1914, presumably on the same grounds, that news of such a disaster to their Russian ally would dishearten the British and the French. The battle received some coverage in *The Times History of the War*, published in the spring of 1915, but, again, it was not until after the war that the full story emerged.[16]

German newspaper readers fared little better. A propaganda campaign, the theme of which was that Russia had mobilised first, the French had invaded German territory, and the envious English had seized the opportunity to crush a competitor whose commercial and naval superiority had to be forestalled, made the war generally acceptable. The high command fed the newspapers streams of stories about German advances, captured soldiers, captured guns, captured flags. The fall of Paris, in that early period of delirium, was said to be only a matter of days.

In Belgium and France, Philip Gibbs and his colleagues battled on. They set out for towns the Germans had already taken. They escaped from others only hours before the Germans arrived. Gibbs switched to the Battle of the Marne and for the first time saw the Germans in retreat. This short extract from one of his dispatches captures the mood.

> All day long on this Sunday in September I trudged over battlefields still littered with the horrors of recent fighting...My comrade of this day was a grave digger. With other peasants enrolled for the same tragic task he had followed the line of battle for twenty kilometers from his own village, helping to bury the German corpses...Dig as hard as he could, my friendly grave digger had been unable to cover up all those brothers in arms who lay out in the wind and the rain...My guide grasped my arm and pointed to a dip in the ground beyond the abandoned village of Levignen. 'See there', he said, 'they take some time to burn'. He spoke in a matter of fact way, like a gardener pointing to a bonfire of autumn leaves. But there in line with his forefinger, rose a heavy rolling smoke, sluggish in the rain under a leaden sky, and I knew that those leaves yonder had fallen from the great tree of human life, and that this bonfire was made from an unnatural harvesting.[17]

Gibbs was getting his copy back to his office by any means he could, including, for a brief but glorious spell, a War Office messenger. Reasoning that the lower echelons of the War Office would not know of the official ban on war correspondents, he simply waylaid a War Office courier and ordered him to take an envelope back to London. The envelope was addressed "The *Daily Chronicle*, Care of the War Office—URGENT." When the envelope arrived in London, the War Office (until someone woke up to what was happening) duly ordered another messenger to rush it to the *Chronicle*.

But by early 1915 the net to prevent war correspondents from getting anywhere near the war was drawing tighter. Kitchener had put out orders for the arrest in France of a number of correspondents mentioned by name. Gibbs tried another ploy. He had himself appointed as a special commissioner of the Red Cross to report on field hospitals in France. At this stage, there were dozens of relief organisations across the Channel (including a group of women from the eastern counties of England—the First Aid Nursing Yeomanry Service—who called themselves FANYS and were, naturally enough, known as "Fannies"), and Gibbs reasoned that one correspondent with the right papers could lose himself easily. He was arrested before he had even left the boat at Le Havre. Kept under open arrest for ten days, Gibbs was solemnly warned that

Kitchener was *very* angry with him and that if he returned to France again he would be put against a wall and shot.

Obviously matters could not go on like this. The government was now under some pressure to make a few changes. There was no danger of anything slipping through that might create public criticism of the conduct of the war or depress the nation, because the Defence of the Realm Act could be used to manipulate the press to fall in with the government's wishes.* Not that most newspapers would need more than a light touch of the rein now and then, since they had already made it clear that they would back the war effort wholeheartedly. "Trust the generals," Lord Northcliffe said.

But the opinion that carried the most weight, and was probably responsible for persuading the Cabinet to accredit at least some war correspondents, came not from within Britain but from America. On January 22, 1915, in a little-known letter to the Foreign Secretary, Sir Edward Grey, the former American president Theodore Roosevelt said bluntly that the British government's refusal to allow war correspondents to pursue their tasks was harming Britain's cause in the United States. "There has been a very striking contrast between the lavish attention showered on war correspondents by the German military authorities and the point-blank refusal to have anything to do with them by the British and French governments ...the only real war news, written by Americans who are known to and trusted by the American public comes from the German side.* If you think [American] public opinion should be taken into account, then it is worth your while considering whether much of your censorship work and much of your refusal to allow correspondents at the front has not been a danger to your cause from the standpoint of the effect on public opinion without any corresponding military gains."[18]

The Cabinet began to press the high command, and GHQ agreed to have a few "writing chappies" with the armies in the field. It spent weeks drawing up regulations to govern war correspondents and laying down rules of field censorship. Obviously,

---

* Churchill, in fact, recommended to Asquith that *The Times* be commandeered and converted into an official British gazette, which, he said, "would have afforded the administration a sure and authoritative means of guiding public opinion." Asquith ignored this advice.

** In an attempt to help win opinion in neutral countries to her cause, Germany had welcomed American correspondents and had given them every assistance.

there could not be any mention of regiments by name, and no mention of places, either, except in the vaguest manner, and no "writing up" of any officers other than the commander-in-chief. But would it be safe to allow any mention of the weather? And who was to decide what would encourage recruiting and what might discourage it? These remained problems until the end of the war, but a rough rule-of-thumb was indicated by a remark of General J. V. Charteris, Chief of Intelligence, when asked by a correspondent how much of an action he would be allowed to report: "Say what you like, old man. But don't mention any places or people."[19] What it came down to in the end was that in the eyes of GHQ the ideal war correspondent would be one who wrote what he had been told was true, or even what he thought was true, but never what he knew to be true. Given these restrictions, the war correspondents might just as well have stayed in London.

Instead, they arrived at GHQ in June 1915, where they were greeted by the commander-in-chief, Sir John French, who was wearing his top boots and spurs. Sir John made a little speech saying he was pleased to welcome the correspondents to his army and that he trusted their honour and loyalty. The correspondents were: Philip Gibbs, representing the *Daily Telegraph* and the *Daily Chronicle*; Percival Phillips, a deep thinker on war, who had been a correspondent since the age of twenty, and represented the *Daily Express* and the *Morning Post*; William Beach Thomas, a classics scholar, representing the *Daily Mail* and the *Daily Mirror*; H. Perry Robinson, the oldest of the team, who was fanatical about detail, representing *The Times* and the *Daily News*; Herbert Russell, representing the Reuters news agency; and Basil Clarke, representing the Amalgamated Press. From time to time these numbers were swelled by H. W. Nevinson, Filson Young, Percival Gibbon, George Dewar, and H. M. Tomlinson, but this first group saw the war through to the end.

They were in officers' uniform, without badges or insignia of rank (although they had honorary status as captains), and wore a green band on the right arm. They were given an old house in the village of Tatinghein as their headquarters and were provided with orderlies, lorries, cars, conducting officers, and censors. Almost the first thing they learned was that, although GHQ had agreed to have them, they were by no means welcome. Lower-ranking regular officers were extremely hostile to the idea that there would be war correspondents "prying around" and "giving the whole show away." So they were to be allowed to go nowhere without a conducting officer, and it did not take long to learn that these officers had been discreetly instructed to waste the correspondents' time as much as possible. These travelling censors went wherever the correspondents went, lived with them, ate with them, read their dispatches, and even examined their private letters, with authority to use, if they considered it necessary, chemical tests to look for invisible ink. It was not a job they greatly enjoyed, coming, as they mostly did, from adventurous parts of the Empire and in expectation of greater glory than being conducting officers or censors. There was Colonel John Faunthorpe, cavalry officer, pig-sticker, tiger hunter, judge, and poet, open in his ridicule of journalism in general and war correspondents in particular. There was Hesketh Pritchard, big-game hunter, cricketer, all-round sportsman, and author of stirring books on Empire. Later there was Colonel the Honourable Neville Lytton, painter, musician, and diplomat, a man who valued "form" above all else. This elegant, intelligent, but insensitive officer spent his leisure time at the front playing Bach on an eighteenth-century ivory flute and doing remarkable imitations of the noise ducks make when lapping up weeds on a pond. And there was Colonel Hutton Wilson, a debonair staff officer, who became thoroughly convinced that war correspondents, "even *The Times* man, by God," were all Bolsheviks.

The correspondents soon settled down into a routine. On the day that an attack was scheduled, they drew lots to see who would cover which area. Each then set out in his chauffeur-driven car, accompanied by his conducting officer. They went as close to the front as possible, watched the preliminary bombardment, got into the backwash of prisoners and walking wounded, interviewed anyone they could, and tried to piece together a story. Back at their quarters, the correspondents held a meeting, and each man outlined the narrative part of his story, keeping any personal impressions for his own dispatch. They then retired to their own rooms, wrote their pieces, and submitted them to the waiting censors. What the censors left was given to a dispatch rider, who took the messages to Signals at GHQ, where they were telephoned to the War Office and sent from there by hand to the various newspaper offices. The War Office had no right to touch a message once it had been censored in France, and the newspapers were not allowed to alter or cut anything the correspondents wrote. Once they had appeared in Britain, the dispatches were distributed throughout the Empire, under the direction of the Newspaper Proprietors' Association.

It was a routine designed with two ostensible ends in view: to enable the public to have a picture of its army at the front, but at the same time to prevent the publication of any information that might be of use to the enemy. But, of course, these were not the real aims. The real aims were, first, to provide colourful stories of heroism and glory calculated to sustain enthusiasm for the war and ensure a supply of recruits for the front and, second, to cover any mistakes the high command might make, preserve it from criticism in its conduct of the war, and safeguard the reputations of its generals. The smarter war correspondents realised this very early on, but for various reasons decided not to confront the system. Some hoped that as the war progressed things would change. Some thought that the high command had the right idea. Others were worried about the reaction of their editors. Had the correspondents had the moral courage to refuse to play their part in the charade, the government might have been forced to reconsider its attitude. (On one occasion, all the correspondents went on strike because of the excessive repression of one censor and won their case.) But they went along with the system, grumbling sometimes, it is true, but saving their protests for the memoirs they published after the war, when it was too late. The justifications and rationalisations they offered, both at the time and later, for permitting themselves to serve as propagandists, to be used in a manner that allowed nothing of the real picture of the war on the Western Front to emerge, go a long way towards explaining why, as one historian said, "there was no more discreditable period in the history of journalism than the four years of the Great War."[20]

Sir Philip Gibbs wrote, in 1923: "We identified ourselves absolutely with the Armies in the field…We wiped out of our minds all thought of personal scoops and all temptation to write one word which would make the task of officers and men more difficult or dangerous. There was no need of censorship of our despatches. We were our own censors."[21]

Naturally, *The Times*, above all other newspapers, approved this view: "Throughout the war the commentators of *The Times* could seldom be anything but *laudatores temporis acti*. They felt that their task was to sustain the morale of the nation in mortal combat; therefore they praised victories no less highly than they deserved; in stalemates they found elements of advantage; and defeats they minimised, excused, or ignored."[22]

Once they realised that the war correspondents were on their side, the attitude of the GHQ staff began to change. Some of the officers actually came to like some correspondents and to treat them, as the Honourable Neville Lytton said, "as officers, *i.e.*, with complete confidence and trust." But the closeness of this relationship between the staff and correspondents was disastrous to the correspondents' work. If the staff was their friend, their confidant, their censor, then how could they write about it when it failed? For their part in keeping quiet, the six major correspondents were received by King George V when he visited the front, were met on the great bridge over the Rhine by Haig, the commander-in-chief, who made a little speech of praise and thanks, and finally, at the war's end, were offered knighthoods. Gibbs, the most sensitive of them, had occasional nagging doubts. After the slaughter at Loos in September 1915, General G.M. W. Macdonough, of Army Intelligence, personally cut forty pages from Gibbs' story. The idea appeared to be, Gibbs said, to conceal the truth not from the enemy but from the nation, "in defence of the British High Command and its tragic blundering."

It is instructive to compare a soldier's description of trench warfare with what the correspondents sent. The French Socialist author René Naegelen wrote, after the war:

> Three of us were crouching in a hole under the barrage of artillery fire. Then a flame, a blast; then darkness and smoke, the acrid smell of gunpowder. Was I killed or wounded? I cautiously moved my arms and legs. Nothing. My two friends, however, lying one upon the other, were bleeding. The bowels of one were oozing out. The other had a broken leg; there was a red spot spreading on his breast, and he was rolling his panic-stricken eyes. He looked at me silently, imploringly; then unconsciously he unbuttoned his trousers and died urinating on the gaping wound of his comrade. [23]

The correspondents preferred lines of stalwart soldiers burning to go like greyhounds on the leash, impatient to leap out of the trenches and charge from shell-hole to shell-hole, from cheer to cheer. C. E. Montague, an assistant editor of the *Manchester Guardian*, first a soldier, then a censor, was caustically critical of the correspondents.

> They would visit the front now and then, as many staff officers did, but it could only be as afternoon callers from one of the many mansions of GHQ, that haven of security and comfort. When autumn twilight came down on the haggard trench world, of which they caught a quiet noon-day glimpse, they would be speeding west in Vauxhall cars to lighted chateaux.... The average war correspondent—there were golden exceptions—insensibly acquired [a] cheerfulness in the face of vicarious torment and danger. In his work it came out at times in a certain jauntiness of tone that roused

the fighting troops to fury against the writer. Through his despatches there ran a brisk implication that the regimental officers and men enjoyed nothing better than 'going over the top'; that a battle was just a rough jovial picnic, that a fight never went on long enough for the men, that their only fear was lest the war should end this side of the Rhine. This, the men reflected, in helpless anger, was what people at home were offered as faithful accounts of what their friends in the field were thinking and suffering. [24]

The effect of this distortion was immense. The average Englishman had been accepting it all his life that if something was printed in the newspapers, then it was true. Now, in the biggest event of his life, he was able to check what the press said against what he knew to be the truth. He felt he had found the press out, and as a result he lost confidence in his newspapers, a confidence to this day never entirely recovered.

Photographers, too, were hamstrung. First, only two photographers, both army officers, had been assigned to cover the Western Front, and since their main task was considered to be that of compiling a historical record, not providing newspapers with material, none of their "realistic" photographs was released. The penalty for anyone else caught taking a photograph at the front was the firing squad.* If not photographers, then how about artists? Artists were not allowed to go to the front until 1916, when Charles Masterman, a former MP working in propaganda, convinced the War Office that some suitably softened sketches would improve his propaganda publications. Muirhead Bone was the first. He arrived in France in July 1916, and was followed by Eric Kennington, Francis Dodd, James McBey, William Orpen, Paul Nash, C. R. W. Nevinson, Adrian Hill, William Rothenstein, Wyndham Lewis, William Roberts, John Sargent, Stanley Spencer, and many others, so that by 1918 there were more than ninety of them. They were not much more successful than the war correspondents in presenting a true picture of the war. Paul Nash protested at the limitations placed on the artists—"I am not allowed to put dead men into my pictures because apparently they don't exist"—and, with Nevinson, appeared more moved than most by what he saw, saying, "I am no longer an artist. I am a messenger who will bring back word from the men who are fighting to those who want the war to go on for ever. Feeble,

---

*One soldier risked it. F. A. Fyfe, a press photographer who had enlisted as a private, concealed a small camera in his bandolier and took a photograph of a dawn attack on German trenches.

inarticulate will be my message, but it will have a bitter truth and may it burn their lousy souls."[25]

It was but a small step from concealing conditions at the front to ignoring German victories. Retreats became strategic retirements, evacuations were rectifications of the line, and a defeat such as that at the Somme in July 1916—perhaps the most bloody defeat in Britain's history—brought only bland, innocuous reports, with nothing to show that the Allies had not had a good day, or even a victory. Gibbs, in fact, wrote in his dispatch: "It is, on balance, a good day for England and France. It is a day of promise in this war..." Gibbs excused himself later with this explanation: "I have had to spare the feelings of men and women, who have sons and husbands still fighting in France."[26] Beach Thomas confessed after the war what had really happened about the correspondents' reports at the Somme. Just before the battle, the Chief of Intelligence, General Charteris, arrived at the correspondents' quarters and briefed them on the Allied plans. During the battle, dispatch riders came up at regular intervals with progress reports, and on the authority of these "we sent off in common a short cable message to say all went well for England and France." But, as Beach Thomas and the others quickly realised, the message was untrue, and the great part of the intelligence supplied to them had been utterly wrong and misleading. "I was thoroughly and deeply ashamed of what I had written," Beach Thomas confessed, "for the good reason that it was untrue ...the vulgarity of enormous headlines and the enormity of one's own name did not lessen the shame."[27]

But an incident involving Keith Murdoch, a young Australian newspaperman, father of the present media magnate Rupert Murdoch, shows that a determined correspondent could make his protest heard. Suspect though Murdoch's motives might have been, his report on the bungling at Gallipoli cost a general his job, contributed to the decision to abandon the campaign, and confirmed the opinion of the general staff that war correspondents were dangerous meddlers and that it had been a mistake ever to have imagined otherwise.

What happened was this: Murdoch, at the age of twenty-nine, was sent in August 1915 to London, to act as representative there for a group of Australian newspapers. It was arranged that he should stop in Cairo, en route to London, and report on the postal arrangements for the Australian troops. While in Cairo, Murdoch, who was anxious to visit the battlefront, wrote for permission to do so to General Sir Ian Hamilton, who was in command of the mixed force that had landed at Gallipoli in April to attack Constantinople and knock Turkey out of the war. Hamilton was reluctant to allow Murdoch to go. Everything had gone wrong at the front, and the British and the Anzacs (Australian and New Zealand Army Corps) were hemmed into a few terrible areas of beach and hillside that were permanently under shell-fire. So Hamilton took the precaution of getting Murdoch to sign the war correspondent's declaration undertaking "not to attempt to correspond by any other route or by any other means than that officially sanctioned" and promising that for the duration of the war he would not "impart to anyone military information of a confidential nature…unless first submitted to the Chief Field Censor."[28]

Murdoch arrived on September 2, made a brief visit to the Anzac bridgehead, declined Hamilton's offer to provide him with transport to go anywhere and see anything, and then returned to GHQ, on the island of Imbros, and sought accommodation at the press camp. The camp, in an olive grove just outside Hamilton's headquarters, housed an interesting collection of war correspondents, including G. Ward Price of the *Daily Mail*, Charles Bean, the official Australian war correspondent, and Ellis Ashmead-Bartlett of the *Daily Telegraph*, the most interesting and dominating personality of them all. Ashmead-Bartlett had covered the Russo-Japanese War and was an experienced and highly competent correspondent. He appeared to have an unlimited expense account and used a large portion of it to purchase liquor from the navy. One of the sights of Imbros was the regular line of Greek porters staggering up the hill to the press camp loaded with supplies for Ashmead-Bartlett. He hated the restraints GHQ imposed upon him, especially that imposed by the censor, Captain William Maxwell, and had been fighting a losing battle, since the first landings, to try to tell the British public what was happening. Maxwell, on instructions from Hamilton, would allow no criticism of the conduct of the operation, no indication of set-backs or delays, and no mention of casualty figures; finally, he refused to give permission for any of Ashmead-Bartlett's messages to be transmitted until Hamilton's own official cables had reached London. This meant that, at a time when there was more interest in the fighting in France, Ashmead-Bartlett's Gallipoli dispatches, days late and heavily censored, often failed to appear in print.

Over the months, Ashmead-Bartlett had grown sour, hostile, and pessimistic. The Australians had arrested him in civilian clothes and had nearly shot him as an English-speaking Turkish spy; he had been torpedoed in the *Majestic*; and he was extremely unpopular with the young officers at GHQ because he was always predicting disaster. He was in the middle of one of his more despondent moods when Keith Murdoch arrived and fell quickly under his influence. Ashmead-Bartlett poured out to Murdoch's sympathetic ear all the frustration he had accumulated over his difficulties in filing stories, spun a gloomy description of the way the campaign was being conducted, and convinced Murdoch that a major disaster would occur during the winter unless the British government and the British people could be told the truth. Murdoch must have realised that almost by accident he was in possession of information that would certainly rank as one of the great stories of the war. He agreed with Ashmead-Bartlett that the only way to get the story out would be to break the rules and get an uncensored dispatch back to Britain. Ashmead-Bartlett wrote it, and Murdoch set out to take it to London.

He got as far as Marseilles, but there was detained by a British officer with an escort and warned that he would be kept in custody until he handed over the letter. He had been betrayed to Hamilton by H. W. Nevinson, the correspondent for the *Guardian*. Nevinson had either overheard Ashmead-Bartlett and Murdoch talking or had been tipped off by one of the batmen, who, the correspondents suspected, was a spy for GHQ.[29] Hamilton, although at first amused by Murdoch's gall, had acted quickly. He had alerted the War Office, which arranged for Murdoch's arrest, and had then withdrawn Ashmead-Bartlett's accreditation and ordered him back to London. Murdoch went on to London and on September 23, 1915, sat down in a room in the office of the Australian high commissioner and dictated everything he could remember of Ashmead-Bartlett's dispatch and what Ashmead-Bartlett had told him during their all-night conversation. His account was in the form of a letter addressed to the Australian Prime Minister, Andrew Fisher, but the presentation had strong journalistic overtones, with the data marshalled in a brisk and attractive way. It was an amazing document, a mixture of error, fact, exaggeration, prejudice, and the most sentimental patriotism, which made highly damaging charges against the British general staff and Hamilton, many of them untrue. But the basis of the charges—that the Gallipoli expedition was in danger of disaster—was correct, and Murdoch's action, questionable though it may have been, had resounding consequences.

Murdoch could see no solution to the problems of Gallipoli

while Hamilton remained in command: "Undoubtedly the essential and first step to restore the morale of the shaken forces is to recall [Hamilton] and his Chief of Staff [Lieutenant General Sir W. P. Braithwaite], a man more cordially detested in our forces than Enver Pasha [the Turkish War Minister]…It is not for me to judge Hamilton, but it is plain that when an Army has completely lost faith in its General, and he has on numerous occasions proved his weaknesses, only one thing can be done."[30]

These were obviously Ashmead-Bartlett's sentiments Murdoch was expressing, since Murdoch's visit had been too brief for him to reach so dogmatic a conclusion. Murdoch would no doubt have felt it necessary to check his accusations much more thoroughly had he ever imagined he was writing more than a private letter to his Prime Minister, and so it must have placed him in a rather awkward position when, three days later, Lloyd George, who opposed the Gallipoli campaign, read the letter and immediately urged that Murdoch send a copy of it to the British Prime Minister, Asquith. Murdoch could hardly have declined, but in a covering note he tried to tone down the virulence of his criticism.

Asquith used the weapon Murdoch sent him in an inexcusable manner. Without waiting until Kitchener had studied it, without checking its more outrageous allegations, and without even asking Hamilton for his comments, he had it printed as a state paper and circulated to the members of the Dardanelles Committee, which was in charge of the campaign. While the committee was still studying it, Ashmead-Bartlett arrived in London, and he and Murdoch began lobbying against Hamilton, Ashmead-Bartlett substantiating the substance of Murdoch's letter with an article of his own in the Sunday edition of *The Times*. This made it clear that they had Northcliffe's backing, and when the Dardanelles Committee met, on October 14, Hamilton's active career was brought to an end and Kitchener was deputed to break the news to him. The evacuation of Gallipoli began on December 12, 1915. A Royal Commission that began sitting in August 1916 (Murdoch and Ashmead-Bartlett both gave evidence) found that the campaign had been a mistake.*

*Hamilton was never asked to serve in the field again, but went on to another career, as an author; the shadow of Gallipoli—and what he regarded as a slanderous and unjust attack by Murdoch—remained with him until his death in 1947. Murdoch became an Australian newspaper magnate, a man of power, wealth, and influence, confidant of prime ministers, and a staunch Australian patriot until his death in 1952.

Here what concerns us is that, although the war correspondents in Gallipoli faced the same difficulties over censorship and were subjected to the same pressures from the general staff as on the Western Front, one, Ashmead-Bartlett, helped by Keith Murdoch, succeeded in getting out a fresh eye-witness account of what was happening there. If the war correspondents in France had only been as enterprising, the war might not have continued on its ghastly course.

By 1917, the elation of the early war years on the British home front had given way to bitter apathy. Hardly a family in Britain numbered all its sons among the living. During the Battle of the Somme the casualty lists had lengthened to include entire divisions that had been virtually destroyed. The system of recruiting battalions from one locality meant that heavy casualties were often sustained by particular areas, and town after town went into mourning.** Inflation was climbing, the economic burden continued to be shared unequally, and big business continued to make huge profits.

Mutinies occurred in sixty-eight out of 112 divisions in the French army. A complete breakdown of morale was averted only by suspending offensives, condemning 629 men, and sending to the firing squad at least 50 innocent, brave, and experienced soldiers. A dreadful suspicion of the truth, of sacrifice unequally shared, began to spread throughout Britain and France.

For the war to continue, it became necessary, as Robert Graves described it, "to make the English hate the Germans as they had never hated anyone before."[31] Propaganda was intensified. The atrocity story was re-employed to fortify the mind of the nation with proof of the depravity of the enemy, of his cruel and degenerate conduct of the war. Prominent people were pressed into service, taken on conducted tours of the front, and asked to do their bit to renew the nation's strength of purpose to win the war. A guest house was established near GHQ through which passed politicians, labour leaders, bishops, representatives of neutral countries, and distinguished writers. None of them saw much of the real thing, but they all seemed to enjoy the experience. Sir Arthur Conan Doyle turned up in the uniform of a county lieutenant so heavy with gold lace that colonels and brigadiers saluted him as he passed. George Bernard Shaw, invited at the suggestion of Philip Gibbs

**It was worse in France, where the entire male population of whole towns and villages was virtually wiped out.

("It seemed to me that Shaw of all men would be useful for propaganda, if the genius of his pen were inspired by the valour and endurance of our fighting men"), did a quick tour and offered a pragmatic view: "There is no need of censorship. While the war lasts we must be our own censors. All one's ideas of the war are divided into two planes of thought which never meet. One plane deals with the folly and wickedness of war. The other plane is the immediate necessity of beating the Boche."[32]

H. G. Wells performed best of all, employing emotive phrases like "Frankenstein Germany" and referring to the Germans' "intellectual inferiority." He turned his considerable talent to scourging the pacifists and tried to convince his readers that war was not as horrible as they had imagined. "I knew my chances of being hit by a bullet were infinitesimal, but I was extremely afraid of being hit by some too vivid impression. I was afraid that I might see some horribly wounded man or some decayed dead body that would so sear my memory and stamp such horror into me as to reduce me to a mere useless gibbering stop-the-war-at-any-price pacifist...but although I have had glimpses of much death and seen many wounded men, I have had no really horrible impressions at all. That side of the business has, I think, been overwritten."[33]

But now a reaction to atrocity stories set in. The man at the front, often the witness to the alleged atrocity, compared what he had seen with what he had read, and the result was a deep disillusionment with his country's honesty and a growing anger against war correspondents. (G. H. Mair of the *Sunday Chronicle* said later that by this time a soldier had "a very much larger detestation for the institution of war correspondent than he had even for the Staff.")[34] There was also an understandable reluctance to believe those few atrocity stories that *were* true. Henri Barby of *Le Journal*, Paris, and Edmund Candler of *The Times* both wrote horrifying stories about the atrocities the Turks were committing against the Armenians, but their detailed and damning accusations were lost in the welter of false and exaggerated propaganda of the period.

Even the most popular atrocity story of all—the German corpse factory—turned out to be another war correspondents' invention. This particular story had a long and highly successful run. It had several variations, but basically it was that close behind their front line the Germans had established factories for boiling down the corpses of their soldiers, from which to distill glycerine for munitions. *The Times* initiated the story, on April 16, 1917, with a suspiciously vague paragraph that said baldly: "One of the United States consuls, on leaving Germany in February, stated in Switzerland that the Germans were distilling glycerine from the bodies of their dead." The account quickly blossomed. *The Times* expanded the original report by reproducing a dispatch by a German correspondent, Karl Rosner, in which he referred to the German army's *Kadaververwertungsanstalt*, which *The Times* translated as "Corpse Exploitation Establishment." Foreign newspapers picked up the story. It appeared in *L'Indépendance* and *La Belge*, two Belgian newspapers published in France and Holland. French correspondents were instructed by their army authorities to send dispatches to their newspapers over their own signatures detailing what was known about the corpse factories. The matter came up in the House of Commons on April 30, when the Prime Minister was asked if he would make the story known as widely as possible in Egypt, India, and the East generally. A corpse-factory cartoon appeared in *Punch*, and in general the affair had world-wide circulation and considerable propaganda value.

The Germans protested in vain that the report was "loathsome and ridiculous" and that *The Times* had mistranslated Rosner's report, the word *Kadaver* not being used for a human body. In vain a British MP tried to get the government to clarify the matter. He said it was perfectly clear, from accounts published in the *Frankfurter Zeitung* and other leading German papers, that the factories were for boiling down the corpses of horses and other animals from the battlefield. Would the government therefore try to find out whether the story published in Britain was true or absolutely false? The government, of course, had no such intention. Lord Robert Cecil, Under Secretary for Foreign Affairs, replied that the government knew no more than had been published, but "in view of other actions by German military authorities there is nothing incredible in the present charge against them"—a typical case of appearing to lend substance to the report without the responsibility of actually doing so.

Germany had to live with the accusation until 1925, when, according to an American newspaper report, Brigadier-General Charteris, who had been in charge of British military intelligence, first admitted that he had been responsible for starting the canard. Two photographs captured from German sources had turned up on his desk. One showed German corpses being hauled away for burial behind the lines; the other showed dead horses on their way to a soap factory. Charteris, so the report said, told the guests at a private dinner party in New York that he had simply interchanged the captions and then, knowing the reverence of the Chinese for ancestors and the uncertainty of Chinese opinion towards the Germans, had sent the photographs to Shanghai for release, hoping the story would be "played back" to Europe. To support the story, what purported to be the diary of a German soldier had been forged, and it was planned to feed this to a British war correspondent with a passion for German diaries. The plan, General Charteris said, was never carried out, and the diary was now in the Imperial War Museum in London.*

On his return to England, Charteris denied his confession, which had been reported in the *New York Times*, and said he had not altered the captions on any photographs and had not been responsible for the fictitious diary. In fact, he said, when the diary had been submitted to GHQ in France it had been discovered to be fictitious and had been rejected. "I should be as interested as the general public to know what was the true origin of the *Kadaver* story."[35]

That the story was untrue was finally admitted officially on December 2, 1925. A statement in the House of Commons made it clear that there had never been any foundation for the story, and Germany was vindicated. Not that she was entirely innocent in such propaganda techniques herself. The German press abounded with stories of hospitals filled with German soldiers who had had their eyes gouged out. The *Weser Zeitung* reported that a ten-year-old boy had seen "a whole bucketful of soldiers' eyes," an atrocity story as old as the Crusades. *Die Zeit in Bild* ran an account of a French priest who wore around his neck a chain of rings taken from fingers he had cut off. The *Hamburger Fremdenblatt* said that Belgians gave German troops cigars filled with gunpowder. But these all appear to have been government-inspired propaganda stories, rather than, like the Courbeck Loo atrocity, deliberate pieces of invention by war correspondents.

The correspondent in question was Captain F. W. Wilson of the *Daily Mail*, who was in Brussels when war broke out. The first message from his office asked for an article on atrocities. Wilson said that he could find no evidence of atrocities, whereupon his office replied that a piece on refugees would do. As Wilson said later:

> There was a little town outside Brussels where one went to get dinner. I heard the Hun had been there. I suppose that there must have been a baby there. So I wrote a heart-rending story about the baby of Courbeck Loo being rescued from the Hun in the light of burning homesteads.

*It may have been then, but it is not today. The museum believes that it was probably among a number of boxes of papers that military intelligence first lodged with the museum after the war and then, on second thought, took back again.

Wilson's story was a great success. The *Daily Mail* had thousands of letters offering to adopt the baby, and parcels of clothes, including a gift from Queen Alexandra, poured into its offices. So the *Daily Mail* instructed Wilson to send the baby to London. Wilson handled the situation with aplomb. "I arranged with the doctor that took care of refugees that the blessed baby died of some very contagious disease, so it couldn't even have a public burial. And we got Lady Northcliffe to start a crèche with all the baby clothes."[36]

The best French effort in this area of false atrocities concerned the Belgian-baby-without-hands. Although the story was started by a *Times* war correspondent in August 1914, it was refined and disseminated by the French. The *Times* man reported: "One man whom I did not see told an official of the Catholic Society that he had seen with his own eyes German soldiery chop off the arms of a baby which clung to its mother's skirts."[37] By 1915, the Bureau de la Presse, the French government propaganda unit, had produced a photograph of the handless baby, and on September 18, 1915, *La Rive Rouge* published it, later making the story even more lurid by carrying a drawing showing German soldiers eating the hands. No one asked how long a baby would live if its hands were hacked off. The Belgian prelate Cardinal Mercier held an enquiry, but he was unable to substantiate the story, and after the war a series of investigations failed to find a single case of this nature.

But by the time the atrocity story was discredited it had served its rôle. It had not only rallied opinion on the home front and strengthened the resolution of Britain and France to prosecute the war to a finish, but had also achieved the important task of lowering resistance to the war in the United States.

If war correspondents had not become part of the propaganda machine, if censorship had not been so complete, what could they have written? What were the great unwritten stories of the First World War? After the Battle of the Marne, each side began to grope for an open flank by successive side-steps, until by October 1914 the movement had come to rest by the sea and the trenches stretched from the Swiss frontier to the English Channel. A new and radical thinking on the art of warfare was necessary to break this deadlock. It was not forthcoming in Britain. "I don't know what is to be done," Kitchener said. "*This* isn't war."[38] And, in France, President Poincaré pointed out that "there really seems no reason why the Germans and ourselves should not stand facing one another for all eternity." The stalemate had caught the Allies unprepared, but, of course, this was not the story a war correspondent could write. Their editors campaigned over the shortage of shells, but no one wrote that at the end of 1915 there were still 160,000 men in the line without arms, or that the Russians were short of no fewer than 1 million rifles.

While shells, arms, and ammunition were short, men were overplentiful. On August 7, 1914, the day after Kitchener took office as Secretary for War, he issued his famous call for 1 million volunteers. Recruiting offices were overwhelmed, and recruits had to be billeted in shops and factories and trained in civilian clothes and with broom handles instead of rifles. There were not enough regular officers to spare for instructors' duties. One typical new battalion had three trained officers: a commanding officer of sixty-three who had retired before the Boer War, a subaltern with a broken leg, and a retired quartermaster who was totally deaf. But the French were demanding that Britain shoulder a larger burden of holding the line, and these new, raw, poorly trained divisions had to be committed. Some are said to have marched towards the front line baaing like sheep. The French, for their part, were equally free with soldiers' lives. Black troops from the French colonies were thrown into exposed positions in order to save white troops from slaughter, "attack fodder so numbed that they could not fix bayonets or throw hand grenades."[39] What stories these could have made!

And what of the staff officers, the men of the red badge, known later to the fighting troops as "the red badge of funk"? Scions of wealthy and aristocratic houses, they considered Kitchener's volunteer army to be made up of useless, shiftless men and treated them as such.* Generals, overwhelmed by the size of their forces, became increasingly sensitive to criticism and increasingly isolated from the men under their command. Secure in their headquarters, where a band played ragtime and light music during dinner, and where the diners were at one time served by little Waacs with the GHQ colours in bows in their hair,[40] most generals came to view the slaughter at the front with equanimity. This did not pass unnoticed, and by 1916 antagonism between staff and combat troops had become so bitter that at the front "a young staff officer with red tabs was like a red flag to battalion officers and men and they desired his death intensely."[41] For by that time a soldier in one of

---

* The author Frank Richards writes of his commanding officer, "Buffalo Bill"—so called because he was always drawing his revolver and threatening to blow his men's brains out: "I never remember him having any favourites. He treated all the men the same way—like dirt."

the better divisions could count on a maximum of three months' service without being killed or wounded, and the life expectancy for an officer at the front was down to five months in an ordinary regiment and six weeks in a crack one.

It cannot be too strongly emphasized that the British public—*and* the French *and* the German—did not know or understand the full extent of the casualties until after the war. Even today, many figures are still disputed. (The Germans began to fake their figures in 1916, and became so muddled by their own lies that the truth will probably never emerge.) In any case, the figures that are known defy real comprehension. Who can comprehend that half a million Frenchmen were lost in the first four months of war, 1 million lost by the end of 1915,[42] and 5 million by 1918? Who can imagine that the Allies lost 600,000 men in one battle, the Somme,[43] and the British more officers in the first few months than in all wars of the previous hundred years put together?

At Stalingrad, in the Second World War, the Wehrmacht had 230,000 men in the field. The German *losses* at Verdun alone were 325,000 killed or wounded. For every British serviceman killed in the Second World War, three were killed in the First World War. The *Daily Mail*, on April 20, 1915, received from its Copenhagen correspondent the latest German casualty figures, which brought, after only eight months of war, the total number of German soldiers killed, wounded, and missing to *two and three quarters million*. The item was given one inch of space at the bottom of page five.

Casualty figures became debased and lost their real meaning. But there is evidence that, among the correspondents, Gibbs, at least, was aware of the magnitude of the killing. After the war, he wrote that the correspondents had seen more than most men of the wide sweep of war on the Western Front. "We saw the whole organisation of that great machine of slaughter...the effect of such a vision, year in, year out, can hardly be calculated in psychological effect unless a man has a mind like a sieve and a soul like a sink."[44] Why did he not write about it at the time?

Lloyd George, then Prime Minister, provides the answer. On December 28, 1917, he invited C. P. Scott, editor of the *Manchester Guardian*, to breakfast and told him: "I listened last night, at a dinner given to Philip Gibbs on his return from the front, to the most impressive and moving description from him of what the war in the West really means, that I have heard. Even an audience of hardened politicians and journalists was strongly affected. *If people really knew, the war would be stopped tomorrow*. But of course they

116

don't know and can't know. *The correspondents don't write and the censorship would not pass the truth* [emphasis added]…The thing is horrible beyond human nature to bear and I feel I can't go on with the bloody business: I would rather resign."[45] Here we have it in a nutshell: "The correspondents don't write and the censorship would not pass the truth." So the whole sordid conspiracy to keep the truth from the people was allowed to grow. *The Times* offers an explanation for this terrible failure of the war correspondents.

> The first reason for the inadequacy of the [war] correspondents was that they did not themselves understand what was happening. Obstacles were not eventually put in their way of getting right up to the front line—provided they did not try to go there when anything in particular was happening; no limits were placed on the people to whom they could talk—provided they did not talk to anyone who was busy!…Press officers directed their movements so closely that they hardly had any initiative in choosing where they should go. The man who came out from a spell in the line never wanted to describe what it was like. Even if correspondents did get any inkling of what conditions for the fighting soldier were really like, they were not necessarily encouraged to send them home: *indeed such knowledge as was theirs inspired silence* [emphasis added].*[46]

Only one correspondent did not remain silent, and his criticism was muted by his intense nationalism. This was Charles Bean, the official Australian war correspondent. Bean was concerned not so much with news as with a record of the war, for the official history he later wrote. Somewhat to the amazement of the British correspondents, he set himself the task of visiting, on the day of the battle or soon afterwards, every important trench or position occupied by Australian troops in Gallipoli and France. He accepted little second-hand information. "He regarded it as his bounden duty," Gibbs wrote, "to see everything with his own eyes." He became known by sight to almost every Australian soldier, not just as a correspondent, but as a civilian who was prepared to share their discomfort and their risks. Although he did not question the war itself, he did ask whether Britain was making the best use of Australian

---

* If *The Times* knew all this, then why did it not speak out, if not on behalf of all correspondents, then at least on behalf of its own? The answer, from *The Times*' own account, is a damning one: "A principal aim of the war policy of Printing House Square was to increase the flow of recruits. It was an aim that would get little help from accounts of what happened to recruits once they became soldiers."

troops in seeking to win it. The British accused him of excessive partiality, but the chief censor agreed that "most of his criticisms of the Mother country were justified" and that he was motivated by "high-minded patriotism."[47]

The American entry into the war in April 1917 was the beginning of the end for Germany. The Allies would now have virtually unlimited manpower and supplies, while Germany, bled white of her men, felt, as well, the increasing grip of the Allied blockade. The threat of starvation grew day by day. There were bread riots in Vienna and strikes in Berlin, and the possibility of revolution overtaking Germany alarmed not only the German leaders but the Allies as well.

British correspondents saw only the military side to this German collapse. After the storming of the Hindenburg Line in September 1918, Gibbs wrote: "I saw the Second German Guards coming along in batches like companies, and after they had been put in barbed wire enclosures, they laughed and clapped at the sight of other crowds of comrades coming down as prisoners. I thought then, something has broken in the German spirit."[48] The real story, however, was what was happening inside civilian Germany. Rumours of successful revolution, of communes of soldiers and workers running large parts of the country, began to circulate even before the Armistice on November 11. So while the British correspondents were being photographed in their cavalry-officer-style uniforms on the bridges over the Rhine and were receiving congratulations from the military for staying on side throughout the war, five American correspondents simply defied army orders and took off on their own into Germany.

They were Lincoln Eyre of the *New York World*, Herbert Corey of Associated Newspapers, Fred E. Smith of the *Chicago Tribune*, Cal Lyon of Newspaper Enterprise Association, and George Seldes of the Marshall Syndicate. After crossing the Moselle, they overtook a retreating German column and were threatened with arrest by the colonel in charge. But then they received the first indication that some of the rumours were true. An English-speaking German shouted a welcome on behalf of a newly formed communal organisation, the Soldiers and Workers Council, of Borg. The correspondents explained that they were on a mission to investigate the food situation, and the council gave them introductions to other communes, guaranteeing their safe-conduct. The council at Trier offered them transport, so the correspondents sent their army drivers back to Bar-le-Duc, the American press division headquarters, with a note to the press office saying that they had an opportunity to visit the interior of Germany and were taking advantage of it because it was "of the greatest importance at the present time that the world learned what was happening there"—a perfectly correct judgement. The letter created an uproar, and for a while the army even considered whether charges of treason could be preferred against the five correspondents, if they were ever found.

Oblivious to this, the correspondents reached Frankfurt, where, as the "American Food Mission," they were welcomed by the new government at a special dinner. From there they went to Kassel, where they were given an interview with Field-Marshal von Hindenburg, who received them reluctantly and only because the government ordered him to do so. They were met by Hindenburg's chief of staff, General Wilhelm Groener, whose head was bandaged. Prompted by his colleagues, Eyre, who spoke German, asked whether Groener had been wounded. He translated the reply: "The general says he has not been wounded. He says he has just lost a world war and has a headache."[49]

Now that they had their story, there arose the problem of how to get it back to their newspapers. The correspondents decided to split up. Seldes had run out of money, and this was not an occasion to borrow from his colleagues. In the lining of his coat he had sewn a twenty-dollar gold piece, in case of emergency. He now cut it out and began a four-day trek back to Luxembourg, where he surrendered to the provost-marshal's guard and asked to be returned to press divisional headquarters. Eyre took a plane to Berlin; the others went by train. In Berlin, they were all picked up by the army and returned to the American press division. All five were now subjected to court-martial interrogation by the judge-advocate-general, who said that in his opinion they were guilty of violating the rules of war and the regulations concerning correspondents. He was still considering presenting a case against them when President Wilson's aide, Colonel House, wrote to Eyre expressing his unofficial view that an investigation into conditions in Germany by American correspondents would have interest and value for the people of the United States. This mollified the army, and the correspondents were restored to their former status and allowed to submit for censorship the stories they had gathered on their trip. But by now so much time had elapsed, and other correspondents had written so much about Germany under the Allied Army of Occupation, that the accounts of the five runaway correspondents were considered stale and were never printed.

The initiative shown by the American correspondents on this occasion and their courage in defying the military to chase what was clearly a story of considerable importance suggest that all the First World War correspondents were not like the British and the French. We now go back to see how the war was reported in its early stages by American and other neutral correspondents, and how the Americans fared when they, too, became involved.

## Chapter Six

# Enter America
# 1917–1918

Once lead this people into war and they'll forget there ever was
such a thing as tolerance. To fight you must be brutal and ruthless
and the spirit of ruthless brutality will enter into the very fiber of
our national life, infecting Congress, the courts, the policeman on
the beat, the man in the street.

—President Woodrow Wilson, on April 1, 1917

---

The outbreak of war in 1914 had taken the American people by
surprise. Their immediate reaction was one of revulsion and
amazement, but they were quick to make their position clear. Historically reluctant to be drawn into Europe's troubles, they reaf-
firmed their neutrality, a neutrality, as President Wilson emphasised
on August 19, 1914, "'in fact as well as in name." But it was felt,
even at this early stage, that the war would be more than one of
Europe's petty squabbles (General Nelson A. Miles saw it as
becoming "the world's most destructive conflict") and that the
American public would want to be well informed of its progress.
Carr Van Anda, editor of the *New York Times*, who was to arrange
a coverage larger than any British newspaper's, papered his office
with maps, and the first wave of American war correspondents, who
were eventually to total ninety, set out for Europe.

There they joined all the other neutral correspondents—Swiss,
Swedish, Danish, Dutch, Spanish, and South American—searching for ways to report the war. At first the German side seemed to

offer greater opportunities. The Germans were winning, and during a brief but fruitful period they allowed the neutral correspondents to go to the front, provided them with every facility, and allowed them to write virtually what they liked. As a result, neutral newspapers often carried vivid descriptions of battles days before the British and German censors released the news to their own people, and a Swedish correspondent, Sven Hedin, was able to write a long and comprehensive account of the early campaign.

On the Austrian front, neutral correspondents appear to have been given even better treatment. Billeted in a small Hungarian village, each assigned a batman, given free wine and cigarettes, dined lavishly, and promised early trips to the fighting areas, they took some time to realise that they were being fooled. The trips to the front seldom materialised, and when they did the correspondents were allowed to see little of real interest. When William G. Shepherd of the United Press arrived to assess the opportunities, he quickly decided that the correspondents had everything they wanted—except news.

On the Russian front, Grand Duke Nicholas arranged for two railway cars to take the neutral correspondents on a tour of the battlefields. But the war was not going well for the Russians, and after a rapid visit to the rear lines in Galicia the party returned to headquarters with nothing of interest to report. The correspondents then moved to Warsaw, where they exchanged rumours and read the uninformative army communiqués.

The French treated neutral correspondents as they treated their own: if they were found near the front, they were seized. Luigi Barzini, after his early successful reporting, was deterred from further excursions to the French front by being arrested and held in a stable for several days, receiving only such food as he could beg from his French guards. The British were almost as unhelpful. They had a system of conducted tours designed to show neutral correspondents everything except what the war was really like. There was also a nasty condition attached to being a neutral correspondent accredited to the British army: if the correspondent later reported from the German side and was captured by the British, he would be summarily executed as a spy. The Germans eventually introduced similar strictures. This tended to force a neutral correspondent to make a commitment to one side for the duration of the war and usually resulted in his being as fully absorbed into the propaganda machine as his British or German colleagues.

So any early reporting successes that neutral correspondents achieved soon became happy memories, as the fighting settled into a stalemate and censorship moulded the reporting of the war the way the military wanted it.

The Americans fought hardest against this, and the history of their rôle in the First World War is of one long battle to report the war as they saw it, not as the British or the German or—later—the American censor wanted it. With courage that must be admired, some refused to compromise their professional integrity. They packed up and went home, forfeiting their accreditation, rather than remain silent.

In 1914, when Richard Harding Davis sailed on the *Lusitania*, he foresaw none of these problems. Davis, who occupied a $1,000-a-day suite with his wife, was the most experienced and most respected of the American War correspondents. He was also the richest (his contract for reporting the war in Europe for the Wheeler syndicate stipulated a salary of $32,000 a year and expenses, an immense sum in 1914), and one of the more pro-British. Davis went straight to Brussels and was there when the first German forces entered the city. "I saw it first in the Grand Place in front of the Hotel de Ville," Davis wrote in his dispatch that night. "It was impossible to tell if in that noble square there was a regiment or a brigade. You saw only a fog that melted into the stones, blended with the ancient house fronts, that shifted and drifted, but left you nothing at which you could point. Later, as the army passed below my window, under the trees of the Botanical Park, it merged and was lost against the green leaves. It is no exaggeration to say that at a hundred yards you can see the horses on which the Uhlans ride, but you cannot see the men who ride them...like a river of steel it flowed, gray and ghostlike."[1]

One morning Davis hired a taxi and drove as far as Hal, where he was arrested and put under guard. After an hour, the sentry guarding him decided to rejoin his regiment. Davis took the road to Ath, where, unknown to him, the British were making a stand. Caught up by a German detachment making a forced march in preparation for a surprise attack on the British right flank, he was compelled to trot with them for five hours—a punishing ordeal for a man his age. Then he was taken to divisional headquarters, searched, and interrogated. The Germans found in his pocket a photograph showing him wearing a British military tunic complete with campaign ribbon, which he had had copied from a uniform worn in the Boer War. His American passport had been issued in

London, not Washington. His *laissez-passer* from the German commandant in Brussels was not signed, only initialled. And—as he said afterwards, the cruellest blow of all—none of the Germans had ever heard of him or of his writings. The German officer said, "It is clear that you are a British officer out of uniform, taken inside our lines. You know what that means." A summary court-martial consisting of eight officers was convened, heard the evidence, and postponed sentence overnight.

At midnight Davis was awakened and told of an impending British attack. If he agreed to head back to Brussels, fifty miles away along the main road, under pain of immediate execution if he was found off the road or outside the city within the next forty-eight hours, he would be released. Davis accepted the terms and, limping from a bruised ankle, set out for the city. A few hours later he hailed a German general's car heading for Brussels and talked his way into getting a lift. In five previous wars, he told the American Ambassador, Brand Whitlock, that evening, he had never been so frightened. Davis lasted another year; then, disgusted at not being allowed by the British or French to visit the front lines, he returned home. "I'm not about to write sidelights," he said. He died, aged only fifty-two, in 1916.

Irvin S. Cobb, war correspondent for the *Saturday Evening Post*, a huge man and a prolific writer, had a similar experience and, like Davis, was saved because the Germans realised the propaganda value of remaining on good terms with American correspondents. Cobb, Harry Hansen of the *Chicago Daily News*, Roger Lewis of Associated Press, and two *Chicago Tribune* men, James O'Donnell Bennett and John T. McCutcheon, set out from Brussels for Waterloo, where a battle was said to be in progress. The Americans travelled in two horse-drawn cabs complete with top-hatted coachmen. But at Waterloo there was no sign of either French or German forces. The Americans thereupon hired a pony trap and drove themselves to Beaumont, headquarters of a German army corps. They sought out an English-speaking colonel and presented their credentials. "But we have no correspondents with our forces," the colonel said. "You have now," said Cobb. The German was not convinced. The correspondents could remain overnight, he said, but would be put on a train for Brussels in the morning, because "it is not permitted to have correspondents with our armies."

The next morning, the Americans found that a British advance during the night had upset arrangements, and the train took them and a coachload of Allied prisoners to Aix-la-Chappelle. There the

German army hierarchy, alert to the opportunity the Americans presented, offered to show them the German army machine. Cobb went up in an artillery spotter balloon, from which he inspected artillery batteries, and finally was taken to the fort at Liège, which had been captured earlier. His escort exulted in the wreckage that the German forty-two-centimetre guns had caused and attempted to impress Cobb with details about them. Cobb, in his flowery but descriptive style, said in his dispatch:

> Had I not already gathered some notion of the powers of destruction of those one-ton, four-foot long shells I should have said that the spot where we halted had been battered and crashed at for hours...Now, though, I was prepared to believe the German captain when he said that probably not more than five or six of the devil devices had struck this target...Conceive of each of the six as having been dammed by a hurricane and sired by an earthquake, and as having been related to an active volcano on one side of the family and to a flaming meteor on the other. Conceive it as having fallen upon a man-made masonry-walled burrow in the earth, and being followed in rapid succession by five or six of its blood brethren; and then you will get some fashion of mental photograph of the result.[2]

Cobb and his colleagues stayed with the German army for two weeks and were then put on board a train for Paris.

Cobb's other big story on this first tour was of an interview with Kitchener. Kitchener's interviews were highly formal; questions had to be submitted in writing, and the correspondent attended later to hear the answers. No one told Cobb the most important condition: Kitchener was not to be quoted. Cobb's story in the *Saturday Evening Post* quoted him liberally, and Kitchener replied by denying point blank that he had ever given the interview. Cobb enjoyed the brief sensation all this caused, but realised he would find it impossible to operate under such strictures, and so he, too, packed up and went back to the United States.

William G. Shepherd was much more successful, mainly because of the ingenuity he and his office displayed in their battles with the British censor. Shepherd had come over to join his agency's hard-pressed London bureau soon after the outbreak of war, and got away to a splendid start by interviewing Winston Churchill, then First Lord of the Admiralty. Churchill, well aware of the benefits of a favourable press in the United States, dictated what he wanted to say and then later, after speaking with the King and the Prime Minister, Asquith, added new material. The story was a major news break, and British newspapers had the disappointment of having to use it, under a United Press dateline, twenty-four hours after it had appeared in America.[3]

Shepherd was visiting GHQ at Saint-Omer on April 22, 1915, on a beautiful spring morning, when the Germans launched the first poison-gas attack on the Western Front. (They had tried gas earlier against the Russians, but the Russians had failed to report it to their allies.) Shepherd hurried to Ypres and arrived in time to see the casualties and to describe their agonising condition. This was one story the censor did not want to kill, and Shepherd's flat, unemotional account of the incident weighed heavily against the Germans in the propaganda battle that was developing in the United States.

But the scoop by which Shepherd is best remembered is his account of the first Zeppelin raid on London, on September 8, 1915. Before the last bomb had fallen and while the fires still raged, the censor issued a general proscription: nothing was to be written about the attack. Shepherd spent a few hours experimenting with his copy and then filed a remarkable story. Though nothing could be written about the bombing itself, there was no ban on writing about the heroism of Londoners. "These civilians, not privileged to fight at the front, had proved their mettle *now that the war had reached their home area. They had fought fires, rescued wounded, shrugged off an entirely new type of warfare and patching together their houses and shops had carried on as usual* [emphasis added]."[4] The censor could find no reason to delete even a word, and there was probably not a single United Press reader the next day who failed to get the message.

The United Press also scored well in France and Germany. Karl H. von Wiegand, a German-speaking American, who was representing the UP in Berlin, wrote a story from Wirballen, in Russian Poland, on October 8, 1914, in which he gave the first description of the effect of concentrated German machine-gun fire on closely packed troops: "The [Russians] literally went down like dominoes in a row. Those who had kept their feet were hurled back as though by a terrible gust of wind...the withering fire raking them even as they faltered, the lines broke. Panic ensued."[5] The Germans liked Wiegand's portrayal of their armed might, and they rushed him to the Western Front to report on the German advance on Paris. On November 20 he was given an interview with the officer commanding one of the attacking armies, Crown Prince Wilhelm. It was the first interview Wilhelm had given to a foreign war correspondent, and the first direct statement to the press by any member of the German royal family since the war had started. Wiegand sent it by a courier, who travelled via Namur, Aix-la-Chapelle, and The Hague to London, and there it was cabled by the United Press to New York. It made front-page headlines in all UP newspapers in the United States. The Crown Prince pleaded the German case, in the same way that Churchill had pleaded Britain's case in his interview with Shepherd, and begged for understanding in America.

> "Undoubtedly this is the most stupid, senseless and unnecessary war of modern times. It is a war not wanted by Germany, I can assure you, but it was forced on us and the fact that we were so effectually prepared to defend ourselves is now being used as an argument to convince the world that we desire conflict."[6]

In Paris, William Simms, the United Press representative, refused to allow the German advance to disturb his daily ritual of morning coffee at the Café Viennoise on the Boulevard Montmartre. He was sitting there when a little German monoplane flew over the city at an altitude of less than a thousand feet. It was so low that Simms could see the pilot quite clearly as he leaned over the side of the cockpit and hurled a bomb towards the ground. It fell in a courtyard across the boulevard from Simms, tore a hole in the ground, and shattered all the windows in the building. Simms hurried back to his office and wrote an eye-witness story of the first bombing raid ever to take place on a large city. But when he tried to join the French armies at the front, an officer tore up his credentials and said, "Get out. We don't want you." Simms wrote, "The old-time war correspondent with freedom of movement passed out in the first month of the war."[7]

Nevertheless, the over-all picture that the American newspaper reader received in the first months of the war was certainly better than that given in British, French, or German newspapers. It was a comprehensive coverage, and at first it was presented with reasonable impartiality. A poll taken late in 1914, in which 367 newspaper proprietors were asked which side had their sympathy, showed that 242, or about two-thirds, expressed no particular preference, and it is clear from reading the newspapers of the early war period that the editors were careful to preserve this neutrality in the selection and display of war news. The *Los Angeles Examiner*, for example, in its issue of September 23, 1914, carried an article written especially for it by Dr. Bernhard Dernburg, a former director of the German Colonial Office, a story by Ellis Ashmead-Bartlett of the *London Daily Telegraph* describing what he saw in Reims after a German bombardment, and a dispatch by W. M. Duckworth of the International News Service and the *London Daily News*, datelined Copenhagen (where Duckworth monitored the Berlin papers), describing the Kaiser's visit to a German military hospital.

Such was the desire at this time to maintain a neutral coverage that the *New York Times* took action to stop a rumour that it was partially controlled by *The Times* of London and that Lord Northcliffe was dictating the *New York Times'* policy to make it friendly towards Britain and hostile to Germany. The *New York Times'* publisher, who had one of his senior staff check the newspaper's reporting of the war, came to the conclusion that there *was* an anti-German slant to the paper. He never succeeded in pinning down exactly how this occurred, but he offered a suggestion: there were a number of pro-British editors on the staff of the paper and at least one British citizen, Frederick T. Birchall. The anti-German slant to the paper came, it was reported to the publisher, "from a cumulative typographical effect." Pro-British stories had been getting big headlines and prominent positions, while pro-German stories had been buried on the back pages. The publisher took steps to correct this practice and restore the newspaper's reputation for impartiality.[8]

This desire for neutrality in reporting extended to most American war correspondents. They were less susceptible to atrocity stories, no matter from which side they emanated. While British and French newspaper readers were being fed with accounts of German atrocities in Belgium, American readers were presented with a declaration signed by the same five influential American correspondents who had persuaded the Germans to allow them to accompany their army for two weeks. The declaration said that, from what the correspondents had been able to observe, the atrocity stories were untrue.[9] None of the correspondents ever retracted this statement, and Cobb later offered it as his considered opinion that only about 10 per cent of atrocity stories were genuine. The Associated Press correspondent on the German front in Belgium, Dr. Hendrik Willem van Loon, arrived in New York in January 1915, after the Germans had expelled him, and said the atrocity reports were "indecent lies." William Shepherd, the United Press man, wrote in 1917 that he had spent a considerable amount of time in Belgium in late 1914 trying to find an authenticated atrocity story and had failed to do so. Donald Thompson, an American photographer working for the *London Daily Mail* and the *New York World*, was

promised handsome payment for photographs of a German atrocity, but was unable to find a single one. The *New York World* of January 27, 1915, quoted a State Department report which said that,
of the thousands of Belgian refugees in Britain, not one had been
subjected to atrocities by German soldiers.

But the stalemate on the Western Front made the Allies realise
that they were in for a long war, and that the drain on their
resources might be so great that they would require the help of the
United States to finish Germany off. The British propaganda
bureau, financed from secret-service funds, had an American section, headed by the popular novelist Sir Gilbert Parker, a Canadian
by birth, who had been a British MP since 1900. Parker spent the
early months of the war analysing the American press and deciding
on ways of influencing it. He then compiled a mailing list of Americans likely to be able to sway public opinion, and he used this as a
basis for a propaganda campaign. Under Parker's direction, British
efforts to bring the United States into the war on the Allied side
penetrated every phase of American life, from the pulpit to the
classroom, from the factory to the office. It was one of the major
propaganda efforts of history, and it was conducted so well and so
secretly that little about it emerged until the eve of the Second
World War, and the full story is yet to be told.[10]

Parker's success turned on the attitude of the American newspapers, which then constituted the sole reading material of 90 per
cent of the American people. Relations between the American and
the British press had always been good, particularly since American
newspapers relied to a large extent for their news from Europe on
London-based correspondents, who either were of British nationality or had lived so long in London that they tended to be pro-
British in outlook. At Wellington House, the headquarters of Masterman's propaganda bureau, every effort was made to win these
correspondents over to the British cause. Wickham Steed, the foreign editor of *The Times* of London, held regular meetings with
them and explained the British view of the war.[11] Frederick Palmer,
representing all three major American news agencies, became the
one non-British war correspondent in the original group accredited to the British Expeditionary Force in France. Other American
correspondents were taken on conducted tours of the front, chap-
eroned by attentive and diplomatic officers. They were then wined
and dined at the headquarters château and quietly briefed about the
British case. The influencing of correspondents of the calibre of

Palmer was done subtly, yet with marked success. Palmer apparently did not see through it until after the war, when he admitted that British propaganda "had much to do with bringing the United States into the war" and yet confessed that he himself had written propaganda "in the illusion of the moment."[12]

The almost complete capture of American correspondents in this way ensured that in American newspapers the war would be seen as if through British eyes. Through his secret *American Press Review*, Sir Gilbert Parker was regularly able to report to the Cabinet on his success, as witness the issue of October 11, 1916: "This week supplies satisfactory evidence of the permeation of the American Press by British influence."

The wisdom of Parker's campaign to win American support for the Allies became strikingly evident in 1917. In that year, Russia dropped out of the war, Italy suffered her overwhelming defeat at Caporetto, England was within six weeks of starvation, there were mutinies in the French army, and Bob Pasha, a Turk who dealt in pacifist intrigue, was arrested in Paris and later executed for using 10 million francs given to him by the Germans to try to "persuade" the French press to advocate an early peace. France was virtually finished and the government, it was said, had secretly fixed November 1, 1917, as France's last day if the United States had not entered the war by then.

When, on April 6, 1917, America did enter the war, there were a number of factors that appeared to have caused that decision. There was the sinking of the liner *Lusitania* on May 7, 1915, which had been carefully fostered into an anti-American act. (BRITISH AND AMERICAN BABIES MURDERED BY THE KAISER, said the *Daily Mail* on May 10.) There was the German decision to go ahead with unrestricted submarine warfare from February 1, 1917.* And, finally, there was the Zimmermann telegram: a message from Arthur Zimmermann, head of the German Foreign Office, to the German minister in Mexico, instructing him to propose an alliance if the United States entered the war and to offer, if this occurred, German support for Mexico to regain New Mexico, Texas, and Arizona.

But it is suggested here that these events were only products of a policy under which the United States had gradually surrendered its neutrality by giving the Allies its material, financial, and moral

---

* It was nearly successful; in the first month, German submarines sank 781,000 tons of shipping, and all that was needed was a rate of 600,000 tons a month to be fatal to Britain.

support, and that this policy in turn was the result of Britain's propaganda campaign. Under the influence of what they read in their newspapers, Americans came to regard the war as a simple battle between good and evil, and, despite the fact that the 1916 presidential election showed that the great majority of the people wanted the United States' neutrality to be maintained, there developed in the minds of America's leaders such a blind hatred of everything German that war became inevitable.

Even when war had been declared, the American people showed a marked reluctance to take up arms. Enlistments were so poor—in the first six weeks only 73,000 men volunteered—that it became necessary for the government to raise a conscript army. To inspire the nation to fight, a new, home-grown propaganda campaign was needed in order to whip up what President Wilson's private secretary, Joseph Tumulty, called "the people's righteous wrath." To this end, President Wilson set up, on April 14, a Committee on Public Information, under the chairmanship of a journalist, George Creel, which was financed to the extent of $5 million from a $100 million fund granted to the President for the general defence of the country. Its aims were helped by Lord Northcliffe, owner of *The Times* and the *Daily Mail* and a member of the Advisory Committee of the Department of Information, who headed a mission to America and established the British Bureau of Information in New York. This mission took over Parker's work (he had resigned, on grounds of ill health, in February 1917, as soon as it was clear that America was going to enter the war), and at its strongest had 500 officials with 10,000 assistants working in the United States.[13]

Hatred of the Germans was now whipped to fever pitch. All the propaganda stories that had worked best in Europe were revived: Germany's sole responsibility, the rape of Belgium, the outraging of nuns, the unmentionable atrocities, the criminal Kaiser. New stories were created; one, a book called *Christine*, by Alice Cholmondeley, a collection of letters purporting to have been written by a music student in Germany to her mother in Britain until her death in Stuttgart on August 8, 1914, mingled a damning catalogue of German character faults with emotional gush about music and filial feeling. The book had a wide circulation, and the Germans rated it as perhaps the best individual piece of propaganda during the war.[14]

The Creel committee sponsored 75,000 speakers, who, in some 750,000 four-minute speeches in 5,000 American cities and towns, aroused the "righteous wrath" of the people against the Hun and the Boche. It sent Lowell Thomas, the author and traveller, to gather stirring stories in Europe to stimulate more enthusiasm. Thomas soon realised that what he saw on the Western Front was hardly likely to bring recruits flocking to the American army, and so he went instead to the Middle East, where he met T. E. Lawrence, who was with the Arabs fighting the Turks. The romanticised dispatches Thomas produced about Lawrence of Arabia not only became brilliant propaganda, but also grew into one of the most enduring myths of the war, turning Lawrence into a national hero and Thomas—"the American who made my vulgar reputation; a well-intentioned, intensely crude and pushful fellow"[15]—into a millionaire.

The influence of this barrage of propaganda on the American public cannot be overemphasised. The war historian J. F. C. Fuller writes of a "propaganda-demented people" and says flatly that there can be little doubt that President Wilson would have remained neutral "had it not been for the octopus of propaganda, whose tentacles gripped him like a vice."[16] Raymond B. Fosdick, in an article titled "America at War," summarised the ecstasy of hate that gripped the American people. "We hated with a common hate that was exhilarating. The writer of this review remembers attending a great meeting in New England, held under the auspices of a Christian Church—God save the mark! A speaker demanded that the Kaiser, when captured, be boiled in oil, and the entire audience stood on chairs to scream its hysterical approval. This was the mood we were in. This was the kind of madness that had seized us."[17]

Those who did not accept the need for America to go to war or who felt she could best contribute by using her influence for a negotiated armistice were shouted down, and the nation united to defeat Germany.

In these circumstances, American war correspondents faced an almost impossible task. The Constitution guaranteed the freedom of the press. The public was hungry for news, there was no censorship within the United States, and, as one congressman put it, "There is no public opinion in the world which ought to be so well informed with regard to the causes of the war, or the incidents of this war, or the principles of this war, as the opinion of the USA." But the principles of a nation at war demanded control not only of the way people fought, but also of the way they thought. Such influential opinion makers as war correspondents could not be allowed to write freely lest they create unproductive reactions, and so the whole apparatus of censorship at the front and the control and manipulation of news that had crippled the British war correspondent was now reproduced for his American colleagues.

The rules for accreditation of a war correspondent to the American Expeditionary Force have to be read to be believed. First, the correspondent had to appear personally before the Secretary of War or his authorised representative and swear that he would "convey the truth to the people of the United States" but refrain from disclosing facts that might aid the enemy. Then he had to write—and the authorities defined "write" to mean with a pen, not a typewriter—an autobiographical sketch, which had to include an account of his work, his experience, his character, and his health. He had to say what he planned to do when he reached Europe and where he planned to go. Then he or his paper had to pay $1,000 to the army to cover his equipment and maintenance and post a $10,000 bond to ensure that he would comport himself "as a gentleman of the Press." If he were sent back for any infraction of the rules, the $10,000 would be forfeited and given to charity. He was allowed to take an assistant—for a further $500 maintenance fee—and if he did not wish to use army transport he could buy a car or ship one overseas for his personal use. Correspondents wore no uniforms, but were obliged to wear a green armband with a large red "C."[18]

Frederick Palmer, who had been the only American war correspondent accredited to the British army, where, because of his pro-British dispatches, he had been treated better than any British correspondent, was commissioned to organise and direct the American correspondents as part of Colonel Dennis E. Nolan's staff at G-2 (Intelligence). Palmer, who was a personal friend of the commander-in-chief of the American forces, General Pershing, had turned down an offer of $40,000 a year to cover the American force for the *New York Herald* syndicate and instead had signed on with Pershing as a major, at $2,400 a year plus allowances. Palmer was a highly experienced war correspondent. He had covered the Greco-Turkish clash, the Boxer Rebellion, the Moro insurrection in the Philippines, the Russo-Japanese War, and Pershing's expedition against Pancho Villa in Mexico. He had been impressed by his experiences with the British army in France and by its method of controlling correspondents. He now made the mistake of trying to impose the same restrictions on his American colleagues, a different group altogether.

They were flamboyant, energetic news seekers, whose very presence seemed to attract trouble. Floyd Gibbons of the *Chicago Tribune* sailed for Europe in February, a few days after the severance of diplomatic relations between the United States and Germany, deliberately choosing the *Laconia*, an 18,000-ton Cunard liner, because he reasoned she would attract German submarines. Gibbons was absolutely right. The *Laconia* was torpedoed off southern Ireland at 10:55 P.M. on February 25, 1917, and sank twenty minutes later. Gibbons had his first big story. He took to a lifeboat, where the other passengers—including a French-Polish actress with the amazing name of Titsie Siklosi—described him later as appearing "cheerful and busy." He passed out cigarettes, offered to help the crew with the oars, and kept a look-out for swimmers.

Early next morning Gibbons was landed at Queenstown, soaking wet, half-paralysed with cold, and with eyes bloodshot from wind and lack of sleep. He got off a quick cable to the *Tribune*, saying where he was and what had happened, and asking for two hours to thaw out and get his story down. He began typing almost immediately, and wrote one of the most vivid, arresting, and detailed dispatches of the war. He not only managed to produce an early casualty list that varied little from the final one, but he also interviewed many survivors, including a member of Lifeboat 3, who gave Gibbons the facts for this intriguing exchange.

> As the boat's crew steadied its head to the wind, a black hulk, glistening wet and standing about eight feet above the surface of the water, approached slowly and came to a stop opposite the boat and not six feet from the side of it. "What ship was dat?" The correct words in throaty English with a German accent came from the dark hull, according to Chief Steward Ballyn's statement to me later.
>
> "The *Laconia*, Cunard Line," responded the steward.
>
> "Vot did she weight?" was the next question from the submarine.
>
> "Eighteen thousand tons."
>
> "Any passengers?"
>
> "Seventy-three," replied Ballyn, "men, women and children, some of them in this boat. She had over two hundred in the crew."
>
> "Did she carry cargo?"
>
> "Yes."
>
> "Vell, you'll be all right. The patrol will pick you up soon," and without further sound, save for the almost silent fixing of the conning tower lid, the submarine moved off.[19]

The appearance of Gibbons' story caused a sensation throughout the United States. It was acclaimed as one of the finest war-correspondence pieces of the period and was read from the floor of both houses of Congress, special emphasis being made of the point that the U-boat captain's query as to the identity of his victim proved that Germany's unrestricted-submarine-warfare policy really meant what it said.

With this reputation behind him, Gibbons was not content to sit around at AEF headquarters at Neufchâteau, and he frequently clashed with Palmer over his unauthorised trips and with other, less energetic correspondents over his opinion of them—"lazy louts who won't get out after their own news." He was always intent on being where "the real action" was, and inevitably he succeeded. In June 1918, with a company of Marines attacking across an open field near Belleau Wood, he raised his head to see what was happening and received a machine-gun bullet through his shoulder and another through his left eye. He recovered in the American Hospital in Paris and thereafter wore the black eyepatch that became his trademark. But the experience had sobered him. He took fewer risks, and the *Laconia* story remained his best effort of the war.

Jimmy Hopper, a shy, small man, who wrote for *Collier's Weekly*, not only got into battle with the Twenty-sixth Infantry, but took fifteen German prisoners as well. He was attempting to enter Cantigny when the Germans, mistaking him for an officer, surrendered. Hopper said he did the only thing that occurred to him—he marched the Germans back to the American lines, bellowing orders like a sergeant-major. But then he failed to write the story. His custom, he explained to his colleagues, was to schedule his stories in a methodical fashion in his notebook, and he had yet to write a piece about the personal heroism of a nun.

Peggy Hull, a woman war correspondent, paid her own way to Europe because her newspaper, the *El Paso Times*, could not afford to send her. She was not accredited, but she had one major advantage —she knew General Pershing, having met him while covering his border skirmishes with Pancho Villa, and having won his admiration by marching where the troops marched, sleeping on the ground in a poncho, and yet keeping her blond, brown-eyed femininity. So when she reported at his headquarters in France, the usually austere general broke into a big smile, put out two welcoming hands, and said, "Well, well, Peggy. You're like a breath from home." Soon afterwards a series of articles by-lined only "Peggy" appeared in the Paris edition of the *Chicago Tribune* and its parent paper in the United States. They dealt with visits to army training camps, and made it clear that at one camp the writer had been the personal guest of the commanding general, with the permission of Pershing himself. They were neat, off-beat pieces, and other newspapers began to pick up the stories from the *Tribune*. At first the correspondents at the press division headquarters in Neufchâteau were intrigued, and then angry. They pushed their protest—at an unaccredited correspondent's being accorded favours—as far as GHQ at Chaumont, and then to Washington. Neither Peggy Hull's friendship with Pershing nor her popularity with the troops (she wrote the way Ernie Pyle did in the Second World War: low-keyed stories about events in the daily lives of ordinary GIs) could get her properly accredited. For some months she managed by sharing his vital pink pass with Joseph Pierson, a business representative of the *Chicago Tribune*. Then the army forbade this, also, and Peggy Hull, a victim of her male rivals, was forced to spend the rest of the war in Paris.

Irvin Cobb made a second appearance, again for the *Saturday Evening Post*. His earlier dispatches had made him one of the most widely read American journalists, and as a result he enjoyed more freedom at the front than most of his colleagues did. His appearance—melancholy expression, apple-red cheeks, alligator jaw, fierce eyebrows, and a permanent cigar—made him easily recognisable, and the American troops regularly mobbed him. Without exception, they would tell him that they had read his book on his earlier war experiences, *Speaking of Operations*, which caused Cobb to remark, "If you guys are telling the truth, then my publishers have held out on me."

Cobb, scrupulous about important facts, was not above altering minor ones if it was to his advantage. Harry Hansen of the *Chicago Daily News* was often with him, but kept quiet for more than fifty years about Cobb's professional methods. "We were associated in the march to the Marne (almost) and as I was the only man present who could talk with German officers, Cobb would come over and ask, 'What did he say?' When I translated he would laugh heartily. Later on, when I read his reports in the *Saturday Evening Post*, I discovered that all the remarks had been addressed to him. In one of his books…he describes 'the most interesting thing that happened to me.' Actually it happened to me. But I bore him no ill will, for I learned much from him about building a readable story. When he wrote his autobiography, *Exit Laughing*, in 1941, he did give me an oblique credit line. He wrote: 'One young man whose name I can't recall...' and I believe him."[20]

Any attempt to regiment such highly individual journalists as these was clearly going to be difficult, but Palmer, backed by General Pershing, was determined to do so. Since a lot of the difficulties the First World War corps of American war correspondents encountered were due to the personalities of these two men, it is worth pausing to look a little further at them. Pershing, a West Point graduate, was a martinet who grew furious at the slightest infraction of military regulations. Partly of German descent, he admired both the discipline and the war skills of the Germans and tried to make his troops emulate them. Yet he was a sentimental family man, whose letters to his wife, Frances, usually began "My darling Frankie" and were generally signed "Jackie." It was perhaps his devotion to his wife and children that caused the cold aloofness he had developed by the time he arrived as commander-in-chief of the American Expeditionary Force. In 1915, one week before his wife, their three daughters, and their son were due to join him in El Paso, from where he was conducting his campaign against the Mexican Pancho Villa, he was told by telegram that a fire had destroyed his house in the officers' quarters at the Presidio in San Francisco and that his entire family except his son, Francis, aged six, had died in it. Pershing took the news without any visible emotion, but within days his hair whitened and his mouth acquired a tightness that marked it henceforth. He had few intimates in France, and gave few press conferences and no individual interviews. His treatment of Westbrook Pegler, later to be a famous columnist, was typical. At the time, Pegler, with United Press, was, at twenty-three, the youngest war correspondent at American press headquarters. So when he announced that he was going across to GHQ to demand a personal interview with Pershing, his colleagues merely grinned. Half an hour later Pegler was back and busy tapping at his typewriter. At length, one of the senior correspondents could contain himself no longer and casually asked Pegler what Pershing had said. Pegler pulled the paper from his typewriter and handed it over. It read: "This correspondent had an interview with General Pershing today. The General said, 'Pegler, get the hell out of my office.'" Pegler's colleagues learned later that this was an entirely accurate report of what had occurred.[21]

Meanwhile, Palmer became more and more the army officer, dispensing only the sparsest information in releases and then usually confining them to laudatory reports on American operations. Since the correspondents were determined to give their reading public the facts about what was happening to their sons, husbands, and brothers in France, trouble was inevitable.

It began with the arrival of the first units of the AEF at Saint-Nazaire, on the coast of Brittany. Palmer had imposed certain restrictions on American correspondents, including a ban on mentioning the name of the port of arrival until the troops had all landed. *Paris Soir*, however, carried a headline announcing the port as Saint-Nazaire. Although the censor had deleted every word from the story underneath, leaving only a blank column, the headline was, of course, enough. It was picked up in London and published there, a clean beat on all the American war correspondents, who began to receive angry cables from their editors. Heywood Broun of the *New York Tribune* sought to make the best of the situation by sending a descriptive article. He submitted to the censor a dispatch in which the first American soldier down the gangplank was quoted as saying, "Do they allow enlisted men in the saloons in this town?" Palmer's censors insisted that this was fiction and refused to clear it. Broun admitted that he had used a paraphrase, but argued that this or something like it had happened, or could have. Since the censors were in no position to disprove the story, they reluctantly passed it, but made a note to watch everything Broun sent with particular care. For his part, Broun went about expressing open contempt for the way the army was running things—"all spit and polish." He succeeded in getting stories passed, even when they included unflattering references to General Pershing, by using phrases that, although cutting, did not violate anything in the censors' handbook. For instance, after it became known that the French soldiers affectionately referred to Marshal Joffre as "Papa," Broun sent a cable saying, "Soldiers of the AEF will never call Pershing 'Papa,'" and he followed this up with his own comment on GHQ at Chaumont: "The American army is doing as well as can be expected."[22]

When Palmer pointed out that this sort of remark infringed the spirit, if not the letter, of the censorship regulations, Broun replied bluntly that he did not consider himself bound in conscience to respect the censorship, since he had signed the correspondents' agreement under compulsion; if he had not signed, he would not have been allowed to accompany the army.

The feud continued, but Palmer was too busy with another problem to give it his full attention. Some of the senior and most influential war correspondents were threatening to break the story of the supply scandal that had hampered the AEF ever since its landing. Although the full extent of the monumental blunders in supplying the American army did not come to light until after the war, several correspondents knew enough to make things uncomfortable for Pershing and Palmer. The truth was that, although the AEF might not have been the worst-armed, worst-supplied American army ever fielded, it was certainly in contention for the title. The mobilisation effort, begun with such ballyhoo, had failed on most counts. The United States finished the war without forwarding a single aircraft to the battle zone; of 4,400 tanks put under contract for building, only fifteen reached France, and they arrived after the Armistice; by January 1918, eight months after entering the war, America had not turned out a single heavy gun, because she had neither the tools nor the workmen. But for the arsenals of her allies, the United States would have been unable to fight.[23]

Palmer discovered that Jannis Wood of the *Chicago Daily News*, Tom Johnson of the *New York Sun*, and Herbert Corey of Associated Newspapers had found out about supply shortages. He therefore invited them to Chaumont for a frank talk with Pershing. In front of the three correspondents, Pershing drafted a carefully worded cable to the War Department suggesting that some moderate criticism of the supply difficulties would be preferable to the loss of confidence by the public if the whole story were broken by hostile instead of friendly sources. Pershing's ploy was a clever one. If the department approved, then he planned to allow the three correspondents to write, under Palmer's control, a watered-down story on the supply muddle. If the department did not agree, the correspondents would at least see that it was not Pershing who was muzzling them. The Secretary of War, Newton D. Baker, rejected Pershing's request. His view, suavely conveyed, was that such stories, no matter how moderate in their criticism, would tend to shake confidence in Pershing and his staff. The correspondents could do nothing, and the matter appeared settled.

Then, in December 1917, Broun broke the scandal wide open. He packed his bags, returned to New York, and, breaking his correspondent's undertaking, wrote a series of bitter articles for the *New York World*, the first of which was headlined SUPPLY BLUNDERS HAMPER FIRST U.S. UNITS IN FRANCE It told of tractors delivered where motorcycles were needed, mules disembarked without harnesses, trucks landed without motors, and urgently needed equipment left behind on the docks. The War Department immediately withdrew Broun's accreditation, and he was fined the $10,000 his paper had deposited on his behalf. Pershing was furious and for a time considered what further action he could take against Broun. Palmer, however, persuaded him that it would be better to let the matter drop.[24]

Censorship was now under heavy attack. Westbrook Pegler, although never able to get an interview with Pershing, had found a far more important story. In the harsh winter of 1917–18, he noted with increasing anger the daily funeral processions that moved out of American billets and across the hills around Neufchâteau. He soon found out what caused them. Straggling back from the front line, weary and soaked from chill rains, the American troops had no warm or dry clothing into which to change. The former sheep barns that housed most of the troops were old and in poor repair. The only heat came from small oil stoves, which burned so poorly that the windows had to be kept open for ventilation. Colds turned to pneumonia, and the death rate rose steadily.

Pegler decided that this story would justify breaking censorship, and so, at the suggestion of the United Press' Paris bureau chief, Lowell Mellett, he typed out a long and detailed report listing not only the pneumonia scandal, but every censorship blunder that had occurred since the Saint-Nazaire landing. "Censorship," Pegler wrote, "is developing more in the news interests of the military than in that of the American reader." Mellett took the report to London personally and gave it to the United Press manager there, Edward L. Keen. Keen backed Pegler's view that this was something the American public should know about and put a summary of the report on the wire, addressed to the United Press manager, Roy Howard, in New York. British censors not only stopped the message, but forwarded it to Pershing at Chaumont. Pershing handled the affair carefully. He used Pegler's age as a lever and simply made an official request to the United Press to replace him. At twenty-three he was, Pershing wrote, too youthful and inexperienced. United Press had little choice in the matter, and Pegler was recalled.[25]

By now censorship had reached almost ludicrous proportions. The correspondents tried to send a story about cases of wine presented to the Americans by the French as a gesture of goodwill. The censors vetoed it on the ground that "it suggests bibulous indulgence by American soldiers which might offend temperance forces in the United States." Daniel Dillon of the International News Service submitted an expense account to his office and, unable to remember where the money had gone, wrote "entertaining General Pershing: $250." The money was not reimbursed, and Dillon, checking to see what had happened, found that Palmer had taken to censoring expense accounts and had deleted the item.

Like Shepherd with his story of the Zeppelin raid on London, the American correspondents became adept at beating the censor, by turning his own rules against him or by the use of esoteric codes. Wythe Williams of the *New York Times* was brilliant at this, and his inventiveness gave the *Times* two notable scoops. The first, late in November 1916, began with a cryptic cable he sent the paper's managing editor, Carr Van Anda, suggesting he should read a recent article by Alden Brooks in *Collier's Weekly*. Van Anda did so. The article covered the career of General Henri Pétain. Van Anda pondered a while and then queried Williams by cable: DOES BROOKS MAN WANT JOB WITH US? Williams answered promptly:YES, WE DICKERING WITH HIM NOW. Van Anda easily deduced that Pétain was involved in some change of command. But what? He cabled Williams again: IS BROOKS MAN TO HAVE ONLY FRENCH BRANCH HOUSE OR ENTIRE FIRM? IN ANY CASE WILL PRESENT LOCAL MANAGER BE PROVIDED WITH ANOTHER PLACE, POSSIBLY ADMINISTRATIVE? Williams replied: HE WANTS BOTH OFFICES.The censors read the exchange with some boredom. Obviously the *Times* was dickering for the services of some writer. Then the negotiations broke down. Williams cabled again: THINK BROOKS MAN DEMANDS TOO MUCH. CANNOT GIVE IT TO HIM. Van Anda had almost all he needed. Pétain aspired to lead not only the French high command, but also the British and Belgian forces on the Western Front. However, the Allies were not prepared to give him such wide powers. Another cable from Williams took the story a stage further: BROOKS MAN WANTS TOO MUCH THINK IT BEST CONSIDER HIS ASSISTANT. A few hours later he cabled the last link: ASSISTANT ACCEPTS. Van Anda knew the assistant could only be General Robert Nivelle, the commander at Verdun, so he prepared a story—date-lined Washington, to protect Williams—and ran it on December 7, 1916. The story said General Joffre's retirement was under consideration and that Nivelle would succeed him. Pétain had initially been considered, but had demanded larger control than France alone could give him. There were furious denials, but the *Times* stood firm, and five days after it had broken the story Paris announced officially Joffre's retirement and Nivelle's appointment as his successor.[26]

By mid-April 1917, Williams was ready for his second scoop. Disillusion with Nivelle's leadership had become apparent, so

Williams revived the "Brooks man" code for an exchange with Van Anda and tipped him off that there had been a renewed offer of the French high command to Pétain. Pétain had accepted the appointment, and the *Times* carried the story on April 29. This time, denials were fewer, competitors having become wary after the first story, and, as was expected, Pétain's promotion was officially announced on May 15. Both Williams and Van Anda kept the secret of how the stories had been obtained until some time after the war.

Fred Ferguson, a quiet-spoken United Press correspondent, sent to France to replace Westbrook Pegler, specialised in using the censorship regulations for his own ends. In May 1918 the press division learned that Captain Archie Roosevelt, a son of the former President, had been wounded in action. Just as quickly, the reporters learned that they were not to publish a word about it until an announcement had been made in Washington. The group of disappointed correspondents broke up and went away. One, Ferguson, lingered. He asked the censor whether, as had happened in similar cases, Roosevelt had been awarded the Croix de Guerre. The censor confirmed that he had. "Well," Ferguson said, "I'm going to send that." When the censor protested, Ferguson quoted Regulation 3 of the censorship instructions: "Decorations...are considered news. Can be published by American correspondents." The censor checked with GHQ, which confirmed that Ferguson was within his rights in asking to send such a cable, and his brief message was passed uncut. The story made headlines, and the belated official announcement of Captain Roosevelt's wounding passed almost unnoticed.

But Ferguson's biggest scoop—a masterpiece of organisation, rather than observation or good writing—came after Palmer had given up the post of press chief and his much more co-operative assistant, Gerald Morgan, had taken over. Congress had started to press for more realistic reporting from the front, and gradually Pershing had been persuaded to accept this view. By this time Palmer had come to be regarded by his former colleagues as stuffy and out-of-date, as well as overrated in his earlier eminence as a war correspondent. Palmer, who was in Washington, returned to Chaumont to find that he had been "kicked upstairs" by being appointed to Pershing's personal staff as an adviser and that Morgan had been made acting field press chief.

Morgan was much more receptive to an unusual idea, and so Ferguson was not worried when he woke Morgan in the early hours of the day the Americans were to attack the Saint-Mihiel salient, the first really big operation planned and executed entirely by Americans. Ferguson, the correspondent, and Morgan, the censor, had both attended, a few hours earlier, a detailed briefing on the attack given by Colonel Dennis Nolan, the American intelligence chief. Nolan had described exactly how the attack would be made, hour by hour. It was clear that every precaution had been taken to make certain that it would succeed, and this gave Ferguson an idea. While the other correspondents turned in, to be ready for a busy day, Ferguson sat down and wrote the story of the battle as if it had already happened. He wrote it, following Nolan's outline, in brief sections, none longer than about fifty words. Then he took his story to Morgan and asked him to censor it then and there. "What's the idea?" Morgan said. Ferguson explained. He would leave the already censored copy with Morgan. As intelligence reports came through indicating that each phase of the attack had gone according to plan, all Morgan had to do was to file Ferguson's pre-written section, or "take," for him. If something went wrong, Morgan could tear up the brief "take" that referred to it. Even if half of Ferguson's messages could not be sent, the other half would provide his New York office with enough material to build up a story.

In case the special Signal Corps wire to Paris became overloaded, Ferguson had made other arrangements. His copy was to go at "urgent" rates via the post-office at Nancy and then by four different world cable routes. If delays or breakdowns stopped any of them, there was a good chance that the others would fill in the gaps at their destination in New York. It was an ingenious if unusual plan, and Morgan could find no real reason why he should not go along with it.

It worked even better than expected. A press officer conducting two correspondents from the Associated Press, Ferguson's rival organisation, went off on his own during the battle and left the two AP men in Ferguson's car. Ferguson, naturally, decided that he wanted to see every sector the Americans had captured, and it was 7:00 P.M. before the worried AP men got back to the telegraph office at Nancy. Their only consoling thought all this time was that their rival, Ferguson, had not been able to send a story, either. But when they arrived at the press office the correspondents already there shouted good-natured abuse at Ferguson. His story had got through, take by take, and had been pushed out to United Press subscribers within a few hours of each phase of the battle. A cable, which every correspondent had already read, awaited Ferguson inside the office. It was from Roy Howard, the United Press' general manager,

143

and it read: CONGRATULATIONS ON YOUR GREATEST BEAT.[27]

The end of the war came as a tremendous shock to many Germans. The government had concealed casualties from the public, minimised the effect of America's intervention, and exaggerated the extent of Germany's resources, so that the news of Germany's surrender was difficult to believe. Many Germans, feeling tricked and betrayed, tried to rationalise what had occurred. Philip Gibbs noticed it: "I became aware of a myth which persisted in the minds of most Germans, and which nothing would alter. 'Our armies, of course, were never defeated in the field', I heard. 'It was a stab in the back which betrayed them. Revolution from behind by Communists and Jews'."[28]

By 1919, when the peace conference assembled at Versailles, this legend—on which the Nazis were to flourish—had become intertwined with German policy: Germany was not going to forget the betrayal; the Fatherland would rise from shame. One correspondent saw this attitude at close quarters. He was Burnett Hershey, a Paris representative of the *New York Sun*.

Every newspaper editor in the world wanted a first-hand story of how the Germans were taking their defeat. But the German delegation to the conference, headed by Count Ulrich von Brockdorff-Rantzau, was restricted to the old Hôtel des Réservoirs in Versailles, which was surrounded by a high stockade and guarded by sentries. The stockade connected with another hotel, the Vatel, which housed the German press corps. Every morning the German correspondents would march from the Hôtel Vatel to the Hôtel des Réservoirs and vanish inside. Hershey devised a scheme for joining them. He bought a pair of striped trousers, a frock-coat, a Tyrolean hat, a pair of heavy spectacles, and a shabby dispatch case. In this disguise, he walked up to the sentry at the entrance to the stockade, flashed his Allied press pass, and walked boldly through. Once inside, he waited for the German press corps to come marching past, fell into step with them, and introduced himself to the nearest correspondent. This was a man named Wolff, of the *Berliner Tageblatt*. Wolff had a fellow correspondent's admiration for Hershey's nerve and smuggled him past the guard outside the Hôtel des Réservoirs and into the press room, where he chatted with the Germans for two hours and promised, when he left, to do some shopping for them and to return another day. Hershey brought off his bluff a second time, but still did not succeed in getting what he really needed to round off his story—an interview with Count von Brockdorff-Rantzau.

On the day the peace treaty was handed to the Germans, every correspondent in Paris was present. They heard Count von Brockdorff-Rantzau, remaining seated and speaking with a defiance and bitterness that angered the Allies, refuse to admit Germany's sole guilt for the war. While the other correspondents returned to write about this, Hershey hurried to the Hôtel des Réservoirs in his disguise, smuggled himself into a meeting between the German delegation and the German press corps, and got one of the few scoops of the whole peace conference.

By accident, he chose a table at what he thought was the back of the room, only to find that arrangements were reversed and that the seat next to him was occupied by Count von Brockdorff-Rantzau himself. This probably saved him. The Count looked straight ahead and, without realising that there was an American correspondent in the room, crowded as it was with Germans, made a brief speech. "Clemenceau, that senile old man, hurling insults at our people," he said, "we are not so to be treated. The only way for me to articulate my feelings was deliberately to remain seated…The Fatherland has been dealt a heavy blow. There is work to be done. We are Germans. We will not forget. We will rise from this shame." Hershey waited apprehensively until the Count had finished and then left. He hurried back to the press room at the Hôtel Crillon in Paris and, sitting in his frock-coat and Tyrolean hat—"to keep the mood"— he wrote his story.[29]

## Chapter Seven

# The Remedy for
# Bolshevism is Bullets
# 1917–1919

If we are, in the end, forced to go, we shall slam the door behind us
in such a way that the echo shall be felt throughout the world.

—Leon Trotsky

No matter what one thinks of Bolshevism, it is undeniable that the
Russian Revolution is one of the great events of human history, and
the rise of the Bolsheviki a phenomenon of world-wide importance.
Just as historians search the records for the minutest details of the
story of the Paris Commune, so they will want to know what happened in Petrograd in November 1917, the spirit which animated
the people, and how the leaders looked, talked, and acted...In the
struggle my sympathies were not neutral. But in telling the story of
those great days I have tried to see events with the eye of a conscientious reporter, interested in setting down the truth.

—John Reed in
*Ten Days That Shook the World*

———

The Russian Revolution and the subsequent Allied intervention
to try to overthrow the Bolsheviks, a campaign that established
the pattern for the relations that have existed between the Soviet
Union and the West ever since, must rank as two of the major
events in this century's history. Yet the public was not kept
informed as to what was happening in Russia in those momentous

days in 1917; nor of the intervention and progress of the Allied forces in 1918-19. In both matters, correspondents in Russia—with three exceptions—failed lamentably to meet the challenge. Most of them, in common with their editors, had no idea what Bolshevism was and had no intention of learning. The few who did realise the impact that the Revolution would have on world affairs, and who took a line different from that of their governments, were silenced—by the censor or some other authority. The others made little effort to see beyond what they were told to see. They accepted as fact not only the propaganda of their own governments, but also the obviously suspect reports of the Czarist agencies in exile. One journalist, Harold Williams, who was in southern Russia for *The Times* of London and the *New York Times*, and therefore a correspondent of immense influence, was so personally involved with the anti-Bolshevist forces that he should never have been given the assignment. Others translated wishful thinking into fact; the *New York Times*, in the two years from November 1917 to November 1919, reported no fewer than ninety-one times that the Bolsheviks were about to fall or, indeed, had already fallen.[1] And when, despite the reservations of President Wilson, the Allies went ahead with intervention—at first to "stop the Germans walking through Russia" and then, after the war ended, to "stop the Red peril"—the correspondents reported either grossly exaggerated successes or nothing at all. Yet what a story awaited their telling!

Three hundred thousand Allied soldiers marched into Russia to fight the Germans and stayed to fight the Red Army. There were Frenchmen, Britons, Americans, and Italians. There were Canadians, Australians, and Japanese. There were Balts, Poles, Greeks, and Finns. And there were Czechs, Slovaks, Estonians, and Latvians. They drew a ring around Moscow and Petrograd that threatened to strangle the Russian Revolution in its infancy, and their actions, coupled with the Allied economic blockade, increased Russian casualties from famine, disease, and civil war to close to 14 million.

Then the war against Germany ended. The months passed, and when the Allied governments kept their soldiers fighting in Russia, for a cause they neither understood nor believed in, the soldiers mutinied. The French, the Americans, the Canadians, and the British all mutinied. Some shot their officers and surrendered to the Bolsheviks. Some raised red flags, sang revolutionary songs, and refused to obey orders. So little of all this appeared in print that not only was the newspaper reader at the time kept in ignorance of the role his countrymen were playing in the intervention, but a student today can find little reference to it in his country's history books. What can only be described as a conspiracy—in which war correspondents were major participants—kept from public scrutiny events in Russia that were unfavourable to the Allies. A few correspondents refused to keep quiet, but in general the Russian Revolution posed a challenge that they were unable to meet. At a time when objective reporting was vital, and could even have influenced the course of history, their contribution to public knowledge on this matter of world importance was, to quote Walter Lippmann, "about as useful as that of an astrologer or an alchemist."[2]

When Russia went to war against Germany in 1914, it was without any foreboding of disaster. The army, as it creaked into mobilisation, was the largest in the world. The peasants and the workers, inspired by an emotional love of Mother Russia, and the chance to eat regularly, responded willingly to the first call-up, only to find that they were led by a minister for war who had not read a military manual in twenty-five years. Many were sent to the trenches without boots, without proper clothing, and sometimes without even rifles. A front of ten miles would have one machine gun. Batteries of six-inch guns would be supplied with four-inch shells. The tactics of the Czarist officers were to send their troops against the Germans in wave after wave, in the hope that what could not be won any other way could be won by sheer weight of numbers.

Russian casualties were unbelievable, even by First World War standards. The garrison regiment of Kiev, the 165th, consisting of about 4,000 men, had such a high casualty rate that *36,000 replacements passed through it in one year*.[3] Hindenburg, the German commander, estimated total Russian casualties at 5 million to 8 million, and he complained about a new military problem: how to use machine guns when the field of fire was blocked by mounds of Russian corpses. By late in 1916, when 15 million Russians had been mobilised, the army was reeling before the Germans on the 1,000-mile northern front and struggling desperately with the Turks in the Caucasus. The industrial and transport system could no longer cope with an army as large as this, and the Allied landing at Gallipoli, designed both to ease the pressure and to open a route through the Black Sea for food and supplies, had failed miserably. The Allies found themselves facing the bitter prospect that Russia was losing her will to fight.

Little of this background to the Russian Revolution found its way into the Allied press. Following their initial victories, the Russians refused to allow war correspondents at the front, except for occasional conducted tours *after* a battle had been fought, and such a decisive engagement as the Battle of Tannenberg, in August 1914, was not reported at all at the time, received only incomplete mention in 1915, and was not fully reported until after the war.

There was, however, one British war correspondent who managed to get to the Russian front and stay there for two years, and yet who, although he saw a lot of this, did not report it. Robert Liddell, representing the illustrated weekly *The Sphere*, made his way to the Polish front as a member of the Red Cross. Once there, he overcame the ban on war correspondents by persuading the 165th Regiment to make him an honorary officer, not too difficult for a Russian-speaking Englishman with good connections to arrange. He got his dispatches and his photographs, taken with a £4 Kodak camera, back to London uncensored by the simple expedient of attaching ten roubles to each packet he submitted to the Russian censor. Liddell has said he witnessed the terrible state of the Russian army and its unbelievable casualty rate, "but I didn't write about it. My position was rather irregular, so I was careful not to write anything that was too controversial."⁴ Liddell was not alone.

All the major Western newspapers and press agencies had resident correspondents in Petrograd, but, with a few exceptions, what they wrote bore little relation to what was actually occurring. There were two important reasons for this. The first was that the alliance with Russia was an embarrassment to the Allies in the propaganda field, challenging the basic ideals for which they claimed the war was being fought. If this was a war between the forces of good and evil, between light and dark, between democracy and absolutism, then what were the Allies doing fighting alongside Imperial Russia, a by-word for the ruthlessness and cruelty of its tyrants? It was obvious, therefore, that dispatches dealing with the corruption, muddle, and incompetence of the Russian army would not find space in the Allied press and that the shortcomings of the Russian autocracy would remain an undiscussed subject until the end of the war. Moreover, the majority of the foreign correspondents in Petrograd were British or French, and to them the thought that the Russian military machine was running down and might actually stop was too painful to contemplate. If the Russians stopped fighting, the German divisions on the Eastern Front could be switched to Flanders, and the whole might of a united German army could roll across France to the Channel, and perhaps beyond. So while the evidence that Russia was reaching the end of her military resources mounted daily, the British and French newspapers, with the exception of the *Manchester Guardian*, toed the official line: Russia could carry on the war indefinitely.

Credit for the *Guardian*'s having been the only newspaper to realise and to print the truth belongs largely to the best British war correspondent to emerge from this period, Morgan Philips Price. The Price family had been in the Gloucestershire timber trade since the eighteenth century and in the 1850's had started to import timber from Russia. Philips Price, having learnt Russian, went to Siberia in 1910 on a scientific expedition, and generally interested himself in Russian affairs. When the war began, he was appalled at the alliance with Russia. C. P. Scott, the *Guardian*'s, great editor, took the same view, and, since any information about what was happening in war-time Russia was scarce, he decided, in the winter of 1914, to send Philips Price there. His brief was not only to send dispatches, but also to keep Scott privately informed, so as to help him to formulate the newspaper's policy. Philips Price stayed on, saw the war, the Revolution, and the start of the subsequent Allied intervention, and, with the American John Reed, stands head and shoulders above any other war correspondent of the time.

The blame for Britain's state of public ignorance about Russia must rest largely with *The Times*, whose correspondent in Petrograd was Robert Wilton, a man of nearly fifty, who had been in Russia from an early age and who, before joining *The Times*, had for fourteen years been a correspondent for the *New York Herald*. Wilton, whose son was serving in a Russian regiment, had visited the front early in the war, but was now concentrating on political news. On November 16, 1916, Wilton took a hard look at what was happening in Petrograd and then wrote to Wickham Steed, the foreign editor of *The Times*, in some alarm. The dynasty was in peril, Wilton said, and the morale of the people low; blundering had marked every act of the Russian ministers since the war started, and "in a country teeming with food...we are bereft of the most elementary necessities of life."[5]

Not only did *The Times* completely ignore this message from its own correspondent, but on December 11 it carried a leading article—based on a Reuters message—headed RUSSIA FIRM AND UNITED. On December 29 Rasputin was murdered. *The Times* carried nothing beyond the bare facts of the murder. Wilton cabled the details, the background, and an assessment of the murder's probable effect on Russian affairs, but, as *The Times* later admitted, "the editor, influenced to some degree by a hint from the Foreign Office, decided that the details, though of a lurid interest, were not fit for the columns of *The Times*." [6]

In some desperation, Wilton wrote to Steed on January 19, 1917, pleading with him to recognise how serious the situation in Russia was. "Things are in an appalling state...chaos has poisoned all the lower branches of the administrations...I hear from all sides that there is a plot to get rid of the Emperor and Empress."[7] The letter reached *The Times* by the end of January, two months before the March Revolution overthrew the Czar and ended the monarchy in Russia for ever. *The Times* ignored it. Its Russian expert, Sir Donald Mackenzie Wallace, had retired, and "there was no one in Printing House Square who was informed about the Russian situation adequately to propound or carry out a Russian policy."[8] Might not *The Times* have taken its own correspondent's word for what was happening or have consulted experts? After the war, *The Times* excused itself on these two counts by saying that Wilton "did not command full confidence" and that the newspaper's foreign department was "too exhausted by routine to inspire articles on a disaster which its correspondent predicted."[9]

It was not until Lord Milner, then Minister without Portfolio, and later Secretary for War, came back from Russia on March 3, after arranging for the Russians to receive supplies of munitions to encourage them to fight on, that *The Times* realised Wilton had been right. Milner saw the editor two days after his return and warned him of impending trouble, but before *The Times* could correct the impression resulting from its failure to report the situation in Russia, the March Revolution occurred.

Beginning with a series of strikes, the revolution spread rapidly. By March 15 a provisional government was formed and the Czar abdicated. All this happened completely unexpectedly and without any co-ordination.* The confusion provides a small measure of excuse for those correspondents on the spot who failed to report what was going on.

On the night of March 12 the telegraph office in Petrograd closed down, so that British newspapers received no reports of what was happening until three days later. The Foreign Office, however, remained fully informed, but decided to release no news to the British press until matters became clearer. Then, overnight on March 15–16, eighteen telegrams from Wilton poured into *The*

---

* To his extreme annoyance, it interrupted the British Ambassador, Sir George Buchanan, on holiday.

*Times*' office. He was able to describe vividly all that was happening, because *The Times*' Petrograd office was alongside the Prefecture, where all the Czar's ministers had taken shelter.

> On a rough computation, four-fifths of the city is in the hands of the troops who have gone over to the Duma [parliament]. Moreover, a huge number of the inhabitants are armed with rifles, revolvers and swords. There is still a good deal of casual firing, but on the whole the armed crowds behave well. They successively stormed and gutted all the police stations, carefully destroying all papers, and releasing prisoners.[10]

Wilton's political comment in one telegram showed that he realised power had passed from the autocracy, but he saw no danger "of the Commune," and he hoped the new Russia would "prosecute the war with unparalleled vigour." *The Times* backed him, warning that a democratic republic in Russia "in present conditions would inevitably result in disruption…wholesale bloodshed and ultimately, in reaction."

The March Revolution occurred while Philips Price was in Tiflis, in the Caucasus, where Grand Duke Nicholas, the Czar's uncle, was viceroy. A few hours after news of the Czar's abdication was received, the Grand Duke summoned Philips Price to an audience and to receive "an important communication." Philips Price found the Grand Duke looking haggard. His eyes were red and his cheeks pale. He had clearly not slept for several nights. "I want to tell you," he said to Philips Price, "that what has happened in Russia in the last twenty-four hours is final and cannot be reversed. I would regard anyone who tries to do so as an enemy of our Fatherland."[11]

Clearly, the Grand Duke thought the chances of restoring the Romanov dynasty were hopeless, and Philips Price telegraphed a message to the *Manchester Guardian* on these lines, quoting the Grand Duke in full. The dispatch appeared in the *Guardian* six days later—but in one edition only. The reason for this remains unknown, but Philips Price believed that his dispatch somehow got past the censor and that after it had appeared in the first edition of the paper the censor must have ordered it to be deleted.

The Americans were openly jubilant about the overthrow of Imperial Russia. The Secretary of State, Robert E. Lansing, said the revolution had removed the one objection to affirming that the battle was between democracy and absolutism. America could now go to war alongside Russia with a clear conscience. President Wilson was lyrical: "The great, generous, Russian people have been added in all their naive majesty and might to the forces that are fighting for freedom in the world, for justice and peace." In many circles in Britain there was equal enthusiasm. The *Manchester Guardian* said, "The sympathy of every man in this country will go out to the Russian people in this supreme hour," and deplored the tendency in other newspapers to take sides over the future government of Russia.[12]

What no one wanted to doubt at this stage was that the new Russia would continue to prosecute the war. The way the *New York Times* handled the news best expressed the desperate wish to believe that Russia would not leave the Allies. In its issue of March 16 it published on the front page a paragraph from London saying, "As the situation is explained to the *New York Times* correspondent, the revolution simply means that German sympathizers in the Russian government have been overthrown and that no chance remains for a separate peace being secretly arranged with Germany." But in the same issue it buried at the foot of the fifth column on page four an interview with Leon Trotsky, who was then in New York. "The cause of the revolution," said Trotsky, "was the unrest of the mass of the people, who were tired of war and the real object was to end the war throughout Europe."

Evidence that Trotsky was right was not long in appearing. Philips Price gave the first indication of the real feeling in Russia against the war. In Moscow, he interviewed the new Foreign Minister, M. Miliukov, who took the Allied line and said bluntly that nothing would satisfy the new government but the end of the Austrian and Turkish empires and Russian annexation of Constantinople. This interview was published in the *Manchester Guardian* on April 26 and then was telegraphed back to Russia, where it caused a sensation. Factory workers and soldiers paraded in the streets with banners proclaiming, "Down with Miliukov. Long live peace between workers of all lands," and a few days later Miliukov was forced to resign.

In April came Lenin's historic journey across Germany from exile—"transported," Churchill wrote later, "in a sealed truck like a plague bacillus from Switzerland into Russia." Few correspondents bothered to report Lenin's arrival. Wilton was visiting the northern front, and so *The Times* had to carry, on April 20, a report on Lenin's passage based on a Reuters telegram. Ten days later, again on the basis of information in a telegram from Reuters, it reported a demonstration in Petrograd at which workmen carried banners demanding that Lenin should "get back to William."

Lenin had made little impression at first, and the Allies remained convinced, against the growing weight of evidence, that Russia could be persuaded actively to continue the war. They embarked on a campaign of propaganda to promote this. They set up press departments in their embassies in Petrograd and asked correspondents to write articles saying that the Russians were eager for a further offensive against Germany. Philips Price refused to do so and told a British embassy official who came to see him that his own evidence was that the Russian army was in no condition to fight and would begin to melt away with the approach of winter. He reported these views to Scott, the *Guardian*'s editor, who went up to London once a week to see the Prime Minister, Lloyd George. Philips Price's views were so different from those the government was receiving that the Foreign Office suggested to Scott that he reassure himself about Philips Price's reliability by sending out another correspondent. Scott sent David Soskice, a British subject of Russian emigrant stock, who compromised his professional objectivity immediately by becoming secretary to the future Prime Minister, Alexander Kerensky.

In July, the Russian army began a major offensive on the southern front and for a while drove the Austrians back. But the Austrians counter-attacked, and the Russians collapsed.

By August, the great garrison towns in Galicia were in uproar and confusion as a million Russian soldiers deserted and started for home. The Allies simply refused to believe this. In Britain, a photograph showing Russian troops packed onto the roofs of railway carriages on their way back to their villages was published in the *Daily Mirror* under the heading RUSSIAN TROOPS HASTEN TO THE FRONT.[13] In the United States, the *New York Times* published a series of dispatches in the first three weeks of August that were, to say the least, decidedly optimistic The headlines varied from RUSSIANS THROW GERMANS BACK to RUSSIANS REPULSE ATTACKS EVERYWHERE, but the theme was the same: the Russians were winning. Unfortunately, this was completely untrue Even Harold Williams, a free-lance journalist who wrote for *New Europe* and other newspapers, and who later, as *The Times* representative, was to emerge as by far the worst war correspondent in Russia, saw the Galician Operation as "a shameful collapse...an hour of national disgrace."

By now the Russian Prime Minister, Kerensky, had begun to lose control, and it was clear that unless the Allies did something drastic Russia would soon be out of the war for good. Then, for light relief, there arrived on the Russian scene one of those larger-than-life Englishmen, who was to establish the precedent for British intervention in Russian affairs. He was the forerunner of the scores of adventurers, spies, and soldiers-of-fortune who were to appear in Russia in the next few years. His name was Oliver Stillingfleet Locker-Lampson, and he was a member of Parliament. His family, which was descended from Oliver Cromwell, had lived at "Rowfant," Sussex, for more than four centuries. The family had its own private railway station and the right to stop a certain number of trains each day so that the Locker-Lampsons could get on or off. Oliver Locker-Lampson had gone to Russia with a British armoured-car squadron, which had been sent as a gesture of Allied solidarity in the fight against Germany, and had been wounded. This eccentric but admittedly brave man involved himself in political intrigues from the moment he arrived in the country, even to the extent of, so he claimed, being invited to help to murder Rasputin. It was not surprising, therefore, that the commander-in-chief of the Russian army, a tough Cossack called Lavr Kornilov, strongly urged Locker-Lampson to help him stage a counter-revolution. Locker-Lampson agreed, and plans were finalised. The British Ambassador, Sir George Buchanan, knew about the plot, did nothing to stop it, and got himself well out of the way by arranging to spend the day on the British residents' golf course.

But the coup went wrong. Kerensky armed the Petrograd workmen and ordered Kornilov to resign his command. By the afternoon of September 11, the counter-revolution was all over and Kornilov was in flight. Locker-Lampson had to take his squadron straight to Archangel, where it was shipped back to Britain. The result of the whole comic mess was that Britain, thanks to Locker-Lampson, was hopelessly compromised in Bolshevik eyes two months before the October Revolution.

*The Times* regretted the failure of the coup, and the Petrograd Society of Journalists wrote an open letter to the Union of English Journalists complaining about the bias in Wilton's reports. *The Times* was also attacked by the *Manchester Guardian* for its general attitude to Russia, the *Guardian* arguing that, although *The Times* might be regarded abroad as the semi-official organ of the Foreign Office, it had no right to criticise those British papers that did not want to see the new government in Russia overthrown.

The follies were to multiply. Correspondents had found the demands of reporting what had occurred in Russia up to October

1917 beyond them; the Bolshevik Revolution now overwhelmed them. Unable to comprehend what was happening, at a loss to explain the strength of Bolshevism, and ignorant of the forces of the extreme Left, most correspondents simply gave up.

Looking back on its own coverage of the Russian Revolution thirty-five years later, *The Times* admitted its shortcomings: "The idea of a campaign *ad majorem proletariatis gloriam* was so foreign to Wilton that he never understood it…More unfortunately still, the idea was equally foreign to Steed [the foreign editor], Dawson [the editor], Northcliffe [the proprietor], to Lloyd George [Prime Minister] and to Milner [soon to be Minister for War]. No one had heard of the forces of the Left except in terms that indicated them to be madmen."[14]

This explains why the rise of the Bolsheviks was not reported, and why their sudden arrival in the corridors of power left most correspondents, and hence their readers, bewildered. Harold Williams had an inkling of what was coming, and in a dispatch sent to the *New York Times* on September 26 he said: "Whatever power there is, is again concentrated in the hands of the Soviets and…the influence of the Bolsheviks has increased enormously." But most correspondents and most newspaper editors refused to take the Bolsheviks seriously. By mid-September, Wilton felt sufficiently confident that nothing earth-shaking was about to happen that he left for London, thus completely missing the Revolution and leaving *The Times* without anyone at all in Russia.*

Of course, events very earth-shaking indeed were occurring. Lenin had returned from hiding in Finland. Kerensky had declared a state of emergency, declared illegal the Soviet's Military Revolutionary Committee, ordered the arrest of Trotsky and other Bolshevik leaders, and banned Bolshevik newspapers. In Petrograd, the Bolsheviks seized the railway stations, the state bank, the power station, the bridges across the river, and the telephone exchange, all without serious resistance. Military reinforcements sent for by Kerensky had not turned up, so he left Petrograd to try to rally the Third Cavalry Corps. During his absence he lost the city. Trotsky's Military Revolutionary Committee announced that the government had fallen and that power had passed to the committee itself. The Winter Palace, where Kerensky's ministers were sheltering, was stormed, and Trotsky

---

*It was to be twenty-two years before *The Times* managed to get a permanent correspondent back into the country.

telegraphed from the front that Kerensky, who had rallied a small force of Cossacks, had been decisively repulsed. When the government's forces in the Kremlin surrendered, it was virtually all over: the Bolsheviks were in power.

Few correspondents witnessed these momentous events, and even fewer understood enough of what was happening to appreciate their significance. High among these few stand the American journalist and poet John Reed, correspondent for *The Masses*, a radical liberal publication in the United States, who had been in Petrograd since August, and Morgan Philips Price, the *Manchester Guardian*'s correspondent. Reed later became a founder member of the Communist Party of America, and his sympathies from the beginning were with the Bolsheviks. But he saw the Revolution with the clear eye of a good and conscientious reporter, and his description of the events in Petrograd in November 1917 is unequalled. Reed, Philips Price, and Arthur Ransome of the *London Daily News* were the only Western correspondents allowed into the Bolshevik headquarters in the Smolny Institute, a girls' school. Reed describes the historic meeting of the Second Congress of Soviets as Lenin's turn came to speak.

> Now Lenin, gripping the edge of the reading stand, letting his little winking eyes travel over the crowd as he stood there waiting, apparently oblivious to the long-rolling ovation, which lasted several minutes. When it finished he said simply, 'We shall now proceed to construct the Socialist order!' Again that overwhelming roar.[15]

The congress later voted on Lenin's motion to end the war—"If the German proletariat realises that we are ready to consider all offers of peace, that will perhaps be the last drop which overflows the bowl; revolution will break out in Germany." The motion was carried unanimously. Reed writes:

> Suddenly, by common impulse, we found ourselves on our feet, mumbling together into the smooth lifting unison of the Internationale. A grizzled old soldier was sobbing like a child. The immense sound rolled through the hall, burst windows and doors and soared into the quiet sky. 'The war is ended! The war is ended!', said a young workman near me, his face shining. And when it was over, as we stood there in a kind of awkward hush, someone in the back of the room shouted 'Comrades! Let us remember those who have died for liberty!' So we began to sing the Funeral March, that slow, melancholy, and yet triumphant chant, so Russian and so

moving. The Funeral March seemed the very soul of those dark masses whose delegates sat in this hall, building from their obscure visions a new Russia—and perhaps more.[16]

How much of all this could newspaper readers in the rest of the world have learnt at the time? *The Times*' Petrograd correspondent was in London, so *The Times* had to report the Revolution by courtesy of Reuters, as did most British newspapers. But the Reuters correspondent in Petrograd, Guy Beringer, was, like other news agency men, operating under great difficulty, and he fled to Finland as soon as he could. His dispatches showed that he failed to understand what was happening. On the day the Bolsheviks took power, he reported that naval troops under "Maximalist orders" had seized a few important points but "street traffic and the general life of the city remain normal."[17] The Associated Press' bureau chief, Charles Smith, was knocked out by a soldier swinging a rifle butt, and another AP reporter was shot in the knee by a sniper.*

Reed and Philips Price were the only correspondents to describe what had happened. Reed cabled a short statement from Lenin on November 15 and a long story on the Revolution to the *New York Call* on November 21. But it was Philips Price, using the Danish telegraph agency, who sent to the *Manchester Guardian* the first account of the Bolsheviks' seizure of power.

> The Government of Kerensky fell before the Bolshevik insurgents because it had no supporters in the country. The bourgeois parties and the generals and the staff disliked it because it would not establish a military dictatorship. The Revolutionary Democracy lost faith in it because after eight months it had neither given land to the peasants, nor established State control of industries, nor advanced the cause of the Russian peace programme. Instead it brought off the July advance without any guarantee that the Allies had agreed to reconsider war aims...the Bolsheviks thus acquired great support all over the country.[18]

The Bolshevik Revolution might have taken newspapers by surprise, but they recovered quickly. Since they lacked the knowledge that Reed, Philips Price, and Ransome had acquired, they were able to state categorically that the Bolsheviks would not survive. This—

---

*Robert Liddell abandoned journalism and, instead, proposed to the British military attaché a scheme to persuade a crack Russian regiment to fight against the Bolsheviks. The attaché lost interest when Liddell said he would need about a million pounds in gold for bribes. Liddell then made his way back to London.

and abuse of the Bolshevik leaders—was the theme of all the dispatches and comment in the days following the Revolution. David Soskice, the man the *Manchester Guardian* had sent to check on Philips Price's accuracy, had fled from the Winter Palace across the frontier to Finland. *The Guardian* ran his dispatches, even though they directly contradicted those from his colleague. "The Bolsheviks must fall," Soskice wrote from Oslo on November 24. *The Times* as early as November 12 had Lenin losing control. The *Observer* was certain that Bolshevism would soon perish, and the *Daily News* felt that all Bolsheviks were doomed, thus ignoring the opinion of its man-on-the-spot, Arthur Ransome, one of the few voices of accuracy and reason in the hysteria, who wrote: "It is folly to deny the actual fact that the Bolsheviks do hold a majority of the politically-active population."[19]

The newspaper reader in the United States, like his counterpart in Britain, could have been forgiven for believing that it was only a matter of days before the Bolsheviks were overthrown. The insistent theme of Russian news in the *New York Times* was that the Bolsheviks could last for only a moment. In the next two years this belief was faithfully fostered. Four times Lenin and Trotsky were planning flight, three times they had already fled; twice Lenin was planning retirement, once he had been killed, and three times he was in prison.

One of the main reasons for the gross misinformation that these reports spread was a growing apprehension as to the nature of Bolshevism, which encouraged wishful thinking about its early demise. As details of Lenin's new social order filtered through to the West, the first signs appeared of the strong anti-Bolshevik sentiment that was soon to become fanatical. It was bad enough for the landed gentry of Britain and France that the Bolsheviks had overthrown their betters in Russia; it was terrifying that they now spoke of spreading this appalling political dogma throughout Europe and perhaps the rest of the world. So when the delegates at the Soviet Congress spoke of "the coming world revolution, of which we are the advance-guard," *The Times* responded with an editorial saying, "The remedy for Bolshevism is bullets,"[20] and *The Times'* readers began to regard the Bolsheviks as a gang of murderers, thieves, and blasphemers whom it was almost a sacred duty to destroy as vermin.

This was confirmed by the Russian release of all the secret treaties negotiated between the Czarist regime and the Allies. Philips Price scooped the world here by calling on Trotsky and asking if he could print the treaties in the *Guardian*. Trotsky could not see Philips Price, but sent his secretary out with a bundle of documents and a message that he could borrow them overnight. A quick look convinced Philips Price that he had the original treaties and that they were political dynamite. There was an agreement giving France a free hand in western Europe on condition that Russia had a similar free hand in Poland; there was a cynical bribe for Rumania, if she would enter the war, by the offer of the Banat with its Yugoslavs, the Bukovina with its Ukrainian population, and Transylvania with its Magyars; there was an agreement splitting Persia between Britain and Russia; and, finally, there was the infamous Sykes-Picot agreement, dividing much of the Arab world among the Allies.* Philips Price translated the documents, working through the night, and then telegraphed them in four or five dispatches to the *Manchester Guardian*, in which they were published in some detail at the end of November.[21]

Compare the *Guardian*'s treatment of what was without doubt a major story with the attitude of *The Times*. *The Times* received a summary of the treaties from J. D. Bourchier, its Balkans man, who had stopped in Petrograd on his way to Japan. It published the summary, but made the amazing decision "not to inconvenience the British, French and Italian Governments, and to maintain silence about the Secret Treaties; also, as far as possible, to curtail its Petrograd correspondent's despatches on the subject... As the governments themselves were bound by the Treaties to be silent, *The Times* decided it could only follow their example."[22]

The release of the treaties added to the growing mistrust the Allies felt towards the Bolsheviks. But much could have been forgiven if Russia had been willing to continue the fight against the Germans. In mid-winter of 1917–18 this became the dominant question in dispatches from Russia and in interviews with "Russian experts" in the West. The first firm indication that the Russians were working towards ending their rôle in the war came from *The Times'* man Bourchier, but his office ruined a first-class scoop. On November 22, to beat the censor, Bourchier sent a coded telegram to *The Times* through the British Embassy and signed it with the name of the Ambassador, Sir George Buchanan. The telegram reached *The Times* two days later. It read: ARE TELEGRAMS ARRIVING

* The release of the latter agreement caused Britain great embarrassment, since she had already promised the Arabs independence in return for raising the Arab Revolt. T. E. Lawrence had to try to explain to the Arabs why the British had double-crossed them.

SENT ABOUT 4,500 WORDS UP YESTERDAY STOP GOVERNMENT INSTRUCTED COMMANDER CHIEF ARRANGE ARMISTICE ALL FRONTS. *The Times* sat on the message for six days, apparently unable to believe it was true, until the German radio carried the Chancellor's announcement to the Reichstag that peace negotiations with the Russians were well under way.[23]

Even now the Allies refused to lose hope that Russia might still fight on. Dispatches sounded a friendly, optimistic note, the *New York Times* going so far as to say in one headline, BOLSHEVIKI MAY HELP ALLIES BEST—and even correspondents who had seen for themselves the war-weariness of the Russians patriotically wrote that the war against Germany might indeed continue. This hope vanished abruptly on February 12, 1918, when the Soviet government announced that as far as it was concerned the war was over.

Immediately a new period began: the preparation of public opinion for Allied intervention. The newspapers were loud in their condemnation of Russia's treachery in leaving the Allies faced with a Germany freed from Russian pressure on the Eastern Front; RUSSIANS SELL OUT TO THE GERMANS AND BOLSHEVIKI YIELD RUSSIA'S RICHES TO BERLIN were typical headlines in the *New York Times*. * So intervention was justified at the beginning on the grounds of the German peril. "It did not originate in hostility to the social aims of Bolshevism," said *The History of The Times* in 1951.

This was not entirely true. Lenin's revolutionary decrees were still being announced when the British Secret Intelligence Service (SIS) sent its first agents into Russia, with the express aim of overthrowing the Bolsheviks. They were involved in an abortive plot to assassinate Lenin.** And there was soon in existence an SIS dining circle called the Bolo (for Bolshevik) Liquidation Club. So it is clear that at least one section of the Allies was determined to achieve what Churchill said later would have been a blessing to the human race: "the strangling of Bolshevism at birth."

Two correspondents, Philips Price and Ransome, saw the other side of the picture and did their best to inform the British public. Philips Price pointed out that a Russia benevolently neutral to the

---

* Russia yielded to Germany 34 per cent of her population, 32 per cent of her agricultural land, 54 per cent of her industry, and 89 per cent of her coal mines.
** On August 31, 1918, a social revolutionary named Dora Kaplan shot Lenin twice. The plot envisaged that his assassination should coincide with risings in Moscow and Petrograd organised by the notorious British spy Sidney Reilly. Reilly was late and Dora Kaplan shot too soon, but Lenin nearly died.

West but bitterly hostile to Prussia would force Germany to keep more troops in the East. Ransome, like many foreign correspondents in those days—especially *The Times*' men—had had some connection with the SIS, but had decided he could not in all conscience continue it. He now tried to explain to his readers that the Allies' attitude only encouraged the Bolsheviks to believe that the Allies planned to buy off Germany by encouraging her in Russia—a fear only too justified. Philips Price and Ransome felt so strongly that the Allies were mishandling the situation that they got together with Colonel Raymond Robbins, head of the American Red Cross in Russia and a personal representative of President Wilson, and sent off messages expressing the view that the Bolsheviks were bound to resist the German generals in the long run, however impotent they might be at the moment. Scott backed them in the *Manchester Guardian.*

It was no use. The Allies were expecting a massive German offensive—it materialised in March—and were in no mood to see beyond the fact that the Bolsheviks had made peace with Germany. Indeed, the Allies reasoned, the Bolsheviks were probably German agents working for the Kaiser. Preparations for intervention went ahead. The Allies were encouraged to believe, from earlier reports of correspondents like Wilton of *The Times*, that all Russia would rise to meet them. ("From Lake Baikal to the Driester, from the Don to the Persian border," wrote Wilton in 1917, "loyal sons of Russia are ready to rise against the forces of disintegration and defeat.")[24] The French, too, had been thinking of intervention in 1917. General Foch, in an interview in the *New York Times*, said: "Germany is walking through Russia. America and Japan, who are in a position to do so, should go to meet her in Siberia."[25]

The stage was thus set for what was perhaps the greatest act of folly the Allies committed in the First World War, an act that poisons relations with Russia to this day. "We remember," Nikita Khrushchev said in Los Angeles in 1959, "the grim days when...all the countries of Europe and America marched on our country to strangle the new revolution."

The only Western correspondent to report the intervention from the Russian side was Philips Price, who had remained in Petrograd, in desperate circumstances.* "*The Guardian* could not send me any

---

* Reed had joined a Soviet propaganda bureau, and Ransome returned to Britain in April 1918.

money," he said some years later, "because the banks had been closed to prevent any cash reaching the counter-revolutionaries. I had to live on one-eighth of a pound of bread a day, potato skins, and tea. I lost twenty pounds in three weeks. As well, there was the risk that if the Bolsheviks were overthrown, then I would be shot. I weighed the choices. I decided I was in the middle of perhaps the biggest thing that had happened to the world and that it was worth risking my life to stay on."[26]

He was down to 112 pounds when the arrival in Petrograd of G. V. Chicherin, a Bolshevik leader (later Commissar for Foreign Affairs) who had been in exile in Britain, saved him. Chicherin had been to Lenin and said that the only fair and objective reports on Russia appearing in the West were those of Philips Price and Ransome, and where could he find them? He was horrified at Philips Price's condition and made immediate arrangements for him to be allowed money from London.

The fact that the burden of providing the bulk of the news from Bolshevik Russia fell on one correspondent, who has freely admitted that disgust with British censorship and the short-sightedness of British policy made him eventually abandon his objectivity, is of even greater significance when the correspondents with the interventionist forces are scrutinised.

*The Times*, without a man inside Russia, had to get by as best it could, which was poorly. Hardly any of the reforms introduced by the Bolsheviks were reported, with the significant exception of measures affecting banks and banking. Nothing was reported of any projects of socialisation, nothing of the nationalisation of the land, nothing even of the reform of the calendar, which took place in February 1918, and so ended the confusion between Old Style and New Style dating. The dark silence maintained by *The Times* was broken only occasionally by the publication of a letter from some such dubious source as "a correspondent in Petrograd with unusual opportunities for assessing the situation."

Looking back in 1951, *The Times* had the grace to admit how poor its coverage had been. "It was hardly guessed that there was nothing ninety-nine out of every hundred Russians wanted except peace. Still less it was appreciated that the one thing that might induce Russians to remain in arms was foreign intervention...The fundamental British error was the belief that local forces could be raised in opposition to the Bolshevik regime. *The Times* perhaps bears the responsibility of having failed to provide a correspondence from Bolshevik Russia which could have convinced the

Government of this error."[27]

So Britain, France, Japan, and the United States—the latter reluctantly—committed themselves to the intervention in Russia, and before it was over it must have seemed to the Russians that half the world was against them.

The intervention can be divided into two parts: that before the Armistice was signed with Germany on November 11, 1918, and that which carried on after the war was over. The first period, which began with a token landing of British and Japanese troops at Vladivostok in April 1918, received scant coverage in the Allied press, because of censorship and preoccupation with the Western Front. On March 21, 1918, the Germans had launched a massive offensive in France, overwhelming the British army. Haig's "backs to the wall" order of the day had been published on April 13, and the great battle in France and Flanders monopolised space in all the newspapers in Britain. The situation was so serious that a plan was discussed to end the war, as Trotsky had feared, by giving the Germans a free hand in Russia. The Prime Minister, Lloyd George, and various ministers and ex-ministers, including members of the War Cabinet and some members of the Labour Party, met privately to discuss such a scheme. Nothing came of it, but it showed that the Bolsheviks' fears about Allied intentions were not unfounded, and their suspicions grew.

Philips Price has confirmed this suspiciousness towards the Allies. He, too, began to feel it, because nearly everything he wrote on the Russian view of events was killed by the British censor. He sent a dispatch reporting a revolt throughout the country by the Left Socialist Revolutionaries and the Anarchists, explaining how it was suppressed and quoting Lenin: "The Left SR's have committed political suicide by striking against revolutionary Realpolitik …Henceforth we, Bolsheviks…must bear the sole burden of the Revolution." This was a dispatch of some historic importance, revealing the sweeping away of the debris of the past that had still remained inside the Russian revolutionary movement and the confirming of the Bolsheviks in power. The British censor suppressed it.[28]

On June 6 he telegraphed to the *Manchester Guardian* a statement by the Bolsheviks on the efforts they were making to return to the Allies a Czech army that had been fighting the Germans on the Eastern Front, and on the obstructions that were being put in the way of this plan by French agents, who, the statement said, were trying to turn the Czechs against the Bolsheviks. The censor in Britain, Sir Frank Swettenham, stopped the telegram and ordered the *Guardian* not to publish it. Philips Price wrote an article of his own, pointing out that when the Czechs marched into a Russian town they arrested the local Soviet and set up an authority relying on cadets and Cossack officers. Since they were acting under the protection of the French military mission and were unofficial representatives of the Allies, the Allies could not "sanctimoniously pretend they are not intervening in Russia's internal affairs and are not helping one of the two political forces in the country against the other."[29]

The message by some chance escaped the censor, and the *Guardian*'s editor, Scott, after reading it, telegraphed Philips Price asking him to find out whether the Bolshevik government would enter into economic relations with Britain. Philips Price interviewed the Commissar for Foreign Affairs, Chicherin, and reported his request for agricultural implements and machinery for repairing railways, for which he was prepared to trade forestry concessions and contracts for railroad construction. Nine days later, on June 29, an economic commission from Britain arrived in Moscow to begin talks with the Soviet government. These negotiations did not last long, for the Allied intervention was intensifying and the Bolsheviks saw little sense in talking trade with a country that was moving troops against them.

Philips Price telegraphed to the *Guardian*: "The Allies are sowing dragon's teeth in Eastern Europe. Some day they will grow into bayonets and will be turned into directions that we least desire." The British censor refused to pass the telegram. Philips Price says he realised by this time that "a conspiracy of silence had been decided on about the war of intervention which the Western Allies were waging against Soviet Russia. Only reports favourable to the intervention were allowed and these were being retailed extensively in the press of Lord Northcliffe and Horatio Bottomley."[30]

Northcliffe was convinced that the Bolsheviks were murderous German agents working for the Kaiser, a view no doubt bolstered by a report in the *Observer* of Bolshevik proposals "that all capitalists over eight years of age should be killed." The credence that should have been given this allegation can be assessed by the source the *Observer* gave: the dispatch came from Copenhagen, but it quoted a message from Stockholm, which in turn quoted "travellers" who had, in their turn, heard the story in Helsinki.[31] Horatio Bottomley, a notorious MP, financier, and yellow-press journalist, wrote in his magazine, *John Bull*, that there was a group of debased creatures in Britain who called themselves "the 47,000." The Germans were behind the social and sexual depravities of these 47,000. The result was to weaken the moral fibre of Britain and to allow British Bolsheviks "to foment anarchy and propagate vice throughout the land."

Philips Price did his best to counteract this hysterical anti-Bolshevist reporting. He had seen the effect of the Allied intervention: that foreign assistance to the Whites had provoked intense bitterness, which made excesses on both sides inevitable. He had seen Trotsky's creation of the Red Army. He had interviewed Lenin and had noted Lenin's change of emphasis from promoting world revolution to concentrating on saving the Russian Revolution. He had taken a job as a translator in the Bolshevist Foreign Office. He had written a pamphlet called *The Truth About the Allied Intervention in Russia*, and he had become a paying guest in the house of Count Sergei Tolstoy, the eldest son of the great Russian writer.* He had met and talked with Alfons Pacquet, correspondent for the German liberal newspaper *Frankfurter Zeitung*, who had arrived in Russia after the peace treaty between Russia and Germany. He was, therefore, remarkably well placed to present a first-hand account of life in Russia under the Bolsheviks and, because of his conversations with Pacquet, of German thinking on Russia. On October 31 he sent a 1,200-word dispatch to the *Manchester Guardian* attacking stories appearing in the British press about the Revolution. He said dispatches about a Red reign of terror were absurd exaggerations. Conditions in general were not too bad. Food rations were good and equal. The main danger to the new regime was that a probable bridge between the Allies and Germany would be found in a common need for opposing Bolshevism.

Philips Price might have got this into his paper but for Pacquet. After meeting Philips Price and Ransome in Russia, Pacquet wrote an article for the *Frankfurter Zeitung* in which he said that these two British correspondents were against the intervention. *The Times* picked up Pacquet's story and reprinted it, saying that Pacquet had charged Philips Price and Ransome with disseminating pro-Bolshevik views. So when Philips Price's October dispatch went before the censor, he killed it, on the ground that it was a piece of "Bolshevist propaganda."[32]

---

* Philips Price has said that one of the strengths of Boris Pasternak's *Doctor Zhivago* is that it portrays so well the suffering during this period of middle-class families like the Tolstoys.

It is true, as Philips Price has readily admitted, that by now he was no longer completely objective and that Marxist jargon had crept into his writing. "It was a pity, but understandable. I was young and impressionable and it was natural that I should start to write as I heard Lenin and Trotsky speak. If I could have kept the old *Manchester Guardian* objectivity, then my dispatches would have had more influence."[33] But it is also true that his dispatch would have been a healthy antidote to the sort of rubbish that Bottomley and his kind were publishing about Russia.

The attitude of American newspapers was more restrained than that of the British, but equally distorted. It was devoted mainly to justifying intervention. The Russian Information Bureau, the official press office of the Russian Embassy (anti-Bolshevik) in Washington, plugged the need to distinguish between the Bolsheviks and the Russian people. The *New York Times* insisted that the true voice of Russia had sought the help of the Allies and the Allies could not continue deaf to that appeal. It even tried to persuade its readers that intervention would have a quietening effect on the situation.

All this propaganda underwent a sudden transformation when, on November 11, 1918, the war between Germany and the Allies officially ended. The troops that had gone to Russia to fight the Germans remained to fight Russians, and what was in reality a new war began: the Allies, with troops from some sixteen countries, against the Bolsheviks.

Historically, this is a period of immense importance, yet little is generally known about it. No full understanding of the Cold War is possible without taking it into account; yet when Khrushchev said, in Los Angeles in September 1959, "Never have any of our soldiers been on American soil, but your soldiers were on Russian soil," most of his listeners did not know what he was talking about. Their ignorance can be forgiven. In 1943, E. M. Halliday, a reporter for *Yank*, the American army magazine, tried to write a story about the fighting between American and Russian troops during the Allied intervention in 1918–19. He found little about it in the *Encyclopaedia Britannica*, and the *Columbia Encyclopedia* stated flatly: "American forces did not participate in the fighting between the Allies and the Bolsheviks."[34]

Contemporary reports were equally misleading. In Britain, with preparations for a general election under way, a war-weary public did not notice the silence that descended around the Allied forces still in Russia. Day after day passed with no news from either Petrograd or the intervention fronts. Then, on December 19, 1918, *The Times* published a letter from the Minister for War, Lord Milner, justifying the continuing presence of Allied troops in Russia. Milner claimed that only the highest motives kept the Allies fighting the Bolsheviks. As a result of Allied efforts, he said, millions of people friendly to the Allies had been spared the horrors of Bolshevik rule.

This was the signal for the Red-peril scare, which became the dominant theme of the Allied press until the intervention ended. Aided by the Bolsheviks' murder of the Czar and his family (news of which had reached the West in the autumn of 1918), British and American newspapers succeeded in convincing many of their readers that no infamy was too great for the Bolsheviks and that, unless checked in Russia, this foul political creed would spread over Europe. The *Daily Mirror* reported a REIGN OF BLOOD AND TERROR. The *New York Times* was more dignified. Bolshevism was spreading in Europe, it said, and "all neutral countries were feeling the infection." Even the United States was threatened. An Associated Press dispatch from Berlin quoted a Bolshevik leader as having stated that the money sent to Berlin to finance the Revolution was nothing compared with the funds transmitted to New York for the purpose of spreading Bolshevism in the United States. Since the aims of the Bolsheviks were anti-American, the *New York Times* felt justified in asking editorially: "Having entered Russia for a purpose, why not carry out that purpose? Start a real movement to drive the Bolsheviki out."[35] The Red peril, hitherto a minor item in the news as against the peril of a Russia dominated by Germany, now became dominant, and the newspapers felt it was acceptable to send war correspondents to report on how the Allied troops, aided by the real people of Russia, were making out in the crusade against Bolshevism.

The spearhead of the Allied intervention was from the east through Siberia, where the White Russian Alexander Kolchak, a fine admiral but a neurotic politician, stood at the head of "the All-Russian Government of Omsk." In the north, from Archangel, the British general F. C. Poole, a cheery womaniser with a taste for Russian gypsy girls, was at first in command, later to be replaced by William Edmund Ironside, a dashing six foot-four-inch veteran of the Boer War, where, it was said he had crushed a Boer soldier to death in his tremendous arms. In the west, General Nicholas Yudenitch, who was so fat he had to be lifted out of his staff car, commanded the "Northwestern Army" against the Bolsheviks. In the south, General Anton Ivanovich Denikin, a soldier who had risen from the ranks to become the Czar's chief of staff, led the anti-Bolshevik forces.

The coverage accorded General Denikin's army in the south not only was an example of biased, inaccurate reporting at its worst, but the reasons for it indicate the general shortcomings in the whole newspaper approach to the intervention on all fronts. The principal war correspondent with General Denikin was Harold Williams, whose reports appeared in *The Times* and the *New York Times*. Williams, the son of a New Zealand Wesleyan minister, was a known admirer of the old Russia and believed the Russian people had been enthusiastic for the war against Germany. He was married to a prominent anti-Bolshevik and was strongly anti-Bolshevik himself, and he and his wife had fled Russia for England, where they both joined the anti-Bolshevik campaign. Williams was convinced that the downfall of the Bolsheviks was only a matter of weeks. Yet this was the man *The Times* and the *New York Times* picked to cover General Denikin's march on Moscow. Williams was certain that local support for Denikin was overwhelming: "When Denikin passed in his car through the streets of Kharkov women weeping for joy pressed forward to kiss his hand and those who could not do that, kissed even the mudguards of his car."[36]

Denikin began well. During July and August 1919 his troops took several cities of importance from the Red Army, including Odessa. Williams saw victory just around the corner, and on July 16 the *New York Times* carried his dispatch under this headline: COULDN'T FIND FRONT OF DENIKIN'S ARMIES—ADVANCED SO FAST DR. WILLIAMS AND BRITISH OFFICERS WERE UNABLE TO CATCH UP. From the captured towns Williams sent messages with impressive lists of prisoners captured and war materials taken—between April and October, over 1,000 guns and 245,000 Bolsheviks—which makes what happened next all the more remarkable. In late October the tide turned, and the Red Army began to roll up the White forces; by mid-December they were back in Kiev and Kharkov, and by the end of February 1920 Denikin was defeated and the campaign was over.

Yet on December 16 Williams had telegraphed an account of the Red Army's recapture of Kharkov: "In Denikin's armies there is no impression or expectation of defeat"; on January 12: "The position at the front is steadily improving...the morale of the Bolshevist troops seems suddenly to have collapsed." By the time this last message got into print the exact opposite had occurred:

*Denikin's* troops had collapsed, and the war on the southern front was as good as over. The evidence of Williams' failure to inform his readers of what was happening becomes even more damning on examination of the stories he did *not* write. The morale of the Allied troops supporting Denikin was extremely poor. They were resentful that they were still in action when the war had already ended, given no information as to how long they would be there, fearful of typhus, and annoyed by the unwillingness of the Russians to support them, and their discipline steadily declined. On the first week that the British troops were in Batum, a drunken Scotsman shot a Russian general dead in the street. The French troops mutinied, and, as one correspondent wrote in 1921, "the conduct of the French ships and their officers and crews was so amazing that no Allied government has yet dared to publish an account of it."[37] Theft, rape, and murder were common, and the British army had to resort to public executions to try to restore order. Needless to say, Williams wrote not a word about this.

The general bungling and black-marketeering were unbelievable. There were five time scales in operation: local time, ship's time, Petrograd time (used by the railways and the army), cement-works time, and British Military Mission time. The mission frequently received contradictory orders from the pro-Denikin and anti-Denikin sections of the Foreign Office, whose influence was about equally matched. Russians who had been pressed into Denikin's army melted away unless watched constantly. One officer who succeeded in getting eighteen machine-gunners into position went to a nearby building to report his arrival by telephone and returned to find that all eighteen soldiers had decamped. The only really reliable soldiers were cadets from military schools and training colleges, most of whom were not more than fifteen years old. Not a mention of this appeared in Williams' dispatches.

So, with his wishful thinking, his unjustified optimism, his prejudice, and his deliberate omissions, Williams got it all wrong. There was no local enthusiasm for Denikin, he could not march to Moscow, Allied support was bungled, and the "demoralised" Red Army of the "tottering" Bolshevik government—according to Williams, almost devoid of guns and troops—drove the Whites into the sea, with Williams shouting to the end, "This can't be true."

In the east the bungling was even worse. Robert Wilton, *The Times*' correspondent in Petrograd, who had made the mistake of going to London three weeks before the October Revolution, had been trying in vain to get back; the Bolsheviks had, understandably, refused him a visa. Now, seeing a chance to return via the back door, as it were, he joined the British interventionary force to Vladivostok as a war correspondent and with some vague assignment from the Foreign Office. Wilton, strongly anti-Bolshevik, and a firm supporter of intervention, was shocked by what he saw and wrote privately to his editor: "It is a truly appalling situation here, far worse than anything we can conceive—almost all due to the divided counsels that prevail among the Allies…One wonders if the world is going mad and one is less surprised at the ridiculous things that are being done regarding Russia."[38]

*The Times* published nothing of this, because, as it admitted, "British public opinion had been roused, very largely by *The Times*, into active animosity to [the Bolsheviks] who were regarded as conspirators with but a short expectation of power."[39] Anything, therefore, that suggested the intervention was a mistake or was being badly handled found no place in the paper.

What had gone wrong in Siberia was the lack of any policy on the part of the Allies, with each country pursuing intervention for its own reasons and few of the reasons tallying. Japan, for example, jumped at the chance to establish herself in Siberia, and under the protection of her military forces she sent thousands of businessmen there to try to create a Japanese monopoly. One section of the American government recognised the threat that this Japanese initiative posed—the United States also had strong commercial ties with Russia—while another section felt that intervention was wrong and that the best means of influencing the Bolsheviks was by economic aid. President Wilson eventually agreed to the dispatch of an American interventionary force, by a formula he set out in an *aide-mémoire* for the commander, General William S. Graves, a cautious officer with no taste for his assignment. The document was vague, contradictory, unrealistic. Its usefulness can be judged by Wilson's proposals that the American force include representatives of the Young Men's Christian Association, presumably, as Churchill wrote later, "to offer moral guidance to the Russian people." The State Department and the War Department each decided that the *aide-mémoire* gave them control of American operations in Siberia, and they argued with each other until the end of the mission.

This force of mixed nationalities with mixed motives found itself supporting Admiral Kolchak and a bunch of minor war lords who behaved little better than gangsters.* Only one correspondent, Carl W. Ackerman, appeared to feel that in backing Kolchak the Allies might discredit their professed cause. Quoting a Czech general, he reported in the *New York Times*: "The change of government has killed our soldiers. They say that for four years they have been fighting for democracy and now that a dictatorship ruled in Omsk they are no longer fighting for democracy."[40]

Militarily, the intervention became a fiasco. General Graves interpreted President Wilson's *aide-mémoire* as an order to be in Siberia but to *do* nothing until a democratic Russian government came into being and asked for help. Consequently, he refused military aid to the other Allied forces and tried to remain strictly neutral in clashes between the Russians. The other Allies soon marked him down as a Bolshevik sympathiser, and Kolchak said openly that Graves and his troops "spread Bolshevik ideas and supported Bolsheviks." With this sort of dissension, it is a wonder Kolchak got as far as he did. His spring offensive began on March 25, 1919, and by May had reached a point some 400 miles from Moscow. Then Trotsky's newly organised Red Army turned Kolchak around, and by November his offensive was 2,000 miles behind the line from which it had started. So the Czechs, with French connivance, handed Kolchak over to the Bolsheviks, together with the Russian imperial treasure, worth some £ 100 million, to ensure free transit for Czech troops to Vladivostok. The Bolsheviks shot him by firing squad on February 7, 1920.

The Canadians, who had protested from the beginning about being drawn into a war that they felt was not their concern, had pulled out in June 1919, despite protests from Churchill, then Minister for War.** Without the Canadians to provide administrative

* Koichak was an honourable man compared with Grigori Mikhailovitch Semenov, who raised a private army of 60,000 men, officered largely by supporters of the old imperial regime. Supplied and financed by the Japanese, Semenov terrorised a large part of Siberia, robbing, pillaging, torturing, and shooting. The situation became so bad that at one stage General Graves refused to hand over any more rifles, because he believed that Semenov planned to use them to attack the United States troops. Before the Americans finally withdrew, fighting between an American detachment and one of Semenov's armoured trains cost two American soldiers their lives. Twenty-six years later, at the end of the Second World War, the Bolsheviks, who have long memories in these matters, finally caught up with Semenov and hanged him

** The Canadian force contained men conscripted under the Military Service Act for the defence of Canada only, and the *Toronto Globe* claimed that "sixty to seventy per cent of the Force despatched to Siberia went unwillingly because they did not believe in the expedition."

support, the two British battalions had been forced to withdraw in September and November. The other Allied forces—Poles, Serbs, Italians, and Czechs—had all gone by September. The Americans left on April 1, 1920, seen off by a Japanese band on the dock at Vladivostok playing "Hard Times Come Again No More." The Japanese clung on until October 25, 1922, and left then only under such pressure from the United States that war seemed not unlikely. "The threat which led to Pearl Harbour," wrote John Swettenham, "could already be discerned."[41]

By any standards, the Siberian fiasco was highly newsworthy. A British soldier, Captain (later Lieutenant-General Sir) Brian Horrocks, was among volunteers to train the White Army. Extracts from his account give some idea of what it was like to be there.

> We landed at Vladivostok, passing at once...to the filth and degradation of this Siberian port, swarming with people who had fled eastwards from the Bolshevik revolution...Our help and our presence was resented, and one wise old British Colonel remarked: 'We shall rue this business for many years. It is always unwise to intervene in the domestic affairs of any country. The Reds are bound to win, and our present policy will cause bitterness between us for a long time...The White Russians were some of the most charming people I have ever met in my life, but they were totally inconsequential and when it came to a serious job of work, quite hopeless. One day, when I was attached to the First White Army staff, I returned to my headquarters, after visiting the front where the White Army was carrying out a most important counter-attack, to find the chief of the Military Operations Branch lying drunk on the floor of the railway wagon where I lived. I could mention numerous instances of a similar nature...The battle-front suddenly disintegrated and we found ourselves amidst a seething mass of terrified people all mad to get away from the Red terror spreading Eastwards. Civil wars are always cruel. We were always being shown photographs of atrocities committed by the Reds. But later we were to see identical photographs shown as examples of atrocities committed by the Whites. There were sinister stories of Red soldiers hammering nails into the shoulders of White officers, one for each star on the epaulettes.

Horrocks was taken prisoner by the Fifth Red Army at Krasnoyarsk, 2,000 miles west of Vladivostok. Typhus was sweeping Russia, helping to bring the Revolution and civil-war casualties to an unbelievable 14 million.

> There were reputed to be 30,000 cases in Krasnoyarsk alone.

For long we had been living surrounded by dead. Naked corpses stacked on the railway platforms, sleighs packed with frozen bodies —these were common sights.[42]

What could the readers of British, American, or Canadian newspapers have gathered of this immense upheaval? Which war correspondents covered this story, and what did they write? Wilton, the *Times* man, sent a message saying that he was setting off on horseback from Vladivostok "to join the cavalry raiders to the interior"—presumably with a vision of eventually riding in triumph into Moscow. His lines of communication with his office were rather tenuous, and he compromised any claim to objective reporting by joining the staff of one of the White Russian generals. His journalism took second place to political intrigue, until finally the chief of the British Military Mission, Major-General Alfred Knox, wrote him an extremely rude letter,* and the War Office backed Knox's request that Wilton be recalled. Wilton complained to *The Times* that there was a conspiracy against him, but it is clear that his active part in the intervention on behalf of various White Russian elements made his value as a war correspondent virtually nil.[43]

Captain W. E. Playfair, technically a Canadian army public-relations officer, rather than a war correspondent, and the French correspondent of *Petit Parisien* both interviewed Admiral Kolchak. But this was not the best way of learning what was happening in the interior of eastern Russia.

Tokyo turned out to be a better listening post for news, and the Associated Press bureau there got a fairly accurate picture from Japanese army sources of the steady collapse of the intervention. But newspapers preferred to print the unfailingly optimistic views of a string of sources such as "well-informed areas in London," "army officers in Washington," "the Russian Embassy in the United

---

*Mr. Robert Wilton:

I would be obliged if you would mind your own business as Correspondent of the "Times" and avoid interference in my work, for which I alone am responsible.

You have given your opinion on me and on my work on several occasions to members of my Mission. Yesterday you visited my Red Cross Stores and gave your ideas unasked as to the proper method of distribution of the articles there. You had no right to go near these Stores. It is impertinence on your part to criticise my orders to people working under me.

It is a matter of indifference to me what you write in your paper, but if I hear of another instance of your agitating against me in my Mission I will report all details home.

Alfred Knox

States," and the Russian Committee in Paris—all White Russian exiles, all emotionally involved, and all highly subjective.

Northern Russia was the most newsworthy of all the fronts, because the Allied forces there were more actively involved in trying to overthrow the Bolsheviks. Whereas in Siberia General Graves had interpreted President Wilson's *aide-mémoire* as an instruction to remain neutral, the American rôle in northern Russia was largely determined by the United States Ambassador, David R. Francis, a bar-room politician who knew little of Russia and to whom Bolshevism was "a foul monster." After leaving Petrograd during the Revolution, Francis ended up in Archangel. When the main body of American troops—disappointingly, only about 5,500 men—landed in September 1918, Francis encouraged them to push into the Russian hinterland and try to take Petrograd and Moscow. His enthusiasm was matched by that of the British commanding officer, General F. C. Poole, and the mixed Allied force—British, American, Canadian, French, Australian, Polish, Czech, Italian, Serb, and Finnish—proceeded to try to march through the interior of Russia, fighting all the way, before the dreaded winter froze the entire venture.

It would be an understatement to say that the Allied force was ill-equipped to tackle such a task. Most of the British force was physically in category C-3, fit only for limited operations, such as guard duty. General Poole kept no accurate maps of current troop positions and no written records, and he issued most orders verbally. The Americans were mostly middle-western draftees, led by reserve officers and armed, for reasons never properly explained, with rifles that had been manufactured in the United States for export to the old Imperial Russian Army. They were planning a campaign in an area where the winter temperature seldom went above zero and readings of thirty to forty below were not unusual. Huge supplies of food, intended to feed both the troops and the civilian population, were diverted to a thriving free market, and even British officers were caught bartering goods in the streets. The area swarmed with SIS officers in improbable disguises and with adventurers like Lieutenant-Colonel Woods, an Irishman who organised the White Russians into a regiment that became known as the "Royal Irish Karelians" and whose men wore shamrocks cut from Shamrock Plug tobacco tins.

If it had not been for the loss of life, it would have been all a comic opera. A British colonel misconstrued a telephone report and shelled an American column, killing two and wounding eight, and then called for another bottle of whisky to steady his nerves before altering the range. Two American companies attacked a Bolshevik position without the expected support from a White Russian and a British detachment. The Russian commander had decided it was "not the right kind of day" for an attack, and the British colonel had, as the official enquiry found, "succumbed to the festivities of the season." An American officer surrounded by Bolshevik forces was happy to see a signal light blinking from a distant British position—until he read the message. It was a demand for him to account for six dozen Red Cross scarves sent to his detachment and not properly acknowledged.[44]

None of this was reported in Britain or America, because up to this time there had been no war correspondents there at all. But when General Poole was replaced, in October 1918, by General Ironside, Andrew Soutar of *The Times* went out to join him. Soutar had been a serving officer in France and was one of the blood-and-glory-for-Britain school. He arrived just as the First World War ended and the reasons for the intervention disappeared. Typically, there was no new declaration of Allied policy, and through the long winter nights the troops sat huddled in their blockhouses wondering why they had been forgotten. Their mail pointed out that the war was over and asked when they were coming home.

Morale slumped, and in February 1919, with still no news of when they were to be withdrawn, the troops started to mutiny. On February 26 a Yorkshire regiment refused to proceed to the front. A company of French colonials followed suit and had to be shipped home. In March, a section of the Canadian Field Brigade refused to obey orders, and an American company objected when ordered to return to forward posts. The Americans later changed their minds, but the War Department, which until then had ignored the northern Russia operation, issued a press release in Washington describing the incident. Newspapers pounced on the story and gave it a prominent display, thus fuelling the growing clamour for the withdrawal of the Americans. General Ironside reported: "We were drawing terribly near the end of our tether as an efficient fighting force."[45]

At first Soutar wrote nothing of this. He believed Britain was in northern Russia as a matter of honour: "When Britain gives her word to a foreign people she abides by that word." He saw himself more in the rôle of a regimental historian than of a war correspondent. He started a newspaper for the troops, lunched with General

Ironside, and made friends with fellow officers (he had the honorary rank of major). When he felt he had some news, Soutar filed as much as the censor would allow via Army Signals, which had taken over the post-office. Soutar was politically ignorant of what intervention involved and freely admitted that he did not know the meaning of Bolshevism or what the Russian Revolution had been about.[46] His dispatches tended to be on these lines:

Archangel, May 14, 1919, by mail:

The work of the medical profession in Russia since this expedition set out from England may never be rightly appreciated by those at home who have not travelled in Russia—Russia that seems to stretch across the world and hang disconsolately over the edge, so that the word "distance" takes to itself the horror of a nightmare.[47]

He permitted himself an occasional grumble: "The Cockney batman-cook-infantryman...placed before me a bundle of mail—letters and newspapers from home...The newspapers were precious, even if there wasn't a word in them about our operations in Russia. Not a word."*[48]

Some idea of the crisis in morale filtered back to Britain, and, lest it become too public, the War Office acted. It issued a stirring message to the troops by Churchill, the newly arrived Secretary for War: "Although cut off from your country you are not forgotten...You will be back home in time to see this year's harvest gathered in, if you continue to display that undaunted British spirit which has so often got us through in spite of heavy odds and great hardship."[49]

This was accompanied by a call for volunteers to help ensure the safe withdrawal of the tired troops. Newspapers took up the campaign to help silence the "bring-our-boys-home" clamour. "We could not withdraw if we would," said *The Times*, "for our Army at Archangel is frozen in." Eight thousand men were formed into two brigades and went into intensive training. Although the expedition was being billed as a noble rescue operation, it was clearly more than that: Churchill, itching for battle, had, in fact, decided to have one last throw at the Bolsheviks.

* The United States was just as ludicrously served. News from northern Russia was limited to brief reports of military engagements. Walter Lippmann and Charles Merz, attempting an assessment in 1920 of American coverage of the intervention, were unable to include a study of the northern Russia press coverage because there were not enough reports on which to base a judgement.

In northern Russia, propaganda to keep the troops fighting was intensified. The theme was mostly the barbaric nature of the Bolsheviks, but sometimes it included a crude anti-Semitic line, presumably on the ground that if the troops did not know any Bolsheviks, they at least knew some Jews.

This sort of thing was no match for the skillful Bolshevist propaganda pamphlets that were circulating in northern Russia. They offered good treatment to prisoners.* The pamphlets appeared everywhere. General Ironside reported: "They were stuffed in letter boxes of officers and private houses. They were well written . . . and one of the cleverest appeared over the name of an Englishman." This was Morgan Philips Price's small tract called *The Truth About the Allied Intervention in Russia*. The Soviet Foreign Office had printed 50,000 copies, which were distributed as widely as possible. The pamphlet began: "One of the most deadly weapons wielded by the ruling classes of all countries is their power to censor the press; for thereby they are able to create under the pretext of military necessity an artificial public opinion with the object of hiding their fell designs...One cannot be surprised of course that the governments of England, France, and Germany should, through the official agencies and their press censors, endeavour to blacken the work of the Russian Revolution...[but] knowing the love of freedom and the sense of justice of the British working man, I am in these few lines appealing to him to understand the facts that I have here set before me."

Philips Price went on to sum up his four years in Russia, to accuse the British censor of stopping all but two or three of his dispatches since the intervention, and to explain the Revolution as he had seen it. He concluded: "Today the banking oligarchies in London try to strangle by isolation and spread of famine the great movement for freedom that has sprung up in Eastern Europe. They will not succeed...and the conquests of the Russian revolution will endure, as did the conquests of the French revolution last century. But to bring this about the workers of England must know the truth and knowing it must dare act."[50]

The arguments in this pamphlet and in other Russian propaganda pieces made a lot more sense to the soldiers in northern

---

* This offer was apparently genuine. A dozen or so prisoners were sent to Moscow, where they were lectured on the evils of capitalism but were allowed to wander freely about the streets. Frank Taylor, a United Press correspondent, who, to his surprise, was allowed into Russia in the middle of the intervention, interviewed them.

Russia than did exhortations to continue fighting, and morale grew worse. The Americans, still with no idea why they were fighting the Red Army, believed that the War Department had forgotten them, and a rash of self-inflicted wounds began to occur. In April 1919 a White Russian battalion mutinied, murdering seven of its officers, and 300 men went over to the Bolsheviks. In June the Canadians went home and were followed by the Americans. On July 7 Dyer's battalion of the Slavo-British Legion—a White Russian force with British senior officers—mutinied, killing five British officers and four Russians. Soutar now stirred himself and wrote a vivid report about this. Although it was delayed by the censor, it had considerable impact when eventually published in London. On July 20 the Fifth Russian Infantry Regiment surrendered a whole front to the Bolsheviks, and the same day an attempted revolt by the Sixth Russian Infantry Regiment was prevented by the use of Australian and Polish troops with fixed bayonets. The Seventh Russian Infantry Regiment also planned a mutiny, but was subdued before it could act.

The incident that really convinced General Ironside he would be wise to evacuate the British force as soon as possible concerned a young battalion commander, Lieutenant-Colonel John Sherwood-Kelly, and the *Daily Express*. Ironside had sent Sherwood-Kelly's men into action against the Bolsheviks, and was angry and bewildered when Sherwood-Kelly withdrew them at the crucial moment without their having fired a shot. Sherwood-Kelly, a South African, had been wounded five times, and awarded the Companion of St. Michael and St. George, the Distinguished Service Order, and, at Cambrai in 1917, the Victoria Cross. Ironside, having failed to get a satisfactory explanation from Sherwood-Kelly of his detachment's conduct, decided he had no alternative but to send him back to Britain. There, on September 6, 1919, Sherwood-Kelly wrote an explosive letter to the *Daily Express* blowing Churchill's "last-throw" scheme wide open.

"I volunteered for service with the North Russian Relief Force in the sincere belief that relief was urgently needed in order to make possible the withdrawal of low category troops in the last stages of exhaustion," wrote Kelly. "Immediately on arrival in Archangel, however, I received the impression that the policy of the authorities was not what it was stated to be...I was reluctantly driven to the conclusion that the troops of the Relief Forces, which we were told had been sent out for purely defensive purposes, were being used for offensive purposes in furtherance of some ambitious plan of campaign, the nature of which we were not allowed to know…The much vaunted 'loyal Russian Army', composed largely of Bolshevik prisoners dressed in khaki, was utterly unreliable, always disposed to mutiny…I formed the opinion that the puppet-Government set up by us in Archangel rested on no basis of public confidence and support, and would fall to pieces the moment the protection of British bayonets was withdrawn. At the same time I saw British money poured out like water and invaluable British lives sacrificed in backing up this worthless army and in keeping in power this worthless Government and I became convinced that my duty to my country lay not in helping to forward a mistaken policy but in exposing it to the British public."* 51

Here they were, out in the open, the facts about the northern Russia intervention, which *The Times'* correspondent Soutar had not sent and which, if he had, the censor would no doubt have killed. Withdrawal was now not only militarily but also politically expedient. The British force, plus 6,000 White Russians who elected to go, was evacuated in September, and the last Allied troops left the following month. The responsibility for the fate of the White Russians who remained rested, said Churchill bitterly, "upon the mighty and resplendent nations who had won the war, but left their task unfinished." Writing about the northern Russia intervention later, John Cudahy, a noted American ambassador, summed up the situation in these words: "When the last battalion set sail from Archangel, not a soldier knew no, not even vaguely, why he had fought or why he was going now, and why his comrades were left behind, so many of them beneath wooden crosses."52

In the west, the Finns, Letts, and other border people, assisted by White Russians, advised by the French, and supplied by the British, tried to capture Petrograd. The main coverage on this front came from exiled Russian sources and was as wildly inaccurate as it was unjustifiably optimistic. The *New York Times*, which by then should have known better, published, on four days in October 1919, accounts of progress on this front. They began with the headline

---

* Churchill declared that Sherwood-Kelly had been guilty of a serious military offence—communicating to the press his views on a military subject. He was court-martialled and convicted, and, although sentenced to only a severe reprimand, he retired soon afterwards. He later tried several times to re-enlist, but was always rejected. He died in a nursing home in 1931, virtually friendless and aged only fifty-one. Ironically, he was buried with full military honours, the army providing two buglers to play the last post.

ANTI-RED FORCES NOW IN PETROGRAD on October 18 and ended on October 21 with ANTI-RED FORCES NEAR PETROGRAD, an advance that had moved backwards. The *New York Times*, which itself lamented the inaccuracy of its information, should have looked more closely at its sources. The first item came from "a dispatch received in Stockholm," the second from "the latest official advices received in London," the third from "a telegram received at the Russian Embassy in Paris," and the fourth from "a message from Helsingfors." The only accurate report came on November 24, when the Estonian chief of staff confirmed that the north-western interventionary army "had virtually gone out of existence."

It is worth mentioning one more encounter between the Bolshevik and the anti-Bolshevik forces, the Battle of Warsaw. If Warsaw had fallen to the powerful Red Army, under the brilliant tactician Mikhail Tukhachevski, this could have been a chance for the Red Army to arouse the working class of Poland, push on to Berlin, already shaken by revolution, and realise Lenin's aim "to unite the proletariat of industrial Germany, Austria and Czechoslovakia with the proletariat of Russia...[and] confront the reactionary capitalism of Britain with a revolutionary giant."[53]

However, this historically decisive battle was scarcely reported at all. I have been unable to find a single contemporary report in any Western newspaper of the battle's significance. The only eye-witness account of any value did not appear until August 17, 1930, when Lord D'Abernon, the British Ambassador to Germany, who had watched the battle, wrote an article on it for the Polish newspaper *Gazeta Polska*. This omission provides a fitting conclusion to the abysmally poor war reporting of the previous years.

The three correspondents who did have the ability and the courage to report events as they saw them eventually won recognition. When John Reed, the American reporter for *The Masses*, and a Harvard classmate of Walter Lippmann, caught typhus in Moscow in 1920 and died, just before his thirty-third birthday, the Russians buried him in Red Square, in the Heroes' Grave, and later placed a plaque in the Kremlin wall to commemorate him. His *Ten Days That Shook the World* still holds its own as a classic of reporting and remains required reading for students of Russian affairs.

Philips Price of the *Manchester Guardian* left Russia soon after the Armistice, so as to be the first Western war correspondent in Germany from the east. In Berlin, he became the correspondent for the new British socialist newspaper, the *Daily Herald*. He did not return to Britain until 1922, having been advised by friends in the

Foreign Office to stay away until ill feeling against him had died down.* Philips Price became a Labour MP in 1929 and was in Parliament almost continuously for thirty years. He died in 1973, absolutely convinced that he had acted correctly in 1917, one of the last witnesses to the Revolution and the intervention.

The third, Arthur Ransome of the *Daily News*, the only other British correspondent in Petrograd during the Revolution, wrote two books on his experiences. In one, *The Crisis in Russia*, a full defence of the Revolution, he pleaded for a more objective assessment of Bolshevist aims. He contributed extensively to the *Manchester Guardian* and became one of the most felicitous authors of children's stories. He married Trotsky's secretary, Eugenia Shelepin, and died, aged eighty-three, in 1967.

Robert Liddell of *The Sphere* went on to become the press censor with the Allied interventionary forces stationed in Tiflis, Georgia. After the war he worked for the *Weekly Graphic* and then became a novelist. His book *On the Russian Front* covers events there up to 1916. He died in London, aged eighty-seven, in 1973.

Robert Wilton, *The Times*' correspondent who missed the October Revolution, got hold of the official White Russian report on the death of the Czar and his family, but would not allow *The Times* to publish it "until a certain eventuality occurred."** Before *The Times* could publish his report, some of it appeared in America. Northcliffe was angry at being scooped, and Wilton was sacked—"flung out on the streets practically penniless...after giving the best years of my life to the service of *The Times*."[54] He went to Paris, rejoined the *New York Herald*, and died in 1925.

Harold Williams, the worst of the war correspondents, whose dispatches from southern Russia consistently misled readers of *The Times* and the *New York Times*, was appointed foreign editor of *The Times* in 1922. He bitterly opposed any recognition of Russia or, indeed, any trade with her, and continued to forecast the imminent downfall of the Bolsheviks until his death in 1928.

Coming so soon after their sell-out in the First World War, the Russian Revolution marked the war correspondents' nadir. The

---

* At one stage, soon after his pamphlet on the Revolution was issued, there had been a move to try him for treason. The Commons discussed whether it would be possible to prevent money from being sent to him, and the Daily Sketch ran a story on him headlined SQUIRE TURNS BOLSHEVIST—DESERTS HOME AND RICHES FOR RAGS IN RUSSIA.

** The "Czar-did-not-die" school has interpreted this phrase to mean that Wilton was involved in an alleged plot to get the royal family out of Russia.

post mortems that followed—the one by Walter Lippmann and Charles Merz in the *New Republic* is a classic in this field—ensured that there would be some effort to improve standards. There now began to emerge, particularly in the United States, a new style of war correspondent. Stimulated by Ernest Hemingway's fictional examination of his experiences in the war on the Austro-Italian front, this school believed that the public should be told about every facet of war and its effects on the individual. The aim of the new style of correspondent was to report with truth and objectivity. None realised how difficult this would prove to be.

## Chapter Eight
# The Real Scoop
# 1935–1936

You know, when I first started in journalism I used to think that foreign correspondents spoke every language under the sun and spent
their lives studying international conditions. Brother, look at us. On
Monday afternoon I was in East Sheen breaking the news to a
widow of her husband's death leap with a champion girl cyclist.
Next day the chief has me in and says, "Corker, you're off to Ishmaelia." "Out of town job?" I asked. "East Africa," he said, just like
that, "pack your traps." "What's the story?" I asked. "Well," he
said, "a lot of niggers are having a war. I don't see anything in it
myself, but the other agencies are sending feature men, so we've got
to do something."

—Corker of Universal News,
in *Scoop*, by Evelyn Waugh

———

The secret treaties of the First World War had promised Italy
economic control of Abyssinia. The treaty of friendship
between the two countries, signed in 1928, was seen by the Italians
as a charter for economic and cultural domination of Abyssinia.
The Abyssinians saw it as simply another stage in their game of
nations, their exploitation of the rivalries of the European powers,
and they observed neither the text nor the spirit of the treaty. Italy
was confident that since the other powers in the League of Nations
had themselves used force to impose their rule in Africa, they
would understand its necessity in Abyssinia. Abyssinia, in turn,

believed that since she was a member of the League of Nations, by which her territory was guaranteed absolutely and explicitly, her fellow members would quickly bring Italy to heel. So both sides confidently prepared for war.

In Britain, the United States, and most of Europe, public sympathy was firmly with Abyssinia. Mussolini was regarded as a bombastic braggart trying to prove his country's new-found virility; Haile Selassie, the Emperor of Abyssinia, the Lion of Judah, as a quiet, modest, and romantic primitive. Troops and war materials were being shipped daily from Italy to Africa with the maximum of ostentation; the Abyssinians moved barefoot through the mountains armed only with sword and dagger. Although the outcome of such an encounter should have been obvious from the start, the pro-Abyssinian sentiments of the public blinded it to the obvious probability that the Italians would win. The Abyssinians would conduct a brilliant guerrilla campaign, trapping the advancing Italians in lion pits, and, if given guns, would, according to a widely held view in the United States, be able to fire them both with hands and with feet.

As tension increased and the world's major newspapers selected their correspondents for the war that now seemed inevitable, it became apparent that the ignorance about Abyssinia and its people extended to the press. "There is little known in the U.K. about this dispute," wrote the foreign editor of *The Times*, "and even we must admit our deficiency in this area."[1] Evelyn Waugh, who covered the war for the *Daily Mail*, put it better: "Few [editors] could find Abyssinia on the map or had the faintest conception of its character. Those who had read Nesbitt believed that it lay below sea-level in stupefying heat, a waterless plain of rock and salt, sparsely inhabited by naked homicidal lunatics, those who glanced through Budge pictured an African Thibet, a land where ancient inviolable palaces jutted on to glaciers…the editor of one great English paper believed…that the inhabitants spoke classical Greek."[2] The *Daily Express* chose its war correspondent, O. D. Gallagher, mainly because he was from South Africa; and Waugh, with no real experience in journalism, much less in reporting wars—"I didn't know the first thing about being a war correspondent"—got the job with the *Daily Mail*, after being turned down by the *Daily Express*, because he had actually spent a few weeks in the Abyssinian capital, Addis Ababa, some years earlier.

Correspondents with the Italian army wore heavy woollen belly-bands, on the advice of the army medical chief, as a means of preventing cholera, while silk pyjamas worn under the clothing were said to prevent typhus. None of this saved Wilfred Barber of the *Chicago Tribune*, who died in Addis Ababa of fever. Other correspondents, determined to be prepared for anything, went with rifles, telescopes, gas masks, pack saddles, and tents. Gallagher bought a mule train. Laurence Stallings of Fox Movietone took a large Red Indian motorcycle and sidecar. No one knew what to expect. Ernest Hemingway warned the American correspondents, before they left, that if they were wounded the vultures would first peck out their eyes and then tear out their livers.

But nothing that the correspondents imagined about covering the war in Abyssinia could match the hilarious reality. When *Scoop*, Evelyn Waugh's irreverent novel of Fleet Street and the hectic pursuit of hot news in "Ishmaelia" by the newly appointed war correspondent William Boot, was published in 1938, it was hailed as a "brilliant parody" of his experiences in Abyssinia. What only the war correspondents present at the time knew was that *Scoop* was actually a piece of straight reportage, thinly disguised as a novel to protect the author from libel actions.

The correspondents began arriving in Addis Ababa in May 1935. By the time war broke out in October there were 120 of them. The British correspondents included George Steer, a young South African from a well-known newspaper-owning family in East London, covering for *The Times* and the *New York Times*; Sir Percival Phillips, covering for the *Daily Telegraph*; O. D. Gallagher, another South African, aged only twenty-two, covering for the *Daily Express*; and Evelyn Waugh for the *Daily Mail*. The Americans included H. R. Knickerbocker of the Hearst chain; Karl H. von Wiegand, another Hearst man, of Universal Service; Jim Mills of Associated Press; the ill-fated Wilfred Barber of the *Chicago Tribune*; and Ladislas Farago, with the photographer Alfred Eisenstaedt. Havas, the French agency, Tass, the Russian, Reuters, and the United Press were there also. It was a distinguished international collection of correspondents, and the Abyssinians were completely unprepared to receive them.

Addis Ababa was little more than a ramshackle town, a shabby, dirty, dusty place, with lepers and eunuchs and slaves. It had a palace with two rows of lions in the drive, one hotel, a railway station, a post-office, two cinemas, a radio transmitting station, a few plaster-covered Indian shops, and a collection of mud, wattle, and corrugated-iron huts. To get there, the correspondents took a ship to Djibouti, in French Somaliland, and then a train with wooden coaches and slatted windows to keep out the terrible heat. They stayed at the Hotel Imperial, which looked as if it had been transported whole from the gold rush in the Yukon, and which had about thirty rooms, so that at the peak of the war there were three or four correspondents to a room. The Abyssinian Foreign Office had established a press section, and accreditation involved getting the newspaper to guarantee a sum of money for its correspondent's repatriation "should he for any reason be required to leave the country by reason of a misdemeanour."

A war correspondent is only as good as his lines of communication with his newspaper, and the first thing the newly arrived correspondents did was to see how they would be able to file the exciting stories they planned to write; how, in the words of the *Daily Express*, they would "lay the truth about the fighting on the readers' breakfast tables." It did not take them long to find out that filing facilities were not only primitive, but laughable as well. To begin with, the cable rate was three-fourths of a (gold) karat per word, about half a crown in British currency, one of the dearest rates in the world at that time. This led the correspondents to invent the most complicated "cablese" in a desperate attempt to cram as much as possible into a message—for instance, SLONGS for "as long as." Since the cable clerk, tapping away at his Morse key, did not understand half the languages in which he was so laboriously transmitting the correspondents' messages, the cablese served further to bewilder him. Cables arrived in London and New York so garbled as to be nearly unintelligible. *The Times* at first put this down to the influence of American correspondents. "The telegraphic influence of the American tyros assembled at Addis has been amazing," complained *The Times*' foreign news editor, Ralph Deakin. "Even with a desire to condense news in the interests of economy it should be quite easy to frame messages so that they mean *something* at this end."[3] Gallagher has said that when the correspondents received clippings of their stories, as "decoded" by puzzled sub-editors at home, they not only were amazed at what had emerged, but also were often unable to understand what the stories had been about. Before censorship was officially imposed, a story went around among the correspondents that the garbling of their cables was deliberate, and intended instead of censorship because it was cheaper and less likely to cause protests.

Incoming communications were, if anything, worse. The system of delivery was completely haphazard. The cable clerk waited until he had enough cables to justify engaging a delivery boy, and the boy then set off with anything up to fifty cables and headed for the Hotel Imperial. Since he could not read, his delivery technique was to hand all the cables to the first European he met at the hotel and ask him to pass them on. This enabled just about every correspondent in the hotel to read, at one time or another, his rivals' messages, and led to some heavy practical jokes. To relieve the tedium, Gallagher concocted a cable purporting to be for George Steer of *The Times*, and at the next opportunity he inserted it into the messenger's bundle. It read, STEER TIMES ADDIS ABABA WE NATION PROUD YOUR WORK STOP CARRY ON IN NAME YOUR KING AND COUNTRY—ASTOR (proprietor of *The Times*).[4] Naturally, word of the cable reached the palace, where it was accepted as being true, and Steer was able to write to *The Times*: "The Emperor has given me the longest interview on record—eighty minutes—and also broke a precedent to invite me to interview him instead of waiting for a request from *The Times*. He has given me the free run of his ministries and seems to be highly satisfied with the attitude of your great paper."[5] (Gallagher says he then thought seriously of sending himself a similar fake cable.)

Unfortunately, the patronage of even the Emperor himself was of no help in getting any real news. As Gallagher noted, "a reporter who cannot speak the language of the country he is working in can never get at the facts because he is completely at the mercy of either his interpreter or the official handouts. Not one correspondent in Addis spoke Amharic except a Lithuanian, who was general assistant to Jim Mills of Associated Press. The rest of us had to rely on what our Abyssinian interpreters told us in their poor English or on official handouts."[6]

The interpreters/assistants/personal spies, as they were variously called, were cashing in on their ability to speak English and on the strength of their salesmanship. Waugh secretly employed an Abyssinian called Wazir Ali Bey, until, so he said, he found that Ali Bey was also secretly employed by nearly every other correspondent in the capital. It was no use for a correspondent to decide to dispense with an assistant and set out to find news for himself. For one thing, there was the language problem, and, still more important, the Emperor refused to allow the correspondents to leave Addis Ababa, claiming, probably with reason, that, since his tribesmen could not distinguish between an Italian and any other European, he could not be responsible for their safety. He also no doubt suspected that some of the correspondents might well be spies. The remarkable Haroun al Raschid, a German, who said he had fought with the Turks in 1914–18 and had taken a Muslim name, and who now claimed to be representing the *Stuttgart Zeitung*, must have appeared very suspicious indeed. Haroun al Raschid, who had shaved his head, had an attractive blond wife, a manservant called Fritz, and a fine custom-built car. He and his entourage disappeared in the last stages of the war, and afterwards the Abyssinians claimed that he was really a Wehrmacht colonel, his wife a coding clerk, and Fritz a German navy radio operator. This claim was never proved, but the Germans definitely had observers with the Italian troops, sometimes under the cover of being war correspondents, and so it seems quite likely that there were German observers in Addis Ababa, also.

All these strictures—being confined to Addis, being forced to rely on paid informers, and having no regular sources of information except official handouts—dictated the coverage of the war from the Abyssinian side and enabled the Abyssinians to present to the world the situation as they wanted it to be seen: themselves as a gallant little nation with an army equipped mainly with spears and antique weapons, and relying on justice from the world powers to prevent its having to go to war. If, however, war were forced upon it, all its tribes, loyal to the last to Emperor Haile Selassie, would rise as one and, conducting a brilliant guerrilla campaign, would drive the invading Italians from Abyssinia, inflicting on them a defeat comparable to that of Adowa in 1896. Unfortunately, this picture bore little relation to the facts and was largely responsible for the misplaced optimism about Abyssinia's chances that persisted right to the end. It also resulted in a rash of invented reports, the product of frustration and of the arrival of one correspondent who was determined not to allow the Abyssinians' restrictions to prevent him from getting exclusive and newsworthy stories.

The correspondent was the veteran Sir Percival Phillips, of the *Daily Telegraph*. Sir Percival, knighted for his services to his country, if not to journalism, in the First World War, took all the problems of the situation in his stride. He and Jim Mills, an old-style Associated Press correspondent, known to his colleagues in Addis as "the Silver Fox" because of his silver hair and professional cunning, scooped everyone with the Rickett oil-concession story. Haile Selassie, in a desperate attempt to forestall Mussolini's invasion, signed over to Francis W. Rickett, a British entrepreneur representing American oil interests, exclusive concessions to a large part of Abyssinia. Phillips and Mills had followed Rickett throughout his stay in Addis Ababa, and they broke the story on August 30,

1935. Phillips could probably have rested his reputation on this one scoop, but he went on to seek further glory. What happened is best described by the series of cables O. D. Gallagher received from his newspaper, the *Daily Express*, soon after Sir Percival arrived.

PHILLIPS IN TELEGRAPH SAYS ABYSSINIAN SPEARSMEN MASSING ON TIGRE FRONT STOP WHAT FOLLOW UP EXYOU.

The second read:

DANAKIL TRIBESMEN MUTILATED ITALIAN SCOUTING PARTY ACCORDING PHILLIPS IN TELEGRAPH STOP AWAIT ACTION REPORT EXYOU.

The third:

PHILLIPS DESCRIBES HAILE SELASSIE SQUARE AS PICCADILLY CIR-CUS OF ADDIS STOP THIS GREAT STUFF STOP LETS HAVE YOUR COM-PARISONS HAILE SELASSIES CAPITAL WITH LONDON.

The fourth shows the *Express'* concern at being regularly scooped by the *Daily Telegraph*.

BEG YOU EMULATE PHILLIPS STOP YOUR LACK CABLES MOST DIS-CONCERTING STOP NOT ONLY YOUR JOB BUT MINE AT STAKE SAYS CHRISTIANSEN [the editor] BECAUSE EYE SENT YOU ABYSSINIA— SUTTON [the foreign editor].

Gallagher remembers well his reaction to the series of cables. "I went straight out to check the spearsmen story. No one seemed to know anything about this except Sir Percival. Again, no one had heard of the mutilation of the Italian scouting party. The compari-son of the squalid Haile Selassie Square to Piccadilly Circus was ridiculous and not worth rebutting. I had been brought up on colo-nial standards of reporting, where we had to be much more accu-rate because, in a small town, people *knew* what we were writing about. This sort of wild romancing I was now witnessing actually shocked me, but in my youthful enthusiasm to save the foreign edi-tor's job I was not going to let Phillips get away with it—especially when I found out that some of his best passages had been para-phrased from an old book called *In the Country of the Blue Nile*, by Colonel C. F. Rey. So with help from Noel Monks [an Australian colleague] I wrote a piece based on Colonel Rey's travels, up-dating it and using it in the terms and situations of the Abyssinian War, and sent it off. The *Express* liked it, so, pleased with my success in this new style of journalism, I did some descriptive stuff about the country, the tribes and their customs, the wild life that the Italians would encounter when they advanced into Abyssinia. I got congratulations each day for a week and the final one came on a Saturday. It said, 'PHILLIPS BRILLIANT IN TELEGRAGH BUT YOU EXCEL HIM STOP KEEP IT UP.' " Gallagher and Monks were astounded. "Well, now we know," Monks said. "It's entertainment they want."[7]

But there was a limit to the material Phillips or Gallagher could get from Colonel Rey's book, and the situation changed dramatically when, after months of preparation, the Italians attacked on October 2, 1935.


The correspondents who had decided—against general advice—to cover the war from the Italian side did not at first fare much better than their colleagues in Addis Ababa. The Ministry of Press and Propaganda in Rome appeared unable to make up its mind whether correspondents would be allowed to accompany the Italian army. Actually, the ministry, which had some knowledge of how to influence the press and win support, wanted war correspondents, but the army did not. The army would have preferred to confine its press rôle to the series of communiqués it issued through the ministry. These listed the progress of Italian troops, engagements, and the numbers of dead, wounded, and sick. As far as they went, they appear to have been reasonably accurate, but only the correspondents on the spot were in a position to know what the communiqués omitted.

The first of these was the United Press correspondent Webb Miller, who had not wanted the job. "I was disgusted by the hypocrisy, two-faced manoeuvring, and double-dealing of the British, French and Italian statesmen and by the prospect of watching the aggression of a nation with all the modern resources for slaughter upon an ignorant, backward, comparatively defenceless people...I told myself that my duty as an objective reporter compelled me to stifle my personal opinions and sit in the grand stand, watching and describing the parade, not to join the procession carrying the banner. And I knew that a writer who detested war made the best correspondent because the scenes impinged more vividly upon his senses."[8] So Miller chose the Italian side, and, like at least one other correspondent, Herbert Matthews of the *New York Times*, came to understand and even sympathise with the Italian attitude to the war.

Miller spent a month in Rome waiting for accreditation and suffering from the same procrastination that had made many other correspondents give up and go home. But Miller was not only a famous correspondent; he was also persistent. By badgering the ministry, he was finally accredited and issued with press card No. 1. He left immediately by ship from Naples, sailed to Alexandria, then went in a British plane to Khartoum, then by an Italian plane to Asmara, the capital of Italian Eritrea, where the northern Italian army was massed for the invasion of Abyssinia. At the press head-quarters, formerly the local Fascist club, he found Floyd Gibbons, another American veteran of 1917–18, who, with a special dispensation from Mussolini, had managed to beat Miller to Asmara by a day. These two men were the only war correspondents to witness the start of the war (there was not even an Italian correspondent present), and Miller rated his six-word message, sent on October 2, 1935—ITALIANS COMMENCE INVASION ETHIOPIA 5 AM—as the greatest newspaper scoop since the First World War.

Other correspondents—including the military commentator General J. F. C. Fuller—now came pouring in from all over the world. There were British, American, Italian, French, Spanish, Austrian, Hungarian, German, Polish, Japanese, and even Latvian newsmen. The press office was overwhelmed. It began a system of news releases fit only for the wastepaper basket. When the corre-spondents themselves set out, found news, and returned to Asmara to transmit it, they first had to submit their stories to censors, who tended to remove everything worth reading. As Matthews remem-bered it, "the stupid Censorship, bad living conditions, the alti-tude, the crazy climate, the strain on heart, lungs and nerves, all combined to create a colony of half-mad correspondents rushing frantically about in a state of chronic hysteria."[9] The Italian com-manding general, Emilio de Bono, did not improve matters by asking the correspondents to a pre-luncheon cocktail party in the officers' club and then saying to them, "Of course I don't like newspapermen or the Press, but I suppose we'll have to get along with each other."[10]

The results of the Italian official attitude were far-reaching. The clamp-down on news from the Italian army coincided with the flush of invented stories from Addis Ababa. Since an invented story, unhampered by facts, makes more exciting reading than a heavily censored account of a minor engagement, newspapers plumped for the stories from Addis Ababa, and this created a false impression of what was happening in Abyssinia.

Towns formerly held by the Italians were reported captured.* Casualty figures were grossly exaggerated.** Matthews has said he tried to tell the *New York Times* that lurid accounts from Addis Ababa should be treated with the utmost caution, but no one in New York appeared to pay any attention to this warning. What Matthews was up against, of course, was that the truth, that the Abyssinians stood no chance against the Italians' mechanised army, was unpalatable; sympathy suspended the reader's critical judgement, and he preferred optimistic but fake reports from Abyssinia to more factual reports from correspondents with the Italian army. Editors were not slow to sense this. "The commands of Fleet Street became more and more fantastically inappropriate to the situation," Evelyn Waugh wrote. And as Wazir Ali Bey, the most active of the interpreter-assistants in Addis Ababa, retailed reports of more and more clashes in which the Italians suffered heavy casualties, "Wazir Ali Bey's news service formed an ever-increasing part of the morning reading of French, English and American newspaper publics."[11]

While the correspondents with the Italians were fighting with the censors and among themselves, and going steadily downhill from the combined effects of fleas, flies, malaria, dysentery, and the altitude, what had the outbreak of war brought for their colleagues in Addis Ababa?

Early in the crisis, the correspondents with the Abyssinians had taken two steps to protect their interests. Both proved to be their undoing. The first was to form themselves into an association, in the mistaken belief that this would improve their bargaining power with the Abyssinian authorities. The association had an important-sounding name—Association de la Presse Etrangère—and was dominated by the British and the French, both because they had been the main movers of the idea and because correspondents of other nationalities were impressed by their enthusiasm. The other move was to suggest to the Abyssinian Press Bureau that it impose some sort of military censorship. It is difficult to imagine why any war correspondent would actually ask to have his copy censored, and the reason advanced in this instance goes a long way towards explaining what was wrong with the coverage from Addis Ababa. "We were assessing in our dispatches the chances of Abyssinia should it come to a shooting war," wrote the Australian Noel Monks.

* Havas, the French news agency, was particularly guilty in this respect.
** At Adowa, early in October, Abyssinian reports claimed that 700 Italians had been killed; the actual figure was six.

194

"All Italian intelligence officers had to do was to read their newspapers...the very hopelessness of Abyssinia's plight won one's natural sympathy [and] because most of us had just that sympathy, it was we who suggested that some sort of military censorship be imposed on our dispatches."[12]

Once the Abyssinians realised that they could censor the news, it was but a short step to trying to manipulate it. Joseph Israels II, an American who had for a brief period acted as correspondent in Addis Ababa for *The Times* and the *New York Times* while Steer was trying to find out what was happening outside the capital, went off to New York to become Haile Selassie's "public relations counsel," dispensing slanted news for the Abyssinian side.[13] In Addis Ababa, the Emperor's American adviser, Everett A. Colson, sorted out the most sympathetic correspondents, showing particular attention to Steer of *The Times*, and would regularly reveal to them the government communiqués the day before they were officially issued. Months of being without information had dulled the correspondents' ability to assess the significance of what they now received, and those honoured by being leaked official information raced each other to the cable office to lodge their messages, under the mistaken impression that what they were sending was news.

In London and New York, the foreign editors despaired. The service from Addis Ababa was costing a fortune, and it was producing little or nothing worth printing. Deakin, the foreign news editor of *The Times*, complained that "only a small fraction of the messages reaching London from the many correspondents in Abyssinia are what is wanted...the flood of trivialities that have been put on to the wire are no substitutes."[14] Steer, whose main source of information was Colonel Kornivaloff, a White Russian who was in Haile Selassie's service, wrote that the Press Bureau had become an instrument of internal propaganda and asked to be allowed to change to the Italian side. Deakin refused. Steer's dispatches and those of the other correspondents who were sending information leaked to them by the Abyssinians did have one value—they revealed what the Abyssinians *thought* was happening: "thought," because it rapidly became clear, once the war started, that the authorities in Addis Ababa had no idea of what was happening at the front and had no intention of letting anyone, especially war correspondents, find out. By mid-October censorship had so stifled reports on the progress of the war that the Newspaper Proprietors' Association in London decided on a collective protest. It cabled the Association de la Presse Etrangère and asked it to convey the proprietors' disquiet to the Emperor. The Abyssinian authorities had never paid any attention to the foreign press association, and now they took not the slightest notice of the more august body of newspaper proprietors.[15] In fact, censorship grew worse, because of a bombing incident involving the Emperor.

From the outbreak of war, the one story that had kept every correspondent from despair during the frustrating weeks of waiting was the Emperor's projected departure for the front to take personal command of his troops. Now correspondents were notified that the censors would pass no copy dealing with the Emperor's departure, the route he would travel, or his subsequent whereabouts. Although the Abyssinians' reason, that the Italians might try to bomb the Emperor, was understandable, it was galling for the correspondents to see the Emperor and his party leave Addis Ababa in mid-November and not be able to report it. The Associated Press, however, managed to do so. Using a code disguised as inter-office messages, the AP's Al Wilson cabled to New York that the Emperor had left for the front, travelling overland via Dessye. The message had two direct results. The Associated Press was denied further cable facilities (the ban was lifted after a week, probably because AP's tolls often amounted to $1,000 a day), and, as the Abyssinians had feared, on December 6 the Italians bombed the Emperor's headquarters.[16]

There were two reported versions of the bombing. The Abyssinian version was that fifty-three people were killed and 200 injured, that the American hospital had been hit, although clearly marked with a red cross, and that the Emperor and several correspondents accompanying him had had narrow escapes. The Italian version was that the bombing had been confined to the military encampment and the Emperor's fortified enclosure; the hospital and the correspondents could have been in danger only if they had been located in the military camp.

The significance of the attack was that the Emperor ordered all the correspondents back to Addis Ababa, and there they were confined—those who chose to remain—until the end of the war. Few were prepared to endure this prospect, and the exodus that had started in November became a stampede. By January, of the 120 who had been in Addis Ababa at the start of the war only twelve were left. Some went quickly: Waugh was sacked, complaining to the end that his instruction to send sensational but exclusive accounts was a paradox. He was a failure as a war correspondent and had sent little since he arrived, except a long cable predicting that the Italian invasion was imminent. To keep the story from his colleagues' prying eyes, Waugh had sent it in Latin, and a puzzled sub-editor on the *Daily Mail* was still trying to work out what Waugh was writing about when the war started and the scoop was lost.[17] Others went in a rage. Stallings, the Fox Movietone man with the Red Indian motorcycle—the correspondent Movietone had promoted by distributing posters reading, "OK boys, you can start the war now, Stallings is there"—went out roaring, "I've spent one hundred thousand dollars US and I haven't got one shot of the war."[18] Stallings and other correspondents who left voiced their complaints to *Time* magazine.

*Time* had been openly pro-Mussolini in its sentiments, and so the magazine was delighted to express the fury of the correspondents who had tried to cover the Abyssinian side. Now *Time* said that the Abyssinians had "cheated the pants off the correspondents." It quoted Stallings as saying that at the first sound of an Italian plane Abyssinian officers dived for the nearest Red Cross shelter, and that Haile Selassie's younger son had a palace that flew the Red Cross flag, although it was not being used for any Red Cross purpose. These statements should be weighed against *Time*'s anti-Abyssinian attitude and Stallings' frustration from his time in Addis Ababa. But there is no doubting the truth of *Time*'s conclusion: "It remains impossible to obtain for love or money anything remotely approaching an accurate day by day account of the war on Ethiopia's fronts...correspondents and cameramen at Addis know less about the fighting they are supposed to be covering than the newspaper reader in New York."[19]

The reason the American reader was better informed was that in November the Italians had finally let their war correspondents loose, and two of the better ones, Herbert Matthews of the *New York Times* and Luigi Barzini, Jr., son of Luigi Barzini, of *Corriere della Sera*, had been sending excellent eye-witness reports. Easily the best of these was of the first main action of the war, fought by an Italian flying column under General Oreste Mariotti after it had been ambushed in Ende Gorge by the Abyssinians under Kassa Sebat. The Italians had expected Kassa Sebat to defend his mountain stronghold of Azbi from an almost impregnable position overlooking the only means of access, a mule track. Instead, the Abyssinians ambushed the Italian troops farther down the valley.

The Italian advance guard consisted mainly of Massauan tribesmen recruited along the coast; then came the Italian officers, then

Matthews and Barzini on mules, then camels carrying artillery and provisions, flanked by another native battalion. When the Abyssinians sprang their ambush, the two correspondents dropped into a natural trench beside the track. The main firing came from the left flank, but other Abyssinians were harassing the column from the right and from directly in front. Matthews and Barzini could not see properly, so they climbed back onto the mule track and crouched with some officers behind a tree. There they came under fire. Bullets, as Barzini wrote in *Corriere della Sera*, "dug into the earth with a puff of dust and into the tree with a small crash."

While they were in the shelter of the tree, the first wounded soldier arrived. He was a Massauan, barely eighteen years old. Machine-gun bullets had riddled the calves of his legs, but he appeared indifferent to the pain he must have been suffering. "The blood which caked his trousers could have been mud," Barzini wrote. "He stood at attention and asked timidly for the doctor, as if afraid to disturb him."[20] Matthews, with a correspondent's instinct, had taken out his notebook and was jotting down times and ideas. But even his *sang-froid* gave way when, fourteen minutes after the ambush had started, the Italian artillery opened fire with its seventy-millimetre guns. "That'll put the fear of God into them," he shouted to Barzini, and began to crawl higher up the slopes to get a better view of the action. It was a dangerous move. A lieutenant was hit in the face and a sergeant-major in the head, and a bullet ripped through Barzini's puttees. For a moment it appeared as if the position were about to be overrun, and an Italian officer advised the two correspondents to take a couple of hand-grenades each for the final clash. But the Italian troops counter-attacked, routed the snipers who had been shooting down on the correspondents from the peak, and forced the Abyssinians back into Azbi.

In the cold dawn the Italians advanced on the fortress, prepared to fight all the way. Barking monkeys watched the column, and white vultures wheeled above the troops as they picked their way over the corpses of men and animals from the previous day. "It was my first sight of dead during that war," Matthews wrote. "Yet I remember looking at them almost indifferently, as if I, who had undergone my baptism of fire the previous day, were accustomed to seeing dead bodies, and so riding by them unmoved. In the back of my mind there was a lurking wonder that I was not filled with pity and revolted by the terrible spectacle."[21]

The following day the Italians occupied Azbi without resistance. Matthews and Barzini visited the fortress from which Kassa Sebat had controlled the town; it was like that of a baron of the early Middle Ages. Built of stone and mud, it had no furniture apart from a few packing-cases. Kassa Sebat had slept on straw. The only decoration in the main room was ox-horns fixed to the walls as hooks for rifles.

All this was excellent material: the testing of Italian native troops under fire, the Abyssinian tactics, the nature of the engagement, the physical surroundings, the primitive Abyssinian fortress, the inexplicable disappearance of the Abyssinian troops. Matthews and Barzini accompanied the wounded back to a field hospital, and from there they hurried to Asmara to file their stories. Barzini telephoned a short account to *Corriere della Sera*, which printed it on November 19. Matthews, who still considers this his best story of the war, wrote non-stop for eleven hours. It took the inadequate Italian radio two days to transmit his report, cost $1,500 in cable tolls, and on November 23 was spread over sixteen columns on the front page and two whole inside pages—the longest single story by a correspondent the *New York Times* had ever published.

This, and other pieces Matthews wrote during the same period, carried a clear indication of his sympathies, and he was promptly accused of being a Fascist. First, it is important to remember that in 1935 Fascism was a respectable political philosophy and that Mussolini had many admirers, including, for example, Winston Churchill. Matthews' attitude, which he is still prepared frankly to admit, was that he admired the Italians, admired the Fascists, and knew that they were going to win. "The right or the wrong of it did not interest me greatly—not any more, let us say, than they did Laval [the French Foreign Minister], Eden, and the Standard Oil Company...If you start from the premise that a lot of rascals are having a fight, it is not unnatural to want to see the victory of the rascal you like, and I liked the Italians during that scrimmage more than I did the British or the Abyssinians."[22] (Webb Miller of the United Press, who was originally bitter about the Italian invasion, came to feel the same, and included in his book on the war a chapter called "The Case for the Aggressor.")

Then, it should be remembered that there was, in the attitude of many correspondents covering the war, a flavour of the grand adventure, of a European civilising mission to a barbaric and backward country. Even the cool-headed Matthews succumbed. He was thirty-five years old—as he wrote, "*nel mezzo del cammin di nostra vita*" ("in the midst of this our mortal life")—and he was attracted by the glamorous image of war: "...stepping out of my tent under the over-full moon while the camp was fast asleep, except for the sentries whose fires twinkled along the crests of the surrounding hills, I was conscious only of the extraordinary beauty of the scene. A sense of timelessness of what I saw came over me. Caesar's legions had made just such marches in conquering Gaul, and set up just such camps with sentry fires gleaming around them. There was the same moon, the same urge to conquest, the same thrill of adventure—life and death and history in the making, whether it be De Bello Gallico, or just a hasty narrative for one day's newspaper."

Matthews has admitted, "I was not concerned then with moral or ethical problems. They grew with time and experience and thought, as the wars took on a political shape and the wanton, wicked, vicious quality of the suffering imposed on others, seared its way into my heart."[23] But in 1935–36, in sympathy with the Italians and moved by war's glamour, what did he report?

For the two months following his Ende Gorge experience, he was unable to report anything. The new commander, Marshal Pietro Badoglio, decided to impose a rigid censorship, which he enforced by keeping the correspondents cooped up in Asmara for ten long weeks, until he was ready to move against the Abyssinians again. There were no facilities for sports and, in any case, the altitude made any form of exercise difficult. There were no cabarets, night-clubs, or English cinemas. There were no English books, newspapers, or magazines. The press corps dwindled. Some left in time to avoid breakdowns, others were recalled by their newspapers, others fell ill and had to be evacuated. Matthews, Reynolds Packard, who had replaced Webb Miller for the United Press, Christopher Holme of Reuters, and Eddie Neil of the Associated Press made up a bridge four and played from 10:00 A.M. to 10:00 P.M., "to stop us from going mad."[24] By Christmas, of the 150 correspondents who had originally been with the Italians only twenty-four were left. Mostly they were Italians; the rest comprised three Americans and one Englishman.

Then, late in January 1936, Marshal Badoglio was ready for a new push. Matthews sent to the *New York Times* dispatches that said the Italians were going to win. Due weight was not given to his opinion, because of his sympathies, while undue weight was given to reports from Addis Ababa, because most newspaper editors wanted the Abyssinians to win and they allowed their professional judgement to be weakened by their emotions.

The Battle of Enderta, fought on February 15, 1936, was a typical example. It was a clear Italian victory and marked the beginning of the Abyssinian collapse. Matthews was there, and he wrote of what he saw. Steer, who represented the *New York Times* through an arrangement with *The Times*, was in Addis Ababa. He wrote a dispatch, quoting Abyssinian sources, which said that there had been several local engagements but no battle. Steer's story was believed; Matthews' was not. As he said later, "I thought that since I had seen the battle and Steer had not, my account would be accepted, and that it would be clear that this was going to be the fate of Haile Selassie's other armies. I was wrong."[25] Even the British military expert Captain (later Sir) Basil Liddell Hart, in assessing the significance of the battle in articles for *The Times* and the *New York Times*, spoke of the lack of any impartial witnesses and the need to "penetrate the present rosy haze by the cold light of reason." He then went on to write that there was "no hint of a decisive victory."[26] Within ten weeks the Italians were in Addis Ababa, and the war was over.

The refusal to believe correspondents who wrote that the Italians were winning led to a frantic search for explanations when it became clear that they were. The easiest and most feasible explanation to hand was that the Italians were using gas and were bombing hospitals, Red Cross stations, and civilian targets. There is no doubt that the Italians used mustard gas on several occasions. But so confusing were the reports of its use, and so vehement were the Italian official denials, that as late as 1939—four years after the war—Evelyn Waugh was still successfully putting down anyone who suggested that gas had been employed.*

Yet Ladislas Farago, on a free-lance assignment for the *New York Times*, reported having seen the victims of an Italian gas attack in northern Abyssinia, and various Red Cross officials examined gas victims and submitted evidence to the League of Nations in Geneva. Italian officers told Herbert Matthews that the Italian army was using gas; Captain Roland Strunk, an officer of the German high command, who was an observer with the Italian forces, saw gas used and wrote a report; and Waugh, despite his later attitude, wrote in 1936: "Gas was used but accounted for only eighteen lives."

* Waugh was attending an officers' course at Deal in the winter of 1939–40. At a lecture on "passive air defence," the instructor said, "This gas was used by the Italians in Abyssinia." "What evidence have you got that the Italians used gas?" Waugh demanded, and the instructor was forced to admit that he had none.

George Steer, writing for *The Times* and the *New York Times*, reported the statements of Red Cross officials in some detail on March 25 and again on April 3 and 4. The April 3 report was perhaps the most damning: "Dr J. W. S. MacFie...stated yesterday that he had personally seen and treated between March 1 and 18 several hundred men, women and children suffering from mustard gas burns. This writer and correspondents of British newspapers have seen and photographed gas cases in the Quorain area." More photographic evidence would undoubtedly have helped prove the Abyssinian charge, but the photographers covering the war worked under great difficulties. Without freedom of movement, they were forced to pose photographs behind the lines.* Matthews has estimated that of all the photographs published of the war, ninety-nine out of a hundred had been faked.[27]

As was seen in the First World War, atrocity stories about the bombing of hospitals and Red Cross units are easy to level and hard to disprove. Hospitals *are* shelled and bombed in war-time, but how often this is done deliberately is another matter. In Abyssinia the question was complicated by three main factors. In sparsely inhabited terrain, Red Cross stations were inevitably near or within a military encampment. Then, the bombing techniques the Italians used were far from accurate. Moreover, the Abyssinians did not have the strict respect for the Red Cross emblem necessary to make conventions about its use workable, no doubt due to the fact that in Abyssinia a red cross had for centuries been used to designate a brothel. When the Abyssinians learned that the Red Cross emblem conferred some immunity from bombing, they took to sheltering in Red Cross tents during attacks and, as the next logical step, to flying Red Cross flags over their officers' quarters. In turn, the Italians felt justified in attacking such encampments, especially when they were fired upon, even though the tents may have been marked by a red cross.

Steer and his colleagues in Addis Ababa regularly filed details of these attacks, and Matthews and his colleagues regularly filed the Italian versions of what had occurred and Italian counter-charges that the Abyssinians were using dum-dum bullets and had decapitated prisoners, both allegations probably being true. But, in the emotional atmosphere surrounding the Abyssinian cause, the Italian case always passed unnoticed.

* Joe Caneva of the Associated Press persuaded the Italians to manoeuvre about fifty tanks and several companies of soldiers for his benefit, and his photograph of this later appeared in many publications throughout the world as an actual tank charge against the Abyssinians.

It is clear in retrospect what Emperor Haile Selassie's strategy was. He knew from the beginning that Abyssinia would be no match for Mussolini and that his main chance of avoiding Italian occupation of his country would be to arouse international public opinion, principally represented by the League of Nations, by projecting an image of a brave but primitive country resisting to the last the mechanised might of Italy. In this strategy, every bombing of a Red Cross camp—it is significant that the Emperor complained to the League about this on the *first* day of the war—every mustard-gas victim, every civilian casualty, was a weapon in the campaign. When it became apparent that the League was powerless and that sanctions, ignored by the major American oil companies, would not work, and that none of the major powers, although they might be shocked by Italian atrocity stories, were prepared to intervene, Abyssinia, unable to resist the Italians militarily, collapsed, and the Emperor went down to the railway station in Addis Ababa and took a train into exile.

The last stages of the war caught the correspondents in Addis Ababa unawares. In March 1936, British and American newspapers had started to give preference to reports from the Italian front, realising at long last that these gave a more accurate version of the progress of the war. But in Addis Ababa the Abyssinians had continued to put out optimistic statements, for local if not international consumption, *Time* magazine, for example, quoting the Abyssinian authorities as saying that 300,000 warriors were assembling for a massive counter-attack.[28]

When the Emperor fled on May 2, the inhabitants of Addis Ababa, realising that they had been betrayed by the major powers, began rioting and turned on all the Europeans in the capital. Steer, who had become so involved with the Abyssinian side that he went with an official of the British Legation to distribute gas masks on the northern front,[29] and a few other correspondents sought refuge in the legation, and there, while mobs raged in the streets, he was married to Mademoiselle Marguerite de Herrero, a fellow war correspondent, who had represented the Paris newspaper *Le Journal*.* They spent their honeymoon behind the barbed-wire defences of the legation, awaiting, with some trepidation, the arrival of the Italians.

Fifteen correspondents entered Addis Ababa with the conquer-

* She died in childbirth less than a year later.

ing Italian forces on May 5. Matthews, who was one of them, broke the news of the end of the war with a cable to the *New York Times*.

TIMES ROMA MAY FIFTH DATE ADDIS ABABA MATTHEWS ERA OF INDEPENDENCE THAT LASTED SINCE BIBLICAL TIMES ENDED FOUR THIS AFTERNOON WHEN ITALIANS OCCUPIED ADDIS ABABA.

The Italians quickly restored order, and then exacted mild revenge on the correspondents who had reported the war from the Abyssinian side. They announced that only the correspondents who had arrived with them would be allowed to send dispatches. Anyone else who wished to send reports should apply to Rome, in writing, requesting accreditation. The four British correspondents had managed to send a joint dispatch on the last two days of the war by using the legation's radio link with the Foreign Office. They now pressed the Italians for facilities to report to their papers. These the Italians refused, and on May 17 they expelled all four. Within ten days Abyssinia had virtually disappeared from the newspapers. By then it was the German occupation of the Rhine frontier and events in Spain that occupied the headlines.

There remains one story to recount, because it captures perhaps best of all the whole Abyssinian fiasco. O. D. Gallagher, the young *Daily Express* reporter, had been recalled late in April, and when the war was over he was sent to Jerusalem, where Emperor Haile Selassie was beginning his exile. His assignment was to see the Emperor and offer him £6,000 for his exclusive story—"How I Lost the War, by Haile Selassie."

The Emperor received Gallagher sitting on a temporary throne of satin, silver, and gilt, which had been provided by the Swiss manager of the King David Hotel. As Gallagher recalled later, "His hand was in bandages, a result, he said, of Italian mustard gas. I had to share the interview with a cameraman from Pathé or Paramount." The *Daily Express* used the interview on most of its front page, with illustrations from stills of the newsreel. The *Express*, getting the precedence right for its readers, if not for those who formulate royal protocol, headlined the story: GALLAGHER SEES EMPEROR. On the question of buying Haile Selassie's personal story of how he lost the war, there was no deal. Gallagher made his offer through the Emperor's personal secretary, Ato Wolde Georgis. Georgis laughed. "My dear Mr. Gallagher," he said, "His Majesty has just refused twenty thousand pounds to appear at the Dallas State Fair."[30]

To round off the Abyssinian affair, it is pleasant to record one of those historical acts of justice that seem to occur more often in fiction than in real life. Haile Selassie remained in exile until 1940, when the British government decided that the Emperor should be restored to his throne. To encourage the Abyssinians to rise against the Italians, a British army intelligence unit, under the command of Colonel (later Major-General) Orde Wingate, mounted what was called an "offensive propaganda operation" from the Sudan. As part of this operation, a British officer was delegated to accompany Haile Selassie in triumph back to Addis Ababa. The officer was George L. Steer, formerly the correspondent in the Abyssinian War for *The Times*. In 1936 Steer could not have known that he would live to see Mussolini kicked out of Abyssinia. Bitter at the Italian victory, he had returned to London to write a book exposing the Italian conduct of the war.

Steer, Gallagher, Matthews, and other correspondents who have appeared in this chapter will reappear later in this book, for the Abyssinian War was the blooding of a generation of young journalists soon to become famous. Gallagher went back to the *Daily Express* and local news again, and Matthews returned to Paris for the *New York Times*. None of them was home for long. In July foreign legionnaires in Morocco revolted, and the bloody Spanish Civil War was under way.

# Chapter Nine

# Commitment in Spain
# 1936–1939

Early in life I had noticed that no event is ever correctly reported in a newspaper, but in Spain, for the first time, I saw newspaper reports which did not bear any relation to the facts, not even the relationship which is implied in an ordinary lie.

—George Orwell in
*Looking Back on the Spanish War*

————

No other war in recent times, with the possible exception of Vietnam, aroused such intense emotion, such deep commitment, such violent partisanship as the Civil War in Spain. On one side were ranged the representatives of the old order: bankers, landlords, clergy, and army. Against them stood the peasants, the workers, the best of Spanish writers and poets, and a democratically elected government. Both sides saw the war as a crusade. The old order, the Nationalists, fought to purge their country of the Reds, to resurrect their ideal of a pure, Christian Spain. The Republicans fought for a new age, the New Jerusalem or, in the case of the Communists, a Marxist utopia. Most saw it as something far wider than a civil conflict. "In essence it was a class war," wrote George Orwell. "If it had been won, the cause of the common people everywhere would have been strengthened. It was lost, and the dividend-drawers all over the world rubbed their hands."[1]

The intervention of Hitler and Mussolini on the side of the old order and of Russia on the side of the Republic seemed to confirm this view. It became an apocalyptic moment in history, a point in time at which to choose and to make a stand. Thousands of young men from Europe and America came voluntarily to Spain, to fight and die for the Spanish Republic, because they believed in the democratic ideal, Orwell's "cause of the common people everywhere." For those who went to fight—or to write—it was an experience that left none untouched, a period in their lives of major and lasting significance, and one which, nearly forty years later, remains as vivid and as moving as if it had happened yesterday. "Today, wherever in this world I meet a man or woman who fought for Spanish liberty, I meet a kindred soul," wrote Herbert Matthews of the *New York Times*. "In those years we lived our best and what has come after and what there is to come can never carry us to those heights again."[2]

The correspondents committed themselves with passion. "Those of us who championed the cause of the Republican government against the Franco Nationalists were right. It was, on balance, the cause of justice, legality, morality, decency," Matthews says. "We knew, we just *knew*," Martha Gellhorn says, "that Spain was the place to stop Fascism. This was it. It was one of those moments in history when there was no doubt."[3] Most of the Spanish Civil War correspondents who held those views then hold them now. They remain unshakeable, completely convinced that they were right and that actively to support the Republican cause was the only thing to do.

We are concerned here not with the validity of these views, but with whether such complete commitment affected the reporting of the war. Was the reporting a victory for the partisans of truth and justice, or were newspaper readers throughout the world victims of duplicity and dissimulation? And in examining this, we face in perhaps more dramatic form than elsewhere the question at the heart of this book. What is a war correspondent's duty? Is it, as Drew Middleton of the *New York Times* says, "to get the facts and write them with his interpretation of what they mean to the war, without allowing personal feelings about the war to enter into the story. No one can be completely objective but objectivity is the goal"?[4] Or is Matthews closer: "I would always opt for honest, open bias. A newspaperman should work with his heart as well as his mind"?[5]

From all over the world, thousands of young men who saw the war as an ideological one made their way to Spain to fight in the International Brigades, the sort of personal commitment to the fight against Fascism described by Ernest Hemingway in his famous Spanish Civil War novel, *For Whom the Bell Tolls*. This voluntary involvement in a war that really did not directly concern them in turn exercised a fascination for some of the most articulate and talented writers of the period, men like Malraux, Orwell, Dos Passos, Spender, Hemingway, Bessie, and Koestler. Their writing had a direct influence in creating, in the United States, France, Britain, and South America, public concern about the war and persuaded newspapers to send to both sides their best correspondents. Hugh Thomas, the most meticulous historian of the war, notes that the greatest names in world journalism were soon to be found south of the Pyrenees and that "the Spaniards were very conscious of this and were very proud of their fame."[6]

If they had set themselves the aim of reporting the war objectively, then many of these distinguished correspondents, none motivated by patriotism, as in, say, the First World War, went about their assignment in a remarkable manner. Hemingway, representing the North American Newspaper Alliance, had been chairman of the ambulance committee for the American Friends of Spanish Democracy before he accepted the NANA assignment. He took it upon himself to instruct recruits in the International Brigades in weapon drill and made frequent visits to the line, not all of which were appreciated. Jason Gurney, a London sculptor attached to the American Lincoln Battalion, remembers Hemingway loosing off a wave of machine-gun bullets that "provoked a mortar bombardment for which he did not stay."

Claude Cockburn, editor of *The Week*, was on holiday in Spain when war broke out.* He promptly joined the Republican militia, but saw nothing strange in continuing to be a correspondent for his magazine and for the Communist newspaper the *Daily Worker*. He was openly in favour of correspondents' committing themselves to the Republican cause; he said he was tired of sitting in Madrid exhorting other people to fight and felt he should do something himself. George Orwell went to Spain to write articles for the *New Statesman*, but joined a fighting force raised in Barcelona. Mathieu Corman, a Belgian correspondent, covered the Republican advance on Teruel with a live grenade in his left hand and a pistol in his right. Jim Lardner, Ring Lardner's son, went to report for the *New York Herald Tribune*, but left to join an International Brigade, and was

---

* *The Week* was a famous English left-wing weekly, started by Cockburn in 1933. It featured news, rumour, and inside information that never appeared in the regular press. It was banned in 1941 because of its anti-war attitude.

killed. Arthur Koestler went as correspondent for the *London News Chronicle*, but this was a cover for his Comintern activities. H. A. R. ("Kim") Philby went as a correspondent for *The Times* of London on the Nationalist side, but was also a Soviet intelligence agent.

Perhaps the clearest case of complete commitment and almost total abandonment of objectivity was that of Louis Fischer, reporting for the American magazine *The Nation*. No sooner had Fischer arrived in Madrid than he was offering advice on the conduct of the war to the Soviet ambassador. "Write me a memo," the ambassador told him, "and I'll send it to Moscow." Next, Fischer appeared as quartermaster at the International Brigades depot at Albacete, where he remained until he fell out with the chief commissar, the veteran French Communist and hatchet man André Marty. All this time, while on active service for the Republicans, Fischer was filing dispatches for *The Nation*, the *New Statesman*, and newspapers in France, Norway, Sweden, and Czechoslovakia. Finally he became an arms purchaser for the Republic, a job that kept him too busy to do much reporting.

Fischer is an extreme example, and he appeared to see no dichotomy in his role. Other correspondents were aware of the thin line they were treading. When Madrid came under siege by the Nationalist forces, a group of correspondents made the Florida hotel their headquarters. The group included Hemingway, Martha Gellhorn of *Collier's* (later Mrs. Hemingway), Sefton Delmer of the *Daily Express*, Herbert Matthews of the *New York Times*, and Antoine de Saint-Exupéry. Their sympathies were clearly with the Republicans, and Matthews, for one, has continued eloquently to defend their attitude. He had been attracted by the romantic glitter of the Italian army in Abyssinia, where, he freely admits, he had been little interested in the rights and wrongs of the war. Now, in Spain, he saw beyond the immediate conflict: "You who stroll along the Great White Way thinking complacently how far away it all is from peaceful America—you, too, will feel a tap on your shoulder one of these days and will hear the call...War has a long, long, arm and it is reaching out for all of us."[7]

Matthews was thirty-six, and was deeply thoughtful about the duty of war correspondents and the ethics of his calling. "All of us who lived the Spanish Civil War felt deeply emotional about it...I always felt the falseness and hypocrisy of those who claimed to be unbiased and the foolish, if not rank stupidity of editors and readers who demand objectivity or impartiality of correspondents writing about the war...It was the same old error which readers and editors will always make and which forever continues to plague the chronicler who, being human, must have his feelings and opinions; in condemning bias one rejects the only factors which really matter —honesty, understanding and thoroughness. A reader has a right to ask for all the facts; he has no right to ask that a journalist or historian agree with him."[8]

This is a powerful argument, providing—as Matthews did—the correspondent makes his bias clear and *does* provide all the facts. But what can be said to justify the attitude of correspondents who knowingly wrote propaganda and disseminated it as honest reporting? The most glaring examples of this concern the activities of Agitprop (the Agitation and Propaganda Department of the Comintern) in Paris. The war correspondents involved were Arthur Koestler and Claude Cockburn (writing under the name Frank Pitcairn). Koestler had been arrested, after the fall of Málaga, on the orders of the Nationalist press officer, Luis Bolin, who wanted to shoot him as a spy. He was sentenced to death and spent three months in prison before being exchanged for a prisoner in Republican hands. Koestler described his experiences in a series of articles in the *News Chronicle*, and these aroused considerable interest.[9] His *bona fides* as an honest, professional, and compassionate reporter (he had deleted from his articles details that might have prejudiced the chances of other British prisoners) was therefore considered impeccable when, the same year, his book *Spanish Testament* appeared. The book, with its harrowing details of Nationalist atrocities, caused a wave of revulsion against General Franco and his forces.

It was not until 1954—seventeen years later—that readers learned how they had been deceived. Koestler confessed that he had written *Spanish Testament* in Paris, amid frequent interruptions from the Agitprop chief, the German Willie Muenzenberg.* Muenzenberg would burst into Koestler's flat. "He would pick up a few sheets of typescript, scan through them and shout at me: Too weak. Too objective. Hit them! Hit them hard! Tell the world how they run over their prisoners with tanks, how they pour petrol over them and burn them alive. Make the world gasp with horror.

---

* Muenzenberg, a brilliant journalist, had a talent for propaganda, especially for forming Communist front organisations and persuading prominent people to support them—the British Committee for the Relief of the Victims of Fascism was one of his creations. He became too independent for Moscow's liking, broke with the party in late 1937, and was murdered mysteriously in France in 1940.

Hammer it into their heads. Make them wake up…" Muenzenberg showed Koestler a cutting from the Nazi paper *Berliner Nachtausgabe* of a story datelined Madrid, November 4, 1936, which ran: "The Red militia issues vouchers to the value of one peseta. Each voucher is good for one rape. The widow of a high official was found dead in her flat. By her bedside lay 64 of these vouchers." Koestler wrote that Muenzenberg told him admiringly, "That, Arturo, is propaganda."[10] So, against his better judgement, Koestler interpolated in his accounts of authenticated Nationalist atrocities a number of highly doubtful ones provided for him by Muenzenberg, and his readers had no way of knowing one from the other.

The Cockburn episode is even more disturbing. Otto Katz, a Czech, who was Muenzenberg's chief assistant and bodyguard in Paris, was puzzling over ways of putting pressure on the French government to allow delivery of a consignment of arms to the Republicans. He decided that he and Cockburn would report an entirely fictitious battle, to illustrate the gallant but unequal struggle the Republicans were waging. Cockburn confessed later: "Our chief anxiety was that with nothing to go on but the plans in the guide books, which were without contours, we might have democrats and fascists firing at each other from either end of an avenue which some travelling night editor might know had a bump in the middle. The fight accordingly took place in very short streets and open squares …Katz was insistent that we use a lot of names of both heroes and villains, but express uncertainty over them. Thus, in the confusion of the struggle outside the barracks it had been impossible to ascertain whether the Captain Murillo who died gallantly was the same Captain Murillo, who, a few months ago in Madrid…In the end it emerged as one of the most factual, inspiring, and at the same time sober pieces of war reporting I ever saw."[11]

This is hardly a tale to inspire much confidence in the reporting of the war, but then, Cockburn's concept of the duty of a war correspondent differed radically from any so far considered. An incident during the Republican siege of the Alcazar best sums up Cockburn's attitude and, as well, illustrates the Communists' approach to reporting the war. Cockburn and the correspondent of *Pravda* and *Izvestia*, Mikhail Koltzov, were standing on the ramparts overlooking the fortress, when they were joined by Louis Fischer. Koltzov immediately launched into a bitter attack on Fischer for having sent a dispatch saying that the Republican militia was demoralised and bewildered. Koltzov admitted this was true, but he argued that Fischer, with his world-wide reputation, could spread alarm and despondency, and that his dispatch had done "more harm than thirty British MPs working for Franco." Fischer tried to defend himself by arguing that facts were facts and that his readers had a right to read the truth, but both Koltzov and Cockburn would hear none of this. "Who gave [the readers] such a right?" Cockburn told his wife later. "Perhaps when they have exerted themselves enough to alter the policy of their bloody government and the Fascists are beaten in Spain they will have such a right. This isn't an abstract question. It's a shocking war."[12]

There can be no validity in Cockburn's attitude. If readers are to have no right to facts, but only to what a war correspondent feels it is in his side's best interests to reveal, then there is no use for war correspondents at all. A team of Muenzenberg-trained propaganda writers would do a better job in a more honest manner. In the event, the outcome of the war revealed the basic flaw in Cockburn's approach to war reporting. If a correspondent writes not what is true, but what he wishes was true, he has a fifty-per-cent chance that the tide of the war will change and he will be proved right. But, equally, it may not change, and he will be seen to have got the whole thing wrong. That is what happened to Cockburn. Examined today, *The Week*'s reports about Spain appear accurate in detail, but grossly wrong in terms of the over-all situation, misleading in their optimism and in their confidence of an eventual Republican victory. Cockburn remained unrepentant. "There seem to be two pieces to this problem…The extent to which I myself totally believed what I said, and the extent to which I was, more or less consciously, trying to get other people to believe it. But I don't think there is really such a clear line of division."[13] Both reasons rendered Cockburn unfit to report the Spanish Civil War—the first because, as the episode with Koltzov and Fischer showed, believing what one writes is no justification for omitting what is true but incompatible with those beliefs; the second because to try to get other people to believe only part of the story is one definition of a propagandist.

Cockburn's conversion from correspondent to propagandist was perhaps the most clear, fully detailed case, but it was not the only one, and, as in most wars, in no field were the propagandists more active than in that concerning atrocities. Today, no one denies that a series of terrible events took place in Spain during the Civil War. In the first three months, in village after village, town after town behind the Republican lines, the peasants and the workers took over, in the name of Communism, Anarchism, or whatever may have been the local political creed, and went about the settling of old scores. Some 60,000 people are said to have been killed during this period of Republican terror, including twelve bishops, 283 nuns, 4,184 priests, and 2,365 monks. A similar purge was taking place on the Nationalist side, and, although the figures are more difficult to authenticate, it appears that the Nationalists murdered about the same number, including about 3,000 in Majorca alone. The brutality on both sides was extraordinary, and on the Republican side it frequently had religious overtones. "A crucifix was forced down the mouth of the mother of five Jesuits," writes Professor Thomas. "Eight hundred persons were thrown down a mine shaft. And, always, the moment of death would be greeted with applause as if it was the moment of truth in a corrida."[14]

Clearly, killing on this scale and in such a manner was important news, and the reader had a right to know it was occurring on both sides. But the few serious attempts to report massacres and atrocities were buried in an avalanche of reports based on the flimsiest evidence, exaggerated to extract the maximum horror, and disseminated, in many cases, by professional propaganda agencies. We begin with Frederick Voigt, the Berlin representative of the *Manchester Guardian*, because one would have expected a higher standard from such a distinguished correspondent. Voigt arrived in Madrid, on a short visit, in April 1937 and promptly announced to the correspondents in the Florida hotel that a reign of terror gripped the city and that "thousands of bodies are being found." When pressed, he agreed that he had not seen any bodies himself, but he remained convinced that "there is terror here." A day or so later, he gave Martha Gellhorn of *Collier's*, who was leaving Spain for a spell, a sealed envelope to take out for him, assuring her that it was only a carbon copy of an already censored dispatch, which he was sending to the *Manchester Guardian* in case the original did not arrive. Fortunately, Miss Gellhorn told Hemingway what she had agreed to do for Voigt, and Hemingway, suspicious, persuaded her to let him take the letter to the censor's office. When the censor opened the letter, it turned out to be not a carbon copy of an already censored dispatch, but an article that began: "There is a terror here in Madrid. Thousands of bodies..." Miss Gellhorn has said that Hemingway was so angry with Voigt for having exposed her to the risk of being caught smuggling an uncensored dispatch that it was difficult to prevent Hemingway from punching him.[15]

Edward Knoblaugh of the Associated Press was in Madrid in the early months of the war and was appalled by the Republican excesses. He wrote *Correspondent in Spain*, published while the war was still on and therefore a work of reportage. In one significant passage, Knoblaugh brings together sex and violence in a way that epitomised the very worst of the pro-Franco atrocity propaganda and helps explain the attitudes adopted by many Catholic leaders. Knoblaugh records how he sat at dinner with five Anarchists. One of them, he says, boasted of how he made two priests dig their own grave, emasculated them, and then "forced the severed organs into the dying victims' mouths before finally shooting them."[16] The point about this story is not whether it was true or false, but simply that Knoblaugh tells it, and by telling it invites his readers—without ever endorsing it himself—to accept it as true.

For Roman Catholics, the killing of a priest is a sacrilege, a wound in the body of Christ, a matter of far greater importance than the death of an Anarchist or a Communist. So the Catholic press, especially in the United States, was prepared to print, on the flimsiest evidence, stories like the one just quoted. A daily news service run by the National Catholic Welfare Conference provided the Catholic press with news, pictures, features, and editorials on the war. It was as biased in its own way as Muenzenberg's Agitprop was.*

The main target for the Catholic press was Herbert Matthews. His newspaper, the *New York Times*, was determined to cover the war with impartiality and had formulated a plan to achieve this: it would print the news from both sides and would give both equal prominence, equal length, and equal treatment. This scheme, fine in theory, was a disaster and pleased no one. To begin with, the *Times*' correspondent with the Franco forces was William P. Carney, a Catholic, who felt strongly about Republican excesses against the clergy, and who was simply not in Matthews' class as a correspondent. Giving his stories equal length with Matthews' often meant overplaying a bad story and cutting a good one. Next, the *Times*' "bullpen," its group of senior editors who read the news as it comes in and decide how much of it will be printed and where it will appear in the paper, was dominated at that time by Catholics

* In 1956, the American historian F. Jay Taylor wrote, in his book *The United States and the Spanish Civil War*: "A close examination of these dispatches would seem to indicate that factual reporting was circumscribed for the purpose of promoting Catholic interests. All of the dispatches examined were strongly sympathetic to the Nationalist cause with little effort made whatsoever toward objective reporting. Since the NCWC news service was controlled by the Catholic hierarchy and so most Catholic publications relied upon this news service for news coverage in Spain, the hierarchy was in a position to control the political convictions of many Catholics from a central point."

who were known to reflect a Catholic viewpoint when assessing the news, with results ranging from playing down stories about birth control to playing up stories expressing alarm over Communism. And, third, the Catholic opposition to Matthews was much more active in pressing its campaign against him than his admirers were in supporting him.

How the *New York Times*' plan worked out in practice can best be assessed by two examples. In December 1937, the Republicans were clinging to the recently captured Teruel. The Nationalists were so confident that it would soon fall to them that they issued a communiqué announcing its recapture. Carney not only filed the communiqué to the *Times*, but also added a vivid description of how the citizens had joyfully received the Franco troops, cheering and giving the Fascist salute. The *Times* used the story. That very day, Matthews and the photographer Robert Capa were in Teruel, after a difficult two-day journey, and, of course, they found it still in Republican hands. On his return to Barcelona, Matthews filed the story, which included so many eye-witness details that the *Times* had to print it, even though it did little for Carney's credibility.

Earlier, in March of 1937, a large Franco force had struck towards Guadalajara, north of Madrid, but was stopped well short of its objective. Matthews went there and found that the attacking troops had been Italian. They had been routed and had left behind prisoners, rifles, machine guns, and some disabled tanks. Matthews talked to the prisoners (he knew Italian), examined the arms, and watched the dead Italians being buried. Back in Madrid, he filed his story, an important one because it contained the first positive evidence that Mussolini had sent not only arms and advisers but also an expeditionary force—a fact, at that time, of great political and emotional significance. To emphasise this point, Matthews wrote that the attacking troops "were Italian and nothing but Italian." In New York, on the instructions of the assistant managing editor, Raymond McCaw, wherever the word "Italian" appeared in Matthews' copy it was struck out and the word "insurgent"—one used to describe the Franco troops—was substituted. This was done even to the extent of making the quoted phrase read "they were Insurgent and nothing but Insurgent," thus completely distorting Matthews' point. To make matters worse, McCaw sent a cable to Matthews saying that the only papers to emphasise the Italian point had been those in Moscow and pointing out that, as far as the *New York Times* was concerned, "we cannot print obvious propaganda for either side even under bylines."[17]

216

Matthews' attitude then, and now, is that when an accredited correspondent tells his newspaper that he has seen something with his own eyes, the paper *must* believe him—or else discharge him. It *must* trust him more than it trusts his competitors—or his editors 3,000 miles away—or where was the sense in sending him in the first place?[18]

From time to time during the war Matthews reported that the Republican government was seriously considering reopening the churches, and in some dispatches he went so far as to suggest that the Vatican was not keen on this, because it would weaken the case against the Republicans. Matthews turned out to be right, and subsequent evidence confirmed the Vatican's reluctance in the matter. But at the time Catholic readers of the *New York Times* refused to believe that Matthews' reports could be other than propaganda, and a campaign, led by Dr. Joseph Thorning, a Catholic professor of history, was started to persuade the *Times* to recall him. The Catholic press passed a motion of no-confidence in him, and in an address to the American Catholic History Association Dr. Thorning referred to Matthews as that "rabid Red partisan." On the other hand, the campaign praised Carney as having shown "a high degree of journalistic responsibility and personal courage" and for having written only "straight news stories," and in 1939 the Knights of Columbus awarded Carney a gold medal "for distinguished services to journalism in reporting the Spanish Civil War."

Matthews' admirers came to his aid. Eight well-known editors and journalists attacked Carney's reporting and concluded, "We shall continue to read Herbert Matthews to discover what is really going on in Spain." Small wonder that the editor at the *New York Times* responsible for the "Letters" column complained, "No matter who writes the dispatch [from Spain] the other side will accuse him of broadcasting propaganda or downright lying. In all my ten or twelve years' experience with letters to the editor, I have never encountered a situation in which so much absolutely rabid partisanship was manifested. It is partisanship that cannot be reasoned with and which, consequently, gets nowhere."[19]

In the midst of this rabid partisanship, it is refreshing to be able to point to one dispatch dealing with an atrocity that has never been seriously challenged. It concerns the massacre of the prisoners at Badajoz, on the frontier with Portugal, on August 14, 1936, and subsequent days. It was written by Jay Allen, a correspondent for the *Chicago Tribune*, and is, rightly, the most often reprinted newspaper report of the Spanish Civil War. Allen had covered the

217

Asturias uprising in Spain in 1934, had left journalism temporarily to write a book, and went back to work when the war broke out. He knew a lot about Spain and was perhaps the best informed correspondent writing for an American or British newspaper. He was in Lisbon when he heard rumours of what had happened after the Nationalist troops, mostly Moors, took Badajoz, and so, accompanied by a Portuguese friend who knew his way around, he took a taxi to the frontier and crossed into Spain. Allen realised that he was late on the story. Two French journalists and one Portuguese had already sent reports, but Allen felt he could do better—"I believe I was...the first newspaperman who went there knowing what he was looking for."

Allen was looking for evidence that the Nationalists were collecting everyone they suspected of having fought against them when they captured the town, marching them to the bull ring, and shooting them with machine guns. He soon found it. He saw two Nationalists halt a man in a workman's blouse and hold him while a third pulled back his shirt, baring his right shoulder. "The black and blue marks of a rifle butt could be seen. Even after a week they showed...To the bullring with him."

Allen drives to the bull ring, recalling that he had once seen Juan Belmonte there, on just such a night, watching the bulls being brought in for the next day's fight.

> This night the fodder for tomorrow's show was being brought in too. Files of men, arms in the air...At four o'clock in the morning they are turned out into the ring through the gate by which the initial parade of the bullfights enters. There machine guns await them. After the first night the blood was supposed to be palm deep on the far side of the lane. I don't doubt it. Eighteen hundred men—there were women too—were mowed down there in some 12 hours. There is more blood than you would think in 1,800 bodies.* [20]

But for every Allen there was a Cecil Gerahty. Gerahty, reporting for the *Daily Mail* from the Nationalist side, followed the Nationalist troops in the region of Torre Hermosa, looking for Red atrocities and helping himself to anything valuable. "I took away an old English family bible which I thought would be an appropriate present for my small son and a revolver which I gave to my chauf-

---

* The only real dispute over Allen's story has been over the number killed and as to whether they were all killed in the bull ring. Professor Thomas puts the total at below 2,000.

feur...In my nervousness I am afraid I must have slipped an old Cordoba silver cigarette case into my hip pocket, as I found it there some time later." He describes finding "the body of an old lady of seventy-six, her head half chopped off and her poor broken arms lying unnaturally as if trying to reach the bodies of her son and grandson, who were lying beaten to death beside her." And he decides that the Reds and Anarchists have a peculiar smell. "One gets it in the churches that have been occupied by the Reds as well as their houses, but in this building it seemed to be concentrated and left me with the impression that I should never be near a real anarchist again without my nostrils warning me of his presence." Finally, he has a government soldier brought to him for questioning before he is shot. "He has no desire to escape his fate. He had the stoic Spanish indifference to death, his attitude being rather that he had backed the wrong horse and could not grumble at losing his stake. He went off to his death with less fuss than I make going to the dentist."[21]

We can dismiss Gerahty, as a poor correspondent writing for an audience already firm in its belief that the Reds were monsters and the Nationalists were fighting to save Christian civilisation. Much more worrying is what resulted from the understandable desire of correspondents with the Republican side that the democratic ideal should triumph over Fascism, that Matthews' justice, legality, morality, and decency should prevail. This ardent wish for a Republican victory made most of them view the Republican army and the progress of the war through glasses tinted with optimism, and led them, consciously or unconsciously, to distort the reality of the situation. The result was that major defects of the Republican side were ignored, that, as Orwell complained, history was written in terms not of what had happened, but of what ought to have happened according to various party lines, and that enduring symbols of the Republicans' cause turned out, under examination, to be not quite what they had been made out to be. We will begin with what was perhaps the best-known incident of the war, the bombing of Guernica.

Guernica is a small town near the Basque capital of Bilbao, in northern Spain. The Basques, a non-Latin people of uncertain origin, with their own language and culture, had always asserted their right to autonomy. At the start of the war, pressed from all sides, the Republican government had conceded full autonomy to the Basques, who formed an independent republic. The Basque leaders were mostly men of the middle class and devout Catholics, and, although they remained solidly on the side of the Republican government in Madrid, they retained the support of the church. The spectacle, therefore, as the Nationalist forces moved against the Basque state, was a curious one—a deeply respectable, somewhat old-fashioned, and devoutly Catholic republic under attack by another traditionalist group, linked equally closely with the church and fighting in the name of Christ as well as Fascism.

General Emilio Mola, leading the Nationalist forces, began his campaign by issuing, on March 31, 1937, a threat later to be directly linked to the fate of Guernica: "If submission is not immediate I will raze all Vizcaya [a Basque province] to the ground, beginning with the industries of war. I have the means to do so." [22] The means were squadrons of German planes, with German pilots, which helped Mola roll back the ill-organised Basque troops until, by Monday, April 26, 1937, his forces were only ten miles from Guernica. During the next twenty-four hours Guernica was destroyed, levelled by Nationalist bombers. The death roll has never been established, estimates ranging from 1,000 to 2,000.

When news of this appeared in British and American newspapers, it caused a wave of outrage that has never really subsided. Guernica became the point in time at which total war was said to have begun, the indiscriminate bombing of a civilian target as a deliberate experiment in terror. The repercussions were immense. Guernica became a watershed in the war, *Time*, *Life*, and later *Newsweek*, for instance, thereafter taking the Republican side. All the dire predictions of the effects of mass air-raids that dominated thinking early in the Second World War flowed from the bombing in Spain, particularly of Guernica and Barcelona.* And the event passed into the traditions of the Left as a symbol of everything hateful about Fascism, a turning point in history, enshrined in Picasso's masterpiece, and as firmly believed nearly forty years later as on the dreadful day it occurred.

The Guernica story began with one man, George L. Steer, the correspondent for *The Times* of London, who had covered the war in Abyssinia and had been reporting in Spain from the Republican side. On the Monday afternoon of the bombing, Steer was making for Guernica by car, accompanied by Christopher Holme of Reuters. Some miles from the town, at the village of Ambacegui, six

---

* The British Foreign Office had sent observers to Spain to report the effects of bombing.

Heinkel 51 planes appeared from the direction of Guernica and began to bomb and strafe the village. When they spotted Steer and Holme, by now sprawled at the bottom of a bomb crater, they devoted some fifteen minutes to attempting to machine-gun them before flying off. The two Englishmen returned to Bilbao and were having dinner that night, with some other correspondents, when word arrived that all Guernica was burning. At first the correspondents considered this to be a wildly exaggerated rumour, but they decided that they should check it. Steer, Holme, Noel Monks of the *Daily Express*, and the Belgian Mathieu Corman of *Ce Soir*, a new Paris afternoon daily financed by Spanish Republican money, set off together. Steer recorded later, in his book *The Tree of Gernika*, what they saw as they drew near. "Fifteen miles south of Gernika the sky began to impress us. It was not the flat dead sky of night; it seemed to move and carry trembling veins of blood; a bloom of life gave it body, flushed its smooth round skin. Nearer it became a gorgeous pink. The sort of pink that Parisians have dreamed of for centuries. And it seemed enormously fat; it was beginning to disgust us."[23]

What the correspondents learned when they entered Guernica that night appeared in the London evening papers of Tuesday, April 27, in the Reuters report from Holme. Steer's story was in *The Times* and the *New York Times* on the following morning. Steer later said that *The Times*, which was already deep into its appeasement-of-Germany stance, was very unhappy with the story, but felt obliged to run it. In the event, it featured the dispatch as the turnover column of the leading page.

> Guernica, the most ancient town of the Basques and the centre of their cultural tradition, was completely destroyed yesterday by insurgent air raiders. The bombardment of this open town far behind the lines occupied precisely three hours and a quarter, during which a powerful fleet of aeroplanes consisting of three German types—Junkers and Heinkel bombers and Heinkel fighters—did not cease unloading on the town bombs weighing from 1,000 lb downwards, and, it is calculated, more than 3,000 two pounder aluminium incendiary projectiles. The fighters, meanwhile, plunged low from above the centre of the town to machine gun those of the civilian population who had taken refuge in the fields.

There followed a passage indicating that the Casa de Juntas, a building that housed the Basque archives, and the historic oak under which the kings of Spain swore to uphold Basque rights both remained untouched—a fact that could be of some significance, and to which we will return later. Then came the essential detail: "at 2 A.M. today when I visited the town. . ." Steer was being careful not to claim eye-witness status, a precaution that tends to encourage the reader's acceptance of firmer assertions, such as this paragraph, the most important in his account:

> In the form of its execution and the scale of the destruction it wrought, no less than in the selection of its objective, the raid on Guernica is unparalleled in military history. *Guernica was not a military objective.* A factory producing war material lay outside the town and was untouched...*The object of the bombardment was seemingly the demoralisation of the civil population and the destruction of the cradle of the Basque race.* Every fact bears out this appreciation, beginning with the day when the deed was done. Monday was the customary market day in Guernica...[emphasis added].

Next came a further description of the bombing, a very cautious estimate of the number of casualties, and accounts of victims said to be still trapped in shelters. "The tactics of the bombers which may be of interest to students of the new military science," wrote Steer, his outrage burning under the irony, "were as follows..." and he set out in detail the way people were driven into the open, only to be machine-gunned from the air, and then, once they had been driven to take shelter again, the way the town was laid open by high explosives and saturated by incendiary bombs dropped from wave after wave of bombers, which appeared at twenty-minute intervals, methodically quartering the town. Steer's story tallied substantially with those of his colleagues, but his interpretation and his accusations of a new kind of warfare were the most precise, the most thoroughly argued, and the most extreme. Christopher Holme has remembered reading the story and thinking how much better it was than his own account. It was also clear that Steer brought the charge with passion, and it was in this account that the generally accepted version of Guernica had its origins.

The response from the Franco side was an immediate categorical denial of the charge, backed by a statement that no Nationalist planes had been in the air at the time of the attack. This was never taken very seriously, since it left open the possibility that the planes had been German. But what was taken seriously was the simultaneous allegation that the Republicans had set fire to Guernica themselves. "Guernica was destroyed by incendiaries and petrol, was bombed and converted into ruins by the Red hordes," said the official Franco release. The Franco forces said they would prove this allegation the moment they captured Guernica.

That happened three days later, and the evidence for the Franco position was presented by three war correspondents. The first, Pembroke Stephens of the *Daily Telegraph*, entered the town with the Nationalists just one hour after the retreat of the Basque forces. He wrote a very uninformative dispatch, merely describing the desolation and quoting some "excited and distracted women" who told him that their homes had been "destroyed at night by fire," which fitted Steer's original story as well as the Franco counter-charge. Four days later, a party of Nationalist-accredited correspondents was conducted through the town. The most important of these were Carney of the *New York Times* and James Holburn of *The Times* of London. Predictably, Carney's report showed that he had been convinced by the Franco version—"This writer found that most of the destruction could have been the result of the fires and dynamiting." Holburn's report was a different matter. Written from Vitoria and dated May 4, it appeared in *The Times* and in the *New York Times* the following day. It said that the fire had destroyed much of the evidence of its origins, but that the town *had* been bombed intermittently for three hours. Holburn wrote that he had been unable to find many craters and that he had noticed many unmarked façades of burnt-out houses. "In these circumstances," wrote Holburn, "it is difficult to believe that Guernica was a target for a bombardment of exceptional severity and was selected by the Nationalists for an experiment with incendiary bombs."

There are important points to make about this dispatch. First, it was written by Holburn, not, as has been widely believed, by *The Times*' other correspondent with the Nationalists, H. A. R. ("Kim") Philby.* [24] After Philby defected to the Soviet Union in 1963, many authors found particular significance in *The Times*' report on Guernica on May 5 because they mistakenly believed that it had been written by Philby, the KGB agent.** One Spanish writer drew a fundamental historical parallel from the fact that Steer was on one side of Guernica and Philby was on the other. All this has confused the real importance of Holburn's dispatch.

* Philby was in Spain constructing for himself the impeccable façade of a correspondent with quiet but solid pro-Fascist views, so as to get as close as possible to the Franco authorities and to the Germans—not for the benefit of his paper, but for his real employer, the Soviet intelligence service, or KGB. Philby has told me that he never wrote anything from Spain that he knew to be untrue, "but the truth can be looked at through many pairs of spectacles and the pairs I used, for ulterior purposes, were supplied by Franco and the Legion Kondor."
** See, for example, Seale and O'Connell, *Philby—the Long Road to Moscow*, page 90.

Holburn, like most correspondents reporting on the Nationalist side, worked under considerable difficulties. The Nationalist method of handling war correspondents was based on the British system in the First World War as observed by a Spanish correspondent, Luis Bolin. Correspondents were given regular briefings and were allowed to make occasional sorties to the front, but always under the supervision of a Spanish, German, or Italian conducting officer. There was rigorous censorship, and it was made clear to the correspondents where their sympathies were expected to lie. If they co-operated they might be rewarded—Christopher Holme has recalled that correspondents in Salamanca were at one stage offered about $1,000 to record favourable broadcasts for the Italian radio.[25] If, on the other hand, a correspondent did not show sympathy for the Franco cause, he could be in difficulties. At the time of Guernica there was one correspondent of the French news agency, Havas, in a Nationalist prison and another under house arrest. Yet, writing under these difficult circumstances, Holburn managed to get out in his story from Vitoria—almost buried in the propaganda necessary to please the censors—the basic point that the Nationalists *had* bombed Guernica, a fact that until then they had strenuously denied.

The story now gathered momentum, principally in Britain, the United States, and Germany. (In France, Havas had reported the bombing in a dispatch totalling only eighty-seven words. Then, when its Franco-accredited correspondent sent a telegram giving the Nationalist version, the agency ignored a coded prefix—indicating that the story was either false or sent under pressure—and published it.)[26] Steer returned to the attack with another dispatch, in which he produced additional evidence. Colleagues had kept pieces of German bombs; trees had been snapped off at the base; there had been no odour of petrol; the dead had wounds consistent with bomb fragments. He restated his initial conclusion, one that has proved remarkably prophetic: "General Franco's aeroplanes burnt Guernica and the Basques will never forget it."

*The Times* printed Steer's second story with even more reluctance than it had displayed over his first account. The newspaper's record on Spain was patchy. It had successfully resisted a Nationalist attempt to get it to drop the term "insurgent"—"It has never been used in *The Times* in any slighting sense"—and it did not give Luis Bolin much of a hearing when he called several times at Printing House Square to try to persuade the paper to send a senior member of the staff to visit General Franco.[27] But it buckled under to German pressure, and it begrudged Steer its support when he needed it most.

When German newspapers called *The Times* a liar and there were official German complaints about its reporting from Spain, the editor, Geoffrey Dawson, wrote to his former Berlin correspondent: "I did my best, night after night to keep out of the paper anything that might hurt [the Germans'] susceptibilities. No doubt they were annoyed by Steer's first story on the bombing of Guernica but its essential accuracy has never been denied and there has not been any attempt here to rub it in or harp on it."[28] Then, in 1939, when Steer began a libel action against a critic who said he had left *The Times* after a dispute over the accuracy of the Guernica story, the newspaper gave him little help. At first, it stated that Steer had not been representing it at the time of Guernica, and it finally agreed only under pressure that his departure from the paper had had nothing to do with his Guernica reports, but had been for personal reasons.[29]

To this day, there are some who claim that the bombing of Guernica was a myth, a brilliant propaganda coup conjured up by the Republicans, and that Steer was primarily responsible for disseminating it.* The principal supporter of this view was the former press officer, Luis Bolin, who set out his case in his book *Spain, the Vital Years*. Bolin cast doubt on Steer's credibility by noting that Steer became an intelligence officer in the Second World War, that his job included creating and disseminating false reports to discredit, among others, the enemies of Emperor Haile Selassie of Abyssinia, and that, on Steer's own admission, when the Emperor did not approve of this campaign he forged the imperial seal. While this does not add to our confidence in Steer's treatment of fact, it is not evidence that he lied about Guernica. Bolin also produced a series of routine dispatches from the Franco forces in Guernica accusing the Basques of burning and dynamiting the town themselves. Bolin claimed that the fact that the Guernica tree and the building housing the Basque archives were not destroyed lent weight to the Nationalists' version, because if the bombing had been as intense as the Republicans claimed, was it not suspicious that these two venerated objects survived?

Bolin remained, until his death in 1969, a propagandist for the Nationalist cause, but his book, published in 1967, served to rekin-

---

* See, for example, "The Great Guernica Fraud," by Jeffrey Hart, in the *National Review*, January 5, 1973.

dle the controversy. Professor Thomas later re-examined the conclusions he had reached after an investigation in 1959—that "it is difficult not to conclude that the Germans deliberately bombed the town in an attempt to destroy it, observe in a clinical way the effects of such a devastating attack, and thus carry out the instruction of Mola of 31 March."[30] Herbert Southworth, an expert on the Spanish Civil War, formerly a Regents Professor of History at the University of California at San Diego, embarked on the definitive account of Guernica. These two historians must rank as world authorities on the subject, so they were asked what they now believe.

Professor Thomas wrote: "I continue to believe that the town was bombed by the Germans, though a) not necessarily with the knowledge of the Spanish High Command, and b) *probably not as a shock attack on a specially prized city, but as one on a town where the Republican-Basque forces could regroup* [emphasis added]."[31]

Southworth wrote: "Guernica was destroyed by explosive and incendiary bombs dropped from German aeroplanes, piloted by Germans. The bombing was done at the request of the Spanish authorities. It was an operation done by men in the field, and it seems highly probable that the Condor Legion and the Spaniards told the truth to Berlin only later and in dribbles. It was a highly successful military operation which had the advantage of the right wind and the right time to spread the flames. Why was it done? This is more speculative. *There is nothing to show that the Germans wanted to test civilian morale. German documents tend to show that it was a tactical operation* [emphasis added]."[32]

So Steer's original accusations, the birth of the legend of Guernica—that the town was not a military objective and that the purpose of the bombing was the demoralisation of the civilian population—now stand contradicted. Thomas says it was *not* a shock attack, Southworth that there is *nothing* to show the Germans wanted to test civilian morale. Thomas says that Guernica was a town where the Republican-Basque forces could regroup, in other words, a military objective; Southworth, that the bombing was a tactical operation. Thus it is clear that the correspondents made Guernica. If Steer, and, to a lesser extent, Holme, Monks, and Corman, had not been there to write about it, Guernica would have passed unnoticed, just another incident in a brutal civil war. Yet the conclusion must be that Steer, with understandable professional, political, and personal ardour, overreacted to the story. On all the evidence available, Guernica was bombed for tactical military reasons. Then the

Nationalists, instead of saying that war is hell and it is sometimes necessary to bomb towns for military reasons, became apprehensive about the reaction abroad, especially in the United States and Britain.* They panicked and committed themselves first to outright denials that there had been any bombing, and then to the untenable Basque-self-destruction stance.

If Guernica became a symbol of Fascist barbarity, then the symbol of Republican sacrifice was the "moment of death," Robert Capa's moving photograph of a Republican militiaman, falling backwards, arms outflung, onto the soil of the Spain he had tried to defend. Capa was an able and brave photographer, who covered wars in most parts of the world before he was killed, doing his job, when he stepped on a mine while on patrol with the French south of Hanoi in 1954. But before the "moment of death" photograph he was scarcely known, and this single picture marked the beginning of his fame.

It first appeared in two French magazines, in *Vu* in September and in *Regards* in October of 1936, but gained international renown with its publication in *Life* magazine on July 12, 1937. It has since become the most reprinted photograph of the Spanish Civil War and is considered by many professionals to be the best war photograph ever taken, one that cameramen from the Second World War to Vietnam have envied.

Yet the curious thing about it is that it does not tell us anything *as a picture*. It is an essentially ambiguous image. However, as captioned in *Life*—"Robert Capa's camera catches a Spanish soldier the instant he is dropped by a bullet through the head in front of Córdoba"—it *does* tell us something, something beyond the face meaning of the words. It tells us that the picture was taken by someone who must have put himself at great risk, someone who was, perhaps, nearly killed as well. With this caption the photograph thus becomes a famous and valuable property in both political and commercial terms. Yet—and there is nothing in the photograph to deny this—if we were to rewrite the caption to read "A militiaman slips and falls while training for action," the photograph would become worthless in both the above senses.

Since there is something wrong with the values of a journalistic world that accepts as an important image a photograph that so

* One Nationalist officer did indeed say virtually that. In October 1937 he told Virginia Cowles, the correspondent for the *Sunday Times* of London: "We bombed it and bombed it and bombed it, and bueno, why not?"

clearly depends on the caption for its authentication, we set out to discover something more about the circumstances in which the picture was taken. When, and exactly where, did Capa take it? The terrain in the photograph tells us nothing; it could be anywhere. Who is the man? His face is blurred, but there appears to be no sign of a wound, certainly not the explosion of the skull that a bullet in the head (see the *Life* caption) would cause. In fact, he is still wearing his cap. How did Capa come to be alongside him, camera aimed at him, lens reasonably in focus, just as the man was shot dead?

We turned to Capa's own writing for an answer, but, although he gives details of other photographs, he appears to have written nothing about the "moment of death." Since it seemed unlikely that Capa would have gone through life without having told someone the circumstances surrounding the taking of his most famous photograph, we then contacted those people he might have talked with and we asked them if Capa had ever mentioned the matter. *Life* did not reply. Henri Cartier-Bresson, Capa's professional associate in Magnum, the famous photographers' group, said he was making a film on Spanish hospitals at the time and "was not with André [Capa's real name] when he shot the picture." But he suggested that Capa's brother, Cornell, might know more. Stefan Lorant of *Picture Post* said he had "no first-hand knowledge" of how Robert Capa took the photograph, but he forwarded the enquiry to Cornell Capa.

Then Cornell Capa replied, to an earlier letter of the author's, "Strangely enough, real answers are hard to come by. I had never seen or heard from Bob details about that particular photograph or that particular sequence. Neither did he write about it…" But Cornell Capa later sent us what he described as a "tongue in cheek" review by John Hersey, the author and a former war correspondent, in a now defunct magazine, *47*, of Robert Capa's book, *Slightly Out of Focus*. In this review, titled "The Man Who Invented Himself," Hersey gives an account of how Robert Capa took the famous photograph. In reply to our query about his sources, Hersey wrote, "Bob Capa told me the story of the photograph of the Spanish soldier himself. 'The Man Who Invented Himself' was based altogether on material I had straight from him. He was a close friend. I had been through the Sicilian campaign with him."[33]

Robert Capa's account to Hersey was that he went to Andalusia in August 1936, when heavy fighting was taking place. During one battle, he was in a trench with a company of Republican volunteers, "fanatical but ignorant fighters," who shouted "*Viva la República*," jumped over the parapet, and charged a Nationalist machine-gun nest. When the machine gun opened fire, killing many of the men, the rest retreated and from the trench fired at the machine gun. They charged again and again, and each time many were killed. Hersey wrote, "Finally as they charged, the photographer timidly raised his camera to the top of the parapet and, without looking, at the instant of the first machine gun burst, pressed the button. He sent the film to Paris undeveloped. Two months later he [Capa] was notified that Capa was now in truth a famous, talented, and nearly rich photographer, for the random snapshot had turned out to be a clear picture of a brave man in the act of falling dead as he ran and it had been published over the name of Capa in newspapers all over the world."

This is an intriguing account. Some, including Martha Gellhorn, who knew Capa in Spain and later, believed that Capa was pulling Hersey's leg and that this account is not to be taken seriously. Hersey's review gives no indication of this, and there is nothing in his letter to suggest that he took what his close friend told him as other than true and accurate. If this is so, then it shows that Capa's famous photograph was a million-to-one chance: a camera aimed blindly and operated on the sound of firing had not only caught a soldier neatly framed, but had caught him at the very moment he was hit!

Further research produced two other, strange versions of the "moment of death" photograph. It must be stressed immediately that at this distance in time it has so far proved impossible either to confirm or disprove them, and that other people who knew Capa in Spain, including Herbert Matthews and Martha Gellhorn, discount them entirely and firmly believe the photograph to be both Capa's and "without a doubt, authentic." The first account is from Canadian playwright Ted Allan. Allan, then only twenty, was in Spain with a Canadian blood-transfusion unit. He also sent reports for Federated Press, a trade-union news agency in North America. He met Capa in Madrid, became friends with Capa and Gerda Taro, Capa's partner and lifelong love, and was with Gerda when she was killed at Brunete in July 1937. Allan says that after the "moment of death" photograph was published, he was discussing it one day with "Chim" David Seymour, a photographer who was killed in the Suez invasion in 1956. "Chim told me that Capa had not taken that photograph. Whether he then told me that he, Chim, had taken it or that Gerda had taken it, I cannot now remember."[34]

The second account is by O. D. Gallagher, a *London Daily*

*Express* correspondent in Spain, first with the Nationalists and then with the Republicans. Gallagher says that at one stage of the war he and Capa were sharing a hotel room. There had been little action for several days, and Capa and others complained to the Republican officers that he could not get any pictures. Finally, says Gallagher, a Republican officer told them he would detail some troops to go with Capa to some trenches nearby, and they would stage some manoeuvres for them to photograph. Capa came back at the end of the day delighted with what he had taken. When the "moment of death" photograph was published, Gallagher says he remarked to Capa how genuine the picture looked, because it was not quite in focus. "He [Bob] had a good laugh and said, 'If you want to get good action shots, they mustn't be in true focus. If your hand trembles a little, then you get a fine action shot.' "[35]

It is, of course, not unknown for photographers to pose pictures. In fact, Cornell Capa sent us an Italian photography magazine, another Capa photograph of this period, clearly posed, showing nine Republican militiamen standing outside a trench grinning and waving their rifles in the air. The Italian magazine writer confuses matters further by placing the "moment of death" photograph as having been taken near Cadiz. He then adds that, despite similarities in appearance, he has resisted the temptation to conclude that the "moment of death" soldier looks to be the same one "still alive" at the left in the posed group photograph.[36] But was the group photograph taken before or after the "moment of death" picture? If before, then why were the soldiers standing in full view of the Nationalist machine-gun nest?

In the end, the emotive "moment of death" photograph, like so many other aspects of the Spanish Civil War, turns out to be not the clear and simple statement of fact that it at first sight appears.

One other symbol in Spain was Ernest Hemingway, by far the most famous of the English-language writers there during the war, an influential figurehead in the fight against Fascism—"How could this fight be lost now, with Hemingway on our side."[37] Hemingway had already worked on one propaganda film, *Spain in Flames*, and had agreed to help with another, *The Spanish Earth*, when he accepted an offer from the North American Newspaper Alliance to report the war. He arrived in Spain for his first visit in March 1937, and altogether made four trips. He travelled widely, usually with Martha Gellhorn, Herbert Matthews, and Sefton Delmer, saw a lot of the fighting, and got to know many of the Republican leaders and supporters. Yet his performance as a war correspondent was abysmally bad. On a technical level, his descriptions of battle and bombardments are monotonous; his emphasis on his own close location to the action smacks of boastfulness; his accounts of blood, wounds, and severed legs are typical of his desire to shock; and his reporting of conversations is so totally Hemingway in style as to make the reader doubt their authenticity. NANA had to ask him to confine his work to human-interest features and, when that failed, to report only developments of vital importance. As his biographer, Carlos Baker, puts it, "His eye for telling details and individual traits was not nearly so sharp as that of Dos Passos, nor did he commonly rise to the meticulous exactitude and inclusiveness which characterised the best work of Matthews and Delmer."[38]

True, Hemingway grew up politically in Spain and believed it was the place to stop Fascism, before Hitler's Brownshirts and Mussolini's Blackshirts could precipitate a second world war. But he was unjustifiably optimistic about the Republicans' chances of doing this. One of his principal informants was Mikhail Koltzov— the *Pravda* and *Izvestia* correspondent who quarrelled with Louis Fischer over an accurate but pessimistic dispatch Fischer had written—and this might explain the views Hemingway expressed to reporters in New York in June 1938. Franco was short of troops, Hemingway said, and handicapped by friction among the foreign elements in his army; the Republicans were well organised and their chances of winning were good. Actually, at that moment the Republicans were only six months away from defeat. But these criticisms are the least serious of Hemingway's shortcomings as a war correspondent. The most important concerns his total failure to report the Communist persecution, imprisonment, and summary execution of "untrustworthy elements" on the Republican side, when he knew this was happening and when disclosing it might well have prevented further horrors like this.

The principal Communist hatchet man was André Marty, who admitted to some 500 executions. Others would multiply that figure by five or even ten. Marty was gripped by a paranoid suspicion and devoted most of his time to passionate spy hunts. He was convinced that many of the volunteers who came to his headquarters were Fascist spies, and he conducted day-long, soul-destroying interrogations, never shrinking from promptly liquidating doubtful cases, rather than put the Republic at risk from what he called "petty bourgeoise indecision." Gustav Regler, working as a political commissar with the International Brigades, knew about Marty's spy mania and the executions, and he told all he knew to Hemingway. Hemingway never wrote a word of it in his dispatches. Regler believed that Hemingway "respected" the information because, of all the groups fighting for the Republic, the Communist Party was the most active.[39]

There is further evidence that Hemingway knew of the executions. John Dos Passos, working with Hemingway on *The Spanish Earth*, was determined to find out what had happened to Jose Robles Pazos, formerly a teacher at Johns Hopkins University, Dos Passos' Spanish translator, and a friend for twenty years. Robles had joined the Republican army as a colonel, but had been suddenly arrested in December 1936. Hemingway undertook to help Dos Passos in his enquiries about Robles and was soon able to report back that he had obtained the personal word of the head of Republican counter-espionage that Robles would receive a fair trial. But the truth was that Robles had already been summarily executed. According to Carlos Baker, when Hemingway heard this he simply assumed that Robles had been guilty. Then he not only failed to appreciate Dos Passos' shock and anger at the news, but also, later, he even wrote for *Ken*, the leftist magazine launched by the publisher of *Esquire*, an article condemning Dos Passos for the naïveté of "a typical American liberal attitude." Dos Passos never forgave him. Finally, just before his last visit to Spain, in October 1938, Hemingway admitted to his editor, Maxwell Perkins, of Scribner, what he had not written as a correspondent: that there was a "carnival of treachery and rottenness on both sides."[40]

In the end, Hemingway did write it all, in *For Whom the Bell Tolls*, but from a war correspondent the reader has the right to expect all the news the correspondent knows at the time, not as interpolations in a work of romantic fiction published when the war is over. The truth was that Hemingway, for all his compassion for the Spaniards, for all his commitment to the Republican cause, used the war to gain a new lease on his life as a writer. As Baker says, "Refusing to waste the best of his materials in his newspaper dispatches...he had gathered and salted away a body of experience and information which he described to Perkins as 'absolutely invaluable'."[41] For a novelist, this was understandable. For a war correspondent, it was unforgivable.

Madrid surrendered on March 28, 1939. Only one full-time correspondent stayed on to see the Nationalists' triumphant entry into the city, O. D. Gallagher of the *Daily Express*. Hidden in the basement of the Ritz hotel, with a supply of water and tinned food, he was awakened one morning by crowds shouting, "Franco! Franco!" Gallagher's messenger boy managed to get about twenty short reports to the telegraph office before Nationalist press officers found Gallagher, told him he was lucky not to be shot, and ordered him out of Spain. This gesture of professional determination was one of the few bright moments in the closing months of the war. For, as the prospect of defeat came closer, correspondents with the Republicans found it increasingly difficult to overlook the fact that their side was not all they had hoped it would be.

Many of its shortcomings had been present from the early days. In the British International Brigade, the hand-grenades were useless, the Russian rifles not much better. Training was farcical; men were flung into the Battle of Jarama after firing ten rounds at an improvised range. A Russian officer gave orders to advance that amounted to suicide. At the end of two days' fighting, only 100 men were left out of a battalion of over 600.[42] Food was desperately short in Madrid, although supplies from Valencia arrived constantly— only to be inefficiently stored in locked warehouses until they rotted. Weak, unintelligent officers were built up into hero figures, only to collapse at the first major crisis. Brigades on some fronts had an average of only 250 serviceable rifles for 1,600 men, while trucks loaded with arms and ammunition remained marooned because of quarrels between local organisations over who should be responsible for them. During the retreat in Catalonia, the Catalans failed to obey mobilisation orders, officers got into cars and drove away from the front, and Anarchists began putting factories out of action. Factionalism, cruelty, political manoeuvring, and intergroup armed conflict marked the dying days of the Republic.

The failure of correspondents to report the imperfect face of the Republican side does not seem to have been due, except in the case of confessed propagandists, to any policy of duplicity, but to their preoccupation with the effect that the war was having upon them personally. Certainly no other war seems to have left such a profound and lasting impression on those who reported it. Matthews wrote, in his last dispatch from Spain: "And the lessons I had learned. They seemed worth a great deal. Even then, heartsick and discouraged as I was, something sang inside me. I, like the Spaniards, had fought my war and lost, but I could not be persuaded that I had set too bad an example." André Malraux said he attached great importance to the war not only as a struggle, "but also because it was a most profound experience of brotherhood."

Martha Gellhorn has said that to this day she cannot read a book about the Spanish Civil War, because "they might get the facts right but none capture the emotion, the commitment, the feeling that we were all in it together, the certainty that we were *right*."[43]

By Drew Middleton's definition, this personal involvement made the war correspondents unable to fulfill their duty because they had lost their objectivity. Matthews' provision for open, honest bias so long as the reader was still given all the facts did not work out any better. Much of Matthews' Spanish Civil War reporting was brilliant. His battle descriptions, his evocation of the emotion of the period, his honest striving to balance Carney's propaganda and the Nationalist faking justified the praise his American supporters accorded him. He was right in his battles with the *New York Times* over its attitude to the war, and his verdict is justified— it failed its readers because it did not give them "a competent, balanced, complete, journalistic picture of the war."

But, equally, Matthews' open, honest bias, his reporting with his heart as well as his mind, affected his judgement. At the time, he saw the war as "a struggle against the forces of evil." Now he agrees that he was wrong to regard the conflict in straightforward ideological terms, that he oversimplified a very complex situation, and that it was more than anything "a civil war, a Spanish war, a conflict whose primary causes and manifestations were to be found in Spanish history." At the time, he felt that anyone who had lived through that period with the Republicans had experienced something so wonderful that it could not occur again: "Spain was a melting pot in which the dross came out and pure gold remained." Now he says: "My judgment is not as clouded as it was and I know a great deal about the war that I could not have known at the time, especially features derogatory to the Loyalists and to the Internationals."[44]

The drawback of reporting with heart as well as mind is that if the cause is basically just, as the Republican one undoubtedly was, the correspondent tends to write in terms of heroic endeavour, rather than face unpalatable facts, and to mislead his readers with unjustified optimism. Few resisted the temptation. Sefton Delmer was none too enthusiastic about the way the Republicans ran the war, and his dispatches reflected this. Stephen Spender saw that the soldiers hated the heroics of the leftist correspondents and that even the rather restrained reporting of Philip Jordan in the *News Chronicle* was too much for them: "I had the impression that soldiers in a war have an almost pathetic longing to know the truth." Spender also recorded that whereas the war had at first unified the social revolution, in the long run it demanded its own measures, which threatened to engulf the whole social system.[45]

George Orwell stands out. He saw the failure of the liberals and the Left: the refusal to recognise that totalitarianism existed on the Republican side as well as on the Right, that Stalin's real enemy in Spain was the independent Left and the Communists were more concerned with eliminating it than defeating the Fascists. He tried to report this, but the *New Statesman* refused to use his dispatches. He wrote it in *Homage to Catalonia*, only to have the book turned down by left-wing publisher Victor Gollancz. When the book was eventually published in Britain, by Secker and Warburg, it sold only 600 copies in Orwell's lifetime, and it was not published in the United States until after his death.[46]

The cause was lost, and no one could bear to hear why. The Spanish Civil War *was* a crusade, but in many ways it was also a cheat and a delusion. Orwell was able to accept this and still be glad that he had taken part—"Curiously enough the whole experience has left me with not less but more belief in the decency of human beings."[47] For most other correspondents, the myth they had helped create remained preferable to the painful reality.

# Chapter Ten

# "Their Finest Hour"
# 1939–1941

The years of war pile on our heads like lime
And horrors grow impersonal as engines;
Nor can I think in discipline and slime.
Perhaps beside some blue and neutral lake
Another Lenin sorts the real from fake.

—Roy Fuller in
*Winter in Camp, a Lost Season*

The outbreak of war on September 3, 1939, brought to Britain none of that upsurge of jingoism which had characterised the early part of the First World War. Years of heavy unemployment—there were still a million without work in January 1940—lack of a clear understanding of what the war was about, the fact that many Conservatives in high places still admired Hitler, the obvious determination of a substantial section of the wealthier class to escape from any unpleasantness, and pessimistic predictions of the effects of the bombing of large cities, mainly as a result of the Spanish Civil War, combined to cause a general depression of morale. Seventy constituency Labour parties demanded peace, and twenty-two Labour MPs signed a manifesto calling for an early armistice, an event that was scarcely reported.[1]

Yet even in these early months there were indications that Britain was prepared to go further in waging total war than ever before. The first peace-time conscription in British history had been introduced in April 1939 and was later extended to include women, for the first time in the history of any civilised nation.[2] The Emergency Powers (Defence) Act authorised the government to do virtually what it liked to prosecute the war, without reference to Parliament. Every press, commercial, or private message leaving Britain, whether by mail, cable, wireless, or telephone, was censored. Everyone, including newspaper editors, was prohibited from "obtaining, recording, communicating to any other person or publishing information which might be useful to the enemy." *

The Ministry of Information, planned as early as 1936, was brought into being two days before the war and grew in four weeks from a staff of twelve to a notorious 999. Yet, unknown to newspaper editors, the Allied general staffs, alarmed by the development of short-wave radio, had decided in 1938 that as far as they were concerned the war would be a newsless one,[3] and that the system for controlling war correspondents would be exactly the same as in 1914–18. There would be an official known as "Eye-witness," and a limited number of correspondents, escorted by conducting officers, would be tolerated at headquarters and allowed to send back carefully censored dispatches on subjects unlikely to affect morale on the home front.

Accordingly, in Britain a Public Relations Section was hastily created, as part of the Intelligence Section of the British Expeditionary Force, and the War Office urged all the major newspapers to nominate men to accompany the BEF, which would leave for France the moment hostilities began. There was need for haste, the War Office said, so that the correspondents could be vetted, get their commissions, learn the regulations, have their uniforms tailored, and be absorbed as smoothly as possible into the army machine. In the meantime, while arrangements were being completed for accommodating the correspondents—with their batmen, drivers, censors, conducting officers, dispatch riders, and telegraphists—"Eye-witness" would provide basic coverage.

This time "Eye-witness" was not an army officer, as in the First World War, but a journalist, Alexander Clifford, formerly Reuters' chief correspondent in Germany and later to become one of the

---

* This last prohibition led to the charade whereby officially there was no compulsory censorship of British newspapers—censors were merely "consulted" by editors for "advice" on what information might be "useful to the enemy." Technically, an editor could make such a decision himself, guided by copious Defence Notices, but if it proved a wrong decision he could be prosecuted and possibly imprisoned.

better correspondents of the war. Clifford left London on September 19 to join the BEF, advance parties of which had landed in France on the day after war broke out. At the same time, four British correspondents, chosen by ballot to report on a pool basis, were deputed to attach themselves to the French army on the Maginot Line, where early action was expected to occur.

A month passed, during which time nothing of interest or importance appeared in the British press from Clifford, and during which arrangements to send the rest of the press group, chafing up and down Fleet Street, ground almost to a halt because of bitter inter-service rivalry. Clifford nearly went mad trying to find something to write about, and when he did he had the frustrating experience of seeing it chopped to pieces by the censor.

The situation for a British correspondent with the French army was even worse. The French regarded the British plans as dangerously lax and developed a system for handling correspondents' dispatches that made the official French communiqué, with its frequent "nothing to report" or "the army spent a restless night," appear a mine of information. Under the French scheme, which applied until the French surrendered, a British correspondent had to prepare his story in quadruplicate. It was then taken by dispatch rider to army headquarters, where it was censored, and then to French general headquarters, where it was censored again. From French GHQ it went to the Hôtel Continental in Paris, where a representative of the British Ministry of Information took charge of it and passed it to the British officer responsible for communications, who arranged for it to be telephoned to London. As it worked out, all this took at least forty-eight hours, and anything newsworthy left in a dispatch after three censors had handled it was usually ruined by the delay.[4]

In this period, American newspaper readers, fed, as the magazine *Fortune* complained, "a tissue of half truths, edited information...poisoned statistics, doped stories, rumours, and rumours of rumours," were justifiably confused and angry. In American headlines, the French advanced in the Saar daily, but by the end of the week had got nowhere. A second Battle of Jutland was fought, water poured through breaches in the Belgian dykes, the Siegfried Line was pierced, German and British planes had fought a dogfight over Southend—all, it turned out, were fairy stories.[5] No wonder American newspaper offices turned to their correspondents in Germany to learn what was going on. For one thing, it was easier to contact them. When the *New York Times*' man in London was taking eight hours to get through to his office, his counterpart in Berlin, Otto Tolischus, was getting his stories through, via Copenhagen, in forty minutes. It was almost impossible to get a telephone call through from London to Paris—when the army was not using the lines, the Bank of England was. On the news front, the "fourth front" of the war, the Germans were winning hands down.

Germany had learnt a lot from the way Britain managed the news in the First World War. The Ministry of Propaganda, under the brilliant control of Dr. Goebbels, looked after neutral war correspondents via its Foreign Press Department, run by Professor Karl Bonner. Correspondents were given special privileges such as extra rations, a petrol allowance, and a special exchange rate for their currency. Some of them were even paid directly by the ministry itself, although a more discreet procedure was for their bills to be settled for them.

A substantial house, 11 Julienenhof, outside Berlin, was fitted out as a country retreat, and friendly correspondents were invited to stay. There was no censorship as such, and the Germans made a big play with their *freie Berichterstattung*, or freedom of reporting. Of course, there was a catch to all this. The day after publication every word of a correspondent's dispatch was scrutinised by an official of the ministry. A correspondent whose material was not considered favourable was subjected to an escalating scale of harassment, which began with a written warning, moved to the disconnection of his telephone, and could, in theory, end with his arrest and trial for espionage[6]—not a difficult charge to bring, because the dividing line between information gathered by a correspondent and that gathered by a spy is often very finely drawn.*

But a war correspondent's difficulties in Britain and France were far greater than in Germany, so during September and early October about 100 neutral reporters made their way to Berlin, to base themselves there.

Arrangements for German war correspondents, however, were quite different. Goebbels had decided early on that there would be no German war correspondent as such. Instead, journalists, writers, poets, photographers, cameramen, film and radio producers, publishers, printers, painters, and commercial artists—the whole range of occupations belonging to what is now described as the media industry—were simply conscripted into the Propaganda

* Richard C. Hottelet, then a United Press reporter, was charged with espionage, kept in a Berlin jail for a month, and released, the charges having been dropped.

Division of the army, which was under Major-General Hasso von Wedel. There, men of the PK (*Propaganda Kompanien*) did basic training and were expected to fight when necessary—their rate of casualties, some 30 per cent killed or wounded, was about the same as in the German infantry. But their main rôle was to use their civilian skills to "influence the course of the war by psychological control of the mood at home, abroad, at the Front, and in enemy territory."[7] They became a vital part of the German war effort, a combination of straight war correspondent, publicist, and master of what the British later termed "black propaganda." Many of the survivors have since become leading authors, publishers, journalists, and film producers in present-day Germany, and the full story of the part their organisation played in the Second World War is only just coming to light.

While the British were still examining the credentials of applicants for war correspondents' licenses and trying to decide whether the insigne on their uniforms should be a "C" or—more appropriately, said some army officers—a "WC," a PK group advancing with the German armies on a doomed Warsaw had set up a radio station in Dirschau, in East Prussia, which broadcast as "Radio Warsaw" four days before the Polish capital fell, thus causing considerable confusion in Poland. A German PK man with the first wave of troops to cross the Polish border reported on the men's mood: "No hurrah-patriotism, no superficial sentimentality. All of us see the hard necessity of this night." PK *Sonderführer* Albert Cusian, who now lives near Hamburg, stayed in Warsaw to chronicle life in the Warsaw Ghetto, using his Leica with 3.5 Elmar lens to capture the misery and suffering of the ghetto's inhabitants. "I photographed everything in sight. The subject matter was so interesting. I took pictures in the morgue and at the Jewish cemetery. Bodies of Jews who had died during the night were laid out on the pavements for collection in the morning. I'd wait until the collectors came and then take pictures of them."[8]

In the early stages of the invasion of Poland, neutral correspondents in Berlin were fed with a stream of photographs, reports, and newsreels, and in the last stages of the brief campaign a few favoured correspondents were allowed to follow the German army, at a safe distance, to corroborate what they had already been told. American newspapers were full of German photographs. Reports from Berlin dominated the news pages. Newsreels of the Polish campaign appeared in cinemas across the United States.

In Britain there was an outcry. The Ministry of Information, with its staff of 999, was the target for most of the criticism, especially when statements in the Commons revealed that only forty-three of the staff had been journalists. The previous employment of other information experts ranged from a professorship of music to a professorship of world Christian relations. The newspapers were vitriolic. The *Daily Express* said that soon Britain would need leaflet raids on itself to tell its own people how the war was going. The *Manchester Guardian* said that the official communiqués could not help the enemy, but "are they any use to us?" Major-General J. H. Beith (the author Ian Hay), the War Office's director of public relations, took the unusual step of writing to *The Times* to explain why the Germans were being so successful on the propaganda front. Beith said that Hitler, being the aggressor, had an initial advantage and that the Polish campaign had provided opportunities for sensational reporting; Hitler, unlike the British, did not mind telling lies, and secrecy about British troop movements had been essential. However, Beith promised improvements. "A large body of correspondents, including a fully representative American contingent...are now with our forces in France."[9]

This group, which had arrived on October 10, consisted of fifteen British and Commonwealth correspondents, nine American, and eight press and newsreel photographers. They were looked after by conducting officers who had been chosen for their devotion to the army, and because they would not have been much use anywhere else; one, who had been a cavalry officer, boasted of his failure to become trained in tanks. They were, no doubt, brave, loyal soldiers, but they had become relics of a vanished England. There was a Captain Charles Tremayne, Military Cross and bar, Old Etonian ex-regular, pre-First World War cavalry officer, a large landowner in Cornwall and Wiltshire. Tremayne was a one-time chairman of the Duke of Beaufort's hunt committee and captain of the English polo team. He was also seldom sober. The correspondents, well able to handle a lot of liquor themselves, remember him as the heaviest drinker they had ever seen. He drank neat gin for breakfast and was known to have finished six bottles in two days. There was Captain Arthur ("Pilks") Pilkington, Military Cross, another Old Etonian, ex-regular, pre-First World War cavalry officer, and almost as heavy a drinker as Tremayne; and there were Captain Eddie Grant, Military Cross and bar, Old Etonian, ex-regular, etc., Lord Hothfield, Old Etonian, ex-regular, etc., etc. The conducting officers were outwardly polite to the war correspondents, but actually hated them. "Although Charles Tremayne's brain had been pickled by drink," another conducting officer wrote, "he still had five times more brain than the journalists he conducted."[10] When Bernard ("Potato") Gray of the *Daily Mirror*, desperate for a story, wrote one day, "An occasional shell removes the washing from the line," the conducting officers pointed out that not a single gun had yet been fired, and accused Gray of writing a mischievous lie and "sent him to Coventry."

The correspondents reciprocated the conducting officers' feelings. O. D. Gallagher has said, "The conducting officers were such astounding caricatures of British army regular officers and upper classes as to be scarcely credible. They were either drunk half the time or half drunk all the time. Whenever you were out driving with them it was always, 'Let's pull up and have a snifter at that café, old chap' or if there were no cafés then out came a flask from some pocket of their expensively cut uniforms."[11] Gallagher frequently told his editor, and tried to tell his readers, what he thought of the press arrangements at Arras and of the Army Public Relations unit in general. In one dispatch, he pointed out that staffing arrangements at the PR unit were such that it required eighty-seven fully trained servicemen to tend the needs of one war correspondent. Why not abandon the whole PR-war-correspondent concept, Gallagher wrote, and adopt the German Propaganda Company scheme? At least it would be more honest. The army warned Gallagher that this was not the attitude to adopt, but he ignored the warning and was recalled to London. There, his editor said he believed everything that Gallagher had written but he did not feel able to publish any of it, because "we can't fight the army in war-time." Gallagher was packed off on a tour of Britain to write about home defences.

During this period, the war correspondents could claim that they were systematically misled by GHQ as to the true situation; but anyone who allows himself to be misled for eight months must share some of the blame. Only one correspondent, Webb Miller, far gone in drink at the time, foresaw what would happen. "The Germans," he said, "will go through that line like crap through a little tin horn." After the Allied collapse, the correspondents remembered another warning, by the then Minister for War, Anthony Eden. At an off-the-record press conference at Arras, Eden had said, "It would be madness to risk an encounter battle with the Germans in Belgium," which was exactly what the Allies did. Kim Philby, still with *The Times*, also had a hint of things to come, from the Duke of Windsor, who, seeing Philby's war-correspondent shoulder straps and learning that he was from *The Times*, spoke to him in a bar at Metz. "If the Germans do attack," the Duke said, "then there'll be the very devil of a mess." Philby, who went on to become head of the anti-Soviet section of the British Secret Intelligence Service before being unmasked as a long-serving member of the Soviet KGB, has said frankly, "Luckily, apart from my censored dispatches to *The Times*, I was able to transmit news to another quarter which was not the least interested in the optimistic lucubrations of GHQ, only in the hard facts of military life: unit strengths and locations, gun calibres, tank performances, etc. But for that, my time at Arras would have been completely wasted."[12]

The Royal Navy, true to its First World War form, decided that it had no room in its ships for correspondents and would see the war through without them. It later relented a little, but throughout the war naval censorship remained the toughest. One example will suffice. On October 2, 1942, the *Queen Mary* rammed and sank the British light cruiser *Curaçao*, which had cut too sharply across her bow. The *Curaçao* sank in seven minutes, and only 101 of her crew of 439 were saved. Clinton B. Conger of the United Press was on board the *Queen Mary* and sent an eye-witness report to his office. The British Admiralty sat on the story until the end of the war, releasing it on May 15, 1945.[13]

Correspondents with the RAF at first thought that conditions would be much better than in the other services. The RAF had appointed experienced newspapermen as service press officers, under Wing-Commander Stanley Bishop, formerly the chief reporter of the *Daily Express*, and, the army having dithered about finding across-Channel transport for the war correspondents, the RAF offered to fly them. This so infuriated the army that it threatened to withdraw accreditation from any correspondent who accepted the offer. This deterred most British newspapers, including *The Times*, from accepting the RAF's offer, but the *Daily Express*, Allied Newspapers, Reuters, and the BBC refused to be intimidated, and their correspondents joined those representing three American groups—North American Newspaper Alliance, *Collier's Weekly*, and the Columbia Broadcasting System—and the Australian Newspaper Services on a flight to the Advanced Air Striking Force base in France.[14] But, after this promising start, arrangements for the correspondents quickly became even more confused than in the army.

Stories that the field censor at the base in France banned as being a danger to security were given out to newspapers by the Air

Ministry in London. When newspapers cried out for photographs, three photographers were accredited to the RAF for the duration—Stanley Devon of the *Daily Sketch*, Henry Heusser of Keystone, and John Daventry of the Sport and General News Agency. But they were *official* photographers and had to hand over their photographs to the Ministry of Information, which then distributed those it approved. Major stories, such as the King's visit to France, resulted in chaotic arrangements for photographers and correspondents alike, with restrictions on their numbers and a ban—later lifted—on reporting the visit at all. Matters reached a head when Air-Marshal A. S. Barratt, commander-in-chief of the British air forces, issued an order setting out new arrangements for correspondents. Only service press officers were to be allowed to visit air stations. There they would gather news, write it, and later hand it to correspondents, who could then telephone it to their newspapers. Correspondents themselves were banned from bases and prohibited from conversing with officers or men of the RAF under any circumstances. As a means of protest, correspondents contacted their offices and requested to be recalled. The BBC was the first to respond, and its correspondent, Charles Gardner, led the return to London.[35]

The situation, then, in these early months of the war—the Bore War, as it was called—was that for a large contingent of war correspondents in France there was little or nothing to report. And, presumably, if there had been anything to write, the system of field censorship would have made certain that nothing important actually got into print.

In contrast, the German PKs were probably more active during this period than anyone else, although their rôle was markedly different from the traditional one of a war correspondent. It was primarily to try to influence neutral newspapers and correspondents, in the belief that they, in turn, would influence Allied morale. The procedure was two-pronged—to create the illusion that the West Wall, the Siegfried Line, was impregnable, and to establish the belief that the Germans planned no aggression. To this end, PK men churned out reports about the strength of the West Wall, which, in fact, was far from finished. Photographs showed groups of neutral correspondents touring those bunkers that had been completed. American newspapers were soon writing about these "magnificent defense works." A PK film unit put together a documentary for release to neutral distributors. It probably could have safely been shown in Germany, so cleverly did it conceal the pitiful state of preparedness that actually existed along most parts of the wall.

To demonstrate Germany's peaceful intentions on the Western Front, the PK men set up loud speakers aimed at the French troops along the upper Rhine and organised concerts with a French flavour. "*Parlez-moi d'amour*," a hit tune of the period, soon became popular with the Germans as well. Huge posters in French fluttered above the German lines: "French soldiers, we have orders not to shoot, if you don't attack us. Germany has no reason to wage war on you." The Alsatian troops were urged in leaflets not to fire at their German compatriots, and PK officers met French officers in secret and assured them that Germany had nothing against France, only against England, "the common enemy." The PK officers made full use of the fact that it was French troops that manned the front lines while the BEF camped safely in the rear. A radio station called "Camarade du Nord," purporting to be an underground French station, came on the air and, in between long performances of the "*Internationale*," broadcast its support for Soviet-German friendship and called on the French Communist Party to back non-aggression. The station was actually run by the PK from near Lör-rach, in the Black Forest.[16]

All the action was elsewhere—in Finland, Norway, and Den-mark—but for most Allied and neutral correspondents these theatres of war proved as unrewarding as the Western Front. In Fin-land, invaded by the Russians on November 30, 1939, to prevent the country's becoming an anti-Russian base, the Finnish troops had some early successes, and the old delusion of 1918–20—that one combined push, one last intervention, could topple the Bol-sheviks from power—again started to affect Allied leaders.

An astonishing campaign began to "switch the war" away from Germany and against Russia. Major Kermit Roosevelt, who had offered his services to the British army on the outbreak of war, was relieved of his duties and promoted to colonel in command of a British volunteer brigade to fight against the Russians. Lady Astor tried to enlist American war correspondents as recruiting agents, and a British officer told Drew Middleton of the Associated Press: "We'll all be marching against the Russians in the Spring."[17] Britain sent off arms and troops, and the *Sunday Times* suggested that the Baku oil-fields be bombed.

One hundred war correspondents from Germany and from Allied and neutral countries rushed to Helsinki—the Russians refused to have them—to cover the story. They got nothing worthwhile. Despite the presence of such experienced American correspondents as Webb Miller and Leland Stowe, of the *Chicago Daily News*, and the charm of women correspondents like Virginia Cowles of the *Sunday Times* of London, the Finns showed an unshakeable determination to allow no correspondents anywhere near the real fighting. Stowe complained that stringent restrictions were placed on what correspondents could see long before anything they wrote came under the censor's blue pencil: "On the Western front they have war without combat. On the Finnish front we have war without correspondents."[18] Such reports as did appear were strongly pro-Finnish—one newsreel director was so anxious to show Soviet planes bombing Helsinki that when he could obtain no genuine film he used some old Spanish Civil War clips instead and hoped that no one would notice the absence of snow. During this time no one seemed prepared to question the fact that the Allied efforts to help the Finns against the Russians greatly exceeded their efforts to help the Poles against the Germans.

Early Finnish successes were exaggerated—"The Finns have succeeded in repulsing the [Russian] onslaught with some of the most spectacular fighting in history," wrote Miss Cowles.[19] This overoptimistic reporting was unjustified, as the collapse of the Finnish army soon proved.

On April 8, 1940, the Allies mined Norwegian waters—violating Norway's neutrality—in an attempt to cut off Germany's access to Sweden's raw materials. The Germans replied the next day by invading Norway across Denmark. Again, the German correspondents, at the spearhead of the attack and with excellent communications, were at an advantage. There were five PK men on board the heavy cruiser *Blücher*, which was sunk, in the attack on Oslo, by the guns of Oskarsborg fortress. Four were killed, but the fifth, Max Ehlert, a photographer, survived to write his story and to save his pictures. But they were not wanted. It was a firm PK rule throughout the war that dead German servicemen were never to appear in photographs or on film, and Ehlert's shots of the last minutes of the doomed *Blücher* were deemed "negative" and not distributed.[20] By the end of the Norwegian campaign, the German correspondents had turned in 300 dispatches, 250 photographs, and 54,000 feet of documentary film. And a fifth of their detachment had been killed in action. From a propaganda view, the result was well worth the cost. Demand from neutral countries, especially the United States, for PK reports and photographs was exceptional, mainly because of the paucity of material from the Allied side. Dispatches from PK correspondents such as Werner Keller, who flew with the Luftwaffe to bomb Tromsö, north of Narvik, and from Kurt W. Marek, who was with General Wilhelm Keitel in the Narvik region, appeared in many newspapers around the world.* [21] In contrast, Allied reporting was highly misleading, the *Glasgow Evening News*, for example, reporting the campaign as a triumph on May 29, just nine days before all the Allied forces in Norway were evacuated.

It was left to a neutral correspondent, Leland Stowe of the *Chicago Daily News*, fresh from the fiasco in Finland, to report the war in Norway as it really was. Sending his reports from neutral Sweden, so as to avoid censorship, Stowe wrote of "one of the costliest and most inexplicable bungles in military history"—how the British expeditionary force to Norway, expecting to take on crack German troops, found itself at the mercy of the Luftwaffe. "They were dumped into Norway's deep snows and quagmires of April slush without a single anti-aircraft gun, without one squadron of supporting airplanes, without a single piece of field artillery," Stowe wrote. Outnumbered, outgunned, and without air cover, the British force was cut to pieces and forced to withdraw.

As for gallant Norway, Stowe introduced American readers to the leader of a pro-Nazi Norwegian party, Major Vidkun Quisling, whose dubious contribution to the Second World War was to add another word to the English language.** Stowe reported that, far from resisting valiantly against massive odds, "Norway's capital of nearly 300,000 inhabitants was occupied by a German force of approximately 1,500 men…without dropping a bomb, without firing a shot within the city limits." Stowe explained in detail how treason on the part of highly placed Norwegian civilian and defence officials had resulted in Norway's capital, all her principal seaports, and her strategic coastal defences falling into German hands "like an over-ripe plum" in twelve bewildering hours. "This…gigantic conspiracy must undoubtedly rank among the most audacious, most perfectly oiled political plots of the last century."[22]

Stowe's dispatches and the mass of material from the German correspondents dominated the American press. Little came from British sources, and that little was mostly wrong. "There can be no question," Ed Murrow of the Columbia Broadcasting System told his American listeners, in a broadcast from London, "that the

---

*Marek was later well known, under the pseudonym C. W. Ceram, as the author of *Gods, Graves and Scholars*.
** "Quisling, 1940: a collaborationist, traitor to one's country."—*Oxford English Dictionary*.

handling by press and radio in this country of the news from Norway in the past ten days has undermined the confidence of a considerable section of the British public in the integrity and accuracy of its news sources."[23] As for official news, the Ministry of Information found few in the United States prepared to listen. Britain was reaping the results of her propaganda campaign in the First World War, when scant attention was paid to truth. Now every British claim, every story put out by the ministry, was automatically labelled propaganda. Any statement from a British war correspondent that showed Britain in a good light was dismissed as an attempt to influence American opinion, an effort to drag the United States once again into a European war. Complaints from American war correspondents about British censorship and restrictions on their movements were seen as proof of Britain's determination to hide the truth about the war. "America...is certainly hard to please," the *New Statesman and Nation* complained. "We are both required to fight a full-blooded war—sometimes judging from comments, a box office war for the benefit of American correspondents—and also we are expected to be plaster saints."[24]

In May 1940 the Bore War ended. The Germans struck through Belgium, Holland, and Luxembourg, and events moved so fast that communications—for those correspondents not running for their lives—broke down. The Germans again fared best; it is easier to report with a victorious army than with one in rapid retreat. German correspondents were in General Heinz Guderian's tanks as they rolled across France—the young tank generals were well disposed to correspondents and understood, better than old infantry commanders like Rundstedt, Bock, or Leeb, the value of a good image at home.* German correspondents flew in bombers, jumped with parachute troops, and marched with the infantry through the abandoned towns of Belgium and northern France, as the blitzkrieg shoved the Allies back towards the Channel.

As might be expected, their reports were peppered with praise for the heroic warriors of the Third Reich and for their leader, bril-

---

* A top correspondent, an *Operativer*, was able to nominate to the Ministry of Propaganda the paper in which he preferred his stories to be published. By selecting papers that Hitler was known to read—the *Deutsche Allgemeine Zeitung*, the *12-Uhr-Blatt*, the *Berliner Borsenzeitung*, and the *Völkischer Beobachter*—a correspondent was able to exercise considerable persuasion with generals who could see the advantage of being favourably described in dispatches their leader would be certain to see.

liant in battle, magnanimous in victory. "Thus it was that a relatively weak German paratroop unit, inferior in numbers and
weapons, a small body of death-defying men, hurtled from the air
into the midst of iron and fire, and through their boldness and
cold-bloodedness captured this strong bastion of the Belgian
defensive girdle," wrote a PK man, *Kriegsberichter* Mansfield,
describing the fall of the garrison at Eben Emael, then probably the
most strongly fortified post in the world.[25] Another PK reporter,
*Sonderführer* Kiekheben-Schmidt, marched into Paris with the
first German troops: "The soldiers of Greater Germany have
conquered Paris—but only the generosity of German leadership—and that means the Fuehrer, the Commander-in-Chief
himself—protected Paris from the fate of Warsaw." The majority
of the working-class Parisians preferred to stay in their homes
rather than flee, Kiekheben-Schmidt wrote. "In contrast, those
with a bad conscience, such as plutocrats, Jews, and other war-
mongers…had speedily deserted the city."[26]

This report did not tally with what the American correspondents, following hard on the heels of the German advance, found in
the French capital. Louis P. Lochner, writing for the Associated
Press, managed to get his version past the German censor: "Except
for Parisian police standing at street corners there was hardly a soul
in this city of over four million. Everybody had fled before Germany's irresistible advance—seventy per cent to nearby towns and
villages, thirty per cent to the privacy of their homes." The censor
probably passed Lochner's message because it came over as basically sympathetic to the Germans. Explaining Hitler's choice of the
German division to parade up the Champs Elysées, Lochner wrote:
"[They] had covered themselves with military glory during the battle of Kutno in Poland. In the general's own words, 'They have
fought on fifty battlefields. They're sculpted of the best German
oak. Their eyes shine as they go forth to battle, just as they shine
now parading here.'" [27]

The swiftness of the German advance wrecked most American
plans for covering the war. The *Time-Life* scheme, among the most
elaborate of any journalistic enterprises, fell to pieces under the
dual strains of a constantly moving front and implacable French
censorship. Some correspondents were fortunate. C. Brooks Peters
of the *New York Times* accompanied the German forces occupying
the Netherlands and wrote an account of the bombing of Rotterdam.
It was heavily censored, but Peters managed to get across the fact
that, the bombing having taken place after the city had surren-

dered, it had no military justification. M. W. Fodor of the *Chicago Daily News* was with a caravan of Belgian refugees fleeing from the German army yet again. Quentin Reynolds was caught in the civilian exodus from Paris, and William L. Shirer of the Columbia Broadcasting System was in the forest of Compiègne, outside the old railway coach in which the 1918 Armistice had been signed, and described via radio, the new and highly successful medium of war reporting, Hitler and Goering enjoying Germany's revenge.

> Now we get our picture through the dusty windows of the historic old wagon-lit car. Hitler and the other German leaders rise from their seats as the French enter the drawing room. Hitler, we see, gives the Nazi salute, the arm raised. The German officers give the military salute; the French do the same…Hitler, so far as we can see through the windows just in front of here, does not say anything. He nods to General Keitel, adjusting his papers, and then he starts to read. He is reading the preamble of the German armistice terms. The French sit there with marble-like faces…[28]

British correspondents, who had previously had so little to report, had more than they wished for in these hectic days, but either they had no way of sending their messages or they were too busy trying to stay alive to be bothered. Those correspondents who had requested their recall to London as a protest against petty restrictions and censorship had hurried back to France at the first news of the German push. By May 24 most of them were in London again, having been forced to run for Dunkirk by the speed of the German advance. The French were still holding out around Paris, so the War Office agreed to allow a smaller corps of correspondents to go back— six British, each representing two papers, one BBC radio man, two newsreel cameramen, two official photographers, and three Americans, Ed W. Beattie of the United Press, Drew Middleton of the Associated Press, and G. R. Nixon of the International News Service. When Paris fell they were on the run again. The best story of the war, the fall of France, was happening on all sides of them, but there was no way of reporting it. "A whole world was collapsing around us," wrote Noel Monks of the *Daily Mail*, who had been trying to cover the RAF's last stand in France. "But there were no means of getting a line about it to our newspapers, simply because there were no more communications and no censors." Monks had one particular story he wanted to send—the French had refused the RAF survivors any airfield facilities, thus ending all further chance of resistance. But this example of the collapse of Anglo-French relations went unreported as Monks and his colleagues struggled down to Bordeaux. There they were evacuated by ship and arrived back in Britain, the last of the correspondents to return, on June 25.[29]

The bulk of the British army had been evacuated at the beginning of the month from Dunkirk, and Britain was still reflecting the elation that this "snatching of glory out of defeat" had brought. It is worth looking at Dunkirk, because it became the first great myth of the Second World War, perhaps the greatest, the origin of the "Dunkirk spirit" that many believe was crucial to victory, and the way it was reported at the time was a major factor in establishing this myth.

The facts about the evacuation are swiftly spelt out. Just over 338,200 troops (of whom 150,200 were French) were brought out through Dunkirk, mainly between May 26 and June 4, and crossed the Channel to Britain in naval ships and in a flotilla of small craft assembled for the occasion. Churchill, addressing the House of Commons, described the operation, accurately and succinctly, as a "colossal military disaster," and privately General Ironside, chief of the Imperial General Staff, went further; he told Anthony Eden, "This is the end of the British Empire." Nothing had prepared British public opinion for a defeat of this magnitude. *

It would be wrong to suggest that in the face of the disaster of Dunkirk an organised campaign now began to change the evacuation into a victory. But the newspaper reader of the day could certainly be forgiven for thinking that something wonderful had happened to British fortunes in the war. BLOODY MARVELLOUS, said the *Daily Mirror*. The *Sunday Dispatch* suggested that divine intervention had been responsible. It pointed out that Dunkirk had followed a nation-wide service of prayer and that during the evacuation "the English Channel, that notoriously rough stretch of water which has brought distress to so many holiday-makers in happier times, became as calm and smooth as a pond...and while the smooth sea was aiding our ships, a fog was shielding our troops from devastating attack by the enemy's air strength."[30] The staid *New York Times* could not contain its admiration: "So long as the English tongue survives, the word Dunkirk will be spoken with reverence. For in that harbor, in such a hell as never blazed on earth before, at the end of a last battle, the rags and blemishes that have hidden the soul of

* Alexander Werth, a war correspondent for the *Manchester Guardian*, writing after the collapse of France, described his feeling of guilt at the "soft soap" he had been feeding his readers.

252

democracy fell away. There, beaten but unconquered, in shining splendour, she faced the enemy."[31] Ed Murrow of CBS tried to put the evacuation into perspective: "There is a tendency…to call the withdrawal a victory and there will be disagreement on that point."[32] Drew Middleton of the Associated Press wrote on similar lines. The censors did not interfere with their assessments, but in Britain the flow of what Middleton has called "hearts and flowers" writing went on unchecked.

One reason for this was that there were no British war correspondents writing from Dunkirk.* They covered the whole of the evacuation second-hand, from the south-east-coast ports where the troops landed. There the correspondents described the condition of the soldiers—"grimy, unshaven and tired…but there is no dejection"—and did their best to piece together what had happened across the Channel. They were given a lead by government statements. "When the full story can be told it will surprise the world," the Admiralty spokesman said, while the Minister of Shipping, describing the part played by the armada of small boats, said, "It grips our imagination. It inspires our minds and it tears at our heart strings."[33] And it was in this tenor that the correspondents wrote their stories—of a unit of Guards drilling at the water's edge while they waited for embarkation; of officers bringing order to panic-stricken French troops at revolver point; of a sailor digging a bullet out of his leg with a sheath knife; of a company of the Royal Warwicks who refused to leave the beaches until they had had regulation haircuts; of dispatch riders putting on a display of motorcycle acrobatics as the Stukas swooped; of the many games of cricket on the sand. Above all, the stories stressed the high morale of the evacuated troops, itching to get back to France and into the fight again. No doubt much of this reporting was true. There were brave and noble deeds at Dunkirk, and they rightly were written about. But was this the full picture? What of those stories that, for reasons that will become obvious, were not reported at the time?

It was not until the late 1950's and early 1960's—nearly twenty years after the event—that a fuller, truer picture of Dunkirk began to emerge.

In 1961 the author Richard Collier published the results of his long researches into what had really happened at Dunkirk. Collier

---

* David Divine, a free-lance, who had written a few navy propaganda books, persuaded the navy to let him watch the evacuation. Divine was wounded and wrote his well-known book on Dunkirk from his hospital bed. Although Divine later became a war correspondent of note, he was not one at that time.

and his assistants interviewed 1,070 eye-witnesses and had access to the private papers of the commander of the BEF, Lord Gort, who, apart from his official dispatches, had never written a word about Dunkirk. Collier's conclusions caused bitter official reaction, but were never rebutted. He quoted accounts of a hotel cellar in Dunkirk packed with British, French, and Senegalese troops singing, weeping, and screaming drunk; of groups of men, deserted by their officers, prowling the town in a mood of savage violence; of a major shot dead through the forehead by another because it was the only way of preventing him from capsizing an already overloaded rowing boat; of a senior officer refusing to leave a foxhole he had dug in the sand; of a corporal of the Guards who kept order in his boat, filled with fear-crazed troops, by threatening to shoot the first one who disobeyed him. As for the survivors arriving in Britain itching to return for another crack at the enemy, this may have been true of the army as a whole, but Collier found a Kentish police inspector, Richard Butcher, who remembered only too well the sight of dispirited men hurling their rifles from the trains carrying them from Dover.[34]

In 1962, General Sir Harold E. Franklyn, who had been a divisional commander at Dunkirk, complained that the evacuation had been "overglamourised." He said reports of "merciless bombing" and "the hell of Dunkirk" were quite ridiculous. "I walked along the beaches on several occasions and never saw a corpse…there was very little shelling; much the same as Armentières on a quiet day in 1915 or 1916." As for cowardice, General Franklyn wrote: "In every unit there are some men who have no stomach for the fight. There were instances of a few men embarking at Dunkirk when their battalions were fighting near the canal."[35] In 1965, Sir Basil Liddell Hart, the military historian, dealt the legend a body blow by stating that Dunkirk need not have happened—"Never was a great disaster more easily preventable." Liddell Hart pointed out that the German breakthrough that led up to Dunkirk, reported at the time as being due to overwhelming superiority, was actually achieved with armies inferior in numbers to those opposing them. Even in tanks, the Germans had fewer and less powerful ones than the Allies. Hitler's generals had been successful in forcing Dunkirk on the Allies because of the tradition-bound attitude of the Allied officers. Liddell Hart illustrated this view with the story of a French officer who sought permission to block the roads to the German tanks by felling trees across them, only to be told that the roads had to be kept clear for the advance of Allied cavalry![36]

The French rôle at Dunkirk was never properly presented in Britain, and the slanders on French troops reported at the time were never properly redressed. There were, no doubt, incidents of French cowardice, just as there were incidents of British cowardice. But 50,000 French troops stood fast at Lille and, although surrounded, managed to hold off seven German divisions from Dunkirk for four vital days. The French navy, assisting in the evacuation, and complete with its own armada of civilian and fishing craft, lost almost as many ships as the Royal Navy, yet carried some 50,000 troops across the Channel. The French have since complained that not only was this contribution not reported at the time, but it was not really acknowledged in the British official war history.[37] If Dunkirk was a miracle, then it had to be a British miracle.

Almost in a class with Dunkirk among the enduring legends of the Second World War were those events that began with the fall of France in the summer of 1940—the Battle of Britain and the Blitz. Again there is no dispute as to the facts. The Battle of Britain began on July 10 with attacks by the Luftwaffe on convoys passing through the Straits of Dover. The BBC war correspondent Charles Gardner, broadcasting live from "Hellfire Corner" in Kent, set the tone for the reporting that was to follow. His voice raised in high excitement, Gardner described a dogfight in the manner of a football commentator. *

> There's one coming down in flames—there, somebody's hit a German—and he's coming down—there's a long streak—he's coming down completely out of control—a long streak of smoke—ah, the man's bailed out by parachute—the pilot's bailed out by parachute—he's a Junkers 87 and he's going to slap into the sea and there he goes—SMASH...Oh boy, I've never seen anything so good as this—the RAF fighters have really got those boys taped.[38]

By August, when it was clear that the Luftwaffe was about to extend its operations to Britain herself, the RAF had caught something of Gardner's tone, and the order of the day, read aloud to every pilot, contained this stirring passage: "The Battle of Britain is about to begin. Members of the Royal Air Force, the fate of generations is in your hands."

The legend goes like this: while England stood alone, the RAF,

---

* Later, German PK radio reporters broadcasting live from bombers over London were equally enthusiastic.

outnumbered and down to its last cartridge, with brilliant improvisation, skill, and unbelievable bravery, soared into battle with a smile on its lips and shot the Luftwaffe out of the sky. While Spitfires traced patterns over south-eastern England, fighting to save the country from invasion, down below the Cockney newspaper sellers chalked up on their billboards the "ours" and "theirs" losses like cricket scores—BIGGEST RAID EVER—SCORE 78 TO 26 ENGLAND STILL BATTING. When the Germans, frustrated in their attempts to knock out the RAF airfields, switched to attacks on centres with large civilian populations, for seventy-six consecutive nights—excepting November 2, when the weather was bad—London was raided, but, as one American correspondent wrote, "it was thumbs up and carry on." St. Paul's Cathedral and the House of Commons were hit. Flames lit the sky. "Send all the bloody pumps you've got," shouted the fire officer at Surrey Docks; "the whole bloody world's on fire." Cockneys wisecracked as their streets disappeared in a shower of rubble, while the old and the children marched off to air-raid shelters singing "Bless 'Em All." And all the time Britain's war-time leader, Winston Churchill, captured the spirit of his people with his evocative speeches: "so many to so few," "blood, toil, tears and sweat," and "fighting on the beaches."

Like all legends, there is some truth in this. As far as the facts go, the average life expectancy in the air of a British fighter-pilot was only eighty-seven hours; there *were* amazing acts of bravery in the Blitz; it was a battle of an unarmed civilian population against an enemy that they could not hurt; and it probably *was* Britain's finest hour. But this is not the whole picture. It is an unbalanced one, which grew from what was written at the time, and to redress the balance it is necessary to examine the accuracy of the reporting of the Battle of Britain and, even more important, to see what was not reported at all.

The first point to make is that by far the biggest volume of reporting on the Battle of Britain came from American war correspondents. There were 120 top reporters from the United States covering the story. Their communications were good; they had the space in their newspapers, the time on their radio networks; and the British Ministry of Information did everything in its power to help them.* To a man, the American correspondents were pro-British—"We

---

* By contrast, with the possible exception of Ritchie Calder (later Lord Ritchie Calder) and his paper, the *Daily Herald*, British war correspondents were slow to see the Blitz as more than a running disaster story. To be fair, they lacked space, and the censor would not allow them to report the one fact every reader wanted to know—what exactly got hit in last night's raid?

saw the indisputable danger to the United States if England were occupied by the enemy," wrote Mary Welsh of *Time* and *Life*, "and we cabled our views as plainly as British censorship then permitted."[39] This pro-British sentiment naturally coloured American reporting, and it prevented most correspondents from giving their readers a balanced view.

To begin with, Britain was not the underdog; the odds were about even. The Germans attacked Britain with 702 single-seater and 261 heavy fighters—a total of 963. They had 1,000 long-range bombers and about 300 dive-bombers. RAF Fighter Command at this time had a tactical strength of 666 aircraft, plus nearly 750 grounded temporarily for repairs or held in reserve—a total of 1,416.[40] True, the RAF was seriously short of trained pilots, but British aircraft production was expanding on a growing base, while German production was geared to short wars during which there would be bursts of intensive economic effort followed by periods of recuperation.* Since most of the fighting was over British soil, German pilots and planes shot down were irretrievably lost. British pilots might survive, and their planes could often be salvaged. The odds were roughly even, yet throughout the battle the RAF regularly lost more fighters than the Luftwaffe—it was the German bombers that swelled the British score, and to break even the RAF had to shoot down a great many of them. This was made possible not by brilliant British improvisation, but by radio-direction-finding (later called radar) stations, which Britain had decided to start building *four years* before the outbreak of war. So much for the lack of preparation. Throughout the Battle of Britain, radar enabled the RAF to know when the Germans were coming and approximately where—a major factor in its victory.

The young pilots of the Hurricanes—the RAF's principal weapon, not, as legend would have it, the Spitfires—were under no illusions about the glamour of their task, and many found Churchill's rhetoric—"Knights of the Round Table," "Crusaders" who "grin when they fight"—embarrassing. Air combat in the Battle of Britain "was a matter of calculating the apparently improbable co-incidence of small pieces of machinery in very large air spaces, with the aim of placing one group of men in a position to shoot another group of men in the back with as little risk as possible to themselves."[41]

There was nothing glamorous in the theory and nothing glam-

* Germany believed she could have guns *and* butter. In 1944 she was still producing domestic refrigerators.

orous in the practice. The Germans fired on British pilots floating helplessly beneath their parachutes because they could, after all, be back in battle the same afternoon shooting down Germans. The RAF, equally calculating, had no compunction about destroying a Heinkel 59 seaplane with civilian markings as it was engaged in rescuing German pilots floating in the Channel, or another Heinkel 59 marked with the Red Cross. True, Air Chief Marshal Sir Hugh Dowding forbade British pilots to shoot at Germans who parachuted to safety over Britain, since it was necessary to wait only a few seconds for them to be captured, but the British pilots interpreted this order as allowing them to give the German all they had while he was still struggling out of his cockpit. And there was nothing to stop the Home Guard from blazing away at a German if his parachute dropped within range. Flight-Lieutenant J. B. Nicholson, the only RAF fighter-pilot to win a Victoria Cross, was wounded in this manner when the Home Guard mistook him for a German.[42]

As far as the daily tally of comparative losses was concerned, the correspondents had little choice but to accept the figures in the official communiqués, and these turned out to be hopelessly wrong and—as the pilots themselves knew—exaggerated to maintain civilian morale. On September 9, for example, *The Times*, in a long story about a raid on London two days earlier, said that 107 German planes had been shot down. In fact, the figure was forty-one. On September 15, the Air Ministry announced 185 German planes destroyed, the "greatest day" in the whole battle: 185 DOWN AND WE'RE STILL BATTING, the billboards said. The real German loss was only sixty. The Air Ministry's total for the period July 10 to October 31, 1940, was 2,698. Actually the Germans lost 1,733. At the end of the war, the Air Ministry admitted, with a touch of British humour, that it had exaggerated its score by only 55 per cent, whereas the Germans had done so by 224 per cent.[43]

Could a conscientious correspondent have checked the official count? It is hard to see how. O. D. Gallagher, who raced around Kent in a tenth-hand Pontiac for the *Daily Express*, has said, "You watched a dogfight. You saw a spurt of smoke that grew and one aircraft began to fall and it was nose-first buried in the earth below in two minutes. How could you hope to know where it came down?"[44] I have been able to discover only one correspondent who at least tried to check the Air Ministry's figures. Barry Cornwell, the south-eastern regional press and liaison officer of the Ministry of Information, used to shepherd neutral war correspondents around the defence area—that part of the south-east coast where neutral correspondents were allowed to go if accompanied by a ministry official. One day Gottfried Keller, president of the Foreign Press Association in London, turned up and announced that he planned to check the British score. The official communiqué claimed that the RAF had shot down twenty-six German planes the previous day. Keller thought that this was exaggerated. "I want to see the wrecks," he said, "and count them myself." Cornwell had been told that nothing was too much trouble for a neutral war correspondent, so off they went, chasing all over Kent, Sussex, and Surrey, climbing fences and tramping through woods, until the count reached fourteen. By this time they were both exhausted, and Keller cried a halt. "That's enough. I believe you."[45] But the majority of the correspondents were prepared to accept the British figures without question, without giving their readers any warning that, although official, the daily tally might well be inflated.

The reporting of the Blitz was much the same. The tenor of the American and Commonwealth correspondents' dispatches was one of bravery, fortitude, and determination—all true, but far from the whole picture. There is evidence that not everyone in Britain at that time shared Churchill's determination to fight to the last. The Duke of Windsor was appointed governor of the Bahamas. The gold reserves of the Bank of England were shipped off to Ottawa. The Minister of Information, Alfred Duff Cooper, sent his son John Julius to Canada, and only Churchill's intervention prevented the departure of his great-niece Sally Churchill to the United States. Parents who could afford to do so started shipping their families to safety in America or the Commonwealth. In June, July, and August of 1940, over 6,000 children took part in this exodus of the rich.[46] The Swedish minister in London told Stockholm that some MPs were in favour of an early peace with Hitler, and the British Ambassador in Washington, Lord Lothian, argued that nothing should be said that might close this door to negotiations. The working class began to feel, with some justification, that the rich had plans to get out while the going was good.

Churchill was obsessed with getting America into the war. He tried to frighten Roosevelt with the prospect of an early German victory. He searched for an outrage, such as the sinking of the *Lusitania* in the First World War, that would arouse American public opinion. German bombing of British civilians might well achieve this. But for weeks it looked as if the Germans had no intention of being so obliging. The Luftwaffe's job was to destroy the RAF, and, apart from the bombing of the aircraft industry's scattered factories, this brief did not include the bombing of civilian areas.

Then, on the night of August 24–25, the German bombers made a crucial mistake. Their target was the oil storage depot at Thames Haven. Their bombs fell, instead, on the City and parts of the East End of London. The German crews were punished for this error by being posted to infantry regiments, so it is reasonable to conclude that the raid was not intended as the first stage of a campaign against civilians.[47] But Churchill's immediate reaction was to order the RAF to carry out, on August 25, a reprisal raid on Berlin, despite the unanimous advice of the RAF chiefs of staff not to do so. *The Times* on August 28 described this raid not as a reprisal, but as an attack on "clearly defined military objectives which had been selected a long time before." A day earlier, *The Times* published a report of the raid, written by one of the pilots, in which he described finding a gap in the clouds over Berlin, locating one of these "clearly defined military objectives," and bombing it. But this report does not tally with the official account, written by Squadron-Leader Russell J. Oxley, who led the raid. Unable to identify his target, Oxley made a crucial decision: "I could have brought my bombs back, of course, but I didn't, I left them in Berlin."[48] London was bombed on August 24, Berlin on August 25—these two futile raids were the shoddy origins of the Blitz.

Once it had started, it was hard to cry a halt. The Luftwaffe bombed British cities, the RAF German ones, to little real strategic end. (A survey in August 1941 showed that one-third of the RAF bombers sent over Germany failed to attack the target, and only a third of the rest got within five miles of it. In these raids more British airmen were killed than German civilians. Equally, Britain's anti-aircraft defences in their early days killed more Londoners than German airmen.)[49] Naturally, none of this was published at the time, but one American correspondent, Raymond Daniell of the *New York Times*, who wrote his share of "finest hour" copy, took a more objective view of the bombing when he returned to the United States in March 1941. "The futility of it all was depressing at times…It was a simple cockney who reduced the whole thing to the ultimate in absurdity for me one night. 'It's a crazy war, guv'nor,' he said, 'I don't see why Jerry doesn't bomb Berlin and let the RAF take care of London. We'd both save petrol and we'd be none the worse.'"[50]

The whole story of what happened as Britain shook to the Luftwaffe's pounding was, of course, not written in British newspapers. If a correspondent had tried to write it, the censor would not have passed it.* American and Commonwealth newspapers concentrated on the courage and self-sacrifice, the cheerfulness, the Britain-can-take-it side to the story, probably best summed up in the song "Mr. Brown of London Town." This is the version of the Blitz that has survived, and it is still preferred to the other side, not reported at the time and painful to admit since.

The Blitz was not the great social leveller. The protection a Londoner got from German bombs depended on how much money he had. When the sirens sounded, residents of the Dorchester went down into the basement, where a neat row of cots, some labelled with their owners' names, offered a safe refuge and even the possibility of sleep. All-night shelter was offered as part of the service at most expensive West End restaurants. In the East End, however, thousands crowded into stifling, insanitary shelters. Yielding to public pressure, the authorities allowed Underground stations to be used, but many of these became terrible slums, foul with the smell of urine, excrement, sweat, carbolic, and unwashed bodies. Lice and fleas flourished, and, justifying to some extent the government's fears about "deep shelter mentality," some people stayed down for weeks on end, while others liked it so much that they continued bedding down there long after the Blitz was over.[51]

The feeling that "we're all in this together" was not unanimous. When the Café de Paris was hit in March 1941, thieves took rings from the fingers of the dead and wounded. Auxiliary Fire Service men appeared before the courts on looting charges. When damaged houses were unattended, often because their owners were in hospital with bomb injuries, looters stole the best furniture.[52] Organisation was not superb. When Liverpool was hit, some groups of fire-fighting parties had no equipment at all; others had pumps, but no vehicles to tow them. When the government did send vehicles, many turned out to be unroadworthy. Warehouses burned to the ground because there was no water for fire-fighting—in a city situated along a great river.[53]

The people could not always take it. When Coventry was badly bombed, Hilde Marchant of the *Daily Express* said the city was stricken, "but keeps its courage and sanity." In fact, the German

---

* Several British correspondents wrote more freely and objectively in books that were rushed to publication in late 1941—for example, *The Lesson of London*, by Ritchie Calder, and *Women and Children Last*, by Hilde Marchant. Censorship of books was not as stringent as of newspapers; also, the worst appeared to be over by then.

attack created panic. Thousands fled from the town in an unorganised rout. The army wanted to impose martial law, and an official report described the general mood by repeating what a survivor said: "Coventry is finished."[54] *The Times* spoke of the "butchery at Coventry...the wanton slaughter by a people pretending to be civilised who, it would seem, kill mostly for the joy of destroying."[55] Coventry was actually a legitimate military target, one of the keys to the British war effort, and the German bombers damaged twenty-one important factories, including the Standard Motor Company, the Coventry Radiator and Press Company, the British Piston Ring Company, the Daimler Motor works, and the Alvis Aero-engine factory. "Here tools and motors were made for British aircraft," the German PK reporter who flew with the Luftwaffe on the attack quite accurately told his readers.[56] The fact that the cathedral was hit and that industrial production in Coventry *rose* after the attack are two indictments of bombing as a weapon of war. Yet, instead, Coventry has gone down in history as a monument to German frightfulness.

Some British and some American war correspondents did their best to show all sides of Britain under siege. Ritchie Calder, in cold, angry terms, reported civil defence failures in the East End, as well as confusion, overlapping, and buck-passing in the various ministries. Hilde Marchant spent days and nights in communal shelters and wrote about the appalling conditions. (For their efforts, ministers accused them of "giving comfort to the enemy.") But, in general, few correspondents or newspaper owners were prepared to risk suppression by defying the censor. So the dropping of parachute mines was kept out of the press for the duration of the war. The names and localities of damaged buildings were not mentioned until twenty-eight days after the raid. All references to raids on factories were avoided, no casualty lists were published, and newsreels that showed the worst were censored. There were no reports of unexploded bombs, no suggestions of panic or chaos anywhere, and anything that might create alarm or despondency was avoided.

The so-called Battle of the Atlantic, for example, a continuous struggle to prevent the Germans from starving Britain into submission, which only really ended when the war did, was reported in terms of heroic endeavour. It was indeed this, as the deaths of some 30,000 British merchant seamen, volunteers at £9 a month, and two shillings and sixpence a day danger money, so eloquently attest. But the crucial information, the rate at which British ships bringing supplies across the Atlantic were being sunk by German submarines, was suppressed, on an order from Churchill on April 14, 1941.[57]  Ed Murrow complained bitterly in a broadcast in May: "The curious thing about the Battle of the Atlantic is that no one knows anything about it. No information—not even general information concerning the sinking of American supplies—is permitted to be revealed...Efforts by official American representatives to secure the release of information...have been unavailing. Nothing may be said either to the Americans or to the British public about this battle which, we are told, will determine the destinies of free men for centuries."[58]

The fact that Murrow was able to get this criticism past the censor shows that American correspondents were given a freer hand than their British colleagues. Murrow and others made good use of this. In another broadcast, Murrow told Americans that the old Britain was dying and that ordinary people were asking awkward questions: "Why must there be 800,000 unemployed when we need shelters? Why are new buildings being constructed when the need is that the wreckage of bombed buildings be removed from the streets? What shall we do with victory when it is won?"[59] Drew Middleton wrote, in November 1940, a story about Britain that was a contradiction of the line the Ministry of Information was taking at the time, what Middleton has described as the "come-on-Hitler-we're-ready-stuff." And in March 1941 he sent home a dispatch saying that the British might trust Churchill to get them through the war, but that there were plenty of Opposition MPs and members of his own party who wanted to get rid of him as soon as possible. "We became aware of the enormous propaganda machine pumping out the government view," Middleton has said, "and the reaction in my case was to take a harder line."[60]

So it was not all a period of glory. Churchillian rhetoric, J. B. Priestley's cosy radio chats about war aims and post-war Britain, the heroism of the ordinary Englishman, all transmitted by the correspondents to an American audience that gobbled it up and asked for more. "And why not?" asks Malcolm Muggeridge. "It was all true, all heroic, all forever memorable. By the same token, all false, all squalid, all eminently forgettable—the heroism no more than indifference, Churchillian rhetoric as empty as Laurence Olivier pounding out Henry V's peroration before Agincourt, Priestley's down-to-earth good sense the purest fantasy."[61]

*Chapter Eleven*

# The Struggle For Mother Russia 1941–1945

Look carefully at these dead Tartars, these dead Russians. They are new corpses, brand new, just out of the factory of the five-year plan. Look how clear their eyes are. Narrow foreheads, thick-lipped mouths. Peasants? They are workers, specialists, *udarniki*, from one of the thousands of *Kolkhoz*, from one of the thousands of workshops in the Soviet Union. Look carefully at their foreheads: narrow, hard, obstinate. They are all like that. All mass produced. It's a new race, a hard race.

—Curzio Malaparte,
correspondent of *Corriere della Sera*,
with the German army on the Eastern Front, July 1941

———

The war between Germany and the Soviet Union began on June 22, 1941, with the clash of two of the greatest armies the world had ever seen. This was the decisive battlefront of the Second World War, and if ever a campaign deserved the fullest possible coverage, from the best war correspondents, surely this was it. Yet the Eastern Front remained throughout the most poorly reported part of the Second World War.

Fifty of the most famous names in newspaper and radio were in Russia at one time or another. Yet the story of those incredible early days when the German army stormed across the border was not fully reported until after the war, and events like the Battle of

Moscow, the siege of Leningrad, Stalingrad, the Battle of Sevastopol, and the Battle of Kursk never received proper attention. Other major stories—from 800,000 Russians who fought for the Germans, to the Katyn Forest massacre—either were not written at all or were written as virtual propaganda handouts. As a result, the reader in the West remained largely ignorant of what was going on in the Soviet Union, the Russians themselves knew not much more, and some of the best reporting came from the Axis side.

The start of war on the Eastern Front caught Western war correspondents unprepared, despite the fact that everyone knew that the two greatest powers of continental Europe were about to come to grips. Newspapers in the United States and Britain had carried reports day after day that Germany was about to attack the Soviet Union, yet June 22 found only seven Western correspondents in Russia, two of whom—Erskine Caldwell and his wife, the photographer Margaret Bourke-White—were there doing a feature for *Life* about the countryside. *The Times* of London and the *New York Times* had no one in Russia at all. The other correspondents— Henry Shapiro of United Press, Henry Cassidy of Associated Press, Maurice Lovell of Reuters, Jean Champenois of Havas, and A. T. Cholerton of the *Daily Telegraph*—had no idea war was about to break out (Cassidy was actually away on a holiday), and so the first news came from Germany. There, correspondents had been on the alert since Saturday, June 14, when all telephone communications out of Berlin had suddenly been cut. This, plus the fact that they had been forbidden to write on Russo-German relations, on penalty of expulsion, made it obvious to most correspondents that war was imminent.[1] The announcement came from von Ribbentrop himself at a press conference at the German Foreign Office at 6:00 A.M. on Sunday, June 22. Correspondents were allowed to send their stories immediately. The news was broadcast on short wave by Radio Berlin within the hour, picked up in London and New York, and printed that day.

The Germans maintained their early lead. A PK reporter, Karl Heinz Seiss, flew over the battlefront in a Luftwaffe plane during the early hours, and the *Frankfurter Zeitung* carried his story on Monday, June 23, the first account of the fighting. "The attack against the enemy begins. There is a target just below. A marvellous sight to see...there are many large hangars and at the edge of the airstrip, lined up as if on parade, there is a mass of Soviet Russian fighter planes. The bombs from our plane fall accurately and with excellent results. Right on the nose! The enemy craft on the ground burst into flames, and the fires spring from one to the other."

On the Soviet side all was confusion. Bombs showered on Kiev, Sevastopol, Kaunas, and other cities to the rear of the fighting. Border posts were overwhelmed. Brest-Litovsk and other frontier towns were shelled. In those first few days, 2,000 planes, the greater part of the Russian air force, were destroyed. The Russians lost thousands of tanks, half a million men killed, and perhaps as many as a million taken prisoner. The basic trouble—as the official war history later revealed—was that the Russians had made the mistake of believing their own propaganda: any Fascist or imperialist state that attacked the Soviet Union would collapse at the very first shots because its workers would rebel against their government.[2]

But as 2 million Germans, supported by thousands of tanks and planes, pushed into the Soviet Union, no Russian knew at first how serious the situation was. The first communiqué, published at 10:00 P.M. on June 22, showed that even the Soviet leaders had no idea of what was happening: "In the course of the day, regular German troops fought our frontier troops and achieved minor success in a number of sectors." The confusion grew. The next day the Red Army announced the fall of Brest-Litovsk. It did not fall, in fact, until a month later, July 24. Then, on July 3, Stalin broadcast a warning to his "comrades, citizens, brothers and sisters, fighters of our army and navy" of the serious threat to Mother Russia and announced the "scorched earth" policy that appalled the world, yet captured its admiration. But he did not explain what had happened.*

It is clear the Soviet leaders decided very early on that the Russians should be told nothing about the war that might damage morale. The danger could not be minimised, but, if presented in the right way, it could arouse the patriotic fervour necessary for eventual victory. Therefore, only "official" news would be tolerated. All private radios had to be handed to the militia, and loud speakers giving the Moscow programme became for most Russians their main source of information—apart from news filtering back from the front by word of mouth. The official communiqués, broadcast regularly, never mentioned the real number of Russian casualties, avoided major disasters, and gave only the vaguest indications of where the fighting was actually taking place. But, since the communiqués were compiled by non-literary figures of limited

---

* It was not until 1967, on the fiftieth anniversary of the Revolution, that a Soviet film, *If Your Home Is Dear To You*, showed shocked Russian audiences what had gone wrong in those first terrible weeks of the war.

creative ability and with strong bureaucratic tendencies, the same phrases began to recur, and it did not take the Soviet citizen long to work out the nuances of the communiqués.[3] In the phrase "fighting in the Smolensk direction" or "the Minsk direction," the key word was "direction," and meant that Smolensk or Minsk had already been lost. "Heavy defensive battles against superior enemy forces" was the worst possible news, and meant that the Russians were in full retreat; a "complex" situation was one of utmost gravity; "nothing of consequence occurred" could mean either that nothing had happened or that there was nothing the military leaders were prepared to talk about. But what could anyone have made from this sentence from a *Times* report, taken from Reuters, which had in turn taken it from *Pravda* or *Izvestia*: "Particularly fierce fighting has developed in the areas 'D' and 'B' where the situation remains grave"?[4]

There was no way of checking the figures of losses. It emerged much later that these had been wildly inflated, as the following example indicates. In *The Times*, on August 23, 1941, the Russian high command claimed that in the first two months of the war the Germans had lost 2 million men killed, wounded, or taken prisoner (this was actually the strength of the whole German army on the Eastern Front) and that 8,000 tanks had been destroyed (more than double the number of tanks in the entire German army in Russia). As the war progressed, the Soviet Union knew very well what was happening on all fronts, but it gave out its version to its people anything from five days to five years later. It could be argued that this kept information from the enemy and did the people at home no harm. On the other hand, in a struggle for existence, if the people actually doing the fighting have not the right to know how the war is really going, who has?

Apart from communiqués, there were the Russian newspapers, with their "country-in-danger" propaganda, their outcry against cowardice, their appeals to patriotism, their astronomical figures of German losses, and their scanty war reports. These reports were written not by regular journalists who had turned to war reporting, but, more often, by well-known writers, who gave a somewhat unreal literary style to the news. The best known of these was Ilya Ehrenburg, who wrote for *Red Star*, and whose bitterly anti-German articles were often reprinted in the West. Others included Vassily Grossman, also of *Red Star*, Alexei Surkov, a poet, Konstantin Simonov, Mikhail Sholokhov, and Boris Mikhailov. Their stories make curious reading for Western eyes and might more properly be termed propaganda essays than reports. Ehrenburg, for example, writing in 1942 on the anniversary of the Revolution, began his article: "We did not create our life easily. But this rough unpolished life was our own way of life. It reminded one of the rough draft of an astounding poem, all blotted and scratched. When we were building nurseries, evil news came to us from the West: there they were building bombers which would kill hundreds of children in one night. The smell of Germany's animal breath was wafted to us and we said to our wives, 'You'll have to wear the old wedding dress another winter.' "[5] These Russian war correspondents were not meant to report battles—although, as shall be seen, one of them was present throughout the siege of Stalingrad—or to build up individual war personalities. The first stricture was because the Russians felt that the official communiqué gave sufficient news of the fighting; the second because Communist ideology held that what was important was not the individual but what he did.

Henry Cassidy, on his way back to Moscow from a Black Sea holiday resort, where he had been at the outbreak of the war, had seen the gigantic machinery of the Soviet Union's mobilisation scheme grind into action. His report, "Ivan Goes Calmly to War," escaped the censor's attention and was the first war-time descriptive article sent from Moscow.[6] This article, and the fact that it was becoming clear that the Russians were not going to be beaten in ten days, as had been predicted in the West, stimulated the news sense of editors around the world, and late in June and early in July their best men were sent hurrying to Russia. The United States group was soon to include such correspondents as C. L. Sulzberger, A. T. Steele, Wallace Carroll, and Alice Leone Moats; later, Edgar Snow, Leland Stowe, Walter Kerr, and Larry Lesueur arrived. From Britain there were Philip Jordan, Vernon Bartlett, Charlotte Haldane, Ralph Parker, Alexander Werth, and, later, Paul Holt. Eventually there were also three Australians, Eric McLoughlin, Jeff Blunden, and James Aldridge (of *Time* magazine, later to be relieved by Dick Lauter).

The newcomers arrived in Moscow by roundabout plane and ship routes, firmly believing that they were heading for the front. Instead, they found that the Russians had quickly created a system especially for them, a system so diabolical that to this day old war correspondents shudder when they recall it. To understand why the Russians behaved the way they did, it must be remembered that in 1918–19 Britain and the United States, along with nearly every other major power in the world at that time, had done their best to strangle the Russian Communist state at birth. Then, the move in Britain at the time of the Russo–Finnish conflict to switch the war away from Germany to Russia had not passed unnoticed in Moscow, nor had the banning, in January 1941, of the British Communist paper, the *Daily Worker*. Moreover, the Russians were suspicious that the Western war correspondents might be intelligence agents, a suspicion that was not without justification.

The Western war correspondents were placed under the care of Solomon Abramovich Lozovsky, Vice-Commissar for Foreign Affairs and official spokesman for the Soviet Information Bureau. A suave man of sixty-three, Lozovsky had begun life selling matches and lemons in the street and had risen to become a teacher of social philosophy. Later he went into exile in Paris, where he met Lenin, and afterwards he took part in the 1917 Revolution. Eventually he emerged as secretary of the Railway Workers' Union. As well as speaking cultured Russian, Lozovsky spoke good French and German and adequate English and Spanish. For the Western war correspondents he was the voice of Russia, their principal source of information, their passport to the front. Under Lozovsky worked Nikolai Palgunov, a former director of Tass, who was chief of the Press Department of the Foreign Commissariat and the head censor, and two assistants, Pietr Amirov and Viktor Khozhemiako. This team successfully crushed any hopes the war correspondents might have had of telling the whole story of the war in Russia.

Lozovsky held a press conference at least twice a week, at which he would parry brilliantly every effort to extract any real information. Could he identify the unnamed city that the communiqué reported had been retaken by the Red Army? "My dear Sir. If the army wanted you to know the name of the city, then the communiqué would have said it." The BBC had reported some Japanese ships blown up by Russian mines. Could Comrade Lozovsky comment? "Ah, well, what do the Japanese newspapers say?" Questioner: "I'm afraid I don't know." Lozovsky: "I'm afraid I don't know either." When could the correspondents go to the front? "In good time, I hope." Lozovsky never refused to answer a question, but at the end of the conference, when the correspondents checked their notes, there was seldom a thing they could write. Such information as he did give was frequently unreliable; he would insist that the Germans were far from some particular point, the fall of which would then be announced in the next communiqué.[7]

On the rare occasions when the correspondents did manage to

discover something for themselves and proceeded to write it, Palgunov or one of his censors would kill it at once. No individual opinions, no speculation, no predictions were allowed. The reasoning here was that because the world knew censorship existed in Russia, it followed that every dispatch a correspondent was allowed to send had, in effect, an official stamp of approval. In vain the correspondents argued that the stories would appear under their own names and would be read as *their* opinions. No, Lozovsky said. If it had been passed by the Soviet Union, the opinion must also be that of the Soviet Union. The only positive point about this was that the censor's blue pencil also fell on what the censor knew to be incorrect. This enabled a correspondent to get some slight idea of what was going on at the front by including the latest rumours in his dispatch. If the censor passed it, then the rumours were true. It was a hit-or-miss method, scarcely worthy of the stories that should have been written, but it was better than nothing. Because, if Palgunov had had his way, nothing was what the correspondents would have sent.

All photography was banned, to the horror of Margaret Bourke-White: "The biggest country enters the biggest war in the world and I was the only photographer on the spot."[8] (But with cajolery and the help of Harry Hopkins, Roosevelt's personal envoy to Stalin, Miss Bourke-White managed to get out photographs of Moscow under a night bombing attack, and even a portrait of Stalin himself.) Descriptive stories, such as one that Cassidy of the Associated Press wanted to send on how Moscow looked under camouflage— "Lenin's red and black marble mausoleum in Red Square was...decorated like a country cottage'"[9]—were forbidden because they might have been of use to German bombers. Human-interest stories bewildered the Russians, who became convinced that the American press was interested only in trivia.

That there was some justification for this belief is illustrated by a story about Eddy Gilmore of the Associated Press. He sent from Moscow whatever he could learn about the progress of the war, but he never received more than a lukewarm response from his office, or any indication that it appreciated his difficulties, and he was on the same pay as when he had left New York a year earlier. Then, from Kuibyshev, on the Volga River, he sent in some desperation a story the substance of which can be gauged from the theme: "The Volga boatmen have never heard of the Song of the Volga Boatmen, the tune that made the Volga famous in the U.S.A." Reaction from New York was an ecstatic cable: YOUR VOLGA BOATMEN STORY MAGNIFICENT STOP YOUR SALARY RAISED STOP REGARDS CONGRAT-

ULATIONS. Quentin Reynolds of *Collier's*, fresh from reporting the Blitz in Britain, wrote a story about the life of a Western war correspondent in Russia that ran to 2,500 words. The censor left only 400. "People are not interested in what you eat and drink," Lozovsky said. "Save such stories for after the war. Important things are happening. Write about the daily communique."[10]

The Russians were not impressed by reputations and were soon handing out this sort of treatment to some of the best-known correspondents in the world, relenting only when it suited them to do so—the visit to the Red Army on September 15, 1941, for example. This was an historic occasion, the first formal visit ever paid to the Red Army by foreign correspondents. It was done on the group-conducted-tour system developed by the British during the First World War, the correspondents being accompanied by an army officer, a brigade commissar, and a censor. They met a general who gave them an interview, traced a Russian victory on a now deserted battlefield, talked to some German prisoners, drank vodka in the army mess, and saw the German lines from a safe distance. This tour set the pattern for the many that followed, a sort of Intourist model: "war correspondents and distinguished visitors." But as the first, which yielded stories that began "With the Red Army," it made news all over the world.

Earlier news had been mainly concerned with the prospect of a quick Russian defeat. But when the Germans started bombing Moscow, on July 21, the reaction of the Russians impressed even those correspondents who had believed that their biggest story would be to cover the German army marching through Red Square. A mood of grim determination replaced the shock of early defeats. Alexander Werth of the *Sunday Times* wrote that when a character in a play at the Malyi Theatre spoke the lines "If war comes, we shall fight with a fierceness and anger the like of which the world has never seen," he brought the house to its feet clapping and cheering.[11] But all this did not stop the Germans from closing on Moscow from all directions.

On October 12 *Pravda* spoke of the "terrible danger" threatening the country, and the following day it was decided to evacuate to Kuibyshev, 1,000 miles east of Moscow, many government offices, the most important armaments works, the entire diplomatic corps, and all the foreign war correspondents. Because they were swept up in it themselves—and it must be emphasised that they had no choice in the matter—the correspondents were unable to report what those who remained derisively termed "the *bolshoi drap*," "the big skedaddle," with looting, stampedes to the railway station, officials fleeing in their cars, and all the time a smell of burning documents. The Germans managed to reach the gates of the city, but that was as far as they got. Stalin made his famous "Holy Russia" speech, an appeal to the people's specifically *Russian* national pride. Erskine Caldwell, who returned to London rather than go to Kuibyshev, wrote for the *Sunday Chronicle* an article confidently asserting that Moscow would survive —"no one can conquer people like these."[12]

Marooned in Kuibyshev, the correspondents passed their time playing poker and fighting with the censor and each other, well aware that as the battle for Moscow raged they were missing one of the great stories of the war. The *Daily Telegraph* had to use its correspondent in Ankara; the *Daily Dispatch* quoted "circles in Istanbul"; *The Times* was forced to quote Reuters quoting *Pravda* and *Izvestia* or to use its London-based military correspondent. But by December 22 the correspondents were back in Moscow, with the veteran A. T. Cholerton writing a long descriptive article from eyewitness accounts and other newspapers running pieces as the news emerged throughout December and January.*

Kuibyshev was a chastening experience. Some correspondents abandoned any hope of ever overcoming the Russian distrust of foreign war correspondents and moved off to the war in North Africa, where, by comparison, they felt free to do and write what they liked. The problem was that the distrust extended even to those correspondents who were so pro-Russian as to make them unfit to send objective reports had they been allowed to do so. Quentin Reynolds, for example, said frankly that being bombed "will rub the ridiculous veneer of neutrality off any hitherto objective reporter." Reynolds had let the Soviet authorities know where his sympathies were by doing the English commentary for their propaganda film *A Day in the Life of Soviet Russia*. He went to work for them in Russia on *Moscow Fights Back* and, to the annoyance of other correspondents, was appointed press attaché for the three-power Moscow conference, when Averell Harriman and Lord Beaverbrook went to see Stalin. It did not help him. "We were all anxious to glorify the Red heroes at the front, anxious to get under the skin of those magnificent people, anxious to get behind the

---

* The full story—or as full a story as it was possible to write while the war was still on—came out only a year later, on the first anniversary of the Russian victory.

scenes so we could get the feel of the whole wonderful battle the Red Army was putting up. But [nothing] could break down the distrust which Soviet officialdom felt for the American and British press."[13]

Another factor was that the Western system of a press divorced from government control was completely incomprehensible to the Soviet authorities. They believed that every foreign war correspondent was also an intelligence agent. In fact, there was ample justification for this belief. At the outbreak of the war, various British intelligence organisations recruited new staff from the ranks of journalists—in particular, from those on *The Times*. Ewan Butler, *The Times*' correspondent in Berlin before the war, and later in military intelligence himself, has said, "In those days journalists and intelligence agents were practically interchangeable."[14] Ralph Parker, war correspondent in Moscow for *The Times* and the *New York Times*, had worked for the Foreign Office's Intelligence Section in Czechoslovakia before the war, and while he was in Russia he reported to the British Ministry of Information (Soviet Relations Section) on the effectiveness of British propaganda efforts there. This was probably an innocent enough operation, but the fact that Parker used the British Embassy cipher facilities to do so must have made the Russians wonder what exactly he was up to.[15]

There is nothing intrinsically wrong with a war correspondent's deciding that he would prefer to serve his country as an intelligence agent. But to try to combine the two jobs must lead to his compromising his own journalistic integrity, endangering his journalist colleagues, and interfering with their ability to carry out their duties. The Russians, with no way of knowing which correspondents were also intelligence agents, played safe and trusted none of them.

The Battle of Moscow made it clear to many correspondents that their staying in Russia would not be worth the trouble and the expense that it would cost their newspapers. If the Russians were not even going to allow them to report what Cassidy described as "some of the best propaganda of the war," then it was useless returning to Moscow. As a result, the war correspondents' corps was eventually reduced to a handful of men determined, for various reasons, to stick it out until the end of the war, supplemented at intervals by visiting celebrities who hoped to get an interview with Stalin or a glimpse of the front. There were the agency men, who had to stay anyway to provide basic coverage—Henry Shapiro of United Press, Henry Cassidy of Associated Press, and Harold King of Reuters. And there were three others, who remained because of Russian connections—Ralph Parker of *The Times* and the *New York Times* (whose wife was Russian), Alexander Werth of the BBC and the *Sunday Times* (who was born in Leningrad), and A. T. Cholerton of the *Daily Telegraph* (who had been in Moscow for a long while before the war). Another correspondent, whose war-time term was short but distinguished, was Ed Stevens of the *Christian Science Monitor*, who had lived in Russia from 1934 to 1939 and who was married to a Russian.

These seven correspondents had one important advantage over the rest: they all spoke Russian. So although, as Stevens has said, "we got the same trips, the same touristic excursions as the others," they were far better placed to get the most from these conducted tours. Soviet citizens were forbidden during war-time to fraternise with foreigners. The first distinguishing mark of a foreigner was his inability to speak Russian. But when the seven Russian-speaking war correspondents got anywhere near the front, they grabbed any soldier they could find and questioned him for as long as he was prepared to answer. In Moscow, they were better able to appreciate the mood of the people, better able to argue with Lozovsky or the censors, better able to interpret the official communiqués, understand nuances in the Russian newspapers, and even plead for the occasional special privilege. Thus Shapiro and Werth were the first correspondents allowed into Leningrad when the siege was lifted, Cassidy wrote twice to Stalin and got an answer each time, and Parker, despite his earlier work for the British Ministry of Information, was supplied with so much inside material in Moscow that *The Times* felt it necessary to ask him to revert to reporting the Russian scene with detachment.[16] But none of them felt that they were reporting in other than a circumscribed manner or were able, as Stevens said, "to give our readers a vivid picture of Russia at war."[17] To appreciate just how circumscribed the reporting was, it is necessary to examine how these seven correspondents, acknowledged as the best of those who worked in Russia, handled the turning points of the war and, further, to look at stories that were not, at the time, reported at all.

None of these correspondents were able to write what had really happened to the German army attacking Moscow, because only the Germans knew and, for a change, they were not telling. The legend of the might of Germany's mechanised army, backed by a highly industrialised society and run with ruthless Teutonic efficiency, has been with us for so long that it is difficult to realise how poor were the German preparations for the Russian campaign. The German army invaded Russia with 3,200 tanks, and the monthly output of 80 to 100 was too low even to make good the wastage. Although this rate later went up rapidly, it did not reach its peak until August 1944, when it was already too late, and even then was only a quarter of the Russian output. The Germans had sufficient fuel for only a fraction of their transport to be motorised. The rest was moved by horses! The average German infantry division had about 1,500 horse-drawn vehicles and only about 600 motor-drawn ones, compared with some 3,000 in a British or American infantry division. The German soldier had no winter clothing, and had to make do by wearing large cotton combat overalls over his uniform and stuffing the spaces in between with crumpled newspapers or, since newsprint was scarce, with German propaganda leaflets.[18]

The Russians, on the other hand, began the war with 20,000 tanks, more than were possessed by the rest of the world put together, and they produced no fewer than 100,000 during the war.[19] They, too, used horses, but their motorised transport was adapted for winter conditions, their winter uniforms were white and, being quilted, provided excellent protection against the cold, and they possessed an adaptability to the environment that the Germans lacked. "Give a Russian an axe and a knife and in a few hours he will do anything, run up a sledge, a stretcher, a little igloo …make a stove out of a couple of old oil cans," a German medical officer wrote. "Our men just stand about miserably burning precious petrol to keep warm."[20]

Much was written later about what happened when what the Germans described as the worst winter in 140 years hit the German army in 1941–42, but little has been written about what this intense cold meant in terms of human misery. * Sentries were found frozen to death at their posts. There were 100,000 cases of frost-bite in one month, nearly 15,000 of which required one or more limbs to be amputated. Half drunk on schnapps and wracked by dysentery, the German soldier either faced the humiliation of soiling his trousers or risked death—and many so died—by having his anus congeal when he exposed it to the cold.

Hopes of a quick victory vanished; "the battle worthiness of our infantry was at an end."[21] Despite a spate of rumours in the first weeks of fighting that the German armies were already in sight of Moscow, German war correspondents were writing much more

*The Russians insist that the winter of 1941–42 was not abnormally severe and that the Germans exaggerated it to explain their defeat.

276

cautious articles. The *Frankfurter Zeitung* of July 6 said that the German soldier had for the first time met an opponent who fought back with the same weapons and who was not stunned by German tactics: "Our enemy in the East reacts in a completely different way from the French to the German tactics of wedges and pincer movements." And a correspondent in the *Völkischer Beobachter* paid tribute to the Russian resistance: "The Russian soldier surpasses our adversary in the West in his contempt for death. Endurance and fatalism make him hold out until he is blown up in his trench or falls in hand-to-hand fighting."[22]

Parties of neutral correspondents taken to Lithuania saw that, while the Germans held the cities, Russian partisans were at large in the forests and major operations would be needed to clear them out. So although the German press chief, Dr. Otto Dietrich, announced on October 9 that the war in Russia was practically finished, with only police operations remaining, German readers were unmoved. That this immobility was justified, that the German citizen had correctly interpreted what he had read in his newspapers, was confirmed on December 1, when the German high command admitted that the Russians had retaken Rostov. Neutral correspondents were told that the main bulk of the German army had had no experience of winter warfare. The German public was told nothing.

Yet again, in the same way that war correspondents in Moscow learned to understand the nuances of Soviet communiqués, the German newspaper reader understood the sudden appearance of elaborate articles explaining why there could be no comparison between the set-back to the German army and the fate of Napoleon. "The first ten weeks of war have shown that the resistance of the Russian army is tough and persistent," said a correspondent in the *Frankfurter Zeitung*. "But while the Russian generals who fought Napoleon in 1812 could withdraw to the Urals without getting into a hopeless plight, the Russian generals of today must comply with the dictates of the geographical situation. Industry and munition factories must be defended."[23]

PK correspondents were instructed to send stories and photographs showing the fate the Russians were suffering at German hands.* Restrictions on neutral correspondents now became tougher, new campaigns were launched against listening to foreign

---

* A PK cameraman, Walter Reuschl, had himself photographed with Stalin's son Jacob, captured in July, and copies of the newspaper with the photograph were dropped over the Russian lines. Stalin did not like this, and when Reuschl was taken prisoner by the Russians he disappeared and was never heard of again.

broadcasts, and there was a resumption of the anti-Semitic campaign. (Surprisingly, this produced in Berlin several small demonstrations in *favour* of the Jews.)[24]

While the winter dragged on, war-weariness grew as readers noticed a distinct change in the tone of German war correspondents' reports. A new limited aim for the war in the East was stated—"to effect such a weakening of the Russians that Bolshevism will cease to be a menace to Europe"—and descriptions began to appear of what would happen to Germany should the British and Russians win. There was criticism of "depot mentality," war-profiteers, bartering, black-marketeering, and bureaucracy—"all abominations to the German soldier in Russia."[25] In short, although the German reader was not told in exact terms what was happening on the Eastern Front, he was able to draw his own conclusions from what was reported.

The reader in the West, on the other hand, received mostly a rehash of the Russian official communiqué, which contained only what the Russian leaders felt it expedient to reveal. There would be an advance on this front, a minor set-back on that, sometimes interpreted by a military correspondent in London or by someone in Stockholm or Zurich. Sometimes these essentially military reports would be lightened by any descriptive or interpretative material the Russian-speaking correspondents managed to extract from their infrequent conducted trips to the front. But, as these correspondents would agree, for the reader it all added up to a blur of battle maps, rather than a vivid picture of a huge nation at war.

The finest war reporting of this period, perceptive, analytical, and accurate, came from an Italian, Curzio Malaparte, correspondent on the Eastern Front for *Corriere della Sera*.* Malaparte had covered the German occupation of Poland and had been disgusted by what he had seen in the Warsaw Ghetto: "The dead lay in the hallways, corridors, on the landings, the stairs, or on beds in rooms crowded with pallid and silent people. Their beards were dirty with mud and sleet...They were as hard and rigid as Chagall's dead Jews..."

Malaparte now began what was to be his first brief spell in Russia by telling his readers of the historical importance of the

---

* Malaparte's real name was Kurt Suckert. The son of a German master dyer of Prato, he fought in the First World War and was decorated by both Italy and France. Between the wars he wrote of the menace that Hitler and Stalin presented to Europe. In 1933 he was arrested for anti-Fascist activities and served three years confined to the Lipari Islands, off the coast of Sicily. He was in trouble with the Italian authorities again in 1940 for his anti-Fascist writing.

conflict. He argued that the world was witnessing a social confrontation between bourgeois powers and a working-class nation in which the "workers' ethic" that the Russian leaders had tried to implant after the 1917 Revolution would be decisive: "The Red Army is the quintessential expression of an industrially-transformed nation and will be a tough opponent for the Germans. They are two expressions of the same industrial processes." He returned to these themes again and again as he followed the German army eastwards. On July 7, 1941: "From the way the Soviet soldier fights, it is clear that the moujik of 1941 fights like a modern industrial worker rather than a moujik...the major industrial creation of Communism is not the collective farms, the giant workshops, or heavy industry, but the Red Army." In another dispatch, Malaparte noted that the Mongol tank divisions manoeuvred like Mongol cavalry. "Many young Mongols now work in Russian heavy industry. They have an extraordinary passion for machines. The former passion for horses has been replaced in Soviet Mongolia by an interest in motors, in gears, in instruments."

The Germans did not like this sort of writing and complained to the Italian authorities. In September, Malaparte was recalled to Milan, told that his dispatches were defeatist, and threatened with exile to the Lipari Islands again. But when his predictions of Russian resistance proved correct, his friends interceded on his behalf, and *Corriere della Sera* managed to send him to join the Finnish troops outside Leningrad, where it was thought he would be safely out of the way of the Germans.

Moscow's danger had distracted attention from Leningrad, the fall of which Hitler considered more important than the capture of the capital. Destroy Leningrad and Stalingrad, the breeding grounds of Bolshevism, he had said, and Russian resistance would collapse. Accordingly, General Wilhelm von Leeb's Army Group North, after two months of swift, destructive blitzkrieg, stood outside the city in August 1941 ready for the final blow. Then Hitler changed his mind. Leningrad was to be encircled and starved into submission. So the siege began, 900 days of slow starvation, more than a million dead in a ghost city caught unprepared—a terrible story of corpses, cannibalism, and political manoeuvring never fully revealed until the 1960's. At the time no one outside Leningrad knew about the situation, because the communiqués the Western correspondents received in Moscow were dry, matter-of-fact, and without description.

Germans read in their newspapers in mid-September that all

fortification lines around Leningrad had been pierced, but at the same time it was admitted that the defences were amazingly strong and progress was slow. Then correspondents in Berlin were told that Leningrad was now strategically unimportant, and then nothing more was said. Again it was Malaparte, in *Corriere della Sera*, who first foresaw what was going to happen and succeeded in getting his story into his newspaper. On September 27 he wrote:

> Every one of Leningrad's 100,000 houses has been converted into a fort. The Germans will have to overcome fierce resistance in each one. Russian warships take part in fighting the German artillery. Every day fresh Soviet tank squadrons launch counter-attacks from dawn to dusk. The countryside is a nursery of mines. Mines are placed everywhere—in isolated houses, public buildings and private dwellings. They are in sofas, telephones, drawers, under carpets. They explode when the light is switched on. Three weeks of fighting around the city has only been the beginning.

In his earlier reports from the Ukraine, Malaparte had described finding a map of Leningrad with all the tactical dispositions of the October Revolution marked on it. In April 1942, from the Finnish lines ten miles outside the city, he wrote: "That map could be used today to indicate the fundamental elements of the defence of Leningrad…the physiognomy of the city's defence is more political than military. The exceptional importance of Leningrad as capital of the October revolution and citadel of Communist extremism imposes this special political and social character on its defence."

Leningrad was saved by the "Ladoga Life-line," convoys of food taken across Lake Ladoga by boat in the summer and over the ice in the winter, but the line did not function effectively until February 1942, when the winter famine had already caused immense suffering. Malaparte, working on a novel, *Kaputt*, a vast fresco of Europe in ruins, went out on the lake as the spring thaw of 1942 started and sent an emotional story to *Corriere della Sera* about the cost of opening this life-line to Leningrad. He had been walking over the ice looking down into the lake as though through a window.

> Under my shoes, imprinted in the ice as in transparent crystal, was a line of beautiful human faces, a line of glass masks like a Byzantine icon. They were looking at me, staring at me. The lips were narrow and worn, the hair long, the noses sharp, the eyes large and very clear. They were the images of Soviet soldiers who had fallen in the attempt to cross the lake. Their poor bodies, impris-

oned all winter by the ice, had been swept away by the first spring currents. But their faces remained printed in the pure, green-blue crystal. They watched me serenely and it even seemed as if they tried to follow me with their eyes.

The Russians allowed two Western correspondents to visit Leningrad during the siege—Henry Shapiro and Alexander Werth. Shapiro went in September 1943 and Werth a few weeks later. Werth wrote: "Only the fittest have survived. The weaker have died or gone away. But among the fittest citizens of Leningrad are the many thousands of children who continue to live there."[26]

The German ring around the city was finally broken in January 1944, and the Russians flew in the Western correspondents from Moscow. But even then lack of time, censorship, the pressure of other events, and a Russian unwillingness to give the siege too much prominence—this attitude reached a climax after the war, when Stalin eliminated Leningrad's personality cult by "eliminating" its defence leaders—meant that little of the real story emerged. Harrison E. Salisbury, there for the United Press late in January, wrote in 1962: "This was the greatest and longest siege endured by a modern city, a time of trial, suffering and heroism that reached peaks of tragedy and bravery almost beyond our power to comprehend. Even in the Soviet Union the epic of Leningrad has received only modest attention compared with that devoted to Stalingrad and the Battle of Moscow. And in the West not one person in fifty who thrilled to the courage of the Londoners in the Battle of Britain is cognisant of that of the Leningraders."[27] So in 1969 Salisbury proved his point by writing *The Siege of Leningrad*, a 600-page account embracing 300 to 400 individual Russians' personal experiences. The book was an immediate best seller, and for the first time, a quarter of a century after the event, the full story of what happened in Leningrad during the war finally emerged.

During the period of the war when Russian fortunes were at a low point, the anti-German outpourings of Ilya Ehrenburg reached a peak. He began to write about "two-legged animals who have mastered the technique of war," "ersatz men" who "in outward appearance reminded one of a civilised European, but who in actual fact would offend the morals of an inhabitant of the Sandwich Islands."[28] Alexander Werth saw this later as "near racialist," but he was in no position to criticise Ehrenburg at the time, because Werth himself had written, in the *Sunday Times*, of the "fanaticism, bestiality and lack of normal human reflexes" of the German soldier and had described two German airmen he had seen as "disgusting pieces of inhumanity."[29] Ed Stevens, then the *Christian Science Monitor*'s correspondent, who knew Ehrenburg, has said, "Being Jewish, Ehrenburg felt very strongly about the Nazis, tended to stress their atrocities, and was reluctant to distinguish between good and bad Germans. In this he deviated from the party line."[30] But deviation from the party line over a long period was not possible, and so the only conclusion one can reach is that the Soviet authorities, while officially taking the line that the Fascists, and not the German people, were responsible for the war, felt that a little emotional anti-German propaganda at a time when Russian fortunes were at a low ebb could only help the situation.

At least Western war correspondents had been allowed into Leningrad during the siege; at Stalingrad there were only Russian and German war correspondents. The Germans brought a party of Japanese, Spanish, Italian, French, and Rumanian war correspondents to the rear of the German lines ready to cover the fall of the city, but early in October 1942, after having waited for nearly a month and with Stalingrad holding firm, they took them back to Berlin. Some Russians were in Stalingrad off and on—Konstantin Simonov and Olender of *Red Star* and Rosovsky of *Izvestia*. But one, Vassily Grossman of *Red Star*, was there throughout the entire battle. Grossman's literary style tended to be flowery and his dispatches of little use to Western correspondents hungry for facts. "Our soldiers have conquered the sun, they have conquered the daylight, they have conquered the right to walk erect over Stalingrad soil," Grossman wrote. "The Germans are now hiding among the stone ruins and there is no sun for them. Their food ration is 100 grams of bread and a little horseflesh. There, like savages overgrown with wool, they sit in their stone caves gnawing at a horse's bone—down there in the muddy darkness among the ruins of a beautiful city they have destroyed, among the dead workshops that were once the pride of our Soviet country. Here among the dark, cold ruins, with no water, and only scraps of horseflesh to eat, they will meet with vengeance; they will meet with it under the cruel stars of the Russian winter night."[31] Simonov, who later wrote a best-selling novel about Stalingrad, at the time concentrated on analytical reports for *Red Star*, and these formed the basis of the dispatches most Western correspondents sent on the battle.

German correspondents' reports made up in frankness what

they lacked in facts and description. "The ranks are thinning," one correspondent wrote in mid-September. "Fighting goes on by day and night. Death has ceased to appall the German soldier on the Russian front; he now regards it as his inescapable fate." All the German correspondents wrote of the effectiveness of the Russian artillery, firing from the left bank of the Volga and from the centre of Stalingrad. One said that doctors at field hospitals were so busy that they often collapsed from sheer fatigue.

But the best straight descriptions of the hell of Stalingrad appear not in contemporary reporting from either side, but in the diaries of ordinary soldiers. A German private noted on September 16: "The grain in the elevator is burning. The Russians seem to have set alight to it themselves. Barbarism! The battalion is suffering heavy losses. There are not more than sixty men left in each company. The elevator is occupied not by men, but by devils that no flames or bullets can destroy." And on September 18: "Fighting is going on inside the elevator. If all the buildings of Stalingrad are defended like this, then none of our soldiers will get back to Germany."

The Russians did defend each building like this. In foundries, factories, houses, and shops, the Germans found themselves fighting for each yard of territory. "We have fought fifteen days for a single house," a German lieutenant wrote in October. "Already by the third day, fifty-four German corpses were strewn in the cellars, on the landings and the staircases...Ask any soldier what half-an-hour of hand-to-hand struggle means. Then imagine Stalingrad: eighty days and eighty nights of hand-to-hand struggles. Animals flee this hell; the hardest stones cannot bear it for long; only men endure."

The Germans endured, but they had spent the flower of the Wehrmacht in the attack, and now, battered and exhausted, they could only try to stay alive. A further major offensive was out of the question. The Russians completed their encirclement of Stalingrad and waited for the Germans to grow weak. Throughout December and early January, conditions became deplorable. "Only twenty to thirty cartridges a day were distributed with the order to use them solely to repulse an attack," one German soldier wrote. "The ration of bread was reduced to a slice. Water came from melted snow. A kilogram box of potatoes had to make do for fifteen men. There was no meat. We ate our horses at Christmas."[32]

Sensing that Stalingrad contained this sort of story, the Western correspondents did their best to get there. A party of eleven, including Alexander Werth and Henry Shapiro, was taken on a conducted tour of the area. The closest they were allowed to Stalingrad itself was some sixty miles away. But even to have been *near* Stalingrad was news. The *Daily Dispatch*, one of the Kemsley Group, for which Werth worked, described his story as "one of the most graphic despatches of the war" and splashed it with the headline I TOURED THE STALINGRAD BATTLE AREA. Yet Werth wrote: "It was not possible to visit Stalingrad itself, but we were near it. We heard from some miles south of the city the guns of Stalingrad as, at nightfall, we crossed a pontoon bridge over the half-frozen Volga, and in the sky in the north there was a faint halo of light."[33] This might appear rather thin material to become excited about, but it was an improvement on what the correspondents had been sending earlier. Back in September, Werth had been reduced to writing: "Moscow, Sunday: I have just seen a man who was in Stalingrad on Friday. 'The spirit of the Russian troops is the most inspiring thing I have ever seen,' he told me."[34] And Ralph Parker sent a whole column to *The Times* and the *New York Times* in mid-October that was a verbatim quotation from a *Pravda* correspondent's dispatch. Even the run-up to the Russian victory did not get the coverage it should have. On January 8 the Russians delivered an ultimatum to General Friedrich von Paulus, commander of the German Sixth Army in Stalingrad, calling on him to surrender, but the text of the document was made public only after it was no longer interesting as news.

The actual surrender, on February 2, was reported round the world. The Russian newspapers published photographs of von Paulus signing the terms of surrender and of the 90,000 German prisoners winding their way like long black serpents across the ice-covered Volga. Germany made no attempt to minimise the disaster. The newspapers published the special communiqué from Hitler's headquarters announcing the end of the Sixth Army, four days of mourning were decreed, and the radio played Uhland's moving soldier's song, "*Ich hatt' einen Kamaraden*," at frequent intervals. The idea seems to have been to tell the truth about the loss of the Sixth Army, but to emphasise the line "their sacrifice has not been in vain."[35]

On February 4 the Russians at last took twenty foreign war correspondents, the largest party allowed anywhere since the start of the war, to Stalingrad. Outside the city they were first shown the eight German generals who had surrendered (Hitler had made von Paulus a field-marshal just before the fall of Stalingrad) and were allowed to conduct a rather strange interview with them. The correspondents were told that it would be up to each general to decide whether he wanted to answer questions. In any case, no correspondent would be allowed to enter a general's room, but would have to speak to him from the corridor, through the open door. The stories the correspondents wrote were—quite correctly—lost in the pressure of harder news, but Werth's exchange with the arrogant Dietloff von Arnim is worth recalling. Werth, mindful of reports of German atrocities in occupied Soviet territory and of the treatment of Russian prisoners (2 million died in camps), asked von Arnim how the Russians were treating him. "The officers are correct," von Arnim said. "But the soldiers are impudent, thieving swine. I had four suitcases and they stole them all."[36]

In Stalingrad itself the correspondents were able to get an idea of the story they had missed. Werth wrote:

> At the far end of a yard I caught sight of a human figure. He had been crouching over a cesspool and now, noticing us, he was hastily pulling up his pants, and then he slunk away into the door of a basement. But as he passed I caught a glimpse of the wretch's face—with its mixture of suffering and idiot-like incomprehension. For a moment I wished the whole of Germany were there to see it. The man was perhaps already dying. In that basement into which he slunk there were still 200 Germans—dying of hunger and frostbite. 'We haven't had time to deal with them yet' one of the Russians said. 'They'll be taken away tomorrow, I suppose'. At the end of the yard, behind a low stone wall, the yellow corpses of skinny Germans were piled up—men who had died in that basement— about a dozen wax-like dummies. I remembered the long anxious days of 1942, the nights of the London blitz, the photographs of Hitler smirking as he stood on the steps of the Madeleine in Paris, and the weary days of '38 and '39 when a jittery Europe would tune in to Berlin and hear Hitler's yells accompanied by the roar of the German mob. And there seemed a rough but divine justice in those frozen cesspools with their diarrhoea, and those horses' bones, and those starved yellow corpses in the yard of the Red Army House at Stalingrad.[37]

Was Stalingrad the turning point of the war? It certainly has a greater claim than the side-show at El Alamein, a fact sensed, rather than recognised, in the lavish celebrations for Stalingrad's twenty-fifth anniversary (of its renaming) that went on all over Britain soon after the Russian victory.*

* The Russian ambassador reported, however, that already some sections of the British public were worried that the Russians would now be able to reach Berlin first.

But there was another battle that deserves the title. This is the Battle of Kursk. Sandwiched in time scale between Stalingrad and the Allied invasion of Sicily, this massive struggle, the real military turning point of the war, went unreported and unrealised in the West, and even today is little known. A head-on clash between two mechanised armies, with some 6,000 tanks and 4,000 planes involved, the Battle of Kursk was fought in six days over a narrow front, a tiny area of concentrated carnage that was left littered with burnt-out tanks, wrecked planes, and thousands of German and Russian corpses.

Kursk was a direct trial of strength between the new German tanks, the Tigers and the Panthers, and the Russian T-34s, a colossal battle of attrition in First World War style, in which fire-power and military morale, rather than leadership, were the crucial factors. It was vital for the Germans to win, not only for political reasons—Hitler desperately needed a victory to counter the Russian success at Stalingrad—but for military ones as well. If this enormous concentration of German military might could not break the Russians, nothing would.

On July 5, 1943, the greatest armoured battle in the history of warfare began at sunrise. The first news of the fighting came from Moscow, where the communiqué that evening, flat and unemotional though it was, contained the startling sentence "Preliminary reports show that our troops…have crippled or destroyed 586 enemy tanks…203 enemy planes have been shot down."[38] There had never been anything like this level of success in one day. The final battle, on July 12, was an eight-hour head-on collision between the remaining 600 German tanks and the Soviet Fifth Army. It ended in a Russian victory. The German losses were put at 70,000 men, 2,000 tanks, 1,392 planes, and 5,000 motor vehicles. The Russians have never revealed their losses, but they, too, must have been enormous. A German PK cameraman took some remarkable shots of the battle, but he was captured, and the Russians did not release his film until 1972, when it appeared, for the first time in the West, in a British television documentary.[39]

In this huge battle, remarkable examples of courage and fortitude occurred on both sides, but it was the fate of such stories to be lost until after the war, because the Russians were too busy celebrating with victory salvoes what they now knew to be the beginning of the end and because, in the West, Stalingrad, though still fresh in the mind, gave way to news of the Allied invasion of Sicily. Kursk, in between the two, went unreported.

There were other events of note on the Eastern Front that went unreported. One of the strangest events concerned the fate of the first big shuttle raid by Flying Fortresses of the United States Air Force, in June 1944. The idea was that the giant bombers would fly over Germany from bases in Italy, drop their bombs on Hungarian and Rumanian targets, land at bases the Americans had established in the Ukraine, and then fly back to Italy, dropping more bombs on the way. The Russians did not like this. They did not like the idea of American bases on Russian soil, and they were reluctant to allow Ukrainians in the war-devastated areas around the bases to mix with American servicemen, with their high standard of living.

The principal base was at Poltava, and to witness the beginning of this example of Soviet-American solidarity the foreign correspondents in Moscow were taken on a tour of the base to see the first Fortresses, seventy of them, fly in.

A German spotter plane had trailed the bombers to the base, but, inexplicably, the Russians made no attempt to provide adequate anti-aircraft or fighter cover. So in the surprise night raid the Germans succeeded in knocking out forty-nine Flying Fortresses on the ground and in killing two Americans and thirty Russians. The Russians were embarrassed at having failed to protect the base properly and were relieved when the United States censors agreed that no news of the German raid should be released. Ed Stevens, who had been at Poltava but had left to return to Moscow before the raid, says he managed to write something about it some months later, but the American war commentator Fletcher Pratt claims that it was not until 1945, when W. L. White told the story in *Report on the Russians*, that American readers learned of the extent of the disaster.[40]

The recapture of Sevastopol in 1944 was reported as a "German Dunkirk." Trapped, the Germans surrendered or were blown to pieces, losing between 60,000 and 100,000 men—the first the German figure, the second the Russian. Foreign war correspondents were allowed to make a brief tour of the liberated city. "You couldn't walk more than a yard or two in any direction without stepping on a body," wrote Harrison Salisbury. "The city itself is rubble. In a ninety-minute drive through the streets, I saw only five buildings which appear to be habitable. [The Mayor] estimated that 10,000 civilians remain from the pre-war population of 100,000. I saw only thirty."[41]

But the real story at Sevastopol was of how the Soviet authorities treated collaborators. The Crimean Tartars had welcomed the arrival of the Germans. They had hunted down Russian soldiers in disguise, had formed a police force under German control, had been active in the Gestapo, and had supplied the Wehrmacht with soldiers. Now the moment of reckoning had arrived. The whole Crimean Tartar community of something between 300,000 and 500,000 men, women, and children was rounded up and sent into exile in Central Asia, and they have never been allowed to return.[42]

This episode raises the whole question of collaboration with the Germans by other Soviet communities, a story never reported at the time, for obvious reasons, and even now a highly sensitive issue in Russia. For the fact is that, had Hitler not been so intent on implementing his racist policies in the conquered eastern territories, he might have won the support of Ukrainians and the non-Slav peoples of the Soviet Union and have turned them all against Stalin. If this had happened, then the outcome of the war might well have been different. As it was, some 800,000 members of these and other nationalities, all citizens of the USSR, served with the German forces.

Opposition to Stalin in parts of the Soviet Union was so strong that Red Army prisoners and civilians in German-occupied areas began by helping the Wehrmacht with menial tasks. This presently extended to the bearing of arms against their former comrades, and before long there was hardly a German unit in the forward areas that did not have a number of Russian troops in German uniform on its strength. The Germans used Cossacks to hunt Tito's partisans in Yugoslavia, Ukrainians to man pill-boxes along the Atlantic Wall, and Russians to help suppress anti-Fascist movements in Italy. And early in 1945 they accepted a scheme put forward by a captured Russian general, Andrey Andreyevich Vlasov, for the recruitment of a "Russian Liberation Army" of two divisions, under the command of Vlasov himself, to fight on the Eastern Front. This "army" was defeated and its soldiers either captured by the Red Army or taken by British or American troops, who handed them over to the Russians. In 1946 Vlasov was hanged in Moscow, many thousands of his men having already been shot.[43]

It is understandable, perhaps, that foreign war correspondents who learned of Soviet citizens serving Hitler decided, in the interests of the Allied cause, not to write the story. But it is less easy to explain why one American, Quentin Reynolds, went out of his way to state that there were *no* collaborators in Russia. *

Finally, the story of the Katyn Forest massacre illustrates the extreme difficulty that foreign war correspondents experienced in working in the Soviet Union during the war. On January 15, 1944, a large group of Western correspondents, including Werth and Stevens, accompanied by Kathie Harriman, daughter of the American Ambassador, Averell Harriman, was taken to look at hundreds of bodies in Polish uniforms that had been dug up at Katyn Forest by the Russians. It was said that 10,000 were buried there. The aim of the official investigation by the Russians was ostensibly to establish whether the Poles had been shot when prisoners of the Russians in the spring of 1940 or when prisoners of the Germans in the summer or autumn of 1941.

The correspondents went with the hope of being able to send stories announcing that the truth had been established, or at least to present their own conclusions on the evidence before them. Instead, they were placed in an impossible position. They were allowed to attend only one session of the enquiry, they were not allowed to interview any of the witnesses, and they were prevented from writing any comment or weighing or assessing the evidence in any way at all. Even implied criticism of the way the Russians had conducted the enquiry was censored from their reports. Since the Katyn Forest massacre was not news in itself—the Germans had revealed the existence of the mass graves in April 1943 and had blamed the Russians—all that a Western reader got from the correspondents now was the official Russian version, that the Germans were the killers. And, although many correspondents felt that the evidence supporting the Russian version was not very impressive, it is by no means certain that they would have written this even if they had been at liberty to do so. "To suggest that the Russian case was as bad as Goebbels's case, or even worse," Werth wrote later, "was something one couldn't do in wartime. It was imperative not to play into the Germans' hands."[44]

With the Germans on the run, it was inevitable that the war

---

* In his book *Only the Stars Are Neutral*, written after ten weeks in Russia in 1941, Reynolds said: "Today there is not one Fifth Columnist, not one Quisling at liberty in Soviet Russia. The Germans tried desperately to set up local tribunals with local citizens as nominal heads of the tribunals when they captured cities like Odessa, Kiev and others which fell to them during their successful march through the south last autumn. But in no case were they successful. Potential Quislings were all in the work camps of the far north. Stalin knew what he was doing back in 1938. Russia's magnificent unity today and her completely unbroken spirit after the dreadful tragedy of that German advance is proof of the fact that Russia accepted the purge and approved of Stalin's 'You can't make an omelette without breaking eggs' policy."

correspondents with the PK—12,000 strong at the height of the Russian campaign—had to take on a new rôle. Many had lost the confidence of German readers through their optimistic reports of progress on the Eastern Front. Stalingrad now brought to a head a long-smouldering enmity between the Propaganda Ministry and the Wehrmacht high command. The *Operativer* correspondents, often former reserve officers, resented what they called the "hurrah, hurrah" reporting of the ardent Nazi PK men. After the Stalingrad defeat, Goebbels market-tested each correspondent's reader following. He must have been alarmed to find that the *Operativer* correspondents, mostly journalists of the pre-Nazi era, were both more widely read and considered by their readers to be more trustworthy. So the more influential of these were moved from the Eastern Front, some to France, some to Italy, leaving the Nazi PK men facing the Russians free to concentrate on their new rôle.[45] No longer would they be writing about victories. Their task now would be to play down retreats, minimise losses, and steel the German nation for bitter resistance.

On the Russians' side, the tide of war having turned, one would have also expected changes. Now, surely, the Soviet authorities would allow Western war correspondents to cover the successes of the Red Army. They did not. The Russian authorities remained as suspicious of Western correspondents during the storming of Berlin in 1945 as they had been in the first days of the war. Given this, and the other difficulties of working in the Soviet Union, it is not surprising that the war in Russia was so poorly covered and produced so few worthwhile correspondents. Malcolm Muggeridge, who was a correspondent in Moscow after the war, summed up the difficulties: "Strongly partisan feelings one way or the other are almost unavoidable. The pressure of the regime's own propaganda is so strong you either largely succumb to it, or feel constrained to adopt a position of dedicated opposition."[46] Werth succumbed, but his reporting carried a depth that others' lacked, and his massive book, *Russia at War*, published in 1964, included all the material he had not written or had not been allowed to write in the war years. He was frank about his pro-Russian sentiments, and some of his anger against the Cold War warriors in the West is understandable.*

Ralph Parker succumbed, despite his early war-time work for

---

* Just before he died, in Paris in 1969, he revealed why he had resigned from the *Sunday Times* when his professional status was at its peak. On his return to London in October 1945, Lord Kemsley, the paper's proprietor, asked him to dinner. Werth was expressing his admiration for the Russian war effort when

the British government. The keenness with which he described the Russian struggle attracted the attention of the Soviet authorities, and he decided that his future was in Russia, rather than in the West. The *New York Times* had dropped him in 1943 for "pro-Soviet bias" and had replaced him with Bill Lawrence, and in 1947 *The Times*, too, asked for his resignation. Thereafter he worked as a free-lance for a number of newspapers, including the American and the British *Daily Worker*. At the height of the Cold War, he published a pamphlet accusing British diplomats of spying—an allegation that, no doubt, contained some degree of truth. In his later years he translated Alexander Solzhenitsyn's *One Day in the Life of Ivan Denisovitch* and represented Sol Hurok, the New York theatrical entrepreneur, in Russia. He died in 1964.

Ed Stevens left the Soviet Union in July 1944, went back from 1946 to 1949, spent six years in the fifties as Mediterranean bureau chief, based in Rome, for the *Christian Science Monitor*, and then returned to Moscow, where he represented, among other papers, *The Times* and the *Sunday Times* of London and *Newsday* of Long Island. Henry Shapiro stayed on until 1973, when, after forty years of reporting the Russian scene, he went back to the United States. His final opinion on working in Russia was: "Anyone who believes in advocacy journalism should not work here. If you take sides, become emotionally involved, you become a crusader. Look upon this place as a laboratory. Look on the negative and the positive. But the minute a newsman takes sides, he stops being a reporter."[47] Curzio Malaparte, the Italian correspondent, whose writing on Russia ranked among the best, died in 1957.

Of the Russians, Ehrenburg died in 1967. Some of the other correspondents are still living, but Lozovsky, the Soviet spokesman who had been in control of the correspondents in the early part of the war, fell foul of Stalin and was shot in 1949.

another guest, the Minister of Supply, Sir Andrew Duncan, suddenly said, "The only solution is to drop the atom bomb on Moscow." Werth agreed later "it was not Lord Kemsley's fault that some of his friends cherished such monstrous ideas," but he resigned anyway.

## Chapter Twelve

# Remember Pearl Harbour
# 1937–1945

In this nation of ours, the final political decisions rest with the people. And the people, so that they may make up their minds, must be given the facts, even in time of war, or perhaps especially in time of war...

> —Paul Scott Mowrer, editor of the *Chicago Daily News*
> and one-time war correspondent

I wouldn't tell the people anything until the war is over and then I'd tell them who won.

> —Military censor,
> at a meeting in Washington

———

Japan had been on the offensive in China since 1931. In that year she had invaded Manchuria and had cut off the three north-eastern provinces from the rest of the country.

In 1937 she moved to take over the five northern provinces, but China resisted, and soon the war spread over the length and breadth of the country. For war correspondents, it was a brief return to the Golden Age. The war was ruthless, bloody, and dramatic, and yet, for British and American correspondents, comparatively easy to cover, with expense no object. Once again correspondents set out from London with gold sovereigns in money belts, but this time on chartered flights—London to Shanghai via Singapore, £3,000. The headlines were worth it: CANTON BOMBED— PEOPLE GO MAD WITH TERROR, said the *London Evening News* of September 23, 1937. "The most terrible air-raid in history took place today...The majority of the bombs fell in the densely-packed dwelling areas of the poorer classes, reducing buildings to dust and their occupants to mincemeat," wrote Reuters correspondent Geoffrey Imerson. "Corpses are as thick as flies on fly paper in the summer-time. Limbs and mutilated bodies are piled high in utter confusion...It is as if gigantic ghastly abattoirs have been created."

British and American newspapers clamoured for eye-witness accounts like this. It was all far away from London and New York, and Herbert Matthews' "long, long arm of war" had not yet reached out to the strollers along the Great White Way of peaceful America. The news in China was there for the writing: bombing raids—"the greatest the world has ever known"; attacks on British and American gunboats; poison gas—"green clouds hang over the front"; and, in November 1937, the Battle of Shanghai—"the world's greatest drama," recalled to many even today by the photograph of a Chinese baby sitting in the bombed-out ruins of the railway station.

There were two cities in Shanghai, Greater Shanghai and the European-dominated International Settlement. While nearly a million Japanese and Chinese fought in Greater Shanghai, the war correspondents had a ringside seat in the International Settlement. "It was," wrote Edgar Snow, the American correspondent, working then for the *London Daily Herald*, "as though Verdun had happened on the Seine in full view of a Right-bank Paris that was neutral, as though Gettysburg were fought in Harlem while the rest of Manhattan remained a non-belligerent observer."[1]

In the mornings the correspondents would go out behind the Chinese lines in their cars (the thrifty Swedish correspondent, Eric Nystrom, took a bus). They would return to the Settlement in time for lunch, drive down to the Japanese front in the afternoon, rush back for the evening Chinese and Japanese press conferences, write their copy before dinner, and dispatch it through the Settlement telegraph office, certain that it would reach London or New York in a matter of hours. For a break in this routine, they could sit in the Park Hotel, drinks in hand, and watch the Japanese divebombers, or go up on the roofs of apartment blocks and see Japanese gun batteries in action. It was not entirely without risk, and on November

11, the last day of the Chinese stand, Pembroke Stephens, the *Daily Telegraph* man, who had survived the Spanish Civil War, was shot in the head and groin in the last hour of the battle and died instantly. O. D. Gallagher wrote the story for the *Daily Express* and sent it to Stephens' own paper: "I couldn't scoop him on his own obituary."[2] It all happened at such close quarters that a film cameraman who captured the whole action found that on the screen it looked like a Hollywood movie.

Another correspondent, an Italian Fascist, Sandro Sandri, was killed when Japanese dive-bombers sank the American gunboat *Panay* in the river Yangtze. Luigi Barzini wrote the story for *Corriere della Sera*. "Sandri was lying on the ground with his jacket open and his shirt lifted away from the wounds. There were two red holes but they did not bleed. He said to me: 'They've killed me this time. What an end. In another nation's ship, in this country.' "[3] Barzini's story was given prominence in Italy, and the angry editor of *La Stampa* of Turin cabled his correspondent, Sandro Volta, SANDRI DEAD, BARZINI MAGNIFICENT, WHERE WERE YOU—a cry echoed by many an editor later in the war.

With eye-witness and personal-exploit stories at a premium, only one correspondent looked beyond the immediate story to what was really happening in China—Edgar Snow. Snow had arrived in China in 1928, and in his long spell there he worked at various times for the *China Weekly Review*, the *Chicago Tribune*, the *New York Herald Tribune*, the *Saturday Evening Post*, and the *London Daily Herald*. He was the first foreign correspondent to make the trip to Red Army headquarters, where he met Mao Tse-tung and Chou En-lai, personal contacts that lasted until Snow's death in 1972. His account of the meeting, printed in the *China Weekly Review* and then widely reprinted, gave the world the first news of the Long March and the first idea of the Communist leaders, their life, and their intentions. Snow saw the hypocrisy of the British and American expressions of sympathy at what was occurring in China. Although newspapers gave prominence to the Japanese aggression, they did not write that the United States was the main supplier of war materials to Japan until as late as July 1939. They did not mention the British companies that had contracts to supply the Japanese in China or the common British view that Chinese resistance was delaying a restoration of trade in the area. Snow saw through Chiang Kai-shek's publicity, arranged for him by Hollington K. Tong, a graduate of the Columbia School of Journalism, to the corruption and brutality of the Nationalist regime, and he documented Chiang's ruthless suppression of Chinese trade unions. He even saw beyond the immediate horror of the rape of Nanking (when 300,000 Chinese civilians were murdered by Japanese soldiers in an orgy of rape and plunder) to the fact that this would lessen political antagonisms between various Chinese groups and intensify the opposition to Japan. You cannot disembowel men at one end of the town, he wrote, while preaching Pan-Asianism at the other.

While the war in China puzzled other correspondents, accustomed to war in the West's terms of seeking a quick decision, Snow saw that the very flexibility of the Chinese Communist resistance, its lack of a visible strategy, would turn out to be its strength. He warned that Japan's advance through China would bring her to the doors of the Western colonies, and of the threat of war that this would involve. And, before Pearl Harbor, he warned that the United States would sooner or later have to decide on its war aims: did it plan to line up with its allies' concepts of empire, or was it to fight for democracy for everyone?

When war broke out in Europe, it was doubtful whether the United States would fight at all. There was strong resistance to sending American soldiers overseas again, and, even if this feeling changed, the United States Army was in no state to go, ranking only nineteenth among the world's armed forces, after Portugal but barely ahead of Bulgaria. Furious efforts to improve the country's defence capacity began. Japan was seen as the major danger, but was seriously underrated. General George C. Marshall, Chief of Staff of the United States Army, told the seven correspondents at a secret press conference in Washington on November 15, 1941, that if war started America would be in a position to "set the paper cities of Japan on fire" with massive air-raids. Throughout the conference—which, for obvious reasons, remained unreported until after the war—General Marshall never once mentioned the possibility of a Japanese attack on Pearl Harbor. It was, he later testified, "the one place we felt reasonably secure."[4]

The shock of December 7 can, therefore, be well imagined. When the last Japanese plane roared off, five American battleships had been sunk and three damaged, three cruisers and three destroyers badly hit, 200 planes destroyed, and 2,344 men killed. For the loss of only twenty-nine planes, Japan had virtually crippled the U.S. Pacific Fleet at a single blow.

The American service chiefs immediately decided that news of a disaster of such magnitude would prove unacceptable to the American people, and steps were taken to ensure that they did not learn about it. So effective were these measures that the truth about Pearl Harbor was still being concealed even after the war ended. The cover-up began with an "iron curtain" of censorship that cut off the United Press office in Honolulu from San Francisco in the middle of its first excited telephone report. So drastic was the suppression of news that nothing further, except for official communiqués, came out of Pearl Harbor for another four days.[5] These claimed that only one "old" battleship and a destroyer had been sunk and other ships damaged, and that heavy casualties had been inflicted on the Japanese. It cannot be argued that these lies were necessary to conceal from the Japanese the extent of the disaster they had inflicted on the U.S. Pacific Fleet. The Japanese knew exactly how much damage they had done, and reports in Tokyo newspapers accurately stating the American losses meant that the Americans knew that the Japanese knew. The American censorship was to prevent the American public from learning the gravity of the blow. *

After flying to Hawaii on a tour of inspection, the Secretary of the Navy, Colonel Frank Knox, held a press conference in New York at which, with President Roosevelt's approval, he gave the impression he was revealing the full extent of the American losses at Pearl Harbor. Colonel Knox told correspondents that one United States battleship, the *Arizona*, had been lost and the battleship *Oklahoma* had capsized but could be righted. This must have made strange reading for anyone actually at Pearl Harbor, who had only to lift his eye from his newspaper to see five United States battleship—the *Arizona*, the *Oklahoma*, the *California*, the *Nevada*, and the *West Virginia*—resting on the bottom. Colonel Knox then went on to say that the entire balance of the Pacific Fleet "with its aircraft carriers, heavy cruisers, light cruisers, destroyers and submarines is uninjured and is all at sea seeking contact with the enemy."[6]

This list did not mention battleships because, of the nine in the Pacific Fleet, five had been sunk and three damaged, and one was in a navy shipyard unready for sea. Three battleships from the

---

* British readers were even worse served. Early newspaper reports actually gave the impression that Pearl Harbor had been an American victory. JAP PLANE CARRIER AND FOUR U-BOATS SUNK, said a *Daily Express* headline on December 8. "The main U.S. Pacific Fleet is heavily engaged with a Japanese battle fleet, which includes several carriers, just off Pearl Harbour, its Hawaii base. Washington reports late tonight say that one Japanese aircraft carrier and four submarines have already been destroyed by the American forces off Hawaii."

Atlantic—the *New Mexico*, the *Mississippi*, and the *Idaho*—were still en route to the Pacific Fleet. But when one correspondent asked whether the fleet seeking contact with the Japanese also included battleships, Colonel Knox answered that it did. No one embarrassed Colonel Knox by asking which battleships, and American newspapers allowed Knox's figures to pass unchallenged. In Britain, *The Times* greeted this exercise in deception with warm applause. "The full disclosure of losses made by the Secretary of the Navy has had a wholly steadying effect. Americans are no more afraid of the truth than Britons, and as free men they have the right to know it, secure in the confidence that they are not to be stampeded either by triumph or disaster. It is only tyrants who must keep their people in the dark."[7]

A year later, on the eve of the anniversary of the attack, the United States Navy felt that it could be somewhat more honest, and issued new loss figures. It now said that five battleships had been "sunk or damaged," but this still evaded the issue, because it gave no breakdown of the figure, and the public was still in the dark as to how many of the five had been sunk and how many only damaged. The evasion continued even after the war. In 1945, the semi-official *War in Outline*, published by the *Infantry Journal* for members of the United States armed forces, perpetuated the legend that the only battleship sunk at Pearl Harbor was the *Arizona*. And as late as 1966 *The Reports of General MacArthur* used the confusing "sunk or damaged" formula, but with the figure now increased to eight.* [8]

The way the disaster at Pearl Harbor was concealed was only the beginning, for suddenly Japan appeared to be unstoppable: Singapore, Hong Kong, Manila, Borneo, New Guinea, Java. By May 6, 1942, the last Americans in the Philippines had surrendered at Corregidor; by May 15 the British had been run out of Burma. In five and a half months the Japanese had seized the richest colonial area

---

* News of America's killing in 1943 of Admiral Isoroku Yamamoto, the man who had planned the Pearl Harbor attack, was suppressed until after the war. The United States had cracked the Japanese codes and learnt Yamamoto's exact itinerary. Colonel Knox signalled a fighter group at Guadalcanal, ordering it to kill Yamamoto and adding, "President attaches extreme importance this operation." The American fighters caught Yamamoto's bomber near Bougainville on the morning of April 18 and shot it down in flames. It then became imperative that nothing about the attack be published, because it could reveal to the Japanese that the United States had broken their codes. Several correspondents heard of the story, but each time the censor stepped in, and nothing was published or broadcast until the war was over, American POWs had been freed, and censorship had ended, by which time it was no longer real news.

in the world, snuffing out in the process the British, French, and Dutch empires. In the long struggle ahead to defeat Japan, the main purpose of news would be to render the greatest possible aid to the American war effort. Truth and objectivity would have to yield to a wholehearted patriotic participation in the conflict. "War touches every individual," one American censor wrote, "and no one can remain aloof as a more-or-less interested spectator. Newspapers …and broadcasting stations must be as actively behind the war effort as merchants or manufacturers."[9] To achieve this, a huge apparatus was created to control what Americans could know about the war.

In the First World War, the Creel committee combined the functions of propagandist and censor. The committee originated news favourable to the war effort and blacked out that which was not. But by the Second World War propaganda had become a much more scientific business, and so Roosevelt decided to keep the two functions separate. The Office of Facts and Figures and later the innocent-sounding Office of War Information, with a budget for its first year of nearly $40 million, under Elmer Davis, the author, news analyst, and former *New York Times* journalist, became the medium for publicising the American war effort at home and abroad.

The Office of Censorship, under Byron Price, formerly the executive news editor of the Associated Press, dealt with censorship of all civilian modes of communication: reading millions of letters, checking cables and telegrams, tapping telephone calls, vetting films, and ensuring that newspapers and radio stations followed the Code of Wartime Practices, which the censors compiled and frequently revised. Although the stated task of the Office of Censorship was to keep from the enemy information that might endanger the Allied cause, it tended also to concern itself with morale, and it suppressed private letters that, while containing no military information, painted a gloomy picture of the war. Scenes that showed "labor, class, or other disturbances since 1917" or that "burlesqued or ridiculed" the United States forces were not allowed in films that would be shown abroad, and Hollywood representatives of the Office of War Information put pressure on film producers to introduce certain themes in films intended for the home market.[10] For example, the pluralism and patriotism of the United States were to be emphasised by scenes of roll-calls of ethnically identifiable names in fighting units. (The fact that it was always the Italian/Polish/Irish-American who caught the bullet, while the WASP leader survived, was Hollywood's own touch.) In short, the world was to be given the impression that a just and perfect America was well on the way to swift and total victory. Since free speech within the United States was guaranteed under the Constitution, this led to a ludicrous situation: Congressman Melvin Maas was able to declare over a nation-wide radio network his belief that America was losing the war in the Pacific; total censorship was imposed on British correspondents in the United States who tried to cable Maas' views to London.[11]

Military censorship worked differently. Within the United States, the army and the navy applied "censorship at source"—that is, they tried to prevent correspondents from learning anything they did not want them to know. The criterion was: "Is it a good thing for the army (or the navy) to have this information made public?" Outside America, control was simpler. Correspondents were not allowed in the theatres of war unless they were accredited, and one of the conditions of accreditation was that the correspondent must sign an agreement to submit all his copy to military or naval censorship. The censors were overworked men in a desperate war. They could not get into trouble by cutting out information, but they could find themselves in a lot of difficulty by letting material pass that should have been censored. They had heard army and navy public relations officers warned that they would be judged not on what they got into the newspapers, but on what they managed to keep out. They were accustomed, as military men, to sending and receiving information in the form of military reports, where such things as shades of meaning and subtle qualifications were to be avoided. Their interests and those of the war correspondents were diametrically opposed. Correspondents seek to tell as much as possible as soon as possible; the military seeks to tell as little as possible as late as possible. Since the armed forces and not the correspondents were running the war, censorship was spectacularly successful. As the author and correspondent Fletcher Pratt wrote: "The official censors pretty well succeeded in putting over the legend that the war was won without a single mistake by a command consisting exclusively of geniuses."[12]

War correspondents went along with the official scheme for reporting the war because they were convinced that it was in the national interest to do so. They saw no sharp line of demarcation between the rôle of the press in war-time and that of the government, and they became so accustomed to censorship that when it finally ended, in 1945, one correspondent was heard to say in some bewilderment, "But where will we go now to get our stories cleared?"[13]

There was some heart-searching after the war. John Steinbeck wrote: "We were all part of the war effort. We went along with it, and not only that, we abetted it. Gradually it became a part of us that the truth about anything was automatically secret and that to trifle with it was to interfere with the war effort. By this I don't mean that the correspondents were liars. They were not...It is in the things not mentioned that the untruth lies...Yes, we wrote only a part of the war but at that time we believed, fervently believed, that it was the best thing to do. And perhaps that is why, when the war was over, novels and stories by ex-soldiers, like 'The Naked and the Dead', proved so shocking to a public which had been carefully protected from contact with the crazy, hysterical mess."[14]

In no theatre of the war was the protection of the American public from reality more complete—and in no theatre did it have quite such serious consequences—than in China. There, the reporting of the SinoJapanese War had created a dangerous myth. This was that the Chinese peasant armies, under the control of their beloved leader, Generalissimo Chiang Kai-shek, and his wife, the beautiful American-educated Madame Chiang Kai-shek, had fought the Japanese to a standstill and that, given American money and military supplies, they could actually defeat them. When the Lend-Lease Act, in March 1941, brought aid of every kind pouring into China, Chiang's appetite swelled to the colossal. Few begrudged it; "what [Madame Chiang Kai-shek] wants she wants for the family of man over the entire earth," wrote Carl Sandburg in the *Washington Post*.

In this emotional climate, it would have needed a war correspondent of remarkable calibre to write the truth: that the Chiang Kai-shek regime was massively corrupt, brutal, and inefficient; that Chiang had no intention of pressing the war against the Japanese; that he was stockpiling American military aid to make his rule safe against insurrection. This was not what America wanted to hear; so, instead, correspondents sent the war communiqués issued by Hollington K. Tong, and these bore more resemblance to fairy tales than to reality. The correspondents went off on tours to "battlefields" where they were shown stacks of captured Japanese guns and equipment, and they knew all the time—one correspondent proved it by scratching his initials on a helmet—that it was the same equipment moved from place to place, just as the same token group of Japanese prisoners turned up time and time again.[15]

They wrote stirring stories about the American "Flying Tigers" and their leader, Major-General Claire Chennault, later the commander of the Fourteenth Air Force, the advocate of the aeroplane as the definitive weapon, who believed that he could defeat Japan with a hundred or so fighters and fifty bombers, and who, with the help of his former public relations aide, Joseph Alsop, pressed these amazing views on Washington. They did not write that these opinions brought Chennault into serious conflict with his superior, General Joseph Stilwell, sent to China to reform the Chinese army and ensure that America's aid was used to best advantage. Nor did they report the bitter breach that grew between Stilwell and Chiang Kai-shek because Stilwell saw Chiang for what he was—an incompetent Fascist commander without the wit to act in his own interest—and Chiang knew that Stilwell knew. (Yet the *New York Times*, in an editorial on Stilwell, wrote: "From the Generalissimo down they all like him.") What the correspondents did write from China made Stilwell's job doubly difficult. As he reported to Washington, the correspondents' stories about furious Chinese counter-attacks and heavy Japanese losses raised the question "If the Chinese army is so full of fight and so well-led, what am I here for?"[16]

The correspondents could not claim that Chiang's censorship was entirely to blame, since even when outside China they still did not report the truth, partly because if they were to do so they would not be allowed back, partly because they felt that the truth would help the Japanese, but mainly because of friendship for China. No journalist could visit Chungking, wrote Vincent Sheean in 1943, without going into ecstasies over the beauty of Madame Chiang Kai-shek, the heroic determination of her husband, and the prowess of the Chinese armies.[17]

True, one correspondent did try to shake the United States out of this serious misapprehension and shatter the false image of China's ability to fight. Theodore White wrote, for *Time* magazine, an outraged eye-witness account of the Honan famine of 1942–43, castigating official stupidity, bungling, corruption, and profiteering, and warning of the people's growing hatred of the regime. *Time* published White's report on March 22, 1943, cut to 750 words and omitting all his criticism.[18] And the first honest assessment of China's military capacity came not from a war correspondent on the spot, but from the military correspondent of the *New York Times*, Hanson Baldwin. In the *Reader's Digest* of

August 1943, Baldwin said that China was not winning battles but losing them, she had no real army, and Chiang Kai-shek's communiqués were almost worthless.

It was not until 1944 that Americans began to learn just how bad things were in China. In *Life*, on May 1, Theodore White wrote that the Chiang Kai-shek regime was a "corrupt political clique that combines some of the worst features of Tammany Hall and the Spanish Inquisition." The same month, and again in September, correspondents made the journey to the Communist zone of China, drew a comparison with Chungking, and came back enthusiastic. Fed up with their treatment in Chungking, realising now that the Chiang Kai-shek regime was not what they had hoped it would be, they were in the mood to be impressed by the Communists, and what they saw was at the time no doubt true. They found the troops well clothed and well fed and morale high. Gunther Stein of the *Christian Science Monitor* wrote that any Allied commander would be proud to command these tough, hardened soldiers. Brooks Atkinson of the *New York Times*, who went with the September group, described local theatricals and the generally optimistic atmosphere. The *Times* ran his report under the headline YENAN, A CHINESE WONDERLAND CITY.[19] Disillusionment with Chiang was complete when, back in Chungking, the reports were heavily censored and in some cases suppressed.

Unfortunately, the truth had come too late. When Roosevelt, in an attempt to save the situation, insisted on Chiang's accepting Stilwell as commander of all the Chinese armies, Chiang refused and successfully demanded Stilwell's recall. Brooks Atkinson considered this development so important that he decided to return to the United States and fight to get the background to the story published. He smuggled what he had written past a military policeman at the Cairo airport, who had demanded that he submit all his papers to censorship, but in New York the *Times* had to take the issue to President Roosevelt before the internal censor would agree to publication. The story appeared on the front page on October 31 and caused an uproar. Atkinson described Stilwell as the ablest field commander in China since "Chinese" Gordon and said that his recall represented the "political triumph of a moribund anti-democratic regime" that was unrepresentative of America's Chinese allies.

Atkinson's assessment of Stilwell may have been debatable, but his other conclusions were not. Stilwell's sacking was an admission that a major American war-time policy had failed. What we are concerned with here is that one reason for this failure was that correspondents did not report what was really happening in China until it was too late.

Now, when it was no use, every correspondent or former correspondent in the China theatre rushed into print with the stories he had not written or had not been permitted to write earlier. The Associated Press correspondent Thoburn Wiant, attempting to explain why the American public had not been able to learn the truth about China before, said it was because Washington had kept on hoping it could clear up the mess. Even now the whole story was not allowed to emerge. Stilwell was ordered not to talk, and when he was finally permitted to meet the press, a censor sat alongside him and not only decided which questions the general would be allowed to answer, but also ruled that correspondents could not write about those questions he had forbidden.[20]

If the policy of shielding the nation from reality, maintaining morale by avoiding the truth, and convincing the public that the war was being conducted by a command of geniuses could have been typified in one area and by one commander, that area was the South-West Pacific and that commander was General Douglas MacArthur. MacArthur arrived in Australia in March 1942, after a dramatic escape from the Philippines, to be commander-in-chief of all the Allied armies there. Newspapers in the United States headlined MacArthur's arrival and the fact that Roosevelt had given him command of a mighty American army assembling in Australia to drive the Japanese back to Tokyo. "MacArthur's appointment as United Nations commander for the South Pacific and the knowledge that American troops are here in considerable strength have brought the first sure hope of victory," wrote the *Chicago Sun*'s correspondent, H. R. Knickerbocker, from Melbourne on March 18, 1942. "The United States is in the war with all its power and under the leadership of the best general that the United Nations possess."

The facts were somewhat different. "There was no great army," the commander of the Allied air force, General George Brett, reported, "and the Air Force consisted of a few battered planes and combat-weary men." Of the eleven divisions of the Australian forces, less than two divisions were effective troops, one was approaching combat condition, and the rest were composed of militia, at that time in a very indifferent state of training and equipment. The Royal Australian Air Force was equipped with almost obsolete aircraft and was short of engines and spare parts. The Royal Australian Navy did not have a single aircraft carrier. In short, as MacArthur reported to Roosevelt on May 8, 1942: "At this time there are present [here] all the elements to produce another disaster."[21]

This was no news to Roosevelt. In the spring of the previous year, before Pearl Harbor, Anglo-American staff conferences in Washington had decided that if the United States entered the war, the Allies would first concentrate on the defeat of Germany. Roosevelt and Churchill, at a meeting after the Japanese attack on Pearl Harbor, confirmed this decision, even if it meant the temporary loss of Australia. Until victory was assured in Europe, operations in the Pacific would have to be conducted with the limited resources available.

So much for the myth of the mighty army awaiting MacArthur. What of MacArthur himself, "the best general that the United Nations possess"? The best that can be said of his record in the war to this stage is that it had not been very impressive. Ten hours after Pearl Harbor the Japanese carried out a successful attack on Clark Field, in the Philippines. Although MacArthur had had adequate warning, the Japanese caught his heavy bombers parked wing to wing on the ground for refuelling and wiped them out. MacArthur never made a satisfactory explanation about this defeat. Part of the problem was that three different plans existed for the defence of the Philippines, and MacArthur followed none of them in its entirety when the war started.

There then followed such recriminations, arguments, and discord between the U.S. Army and the U.S. Navy over who had been responsible for the debacle that relations remained soured for the rest of the war. MacArthur's communiqués from the Philippines maintained the cheerful, optimistic strain that had so misled Washington before the war with Japan, and his news releases bore so little resemblance to what was actually happening that they aroused resentment among the troops: "Help is on the way from the United States, thousands of troops and hundreds of planes are being dispatched."[22] He created around himself the legend of a military genius aloof from the day-to-day conduct of the war, busy with matters of strategic importance. Although no one questioned his bravery, he spent so much time underground in the fortress on Corregidor that he became known as "Dug-out Doug." Fresh from the worst defeat American arms had ever suffered, was MacArthur the best general the United Nations possessed?

A highly skilled public relations team, under MacArthur's personal direction, set out to make this true, and there remains the ironic possibility that MacArthur did eventually expand to fill the rôle his publicity created for him. He began brilliantly by announcing, on his arrival in Melbourne, "I have come through and I will return." Tidied up by his publicity staff, this became "I shall return," an historic war-time slogan, which not only was repeated in correspondents' dispatches on every possible occasion, but also was printed or stamped on thousands of match folders, blotters, buttons, and cakes of soap that were then dropped on the Philippines.[23] Never one for understatement, MacArthur addressed Australian leaders in Canberra by telling them: "We shall win or we shall die. To this end I pledge you the full resources and all the mighty power, all the blood of my countrymen."[24] He made his first public appearance wearing thirty-six medal ribbons—nine rows of decorations—and his personal photographer, who had orders always to get the best profile, took pictures of him hard at work on his campaign. At the same time, aided by the Australian authorities, he established almost the tightest censorship of any theatre of the war.*

He ruled that any correspondent who interviewed any member of the Allied forces would be banned from advanced bases and that the soldier would be court-martialed. All dispatches had to pass through MacArthur's headquarters, no matter where they were lodged, and submission to one censorship authority did not exempt the correspondent from obtaining clearance from any other censor whose service might be involved. So when, for instance, Japanese midget submarines attacked Sydney Harbour, correspondents' stories had to be cleared by the Garden Island Naval Base, Sydney; the Navy Board, Melbourne; MacArthur's GHQ; and Commonwealth Security, Canberra. [25]

One reason for such strict censorship was to avoid the alarm and despondency that would have resulted if the correspondents had got to hear of and tried to publish the plans MacArthur had approved to defend Australia from Japanese invasion. Western Australia and everything north of Townsville would have to be surrendered. Perth and Darwin were to be left to their fate, because there were simply not enough troops to hold them against a determined Japanese assault. The First Army was to defend the coast from Brisbane to the Victoria border; the Second Army was to provide

---

* Joseph C. Harsch of the *Christian Science Monitor*, who had been with the German army in the early months of the war, complained to the Australian government that censorship in Australia was stricter than in Germany.

local protection for Melbourne.[26] In case the Japanese should be so foolish as to land in the sparsely populated northern part of Australia, groups of "scorched earth" troops were stationed there, with secret orders to wait until the wind was in the right direction and then start gigantic bush-fires—one of the more bizarre war stories still not fully known, even today.[27] Since civilians in those areas to be abandoned to the Japanese might have shown some resentment about this plan if news of it leaked out, care was taken that it did not, even to the extent of deliberately not withdrawing those troops that were already there. This was done, as the army coyly put it, "for reasons of morale and psychology." None of this emerged until after the war.

But another reason for the strict censorship was to control the image of MacArthur as projected by correspondents. On October 2, 1942, MacArthur flew to New Guinea, where a Japanese attempt at invading Milne Bay had been repulsed by Allied troops, the first land operation to take place under MacArthur's new command. The visit was heavily covered—one Australian officer said he had not known that there were so many photographers in the world— and American, Australian, and British correspondents lodged with the censors 25,000 words. A day later, the correspondents were told that the stories had not been sent because they had said—correctly—that it was MacArthur's *first* visit to New Guinea. The correspondents learned what was expected of them when, five days later, with the stories still not sent, the British correspondents withdrew theirs on the ground that the visit was now stale. They were thus able to see the changes MacArthur's censors had made. Walter Lucas of the *Daily Express* had written, "General MacArthur has returned from his first visit to New Guinea." The censor had crossed this out and substituted "General MacArthur has been seen at the front in New Guinea." When the correspondents protested that their stories were being doctored to create a false impression, the censors cut the 25,000 words down to 10,000 and released them a week after MacArthur's visit.[28]

We are concerned here not to assess MacArthur's status as a military commander, but to look at his influence on the way the war in the Pacific was reported. Due to his total control over the correspondents in his area, no one attempted an assessment of how the General's carefully fostered image measured up to reality or of how his communiqués compared with the truth. In 1969, Gavin Long, a correspondent who later became editor of the Australian official history of the war, wrote of the downright mendacity of

MacArthur's communiqués and suggested that the strategy that won him so much renown—of by-passing enemy strong points and leaving them to "wither on the vine"—originated with the U.S. Navy and was imposed on an unwilling MacArthur by his superiors in Washington.[29] Yet the fact remains that MacArthur not only returned to the Philippines but went on to Tokyo, and that there is no evidence that, even in the darkest days, he ever doubted he would. When Noel Monks decided that the censorship and Hollywood-style publicity of MacArthur's command were not for him and that he was going back to London, MacArthur sent for him, as he did every correspondent who wanted to leave his theatre, and tried to dissuade him. "You're going away from the big front, the big war, son," he said.[30]

It must have caused MacArthur some chagrin that what appeared to be the first striking victory against Japan came at sea. This was the Battle of the Coral Sea, the first naval action in history in which surface ships did not exchange a single shot. The battle was fought entirely in the air, and its significance was reported by the *Chicago Tribune*'s correspondent, Australian-born Stanley Johnston, who was on board the American aircraft carrier *Lexington* until she sank. Johnston wrote that the battle showed how completely the carrier had displaced the battleship in importance in modern war.[31] Johnston's considered conclusion was virtually overlooked in the euphoria. The Americans had sunk the escort carrier *Shoho* and had damaged another, so the result of the battle was about even. But it was presented as a major American victory and the saving of Australia. Quoting figures that bore no relation to reality, the *New York Times* of May 9, 1942, said: "Japanese repulsed in great Pacific battle, with 17 to 22 of their ships sunk or crippled." (Japan also claimed the battle as a victory, the *Japan Times and Advertiser* going right overboard with its headline—U.S. PANIC-STRICKEN.) True the troop convoy escorted by the Japanese naval force, heading for Port Moresby, in New Guinea, turned back, thus lending credence to correspondents who wrote that the battle had saved Australia.

The fact, although of course not known then, was that the Japanese did not intend at the time of the Battle of the Coral Sea to invade Australia, because they were incapable of doing so. The Japanese navy had wanted to occupy such key areas as Sydney, Brisbane, Townsville, and Darwin. But the Japanese army had said that this would require ten to twelve divisions and that it could not risk moving so many troops from Manchuria and other occupied areas at that time.[32] Even a compromise plan to isolate Australia by cutting her supply lines from the United States was postponed, in favour of a large-scale attack on Midway, the fortified American atoll protecting Hawaii.

If there was a single battle in the Pacific that turned the war in America's favour, it was the Battle of Midway, the first decisive defeat inflicted on the Japanese navy in 350 years. It was one of those rare battles in which a numerically inferior fleet, in the space of only minutes, snatched victory from a stronger force and changed the course of history. For the loss of one American carrier and 147 aircraft, the United States Navy sank four Japanese aircraft carriers, two heavy cruisers, three destroyers, and several transports. The result was that Japan had to restrict her plan to isolate Australia, yield the central Pacific to the United States, and go on the defensive. As well as being a great strategic victory, the battle produced notable exploits of bravery and self-sacrifice on both sides. An American torpedo squadron went into the attack without fighter protection and lost every plane and every man but one. A Japanese carrier captain refused to leave his bridge, armed himself to prevent any of his crew from attempting to remove him by force and went down with his ship, calmly singing "*Kimigayo*," the national anthem. Yet this watershed of the war was the worst-reported naval battle in the Pacific. The first attempt to tell the American public about it almost resulted in the correspondent's being charged with espionage, and it was months before anyone would believe that Midway was a victory at all.

The battle was fought on June 4, 5, and 6, 1942. There were no American correspondents present, but during this period Stanley Johnston, the *Chicago Tribune* correspondent who had reported the Battle of the Coral Sea, was en route for the United States on a naval transport, after his rescue from the *Lexington*. Sailors on the transport had heard of Johnston's rescue work when the *Lexington* went down, and they went out of their way to be friendly with him. They spoke freely about the reports coming in of a battle raging around Midway. On arrival in Chicago, Johnston sat down in his office and wrote what he had learned. Then, with Wayne Thomis, one of the *Tribune*'s staff, he went through *Jane's Fighting Ships* and roughed out the likely composition of the two opposing fleets. Finally, a brief communiqué from the navy, announcing the bare details of the battle and estimated Japanese losses, enabled Johnston and Thomis to set out, with remarkable accuracy, an account in which they gave the order of battle of the Japanese fleet in detail. Through an oversight, Johnston had not been asked to sign accreditation papers as a war correspondent attached to the navy, and therefore he was not bound to submit to the naval censors everything he wrote. There was nothing in the censorship code for newspapers that prohibited the disclosure of the names, movements, or location of *enemy* vessels, and so the *Tribune* went ahead and published Johnston's story on its front page on June 7.

It created an uproar. Johnston and Thomis were immediately summoned to Washington and interrogated by Navy Department officials. Johnston freely revealed his sources and said he was bewildered about the fuss—all he had tried to do was to tell the American public about a great American victory.[33] Next, a special federal grand jury was appointed and asked by the attorney general to carry out an investigation into the story, with a view to discovering whether an indictment should be preferred against Johnston on charges of violating the Espionage Act. President Roosevelt was accused of using the case as a means of punishing the *Tribune* and its owner, Colonel Robert R. McCormick, for the neutralist views they had expressed before the war. Nevertheless, the grand jury's investigation, the only one of its kind during the war, went ahead, but found after two months that there were no grounds for issuing an indictment. For Johnston, it could be said that the damage had already been done. Contrary to the usual custom, the grand jury had revealed Johnston's name and the nature of the charges being investigated, and the linking of a war correspondent with espionage allegations could not help his reputation, no matter what the grand jury eventually found.

It was not until the end of the war that Johnston learned the real reason the navy had tried to punish him. The navy had known of the movements and composition of the Japanese force at Midway because it had been reading the Japanese codes, and it was worried that the accuracy of Johnston's story would make the Japanese realise that their codes had been cracked. It did not, but American censorship rules were now extended to restrict all material about enemy as well as friendly ships, and relations between the navy and Johnston remained bitter for the rest of the war. And, probably because of the navy's reaction to the *Tribune* story, editors, politicians, and the public discounted further reports about the American success at Midway as being exaggerated, so that for months its significance went unnoticed. Not until Robert J. Casey, a war correspondent for the *Chicago Daily News*, published, late in 1942, his book *Torpedo Junction*, recording the rise of the United States Navy from the disaster of Pearl Harbor to its triumph only six months later at Midway—"one of the greatest maritime battles of history"—was the importance of the battle at last recognised. But so much information had been suppressed that Paul Scott Mowrer, the *Chicago Daily News'* editor, complained that even in the spring of 1943 "the general public is not clear whether the Coral Sea and Midway battles were different, or the same."[34]

Clearly, American correspondents had fared badly in the early part of the war in the Pacific. As the United Press reported later: "The swiftness of the Japanese conquest in Southwest Asia, the dire plight of the United States Navy, and the blanket of censorship and propaganda that covered military operations made the first months of 1942 a nightmare of confusion for correspondents at the fronts and editors at home."[35] But British war correspondents, in their theatres, did little better, despite a creditable start. Two British correspondents and one American were on board the battle-cruiser *Repulse* when she and the battleship *Prince of Wales* were sunk by the Japanese in the Gulf of Siam on December 10, 1941.

Churchill had sent the two British ships to the East in pursuit of one of his personal strategic fantasies—that it should be possible to bluff the Japanese out of the idea of war altogether or, if that failed, then persuade them to attack the hard-pressed Soviet Union. So, three days after Pearl Harbor, the two most effective ships in the British navy were blundering about in the Gulf of Siam, within easy reach of Japanese bombers and without any air cover.

The three correspondents—O. D. Gallagher of the *Daily Express*, Cecil Brown of the Columbia Broadcasting System, and Lieutenant "Tubby" Abrahams, an official navy photographer—had a close-up view of the worst individual disaster that the Royal Navy suffered during the war and one of the heaviest set-backs to the Allied cause in general. As Yukio Waku, war correspondent for *Yomiuri*, reported: "We succeeded in locating the *Prince of Wales* and the *Repulse* a few miles off Kuantan…Our formations of bombers fell on the two capital ships amidst anti-aircraft fire from the enemy. Our torpedoes hit their mark with incandescent glow flashing amid dark smoke columns. In disorderly wakes ran the *Prince of Wales* and the *Repulse* and in a moment they turned into columns of fire, going to the bottom."[36] Down below, all three correspondents survived the sea and the oil, until they were picked up

by destroyers. The notes Gallagher and Brown had taken also survived, and back in Singapore each wrote his story and got it away
without difficulty. "We were able to tell the truth because we had
seen for ourselves what had happened," Gallagher has recalled.
"There were no public relations officers to gum things up, because
the Royal Navy was in such a mess no one had any time to think
about correspondents and their stories."[37] Gallagher's story was the
front-page lead in the *Daily Express* and dominated the rest of the
paper. Brown's dispatch was broadcast five times in one day.

As a result of their first-hand experience of Japanese fighting
qualities, Gallagher and Brown were now better placed than most
other correspondents in Singapore to assess the base's chances of
resisting a Japanese attack. Both they and Ian Morrison, *The Times*
of London's correspondent, who was the son of "Chinese" Morrison, and had lived and worked in Japan, soon became very pessimistic, while those correspondents who had no reason to doubt
British officials' statements that the Japanese could not be taken
seriously soon became, as the army commander, General Arthur
Percival, reported, "whole-heartedly behind the war effort" and
sent home reams of soothing nonsense. "Singapore, nerve-centre of
Britain's defensive system in the East, is sharpening her teeth,"
wrote Leonard Mosley of the *Daily Sketch*, in a dispatch typical of
reports at the time. "Giant guns [guard] the jungle-fringed
shores...Australian, British and Indian troops in the hot fly-
infested forest are ready for anything, while clouds of planes daily
patrol over neighbouring islands."[38] Mosley and his colleagues can
perhaps be forgiven for misleading reporting such as this, because
they, in turn, were misled by the Ministry of Information and by
service officials, who genuinely believed that Singapore was an
impregnable fortress and that the Japanese were incapable of efficiently waging war with Western inventions like battleships, tanks,
submarines, and aircraft.

The truth was that Singapore was virtually defenceless, and
when the Japanese army came cycling down the main roads of
Malaya, Singapore began to fall apart. The city was bombed, but
there was no one on duty to sound the sirens, and the street lights
remained blazing because no one could find the key to the master
switch. The post-office cut the telephone circuit to the front line
when the regulation three minutes were up. A last-minute attempt
to build defences on the island was delayed ten days by an argument
over the correct wage to pay the coolies. The secretary of the golf
club insisted that no guns could be mounted on the links until he

had consulted the committee. Airfields had been built without any consultation, often could not be defended by the army, and, like everything else, had to be abandoned on the run. British troops retreated from positions the Japanese were not attacking, disobeyed orders to counter-attack, and failed to follow up advantages obtained by the rare ambush. Morale collapsed, and deserters poured into Singapore, to add to the chaos.

In the end, on February 14, 1942, a British army with ample munitions surrendered to a Japanese force barely one-third its strength and down to its last hundred rounds of ammunition per man.[39] The correspondents must accept some of the blame for the shock that the fall of Singapore caused. Once the myth of "the fortress of the East" was established, once the "impenetrable jungle" with its "crocodile-infested creeks" was firm in the reader's mind, it was difficult to erase. To their credit, a few correspondents tried. Theodore White wrote for *Life*, in July 1941, an article saying that in the event of war the Japanese army would attempt to take Singapore by fighting its way down the coast of Malaya. Cecil Brown constantly inveighed against British complacency, and for his pains had his accreditation temporarily taken away from him. O. D. Gallagher attacked the "it-can't-happen-here" attitude of the Singapore civilians. But they were all up against powerful pressure from the Ministry of Information to put out the official view. Gallagher wrote later that each week the official bulletin announced the arrival of yet more reinforcements. "We reporters had to cable these bulletins to various parts of the world. Reinforcements *were* arriving almost weekly, but their arrival did little more than build up an army of reasonable size. Obviously we were unable to explain this in our cables and the result was that the world in general was given the impression that Malaya, and particularly Singapore, was receiving all the attention it rightly deserved. The shock of its collapse was greater than it need have been."[40]

Once the Japanese began their drive down the peninsula, correspondents were largely dependent on the official communiqué, which was remarkably uninformative. When formation after formation of Japanese bombers dropped stick after stick of bombs across airfields, destroying bombers and fighters on the ground, this was described to the correspondents as "the enemy endeavouring to gain a measure of air superiority." When groups of correspondents were sent to the front with a conducting officer, the only stories they could hope to get were interviews with junior staff officers, who tended to describe what would turn out to be a decisive engagement as "a spot of bother," or stories of the bravery of British troops in retreat. Ian Morrison soon realised that this sort of reporting failed to convey what was really happening in Malaya. "I sometimes wonder," he wrote, "if a correspondent does not do a disservice to the general cause by recounting these tales of personal heroism which are so eagerly read by the people at home. The tales are often so stirring that they clamour to be written, but when things are going badly, do they not sometimes obscure the main issues?"[41]

After his escape from Singapore, Morrison succeeded in publishing his view of the debacle: "If the British ran the rest of their Empire as they had run things recently in Singapore, then they did not deserve to have an empire at all."[42] But Cecil Brown told the American public on his return that censorship had done "everything possible to hide the real situation." O. D. Gallagher, whose book *Retreat in the East*, written in 1942, attacked "the guff of the propagandists" at Singapore, went to see the then Minister of Information, Brendan Bracken, to ask for more paper so that his publisher could meet the wide demand for a reprint of the book. Bracken cut short Gallagher's pleas with "You don't really expect me to give you paper to print a journalistic attack on the British government, do you?"[43] Yates McDaniel of the Associated Press, who had been the first American correspondent to arrive in Singapore and was the only one left to witness its fall—he got out on the last boat and turned up in Batavia on February 20, after a week of wild adventure—captured in his dispatches the apocalyptic, almost surrealist nature of the Malayan disorder. Three days before Singapore fell, for example, he wrote a report describing how the white population still firmly refused to believe it was all happening: "In front of the Raffles Hotel cars are depositing patrons of the daily tea dance and outside the theatre people are queuing up to see Joel McCrea and Ellen Drew in the film *Reaching for the Sun*."[44]

On February 15 there were only Japanese correspondents and cameramen around to record the British officers, in their baggy shorts and faintly absurd toothbrush moustaches, signing the surrender and agreeing that British troops would help the Japanese maintain order until the occupation could be completed. This orderly hand-over of power from one imperial regime to another, marked by a display of friendly relations between many British and Japanese soldiers, was the most costly and humiliating defeat in the history of the British Empire. White supremacy had ended, and nothing in the East would ever be the same again.*

In Burma and India, the authorities had no intention of allowing correspondents to record what looked as if it would be the early collapse of the British Empire. Not only was there the question of trying to maintain morale, but there were political considerations as well. The British war aims were to restore everything to the way it had been in 1939. The Burmese were witnessing the Japanese drive the British out of Burma; they would one day witness the British, preferably unaided, drive the Japanese out. So the British administration looked without favour at two Chinese armies, led or advised (no one ever made it clear) by General Stilwell, trying to stem the Japanese advance. Without any effective over-all command, everything went wrong. The Chinese were short of ammunition and supplies, yet, as everyone in Rangoon could see, the docks were choked with American war materials. O. D. Gallagher, fresh from Singapore, and Leland Stowe of the *Chicago Daily News* tried to send this story, but as soon as the censor learned the subject of their messages, he refused even to read them. F. W. R. Stone of the *Rangoon Gazette*, probably realising that he would soon lose his newspaper anyway and that there would be little the censor could do to him, wrote the story, under the headline FAITH IN OUR FIGHTING MEN, BUT PROTECT US FROM NON-BELLIGERENT DOPES. The British abandoned Rangoon, destroying valuable oil installations— £11 million worth went up in flames in seventy minutes—and set out on the long retreat to India.

The British authorities ordered all correspondents to leave, and from then on reports of what was happening in Burma came from official communiqués issued in either Delhi or Chungking. These were interpreted by correspondents in the best possible light, and newspaper readers in the United States and Britain could be forgiven for believing that the Japanese were receiving a lesson they deserved. One headline read CHINESE CAVALRY ROUTS JAP PANZERS IN BURMA,[45] and when Stilwell was making his forced march to India, through a great stretch of jungle bounded by the Irrawaddy River and the Himalayas, Americans were reading INVADING FORCE CRUSHED BY STILWELL and STILWELL'S CHINA TROOPS TRAP JAPS—

---

* Two months later, Churchill, who had ostentatiously taken responsibility for the disaster, was apparently so ill-informed as to its causes that he was unable to explain it to the House of Commons. It was not until the enormously detailed, and admittedly nationalistic, Australian and New Zealand war histories appeared after the war that the awful truth at last began to emerge. Only in the late 1960's and early 1970's, with a spate of histories, memoirs, and biographies, was the full story finally told.

INVASION ARMY IN FULL RETREAT.[46] Stilwell's own comment when he met correspondents on arriving in Delhi—"I claim we got a hell of a beating"—came as a refreshing shaft of honesty.

One correspondent told the truth as he saw it. Jack Belden, a young American adventurer, a romantic and idealist, had jumped ship in Shanghai in 1933, roamed around China, and joined the United Press after the Japanese invasion. He had gone to Burma with Stilwell for *Time* and accompanied Stilwell on his forced march, but before leaving he managed to get off a series of short messages on the last aircraft to India. He began, "This is probably my last message," and ended, "Must go. Goodbye." In between, although he complained that everything was happening so quickly he could not write a co-ordinated story, Belden set out what had gone wrong in Burma and the lessons to be learnt. It was a first-class piece of war reporting, in a period of fantasy and self-delusion.[47]

In the middle of this low point in Allied fortunes, there arrived in the India-Burma theatre one of those English eccentrics whose activities cannot help but be newsworthy and whose value to the war as morale raisers is beyond calculation. Orde Wingate, like Lawrence of Arabia, his distant relation, had unorthodox views about how wars should be fought, and early in 1943 he led his "Chindits," a special force of some 3,000 men, on a guerrilla-type operation hundreds of miles behind the Japanese lines. Three months later only 2,187 returned, and of these no more than 600 were ever fit for active soldiering again. The mission had no strategic objective, except, perhaps, to exhibit British activity and to demonstrate that the Japanese were not invincible in the jungle, and the official army historian decided after the war that the results achieved by Wingate's special group were incommensurate with the forces diverted to it.[48]

But from a public relations point of view Wingate was a godsend. A British force had engaged the Japanese on their own ground and had had a measure of success, the *only* success, at that stage, in the whole of the Far East. So when British correspondents in India went among the survivors and collected their stories, the army did not need much prompting to issue a communiqué and raise censorship to allow the whole episode to emerge. It made an immediate and enormous impression, especially on Churchill, who was drawn to Wingate as he had been drawn to Lawrence. The publicity storm grew in strength. Photographs of haggard Chindits in tattered tropical uniform and Australian slouch hat were in all the newspapers, and Wingate himself, in old-fashioned pith helmet and thick dark beard, became a British hero overnight. "Mastery in the jungle...unforgettable adventure," *The Times* said.[49] Other newspapers described Wingate as a genius and the operation as the greatest jungle epic of the war. The Royal Central Asian Society awarded Wingate its Lawrence of Arabia medal, and Churchill had him flown back to Britain and then took him along to the Quebec Conference, to meet President Roosevelt and the American chiefs of staff.

The extremes to which the British correspondents had gone to glamorise Wingate created a public appetite for more, and when he returned to India, to organise a second Chindit expedition, the army worked out an elaborate plan to make the most of the publicity. The idea was to put out colourless reports to begin with, followed by more detailed ones as public interest was excited, moving towards a climax of sensational dispatches beginning "Now it can be revealed..." No one told Wingate this, and when the early press releases from the South-East Asia Command headquarters on the second operation made no mention of the Chindits or of Wingate, but of "troops of the 14th Army," Wingate was furious, and protested to Lord Mountbatten and later directly to Churchill. Churchill replied promising to mention the Chindits and their commander in his next broadcast to the nation. On March 24, 1944, before Churchill's message reached him, Wingate and two British correspondents, Stuart Emery of the *News Chronicle* and Stanley Wills of the *Daily Herald*, were in a Mitchell bomber that crashed in the Assam hills. They were all killed.

The place Wingate and his Chindits deserve in the history of the war against Japan remains the subject of debate, with Field-Marshal Sir William Slim of the opinion that the press excitement over the expedition was its only justification. But blame for the overglamorising of a comparatively minor and very costly operation in the Burma campaign must lie almost entirely with the correspondents.

As it turned out, Wingate and the Chindits were the journalistic high point in the India-Burma theatre, and the heavy hand of the censor settled on most other aspects of the war there. Unrest in India was largely responsible, and the fact was that the British no longer trusted the will of the Indian army to fight for the Empire. Officers learned by rumour, by whisper, by secret briefing that the Japanese were raising an army of Indian prisoners-of-war to march against the British and were calling on patriotic Indian soldiers to turn on their officers. This was a traumatic shock, which haunted the British throughout the war. "We all knew about it," the Indian war correspondent Frank Moraes said. "But no one tried to write about it. No one dared."*

This highly sensitive area made the censors overly security conscious, as the story of Douglas Wilkie shows. Wilkie, representing a group of Australian and British newspapers, including the *Evening Standard* of London and the *Herald* of Melbourne, made a 2,000-mile tour of the India-Burma theatre in 1943. During his tour, Wilkie wrote twelve articles describing his experiences and assessing the state of the campaign, and sent them back to Delhi for the censor to handle and cable to his newspapers. On his return, Wilkie found that the censor had stopped three articles completely and had sent the others only after cutting them so heavily that they did not make sense. "My final picture of one of the world's main battlefronts...was in large part frivolous references to elephants and tribesmen I had interpolated in more important material," Wilkie wrote to the director of Army Public Relations. "If war correspondents are to be allowed to write only what the Army wants, then it would be easier if you confined your publicity to official handouts ...It is my concern in every sense that my professional reputation should be endangered because of my editor's compulsory ignorance of your [censorship] policy...My articles as dispatched are not a fair index of my industry, views, or conception of the functions of a war correspondent."[50] Wilkie delivered this letter; then, as a protest in which other correspondents should have joined, he packed up and went home.

Japanese correspondents had none of these problems, because Japan made no pretence about the correspondent's rôle. When war broke out, a Board of Information (a Japanese version of the OWI), a Patriotic Critics' Association, and a Patriotic Commentators' Association were set up, to remind people of the reasons for the war and to stress its aims. The Domei news agency, Radio Tokyo, and all the newspapers were reorganised as "public utilities" charged with a "mission" under the war-time structure.

A Board of Censorship, with representatives of the army, navy,

---

* Eventually, *Blitz*, a weekly paper started by the Bombay War Publicity Committee, revealed the existence of the Indian army raised by the Japanese, under the heading THIS QUISLING ARMY. The editor, R. K. Karanjia, told me that the headline made him ashamed, "but how else could I have got the story out?" He was prosecuted under the Subversive Publications Act, but was acquitted.

Home Office, and Ministry of Transport, looked after censorship in Japan, while service censors handled war correspondents' copy in the war theatres. There, the Japanese were as obsessed with secrecy as the Americans were. It was a crime to mention even the routine move of an officer, troops were discouraged from writing letters home, and any criticism of the armed forces, no matter how mild, was not permitted. There was one simple test for a story: would it contribute directly to the Japanese war effort? Nothing else was to be published. Stories from individual war correspondents had to be sent back by air mail, and by the time they reached Tokyo they were hopelessly out of date; so the largest media for information became Radio Tokyo and Domei. Domei not only distributed the news, but also issued orders as to where it should appear in the newspaper and what display it should be given. Correspondents were expected to identify with the services by wearing uniform.[51]

They were present at most of the major events in the war, but what they wrote was predictably patriotic. At Midway, for example, a Japanese navy cameraman, Teichi Makishima, filmed the battle from an escort ship, but when he got back to Japan he learned that his film would not be used. Although the navy had lost all four of the carriers taking part, it was admitting to only one sunk and one damaged and was claiming a victory. Makishima not only had his film confiscated, but also agreed to be held virtually incommunicado until the end of the war, in case he was tempted to tell anyone the truth.[52] Torao Saito of *Asahi Shimbun* used to visit abandoned Allied military camps in South-East Asia, gathering all the wastepaper that had not been burnt. He took this back to Japan and sifted through it, often finding, in service manuals, documents, magazines, or letters, interesting material for his paper. His reports also interested Japanese intelligence, and between 1941 and 1943 Saito spent most of his time on this operation, in interviewing Allied POWs, and in writing reports for the Japanese army and navy.[53]

So Japanese correspondents made no pretence of being other than what they were, an arm of the war effort, and they wrote nothing that did not advance their country's chances of victory. But were Allied correspondents any different? There was one aspect of the war about which correspondents on both sides failed—for patriotic reasons—to write the whole truth: prisoners-of-war and the atrocities inflicted on them.

\*

The war in the Pacific, unlike the war on the Western Front in Europe (the Russian front was another matter), had strong racial overtones. British and American propaganda encouraged the Allied troops and the public at home to think of the Japanese as "apes in uniform," lacking sufficient intelligence to master mechanised warfare, unable to learn to pilot planes because they had been strapped to their mothers' backs as babies and had thus lost their sense of balance. The danger of propaganda like this is that it dehumanises the enemy and makes it easier to treat him like an animal, whose life and feelings are of little value. It was thus inevitable that atrocities occurred, and they occurred on both sides.

A trade sprang up among Australians in New Guinea in providing Japanese ears, usually preserved in spirits, as souvenirs for American troops. Americans knocked gold teeth from Japanese dead, in the mistaken belief that the fillings were valuable and that they could sell them when on leave. President Roosevelt refused the gift of a paper-knife made from the bone of a slain Japanese soldier. MacArthur's intelligence staff had a file, No. 384, which dealt with Allied war crimes, and which included cases of American and Australian cannibalism. One of his officers told me that, whereas Japanese cases of cannibalism were frequently the result of necessity, at least one of those cases of Allied cannibalism which he had investigated was the result of a dare or a bet. It was generally accepted by Australian military intelligence that the Japanese sinking of the Australian hospital ship *Centaur* was in retaliation for the destruction by Australian troops of a Japanese field hospital in New Guinea while the wounded were still in it, but the Australian public was not told this. In Borneo, immediately after the war, Australian troops seeking information about Japanese war crimes made one Japanese dig his own grave and then kneel beside it while a soldier stood over him with an axe, with the apparent intention of beheading him. At the last minute, it was decided that the Japanese knew nothing, and he was returned to the prisoners' compound. Australian troops set upon Japanese working parties at Sandakan, beat the men to the ground, and then rolled full forty-four-gallon fuel drums over them. They beat Japanese sick and wounded with oars and paddles while loading them onto landing craft in Sandakan Harbour.[54]

These individual acts can, perhaps, be excused as excesses after provocation. But there are also well-documented acts of policy, which, had they been known at the time, might have caused some public concern. American submarines sank all Japanese ships on sight, irrespective of whether they were carrying passengers or war materials. Even the fact that one ship that was sunk turned out to be carrying American prisoners-of-war caused no change in the policy. Official communiqués said that American planes bombed only military objectives in Tokyo, and with "pinpoint accuracy." In fact, the fire-raid bombings were indiscriminate and caused more casualties than the atomic bomb at Hiroshima; at least 250,000 were killed and 8 million made homeless. One raid alone—that of March 10, 1945—killed 140,000 people and left 1 million homeless.

Japanese atrocities are well known. The Bataan death march, the Burma railway, overcrowding and starvation in POW camps throughout South-East Asia, the beheading of prisoners, rape, and mass executions were all true. This was due in part to the Japanese code of behaviour about being taken prisoner, in part to the absence of any Japanese organisation to handle POWs, and in part to historical pressures—the Japanese saw prisoners not as people but as provocative symbols of a detested past. "They only had to look at us for this urge of resentment to quicken in their blood to such an extent," wrote a former POW, Laurens Van der Post, "that I still marvel not so much at the excesses they perpetrated as at their restraint."[55] But it was mainly due to the fact that the Japanese, as "sons of Heaven," believed themselves to be racially superior to Westerners and came to regard the Allied soldiers as less than human.

Neither side reported its own atrocities. Throughout the war, there was not a single mention in Japan of any atrocity by a Japanese soldier, and I have been unable to find any report in the Allied press of an atrocity committed by an Allied soldier. Both sides emphasised atrocities committed by the enemy. Here the Allies had an advantage, in that they could use the brutal treatment of Allied POWs to stimulate hatred of the Japanese—it was a joint United States Army and Navy release in 1944 that coined the expression "march of death" to describe what had occurred at Bataan. Japan could not retaliate, even by inventing stories about Allied treatment of Japanese POWs, because the Japanese government had told its people that no Japanese soldier was ever taken prisoner; all died fighting. Even the POW camp riot in Australia in 1944, when 221 Japanese prisoners were either shot by Australian troops or killed themselves, was not reported in Japan, although the Japanese authorities knew about it.*

---

* However, when the Australians cremated with full honours the bodies of the Japanese naval officers killed in the midget-submarine raid on Sydney, and returned the ashes to Japan, this was widely reported in the Japanese press.

When the end of the war produced evidence that not *all* Allied POWs had suffered at the hands of the Japanese, this was ignored. General Percival, captured at Singapore, to his credit wrote in 1949, when passions had cooled, an objective account of his POW experiences. He had shared a bottle of whisky with the camp commandant in Singapore, had travelled in the first officer's cabin on the ship to Japan, because he was sick, and had received Red Cross stores on arrival at the new camp. In 1943 he was moved to a camp near the capital of Formosa. "Each officer had a small room to himself. There was a library of English and American books…table tennis and a gramophone with a good supply of records which we were able to buy locally."[56] The prisoners received letters (they took a long while in transit, sometimes eighteen months to two years), were allowed to write one a month, had for a period two English-language daily papers printed in Japan, and had a radio set, which could receive only Japanese stations. When they were moved to Manchuria, they were given warm clothing and housed in centrally heated barracks.

By the autumn of 1943 the United States had regained its strength. The losses sustained at Pearl Harbor had been made good, and there were now the men, planes, and ships to begin the drive on Japan herself. The Americans decided to start by recapturing the islands on the Japanese defensive perimeter. Since the idea was to gain bases from which their new Superfortress bombers could strike at Japan, the Americans were prepared to lose the lives of many men for the sake of a single runway. Much bloody fighting lay ahead, because the Japanese were a tenacious, fanatical foe, but now that the tide was clearly running in America's favour one would have expected the reporting of the war to improve.

The armed services certainly gave the impression that the correspondent's task would be easier. The United States Pacific Fleet's public relations unit put out a pamphlet addressed to correspondents offering to "put you on the trail of this story gold mine." The unit offered to make arrangements for a correspondent to visit any command, to take photographs, conduct interviews, go to sea in ships, "in short do anything for you that will help to get your yarn."[57] The navy also began to work towards a censorship system under which the press relations division would be headed by an officer of sufficient rank and experience to decide on his own responsibility whether a story could be released.

In the end, it made little difference. When a correspondent was lucky enough to be selected for a major assignment, he found himself part of a "pool," and his story had to be shared with his colleagues. William F. Tyree of the United Press, in a navy Liberator flying over Iwo Jima, represented the whole American press when the Americans put ashore one of the largest forces to take part in a single Marine Corps action, and Webley Edwards of CBS represented all the radio networks.* If, by some chance, a correspondent had a story all to himself, distances in the Pacific were so great and communications presented such a problem that he was almost certain to be beaten by the official communiqué. As *Newsweek* said, "The two most important American war correspondents are the two men who sit in Washington and prepare the Army and Navy communiques."[58] With more and more newspaper commentators and military experts to "interpret" the news for the public, the correspondent found his story becoming a small part of the finished product, and, although he was on the spot, what he contributed was often not allowed to disagree with the official version. It was claimed, for instance, that nineteen Japanese heavy cruisers had been sunk before the Battle of Leyte Gulf, chiefly by the bombers of the MacArthur command. The Japanese had begun the war with eighteen, built none in the intervening period, and yet sailed into the battle with fourteen. The censors struck from correspondents' copy all references to the discrepancy.[59]

Disheartened, some war correspondents gave up the unequal struggle and went back behind a desk to handle copy from men in the field. This left too many "spot news" reporters, competent enough at covering a battle or writing a human-interest story, but unable to write about the broader horizons of the war. Some were content to sit at headquarters and rewrite official handouts. Others, usually under pressure from their offices, went with the troops and wrote the sort of story that began, "I was the first correspondent into Tarawa today as the bullets flew, and this dispatch comes to you by PT boat and short-wave radio." This sort of reporting was cleverly parodied by one Australian correspondent, Allan Dawes of the

---

* Joe Rosenthal of the Associated Press, representing the Wartime Still Pictures Pool, took the best-known photograph of the Pacific war there, "The Raising of the Flag on Iwo Jima," a group of Marines struggling to erect a steel pole with the American flag on the highest point of the island. The photograph was used on a postage stamp, became the symbol of the seventh War Bond drive, was used on 3·5 million posters and 175,000 car cards, and was the inspiration for the hundred-ton bronze memorial to the Marines at the edge of Arlington National Cemetery.

*Melbourne Herald*. Dawes, a fat, slow man, decided that readers might well be fed up with brave and intrepid correspondents, so in 1943 he wrote a dispatch that began, "Somewhere in New Guinea: I was the last correspondent into Lae…" He sealed it in an envelope and put it in the forces mail-box. A month later, his newspaper ran the story, under the headline LAST PRESSMAN INTO LAE POSTS MESSAGE.[60]

Two defences are put forward for the over-all poor reporting of the war in the Pacific. The first is that newspapers demanded battle descriptions, and when a battle correspondent tried to break away from his stereotype his newspaper became restive and wanted him back where the action was. As a result, correspondents' casualties were proportionately greater than those of any combat service. But here we are interested not in bravery, but in effectiveness. Fletcher Pratt, himself a correspondent, and a student of military affairs, has pointed out that the Japanese on Attu lost 99.5 per cent of their force, which would entitle them to still higher praise than the war correspondents, but that they, too, failed to achieve their objective. Pratt's conclusion was: "The war was reported in terms of a social function by the Fifth Street Ladies Club—the names and addresses were correct and all the necessary ones got in. The phrases were the stereotyped, unobjectionable stencils one should employ on such an occasion—there was almost never any sense of the hurry, passion, and continual surprise that are the essence of real fighting, or the ineffable boredom and desperate devices for self-entertainment that are the focus of preparation for battle. These were left for the 'trained seals,' the stunt men like Pyle, La Farge, and Clark Lee."[61]

The second defence is to ask how the correspondent could report what was happening when often the military did not know itself; and when the military did, it often did not tell the correspondent until it was ready to do so. This defence carries more weight. The Battle of Leyte Gulf, in October 1944, for example, was greatly underrated at the time because the United States Navy did not know what a great victory it had won. George E. Jones of the United Press, on board Admiral Marc Mitscher's flagship, wrote: "Today the Japanese fleet submitted itself to the destinies of war and lost. Four enemy carriers have been sunk, eight battleships have been damaged."[62] It was, as Jones learned later, a more sweeping defeat for the Japanese than that. Forty Japanese ships had been sunk, forty-six others damaged, and 405 planes destroyed. The Japanese fleet as an offensive force had been virtually eliminated, in the first and last battle of the Pacific war to be fought by surface warships and in the classical manner. The navy and Jones were not to realise this, but it was unfortunate that the navy delayed even giving a satisfactory account of what it knew of the battle until interest had virtually died.

The navy kept from correspondents the extent to which Japanese suicide pilots, the "Kamikaze Corps," were crippling American ships. These attacks started at Leyte in October 1944 and grew in intensity throughout the spring and summer of 1945. At first, all mention of the attacks was banned, on the ground that it would provide the Japanese with a propaganda weapon. At Okinawa 100 United States ships were lost or damaged in Kamikaze attacks. West Coast shipyards were so glutted with damaged ships that some of the worst ones had to be sent to East Coast yards. Clearly, news of the Kamikaze could no longer be suppressed, so in mid-April Admiral Chester Nimitz officially announced the bare fact of their existence, and censorship was applied only to details of damage.[63]

On May 28, Phelps Adams of the North American Newspaper Alliance wrote the first detailed account of a Kamikaze attack. Adams, on a neighbouring carrier, saw two Japanese planes, each carrying 1,100 pounds of bombs, plunge into the flight deck of the U.S.S. *Bunker Hill*, Admiral Mitscher's flagship, killing nearly 400 officers and men, "and transforming one of our biggest flat-tops into a floating torch, with flames soaring nearly 1,000 feet into the sky."[64] The *Bunker Hill* limped back to the United States for repairs, so there was nothing to be gained by suppressing Adams' story, and the American reader learned at last the full danger of the Kamikaze.*

Censorship also kept from the public the full story of the most bizarre weapon of the war, the 9,300 Japanese paper balloons that drifted with the trade winds across the Pacific to bomb the United States. The balloons, the first inter-continental missiles, were thirty-eight feet in diameter and each carried an anti-personnel bomb weighing thirty-five pounds. They landed as far apart as Alaska and Mexico, and a few reached Iowa. The military results were minor, but they killed six people, caused much anxiety and uncertainty, tied up considerable forces of men, radar, and fighter aircraft, and eventually disappeared only because the B-29 raids on Japan dis-

---

* It is doubtful whether the British reader learned about the attacks until after the war. With the fighting in Europe over and Britain in the middle of a general election campaign, newspapers lost interest in the Pacific until the A-bomb was dropped on Hiroshima.

rupted their supplies of hydrogen gas. Little was published at the time, only brief details after the war, and the full story was not told until 1973.[65]

Another story suppressed by censorship concerned American-Australian relations. Ill feeling between the troops of the two countries reached such an intensity that in the so-called "Battle of Brisbane," in 1942, an American MP shot and killed one Australian soldier and wounded eight others, and in the Rockhampton, Queensland, railway station the following year a trainload of Australian commandos on their way to the battle zone fought a pitched battle with a trainload of GIs returning south on leave. The full story of these events did not emerge until more than thirty years later.

However, there was no holding back news when it involved a publicity-conscious general like MacArthur. When he returned to the Philippines on the morning of October 20, 1944, and waded ashore, not at just one beach but at several in succession, there were correspondents, cameramen, and MacArthur's own personal photographer to make certain that the event was recorded for history and reported widely. Generals and admirals had a right to enjoy their successes, but the picture of the war would have been more balanced—and perhaps more human—if the correspondents had not gone along with the public relations view that the troops were led by the finest soldiers since Alexander the Great and that the United States forces were as nearly perfect as possible—no cowards, no excessive drinking, no immoral behaviour, no black-marketeers, no looting, and no theft. It would have been too much to expect a little debunking, yet after the war John Steinbeck wrote (referring to the European theatre, but no doubt it applied equally to the Pacific): "We knew that a certain very famous general officer constantly changed press agents because he felt he didn't get enough headlines. We knew the commander who broke a Signal Corps sergeant for photographing his wrong profile. Several fine field officers were removed from their commands by the jealousy of their superiors because they aroused too much admiration from the reporters. There were consistent sick-leaves which were gigantic hangovers, spectacular liaisons between Army brass and WAACs, medical discharges for stupidity, brutality, cowardice, and even sex deviation. I don't know of a single reporter who made use of any of this information. Apart from wartime morale it would have been professional suicide to have done it."[66]

But why were there not more newspapers like the *Christian Science Monitor*, which told its correspondents to play down adventure and "home-town-boy-becomes-hero" stories, and concentrate on the significance of the war; to "keep the long-range meaning in view and write about it"?[67] Or more news cameramen like Damien Parer, an Australian, whose determination to convey exactly what the war was like, without glamour, faked shots, or false "look-at-our-happy-boys-at-the-front" propaganda, did not please the Australian Department of Information. It interfered in his work to such an extent that Parer resigned and went to work for Paramount, only to suffer guilt feelings for having, as he put it, "sold out to the Yanks."*

As it was, the failure of the correspondents to see the broader issues of the war, their emphasis on battle, bravery, glory, and adventure, plus the stultifying effects of censorship, meant that two major stories of the latter stages of the Pacific campaign—the United States submarine offensive against Japanese oil tankers, which largely won the war, and the development and use of the atom bomb—were poorly reported.

The success of the United States Navy in denying Japan her vital oil supplies is told in one simple table of figures. Of what was produced in the southern oil-fields that Japan had conquered, the following amounts reached Japan: in 1942, 40 per cent; in 1943, 15 per cent; in 1944, 5 per cent; in 1945, none. This was what really defeated Japan. With or without the atom bomb, the Russian entry into the Pacific war, or the great naval battles, Japan was finished, because her ships, aircraft, tanks, and vehicles could not move. They had no fuel.[68] This classic case of strategic warfare went unreported at the time because of a Navy Department directive that nothing should be written about submarines. Several correspondents wrote long and detailed stories on the daring achievements of American submarines against Japanese shipping, but the Navy Department refused to pass them. After the war, a censor wrote, "Large sections of the material not only contained no security information, but would have given the American people cause for rejoicing over sweeping naval successes."[69]

The atom bomb was a different matter. Its development had been kept secret, and even its testing, in New Mexico on July 16, 1945, was successfully passed off on an unsuspecting public by a lazy press as "an ammunition dump explosion" with no loss of life and little damage to property.[70] But there was no chance of keeping

* Parer was killed by Japanese machine-gun fire in the Palau Islands on September 17, 1944.

secret the use of the bomb on Hiroshima on August 6. President Truman announced the dropping of the bomb sixteen hours later and specified the nature of the weapon: "It is a harnessing of the basic power of the universe. The force from which the sun draws its power has been loosed against those who have brought war to the Far East." Radio Tokyo, on August 8, gave some idea of the bomb's effect: "The impact of the bomb was so terrific that practically all living things, human and animal, were literally seared to death by the tremendous heat and pressure engendered by the blast."[71] The Soviet press reported the bomb in a short item buried away with minor news and did not report the second bomb, at Nagasaki, at all. Bin Nakamura, a reporter with the Domei agency's Hiroshima branch, survived the blast, gathered as much information as he could, and got out the first eye-witness account of what had occurred. He even included a little speculation as to what could have caused such devastation. Fantastic though it must have seemed to him at the time, Nakamura wrote, "It might have been an atomic bomb."[72]

By the first week in September, three weeks after Japan had surrendered and nearly a month after Hiroshima, there still had been no account by a Western correspondent of the effects of the atom bomb on the two Japanese cities. General MacArthur had placed all southern Japan "off-limits" to the press and, instead of ending censorship, had tightened it. The army's press relations division was doing its best to push correspondents north to the newly liberated POW camps for what one correspondent called the "look-Mom-I'm-free" story. But, clearly, even MacArthur could not keep the world's press away from Hiroshima indefinitely.

On September 3, Wilfred Burchett of the *London Daily Express* arrived in Hiroshima, after a twenty-one-hour train journey from Tokyo. Burchett spent the morning surveying the ruins of the city and then handed his story to the Domei agency, which sent it by Morse code to Tokyo, from where it was relayed to London. Later the same day the first American correspondents arrived, flown in by the United States Air Force. The colonel in charge of this group was so annoyed to find Burchett already there that he refused to give him a lift back to Tokyo or even to carry a duplicate copy of Burchett's story. (To their credit, two of the American correspondents, Homer Bigart and Bill Laurence, protested about this treatment of Burchett.) His story, with some of the more horrifying details cut out, appeared in the *Daily Express* on September 5, an historic exclusive.

In Hiroshima, thirty days after the first atom bomb destroyed the city and shook the world, people are still dying, mysteriously and horribly, people who were uninjured in the cataclysm—from an unknown something which I can only describe as the atomic plague. Hiroshima does not look like a bombed city. It looks as if a monster steamroller had passed over it and squashed it out of existence. I write these facts as dispassionately as I can in the hope that they will act as a warning to the world.

Burchett's report was the first to describe radiation sickness. The American authorities reacted quickly. Army press relations called a conference in Tokyo to refute Burchett's account. There was no such thing as radiation sickness, the spokesman said. Burchett arrived back in Tokyo to walk into the conference just in time to hear the spokesman accuse him of "falling victim to Japanese propaganda."[73] Hiroshima was put out of bounds to all correspondents, Burchett was served with an expulsion order (later rescinded, after the U.S. Navy intervened on his behalf), and, in the United States, Major-General Leslie R. Groves, head of the Manhattan Project, as the programme for the development of the bomb had been known, declared flatly, "This talk about radio-activity is so much nonsense."*

But the dropping of the first atom bomb was a story too big to be handled as hard news, too important to be treated solely from a scientific point of view. Over the months, millions of words were written on every aspect except the obvious one: what was it like to be in Hiroshima on August 6, 1945? In May 1946, *The New Yorker* decided to remedy this by sending the author and correspondent John Hersey to find out what had happened at Hiroshima, to describe what survivors had seen and felt and thought, to tell what the coming of the atomic age had meant, not in terms of scientific marvels, but in terms of human suffering. *The New Yorker* devoted its entire issue of August 31 to Hersey's brilliant 30,000-word account, which related, in straight narrative form and in a sober, matter-of-fact style, what happened to six ordinary Hiroshima people on that extraordinary day. The story created a sensation. The issue sold out in hours, and the report was serialised in other

---

* To prove it, he invited a group of correspondents to New Mexico to inspect the site of the test explosion. The correspondents came away far from happy. They had had to wear shields over their shoes, so that radio-active earth would not stick to the soles, they had been followed by men with Geiger counters, and they had been warned not to carry any souvenirs of fused earth unshielded near the skin.

magazines and newspapers, broadcast by ABC in the United States and the BBC in Britain, and published as a book, *Hiroshima*, all over the world. It remains one of the literary classics of the war.

On September 2, 1945, General MacArthur, his hands ostentatiously stuck in his pockets, accepted Japan's surrender in Tokyo Bay on board the U.S.S. *Missouri*, a battleship that had survived Pearl Harbor. While General Stilwell toured the war ruins gloating over the destruction, a Domei correspondent wrote, "We await the will of our new masters."[74] In the euphoria of victory, the war was hailed as the best reported in history, and there was little of the deep soul-searching that had followed the First World War. Yet if we take away the few exceptional correspondents, the ones who believed that in a democracy the people need facts to make decisions, "even in time of war, or perhaps especially in time of war," if we take away the few who felt that if censors were to dictate the coverage then it would be better to have no coverage at all, what are we left with? The war against Japan was waged by a democratic alliance. But the coverage of the war, particularly in its early stages, was not so remarkably better in the United States than it was in Japan. With what were, no doubt, the best of motives, most Allied correspondents in the Pacific acquiesced in a system that gave the illusion of providing a free and open coverage of the war and its conduct. In fact, the result was the same as the system adopted in Japan—the public received only that news of the war which its government considered advisable to tell it.

## Chapter Thirteen

# Never Again
# 1940–1945

It is my earnest hope that…a better world shall emerge…a world
dedicated to the dignity of man.

—General Douglas MacArthur,
Manila, September 2, 1945

There were lots of bodies we never identified. You know what a
direct hit by a shell does to a guy…Sometimes all we have is a leg
or a hunk of arm.

—Technical Sergeant Donald Haguall,
Forty-eighth Quartermaster, Graves Registration,
in *American Treasury*

———

The last months of 1940 saw Britain facing bankruptcy. She had
paid for all her food, munitions, and shipping with cash, but,
as Churchill said in a long letter to Roosevelt, the moment was fast
approaching when the money would run out. Roosevelt replied with
the Lend-Lease Act, turning the United States into "the arsenal of
democracy" and providing Britain with special credits to buy whatever she needed.

The act was a strong indication that the United States would
eventually enter the war, and it was clear that when it did it would
be the dominating partner. So, with Britain stripped of her major
assets abroad and incurring gigantic debts, her continued existence

as a world power from that moment became doubtful.

Churchill must have sensed this, and to some extent it explains his obsession with the two areas where Britain would, for a time, still be able to exercise independent command—North Africa and the bombing of Germany. Thus, although for Hitler it was never more than a side-show, the desert campaign became for Churchill and the British the greatest theatre of war. It attracted the best war correspondents, produced some of the best writing, and was given a disproportionate amount of space in British newspapers. It threw up more heroes, more household names, and more legends than any other front. It became the most romanticised part of the war, "a correspondent's paradise," "the last gentlemen's campaign."

It was certainly true that if a war had to be fought, the North African desert was the place to fight it. The action took place in an empty arena, devoid of those houses, schools, churches, and civilians that elsewhere get in the way of battle. There were few roads, but, since the desert provided firm going for most of the time, armies were as free to manoeuvre as fleets. It was war in its purest form, what Alan Moorehead, there for the *Daily Express*, called a "Knights' tournament in empty space."

The armies rose to this romantic challenge. Erwin Rommel, the German general, became "the Desert Fox," operations were given names like "Crusader," armoured-division officers gave orders from their "chargers" (tanks or armoured cars), supply trucks moved off to rendezvous point on the order "Lead horses!," and an army public relations handout referred to officers "sitting in their tanks like sunburnt gods."

For the correspondents, the war had everything they could desire. They were free to go wherever they wished (for those who, like Quentin Reynolds, had come straight from the Soviet Union, this was scarcely believable). Stories were there for the asking, censorship —with some glaring exceptions—was reasonable, communications were good, and the desert bred a strange spirit of kinship. When Sir Archibald Wavell began his offensive, in December 1940, he announced it to six correspondents. Eighteen months later there were ninety-two, and more were arriving daily. On a personal level, many found the desert campaign the most profound experience of their lives.

Alan Moorehead has described the deep and lasting friendship that developed between him and his professional rival, Alexander Clifford of the *Daily Mail* (formerly "Eye-witness" in France), a friendship so intellectually complex that Moorehead frankly admitted, "Mentally, by this time, I was more married to Alex than I was to Lucy." Like most of the other correspondents, Moorehead and Clifford were young and vigorous, and had a sense of history and of the part they were playing in it, as well as the arrogance of the British, still strong in the approaching twilight. "We were rich and powerful. We believed that we belonged to a superior race of men ...we were constantly moving among coloured men whose territory for many years past had been governed by the British...wherever we went in the Middle East we remained on what we liked to think of as 'British soil'. Like the children of very wealthy parents, it seemed quite natural to us that we should occupy the best houses and hotels, that we should have at our command cars, motor launches, servants and the best of food."[1]

On a professional level, the correspondents were all absorbed into the military machine without much trouble. The Ministry of Information was beginning to consider war correspondents as "an integral and essential part of our fighting activities on land, on the sea and in the air,"[2] and as what General Montgomery was later to describe as "an element of my staff." Few correspondents resented this. Before going to the Middle East, most had thought a lot about their careers. Should they continue as reporters or should they enlist?

Clifford said that surely the answer was to become a war correspondent, presumably because one continued one's career but at the same time made a contribution to the war effort. Clifford and others had difficulty in deciding what a correspondent's duties should be. Clifford's strength as a correspondent—his refusal to be taken in by British propaganda and his recognition of German strength of purpose—made him pessimistic about Britain's future and thus more involved in doing his bit to preserve it. Flying over Sicily with the RAF, he had taken an air-gunner's place when the gunner was wounded and had shot down an enemy fighter, a fact that had to be hushed up, because war correspondents were supposed to be non-combatants. One of Clifford's colleagues, Ronald Monson of the *Daily Telegraph*, who described himself as "a battlefront correspondent by choice and conviction,"[3] had swum the Euphrates during the Iraqi revolt to rescue a badly wounded British private. The two of them having almost reached safety, they were helped by an officer, who was later awarded the Distinguished Service Order. Eye-witnesses to the incident affirmed that Monson should be awarded the Victoria Cross, but, again because war correspondents were accredited *to* the forces and not as part of them, he was merely mentioned in dispatches. This sort of involvement with the military, the correspondents' understandable feeling that they were part of the fighting forces, had a powerful effect on the reporting of the North African campaign.

To begin with, the war was reported very heavily in romantic terms. The enemy was depicted as brave and, in the case of the Italians, if not brave, then chivalrous. Hal Denny of the *New York Times*, who was taken prisoner and later exchanged, described Italians at Taranto pushing forward to offer British prisoners cigarettes and wrote of a fine meal they were given in the first-class section of the passenger liner *Vittoria*, to compensate for the crowded conditions in the Italian cruiser that had brought them from Benghazi. British troops began to sing the Afrika Korps' marching hit-song, "Lilli Marlene." Churchill saluted Rommel—"May I say across the havoc of war, a great general"—and the British public was inclined to treat "the Desert Fox" as its own hero.*

The arrival of General Bernard L. Montgomery as commander of the Eighth Army, a man destined to become one of the more controversial generals of the Second World War, added the one factor missing from this romantic version of the war—a hero-figure. Montgomery turned out to have many of the qualities of that other amazing character of the desert, Lawrence of Arabia. He had Lawrence's keen sense of personal publicity, of getting himself a good press while appearing to hate it, of "backing into the limelight." He, too, adopted unorthodox dress, had the same dislike of too much pomp and formality, and, above all, had the same sense of walking with destiny. In addition, Montgomery was expert at the striking phrase suitable for headlines in tabloid papers—"Hit the enemy for six"—and at memorable, if somewhat bloodthirsty, exhortations to his troops—"Kill Germans, even padres—One per week day and two on Sundays."[4] With "Monty" to write about, the neat, self-contained war in the desert was complete.

What occurred when the vicious, impure war from outside intruded on the desert saga is best illustrated by the treatment afforded Robert St. John. St. John, the Associated Press' man in Belgrade, got caught up in the German push through Yugoslavia, Greece, and finally Crete. He was persuaded by a Greek correspondent, abetted by the British Embassy, to send a story about

---

* Rommel did not deserve it. According to Arvid Fredborg's *Behind the Steel Wall*, he gave an interview in Berlin to neutral correspondents and described the British as cowards, whose methods of fighting were dishonourable.

300,000 British troops in Greece. The story turned out to be a fake —there were actually only 40,000 troops. He was bombed and strafed, and he was horrified by the slaughter he saw all around him—"All Corinth was permeated by the smell of burning human flesh. Human flesh burns with a sickening sweet smell. It's a smell you never forget." He tried to give a lethal dose of morphine to a man whose hands had been blown off and whose intestines were hanging out, and he listened all one night to the whimpering of a five-year-old girl "whose right arm hung in black tattered shreds." In his progress southwards, always just one jump ahead of the Germans, St. John became sick of his own calling. "We were just leeches, reporters trying to suck headlines out of all this death and suffering."

When he got to Cairo, St. John was amazed to learn that all that had been written on Greece had come from completely misleading official dispatches, that the story of what had really happened had not been told, and that no one wanted to know. "It seemed to be a tradition around the better places in Cairo that you mustn't let the sordid side of war creep in." So St. John sat down at his typewriter and tried to put down all he had seen: the horror, the shambles, the sacrifices. When he had finished, he was told he needed a stamp of approval on each page from the British military censor, the British naval censor, the RAF censor, the Egyptian civil censor, the British civil censors, and the telegraph office censor.

But it was already 5:00 P.M., and the censors had gone home. However, he was determined that the world should know what had been happening, so he tracked down all the censors (most of whom were at the Gezira Club) except the RAF one. The problem created by his absence was overcome by striking out all references to aircraft, or, rather, to the lack of them. Then St. John examined what the censors had left of his story. He had written that the evacuation from Greece had not been another Dunkirk; *the Greece evacuation had been much worse*. The censor struck out the second clause, thus completely reversing St. John's meaning. He and his colleagues, by interviews and observation, had conservatively calculated Allied casualties at 20,000 killed, wounded, or captured. The censor had changed this to 3,000. In another story, St. John wrote about an ambulance driver who had been burned to death. The censor changed this to read "shot." He explained that correspondents should try their hardest not to make war seem horrible and that death by being burned alive was not very pleasant to read about, was it? St. John argued that one reason for the debacle in Greece was the lack of aircraft. If Americans were made aware of the death and suffering in Europe, then they might stop buying automobiles and let aeroplanes be made instead. True, the censor said, absolutely true. Horror stories were fine for the United States, but Britain and the Empire must not be told how bad things were, and since the advent of radio it was impossible to keep stories for America and stories for the Empire nicely pigeon-holed. The policy, therefore, was to keep to safe middle ground. St. John gave up, deciding that he was lucky to be able to send anything at all. He waited until he got back to the United States and told the whole story in a book.[5]

Censorship in the Middle East was not always as stupid as this, and after the United States entered the war and the Allied invasion of North Africa took place, American censors showed in general a more liberal attitude to correspondents. Ernie Pyle, later to be famous as the man who chronicled the war of the ordinary soldier, began his spell as a war correspondent in North Africa with a bitter attack on United States policy, involving, as it did, disapproval of the French Committee of National Liberation, with its plans for sweeping reforms and a new status for France's colonies, and recognition of none but the de facto government in France. In practice, this meant keeping in power Vichy officials who had collaborated with the Germans. Pyle, and many others, objected to this. "We have left in office most of the small fry officials put there by the Germans before we came," he wrote. "We are permitting Fascist societies to continue to exist."[6] The American censor passed this. The British censor, on the other hand, allowed Richard Hughes of the *Sydney Daily Telegraph* to report a damning interview with the Vichy government's Resident-General, Auguste Noguès, but struck out Hughes' reference to Noguès' "abominable but appropriate halitosis."[7]

John Steinbeck, reporting for the *New York Herald Tribune*, wrote about three soldiers arrested for dealing in watches and about an American infantryman's deserting to get back to see the World Series, and the censor passed both stories. Drew Middleton, then with the AP, has said, "I covered the Kasserine Pass battle in Tunisia where the U.S. II Corps got its ass kicked, wrote it as a defeat, and the censor passed it."[8] Fletcher Pratt has pointed out, however, that the censor did not permit the mention of any particular officer as being responsible for the set-back. And perhaps the coverage of the political issues raised by the Allies' controversial complicity with the Vichy government in North Africa and by their attitude towards the Free French, led by General de Gaulle, should be assessed in conjunction with the fact that, at the height of the affair, six out of every ten Americans still had no idea who General de Gaulle was.[9]

As the campaign drew to a close, difficulties for the correspondents increased. "From the first to the last, we never 'saw' a battle in the desert," Alan Moorehead wrote. "We were simply conscious of a great deal of dust, noise and confusion. The only way we could gather a coherent picture was by driving hard from one headquarters to another and by picking up the reports from the most forward units as they came through on the radio telephone. Then, when the worst was over, we went forward ourselves to observe the prisoners and the booty and to hear the individual experiences of the soldiers."[10] There was danger, communications bother, and often a gruelling pace.

It is worth recounting a day in the life of one correspondent so as to appreciate some of the problems.

Richard Hughes, then of the *Daily Express*, and some American colleagues were watching the assault on Tunis when they learned that the city had fallen unexpectedly, other correspondents were already there, and a courier plane would leave for Algiers with dispatches at dawn. Hughes and his colleagues bundled into an open car and drove madly into the city, with Hughes, who is large and impressive, standing in the back seat, to try to convince the French traffic police that he was a general.

In one street snipers would still be dangerous, in the next the correspondents would be overwhelmed by people throwing flowers. At 8:00 P.M. Hughes began a nightmare drive back to the correspondents' camp. It was raining, the highway was choked with military traffic, and Hughes had to fight for space along a road still sown on either side with mines. The twelve-mile journey took six hours.

Hughes began writing at 2:00 A.M. and finished at 4:00 A.M., only to learn that the courier plane had been cancelled and that dispatches from the other correspondents had already left by jeep. So Hughes and Dan De Luce of the Associated Press drove to the airport and spent two hours begging the air force to find them a plane going to Algiers. At dawn a courier plane landed unexpectedly and agreed to take their stories. Then Hughes and De Luce drove back to their base, just in time to leave for the last push to Cape Bon.

It was not easy to write distinguished reports under such circumstances. Moorehead is now considered one of the better correspondents of the period, and his piece from the early days about a tank battle is often quoted as a good example of his ability to combine vivid description with tactical analysis. But it is difficult to say whether his North African work would be remembered had he not gone on after the war to become a famous and distinguished author. E. A. Montague of the *Manchester Guardian* mixed fine prose with accuracy and insight, and was, Captain Basil Liddell Hart reported, a reliable source of information for anyone trying to "probe for the truth in the half-truths of official information." Montague saw beyond the victories in North Africa and intelligently drew an unpopular but entirely accurate conclusion from the campaign—"If the Allied armies are called upon to fight the enemy in Europe they will find [only] the grimmest resistance."[11]

Richard Dimbleby and Godfrey Talbot of the BBC showed that radio could provide, in certain circumstances, a sense of participation that much newspaper reporting lacked. The live sound of British tanks going into action at Alamein and the victory skirl of the pipes as the Eighth Army entered Tripoli are easily recalled. Some of the broadcasters' analysis was also first-rate. Chester Wilmot of the Australian Broadcasting Corporation spent three months in Tobruk during the siege and later produced an excellent book on the subject. Wilmot was an unusual correspondent, little interested in reporting the war day by day—although he did this competently—but more in broad issues, the wide survey, an analysis of the campaign from both a military and a political point of view, an early indication of the talent that would make him a leading historian after the war.

But for every Wilmot there were ten or twenty correspondents who preferred lines like these, from a dispatch from Tobruk by a United Press correspondent, Jan H. Yindrich: "A 23-year-old Australian...a former travelling salesman from Sydney, was one of a patrol of seven who routed forty Germans and brought back one prisoner. 'We tore into them with the bayonet. I got the shock of my life, because not one of them wanted to fight. I bayoneted four of them myself and my bayonet stuck in the fifth. He was the only bloke who showed any fight. He grabbed my rifle and pulled me down on top of him...I bashed several other Germans over the head with the butt of my rifle till it broke. Then I picked up a stone...One of them shouted, "Peace, it is peace" and then in French "S'il vous plait." I must have killed about twelve of them altogether.' "[12]

There was plenty of this "blood-and-guts" reporting, and the usual share of overoptimistic dispatches. General Sir Leslie Morshead, who commanded the Australian Ninth Division in Tobruk, allowed Ronald Monson into the town during the siege, because, Morshead told Monson, he "had had enough of lying correspondents" and wanted someone he knew and trusted to report accurately. During the "Crusader" battle, in November 1941, more German tanks were destroyed in correspondents' reports than Rommel had ever possessed.[13] When the British retreat towards Alexandria was halted, the BBC reported that the Eighth Army was now safe because it had reached the "Alamein Line." A rifle-brigade officer wrote later, "When the troops heard this from the suave voice of the BBC announcer…they looked round at the empty desert and commented as only Riflemen can."[14]

There was, in fact, no such thing as an Alamein Line, but some correspondents managed to convey the impression that it stretched like some super Maginot Line across the path of Rommel's advance. The reports actually influenced Rommel, and he delayed his attack to make preparations to cope with it. The reports did not impress British army base personnel in Alexandria, who moved to safer quarters with great speed, and they failed to convince the British navy, which sailed out of Alexandria in such a hurry that it forgot to tell the army it was leaving.[15]

There was not a lot of reporting about looting, probably because many correspondents had discovered the joys of it themselves. "We looted parmesan cheeses as big as cartwheels and tins of strawberries, barrels of wine and cases of chocolate, binoculars and typewriters, ceremonial swords and Italian money galore," wrote Alan Moorehead. Even generals were not above a little theft. The sand-and-sun goggles that became part of Rommel's image as "the Desert Fox" he personally took from a captured British general.[16]

The other purely British battle with Germany, the campaign of the Bomber Command of the RAF, was perhaps the most gruelling continuous operation in military history. It began in 1940, and in those dark days Churchill believed it held the secret of victory. He was convinced that raids of sufficient intensity could destroy Germany's morale, and so his War Cabinet planned a campaign that abandoned the accepted practice of attacking the enemy's armed forces and, instead, made civilians the primary target. Night after night, RAF bombers in ever-increasing numbers struck throughout Germany, usually at working-class housing, because it was more densely packed.[17] Berlin itself became the most-bombed place on earth at that time. In 1943, the United States Air Force joined the RAF in striking, it was hoped at the time, crippling blows at German war industry and at Germany's will to continue the struggle. Yet it was all a delusion; German war production actually increased, and it was discovered too late that air-raids made the German population more, not less, determined.[18] Two raids alone demonstrate this, and also show the part contemporary war reporting played in perpetuating the delusion. The first is the so-called "dam-busters' raid," and the second is "Operation Thunderclap," the attack on Dresden.

The dam-busters' raid, on May 16–17, 1943, by Wing-Commander Guy Gibson and his pilots of 617 Squadron, was conceived as a way of breaching five dams in western Germany, thus disrupting the German war effort. Using a special "skipping bomb," two of the dams, the Moehne and the Eder, were breached, both to their foundations. Reception of the news in Britain was enthusiastic. The *Daily Express*' headline read FLOODS ROAR DOWN RUHR VALLEY. The *Daily Mirror* said, "Hundreds of square miles of devastation have spread through the Ruhr, Germany's most densely-populated industrial area, by the RAF's staggering attack on the Moehne and Eder dams." Guy Gibson, a hero-figure overnight, was awarded a Victoria Cross, to add to his DSO and DFC, and was sent on a tour of the United States.* A book on the raid, *The Dam Busters*, by Paul Brickhill, became Britain's biggest-selling war book and remains popular to this day. Millions have seen the film of the book (same title), and if the British public were asked to name the one war-time story it knew best, it would almost certainly plump for Guy Gibson and the dam-busters.

In 1972, after examining newly released Second World War official documents, the author and journalist Bruce Page wrote, "the truth about the raid is that it was a conjuring trick, virtually devoid of military significance," the "skipping bomb" just a gimmick, and that the real story of the raid was one of sloppy planning, narrow-minded enthusiasm, and misdirected courage. "Apart from the aircrews, the only people to emerge from the story with real credit are a handful of people in the Ministry of Economic Warfare who tried to calculate in advance whether the raid would damage the German war economy. They calculated accurately, that it would not…and they were ignored."[19]

The facts were that the Sorpe, the one dam whose loss would have hit the German war effort, was attacked by only a token force from 617 Squadron, and the bombs were not effective against it

* He was killed in action in 1944.

anyway. The breaching of the Moehne and Eder dams caused flood damage to agricultural land, of which Germany had no lack. It did not affect hydro-electricity, because the Moehne had only negligible electrical capacity and the Eder had none. The largest single group killed in the raid was not Germans, but several hundred Allied servicemen, Russian POWs who had been confined below the Moehne dam. The results of the raid, the official historian wrote in 1961, were "disappointing." But the myth, born in the rapturous press reporting of the raid, triumphed over the reality.

The difficulty for newspapers was that they had no way of checking—even if they had been sceptical, which they were not—whether the RAF's claims of the success of bombing raids were justified. The RAF was extremely reluctant to carry correspondents on missions, for the simple reason that there was little room in a loaded bomber for a non-combatant, especially one who might get in the way. Although, reading them now, one account of a bombing raid is much like another, at the time correspondents felt that they were missing good stories and chafed at the ban. Finally, in January 1943, after a long struggle with the Air Ministry, six reporters, representing the British, American, and Dominion press, and two broadcasters, one British and one American, were allowed to go with the RAF on a night raid on Berlin. A month later, after taking a short course in high-altitude flying, five others joined the United States Eighth Air Force in raids over Germany.

Throughout the war, while area bombing attacks on the civilian population were War Cabinet policy, Britain was officially claiming that she was bombing only military targets.[20] German and some neutral correspondents were writing that the RAF was systematically bombing civilian areas, but these stories were dismissed in Britain and America as propaganda. The Allied correspondents who went on raids in 1943 were the first to have an opportunity to check the truth of the matter. True, it is difficult, in a bomber at high altitude and under attack, to do much more than take the crew's word for where the bombs are falling, but in most cases correspondents went out of their way to stress that they were not falling on civilian targets. For example, James MacDonald of the *New York Times*, in an exciting story of an RAF raid on Berlin, wrote, "I am not permitted to divulge the various targets, but I can assure readers that they were picked for the special purpose of crippling Berlin's war effort."[21] Ed Murrow of CBS was closer to the mark when he reported, on a later Berlin raid: "The work done last night was a massive blow of retribution...this isn't a pleasant kind of warfare—the men doing it speak of a job…Men die in the sky while others are roasted alive in their cellars…This is a calculated, remorseless campaign of destruction."* [22]

By 1944 British bombers were suffering such losses at the hands of German night-fighter pilots that it was the Battle of Britain in reverse. RAF crews dropped enormous quantities of bombs in the North Sea, and an official report to Bomber Command spoke of them as having "balked the jump." [23] All this time, correspondents were fighting a running battle with the Air Ministry over strengths and losses. The ministry deliberately tried to conceal figures, by using phrases like "a strong force" and "a very strong force" and by talking at infrequent intervals of losses not exceeding an average of, say, 5 per cent. Correspondents argued that if the losses on a particular raid had been, say, forty planes and if this was the average loss of 5 per cent, then they were justified in estimating the total number taking part in that raid at 800. [24] But, in arguing their right to say this, the correspondents missed the real point—that the Air Ministry was concealing from them the ratio of losses of planes to numbers taking part not to avoid encouraging the enemy, but to prevent the reader from losing faith in bombing as a means of waging war.

So, unquestioned and unchecked, the theory of area bombing proceeded, in 1945, to its logical conclusion, "Thunderclap," a catastrophic blow against a single city, a raid so great and so terrible that it would precipitate the end of the war before Hitler could deploy his new V-weapons.

Dresden was chosen, and on the night of February 13, 1945, while Churchill, Roosevelt, and Stalin met at Yalta, the RAF struck at the city, crowded with refugees from the Russian advance, and dropped three-quarters of a million incendiary bombs, which created a fire-storm, an artificial tornado in which air is sucked into the fire centre at an ever-increasing speed. At Dresden, winds approaching 100 miles an hour swept debris and people into a fire centre where the temperature exceeded 1,000 degrees centigrade. The flames ate everything organic, everything that would burn. People died by the thousands, cooked, incinerated, or suffocated. Then American planes came the next day to machine-gun survivors as they struggled to the banks of the Elbe. Precise casualty figures

* Murrow later saw the effects of bombing from the ground. On April 22, 1945, he was in Leipzig and broadcast this report: "The shelling had caused no fire. There was nothing left to burn. The city had been killed by bombing. It was merely a dusty, uneven desert."

will never be known. The German authorities stopped counting when the known dead reached 25,000 and 35,000 were still missing. Some post-war sources put the number of dead at from 100,000 to 130,000, which would greatly exceed the number killed in the atom-bombing of Hiroshima and would make the 380 killed at Coventry or the Blitz *total* of 51,500 look small indeed.

Ministry of Defence records show that there were no war correspondents with the planes over Dresden, and so there were no eye-witness accounts of the bombing, except for those of a few air crews interviewed on their return, and they had been given various concocted explanations as to why they were bombing the city— they were attacking German army headquarters, destroying an arms dump, knocking out an industrial area, or even "wiping out a large poison gas plant."[25]

Both British and American newspapers correctly assessed the raid as "one of the most devastating 24-hour periods of aerial warfare ever known." British newspapers at first accepted and published without query the official line, that Dresden was an important military target.[26] Dresden was merely a staging centre for half a million refugees from Silesia. The marshalling yards were not even attacked. There were no ammunition workshops and factories, only a small works making optical lenses for gunsights.[27]

The truth first came out in Sweden. At 10:15 P.M. on February 15 a Swedish news bulletin transmitted in Danish to occupied Denmark said that the death toll in Dresden was already between 20,000 and 35,000. Newspapers in Switzerland and other neutral countries began to print horrifying accounts of the raid. Then, on February 17, after a briefing at Allied Supreme Headquarters in Paris, the Associated Press reported throughout the United States: "Allied Air Chiefs have made the long-awaited decision to adopt deliberate terror bombings of German population centers as a ruthless expedient of hastening Hitler's doom." This decision, of course, had been taken long before, and the bombing of German population centres had been going on for nearly three years. In Britain, the authorities imposed a total ban on the publication of the AP dispatch,[28] and it was not until March 5, nearly three weeks after the event, that the *Manchester Guardian* published an account suggesting that the bombing of Dresden had killed large numbers of civilian refugees in a particularly unpleasant manner.

There was, however, only one prompt, comprehensive, and factual report at this stage of what had happened in Dresden. It was a German one, written by Rudolph Sparing, war correspondent for the German Overseas News Agency. After a short but accurate description of the raid and an early estimate of casualties, Sparing wrote: "The Dresden catastrophe is without precedent. In the inner town not a single block of buildings, not a single detached building, remains intact or even capable of reconstruction. The town area is devoid of human life. A great city has been wiped from the map of Europe."[29]

When the United States entered the war and assumed the major rôle on the Western Front, American methods of dealing with war news began to intrude on the romantic attitude that had so coloured war reporting in the desert. Public relations, of which war correspondents were considered a part, became another cog in the massive military machine the Americans constructed to defeat Hitler. The supreme commander, General Eisenhower, spelt it out very clearly. "Public opinion wins war," he told a meeting of American newspaper editors. "I have always considered as quasi-staff officers, correspondents accredited to my headquarters."[30] So, beginning with the invasion of North Africa, the Allied system for controlling war correspondents grew steadily through the Italian campaign, and by D–Day and the Normandy battles it was as much a part of military planning as, say, logistics was.

Considerable resources were devoted to it. By late 1944 the Allied public relations headquarters in Paris had the staff and facilities to deal each week with 3 million words from nearly 1,000 correspondents, plus 35,000 photographs and 100,000 feet of newsreel film. A more easily understandable example is that the U.S. Ninth Army, which at San Antonio used to see about two journalists a week "only if we called them up," found, on arrival in France, that it was required to provide accommodations and mess facilities for fifty correspondents, a mobile radio link capable of transmitting voice to London, a teletype circuit and technicians to run it, plus fifty vehicles and drivers.[31]

Generals became conscious of the importance of projecting a good image, of knowing what the correspondents wanted and being able to give it to them. The U.S. Ninth Air Force organised an expedition of correspondents to tour the front lines to get a commander's view on tactical air support. The programme included a briefing by Generals Omar Bradley, George S. Patton, Courtney Hodges, and William H. Simpson. Simpson arranged for his public relations men to have on hand a sergeant fresh from the field. "Bring him in mud, beard and all," Simpson ordered. "Don't clean him up." Simpson made a few opening remarks to the correspondents and then said that an ordinary soldier who had sneaked, crawled, and run forward behind Allied skip-bombing and strafing would better be able to describe the fine quality of tactical air support. He then dramatically produced the muddy sergeant, who was seized by the correspondents and featured heavily in their stories.[32]

True, censorship remained, but it is the opinion of at least one noted correspondent of the Second World War that censorship enabled correspondents to be *better* informed about the war than, say, their colleagues in Vietnam would be twenty years later. Drew Middleton writes: "As long as all copy was submitted to censors before transmission, people in the field, from generals down, felt free to discuss top secret material with reporters. On three trips to Vietnam I found generals and everyone else far more wary of talking to reporters precisely because there was no censorship."[33] So we have strong evidence that the military came to consider correspondents as part of the forces, and it is equally clear that many correspondents felt the same way.

Early in the war it had been thought that correspondents, as unarmed non-combatants, were ineligible for decorations. Then General MacArthur broke American army precedent by awarding the Silver Star to Vernon Haughland of the AP for "devotion to duty and fortitude." Harry Gorrell, Jr., of the United Press was awarded the Air Medal for giving first aid to a wounded air-gunner during a bombing raid on Greece. Leo S. Disher of the UP got a Purple Heart after the attack on Oran, and at least five British correspondents were mentioned in dispatches for conduct under fire —Moorehead, Monson, Clifford, Basil Gingell of the *Exchange Telegraph*, and Cyril Ray of the BBC. Ray, who had been "almost a conscientious objector" early on, but then found, to his horror, that "I came to adore the whole business and had a wonderful time," got his mention in dispatches at Ortona, in Italy, for grabbing a gun and leading to safety a platoon of Canadians that had lost all its officers and NCOs—"I like to think that I managed it without killing any Germans."[34]

Some correspondents began to carry guns, and the American and British armies seemed to be preceded at times by jeeploads of journalists, who frequently found themselves taking towns and accepting surrenders. Ernest Hemingway, whose style of war reporting was to take part in the action as if he were an infantry officer and then to write about what had happened to him, reported that he had managed to gather a small combat outfit of his own, mostly French irregulars, and get into Paris almost a day before the official liberation. Evelyn Irons of the *Evening Standard*, accredited to the Free French Army, because Montgomery at first flatly refused to have any women war correspondents with the British forces, captured a village in Bavaria. "We somehow had got ahead of the advance, and four of us in a jeep came to this village and found no Allied troops had arrived. So we took it ourselves. We were armed —the French would have none of this nonsense about war correspondents not carrying weapons—so we held up everyone at gunpoint and accepted their surrender. Then we helped ourselves to all the radios, cameras, and binoculars we could find and drove off."[35] Marguerite Higgins of the *New York Herald Tribune* liberated prisoners at Dachau concentration camp. Kemsley correspondent Leonard Mosley parachuted behind German lines. Ronald Monson became so angry after seeing Belsen concentration camp that, as he said, "I drove my car into a column of German prisoners. My God, did they scream!"[36]

So for bravery and endurance—especially bearing in mind that none of them had to be there—war correspondents emerge with distinction. But what we are concerned with here is not their courage, but the quality of their reporting. It is worth reading the view of a war correspondent himself, Reginald Thompson, a captain in the British Intelligence Corps until he was released, in July 1944, to be a war correspondent for the *Sunday Times*. (He afterwards became a military historian of some renown.) In 1969 he looked back on the Allied campaign in Europe in a book, *Montgomery the Field Marshal*. Thompson concluded: "In the nature of things it was difficult, if not impossible for any man on the spot to write a balanced account of events as they were taking place. Some saw, others listened, and often the events men saw did not match the things to which men listened. Inevitably, prejudices were fed, and I believe that it was impossible for a general reader of a newspaper to form a balanced view of the progress of the war."*

It is possible to illustrate this by taking some of the major stories of the war in Europe and seeing how correspondents handled them. We will begin with the Dieppe raid, in August 1942, not because it was of any great military importance—one history gives it just six lines—but because it shows the lengths to which

---

* Or, as Thompson put it more succinctly to the author: "I'm certain that readers of *The Times* in 1854 had a damned sight better view of the Crimean War than readers of *The Times* in 1939–45 did of the Second World War."

the military establishment went to conceal its failures and how correspondents became involved in this concealment.

Six thousand troops—5,000 Canadians and the rest made up of British commandos, a token force from the United States Rangers battalion, and a few Frenchmen—raided Dieppe on August 19, 1942, for nine hours. What should have been a triumph for Canadian arms turned into a bloody massacre.

British archive papers released in 1972 show that the chief of combined operations, Lord Louis Mountbatten, told the War Cabinet the day after the raid that it had gone off "very satisfactorily." The planning had been excellent, air support faultless, and naval losses extremely light. Of the 6,000 men involved, two-thirds had returned to Britain, and "all I have seen are in great form."[37] Throughout this exercise in self-congratulation, not a word was mentioned about the crippling Canadian losses. How was Mountbatten able to get away with describing Dieppe in terms appropriate to the playing fields, when it would have been more accurate to rank it with the charge of the Light Brigade?

The official communiqués had been remarkable for confusion and contradiction, unable to state definitely the proportion of Canadians taking part. The confusion may have been deliberate, because the records show that the Ministry of Information was making an intensive effort to conceal from the public the extent of the disaster.[38] The United States Army's carefully worded communiqués gave the impression that the Rangers had dominated the raid and that the way back to Europe had been opened by American servicemen, a headline snapped up by American newspapers. WE LAND IN FRANCE, said the *New York Post*; TANKS AND U.S. TROOPS SMASH TO THE FRENCH COAST, said the *New York World-Telegram*.

Nine correspondents went on the Dieppe raid—four were American, three Canadian, and two British. At the pre-raid briefings, they had been told that as "representatives of a Free Press" they could report events as they saw them, "honestly and fearlessly, within the limitations permitted by considerations of security."[39]

A. B. Austin of the *Daily Herald*, who was later killed in the fighting in Italy, covered for the entire London press on a pool basis. Austin wrote an eye-witness report of the British commandos in action. It was a graphic, if bloodthirsty, description of one part of the operation. But it made no mention of the level of casualties and no mention of the Canadian forces, and it gave no indication whatsoever of the success or failure of the mission as a whole. Ross Munro, reporting for the Canadian Press news agency, was in a boat in which casualties reached 80 per cent, so he had some idea of the extent of the slaughter. He opened his story with: "For eight raging hours under intense Nazi fire, from dawn into a sweltering afternoon, I watched Canadian troops fight the blazing, bloody, battle of Dieppe."[40] He mentions later that "the fire was murderous" and that the Canadians' fire-power was reduced by casualties, but the over-all impression he gives is that the raid was a success.*

In fairness, it must be emphasised that the correspondents were labouring under double censorship—Combined Operations first, and then the ordinary censor. This, plus the fact that Lord Mountbatten insisted that no copy could be cleared until the correspondents had first been given a thorough briefing, meant that the first messages were not sent off until nearly thirty hours after the operation and were written by men verging on total exhaustion—Munro kept going on Benzedrine tablets. But the reason he was unable to tell the story of the whole tragic mess at Dieppe is more complicated, and lies closer to the core of the problem that confronted all the Second World War correspondents.

Before becoming a correspondent, Munro had joined the Canadian army and had been commissioned as a lieutenant in the Army Service Corps. "I was committed to the war completely and utterly, right from the start," he said later. "I don't think young people today could ever feel the commitment that we had. Maybe it was just jingoism, chauvinism, and stupidity, but we felt that the Germans were going to wreck this world of ours and that we would have to stop them. The troops were committed to it and I think the correspondents were—I certainly was. But it won't ever happen again. The war we were involved in was very clear cut. It really was a crusade."[41]

In Britain, Munro lived with the Canadian army, went on training courses and manoeuvres, and wrote a few lines about every Canadian soldier he met for the soldier's home-town newspaper. He thus acquired an intimate knowledge of the organisation of the army and, in turn, was widely known both to Canadian soldiers and to their families back in Canada. In these circumstances, it would have been unrealistic to expect him to write the truth about Dieppe

---

* Drew Middleton, one of the American correspondents on the raid, makes the point that the correspondents did not have access to any casualty figures, but he claims that none of his readers could have missed in his story the fact that casualties were heavy and the raid a failure.

at the time (or, later, to write about an incident when Canadian troops shot eight German prisoners-of-war). At Dieppe, it was understandable that, instead, he chose to write about the valour of the troops—"they must rank among Canada's immortals of the battlefields." Munro agrees now that the raid was an utter tactical failure, that practically everything that could have gone wrong did so, that, "looking back, it seems to me to have been an incredibly risky task with only a gambler's chance of success."

But, even if he had wanted to write on these lines immediately after the raid, the censors would not have allowed it. "When you went abroad as a correspondent, you couldn't report all that you liked. You were up against censorship and it was quite rigid. There was a reason for it, of course. If there was a bad action and half the battalion was shot up, it would be weeks before the impact was felt at home, so in a sense the censor protected the public. I can see that now. But you got very deft and skilled at telling the story honestly and validly despite censorship. I never really felt, except maybe on the Dieppe raid, that I was really cheating the public at home." After the raid, Munro was flown back to Canada and sent on a speaking tour of the seven cities that the Dieppe units represented. "I felt then that what I had done had been more useful than if I had stayed on as a lieutenant in the Army Service Corps. I had probably achieved more for my country."[42]

In a way, Munro was right. In a war in which the wickedness of the enemy did not have to be invented, a patriotic war correspondent got on side. But this meant that the war-time reader had to learn to treat most correspondents' dispatches like official communiqués—with some scepticism.

So it turns out that the most accurate summary of Dieppe at the time was actually a German one. Written by a PK man who had been visiting a nearby Luftwaffe station, it appeared in the *Deutsche Allgemeine Zeitung*. "As executed," he wrote, "the venture mocked all rules of military logic and strategy."

The correspondents' commitment to what Steinbeck described as "that huge and gassy thing called the war effort" is probably best illustrated by the Patton slapping incident. General George S. Patton, Jr., commander of the United States Seventh Army, an unhappy combination of a brilliant tank general and a perennial adolescent, known as "Old Blood and Guts," and given to wearing pearl-handled revolvers in cowboy holsters, was visiting a military-hospital evacuation tent in Sicily early in August 1943. He came across a soldier whom he suspected of feigning illness, and in front of the astonished doctors he slapped the soldier on the face. This incident might have passed unrecorded, but five days later, in another hospital tent, Patton came upon another private and again asked the man what ailed him. When the private replied that he thought it must be his nerves, Patton lost control of himself. He called the man a coward, "a yellow bastard," slapped him across the face with a pair of yellow gloves, and, when the soldier moved towards the door of the tent, kicked him in the behind. Patton then began to sob, and as he emerged from the tent he was heard by correspondent Noel Monks to shout, "There's no such thing as shell shock. It's an invention of the Jews."

As it turned out, Patton had picked the wrong soldier. The man had fought throughout the Tunisian and Sicilian campaigns, and his record was excellent. His unit doctor had tried to get him to have treatment a week earlier, but the soldier had refused to leave the front and had continued to fight with his unit until finally he was ordered to hospital.[43]

At the press camp, about twenty correspondents held a meeting and decided that no one would send a story about the incident. Instead, they appointed a courier to fly to Algiers with a petition to General Eisenhower asking that he order Patton to apologise to the soldier. Eisenhower, who had, no doubt, received other reports of the incident, wrote to Patton denouncing his conduct and ordering him to apologise to the two men, to all witnesses of the incidents, and to officers and men of each of his divisions, or be removed from his command. Patton complied, and so the whole story was known to thousands of soldiers, many of whom would be returning to the United States. Edward Kennedy, a senior Associated Press correspondent, asked to see Eisenhower, pointed this out to him, and expressed the view that, since the affair must eventually find its way into print, it would be preferable that war correspondents on the spot write it. Eisenhower told the correspondents that they were perfectly free to write the story if they wished to do so, but that he believed its publication would be of value to the enemy as propaganda and could embarrass the United States Army command.[44] This amounted to a personal request from Eisenhower to suppress the story, and that was what the correspondents on the spot did.

For nearly three months, not a word was published about the incident, although it continued to be widely discussed throughout the United States Army. Then the Washington columnist Drew

Pearson got to hear of it. Pearson was not a war correspondent and was not subject to army censorship. He submitted the story to United States internal censors for their reaction. The censors checked with the War Department, which urged that the story be killed for reasons of morale. Internal censorship felt that its terms of reference did not allow it to act on these tenuous grounds, and it gave Pearson its approval to publish the story.[45]

So a major news story—it concerned whether or not Patton should be removed from his command—was broken not by a war correspondent, but by a columnist who knew news when he heard it.

The reaction at Eisenhower's headquarters was one of confusion. At first, a blanket of censorship dropped over the case. Then an officer of Eisenhower's staff issued a statement, but told correspondents that they would be allowed to send only those facts contained in the statement. Finally, another officer announced that correspondents could send anything on the matter that they knew to be true.

Kennedy, who at least had the satisfaction of knowing that his advice to Eisenhower had been proved correct, got his story of the incident away on November 23. It was considered so important that, although months out of date, it still made headlines around the world, except, perhaps, in Britain, where *The Times* agreed with its correspondent at Allied headquarters in Algiers, Philip D. S. Ure, and his assessment of the matter. In a small item given minor display and headed only AN UNFORTUNATE INCIDENT, Ure wrote that the United States Army's statement had now put the matter in its proper perspective. He concluded with his own advice to Eisenhower: "General Patton is too great a commander to be anywhere but in the field of active service."[46]

This support for the military view of matters extended to most areas. When, at Monte Cassino, on February 15, 1944, the Allies bombed to pieces the 1,400-year-old monastery, parent house of the Benedictine order and one of the most picturesque monuments of Christian culture, they justified the act on the grounds of military necessity—the lives of soldiers mattered more than monasteries. A German PK reporter, writing for the *Deutsche Allgemeine Zeitung*, said, however, that the bombing was "a devilish work of destruction without any military justification whatsoever."[47] Who was right? Most Allied correspondents fell in step with the military argument. The bombing, they wrote, was justified as an act of war; only Roman Catholic bombardiers, all volunteers,

351

had taken part, and the building would be reconstructed when peace came.* Christopher Buckley of the *Daily Telegraph*, who watched the bombers return a month later and, in four hours of almost continuous action, wipe out the town of Cassino as well, admitted that "it was easy, perhaps too easy, to feel compunction." But he simply reminded himself, and his readers, who had started it all: "I was in Warsaw on September 1, 1939 and I remember from the evidence of my own eyes who was responsible for letting loose this terrible weapon."[48]

Correspondents argue that even if they had wanted to challenge the official version of events they were in no position to do so, because they were totally dependent on the military to be able to see the war at all. The arrangements for the press coverage of D-Day, for example, needed complete co-operation from the military, which treated correspondents as just another branch of the services; as part of a broad deception plan, it put them on a train to Scotland a month before the invasion and kept them there for a week. True, it then did everything it could to help them cover the landings, accrediting no fewer than 558 writers, radio reporters, photographers, and cameramen, and providing censors on the assault craft and even on the beaches. A friendly British officer tipped off Ross Munro of the Canadian Press about a destroyer going back to Britain from a Normandy beachhead to pick up General Montgomery, thus enabling Munro to send back the first dispatch from the coast of France and maintain his record—the first eye-witness stories from Spitsbergen, Dieppe, Sicily, and Italy. There were limited radio links, but there were courier planes, speed-boats, and special facilities for those who had to stay in London, and, as the invasion proceeded, the four correspondents with advanced headquarters were given long briefings by Eisenhower himself.

The correspondents sent some 700,000 words on the first day, and yet, reading their reports thirty years later, one cannot escape the impression that the sheer size of the operation overwhelmed most of them. Radio emerges best, partly because, unlike the wartime newspapers with their restricted space, it could give a story as much time as was merited. The BBC assigned forty-eight correspondents for D-Day, including Chester Wilmot in a glider, Richard Dimbleby with the RAF, Robert Dunnett with the United States Army, Stanley Maxted in a minesweeper, and Robert Barr

* It was.

with General Eisenhower at SHAEF. But it was an air force observer, Air-Commodore W. Helmore, in a Mitchell, recording for the BBC under the stress of a bombing attack the first eye-witness account of the Normandy invasion, who had listeners all over the world silent by their radios: "This is history; it is a thing I can't be eloquent about in an aeroplane because I've got engine noises in my ears. But this really is a great moment for us…I feel detached, and that awful feeling that the great history of the world is unfolding before us at this very moment…"

"At this very moment"—that, too, was the feeling George Hicks of CBS conveyed, broadcasting from an American naval flagship in the Channel. He was interrupted by static, the sound of the ship's whistle, explosions, heavy ack-ack, voices cheering, "terrific background noises," and his own excitement—"If you'll excuse me, I'll just take a deep breath for the moment and stop speaking." For dramatic effect, a sense of immediacy, and the involvement of the listener, Hicks' broadcast typifies the lead that radio maintained in its D-Day reporting. Beside it, the newspaper reporting appeared stilted and overly formal, and even the "soft" pieces (articles that are not hard news, but are expected to add to the reader's understanding of an event, to round out the picture, to help tell a fuller story) seemed, for the most part, unsatisfactory.

Perhaps censorship was to blame. W. W. Chaplin of NBC wrote a bitter but illuminating description of General de Gaulle making a political speech in a little village in Normandy before an audience that included a peasant woman with a wheelbarrow holding the body of her child, killed by the Allied bombardment. The censor would not pass it. He wrote about a French town showered from the air with leaflets warning the inhabitants to leave because the Allies would have to shell and bomb the town. The wind carried the leaflets miles away, the people received no warning, and they died in the rubble of their houses. The censor killed the story.[49] Perhaps what was needed was more correspondents of the calibre of A. J. Liebling of *The New Yorker*. Liebling's ability to seize on what appeared to others to be the commonplace and to fit this into its proper context in the war was not part of the equipment of many correspondents. An article he wrote for his magazine after the invasion, with his descriptions of dead cows—"the stench of innocent death"—a crutch in an abandoned farmyard, and the contents of a deserted house—old corsets, a marriage contract dated year 3 of the First Republic, dingy family photographs, a pile of exercise books marked "*Cahier d'Albert Hedouin*," a bundle of letters from Louis

Hedouin of the 336th Infantry beginning on September 25, 1914–brought some idea of what it was like to be advancing with the Allies through Normandy in the summer of 1944.[*][50]

As the war moved closer to the German homeland, it was not only a question of correspondents being dependent on the military. In many cases, it was a matter of correspondents becoming involved in military affairs. Small groups of favoured war correspondents enjoyed easy access to commanding generals and their chiefs of staff. Generals Bradley and Patton played unashamedly to a public that knew of them from correspondents' reports. Public opinion became a new factor in the generals' own power struggle. "At times it constrained, at others it instigated the very tactics of warfare," wrote correspondent Reginald Thompson. Thompson, who was there, says that those correspondents close to a general had considerable glamour and, consequently, an avid readership. They backed their general in his feuds—the "Monty-versus-Bradley" one was notorious—sometimes with serious results. "The differences between Montgomery and Bradley were exacerbated by correspondents' reports," Thompson has said. "As a result the feeling of unity in the Allied army which Eisenhower had done so much to protect was killed and a united effort made impossible."[51]

This breach had its effect on correspondents' judgement. Military successes were exaggerated to boost national pride, set-backs minimised to maintain morale. "Operation Market Garden," Montgomery's overambitious plan to cross the Rhine, strike into the heart of the Ruhr, and "end the war by Christmas," is a good example. When troops of the First British Airborne dropped on Arnhem to seize the bridge there, the British press hailed the operation as an overwhelming success. The BBC described it as "an incredible achievement, certainly one of the outstanding operations of the war." In fact, it was a dreadful muddle, the full extent of which did not emerge until thirty years later, when Cornelius Ryan's book, *A Bridge Too Far*, provoked a re-examination of what had gone wrong. When the British were forced to retreat with heavy losses, the BBC switched to "a valuable stand" by a "depleted, gallant, and undaunted force."[52] This was true, but it missed the main point, that the operation had failed and should never have been undertaken. Correspondent Cyril Ray, who dropped on

---

[*] All of *The New Yorker*'s war reporting was excellent, but its audience infinitesimal; its volume of war news represented less than 1 per cent of the total reaching the United States, and its war-time circulation never exceeded 234,000.

Nijmegen, complained, "We tart up our reverses so heroically that it takes an effort to grasp that Arnhem was not merely a British defeat but a German victory."* [53]

The Americans were equally guilty with their reporting of the German counter-attack in the Ardennes in December 1944. Everyone had thought that the Germans were finished, and it took until the end of January 1945 before they were finally repulsed. The German advance sent correspondents fleeing to Maastricht, where they tried to send their first stories. The censor quickly pulled them into line. What they had written, he said, was "sheer hysteria," and he told his staff to use blue pencils freely. The correspondents were grateful. "What could have been an unholy mess," Wes Gallagher of the Associated Press cabled to his office, "was saved by the good sense of front line field press censors." [54]

Correspondents now emphasised epics of bravery like the American defence of Bastogne, with its tough commander whose reply of "Nuts!" to the German demand for surrender has passed into American military legend. There was some description of roads choked with burnt-out American vehicles and wrecked equipment, but this was attributed to the attempted flight of non-combatant units. The ground troops were fighting huge German Royal Tiger tanks with only rifles and bazookas, and were "so filled with remorse and vindictive revenge that they fall upon the enemy with only knives in their hands and with tears streaming from their eyes." [55]

It was true that many Americans fought bravely and well. But the Ardennes story was incomplete without an account of the panic, confusion, and cowardice the German onslaught produced. One American major-general who had never seen action before had his division taken away from him and died soon afterwards of heart failure. A colonel of an armoured unit handed over to his number two when the attack began and was last seen in a highly nervous state hurrying to the rear "for ammunition." Moves to restore morale were handicapped by the knowledge that, while some American soldiers were fighting for their lives, another 19,000 or so were absent without leave, wandering about in bands stealing petrol, hijacking food trucks and trains on the way to the front,

* Ray did not get a word out, because the British officer in charge of censorship and dispatch stuffed the correspondents' messages into his battledress blouse and produced them several days later, saying, "Terribly sorry, you chaps, but I quite overlooked them." American readers were also in the dark; there were no American correspondents at Arnhem at all.

and making fortunes on the black market.[56] Correspondents wrote nothing about this, and if they had tried, the censor would undoubtedly have killed it.*

Perhaps the answer to a correspondent's dilemma in a war that is basically a just one is not to concern himself with the mainstream of events. Many a Second World War reporter simply opted out. When the war moved on from Paris, it left behind in press head-quarters at the Hôtel Scribe a lot of correspondents who felt that there was nothing to be said for following armies going full tilt through the old battlefields of the First World War when they could pick up enough stories in Paris just by plucking at the sleeves of soldiers on leave. Occasionally, the military wondered where all the correspondents had gone. At one vital stage of the Battle of Nijmegen, a British officer remembers, "there was only one war correspondent present...I asked him which paper he represented and learned that he came from a women's magazine. Heaven knows how he got there; for a certainty, the usual gang of war correspondents, who we got to know quite well in the campaign, were still playing poker in Brussels."[57] According to one of the American public relations officers, correspondents in Brussels were known to take dinner in one of the better restaurants, stroll around the town, return to their deluxe Canterbury Hotel, and begin their stories, "On the Western Front..."[58]

Another possibility was to write the atmospheric, reflective arti-cle that captured the feel of the place and time. If it also conveyed the waste, confusion, and tragic futility of war, then the result was war reporting of the A. J. Liebling level, achieved by very few, unfortunately. Or a correspondent could deliberately choose an unpopular backwater of the war, with the hope that one outstand-ing story would make weeks or months of waiting worth while. Evelyn Irons of the *Evening Standard* was with the French Army: "At this stage the Allies didn't give a damn about the French, but General de Gaulle was determined to restore some of the lost hon-our and glory of France. He was absolutely adamant that even though it might have no military value, French troops would cross the Rhine and occupy part of Germany. The French troops were terribly ill-equipped—the Allies wouldn't let them have anything —and in the middle of February, a bitter winter that year, half of

* Cyril Ray wrote after the war of a major arrested by the provost-marshal of the Seine base area. Before he was caught, the major had sent back to the United States $36,000 from black-market deals. The provost-marshal told Ray, "It's just like Chicago in the Al Capone days."

them were wearing old tennis shoes because there were not enough boots. But de Gaulle had them all lined up and with a band playing and a tricolour fluttering he marched them in their tennis shoes across a pontoon and onto German soil. It was probably France's only great moment in the war."[59]

There was a third course open to correspondents—the Ernie Pyle way. One of the curious facets of the reporting of the Second World War was that the more the importance of the individual soldier was reduced by technology, the more correspondents concentrated on writing about him. Pyle was the master in this field. He was the antithesis of the Hemingway "gung-ho" school of war correspondents. A slight, gnome-like man, he hated the whole business. He knew nothing of strategy or of military affairs, and so he concentrated on human-interest stories. No detail about life for the GI in Europe was too insignificant to report—he once wrote about the colour of the soldiers' foot ointment—no complaint too minor to mention, no message too mundane to relay. His column became the inarticulate GI's letter to his folks back home. He was "the GIs' friend" because he made them feel important; he was on their side. "I love the infantry because they are the underdogs. They are the mud-rain-frost-and-wind boys. They have no comforts, and they even learn to live without the necessities. And in the end they are the guys that wars can't be won without."[60]

When Pyle took up a GI cause, in some 300 daily newspapers and 10,000 weeklies, the military authorities appeared to tremble. On Pyle's demand, all soldiers were allowed to wear stripes on their sleeves for overseas service, and combat infantrymen got $10 a month extra pay. Congress even nicknamed the legislation approving these measures "the Ernie Pyle bill." In fact, the military authorities loved Pyle as much as the GIs did. He was good for morale; General Bradley said, "Our soldiers always seemed to fight a little better when Ernie was around." Various branches of the services competed to have him with them, because his fame rubbed off on whomever he joined. The sad thing was that Pyle genuinely did not understand the magnetism he had for soldiers, and the emotional responsibility it involved became a burden for him.

In August 1944 he had had enough. "If I heard one more shot or saw one more dead man I'd go off my nut." So he went back to the United States for a rest. But the military needed him, and he came under heavy official pressure to move to the Pacific theatre. He did not want to go. "The old romanticism about getting itchy feet to get back to the front is a myth as far as I am concerned." In the Pacific, the military went to great lengths to protect him, and, since his appeal depended so much on mixing with the ordinary fighting man, his writing lost its quality. He resented his new assignment, and he angered the troops there by saying that the real fighting was in Europe and that those in the Pacific theatre had "no conception whatsoever of what our war was like."[61] He had a premonition that he was going to be killed, and he died from a sniper's bullet on the island of Ie Shima, renowned and rich, but lonely and frustrated covering a war theatre he did not want to know.

It is interesting to imagine how someone like Pyle would have covered the last days of Germany, with the looting, the plundering, and the horror of the concentration camps. It was a difficult period for correspondents. The Russians were lyrical. "The night is coming to an end," wrote Vassily Grossman, who was with the Red Army closing on Berlin. "The day will be ours, on from the break of dawn. Let the guilty tremble." His colleague Ilya Ehrenburg continued to ignore the party line and call for vengeance. "The Germans have been punished but not enough...Who can stop us now? The hour of revenge has struck." The note of exultation appeared also in British and American reporting. "This is the greatest armoured joyride in history," wrote Hal Boyle of the United Press, as the Allied military machine rolled into the heart of the Third Reich.

Those German correspondents still surviving were reduced to writing propaganda of the "hang on, hold out, wait for the miracle weapon" variety. The German public had long since stopped believing in newspapers or newsreels; audiences watching films showing the Allied landings in Normandy being repulsed were actually seeing German shots taken of the abortive Dieppe raid. It was thought, however, that readers might still have faith in the astrological column, and so some PK men suffered the indignity of creating horoscopes that spoke of valleys of darkness to be passed through before the final triumph, and these were distributed to newspapers, with orders to publish them.[62]

It was hard for a reader, in April 1945, to find a correspondent prepared to describe the grotesque heap of rubble that once was Germany, a correspondent whose reporting showed either a trace of pity for the conquered or any regret at the loss of compassion that war brings to both sides.

One such man, however, was V. S. Pritchett of the *New Statesman and Nation*. On April 7, 1945, Pritchett wrote:

We have become connoisseurs of ruin in this war. We have learned to distinguish between the bombed, the shelled, the burned, the blasted. But in England we have never seen a town that has been killed, completely written off and abandoned, a place as empty as Pompeii, that has the sour stench of a rubbish heap from one end to another, and where the only sound is the drip of water from the broken roofs. Disgust furs the tongue and sours the stomach. One does not pity the people of the town, nor does one hate them. One says, 'they did it to us', but one is left just staring. The scene has gone beyond argument. The terrible thing is that one has no feeling at all…One is stripped of every feeling, the humane and the inhumane, and curiosity grows feeble. This is negation. The mind and heart have got to begin at the beginning again and learn all they knew once more.

Pritchett described Allied looting in Germany and succeeded in getting his story by the censor. (William H. Stoneman of the *Chicago Daily News* was less successful. A dispatch he wrote about American looting at Jena, where the Zeiss company had its headquarters, was held up until the war was over.)[63] Pritchett cleverly linked the looting to the absent victims. "It occurs to you the street is yours. Any street, any house. You can have the lot. Climb over the wreckage, dig out a motor bicycle, 'Help me with this goddam door, I've seen a lot of tools I want, Boys! Wine glasses! What have you got? Anything in there? Books? Wine? Cameras? Some son of a bitch has been here before.' You go in your boots crunching the glass. You climb gingerly into a bedroom. The wardrobe has fallen on to the bed. What awful hats the woman wore. Why only one evening shoe? She read Tristan and Isolde. She hoarded face powder. Her child had a red engine. She did not finish knitting the jumper."

It required correspondents of exceptional ability to convey the full horror of the concentration camps. The fact that such camps existed was not news. British newspapers had reported in 1942 that over 1 million Jews had been killed since the outbreak of war. Some details of the methods of execution had been published, and the Russian Ilya Ehrenburg had exposed some of the Red Army's terrible discoveries in a report in *PM* in August 1944. But many readers had tended to discount much of Ehrenburg's writing as propaganda, because of his intense emotion over what the Germans had done to his country: "I cannot write calmly about what I see…a Tommy gun not a pen is needed."[64] Even as camp after camp was liberated, it was difficult for readers to believe that this was part of a deliberate and systematic policy of the German government. The disastrous effect of the Allied atrocity propaganda of the First World War was now fully realised. Horror stories about beastly, bloodthirsty Huns mutilating nuns and nurses and using bodies to make soap had appeared in newspapers between 1914 and 1918, and had later turned out to be lies. What guarantee had the reader in 1945 that the stories now about German concentration camps were not equally false? The correspondents did their best. The difficulty was to find a way of conveying the horror in a manner that carried conviction.

Marguerite Higgins of the *New York Herald Tribune*, who, with Sergeant Peter Furst of *Stars and Stripes*, liberated Dachau, tried the hammer-blow approach written as an eye-witness account. She described how the newly liberated inmates beat one of the SS guards to death and how, when they were again confined until they could be screened for typhus, "in a suicidal protest against the quarantine edict they flung themselves against the electrically-charged fences, electrocuting themselves before our eyes."[65]

Ronald Monson, who was with the first troops to enter Belsen (the Wehrmacht had invited them to take the camp, because it did not like what it had seen there, and also because it feared a cholera outbreak), tried flat, unemotional description. But a few days after his article appeared Monson found that a well-known British prisoner-of-war would not give him an interview because, the POW said, "I don't want to talk to a correspondent who could write such lying propaganda about the Germans."[66]

Ed Murrow begged his audience to believe him: "I pray you to believe what I have said about Buchenwald. I reported what I saw and heard but only part of it. For most of it I have no words." Larry Solon of the *London News Chronicle* concentrated on the child inmates of Sandborstel camp—"Their starved bodies and their eyes like coals burning in their starved grey faces bear witness to the greatest mass horror the world has seen."[67]

Gene Currivan of the *New York Times* came closest to writing a convincing report. Currivan arrived at Buchenwald several days after it had been liberated and was considering what was left for him to write about when he learned that the United States military authorities planned to force 1,200 German civilians from the nearby city of Weimar to make a tour of the camp. Currivan wrote about this, and because his report combined a description of what the Germans were seeing with a description of the effect it had upon them, Buchenwald at last seemed real. "The stench, the filth, and the misery defied description," wrote Currivan, and he told how the German civilians fainted, wept, were sick, went white and turned away in horror.[68]

But perhaps the concentration camps were beyond the power of any correspondent to convey fully to his listener or reader. Was Eisenhower, watching Patton walk off to vomit after their tour of Ohrdruf Nord camp, right in his assessment that "this is beyond the American mind to comprehend"?[69] Perhaps the French inmate of Buchenwald, a former Havas reporter, had the answer when he told Murrow, "To write about this you must have been here at least two years, and after that...you don't want to write any more."[70]

Admitting all the problems that correspondents faced, it remains hard to reach any conclusion other than that the war could have been better reported. The main bar to this was the correspondent's excusable identification with the cause and his less excusable incorporation into the military machine. Apart from finding a style of reporting that did not bring a correspondent into conflict with the military authorities, it is not easy to suggest what anyone could have done about this. Organised revolt or individual defiance achieved little. Two examples, Anzio in 1944 and the reporting of the German surrender, will suffice.

An Allied bridgehead at Anzio, on the coast below Rome, established in January 1944, met a heavy German counter-attack. When the Allies were hard pressed, General Alexander, acting on orders from Churchill, closed down the radio transmitter that had been sending correspondents' dispatches and imposed policy, in addition to security, censorship. Alexander said this was done because correspondents had been sending alarmist reports saying that Anzio could become another Dunkirk. Both British and American correspondents cabled protests to their newspapers, to the War Office in London, and to the Office of War Information in Washington. There were editorials of protest in newspapers, and the matter was raised in the House of Commons and taken up at a press conference in Washington with Secretary of War Stimson. But only when the military situation changed in the Allies' favour were transmission facilities restored, and policy censorship remained until the front was stabilised. Correspondents were left in no doubt about their position. To cheers in the Commons, Churchill said: "Such words as 'desperate' ought not to be used about the position in a battle of this kind when they are false. Still less should they be used if they were true."[71] In Washington, Stimson said that correspondents had been too pessimistic: "It would be a good plan in future to remember the old adage, keep your shirt on."[72]

As the fighting in Europe drew to an end, seventeen correspondents were selected by the SHAEF public relations section and on May 6, 1945, were flown to Reims to witness, on behalf of the world's press, Germany's surrender. The SHAEF press officer warned the correspondents that the announcement of the surrender would first be made by the heads of the governments concerned. "I pledge each one of you on his honour as a correspondent and as an assimilated officer of the United States Army not to communicate [the news] until it is released on the order of the Public Relations Director of SHAEF."[73] The surrender was signed in the early hours of May 7. The SHAEF press officer now told the correspondents that orders had come from "a high political level" that the news would not be released until the following day at 8:00 P.M., when it would be announced simultaneously in Paris, London, Moscow, and Washington.

The correspondents were worried by this, particularly the American news agency men. For them, being first, even by only a minute or two, was what the business was all about, and they did not believe that the embargo would hold for such a lengthy period. They protested, but were told that the decision was a political one and could not be changed. Edward Kennedy, an experienced war correspondent, and at the time head of the Associated Press' Paris bureau, was the most disturbed. He had been the first correspondent into Bizerte, in Tunisia, at some risk to his life, but then the army had made him toss a coin with other correspondents for first use of the limited telegraph facilities, and Kennedy had lost. He had been among the first correspondents into Paris, again at some risk, but the area was controlled by the Third Army and Kennedy was with a unit of the Seventh, so the censors would allow him to say nothing about his exploit.[74] He had sat on the Patton slapping story, at Eisenhower's request, only to see it broken in the United States by columnist Drew Pearson. Now he found himself third in the queue for transmission facilities out of press headquarters at the Hôtel Scribe in Paris.

Boyd Lewis of the United Press had been the last man on the press plane at Reims and the first off at Paris. He was on the first jeep away from the airport, was first into the press centre, and was first on not just one but all the telegraph outlets, thus blocking his rivals. James L. Kilgallen of the International News Service was second in line, having beaten Kennedy in the race to the press centre by throwing his typewriter under Kennedy's legs.[75] The final blow came when Kennedy and the other correspondents heard that SHAEF had ordered the German government to announce the signing of the surrender "by all possible means"—and that the German army radio had done so not in its code, but in the clear!

Kennedy decided that the time had come to break the embargo, or, as Boyd Lewis, who still feels strongly about what happened, has put it, "to impose his own ground rules and betray his colleagues." Kennedy went to the chief American censor and said, "I give you warning that I'm going to send the story."[76] Kennedy then used a complicated military telephone link that the censors had overlooked, put through a call to the AP office in London, and at 3:24 P.M. dictated: "Reims, France, May 7—Germany surrendered unconditionally to the Western Allies and the Soviet Union at 2:41 A.M. French time today."[77] The British censors raised no questions, because they had been given no special instructions on surrender stories. Less than ten minutes later, the story was around the world and wild victory celebrations had begun.

For four hours officials were silent. Then the British Ministry of Information stated that the official announcement would be at 3:00 P.M. on Tuesday, May 8, which would be V-E Day. Similar statements were made in Washington and Paris. All this confirmed that Kennedy's story was true, that it had forced the official announcement, and that it was the scoop of the war.

SHAEF, in an unprecedented action, immediately suspended the filing facilities of the Associated Press throughout Europe and withdrew Kennedy's accreditation. Fifty-four of Kennedy's fellow correspondents wrote to Eisenhower: "We have respected the confidence placed in us by SHAEF and as a result have suffered the most disgraceful, deliberate and unethical double cross in the history of journalism."[78] Eisenhower issued a statement deploring Kennedy's action, and the president of the AP apologised to the nation. On May 17 SHAEF served Kennedy with his departure papers. He flew back to New York to a mixed reception. Many newspapers and most readers—who felt that they had a right to know the news and could not see what the fuss was about—supported Kennedy, but his employers did not.

While he waited in solitude in a New York hotel, increasingly morose, the Associated Press reviewed his case and finally offered to let him continue with the agency if he admitted that he had been wrong. Kennedy refused to do so and was fired. In 1948 a proposal was made to the United States Congress that a special decoration be awarded to those correspondents who went with Kennedy to

Reims and who then "displayed the highest ideals of responsible journalism...by keeping inviolate the pledge of confidence and military secrecy imposed upon them."[79] This was the nub of the matter: Kennedy's sin had been to transgress on matters of military confidence and secrecy. If correspondents were allowed to challenge the military in these areas, then their usefulness as "assimilated officers, or "quasi staff officers," to repeat Eisenhower's phrase, would be ended. Edward Kennedy found a place in journalism's history, but when he died, in an automobile accident in 1963, he was still nursing the bitterness he felt at the treatment he had received in 1945.

The early years of victory were no time to assess the rôle correspondents had played in the war. But if sufficient correspondents had undertaken a critical look at their performance, some improvement in the whole standard of war reporting might have followed. Thirty years later, Charles Lynch, a Canadian, who had been accredited to the British army for Reuters, grasped the nettle. "It's humiliating to look back at what we wrote during the war. It was crap—and I don't exclude the Ernie Pyles or the Alan Mooreheads. We were a propaganda arm of our governments. At the start the censors enforced that, but by the end we were our own censors. We were cheerleaders. I suppose there wasn't an alternative at the time. It was total war. But, for God's sake, let's not glorify our rôle. It wasn't good journalism. It wasn't journalism at all."[80]

# Chapter Fourteen

# Korea,
# The United Nations' War
# 1950–1953

It was clear that there was something profoundly disturbing about
this campaign and something profoundly disturbing about its
Commander-in-Chief.

—Reginald Thompson,
British war correspondent, in *Cry Korea*

———

Korea, divided after the Second World War into a Communist
North, supported by Russia, and an anti-Communist South,
supported by the United States, had long been a flash-point in the
Cold War. When hostilities broke out on June 25, 1950, it was automatically assumed in the United States, in the grip of the
McCarthy era, that the Communists were responsible. Who actually attacked whom in those early hours of the war was never properly
established, and the issue soon became academic, as the Communists, in a series of startling successes, nearly wiped out the South
Korean army in the first week's fighting. The United States had little difficulty in persuading the United Nations to begin an official,
collective "police action" in Korea, (a report from two Australian
officers on secondment to the UN, Major F. S. B. Peach and
Squadron Leader R. J. Rankin, said North Korea was prepared for
war). For the first time since the intervention in Russia after the
First World War an allied army was created to confront Communism with force of arms.

The first correspondents on the spot to cover this frustrating action—"a war we can't win, we can't lose, we can't quit"—were the news agency men based in Seoul, but two days later a transport aircraft with fighter cover brought Keyes Beech of the *Chicago Daily News*, Frank Gibney of *Time*, Burton Crane of the *New York Times*, and Marguerite Higgins of the *New York Herald Tribune* into the South Korean capital from Tokyo. They were just in time to flee as Communist troops entered the city. With South Korean troops bolting all around them, blowing up roads and bridges without warning their American advisers, and often killing their own men by mistake, the American correspondents went south to Suwon. Three days later, with newly arrived members of the growing press corps, they were running again as Suwon, too, fell to the Communists.

The early days were a blur of exhaustion—correspondents had to fly to Japan to get their messages out—anger, and fear. At Suwon, only one American officer bothered to warn the correspondents and the enlisted men that the town was in danger. "The events of that evening provided the most appalling example of panic that I have ever seen," Marguerite Higgins wrote later. She quoted a Signal Corps sergeant as complaining that "those sons of bitches are trying to save their own hides—there are planes coming, but the brass won't talk. They're afraid that there won't be room for everybody."[1]

There was worse to come. The retreating correspondents came to a halt in the far south of the peninsula, and on July 5 the first American troops went into action. From a foxhole overlooking the main road near Osan, a United Press correspondent, Peter Kalischer, watched raw American infantry—some were boys of only nineteen or twenty—make contact with a column of twenty Russian-made tanks spearheading the North Korean advance. He did not stay to watch for long. The Americans fell back, then broke and ran, stumbling and sobbing in panic. He joined a file moving south, and on the third day staggered into Taejon to tell the story of how the Communists had clobbered the Americans in their first engagement of the war. Tom Lambert of the Associated Press and Marguerite Higgins witnessed similar debacles as the Americans fled south. "It was routine," Higgins wrote, "to hear comments like 'Just give me a jeep and I'll know which direction I'll go in. This mama's boy ain't cut out to be no hero.'" She also quoted a young lieutenant, his lips trembling with exhaustion and anger, who asked her, "Are you correspondents telling the people back home the truth? Are you telling them that out of one platoon of twenty men, we have three left? Are you telling them that we have nothing to fight with, and that it is an utterly useless war?"[2]

Amazingly, at this stage of the war the correspondents, to the fury of the army, were writing just that. There was no censorship, only a voluntary code of war reporting aimed at preserving military secrecy, and so the correspondents wrote freely of "whipped and frightened GIs," of the panic, of the poor example set by many officers, of the lack of equipment—"you can't get a tank with a carbine"—of the general desperation, horror, and lack of purpose. The army in Korea and at MacArthur's headquarters in Tokyo accused the correspondents of being traitors, of "giving aid and comfort to the enemy." Lambert and Kalischer, in Tokyo to dispatch stories, were told at headquarters that they would not be allowed to return to the Korean front. They had, the public information officer said, failed to observe "discretion and co-operation in the dispatch of their file" and had been guilty of disclosing information that would have "a bad moral and psychological effect" on the United Nations troops. Lambert and Kalischer made representations to MacArthur himself, who lifted the ban but took the opportunity to remind all the correspondents that they had "an important responsibility in the matter of psychological warfare."

The correspondents now did not know where they stood, and when, on July 25, the army extended the voluntary code to rule out any criticism of decisions made by United Nations commanders in the field or of conduct by allied soldiers on the battlefield, their confusion grew. Their motives, they insisted, were entirely patriotic. As Marguerite Higgins wrote, "So long as our government requires the backing of an aroused and informed public opinion...it is necessary to tell the hard bruising truth...It is best to tell graphically the moments of desperation and horror endured by an unprepared army, so that the American public will demand that it does not happen again."[3] So, rather than continue with voluntary censorship—described by one correspondent as "you-write-what-you-like-and-we'll-shoot-you-if-we-don't-like-it"—the correspondents found themselves in the unusual position of imploring the military authorities to introduce full, official, and compulsory censorship. The authorities were not yet ready to do this, but clearly the first round was theirs.

For, as well as having censorship problems, the correspondents were at the mercy of the army for communications, transportation, and housing, and in Korea all these were so poor that Hal Boyle, the Associated Press columnist, wrote, "Never since and including the Civil War have correspondents had so few of the facilities vital to their trade." Press headquarters at Taejon was in a dingy, rat-infested government building. The correspondents had one large room in which to sleep, eat, write, and fight. There was one military telephone line to Tokyo, into which each correspondent shouted his story for his rationed period of a few minutes between midnight and 4:00 A.M. There was no secrecy, there were no exclusives—because everyone could hear what everyone else dictated—and there was no other way to get a story out, short of flying with it to Japan. Rutherford Poats of the United Press borrowed some carrier pigeons from the Japanese newspaper *Mainichi*, but after the first bird took eleven days to fly from Korea to Tokyo he abandoned their use. Repeated representations to the army for better facilities brought the reply that equipment was more urgently needed elsewhere. Higgins wrote: "Colonel Pat Echols, MacArthur's press chief, apparently regarded the press as natural enemies. He couldn't get rid of us completely, but he could make our reporting life very difficult." Clearly, with the war going badly for the allies, the military felt that the fewer correspondents around, the better.

But by now they were rolling in from all over the world. Early August saw 270 correspondents from nineteen countries reporting the war, including Homer Bigart, a top correspondent for the *New York Herald Tribune*, whose personal feud with colleague Marguerite Higgins became news in itself. There were some veterans of the Second World War back in action, but others had had enough. George Johnston, the Australian who had worked for *Time* and *Life*, the *Saturday Evening Post*, and groups of British and Australian newspapers in the Pacific theatre, rejected an offer to go again. "All I remembered of the war was an incredible number of dead human beings and a vast amount of misery. All for what? The answer was certainly not going to be found by running around with a green flash on my shoulder filing urgent press collect."[4]

The correspondents soon sorted themselves out into front-line men—regularly about sixty or so—and headquarters men. Most of the front-line men went armed. Fred Sparks of the *Chicago Daily News* explained his reason: "Suppose a gook suddenly jumps into my foxhole. What do I do then? Say to him, *Chicago Daily News?*" But others had a different reason for carrying guns, and their attitude disgusted the veteran British correspondent Reginald Thompson, of the *Daily Telegraph*. "The dearest wish of a lot of

368

them was to kill a Korean. They'd cradle their weapons in their arms and say, 'Today I'll get me a gook'."[5] Clearly, anyone so itching for action and the chance to spill a little blood should never have been accredited as a correspondent in the first place, but nothing was done about it.

The front-line correspondents wrote the usual "I-was-there" copy, especially Marguerite Higgins and Bigart, who took chances that others rejected and spurred each other on in a private competition to get top billing on the *Herald Tribune*'s front page. "This correspondent was one of three reporters who saw the action," wrote Bigart, "and the only newsman to get out alive." Higgins, an attractive, ambitious woman, who had once told friends that she did not plan to marry "until I find a man who's as exciting as war," matched Bigart shot for shot. "A reinforced American patrol, accompanied by this correspondent, this afternoon barrelled eight miles deep through enemy territory," she wrote. "Snipers picked at the road, but the jeep flew faster than the bullets which nicked just in back of our right rear tire."

Considering the risks that this type of reporting involved, it was surprising that Higgins and Bigart survived. Two British correspondents, Ian Morrison of *The Times* and Christopher Buckley of the *Daily Telegraph*, were not so lucky. Both had got through the Second World War, and, although they had considered retiring from war reporting, both had found its lure too strong. Morrison's career, in particular, reveals the obsession for highly competitive excitement and the willingness to sacrifice personal relationships that mark the dedicated war correspondent. It will be remembered that he had covered the British retreat in Malaya, warned that Singapore would not be held, and spelt out the lessons of the debacle in South-East Asia. In New Guinea, this seemingly frail figure, wandering about the jungle with his equipment in a small petit-point bag slung over his shoulder, at first had appeared to the muscular Australian troops as a laughable example of an effete Englishman. But he was deceptively tough and soon became something of a legend, that mixture of intellectual awareness and physical courage that has produced some of the more remarkable British men of action. His reporting of the war against Japan and his early post-war campaign for the need to understand the new national aspirations in Asia won him a wide reputation. Few knew what the cost had been.

During the war Morrison had contracted dengue fever, tropical ulcers, amoebic dysentery, and recurrent malaria. He was in two

369

plane crashes, suffering fractured vertebrae in the second one, and was slightly wounded in 1943 and again in 1945, in Batavia. He was painfully thin throughout the war, and by V-J Day was down to 130 pounds. Both his children were born while he was away at the war, and at one stage, because he was moving about so much, he had only one letter from his wife in two months. But, he wrote, "fortunately these things don't worry me at all." Contrary to what is generally believed, not all war correspondents are paid huge salaries. During the war Morrison's did not exceed £750 a year. (Later this was increased to nearly £1,000, but Morrison calculated that for the privilege of being a *Times* correspondent he had had to draw on his savings in one two-year period to the extent of £2,000.)

Yet such was the attraction the business held for him that, as the war drew to a close, he wrote to *The Times* pointing out that there would be "scope in China for war correspondents for ten years after the war at least." *The Times* agreed to keep him in the area, based in Singapore, and, although the war with Japan was over, for months on end Morrison was in the midst of fighting in Burma, Indonesia, India, Indo-China, Malaya, and the Chinese mainland. In 1949 he began to feel that he had had enough. His work, he felt, "puts a strain on marriage"; his son was seven, and he wanted the boy to go to school in England. So he wrote to *The Times* asking for a posting in Europe, preferably in Rome or Vienna.

The lure of the craft was too strong. Within months Morrison had changed his mind: "I have no desire to be transferred to a European post when such tremendous things are happening here." He planned a long break in Europe instead. But as soon as news of the war in Korea reached Singapore, Morrison was cabling *The Times* asking to be allowed to cover the front-line fighting: ANXIOUSEST KOREAWARD EARLIESTLY.[6] *The Times* agreed to his request. In Korea, Morrison sent back several first-class reports, mostly objective and accurate descriptions of what was happening in areas overrun by Northern troops, and one penetrating analysis of the weaknesses and excesses of the South Korean regime.

Then, on August 12, Morrison, Buckley, and Colonel Unni Nayar, a former Indian army public relations officer in the North African campaign, who was in Korea as India's representative on the United Nations Commission, went out in a jeep behind the South Korean lines. It should have been a comparatively safe journey, but near Waegwan the jeep struck a land-mine and blew up. Morrison and Nayar were killed instantly. Buckley, who had been planning to give up being a war correspondent and settle down in England, died later in hospital. Morrison was thirty-seven, Buckley forty-five.

On September 15, General MacArthur tried to end the war quickly with an amphibious landing at Inchon, on the west coast of the peninsula, opposite Seoul. It was an outstanding military success, but from the correspondents' point of view it was a disaster. There was little secrecy in allied circles about plans for the landing—it was known in the Tokyo Press Club as "Operation Common Knowledge"—but the army declined to consult the correspondents about their requirements for covering it. As a result, the first assault waves included press barges loaded with magazine writers and columnists, while many daily newspaper correspondents did not get ashore until two or three days later. The only correspondents well cared for were the four news agency chiefs, who were personal guests of General MacArthur on board the command ship *McKinley*. They were provided with special facilities and with telephones direct to Tokyo, so that the official view of events would get quick and wide distribution.[7]

Any attempt to by-pass the official channel in sending home the story of the landing was heavily punished, and Bill Shinn, a young Korean-born Associated Press reporter, who heard of the start of the action from a South Korean general and beat the army's own release by nine hours, was denied any further use of the military telephone between Korea and Tokyo. It needed the sceptical, compassionate eye of a British correspondent, James Cameron of the *Picture Post*, to put all the inflated claims, hyperbole, bungling, and butchery into perspective.

> This was the operation to end the war. This was the pay-off to take the Thirty Billion Dollar Police Action out of the red at last. This was MacArthur's final argument in his personal one-man deal with destiny…Then when it came, it stunned for a while. All the fear came first. Perhaps we shall never understand how it came off as it did, nor why the enemy failed to do any of the three things that could have crippled the whole enterprise. Anyhow, God was on the side of the big battalions; they were even that big.

Cameron, an unequivocal pacifist, a man who believed that *nothing* justifies war, went on to describe the massive build-up of landing craft, marshalling craft, and "things full of cranes and guns and lorries and bulldozers and marines…tall boats and squat boats and bad-dream swimming tanks.

"In the middle of it all, if you can conceive of such a thing, there was a wandering boat, marked in great letters PRESS, full of agitated and contending correspondents, all trying to appear insistently determined to land in Wave One, while contriving desperately to be found in Wave Fifty." Cameron's party lands on the wrong beach, and is followed by the Marines, "blazing in behind us, making retreat quite out of the question." He describes the South Koreans mopping up the town, "rounding up householders, herding them around, ancient crones and baby toddlers too, with the strange venom of the Korean, which is that of the armed adolescent." Cameron concluded that

> the North Koreans lost their beach-head, they lost their town, they lost their lives in numbers, and with them the lives of many simple people who shared the common misfortune of many simple people before them, who had the ill-luck to live in places which people in War Rooms decided to smash...Sitting here, one is glad to be alive—a bit ashamed maybe, but glad.[8]

On September 27 Seoul was recaptured, and after a brief pause the United Nations forces pushed on across the thirty-eighth parallel. Pyong-yang, the capital of North Korea, fell on October 19. Almost all the correspondents saw the war as over and began to make arrangements to return to base. Few thought it significant that the North Koreans had withdrawn with hardly a fight, that they were proving difficult to catch, that each enemy front-line soldier was largely self-sufficient, needing only one man at the rear to support him (compared with the United Nations figure of nine at the rear for every one at the front), or that, under conditions in which the mechanised UN army bogged down, the North Koreans could still move huge loads on their backs with the aid of the H-frame, perhaps the decisive instrument of the war.* Reginald Thompson watched the performance of the United Nations troops with a critical eye, and while most correspondents were writing of the success of MacArthur's drive northwards and forecasting an early peace he sent an air-mail article to his office predicting, with devastating accuracy, that "if China or Russia is provoked...this army will disintegrate, leaving its vast equipment behind it... Against an armed enemy of any quality, we shouldn't have a chance."

---

* This was a wooden frame shaped like the letter H and strapped to the shoulders.

Early in November, Charles R. Moore of the United Press wrote that he had reached the Yalu River, the border of Manchuria, with American forward troops and had spat into the water. Then the Communists struck back, and the dash to the Yalu collapsed at a single stroke. MacArthur's headquarters desperately tried to maintain that the war was still going well, but finally, under the strongest pressure from correspondents of the stature of Lindsay Parrot of the *New York Times* and Howard Handleman of the International News Service, it admitted that "alien" forces had been engaged from across the Yalu River.

Trying to report the war now became close to a farce. The United States Air Force began issuing bulletins in which pilots gave the figures of enemy killed down to the last man. Soon MacArthur's intelligence officers followed suit, and from previously not having known the enemy's strength to within 100,000 or 200,000, they now claimed to know the numbers of Chinese involved down to single figures. MacArthur ordered a counter-attack, made his famous "home for Christmas" promise, and, when the assault failed, claimed it had been conducted only to expose the real plans of the "surreptitious Chinese." As the United Nations troops streamed south again, the briefing conferences for correspondents grew increasingly ridiculous. The "Chinese hordes" were swollen to nearly a million in a few days, though everywhere out of contact. The briefings finally ended when Michael Davidson of the *Observer* asked, with deceptive seriousness, "Will you tell us how many Chinese battalions go to a horde, or vice-versa?"[9]

The approach of Christmas found the United Nations armies in freezing foxholes south of the thirty-eighth parallel, where the war had started. They were no longer singing the current hit tune "Goodnight Irene," and the "Kilroy was here" signs ceased to be amusing. The weather was a nightmare, caught best by *Life*'s photographer David Duncan with his shot of a weary Marine hacking out his breakfast from a frozen tin of beans. The beans were encased in ice crystals, and little ice slivers had formed on the Marine's beard. Duncan snapped the Marine and asked him what he wanted most for Christmas. "Gimme tomorrow," the Marine said, and went back to his beans. Shaken by defeat, badly hit by frost-bite and by respiratory diseases, the troops waited with trepidation for the next Chinese advance.

By now, the more serious war correspondents had taken time off from the retreat to consider the war as a whole, and their conclusions were not calculated to improve morale. What Reginald

Thompson had written about the UN force had proved true. When faced with a determined Chinese attack, many UN troops had broken and run. Rene Cutforth of the BBC saw "young GIs of hardly nineteen or twenty, ill-trained and in total panic, throw down their weapons and run from the front, tears streaming down their faces."[10] True, some troops had fought bravely and well, the Commonwealth Brigade and the Turkish contingent in particular. But the South Koreans had behaved deplorably. An American colonel complained, "South Koreans and North Koreans are identical. Why then do North Koreans fight like tigers and South Koreans run like sheep?" Bitter recriminations began among the allies, with accusations of flanks left unprotected and positions abandoned needlessly and without warning. Correspondents began to write wondering whether South Korea was worth saving.

There was certainly reason to raise the question. Under the government of Syngman Rhee, corruption flourished. The police, who had been trained by the Japanese army, were heavily involved in the black market, in blackmailing citizens with the threat of denouncing them as Communists, with providing destitute refugee girls to the brothels, and with protecting the distillers of the highly dangerous liquor concocted for the allied troops.* It was not unknown for South Korean conscripts to die of starvation in military camps because corrupt officers had profiteered on food supplies. There had been 14,000 political prisoners in gaol awaiting trial at the outbreak of the war. Executions for political reasons began when Seoul was recaptured by the allies, and when the South became threatened again they increased at an alarming rate.

John Colless, an Australian working for AAP-Reuter, reported that the police shot fifty-six political prisoners alongside the Sariwon railway station and then watched American troops give first aid to those who had not died outright. According to historian Peter Gifford, Colless then became obsessed with South Korean atrocities and abused an AAP-Reuter executive claiming that his atrocity stories were not being used. APP-Reuter recalled Colless to Japan and did not allow allow him to return to Korea until later in the war. Peter Webb of the United Press, at British Twenty-ninth Brigade headquarters, wrote: "White-helmeted military police—their

---

* Rene Cutforth has recalled that only the Canadians seemed to succeed in preventing their soldiers from drinking this liquor. They adopted the dramatic expedient of tying to a post the body of a soldier who had died from it and parading the Canadian troops in front of the unfortunate man.

nationality is not known—with orders to keep UN troops at a distance, stood guard today while a South Korean firing squad executed another batch of prisoners on Seoul's 'Execution Hill', according to eye-witnesses. Women and children were among those shot in a previous mass execution." Webb quoted a British soldier as saying, "It was just mass murder."[11] The *Daily Worker* carried a page of photographs, taken by I. R. Lorwin of Pix Incorporated, a New York agency, and distributed in Britain by the Associated Press. The photographs showed a mass execution by South Korean troops at a spot about eight miles from Seoul. The victims, who included some women, were bound together in pairs, shot in the back by firing squads, and then finished off by an officer with a pistol.[12] Rene Cutforth reported a British army officer's story of finding forty to fifty prisoners crammed in a room fourteen feet square and described angry British troops standing guard over another batch of prisoners to prevent the South Koreans from executing them.

One correspondent took direct personal action to stop the executions. He was Alan Dower, of the *Melbourne Herald*. Dower, a former commando officer, was driving into Seoul with Cutforth and a cameraman, Cyril Page, when they passed a column of women, many carrying babies, and wearing straw masks over their heads, being escorted by South Korean policemen. Dower stopped the jeep and asked what was happening. "These Communists," a policeman said. "They go be shot, executed." Dower said, "What? Babies Communist? Who say they Communist?" The policeman looked puzzled. "People say. People in street point and say that person Communist." The three correspondents followed the column to a gaol on a hill at the outskirts of Seoul and watched the heavy gates clang behind it. Then Dower, who was armed, thudded on a peep-hole with the butt of his carbine. When a policeman's face appeared, Dower pointed the gun at him and threatened to shoot him if he did not open the gates. Inside, the correspondents saw the column of women and children kneeling alongside a deep, freshly dug pit. On the other side were two machine guns. "Hell," Dower said, "this is a bloody fine set-up to lose good Australian lives over. I'm going to do something about this." The correspondents stormed into the office of the gaol's governor and found him sitting behind his desk. Dower aimed his carbine and said, "If those machine guns fire I'll shoot you between the eyes." After the governor promised that the guns would not fire and that there would be no executions, Dower threatened that if he failed to keep his word Dower would seek him out and kill him.

In Seoul, Dower went to United Nations officials and told them what had happened. "They pleaded with me not to make an international incident out of it. I told them that I had sent my paper an outline of the story, but if there were any more executions, then I'd send a story that would rock the world. They promised to see that there would be no more women and children death marches and as far as I could find out there weren't."[13] But what had already been published, by Dower and by a few other correspondents, mostly non-American, caused a wave of disillusionment with the South Korean regime and with the war in general. The British Sunday newspaper *Reynolds News* summed up this feeling: "Terrible things are being done in Korea in your name. They are being done by Syngman Rhee's police sheltering behind US and British United Nations troops."[14]

Clearly, if the war was to go on, criticism of the United Nations effort could not be allowed to continue. On December 21 MacArthur's headquarters ended the voluntary censorship system and imposed full military censorship on news messages, broadcasts, magazine articles, and photographs from Korea. Any hope the correspondents had that the new censorship would be applied leniently and with discretion was quickly squashed when, two days later, Peter Webb of the United Press was suspended from working in Korea because of his report on the death of General Walton H. Walker, commander of the United Nations Eighth Army. Webb had been riding in a jeep with David Walker of the London *Daily Mirror* when, near Seoul, they came upon a wrecked jeep, a pool of congealing blood, and a pair of dark glasses—General Walker's "trademark." They hurried to the nearest field hospital and arrived in time to hear a surgeon say to a group of officers, "I'm sorry, gentlemen, we did everything we could, but he's dead." Back in the Seoul press room, Webb telephoned to Tokyo, and while he dictated his story Walker sang loudly, so as to prevent the other correspondents from overhearing. The story was cleared by the censor in Tokyo, but when it appeared Eighth Army headquarters arrested Webb. It was eighteen hours before he was able to prove that he had not violated censorship regulations, and he was then released. The point had nothing to do with military security. It was really over whether correspondents were going to "get on side" and do what the military told them. The Peter Webb incident suggested that they were not.

So, early in January, correspondents were placed under the complete jurisdiction of the army, and for any violation of a long list of instructions they could be punished by a series of measures beginning with a suspension of privileges and extending, in extreme cases, to deportation or even trial by court-martial. The new instructions included the usual limitations on matters involving military security, but had been extended to include "any discussion of allied air power" and "the effect of enemy fire, unless authorised." And it was now forbidden to make any criticism of the allied conduct of the war or "any derogatory comments" about United Nations troops or commanders, quite unprecedented restrictions. Clearly, from now on the war was going to be reported only the way the military wanted it to be. There were protests. The *London Daily Dispatch* said censorship was now so tight that it was no longer officially possible to say anything about United Nations troops other than that they were in Korea. But there is evidence that, even without the new censorship, a backlash had begun against the early critical reporting of the war, a feeling that it was time to "get on side" and stop helping the Reds.

James Cameron and the photographer Bert Hardy were in Korea for the *Picture Post*. They witnessed and photographed the brutality of the South Korean authorities towards political prisoners: "They are roped and manacled. They are compelled to crouch in the classic Oriental attitude of subjection in pools of garbage. They clamber, the lowest common denominator of personal degradation, into trucks with the numb air of men going to their death. Many of them are." Cameron protested to United Nations officials and was told, "We wish you would try to do something about it, we can't." So Cameron wrote an article, which was illustrated by Hardy's photographs. To balance the picture, he included a description of an American POW being guyed through the streets of Pyongyang, a false nose fastened to his face, a swastika on his arm, the Stars and Stripes trailing in the dust. The *Picture Post*'s editor, Tom Hopkinson, spent some weeks checking Cameron's evidence and consulting him on a presentation of the article that would be moderate and calm, yet irrefutable. The issue was actually on the presses when the proprietor of the magazine, Edward Hulton (later Sir Edward Hulton), decided that the article would give "aid and comfort to the enemy" and instructed Hopkinson to withdraw it. Hopkinson said he could not accept Hulton's argument and refused to do so. Hulton then sacked him.[15]

Rene Cutforth witnessed the American use of saturation bombing and napalm in Korea. Napalm was a new weapon, and Cutforth felt that his listeners should know exactly what it did. He described the lazy fall of the canister, the roaring flame of impact, and the rush of heat so intense that, even though he was some distance away, he felt as if his eyebrows had been singed. "Then over this scene of silent desolation crept a reassuring smell that immediately took me back to Sunday dinners in Britain—the smell of roast pork, for that's what a napalmed human being smells like." There was a longer than usual interval after he sent this dispatch before Cutforth had an acknowledgement from the BBC. "When it arrived, it was in the form of a cable so long that it must have cost the BBC about £75 to send. It began: 'This is to explain why we cannot use your M59 [message].' Then there were several hundred words of explanation which made not the slightest case for killing the story. It was a moment of some disillusionment for me."[16]

Ed Murrow of CBS went to Korea in the first summer of the war, even though he "had thought to have seen enough of dead men and wounded buildings, of fear and high courage," during nine years in Europe. Murrow did not like what he saw in Korea and decided that reporting some of the unpleasant facts would help, even though this went against his usual practice—"I have never believed that correspondents who move in and out of the battle area, engage in privileged conversations with commanders and with troops and who have access to public platform, should engage in criticism of command decision or of commanders while the battle is in progress." Murrow set out what he had seen of the war and his pessimism about the outcome, and concluded by quoting a psychological warfare officer: "One thing we must do is to write out our war aims. Tell them what they can look forward to when we've won the war. And then drop that statement in leaflet form on top of them." Murrow wrote: "And a correspondent who shall be nameless added, 'That will take quite a bit of writing and, when the pamphlet is done, maybe we should drop some on the American people, too.'" CBS felt that Murrow's broadcast might hurt the war effort and decided not to use it.[17]

I. F. Stone, then a columnist for the *New York Daily Compass*, noticed, while on an assignment in Paris, that the reports of the Korean War being presented by British and French correspondents differed from those he had read in the American press. His subsequent research led him to reassess his view on the war, and he set out his conclusions in a book. He first sought a publisher in Britain, but by now Britain was rapidly swinging into line with its ally, and Stone was advised to seek a publisher in the United States. There, twenty-eight publishing houses turned the book down, before it was accepted by the Monthly Review Press and published, in the spring of 1952, as *The Hidden History of the Korean War*.

Reginald Thompson, an experienced war correspondent, published in Britain in November 1951 a book called *Cry Korea*, which was critical of the conduct of the war and of the senseless destruction of the country. Although Thompson has since become convinced that the war was "a shattering waste of life, effort, money, and time, a political, military, and strategic blunder," the book was not entirely unsympathetic to American policy. No American publishing house would touch it. "I was warned not to continue to try to find an American publisher," Thompson has recalled. "I was told that the book could endanger the Anglo-American alliance."[18]

So the prospect of the Korean War's being reported fully and truthfully receded rapidly, under a variety of pressures, foremost among which was the political atmosphere in the United States at the time. Not one major daily newspaper opposed the war, and even among left-wing journals the *National Guardian* was almost alone in its anti-war policy. The *New York Daily Mirror* demanded: "Isn't it time to do something about our native communists?"* Alger Hiss had been convicted, the Rosenbergs had been arrested, and Senator Joseph McCarthy was becoming a decisive, dominating Cold War force. Censorship by an army sensitive to its early failures in the field had reached ridiculous lengths.**

The general quality of the correspondents was not very good, particularly in the American group. Thompson, who knew many of them from the Second World War, has said, "With American correspondents the quality is so uneven. At the top you get the very best. Below that you get virtual illiterates."[19] Too many were prepared to go along with whatever the military told them, getting their stories from handouts, which were not military documents but were filled with the phrases of advertising copy writers, not only misleading but often wrong—relying on handouts, the Associated Press put out two flashes announcing the recapture of Seoul on September 22, five days before the town actually fell. Too many became infected by the

---

* Columnist Westbrook Pegler suggested they should all be executed, according to James Aronson's *The Press and the Cold War*.

** A Reuters correspondent who tried to send a message correcting an American news agency report that a Royal Ulster Rifles battalion had been wiped out—a report that the censor admitted had been a mistake—was told he could not send the correction, because it mentioned a specific unit and this was against censorship rules, said the *Daily Dispatch* of January 9, 1951

glamour of danger. "With a shell whistling at you there is not much time to pretend, and a person's qualities are starkly revealed," wrote Marguerite Higgins. "You believe that you can trust what you have seen. It is a feeling that makes old soldiers, old sailors, old airmen and even old war correspondents, humanly close in a way shut off to people who have not shared the same thing."[20] Cutforth wrote of a travelling companion who "was wearing the full panoply of an American correspondent, cartridge belts and a huge automatic in a gangster's shoulder holster." James Cameron described Korea as the war of "mass-produced war correspondents, a prep-school for Vietnam."

British correspondents took a more detached and sceptical view of the war, and thus reported it better than most of their American colleagues did. The Australians were there in force, probably because the Australian government was well aware how important good relations were with the the USA at a time when Britain, the "Mother Country" was beginning its withdrawal east of Suez. The Australians included Denis Warner, a veteran of the Second World War (he had worked with Damien Parer) and an expert on South-East Asian affairs. Warner was with the Americans from the very first day they were in action and he did not shrink from describing the chaos among the South Korean troops and the raw American GIs in the early days of the war.

Norman Macswan, of AAP-Reuter, a top agency man, remained in Korea longer than most and saw a lot of action. His agency colleague, Warren White, was in great demand with other war correspondents because of his languages, which included Japanese. Harry Gordon, of the *Sun News Pictorial* of Melbourne, covered the activities of 3 Battalion of the Royal Australian Regiment, along with Lawson Glassop, author of *We Were the Rats*, a novel about Australian troops in Tobruk.

Correspondents Ronald Monson and Desmond Telfer, along with photographers Laurie Shea (the Sydney *Sun*) and Lloyd Brown (*Sun News Pictorial*), made up the rest of the Australian contingent. They all showed a typical Australian objection to injustice, and, as Alan Dower's action showed, a determination to confront officialdom over specific cases. But many correspondents from all countries were under instructions from their newspapers, magazines and radio stations to play down stories dealing with the sufferings of the Korean people, and only a few, men of the calibre of Cutforth, Colless Cameron, Thompson, and Robert Guillain of *Le Monde*, reported the war primarily in these terms. Thompson noted the racist character of the war, the contemptuous attitude the Americans adopted towards Koreans, North *and* South: "They never spoke of the enemy as though they were people, but as one might speak of apes. If they remarked a dead Korean body of whatever sex, uniformed or un-uniformed, it was simply 'dead Gook' or 'good Gook'. I don't think it ever occurred to them that these Koreans were men, women, and children with homes, loves, hates, aspirations, and often very great courage."[21] All of them wrote of the corruption and brutality of the South Korean regime, the child refugees, the staggering civilian death roll. But, as censorship intensified, there were stories that no one was able to tell.

Cutforth could not write that South Korean racketeers had stolen his jeep, because that would reflect discredit on an ally and so would not pass the censor. He could not write that the United Nations troops blew up the ice over the river at Seoul to prevent South Korean refugees from crossing it and choking the south-bound roads, needed for military traffic in retreat. The censors tried—but failed—to stop the story of the first Americans taken prisoner by the Chinese. They had been well fed, lectured most skilfully by pretty Chinese women, primed with peace propaganda, and then released, a mile or so from their own lines. There they were taken to hospital, under heavy guard, and all contact with them and all mention of their return were forbidden. It was only when it became clear that Roy Macartney, an Australian working for Reuters, was prepared to fly out of Korea, if necessary, to get the story through to his office, that the military abandoned the effort to stifle the news.[22] No correspondent dared ask whether MacArthur had overextended his forces by miscalculating China's reaction and the strength of her intervention, probably because the supreme commander had already expelled some seventeen correspondents from Japan for having criticised his policies. But there were larger and more important events in the Korean War that either were not reported at all or were not given proper attention—the proposed use of the atom bomb, disunity among the allies, the amazing behaviour of the allied POWs, and the farcical conduct of the peace talks.

The question of whether the United Nations should use the atom bomb arose first after the initial set-backs in the war, and by late July 1950 it was being widely argued throughout the United States. Hanson W. Baldwin of the *New York Times* wrote persuasively against the use of the bomb, but he faced a growing body of opinion that felt, as the then Senator Lyndon B. Johnson put it, that "America will use it if and when it can stem the tide of aggression."[23] In Britain, Major P. G. Roberts, a Conservative MP, writing in the *Sunday Graphic*, was all in favour of the bomb's immediate use "to enforce peace." The military historian Major-General J. F. C. Fuller suggested that this would be the height of both political folly and strategic ineptitude, "as futile as bringing up a heavy siege-piece to knock down a sentry box."

Unknown to the general public in either country, there were two occasions during the war when the United Nations came very close indeed to using the bomb. In 1960, the former President Harry S. Truman revealed that when China entered the war he had come under pressure from General MacArthur to use the bomb against "Red China, Eastern Russia, and everything else."[24] Truman denied that this was the main reason he had sacked MacArthur in 1951, but he agreed that it had been one of the reasons. After his dismissal, MacArthur had an interview with the President-elect, General Eisenhower, and impressed him with the necessity of using atomic weapons against strategic targets in North Korea, in Manchuria, and on the Chinese coast. Eisenhower was more receptive to the idea than Truman had been, and in a television interview in 1966 he disclosed that if the North Koreans had not agreed to sign an armistice in 1953, the United States would have used nuclear weapons—"enough to win, and we, of course, would have tried to keep them on military targets, not civil targets."[25]

No war correspondent could have known this at the time, but they all knew about the deplorable state of relations among the allied countries making up the United Nations force in Korea. Some of them wrote some of the story. They reported MacArthur's edict that Red Cross teams from various UN member countries, which arrived in Tokyo in January 1951, would not be allowed to serve in Korea unless they wore American uniforms and had no Red Cross emblem or any indication of the country they came from. This ban was later lifted. They reported that American Shooting Star jets had bombed Greek troops by mistake; that Canada had sacked its commanding officer because he allowed his troops to help Americans to put down a POW camp riot, without first telling his government about it; that MacArthur had accused the British of allowing a flood of strategic material to pour into China through Hong Kong; and that some American senators saw MacArthur's dismissal as "a victory for Great Britain and a triumph for communism." They even hinted at the bitterness some of

382

the member contingents felt over the failure, on many occasions, of American soldiers to hold ground at vital moments and at the sense of solidarity that this engendered in the non-American troops.* But no one reported that British contempt for American fighting qualities and the resulting American resentment had produced deep ill feeling between the troops. Rene Cutforth has said, "Allies always dislike each other, but the British and Americans *hated* each other. In retrospect, I feel that I made too little of this in my reporting. I did so because I thought that relations might improve and because I did not want to do any disservice to the United Nations campaign."[26]

The POW issue was an emotive one, surrounded by allegations of atrocities and brainwashing techniques, and sensitive among the United Nations authorities because of the unprecedented behaviour of American troops. The facts—not revealed until well after the war—were that, although the Chinese and North Koreans kept more than 10,000 United Nations prisoners in "camps" which were without conventional physical defences, not one prisoner managed to escape in three years, and co-operation between prisoner and gaoler was such that nothing occurred in the camps without the Communists knowing of it almost immediately.[27] Of the 7,000 American POWs, about 40 per cent gave up hope and died in captivity. Some 70 per cent collaborated with the enemy to some degree, such as by writing letters home containing favourable statements about their treatment, denouncing the United States, or making broadcasts on behalf of the enemy.[28] The decline in morale was staggering. The Americans refused to take orders from their NCOs, made no effort to adjust themselves to unfamiliar food or the absence of their usual comforts, gave no sympathy—much less help—to their weaker comrades, and even stole food from the sick and injured.

This should be contrasted with the behaviour of prisoners from the Turkish Brigade, the least sophisticated of the United Nations contingent, who flatly refused to speak with their captors, kept strict military discipline, cared for their sick, shared their food, maintained their fierce personal pride, and neither lost a single life in captivity nor gave any comfort to the enemy. In the United Nations camp on Koje Island, on the other hand, Chinese and

---

* According to Rene Cutforth, one Turkish officer, ordered to join an American unit in an attack, refused, saying, "I stay with the British. Then at least I have one flank I can rely on."

North Korean POWs virtually opened a second front; they turned the tables on their captors, took the camp commandant, General Frank Dodd, prisoner, forced him to sign a document agreeing to their demands, and surrendered only when faced with tanks and parachute troops flown in from Japan.

When the exchange of POWs was about to begin, the United States Army announced that military censors would forbid the returning prisoners from revealing their experiences in Communist camps. The former POWs were required to sign a statement binding on them even after their return home and preventing them from talking to journalists not bound by military censorship. The men were lectured by specially trained counter-intelligence officers at rest camps in Korea, on troopships on the way to the United States, and in hospitals after they arrived. This desire to suppress the story of American POW collaboration angered some correspondents. Keyes Beech wrote, in the *San Francisco Chronicle*, of a "fear-ridden atmosphere" on the troopships. "All interviews with repatriates are conducted in the presence of a censor and a counter-intelligence corps agent...Often during the course of the interviews, ex-prisoners have turned to the counter-intelligence men for consent before answering questions."[29]

About a thousand soldiers did talk to correspondents, but the emphasis in most of the stories that appeared in American newspapers was not on collaboration, but on atrocities committed on the POWs by their Chinese captors. Some American correspondents became specialists in atrocity stories—William Miller of the United Press, for example. This willingness on the part of correspondents to write what they believed their editors and readers would find acceptable about the POW issue, instead of the harsh but vital truth, helped delay for years a proper examination of the reasons for a collapse of morale unprecedented in American military history.

Britain handled her POW issue with greater sophistication and far better results. The British war correspondents were allowed to treat the story on its merits, and censorship was applied only to matters of military security. As a result, they got it largely right. Patrick O'Donovan of the *Observer* was sufficiently astute to see that the POWs in Korea had "undergone an experience probably unique in the history of taking and keeping prisoners of war"—a fact that, according to Cyril Cunningham, formerly a senior psychologist in British Prisoner of War Intelligence, is still not generally appreciated today. O'Donovan rejected the standard atrocity story, then being widely printed in the United States. "[The POWs] were greatly surprised at the gentleness of the Chinese. Their punishments were intellectual rather than physical, though for real intransigence a threat of punishment close to torture was implicit. Occasional savage punishments were awarded, but the majority of the prisoners never heard of them." He concluded: "Even after ten days of freedom the 'Progressives' have been having second thoughts and seem driven to explaining their actions not on ideological grounds but on the pleas of the prisoners' necessities. Their confusion is pardonable; it is only a reflection of the moral confusion and muddle about final goals that has clouded the whole war in Korea."[30]

The anger that the military high command had felt throughout the war at the failure of some war correspondents to "get on side" reached a peak during the protracted peace talks that followed the stalemate in the fighting in mid-1951. The U.S. Secretary of State, Dean Acheson, announced at the end of June of that year that a cease-fire based on the thirty-eighth parallel—where the war had started—would be acceptable to the United States and would be considered a victory for the United Nations forces. Since the North Koreans had claimed that they had been invaded by the South, a cease-fire along the thirty-eighth parallel could also be considered a victory for them. There was every reason to believe, therefore, that the peace talks would be swiftly over and the war officially ended.

The correspondents covering the talks soon found that this was not the case. The peace talks appeared endless, and fighting continued all the while, with the United Nations forces losing an average of some 400 troops a month. What had gone wrong? The correspondents despaired of finding out. MacArthur's press policies had been bad enough, but those adopted by his successor, General Matthew Ridgway, were disastrous. Since the correspondents were apparently not prepared to back the war wholeheartedly and without reservation, censorship at the peace talks became total. Correspondents accredited to the United Nations command were forbidden to speak with the UN negotiators. Instead, they were briefed, for several hours after each session, by a United States army officer, who, in turn, had been briefed by officers who had attended the talks. Correspondents were prohibited from inspecting documents presented at the negotiations and were allowed to see only those maps specially prepared for them by the United States Army's public relations section.

The picture the correspondents received in this manner—and which they faithfully reported to their public—was a mixture of lies, half-truths, and serious distortions. While the United Nations was refusing to discuss a cease-fire at the thirty-eighth parallel and demanding one thirty-two miles to the north instead, the correspondents were told that it was the North Koreans who were refusing to accept the thirty-eighth parallel. A map of the precise truce-line positions the United Nations was demanding, which was displayed in the allied press tent, turned out to be faked, and though the North Korean and Chinese delegates proposed a demarcation line along the exact existing battle line, a settlement acceptable to world opinion, the briefing officer flatly denied that any such proposal had ever been made. The United States Army's attitude to all this is clearly illustrated in an exchange between David McConnell of the *New York Herald Tribune* and the chief army public relations officer. A B-26 had strafed the truce-talk zone at Kaesong, and McConnell demanded to know what precautions were being taken to prevent a recurrence. "Don't you forget," the officer said, "which side you're on."[31]

This was not good enough for some correspondents. The British ones were becoming outspokenly critical of the stalling at the peace talks, and some Americans began having angry scenes with the briefing officers. A Reuters correspondent, Sydney Brooks, wrote that the army's method of handling news of the truce negotiations made many believe that the "prestige and integrity" of the United Nations were being reduced. Robert C. Miller of the United Press told a conference of editors in the spring of 1952 that critics of the press coverage of the Korean War had been right: "We are not giving them the true facts about Korea, we haven't been for the past sixteen months and there will be little improvement in the war coverage unless radical changes are made in the military censorship policy." Then Miller, who believed that the press was one of the big guns in the battle against Communism, made a devastating admission for a war correspondent: "There are certain facts and stories from Korea that editors and publishers have printed which were pure fabrication…Many of us who sent the stories knew they were false, but we had to write them because they were official releases from responsible military headquarters and were released for publication even though the people responsible knew they were untrue."

Given this situation, it is understandable that many United Nations correspondents began to turn to the two Western correspondents with the North Korean–Chinese delegation, Wilfred Burchett, now with *Ce Soir*, a Paris left-wing newspaper, and Alan Winnington of the *London Daily Worker*. After his experience at Hiroshima, Burchett had worked in Berlin and Budapest, and then, in 1951, he went to China, mainly to gather material for a book. When the peace talks in Korea began, *Ce Soir* asked him to go there and report them. He thought he would be in Korea for three weeks, but he ended by staying two and a half years. Burchett had met many of the United Nations correspondents during the Pacific war, and after some initial caution most of them renewed the acquaintanceship. The UN correspondents soon discovered that Burchett and Winnington had the complete trust of the North Korean–Chinese delegation and had free access to all the documents, maps, and reports relating to the negotiations. The two became a regular source of information for the UN correspondents, and a cause of much annoyance to UN briefing officers.\* Burchett, at the request of the Associated Press, took a camera to one of the agency's photographers, "Pappy" Noel, who had been taken prisoner, and brought back a film Noel took of GIs in several North Korean POW camps. To placate the United Press for this scoop, he agreed to that agency's scheme for him to photograph General William F. Dean, commander of the U.S. Twenty-fourth Division, also in a North Korean POW camp. Both sets of photographs were widely used.

All this was too much for the United States Army. Correspondents were warned against accepting Burchett or Winnington as a reliable source of news and were requested to behave in a "more loyal" manner. Because *Stars and Stripes*, the United States Army newspaper, carried the United Press photograph of General Dean, the editor was sacked and sent home. General Ridgway himself issued a memorandum prohibiting contacts between United Nations and Communist correspondents: "The UN Command view with growing apprehension the practice of some reporters of excessive social consorting, including the drinking of alcoholic beverages, with communist journalists." Certain allied correspondents were abusing their facilities, the General said, and were "consort-

---

\* It was by comparing the correspondents' map with the one the Communist delegation was using that Burchett discovered the correspondents' map had been faked. (Burchett himself has told this story to the author, and it also appears in Aronson's *The Press and the Cold War*.) It was Burchett and Winnington who gave the correspondents the English text of the Communists' demarcation-line proposal, the one the UN briefing officer insisted had never been made.

ing and trafficking" with the enemy. In future, such contacts would
have to be ended, and journalists would have to behave so as not to
endanger military security. The UN correspondents ignored the
ban, and even those who had avoided Burchett and Winnington in
the past now went out of their way to greet them. Editors supported the correspondents, and with their approval a delegation went to
Japan and prevailed on Ridgway to rescind the order. Many American newsmen disliked fraternising with Burchett and Winnington.
There was no doubt both correspondents supported the communist side and made no secret of this fact. Burchett was later accused
of going further, of playing down North Korean atrocities, painting
a false picture of conditions in North Korean POW camps and,
worse, of assisting in the interrogation of UN POWs in these camps.
Burchett vehemently denied this to me and various court actions in
Australia later failed to resolve conclusively this accusation. But in
Korea, the truth was that Burchett and Winnington were a better
source of news than the UN information officers, and if the allied
reporters did not see them they risked being beaten on stories.

Perhaps the most unsatisfactory story of the war was the charge
that the United States was experimenting with germ warfare. This
was first made by the North Korean Foreign Ministry on February
22, 1952, when it alleged that the United States had been dropping
disease-infected insects over wide areas of North Korea. The United Nations flatly denied the accusation, but when an international
scientific commission, organised by the World Peace Council and
comprising scientists in the fields of bacteriology, parasitology,
microbiology, anatomy, the veterinary sciences, and others, decided
that it was true, its findings were widely reported. Burchett wrote
in *Ce Soir* of finding a large patch of insects, covering an area of
about 200 yards by 50 yards, near the Yalu River on June 6, 1952,
after an American plane had flown low overhead. The insects were
of a type not seen there before. Several American airmen, taken
prisoner after being shot down, gave detailed statements admitting
their involvement in germ warfare in Korea. These were released to
the Western press, but were largely discredited when the airmen,
on repatriation, repudiated their admission. None of the UN correspondents, many in no way sympathetic with the war or the
American forces, reported seeing or hearing anything that might
even have suggested that the United States was waging germ warfare, and twenty years later the issue remains as inconclusive as it
was at the time.

The war in Korea officially ended on July 27, 1953. President Syngman Rhee promptly presented an astonished United Nations with a bill for $90 million, for rent of South Korean land used by the UN forces during the fighting. The total cost of the UN action has never been calculated. There is, of course, no way of calculating the monetary value of the 300,000 allied soldiers killed, wounded, or missing—most of whom never really understood what they were doing in Korea, because the American military was no more successful in "selling" the war to the soldiers than it was in selling it to the nation.

As for the correspondents, one cannot escape the conclusion that, although they showed admirable professional courage on the battlefield, they failed to show equal moral courage in questioning what the war was all about. The Americans constituted the largest single group of correspondents and were the most culpable. Under pressure to prove their patriotism, they got on side and went along with the United States military's view of how the war should be reported. Although it would have required considerable courage and, no doubt, would have put their careers at risk, more correspondents should have been prepared to challenge censorship and misinformation, to question the way in which the war was being conducted, to criticise the dominance of the United States in what was supposed to be a United Nations action, and, above all, to question whether the political aims of the war could justify the misery inflicted on the civilian population.

Instead, too many correspondents became engrossed in describing the war in terms of military gains and losses, rather than standing back, as one or two British correspondents did, and trying to assess whether the intervention was justified, whether its aims were feasible, whether any long-term gains were worth the terrible short-term cost. True, it was easier for non-American correspondents to attempt this, because, being less involved and suffering less from the effects of the McCarthy period, they were less susceptible to the pressures of appeals to patriotism. But if a war correspondent's duty is not to tell the truth as he sees it, even if that truth appears at the time to be against the national interest, then what is it?

So correspondents must accept some of the blame for the fact that 2 million civilians were killed in Korea, more than 100,000 children were left orphaned, and the whole peninsula, says Rene Cutforth, "looked as if a gigantic wind had swept it clean of everything." All for what? It remains difficult to name a single positive thing the war achieved. The best that General James A. Van Fleet, the United Nations commander in the field, could produce in 1952 was: "Korea has been a blessing. There had to be a Korea either here or some place in the world."[32]

## Chapter Fifteen

# Algeria is French
# 1954–1962

My policy? Sir, I am a soldier. I do not have a policy.

—General Henri Giraud,
on being appointed governor of Algiers

---

The Algerian War began on All Saints' Day, November 1, 1954, lasted nearly eight years, and cost the lives of at least half a million Algerian and French soldiers and citizens. It toppled the Fourth Republic, and brought General de Gaulle to power, plastic bombs to Paris, and mutiny to the French army. The Algerian revolt, following the French defeat in Indo-China, marked the dying gasp of France as a colonial power, the ultimate stage in a pattern of serious decline that had begun in the years before 1939. Algeria was a bloody, brutal, and racist war, with torture, atrocities, and the killing of civilians on a large scale, important not only to the two peoples concerned, but also for the lessons it held for the rest of the world.

Yet in 1972, ten years after the fighting ended, the French public suddenly realised that it had been deceived about what was happening during the war, and a hunger became apparent in France for facts that should have been provided at the time. An illustrated weekly magazine devoted entirely to the history of the war sold 400,000 copies per issue. Books describing the fighting became national best sellers. Parisians queued to see a long documentary film, *La Guerre d'Algérie*, that included newsreel footage—suppressed by the censor at the time—of French soldiers shooting down an Algerian peasant for no apparent reason. General Jacques Massu, a former paratroop commander, wrote a book, *La Vraie Bataille d'Alger*, in which he admitted having accepted the use of torture to gain information from those he considered "terrorists" among the Algerians. The *barbouzes*, Gaullist toughs who went secretly to Algeria to wage an underground fight against the extreme right-wing OAS (Organisation de l'Armée Secrète), a settlers' terrorist organisation, published their own unofficial history.

The more that appeared about the war, the more astonished the French public became. A newspaper columnist asked, "Why didn't we know this sort of thing happened?" The answer is that the few correspondents and editors who tried to present the truth at the time were harassed, expelled, gaoled, and, in at least one instance, tortured. Newspapers were seized, books suppressed, newspaper offices bombed. It became easier to forget the truth and to write what was convenient. The French people did not learn what was happening in Algeria because, with a few honourable exceptions, the press failed in its duty. This failure began nine years before the outbreak of the war, at the town of Sétif, south-west of Constantine, on V-E Day, May 8, 1945, the day that Algerian history books say marked the real start of the war.

Accounts still differ as to what happened at Sétif, but most agree that a demonstration of some 8,000 Algerians of assorted nationalist groups, after seeking and obtaining official approval to celebrate the occasion, began to march peacefully through the centre of the town. Some of the banners carried by the Algerians demanded freedom from French rule, and the police decided that the more inflammatory ones should be removed. Violence followed and grew into a riot. The French authorities not only repressed the riot, but also decided to make an example of Sétif, to discourage further nationalist demonstrations.

The French air force, under the political direction of a Communist minister, Charles Tillon, went into action against Algerian villages in the area. Medium and heavy bombers, flying up to 300 sorties a day, flattened entire communities. Senegalese troops and units of the French Foreign Legion were allowed a free hand in the area, and they killed, burned, and looted at leisure. Independent American sources put the number of Algerians killed at 17,000. The nationalists said the figure was nearer 45,000. No matter which is correct, the fact remains that France carried out a large-scale punitive action on an Algerian civilian population after only minor provocation. On the very day set aside to celebrate the successful conclusion of a war fought to safeguard democracy, an Allied power had behaved in a fashion usually associated with the excesses of Nazi Germany. How was this watershed in French-Algerian history reported?

At first, not at all. The killing had been on too large a scale to be ignored, and so the Ministry of the Interior issued, in Paris, an official statement that, although not technically a lie, concealed more than it revealed. Armed bands had attacked the population at Sétif, it said, and the number of casualties had passed the 100 mark. In the elation of the victory celebrations, this passed almost unnoticed, no one bothering to ask which armed bands, or by how many had casualties passed 100.

The French Communist newspaper *L'Humanité*, obsessed with purging Vichyites in North Africa, and yet to develop its anti-colonialist stance, readily accepted the possibility that the affair was the work of Hitlerian elements: "Energetic action was taken in North Africa against Fifth Column criminals." American and British correspondents also accepted the official account. "Rumours of food riots are confirmed in Paris by the Cabinet," said the *New York Times*. "At Sétif what was described by the Governor General as 'Hitlerian elements' attacked the population while it was celebrating VE day. Troops were used."[1] *Reynolds News* even provided details: "Several people were killed when armed bands of Arabs, led by a violently anti-French party known as Manifesto marched down from the mountains on the Town of Sétif and fired on the crowd."[2] Only the *Christian Science Monitor*'s correspondent Egon Karkeline questioned the official version. "Despite the veil of censorship with which the French government has surrounded the recent riots in Algiers," he wrote, "it is manifest that these disturbances had a serious character."[3]

Then, more than a month after the French attack, the United States Army newspaper *Stars and Stripes* blew the whole story wide open. The Rome edition of the paper, quoting sources in Casablanca, gave a reasonably accurate account of what had occurred, hedging only with "the true picture of events and their cause was obscure." The *Stars and Stripes* version was picked up and reprinted in the *New York Times*, the *Manchester Guardian*, the London *Daily Telegraph*, and many other newspapers. This sent Ch.-André Julien of the Socialist official daily, *Le Populaire*, after the story, and on June 28 he wrote the first account in France to give anything like the true picture of what had happened: "Senegalese and Legionnaires were allowed to massacre at will around Sétif. Their path could be followed by trails of fire. In the Jijelti region, where there had been no disorders, other Senegalese murdered and burned at leisure. Planes scattered bombs on Arab tent camps. The military gave the number of victims as between six and eight thousand." This report brought revised figures from the Ministry of the Interior. The "more than 100" casualties now became 1,200, and it was officially admitted that 50,000 Arabs had taken part in the events of May 8.

All this time there had been an eye-witness account of the first trouble in Sétif. Pierre Dubard of *Le Figaro* had watched the demonstration and had seen the police violence, but he was unable to get his story past the censor until July 7, two months after the event. When it finally appeared, it confirmed not only *Le Populaire*'s story, but also most of what had appeared in *Stars and Stripes*. French official sources were completely discredited, the danger of accepting government statements at face value was amply illustrated, and the manner in which each newspaper's political line had influenced its version of the Sétif attack had been clearly shown. Yet nine years later, when the fighting began in earnest, not one of these lessons was remembered.

The tone for the reporting of the war was set by the French government. It began by minimising the uprising, and until the United Nations General Assembly placed the matter on its agenda, in September 1955, France succeeded in passing off the fighting as a minor "internal difficulty." Newspapers fell in with this deception, and, although massive reinforcements were pouring into Algeria from November 1954 onwards, the spasmodic fighting at first made news only on the inside pages. When it became no longer possible to conceal the seriousness of the revolt, France came up with a new line. Through censorship, propaganda, and political pressure, she now sought to convey an impression of French valour on trial. The rebels cutting throats in Algeria were savage barbarians, ungrateful for their years of exposure to the culture of France; they lacked popular support, were devoid of any intellectual base, and had dragged the proud armies of the Republic into a dirty war without rules. But France would stand fast and would surrender not a centimetre of Algeria; France would safeguard Christian civilisation on the soil of Africa, no matter what the cost. "In Algeria," said François Mitterrand, a leading light of the French Left, "the only negotiation is war."[4]

Not only the French reader, but also the American and the British, was receptive to this line of propaganda, because of the poor reporting of the Algerian question that immediately preceded the war. In February, nine months before the outbreak of fighting, the *New York Herald Tribune* accorded the French government's line complete validity: "Algeria is no longer a French colony but an integral part of France...Since World War II it has been perhaps the most important operations centre of a communist effort to gain a real foothold in North Africa."[5] Wayland Young reported in the *Scotsman*, only two months before the war began: "The military insurrectionary nationalism which has swept Tunisia and Morocco does not affect Algeria at all. It is hard to see how any independence movement could make any headway here."[6]

Some French correspondents were more perceptive. Jacques Madaule of *Le Monde*, after a visit to Algeria in May, warned of the gravity of the situation. Under the heading ALL IS CALM IN ALGERIA, Madaule set out the Algerians' case and ended with the telling line "Algeria is calm: the children die without crying."[7] But most correspondents repeated the government line that all was calm in Algeria and that the outbreak of fighting on November 1 came as a complete shock. Only *L'Humanité* pointed out that the French troop reinforcements were shipped to Algeria before the first incidents, which suggests that, if the revolt caught the government unawares, it did not surprise the army. The military now promised a brief but lively mopping-up operation, as 10,000 French paratroopers, legionnaires, and *chasseurs* moved into the mountainous Aurès region of eastern Algeria to confront the terrorists. Almost everyone was optimistic. The *New York Herald Tribune*, for instance, assured its readers that the revolt would make little headway. With the help of two combat-trained divisions, the French would quickly clear the Aurès.[8] Only René Janon, in *Le Figaro*, saw that it would not be as easy as this. The timing of the rebel offensive was such, he wrote, that seasonal rains and then snow would make a mountain campaign very arduous.[9] In fact, the war dragged on for another seven years.

The French troops found themselves chasing an elusive and highly motivated enemy, which would not stand and fight, and which was indistinguishable from the Algerian civilian population. The French army's answer to these tactics was to offer the Algerian population a choice: protection in return for loyalty, or be bombed to pieces for suspicion of harbouring rebels. This soon escalated to encompass a so-called pacification programme (under which the

French resettled the villagers from an area of rebel activity and then bombed anything there that moved), reprisal strikes, counter-terrorism, and the use of torture to extract information and to undermine the enemy's morale. In short, the French army tried in Algeria virtually the same tactics that the Americans were later to use in Vietnam; and since these tactics were incompatible with her "Christian" mission, her desire to "save the free world," her claim to unimpeachable conduct and the morality of a civilised society, all of which France had advanced as her reasons for fighting the war, she was forced to employ a campaign of censorship, repression, and intimidation of correspondents, so as to keep from the French public—and the rest of the world—the truth about the nature of the war in Algeria.

All publications in Algeria were put under the control of the Préfecture, which was given the right to veto any material prior to printing. In France, the authorities used an obscure section of the criminal code to seize all the issues of *Les Nouvelles de Bordeaux*, the first paper to suffer what was to become a popular form of suppression and financial punishment (*France-Observateur* lost 20 million francs as a result of seized issues in one year alone). There was a wave of arrests of journalists. Boudjeroudi Said, assistant to the mayor of Algiers and a contributor to *L'Algérie Libre*, Laurent Salignac of *La Liberté*, and Boualem Khalfa, editor of *Liberté*, were imprisoned and heavily fined. French newspapers that failed to follow the government line were attacked for being unpatriotic, traitors to France. Edgar Faure, the Premier in 1955, found *L'Express* "disgraceful in that a French newspaper should so far lose sight of the national interest."[10] And when Georges Arnaud, who contributed to *Paris-Presse*, reported on a press conference given by a French supporter of the FLN (Front de Libération Nationale), he was arrested, charged with "non-denunciation of an individual exercising activities harmful to national defence," and given a two-year suspended sentence.[11] There appeared no limit to the government's determination to suppress news that it did not like and to discredit or destroy professionally any correspondent who resisted this policy.

On August 22, 1955, Georges Chassagne, a French cameraman employed by Fox Movietone, was taken by the French authorities to see some Algerian prisoners. While Chassagne was filming, an auxiliary policeman dragged one of the prisoners away and, in front of the camera, shot him dead. Chassagne's film was shown in cinemas throughout North America and in other parts of the world, but not in France. Stills from the film were reproduced in *Life* in October, but the issue was banned in France. Then, on December 29, *L'Express* published the *Life* photographs. The Ministry of the Interior immediately called a press conference, at which it agreed that the incident had taken place but said that Chassagne had bribed the policeman to shoot the prisoner while he filmed the scene. The Defence Ministry added that publication of the film harmed the honour and morale of the army. Chassagne denied the bribery allegation and protested that the government was trying to smear him. Four days later, the government, without any apology, withdrew its charge, saying merely that the theory of bribery did not seem to be corroborated by an official enquiry.[12]

The government also failed in its attempts to discredit the reporting of Georges Penchenier of *Le Monde*, one of the best and most courageous correspondents of the war. After a concerted attack by the rebels in August 1955, the French authorities had carried out a series of reprisal raids on Algerian villages. Robert Lambotte of *L'Humanité* accused the legionnaires and the troops of the CRS (Compagnies Républicaines de Sécurité) of killing Algerian women and children—"The forces of repression have gone mad."[13] All copies of *L'Humanité* were seized, and Lambotte was expelled from Algeria. But Penchenier, too, had been accompanying French troops on the raids, and he wrote how, at the village of Zef-Zef, soldiers had executed fifty Algerians, including old people, women, and children. "The ditch outside the village, along the Roman road, contained a thousand corpses," Penchenier wrote. "Here the hour of repression has sounded…This has become a war of race and religion."[14]

The Ministry of the Interior flatly denied Penchenier's story. The rebels had made a stand at Zef-Zef during heavy fighting on the first day of the Algerian attack, and the women and children, the ministry said, had willingly fought alongside their menfolk against the French troops. "The loss of life was solely as a result of the battle of August 20. All those killed were combatants." Penchenier refused to accept this. The dead were clearly non-combatants, and they had been killed *after* the battle. He enlarged on his earlier description of the scene at Zef-Zef: "A dog tied to a post began to whine on seeing us. Some chickens picked quietly among the bodies. I do not recall seeing any adult males. I could distinguish several children of less than ten…a little girl, knees bent, head in hands… an old woman…three other women with babies in their arms. The coagulated blood was still red—it was a fresh slaughter."[15] The ministry foundered: "The Zef-Zef incident was an isolated case that will not recur, an unfortunate consequence of warfare."

The pro-government correspondents rushed to its aid. Claude Delmas of *Combat* decided that the army had chosen the milder of two courses open to it: "After the [Algerian] terrorism of August 20 the authorities had two choices: (a) repression—ten thousand executions give ten years of calm; or (b) limited repression, taking in only the guilty. It was this second solution that was adopted."[16] Olivier Lecamp of *Le Figaro* said that the French in Algeria were reacting with courage to a difficult situation; the pacification teams working in Algerian villages were doing a great job, and the paratroopers were tough but fair. "I met an old friend from Indo-China, a sergeant from the Dien Bien Phu campaign. He told me of a reprisal raid: 'We destroyed the houses one by one. We evacuated the women and children…Then the men definitely identified as rebels were shot. One, before dying, confessed to having the blood of 36 Frenchmen on his hands.' "[17]

This idealised picture of French troops did not match the impressions of Lambotte or, later, of Alexander Werth, writing in the *Scotsman*. Before his expulsion, Lambotte wrote of sharing a compartment in a train with a group of German legionnaires. The legionnaires told him of burning Algerians in their houses, of lining up others and shooting them, and of always "losing" about half their prisoners when taking them to camps. Werth wrote: "I had a long conversation on a cafe terrace in Bone with an almost angelic-looking young German from the Foreign Legion, a worthy heir of the SS, who talked in the most casual and matter-of-fact way about the manner in which his unit tortured and then killed captured Algerians. 'We've got to extract information, *aber ohne Folter geht's nicht*' (but without torture you get nowhere) ."[18]

The torture issue became a major one with the publication, in 1958, of Henri Alleg's book *La Question*. Alleg, the editor of *Alger Républicain*, who was arrested and tortured by paratroopers, described his experiences in a manuscript smuggled out of prison. Published by Les Editions de Minuit, the book sold 60,000 copies in two weeks, before it was seized by the police—the first time a book had been banned in France for political reasons since the eighteenth century. When François Mauriac mentioned the book in *L'Express*, the newspaper was seized in Algeria. When, the following week, *L'Express* published an article on the book by Jean-Paul Sartre, the entire issue was seized by the Paris police. *France-*

*Observateur* tried to publish extracts from the book, but its edition was seized, too. The French publisher then printed the extracts as a pamphlet. This also was seized. Only the *London Observer* and the *Manchester Guardian*, both of which had a limited French readership, were able to publish extracts and remain on sale in France. Everyone, from the Minister-Resident for Algeria, Robert Lacoste, to the farmers in Aveyron, knew that people in Algeria were being tortured regularly and systematically, wrote Sartre in the English edition of *La Question*, but France was almost as mute as during the Occupation.[19]

The weekly *Témoignage Chrétien* took up the issue, and in 1959 it published two controversial articles. The first made public a report to their bishops by thirty-five priests serving as reserve officers in Algeria.[20] The report said that methods were being used in the conduct of the war "which our consciences condemn—arbitrary arrests, torture, summary executions, and the killing of wounded on the battlefield." The second article revealed the existence in Algeria of a special training camp for officers where the conditions under which torture could be practised were taught.[21] *Témoignage Chrétien* said that the school's official name was the Joan of Arc camp and that officers were told the conditions necessary for "humane torture"—it must be clean; it must not be witnessed by young soldiers; it must not happen in the presence of sadists; an officer must be present; it must stop the moment the man talked; and it must cause no permanent injury. Water torture and electric shock were both considered suitable, the article said.

The more the army was attacked, the more its sense of solidarity grew. It entered the information field itself. "The Army possesses a considerable power of action over the Metropolitan Frenchman," wrote Lacoste. Hence, if ordinary soldiers were told the army's view of the situation in Algeria, "they can become excellent informants of French opinion." In other words, to defend itself the military would have to become a propaganda medium. Officers needed little encouragement, and soon generals and colonels were producing pamphlets and small newspapers giving their opinions on the press coverage of the war and setting out the army's view. Soldiers' reading matter was censored, to eliminate newspapers known to be against the war, and even official news releases were vetted, to remove any references to atrocity allegations or to military defeats. Sympathetic correspondents were taken on trips to battle areas and encouraged to write about the bravery and chivalry of the French soldier in the face of a brutal and barbaric enemy.

The correspondent for *Combat* toured paratroop command posts in the Atlas Mountains. "There we saw the paratroopers, magnificent, strapping fellows, gay and affable. The paras possess the prestige without which nothing is possible where Islam governs. Their audacity, their strength, their fighting virtue, reassure the population. These boys, sons of our beautiful people, have found from the start the gestures, the attitudes that go to the hearts of the ordinary people."[22]

Foreign correspondents were issued press kits setting out the French case, stressing France's contributions in Algeria, and complaining of the rebels' lack of gratitude. Some correspondents were impressed. Ian Todd, after a short visit in 1956, wrote in the *Johannesburg Star* that Algeria was a model of democratic rule and that the Algerians were a "host of ferocious fanatics."[23] Thomas Cadett of the BBC, in a broadcast from Paris, lauded the development of Algeria, "towards which France has made a remarkable contribution."[24]

The strangest report came from a British writer and member of Parliament, Lord Lambton. Writing in the *Evening Standard*, he gave his version of rebel recruiting procedures. "They go into a remote village and tell the young men to join them, and if one hides they kill his father. It is an effective system." He then described schools in country districts, where "little girls in multi-colored dresses are happily to be seen singing French songs." He walked around the modern university, visited clinics, watched operations, and inspected French hospitals, where Algerian babies were born and "the oldest patient looked after with tenderness." Then Lord Lambton reached his considered conclusion about France and the Algerian War: "The present troubles spring, in the main, not from her misrule but from the efficiency of her health service which has upset the balance of nature."[25]

French atrocity propaganda was highly organised. Correspondents were given a book of photographs showing the gruesome things the rebels did to French soldiers, and when the entire male population of the village of Melouza was massacred, in May 1957, the French made full use of it for propaganda purposes. They alleged that a rival rebel group was responsible.* They rushed correspondents to the village, arranged interviews with witnesses, encouraged photographs, and did everything possible to ensure

---

* The FLN denied this and called on world leaders, including the Pope, to support an independent enquiry. It has never been established beyond doubt who carried out the killings.

world-wide coverage. President René Coty appeared in an amazing midnight television broadcast, asking Frenchmen to see Melouza as final proof of the bestiality of the enemy in Algeria and calling on "the civilised world" to repudiate Algerian excesses. The *Daily Express* wrote Coty an open letter assuring him of "the support of all the impartial citizens of this country."[26] C. L. Sulzberger, writing from Paris for the *New York Times*, said, "It is not possible for a civilized power like France to strike back with terror against terror such as that employed at Melouza"[27]—a view that Sulzberger no doubt changed when details of French torture and atrocities emerged some months later.

The truth was, of course, that both sides practised atrocities, often of a similar type. An Algerian lieutenant described finding the body of a colleague who had been questioned by French soldiers. "Every time he wouldn't answer they cut off a little piece, starting with the fingers. They got halfway to his elbow before he bled to death...After we buried him we got ourselves a prisoner, tied him in a chair, and sliced him like a loaf of bread...He took quite a while to die too."[25] Both the French and the Algerians went in for crucifixion, burning alive, and the cutting off of genitals to cram into the victim's mouth. Atrocities like these were possible because of the racial nature of the war, helped by a lack of class solidarity between the French worker and his Algerian neighbour, so pronounced that the French Communist Party had to pull its punches and various left-wing politicians became deeply involved in the follies and crimes of the repression.

While the French authorities, helped by pliant French and foreign correspondents, managed to put over the official view of the war and its progress without great difficulty, it was at first impossible for the FLN to have its side heard at all. It tried offering bribes to influential French correspondents, but was rebuffed. It took an Egyptian correspondent on a tour of rebel-held areas, but he was captured by the French, tried in Oran, and sentenced to death. A commando squad of the ALN (Armée de Libération Nationale) managed to rescue him, but his experience deterred other correspondents from risking visits to the rebel side.[29] Then, in the winter of 1956–57, an American free-lance writer, Herb Greer, and a film maker, Peter Throckmorton, were taken into Algeria from Morocco, and they became the first Western reporters to film the war from the FLN side. They filmed ALN training camps and arms dumps, saw action, toured villages razed by legionnaires, and photographed both French and Algerian casualties. They did not enjoy their work. Greer described filming a crude emergency operation on a wounded ALN soldier. The nurse held the soldier's head, watching coldly as Greer crouched over them, camera whirring. "I was sick with shame," he wrote later, "but I worked on."[30]

Their material was televised in the United States, and their reportage was sold in many countries, "to the fury of the French authorities, who attempted to suppress our film in New York and to discredit our photographs and our articles."[31] Greer went back in the winter of 1958, with film equipment and $250 from NBC television. His job was to take pictures of Algerians killing or being killed. "The demand was for gore, corpses, the good dismembered meat easily associated with popular and enjoyable war novels and films…that is, exactly what I had gone dizzy with shame filming in the Atlas mountains the year before. But I was not a missionary; the public in Britain and America was welcome to its taste so long as I was not forced to share it."[32]

Greer found that a flood of correspondents had poured into the rebel areas after he and Throckmorton showed that the Algerians were a serious military organisation and not a gang of bandits. The FLN now had a press office in Tunis, with attachés to conduct correspondents through rebel-held areas. The correspondents were mainly from the United States and Britain, but there was even one from Yugoslavia, Alexander Pryla of the Belgrade newspaper *Politika*. There was also a woman, Dickey Chapelle, who became the first American accredited straight from the United States to the ALN. Dickey Chapelle was a tough, competent writer, who had been in the Second World War and Korea. She found the Algerians both highly motivated and well informed about the war. Conversations with FLN rebels usually began with their asking, "What do your people think about our revolution?" and "When will America stop arming France?"[33]

One of the few to see both sides, first the French and then the Algerian, was Joseph Kraft, formerly of the *New York Times*. Kraft decided to check for himself the French claim that the rebels had no popular support and that they terrorised villagers into helping them. Writing in the *Observer*, Kraft dealt the French case a decisive blow. Wherever he had gone with the ALN, he said, the whole village had turned out to greet them. "While we stayed, nothing was too good for us." Kraft listed all the marks of devotion to the nationalist cause and quoted an old Algerian as saying that the only thing he feared was that the FLN leaders would "settle for peanuts."[34]

The French authorities hated stories like these—Greer said he was warned that it would be advisable for him to stay out of France for the time being—but there were still correspondents who saw the war through different glasses. Richard Neville, writing in the *Sunday Times* about the French army's pacification programme, said: "I have been amazed by the quite unexpected degree of confidence that existed between the soldiers and the Muslim population, wherever the French were in a position to assure protection. A village that perhaps only the week before had been under fellagha domination would change overnight once the threat of terrorism had been removed."[35] Neville concluded that, militarily speaking, the Algerian problem had been contained and victory was within the reach of the French army.

Instead, the military situation for France steadily deteriorated, until by 1961 the objective of victory in the field was being reluctantly supplanted by the prospect of a political settlement. The drawn-out, sporadic struggle between the French army and the ALN in the mountains was replaced by a vicious war in the cities. Now a third force entered the conflict. To the French army, which had fought to keep Algeria French, and the ALN, which had fought for independence, was added the OAS, a European settlers' group determined either to thwart a settlement or to bring Algeria to a Götterdämmerung. The OAS blamed the politicians and the press for what was happening to Algeria, and correspondents became a mark for its anger and abuse.* Sections of the French army, such as the paratroopers and legionnaires, felt equally strongly, and to the usual dangers of a correspondent's profession was added the risk of injury or murder by a fellow European.

Jean Daniel of *L'Express*, a friend of the novelist Albert Camus, was particularly hated. He had written: "These French of Algeria have more than one point in common with the slave masters of the southern United States: courage, dynamism, narrowness of views...they are born to be masters as others are born to be slaves."[36] In the summer of 1961, Daniel, a writer known by sight in Algiers, carrying proper press credentials and going about his business in a legitimate manner, was shot by paratroopers. The

---

* The OAS probably suspected, too, that some of the correspondents were also intelligence agents. The OAS leader, General Raoul Salan, had himself used the cover of being a correspondent for *Le Temps* when he was in Ethiopia in 1939 as a French government intelligence agent.

incident was officially explained as having been an accident, despite eye-witness accounts that the soldiers who shot him had fired over the heads of the stretcher-bearers carrying him to an ambulance and then had emptied their magazines at the ambulance itself as it drove away. In hospital, Daniel, bleeding profusely, was given the wrong blood type, but survived.

John Casserly, an ABC correspondent, was in a bar near the Hôtel Aletti, where most of the correspondents stayed, when two settlers, both armed, told him that his broadcasts were not liked and that he was to leave Algeria within forty-eight hours if he wished to stay alive. Fortunately, another correspondent was already on his way to relieve Casserly, and there was no need to test whether the settlers had been bluffing. But the best-known intimidation incident concerned the Italian press and television corps.

On March 3, 1962, four armed OAS men entered the Hôtel Aletti and seized half the equipment and film belonging to an Italian television team that had been filming the previous day in the Casbah. The OAS men took two Italians as hostages, leaving the others under guard. They returned soon afterwards, collected the rest of the television equipment, and released the hostages. That evening, when the bar of the hotel was crowded with correspondents discussing the incident, two OAS men burst in, sought out Giovanni Giovannini of Turin's *La Stampa*, and led him away at gunpoint. Nicolo Caracciola of *Il Giorno*, Milan, appealed to a French army officer at the bar to intervene. The officer flatly refused, and when Caracciola replied, in disgust, "I compliment the French army," the officer punched him. Clare Hollingworth of the *Guardian* threatened to strike one of the gunmen with her shoe, and then she said she would accompany Giovannini, to ensure his safety, but was restrained from doing so. John Wallis of the *Daily Telegraph*, drinking with Bruno Romani of *Il Messaggero*, was interrupted by a man who began talking to Romani in Italian. Wallis remembers that "I turned around a minute or so later to find Romani leaning against the wall, white-faced. He said he had just been told to leave Algeria within twenty-four hours or he would be shot."[37]

Meanwhile, Giovannini had been taken to the back room of a restaurant in the Telemly quarter, where an OAS "tribunal," presided over by a former French officer, outlined the charges against him—he had written stories hostile to the OAS and, "like most correspondents, you are in the pay of de Gaulle." He was given twenty-four hours to leave Algeria, taking all the other Italian correspondents with him, or he would be shot on sight. He was then returned, unharmed, to the hotel. There he learned that a delegation of correspondents, led by another Italian, Corrado Pizzinelli, had roused the government information officer, Philippe Mestre, to protest at what had happened and to demand protection. Mestre had dismissed the abduction as "a bar-room incident" and had done nothing.

Later in the evening, the OAS passed a message to the Aletti that it wanted to talk to the foreign press. John Wallis and a BBC correspondent, Peter Raleigh, were picked up by two men and escorted to an OAS bar. There, they protested that any attack on the Italians would be regarded as a threat to the world's press and could only harm the OAS cause. The OAS men said they were just carrying out orders. The following morning, eleven of the twelve Italian correspondents in Algeria flew back to Italy, where they wrote indignant accounts of the incident. The one who remained, Caracciola, walked to the regular government press conference that afternoon surrounded by a bodyguard of thirty American, French and British correspondents. Confronted by this display of solidarity, the French authorities gave promises of protection, which they repeated, with greater emphasis, when the Italian press loudly condemned the French official attitude. Giovannini's own article made the point that this attitude appeared to reflect not only official confusion but also indifference, and "gives one an idea of the situation which prevails in the magnificent and tragic country that we have momentarily abandoned." The authorities kept their promise of protection, and there were no further abductions.

There was, however, considerable pressure on the correspondents to refrain from reporting anything to do with the OAS, especially anything to do with those of its members who were French army officers or any details of the vicious underground war it was waging with the *barbouzes*. Any correspondent who interviewed the OAS chief, General Salan, would be expelled, the French authorities warned, and in January 1962 the European edition of *Time* was seized because it carried a picture of Salan on its cover. The issue was released only when the cover was replaced by a blank page. John Rich of NBC was refused permission to re-enter Algeria after he reported on the OAS while on a visit to Washington.[38]

These strictures were aimed mainly at preventing the OAS from putting its case. There was no way of preventing the public from learning about its operations, because they were bloody and public. *Paris-Match* described a typical killing: "On Avenue de la

Bouzareah, in Babel Oued, a Moslem lay wounded, shot. An OAS gunman came up, took aim and fired—but the gun jammed. Lying there, the Moslem, trembling uncontrollably, managed to clutch his jacket to his face. The gunman looked down, studied him and pulled the trigger—but the gun jammed a second time. Finally it went off."[39] Fourteen-year-olds lynched a Muslim with piano wire. Seven Muslim women were shot in the back of the head as they walked to work in settlers' houses where they had been employed for years. A thirteen-year-old boy waited until an Arab and his fiancée came out of a shop and then shot the Arab dead, placing over the man's face a paper cone he had brought along for that purpose.[40] The killing was not all on one side. A car containing several Arabs ran down a European, and as he lay moaning on the road they jumped out, poured petrol over him, and set him alight. Muslim riflemen in the French army, under the command of a young French lieutenant, opened fire on a peaceful settlers' march in Algiers, killing at least thirty-six and wounding more than a hundred, including women. Jean-Pierre Farkas reported the incident for Radio Luxembourg. Farkas, a former soldier, said he returned to his hotel room and vomited—"I had never seen so much blood in my life."[41]

Frenchman also killed Frenchman. A team of agents—mostly Gaullists with service in Indo-China behind them or Vietnamese who had worked with the French forces in Indo-China, all of them chosen mainly on the basis of physical courage and brute strength —had entered Algeria secretly to tackle the OAS on its own ground and with its own methods. They called themselves Le Talion ("retaliation"), but they were popularly known as the *barbouzes*. Their existence was first revealed by a *France Soir* correspondent, Lucien Bodard. He wrote of the new force: "It will be autonomous, not subject to normal authority, acting outside the Army and the police, with its own means of action. Absolutely secret, it will be used for the immediate running down of tips…we are going to see war between OAS networks and anti-OAS networks."[42]

Bodard was absolutely right. Although the French government denied the existence of the *barbouzes*, and then any connection with them, the forces of the OAS and the anti-OAS machine-gunned and bombed each other, threw grenades, fired bazookas, set off plastic-explosive charges at each other's headquarters, and generally waged a war of their own, as the last act of decay, racism, and sudden death was performed in the streets of Algiers. The curtain fell in July 1962. On July 1, of 6H million eligible Algerians,

5,975,581 voted for independence. On July 3 the French Cabinet met in Paris and issued a fourteen-line proclamation. France recognised the independence of Algeria's fifteen departments, and a new nation was born. In Algeria, one of the first decisions of the new government was to rename streets and landmarks after heroes and martyrs of the revolution, so that no one would forget.

In France, no one wanted to remember. The divisions were too bitter, the scars too fresh, for any examination of the rôle of the information media, the effect of political prejudices on newspaper policy, the bias in the reporting of the war. Back in 1957, Tom Brady of the *New York Times* had warned, "All information in Algeria is controlled by the French."[43] Not until the series of post mortems in 1972 revealed the truth did the French public realise how total this control had been.

# Chapter Sixteen

# Vietnam
# 1954–1975

Every government is run by liars and nothing they say should be
believed.

—I. F. Stone, journalist,
in Jerry Buck, Jr.'s documentary film,
*I. F. Stone's Weekly*

———

At the end of the Second World War, in order to help rehabili-
tate the Western alliance, the United States decided to support
France in her efforts to cling to her former colonies in Indo-China.
By 1950, the rise of Mao Tse-tung in China and the outbreak of the
Korean War had, in Washington's eyes, turned the Cold War into a
global ideological struggle. In 1954, following the French defeat at
Dien Bien Phu, Vietnam was divided between a Communist North,
under Ho Chi Minh, and a non-Communist South, under Ngo
Dinh Diem. The United States, as part of its policy of containing
China, supported Diem, and the first of 200 military advisers left
for South Vietnam. This act was to cause the United States to be in-
exorably drawn into the most traumatic war in its history. However, the events in Vietnam that followed the arrival of the advisers
received only modest attention in the American press. There were
few experts on the area, and most articles, in the period from 1954
to 1960, concentrated on the Communist menace and the need for
greater American involvement. "Battered and shunted about by the
war," wrote Leo Cherne in *Look* magazine on January 25, 1955, the

South Vietnamese "are too weary to resist the Reds without us." Diem, later to be recognised as one of the most corrupt leaders in Asia, was hailed by *Newsweek* as "one of Asia's ablest leaders" and by *Time* as "doughty little Diem."[1]

It was only after the revolt of army paratroopers in Saigon in November 1960, when some 400 civilians were killed before the rebels were overcome, that the American press showed the first signs of interest in what was really going on in Vietnam. The *New York Times* sent out a veteran war correspondent, Homer Bigart, formerly with the *Herald Tribune*, who joined a tiny corps of full-time reporters in Saigon. The others were Malcolm Browne of the Associated Press, Ray Herndon of the UPI, Nicholas Turner of Reuters, and Pierre Chauvet of Agence France Presse. *Time* had Jim Wilde as a stringer (a part-time correspondent), and François Sully, a Frenchman, who had been living in Vietnam for thirteen years, was a stringer for *Newsweek*. No British daily newspaper had a full-time correspondent there at this stage. A major story would bring in correspondents like Richard Hughes of the *Sunday Times*, Frank Robertson of the *Daily Telegraph*, Dennis Bloodworth of the *Observer*, Denis Warner, who represented various Australian and American newspapers, and other special correspondents, from Tokyo, Bangkok, Hong Kong, Singapore, or even as far afield as Melbourne.

For Warner, all this was a continuation of a story he had started reporting back in 1953-54 in the last days of the French in Indo-China. Warner, who had been under fire at the siege of Dien Bien Phu, believed that the French were finished and his dispatches to the *Daily Telegraph* in London reflected this view. When he found that the *Telegraph* was censoring his articles, he resigned on a point of journalistic principle—as the man-on-the-spot he knew better than his office in London what was really happening and should be allowed to report it.

But, to the discredit of the world's press, the fact remains that in the crucial years of Diem's decline, with American involvement growing steadily, the only daily newspaper with a full-time correspondent in Saigon was the *New York Times*. The rest relied for their day-by-day coverage on the four news agency men.

These correspondents had a difficult task. To begin with, they were accredited by the Diem government, which saw no reason why it should allow foreign correspondents to write stories critical of its performance. If the correspondents did so, the Diem regime called them spies and Communists, and did its best to censor their copy and, by intimidation, prevent them from repeating the offence. The United States Military Assistance Advisory Group (MAAG) was desperately trying to conceal the full extent of American participation in the war against the Vietcong, and it tried to make the correspondents accomplices in this deception. The correspondents were depressed about it. "[We] seem to be regarded by the American mission as tools of our foreign policy," wrote Homer Bigart in the *New York Times'* house magazine. "Those who baulk are apt to find it a bit lonely, for they are likely to be distrusted and shunned by American and Vietnam officials."[2] Malcolm Browne of the AP decided to put his experiences on public record. He sent in a dispatch complaining that United States officials had concealed from correspondents the extent to which American servicemen were performing combat duties, and his story appeared in, among other newspapers, the *New York Times*, on March 24, 1962.

Diem's government reacted swiftly. At that stage, it did not move against Browne. Instead, it issued expulsion orders against Sully, the *Newsweek* stringer, because of his stories about Diem's corruption and ineptness, and against Bigart for the general tone of his reporting, and in particular for a story he had written about members of a Michigan State University group, who had expressed disgust at the corruption they had encountered.* The expulsion orders were withdrawn when the State Department, alarmed at the uproar that seemed likely to result, put pressure on the United States Mission in Saigon, which in turn put pressure on Diem. But, clearly, matters could not go on like this, and so the State Department arranged for John Mecklin, *Time*'s bureau chief in San Francisco, to have leave for government service, and sent him to Saigon to straighten out the press problem, or the "press mess," as it was known in the mission.

Mecklin had an unenviable job. The basic difficulty was that the mission in Saigon had to keep to the line being given out in Washington, namely, that the American advisers *were* only advisers, that the United States was not actively involved in the war, and that Diem, although a little shaky in his interpretation of democracy, was coming along fine. So, although members of the mission knew the truth about the United States' involvement and about the real nature of the Diem regime, they had to lie to the correspondents. They did not tell "really big falsehoods," Mecklin said, but only "endless little ones." But the correspondents knew they were being

* The group had been sent to advise Diem's police force on administrative matters.

told lies, and were given to storming into the offices of the United States Information Service to make it clear that they knew. The only way out for the American officials was to claim that this deception on the American public was necessary, that the Communists had to be stopped, that the United States had "put all its chips on Diem," and to appeal to the correspondents' patriotism not to damage the national interest.

This appeal failed. The American military authorities were bewildered. Correspondents had been patriotic in the Second World War. They had been on side in Korea. What was wrong in Vietnam? "So you're Browne," said Admiral Harry D. Felt, meeting the Associated Press man at a press conference in Saigon. "Why don't you get on the team?" Mecklin was bitter. "In Vietnam," he wrote later, in *Mission in Torment*, "a major American policy was wrecked, in part, by unadorned reporting of what was going on."[3] So it is clear that American correspondents were doing their best, during this period, to inform their readers of the true situation in Vietnam. Unfortunately, they were not as successful as they could have been. In the early years of the American involvement, the administration misled Washington correspondents to such an extent that many an editor, unable to reconcile what his man in Saigon was reporting with what his man in Washington told him, preferred to use the official version. John Shaw, a *Time* correspondent in Vietnam (now *Time*'s bureau chief in Moscow), says, "For years the press corps in Vietnam was undermined by the White House and the Pentagon. Many American editors ignored what their correspondents in Vietnam were telling them in favor of the Washington version. Yet the Pentagon Papers proved to the hilt that what the correspondents in Saigon had been sending was true."[4]

Perhaps the editors and the Washington correspondents can be excused, on the grounds that President Kennedy's administration itself did everything in its power to ensure that the existence of a real war in Vietnam was kept from the American people, as witness the notorious Cable 1006 from the State Department to its information service in Saigon. This cable warned against providing transport for correspondents on military missions that might result in the correspondents' producing undesirable stories, and it ordered that they be told that any criticism of Diem's regime would make it difficult for the United States to maintain friendly relations with the South Vietnamese government. Assistant Secretary of State Robert Manning went to Vietnam for an on-the-spot survey of the press situation, to try to do something, as he reported, about "the long-standing desire of the United States government to see the American involvement minimised, even represented as something less in reality than it is."[5]

The little corps of correspondents was not co-operative. The smallness of the group and their vulnerability made them stick together, so that, as official sources became closed to them, they could co-operate in pooling what information they could gather. The war was still a leisurely, almost unreal one, something like the phoney-war period in Europe in 1939–40. The correspondents could take a taxi from Saigon in the morning, drive down Route 4 to the Mekong Delta, lunch at a river-bank French seafood restaurant on four courses and three wines, go on to discuss the military situation with a South Vietnamese army officer, and be back in Saigon before dusk; after dark the roads belonged to the Vietcong. The group of full-time correspondents was still so small in 1963 that when they met for lunch, on most days at Brodards, in Tu-do Street, they were all comfortably accommodated at one table.

But interest in Vietnam began to grow. British correspondents, hampered by none of the political difficulties that beset their American colleagues, began to sense the real story there. Richard Hughes wrote bluntly in the *Sunday Times*, as early as March 4, 1962, that the United States military intervention in South Vietnam "has already passed the point where aid can be distinguished from involvement," and the following week Nicholas Turner of Reuters spelt out just what this involvement meant, catching Washington out in a direct lie. "The official United States position...has been that American forces are not taking part in combat missions in South Vietnam, except when their role as advisors brings them under fire," Turner wrote. "A Vietnamese communiqué last Sunday said that about sixty communist guerrillas were killed by attacks by the Vietnamese air force. In fact, careful checking shows that only the co-pilots of the aircraft were Vietnamese. The pilots were Americans."[6] While American newspapers were describing "Operation Sunrise" as a trial resettlement programme, Bruce Rothwell of the *Daily Mail* wrote that whole villages were being burnt down and thousands of peasants forcibly resettled in camps, which had a minimum of barbed wire, "to avoid a concentration camp atmosphere."[7] When the United States Secretary of Defense, Robert McNamara, was quoted in America as saying that he was "tremendously encouraged" by what he had seen in Vietnam, Denis Warner was writing in the *Daily Telegraph* that the Vietcong dominated three-fifths of the land area and about one-third of the population.

Dennis Bloodworth of the *Observer* forecast the failure of the strategic-hamlet operation and was sceptical about the possibility of defeating the Vietcong. In *The Times* of London, John White explained one reason why the American army was not averse to further involvement in Vietnam: "South Vietnam is the only part of the world where the Pentagon's training manuals can be put to the test under conditions of real warfare. In this tropical Salisbury Plain [a British army training area] new techniques are being developed of 'counter-insurgency'."[8]

American correspondents wrote stories like these at their own risk. François Sully wrote an article for *Newsweek* on August 22, 1962, headed VIETNAM: THE UNPLEASANT TRUTH. It said that the war was "a losing proposition" and quoted the historian Bernard Fall as saying that Diem's government was inadequate and the Americans inept at teaching the South Vietnamese army. Diem's regime issued an expulsion order against Sully twelve days after the article appeared, and, despite protests from other correspondents, the order was enforced and Sully had to leave Vietnam. A few weeks later, NBC's South-East Asia correspondent was also expelled—for remarking to a fellow correspondent that an interview with Diem was a waste of time.

Over the next six months, relations between the correspondents, on the one hand, and the American mission and the Diem regime, on the other, deteriorated rapidly. In January 1963 the first significant battle of the war took place. At Ap Bac, in the northern Mekong Delta, a clash between an armoured column of the South Vietnamese army's Seventh Division and a small force of Vietcong turned into a shambles. Three American advisers were killed trying to lead reluctant Vietnamese troops into action; the Vietnamese shelled their own men and narrowly missed American Brigadier-General Robert H. York; 100 Vietnamese troops were killed and five American helicopters were shot down. It was a humiliating defeat, rubbed with salt when David Halberstam, who had succeeded Homer Bigart as correspondent for the *New York Times*, Browne of the Associated Press, Neil Sheehan of United Press International, and Turner of Reuters wrote stories quoting one of the United States advisers, Lieutenant-Colonel John Vann, on how well the Vietcong had fought and how cowardly the South Vietnamese troops had been— an assessment that did little to help Colonel Vann's military career.

The correspondents learned the following month what the American mission thought of this sort of reporting. Mecklin, asked to write a memorandum on the press problem in Vietnam, was blunt. He described the correspondents as inexperienced and unsophisticated, and their reporting as irresponsible" and "sensationalized." Someone leaked a copy of the memorandum to the correspondents, who digested it but, probably correctly, did nothing about it. They no longer had to rely on official sources for information—because there were now many people who were unhappy at the way things were going in Vietnam and who were only too ready to tell the correspondents what they knew.

One such source was the Buddhist community, particularly after Diem's troops fired on Buddhist demonstrators in May 1963. On June 9, the Buddhists told the correspondents that something important would happen that day. This advance information enabled Browne to be on the spot—with his camera—when a monk, Thich Quang Duc, immolated himself while his brother monks threw themselves in front of fire engines to prevent the firemen from halting the suicide. Browne photographed it all and quickly got the pictures and his story on the AP wire to the United States. The pictures became front-page news around the world, and, in many cases for the first time, readers began to wonder what was happening in Vietnam.

Diem's reaction was to accuse Browne of bribing the Buddhist monks to murder their fellow monk. The American mission's reaction was to try to freeze the few official sources that still remained open to correspondents—not an easy task, because the press corps was now a tight, united, and formidable group. Diem's secret police tapped their telephones, monitored their Telex machines, planted agents in their offices, and tried to follow them in the streets. But, by using visitors, airline employees, and even friendly military personnel as couriers, the correspondents continued to get out the story as they saw it. So, having failed to manage the media at the source, Kennedy's administration went higher up the editorial ladder.

In the United States, pressure on editors to "get on the team" had begun after François Sully's expulsion from Saigon in September 1962. Newsweek was bombarded with official complaints about Sully's negative attitude, and in particular about his description of Diem's sister-in-law, the notorious Madame Nhu, as a "detested" figure in Vietnam. Newsweek buckled under the onslaught and sent one of its columnists, Kenneth Crawford, a Roman Catholic liberal, for a fresh appreciation of the Saigon scene. On December 10, Newsweek ran a cover story about Diem's regime praising his strategy and referring to Madame Nhu as that "beautiful and strong-willed woman."

Now it was *Time*'s turn to join the team. In August 1963, Charles Mohr, the magazine's chief correspondent in South-East Asia, and Merton Perry, who had been a *Time* stringer in Saigon since 1962, wrote, at the request of the head office, a long story on the Saigon correspondents and their battle with the American mission and an even longer round-up of the war situation. The latter began: "The war in Vietnam is being lost." When it appeared in *Time*, this line had disappeared. Things were going well in Vietnam, the article said, and "government troops are fighting better than ever." The article on the Saigon press corps did not appear, but on September 20 another article was published. It was a vicious attack on the correspondents, and it began: "For all the light it shed, the news that U.S. newspaper readers got from Saigon might just as well have been printed in Vietnamese." The article accused the correspondents of pooling "their convictions, information, misinformation and grievances," of becoming themselves "a part of Vietnam's confusion," and of producing material that was "prone to distortions."

It transpired that the Saigon press corps had made some powerful enemies. Marguerite Higgins, the *New York Herald Tribune*'s correspondent, who, after her spell as a war correspondent in Korea, had married General William Hall, of the United States Air Force, had visited Vietnam in the summer of 1963 and had been unable to understand the attitude of correspondents like Mohr, Halberstam, and Sheehan. "Reporters here would like to see us lose the war to prove they are right," she wrote. Otto Fuerbringer, then the managing editor of *Time*, agreed, and had discarded the original Mohr-Perry article. He had then called a *Time* writer to his office and dictated the outline of an article to replace it. When the article appeared, *Time*'s chief of correspondents, Richard Clurman, who had tried to have it stopped, called Mohr to placate him. Mohr said that unless he could have equal space to reply personally to Fuerbringer's story, he would resign. *Time* would not agree to this, so Mohr and Perry went.

Washington kept up the pressure. News reports from Vietnam, said Pierre Salinger, the White House press secretary, were emotional and inaccurate.* A stream of highly regarded reporters and

---

* Salinger's attitude on what the press should be told can be judged from an admiring note by McGeorge Bundy, Kennedy's national security adviser, that was found in Kennedy's official White House papers. As quoted in *The Times* of August 3, 1971, Bundy had written in the margin of a communiqué prepared by Salinger: "Champion...a communiqué should say nothing, in such a way as to fool the press without deceiving them."

special writers went out to Vietnam, including several Second World War correspondents, and the columnist Joseph Alsop. All decided that the war was going well. Frank Conniff, a Hearst writer, blamed the pessimistic reporting on American editors. The fact that young reporters, most of them in their twenties, had been assigned to report an involved story reflected little credit on the prescience of their employers, he wrote. President Kennedy felt the same way, and he tried to get rid of his particular bête noire, David Halberstam, by asking the *New York Times'* publisher, "Punch" Sulzberger, to reassign him. Sulzberger not only refused to do so, but also cancelled a two-week holiday Halberstam was about to take, in case it should appear that the *Times* had yielded to Kennedy's pressure.[9] So the impression of these early years of Vietnam is of courageous and skilled correspondents fighting a long and determined action for the right to report the war as they saw it.

There is only one flaw in this: the correspondents were not questioning the American intervention itself, but only its effectiveness. Most correspondents, despite what Washington thought about them, were just as interested in seeing the United States win the war as was the Pentagon.* What the correspondents questioned was not American policy, but the tactics used to implement that policy, in particular the backing of Diem as the "white hope" of Vietnam. "We would have liked nothing better than to believe that the war was going well, and that it would eventually be won," Halberstam wrote later. "But it was impossible to believe these things without denying the evidence of our senses."[10] Mohr was embarrassed when he found that his stand against *Time* had made him something of an anti-war hero. "Everyone thought I left because I was against the war. I just thought it wasn't working. I didn't come to think of it as immoral until the very end."[11]

Sheehan said he had arrived in Vietnam convinced that what the United States was doing was correct—helping the non-Communist Vietnamese to "build a viable and independent nation state and defeat a communist insurgency that would subject them to a dour tyranny."[12] When he left in 1966, to become the *New York Times'* man at the Pentagon (where he broke the great story of the Ellsberg-Pentagon Papers), he still hoped that even if the United States should be unable to score a clear-cut victory, as in 1945, "yet we may well prevail." True, Sheehan wondered whether any nation

* Mohr's commitment was such that, back in Vietnam for the *New York Times*, he took part, armed with an M-16, in the American retaking of Hué Citadel after the Tet offensive.

had the right to inflict suffering on another for its own ends, and he hoped that it would not be necessary to do so again, but after three years in Vietnam he was—like most of the correspondents—basically still a partisan for the American cause.

In August 1964, General William Westmoreland took over command of the rapidly increasing American forces in Vietnam, the first land-based jets arrived, and the United States Seventh Fleet was patrolling international waters off North Vietnam, where it exchanged shots with Northern gunboats. Navy jets bombed selected targets in the North, amidst international uproar, and the United States set out down the rocky road to full-scale war.

It became a war like no other, a war with no front line, no easily identifiable enemy, no simply explained cause, no clearly designated villain on whom to focus the nation's hate, no menace to the homeland, no need for general sacrifice, and, therefore, no nationwide fervour of patriotism. It was a vicious war, in a tiny, distant, devastated, and backward nation, against what Bernard Kalb of CBS described as "the most faceless foe in our history." It was a war in which military success had to be measured in numbers—numbers of incidents, of destruction, defection, weapons lost, weapons captured, villagers relocated, areas searched, areas cleared, and that new American statistic, the body count—until only computers became capable of digesting and understanding it all, and machines took over decisions on life and death. It was a war in which, as the desperate quest for a solution intensified, a new expedient would be mooted, rejected as almost inconceivable, accepted, and then dismissed as inadequate. In this manner, the whole awesome range of American military technology—short only of a nuclear strike or the sowing of a biological plague—was steadily brought to bear on an Asian peasant nation.

At each stage of this escalation, the United States tried either flatly to deny what it was doing or to minimise the effects or to conceal the results behind a torrent of questionable statistics, a bewildering range of euphemisms, and a vocabulary of specially created words that debased the English language. To its credit, it did not attempt to solve the problem by imposing censorship. Instead, it mounted a public relations campaign, under highly professional direction, to get over its version of the war.

Photographers from the smaller American papers were brought across for short conducted tours. Transport was provided for correspondents from Europe and Asia—"so they can see for themselves and get a first hand acquaintance with the facts." United States Information Service agencies throughout the world were told to encourage correspondents to come to Vietnam. If they needed money, the American government did its best to provide it, and up to the end of 1966 about thirty-five non-American correspondents were assisted to visit Vietnam in this questionable way.[13] The pitfalls were obvious. Richard West, a British free-lance journalist, who paid his own fare to Vietnam, wrote in the *New Statesman*: "Even those who come at their newspaper's expense are likely to be overwhelmed by the help and hospitality they receive from the American propaganda machine...[They] are bound to be grateful. Moreover, they feel a natural sympathy for the pleasant and long suffering GIs. In consequence, there is a danger of their becoming simply a part of the military propaganda machine."[14] American correspondents were subjected to repeated appeals to their patriotism and the national interest. "When you speak to the American people," Vice President Hubert Humphrey told correspondents in Chu Lai in November 1967, "give the benefit of the doubt to our side...We're in this together."[15] And Dean Rusk said at a background briefing in February 1968, just after the Tet offensive: "There gets to be a point when the question is, whose side are you on? Now I'm the Secretary of State of the United States and I'm on our side."[16]

The danger Richard West saw was real, as was the pressure on American correspondents. Yet—and it must be said at this stage, so as to put the later criticism into perspective—things did not work out that way. Some correspondents became part of the military propaganda machine, and "got on side," but, largely thanks to those who did not, the whole story of the Vietnam War all came out in the end. Some of it could have been told earlier than it was, some of it was told not by war correspondents but by determined reporters at home, some of it was told first outside the United States and then belatedly picked up by American papers, and some of it was told by correspondents who risked life and reputation to report from the other side. The administration's policy proved self-defeating. By making every facet of the war unusually accessible to any correspondent who turned up in Saigon, it lost control of the situation. When there were eventually nearly 700 war correspondents in South Vietnam, it became inevitable that some of them would refuse to accept the official line at face value and would get out into the field to see things for themselves. So when Barry Zorthian, the public relations chief for the United States Embassy, complained that he had not been able to get over to the American public the real story, his self-reproach was unjustified. The real story finally *did* get over, and it toppled a president, split the country, and caused Americans to make a serious reappraisal of the basic nature of their nation.

British correspondents were better placed to write about Vietnam than were their American colleagues—just as, later, Americans were better placed to write the truth about Northern Ireland. But the British press seemed reluctant to get deeply involved. *The Times* would send a man only infrequently and—until the paper's change of ownership in 1967—would never allow him to stay long enough, a criticism equally valid for the *Observer*. The *Sunday Times* sent someone only at long intervals, the *Daily Mail* hardly ever, the *Guardian* only seldom. The *Daily Telegraph* had the most regular coverage. However, John Draw, the *Daily Telegraph* correspondent in Saigon who reported events leading up to the retreat of the South Vietnamese army in March–April 1975, was actually Captain Nguyen Ngoc Phach, aide to the chief of staff of the South Vietnamese army. With the exception of the *Telegraph* and *The Times*, both of which aimed at producing a daily record of the war, British papers tended to give news coverage to Vietnam only when the war flared up. The *Daily Express* is an example of this. The *Daily Mirror*, like the *Express*, had a man in Saigon at frequent intervals, but from 1966, when the *Mirror* decided that it was against the war, it also sent feature writer John Pilger, once or twice a year, to write his own very personal view of the war.

Pilger's attitude was that Vietnam was a new type of war, "impossible to cover without becoming part of it yourself, and when you become part of it you have to decide where you stand."[17] Pilger made his stand clear in a series of articles on what the war was doing to Vietnamese civilians, which the *Sunday Mirror* launched with the front-page headline HOW CAN BRITAIN SUPPORT A WAR LIKE THIS? When Pilger's Vietnam reporting won two major British awards, his critics said his work was emotional and anti-American. He replied that it was anti-war, rather than anti-American, and that the charge of emotional reporting usually came from correspondents who had been so long exposed to the war that their compassion had been deadened.

British magazines relied for their Vietnam coverage mostly on freelance journalists and photographers, who visited Vietnam for short periods. Although these correspondents were usually not as well informed about the war as the resident men, they did have the advantage of a fresh eye for some of the stranger facets. In 1964, Brian Moynahan, a free-lance writer, interviewed Nguyen Cao Ky, then a not-so-well-known South Vietnamese air force officer, and was so struck by Ky's political views that he took careful note of them for a story. "People ask me who my heroes are," Moynahan quoted Ky as saying. "I have only one hero—Hitler…We need four or five Hitlers in Vietnam." When Ky became premier the following year, Moynahan dug out his earlier story and sold it to the *Sunday Mirror*, which displayed it prominently.[18] At first, no American newspaper picked up the story, but then the *New York Times* carried a report from its office in London quoting the United States Embassy there as saying not only that Ky had never made such a statement about Hitler, but also that he denied ever having spoken to Moynahan. Unfortunately for the embassy and for the *New York Times*, the very day that this report appeared Ky repeated the statement almost verbatim to the Reuters and BBC correspondents in Saigon.

Neither British nor American correspondents did very well in writing about the unimaginable scale of corruption in Vietnam, perhaps because few correspondents could claim to be completely untainted themselves. Most of them changed dollars and pounds on the black market, and many bought stolen army goods, although one British correspondent said he felt things were going a little too far when a United States army captain called on him in his hotel room, within hours of his arrival in Saigon, to ask whether he wanted to buy liquor, clothing, luggage, cameras, or electrical goods. In fact, as Murray Sayle, in 1967 the correspondent for the *Sunday Times* of London, wrote: "Economic activity in the South has practically ceased, except for the war; Saigon is a vast brothel; between the Americans who are trying more or less sincerely to promote a copy of their society on Vietnamese soil, and the mass of the population who are to be 'reconstructed', stand the fat cats of Saigon."[19]

When the full story of the pilfering, theft, hijacking, bribery, smuggling, extortion, and black-market dealings finally emerged—mainly through United States Senate hearings in Washington and, in the case of opium-smuggling, in a series of articles by John Hughes in the *Christian Science Monitor*[20]—the facts were staggering. In one South Vietnam black market, at Qui Nhon, thousands of cases of army C rations, liquor, clothing, television sets, washing machines, and weapons and ammunition worth an unbelievable $11 million changed hands *each month*. Vietnamese dealers offered to supply anything from a heavy-duty truck or an armoured personnel carrier to a helicopter. One American sub-contractor lost through pilfering, over a one-year period, $118 million worth of goods. In 1967, half a million tons of imported American rice simply disappeared. Black-market currency transactions were estimated to run to some $360 million a year. The Central Intelligence Agency allowed Laotian generals to use its private airline, Air America, to smuggle opium. The United States Army's own police force, the Criminal Investigation Division, accused its senior officer, Major-General Carl C. Turner, of refusing to permit it to investigate the dealings of a network of sergeants who personally profited from their operation of clubs for servicemen at army bases.* And, finally, in the three fiscal years 1968–70, $1.7 billion authorised for the Saigon government pacification programme was, according to the General Accounting Office, lost without trace.[21]

Most correspondents considered corruption stories peripheral to the war itself. It seemed to many of them more important to devote their time to the army or the Marine Corps, to attach themselves to a unit going into action and to write about it, usually in simple Second World War terms. When the first Marines landed at Da Nang in 1965, American reporters spent weeks writing about leathernecks "storming ashore," whereas they had walked up the beaches unopposed. Almost any action produced emotive comparisons—"the biggest since Inchon," "the second biggest since Normandy." This sort of reporting—mostly by veteran correspondents—injected a new feeling of badly needed confidence in victory, and was the model the United States authorities wished all correspondents would follow.

Jim G. Lucas of the Scripps-Howard group is an example of this type of correspondent. Lucas, a Marine Corps combat correspondent at Guadalcanal, Iwo Jima, and Tarawa, has eight battle stars, the Bronze Star, the Presidential Unit Citation, and the Distinguished Service Award of the Marine Corps League. He was not very impressed with the other correspondents in Vietnam when he first went there, in 1964: "In the six months I lived in the Delta I was the only correspondent regularly assigned to—working and living with—combat troops." He wrote about the mud in the Mekong Delta, the conversation of GIs, the bravery of the Marines, the smell of cordite, and companionship under fire, in short, snappy sentences interlaced with simple war philosophy: "You know it's war

* The General, who retired in 1969, later had his Distinguished Service Medal revoked by the army.

when you see a young man dead. Young men court danger as they court women, and for much the same reasons...secretly each wants to be a hero, in the finest and best sense of the word, and there's nothing wrong with that, because quiet heroism is the stuff of war."[22]

Some of the correspondents, like Frank Harvey, were fascinated by the technical aspects of the war. Harvey went to Vietnam and wrote a long article for *Flying Magazine* in 1966, which he later expanded into a book. Harvey lived and flew with the Americans piloting the wide range of aircraft involved in the air war in Vietnam, and he described how they operated and what they felt about the war. "Ninety per cent gave me roughly the same answer, 'We have to stop Communism and we'd rather do it here in Vietnam than on the coast of California.' One F-4 fighter-bomber pilot in Danang told me he thought we should start at the DMZ and kill every man, woman and child in North Vietnam."[23] Like Lucas, Harvey saw the war in straightforward terms: "The United States is presently a world leader and I believe we intend to keep it that way...We are prepared to fight, if necessary, to hold onto what we've got and get more. In Vietnam. In South America. Anywhere."[24]

Reporting like this had been quite adequate in the Second World War, where the issues were more clearly discernible. Vietnam was a new kind of war and required a new kind of war correspondent. It was an interdisciplinary war, where complex political issues intruded on the military aspects, where battle success was necessary but where battle success alone was insufficient, a war where unwarranted optimism, propaganda, and news management could deeply obscure the issue. Ward Just of the *Washington Post*, a compassionate and conscientious correspondent, summed it up in this story: "'You will never be any more clear-headed than you are right now,' an American major told a reporter driving in from Tansonnhut airport thirty minutes after his arrival in Vietnam. And the major, according to the reporter, has so far been right."[25]

Assessing the coverage of Vietnam, it seems clear that a primary requisite for this new war was for the correspondent to find some way of protecting his compassion. John Shaw has said, "Things which shocked you when you first went there, six weeks later shocked you no more. It became easier to let horrifying things slide over you. There was lots of cynicism and you could get very hard after a while."[26]

For American correspondents, Vietnam required the courage to face squarely the racist nature of the war and the effect this racism

423

had on their fellow countrymen. It was no accident that the most damning indictments of this important aspect of the war did not come from American correspondents.

All governments realise that to wage war successfully their troops must learn to dehumanise the enemy. The simplest way to achieve this is to inflame nationalistic or racist feelings, or both. Thus, American racism, which had first been aroused on a national scale in the Second World War and then revived in Korea, reached a peak in Vietnam. But Vietnam was an insurgency war. The enemy was physically indistinguishable from the ally. Racist hate directed at Charlie Cong the enemy made no provision for exempting those Vietnamese that the United States had intervened to save. In motivating the GI to fight by appealing to his racist feelings, the United States military discovered that it had liberated an emotion over which it was to lose control. Sartre has written that American racism—anti-Negro, anti-Mexican, anti-Asian—is "a fundamental fact which goes very deep and which existed, potentially, or in fact, long before the Vietnam war."

In Vietnam, racism became a patriotic virtue. *All* Vietnamese became "dinks," "slopes," "slants," or "gooks," and the only good one was a dead one. So the Americans killed them when it was clear that they were Vietcong. "I shot up a Charlie in the paddies today," Frank Harvey quotes an American helicopter pilot as saying. "I ran that little mother all over the place hosing him with guns, but somehow or other we just didn't hit him. Finally, he turned on us and stood there facing us with his rifle. We really busted his ass then. Blew him up like a toy balloon."[27]

And they killed them when it was clear they were not Vietcong. A British free-lance photographer, Philip Jones Griffiths, went out with a platoon from the First Cavalry. The GIs were nervous and opened fire on the first farmer they saw. They missed. Jones Griffiths wrote: "The next farmer was not so lucky. Soon he lay dying among the ripening rice in a corner of the paddy field, the back of his skull blown away. He was somehow conscious, making a whimpering sound and trying to squeeze his eyes more tightly shut. He never spoke and died with the fingers of his left hand clenching his testicles so tightly they could not be undone. 'Got him in the balls, knew I hit him,' cried the boy from Kansas, until someone took him to one side and explained that they do that to relieve the pain elsewhere."[28]

The Americans mutilated bodies. One colonel wanted the hearts cut out of dead Vietcong to feed to his dog. Heads were cut off, arranged in rows, and a lighted cigarette pushed into each mouth. Ears were strung together like beads. Parts of Vietnamese bodies were kept as trophies; skulls were a favourite, and the then Colonel George Patton III—"I do like to see the arms and legs fly"—carried one about at his farewell party.[29] The Americans photographed dead Vietnamese as if they were game trophies—a smiling Marine with his foot on the chest of the nearest corpse or holding a severed ear or two—or, in the case of a dead Vietcong girl, without her pyjama pants and with her legs raised stiffly in the air. The Twenty-fifth Infantry Division left a "visiting card," a torn-off shoulder patch of the division's emblem, stuffed in the mouth of the Vietnamese they killed. Other divisions had similar practices.

Killing Vietnamese became almost mundane, almost like a movie in which the Americans were the cowboys and the Vietnamese the Indians. "Batchelor squeezes off a careful shot. The Marines around him cheer. 'Holy Jesus! You see that? Just like the movies. The guy sagged, then just kinda slowly slid down holding on to the doorway.'"—Ian Adams, in *Maclean's Magazine*, February 1968. Captain Lynn A. Carlson, who flew a Cobra helicopter gunship out of Pleiku, used to drop specially printed visiting cards over his target areas. The cards read: "Congratulations. You have been killed through courtesy of the 361st. Yours truly, Pink Panther 20." On the reverse side were various messages: "Call us for death and destruction night and day." Or, "The Lord giveth and the 20mm [cannon] taketh away. Killing is our business and business is good."[30]

Carlson clearly enjoyed his work. He was not alone in this. The late Nicholas Tomalin of the *Sunday Times* of London spent an afternoon, in June 1966, with General James F. Hollingsworth, and wrote about it in an article headed THE GENERAL GOES ZAPPING CHARLIE CONG. It began: "After a light lunch last Wednesday, General James F. Hollingsworth, of the US 'Big Red I' Division took off in his personal helicopter and killed more Vietnamese than any of the troops he was commanding." Tomalin described how the helicopter covered the landscape beside Routes 13 and 16 while the General blazed away with his personal M-16 carbine at any Vietnamese seen running for cover. He concluded with Hollingsworth's saying: "There's no better way to fight than goin' out to shoot VCs. An' there's nothing I love better than killin' Cong. No, sir."[31] Set beside examples such as this, the fact that many helicopter pilots referred to their missions as "turkey shoots" was not surprising.

However, the attitude of some of the army chaplains remains bewildering. Those at Phu Cat air base went around in a jeep on which was inscribed, in bold white letters, "The God Squad."[32] A Marine who had taken some horrifying photographs after an operation on the Cua Viet River became worried about the morality of having done so and asked his chaplain for advice. Michael Herr reported, in *Esquire* in April 1970, that all the chaplain did was to tell the Marine that it was forgivable. He then put the pictures in his drawer and kept them. James Fox, an American writer based in London, met a Cobra pilot who planned to become a Lutheran missionary when he left Vietnam. Fox asked the pilot whether he felt any conflict between his religion and his gunship work. "Oh you oughta been here with Father Dodge," the pilot replied. "He always used to say, the faster you get 'em the quicker their souls get to heaven. I feel I'm killing to spare souls."[33]

Some of this side of the war appeared in American newspapers and magazines, but not without difficulty. General Hollingsworth's "Cong-zapping" activities were known to American correspondents before Nicholas Tomalin wrote his story—"Jeez, I'm so glad you was along," the General said. "I've been written up time and time again back in the States for shootin' up VCs, but no one's been along with me like you before." Yet when Tomalin's graphic account was passed to the *Washington Post*, the *Post* refused to publish it.[34] It eventually appeared in the *San Francisco Chronicle* and was read into the *Congressional Record*, along with an official explanation from the United States Army. In short, until the My Lai massacre story, American coverage was weak on the racist and brutalising nature of the war and on the way Americans treated the Vietnamese.

Herr offered one explanation in his *Esquire* article. A soldier from the First Infantry Division had just said that he believed that Americans treated the Vietnamese like animals. "You know what we do to animals…kill 'em and hurt 'em and beat on 'em, so's we can train 'em. Shit, we don't treat the Dinks no different than that." Herr wrote: "We knew that he was telling the truth…We mentioned it later to some people who'd been at the Pacification briefings, someone from the [*New York*] *Times* and someone from the AP and they both agreed that the kid from the Big Red One had said more about the Hearts and Minds Programme than they'd heard in over an hour of statistics, but their bureaus could not use his story, they wanted Ambassador

426

Komer's, and they got it and you got it."*

Perhaps the case of Martha Gellhorn deterred correspondents from writing this side of the war. Miss Gellhorn, a famous, experienced, and respected war correspondent (Spain, China, Finland, Britain, Italy, France, Germany), went to Vietnam in 1966–67 as a free-lance. Taking from the indoctrination lecture read to United States troops on their arrival in Vietnam the sentence "To really and truly and finally win this war we must...win the hearts and minds of the *people* of South Vietnam," she determined to see whether this central tenet of American doctrine was in fact being carried out. First, she visited Qui Nhon provincial hospital, where a team of dedicated New Zealand doctors and nurses was caring for wounded non-combatants, "under conditions suitable for the Crimean war." She reached the conclusion that

> we, unintentionally, are killing and wounding three or four times more people than the Vietcong do, so we are told, on purpose. We are not maniacs and monsters, but our planes range the sky all day and all night, and our artillery is lavish and we have much more deadly stuff to kill with. The people are there on the ground, sometimes destroyed by accident, sometimes destroyed because Vietcong are reported to be among them. This is indeed a new kind of war, as the indoctrination lecture stated, and we had better find a new way to fight it. Hearts and minds, after all, live in bodies.

Miss Gellhorn then went to an orphanage in Saigon, where Catholic nuns, desperate for funds to keep their institution going under the stress of new demands, wrote their first and only letter to the U.S. AID (Agency for International Development)—which that year had a budget of $700 million—asking for money to build a rain-water cistern. The letter was not answered. "The [South Vietnamese] Ministry of Social Welfare predicts an average of 2,000 more orphans every month," Miss Gellhorn wrote. "Is it not strange that we count and proclaim only military casualties? These lonely waifs of war should be listed as wounded, and wounded forever." In her final article Miss Gellhorn described a refugee camp, "a dump heap," where just a few of the million or more Vietnamese made refugee *in the previous two years* were housed.

> These peasants had survived the Vietcong since 1957, on whatever terms hostile or friendly, and the war however it came to them. But they cannot survive our bombs. Even the Catholic

* Robert Komer was the deputy ambassador in charge of pacification, and his story was of how well the programme was progressing.

427

refugees did not leave their hamlets until the bombs fell. We are uprooting the people from the lovely land where they have lived for generations; and the uprooted are given not bread but a stone. Is this an honourable way for a great nation to fight a war 8,000 miles from its safe homeland?

No newspaper in the United States would publish the series of articles. "Everywhere I was told that they were too tough for American readers." Eventually, the *St. Louis Post-Dispatch* took the two mildest ones. Miss Gellhorn had to turn to Britain to get all five published. They appeared in the *Guardian*,[35] and ended Miss Gellhorn's career as a war correspondent in Vietnam. When she applied for a visa to return there, her request was refused. She tried over the years since then, applying at various South Vietnamese embassies around the world, and was refused every time. "It appears I am on some sort of black list and I will not be allowed to report from South Vietnam again."[36]

Philip Jones Griffiths, one of the few photographers to concentrate on portraying what the war did to Vietnamese civilians, had great difficulty in finding an outlet for his work in the United States. "I was told time after time that my photographs were too harrowing for the American market."[37] When, eventually, a book of his photographs, *Vietnam Inc.*, was published in the United States, the South Vietnamese government banned his return to Saigon.

It was the racist nature of the fighting, the treating of the Vietnamese "like animals," that led inevitably to My Lai, and it was the reluctance of correspondents to report this racist and atrocious nature of the war that caused the My Lai story to be revealed not by a war correspondent, but by an alert newspaper reporter back in the United States—a major indictment of the coverage of the war.

What happened at My Lai is now well known. C Company, First Battalion, Twentieth Infantry, Eleventh Brigade, Americal Division, entered the village of My Lai on March 16, 1968, and killed between ninety and 130 men, women, and children. Acting, the men said later, under orders from the platoon commander, Lieutenant William L. Calley, Jr., they gathered the villagers into groups and "wasted" them with automatic-weapon fire. Anyone who survived was then picked off. "A really tiny kid—he had only a shirt on—nothing else...came over to the people and held the hand of one of the dead. One of the GIs behind me dropped into a kneeling position thirty metres from this kid and killed him with a single shot."[38]

A little over a year later, Ronald Ridenhour, a former door-gunner in a helicopter, who had heard about the massacre at My Lai from various members of C Company, mailed, from his home in Phoenix, Arizona, thirty letters setting out everything he had heard about My Lai and listing the names of people who had given him the information. The letters went to President Nixon, to various military authorities, and to senators and congressmen who, Ridenhour thought, might be able to exert some sort of pressure on the army to compel it to take action. Most of them never replied, but Congressman Morris Udall, a liberal from Arizona, telephoned to say that he would do everything in his power to see that the matter was investigated. The army began a full-scale investigation on April 23, 1969, and in September, only days before he was due to be discharged from the army, Lieutenant Calley was charged with the murder of 109 "Oriental human beings" (the number was later reduced to 102).

This fact was made public in a small item, of fewer than a hundred words, put out from Fort Benning, Georgia, by the Associated Press on September 6. The item did not say how many murders Calley had been charged with, and it gave no indication of the circumstances. It is not surprising, therefore, that not a single newspaper or broadcasting station called the AP to ask for more information.[39] In fact, the item passed completely unnoticed—the *New York Times*, on September 8, put it at the bottom of page 38—and that might have been the end of the matter had it not been for a freelance reporter called Seymour Hersh.

Hersh, then aged thirty-two, had covered the Pentagon in 1966–67 for the Associated Press, but had hated it—"just one lie after another"—and had left. On October 22—six weeks after the first story about Calley and the murder charge—a contact of Hersh's, a lawyer called Geoff Cowan, said to him, "The army is trying to court-martial some guy in secret for killing seventy-five Vietnamese civilians." It took Hersh two days and twenty-five telephone calls to find out that the civilians numbered 109, and to sense that the story warranted a lot more effort and would require more money than he had. He telephoned Jim Boyd, of the Fund for Investigative Journalism, in Washington, and was promised $1,000. He then flew to Fort Benning and, after an amazing run-around, finally found Calley and on November 11 interviewed him at length. The problem now was where to publish the story. *Life* turned it down, even though it had earlier heard much the same version from Ridenhour. *Look* said that its publication delay was too long. So Hersh turned to a little-known Washington agency, the Dispatch News Service, started only a few months earlier by his neighbour, David Obst, aged twenty-three. Obst telephoned some fifty newspapers, offering the story for $100 if it was used. Subsequently, thirty-six of the fifty—including *The Times* of London, the *San Francisco Chronicle*, the *Boston Globe*, and the *St. Louis Post-Dispatch*—ran the story. It was first printed on November 13. On the same day, the *New York Times*, which had started working on the story six days earlier, ran its own account of My Lai, written by one of its reporters, Bob Smith.

Then, amazingly, the story appeared to die. Throughout the following week, when My Lai was a leading story in British and continental newspapers, it was still on an inside page in the *Washington Post*, and in other newspapers it was given less play than Apollo 12 or Vice President Spiro Agnew's attack on the liberal press. It was revived when the Dispatch News Service sent out Hersh's second story, interviews with members of C Company, and it really made headlines on November 20, when the *Cleveland Plain Dealer* carried photographs of the massacre taken by an army photographer, Ronald L. Haeberle, who had been in My Lai with Calley and C Company, and who had settled in Cleveland after leaving the army. The photographs were a harrowing record. One showed a boy of about seven lying on a pathway with protective arms around a smaller boy, who had been shot but was still alive. Then, according to Haeberle, the GIs had moved in and shot both of them dead. But even now, in spite of Haeberle's detailed account of how he had taken the photographs, and in spite of the evidence of the photographs themselves, obstacles were still put in the way of their world-wide publication.

The first objection came from David Duncan, a photographer who had taken war pictures during the Second World War, in Korea, and in Vietnam. Duncan had been to Vietnam for *Life*. There, his series on the fighting at Con Thieu—"Inside the Cone of Fire"—had won him the Overseas Press Club's Robert Capa Gold Medal. Duncan, who was in Cleveland promoting his latest book, saw an early edition of the *Plain Dealer*, called the newspaper, said he believed the photographs were phoney, and begged the paper to stop the presses in the national interest: "You're doing a disservice to America." The *Plain Dealer* had been uneasy about the authenticity of Haeberle's photographs and had done all it could to check them. Duncan's telephone call went to the night managing editor, a tough home-town newspaperman, who was not

430

impressed by Duncan's arguments and so got rid of him as polite-
ly as he could.[40]

Then, negotiations to sell the photographs nearly foundered.
*Life*, having offered $100,000 for world rights, became worried in
case it should appear in America that the magazine was acting as
"brokers for massacre pictures." The *New York Times* did not want
to be "in the position of buying massacre pictures," but it was prepared to help to sell them.[41] The Japanese made a modest offer of
$500, and when this was declined they announced that they would
simply copy the photographs from the *Plain Dealer*, "because it will
take thirty years in the Japanese courts for the [copyright] case to
come to trial."* The *New York Post* broke the deadlock in the United States by copying the *Plain Dealer*'s pictures, on the ground that
Haeberle's copyright was dubious because he was an army photographer and on duty at the time he took the photographs; therefore,
the photographs were United States government property, and,
since they had been published, they were in the public domain. As
newspapers from all over the world began to carry the pictures,
Haeberle quickly settled for $50,000 from *Life*.

The following week, the outcry in the United States grew
rapidly, until, three weeks after Hersh's original story had
appeared, *Time*, in its issue of December 5, and *Newsweek*, in its
issue of December 8, carried major stories on My Lai. *Time* called
it "an American tragedy." *Newsweek* used the headline A SINGLE
INCIDENT IN A BRUTAL WAR SHOCKS THE AMERICAN CONSCIENCE.
Paul Meadlo, a C Company soldier who had participated in the
attack at My Lai, "sold" by Hersh and the Dispatch News Agency
to CBS for $10,000, appeared on television to say he was sorry for
what he had done. His mother, who appeared with him, blamed the
army. "I sent them a good boy," she said, "and they made him a
murderer." The United States wallowed in weeks of conscience-
searching.

Suddenly, nearly every war correspondent who had been in
Vietnam had an atrocity story to tell. *Time*'s correspondent Frank
McCulloch had had nothing to say about atrocities when, in
December 1967, he had written a farewell assessment of Vietnam
after covering the war for four years.[42] Now, McCulloch recalled
having seen men pushed from aeroplanes, shot with their hands
tied behind their backs, and drowned because they refused to

* The Japanese did copy the pictures, and they were more widely circulated in
Japan than in any other country, including the United States.

answer questions. He recalled having seen Americal Division troops unleash a Doberman pinscher dog on an old man suspected of being a Vietcong and watch it tear the man from head to belly. *Time*'s correspondent Burt Pines related the case of a sergeant on patrol who shouted, "A three day pass for whoever gets that gook." After a moment's hesitation, most of the patrol opened up with their M-16s, ripping an old man, as well as the child he was carrying, into pieces.[43]

If there were atrocities before My Lai, why did not correspondents write about them at the time? And if the answer proves to be that they did but that no one would publish them, then why was it suddenly possible to publish the story of My Lai? The word "atrocity" requires careful handling, but it can be argued that My Lai was *not* an atrocity—at least, if it is argued that an atrocity is taken to be something freakish, something quite apart from the normal events coming before and after it. My Lai, on the contrary, was an unusually pure example of the nature of the war in Vietnam and departed little—if at all—from common American practice.

There were events equally horrifying before My Lai, and massacres on a larger scale occurred afterwards. The war in Vietnam was an unusually frustrating one. The fact that the Americans were able to destroy the enemy's country and yet were not able to win was something new to their experience, and they sought desperately to cope. The destruction of villages and the relocation of the inhabitants in operations like "Cedar Falls"—chillingly described, in July 1967, in "The Village of Ben Suc," a fine piece of war reporting by *The New Yorker*'s correspondent Jonathan Schell—only helped to expose the shortcomings of the American military conduct of the war. In particular, the use of raw young soldiers, on a fixed period of service, bewildered by the faceless nature of the enemy, and encouraged to regard the Vietnamese as less than human, made an event such as My Lai highly likely to occur. The system of evaluating the progress of the war in terms of a body count, which rewarded individuals, units, and whole brigades on the basis of how many Vietcong they had killed, made it inevitable. A Vietnamese taken prisoner might turn out to be an innocent civilian. A Vietnamese shot dead became a Vietcong killed in action.

With no moral restraints against "wasting" Vietnamese, in fact with incentives to do so, and with the understandable desire, above all, to stay alive, the American soldier in Vietnam ended up committing acts that the nation believed impossible. "Some people think that the Japanese committed atrocities, that the Germans committed atrocities, that the Russians committed atrocities, but that the Americans don't commit atrocities," Colonel Robert Rheault, a former commander of the United States Special Forces in Vietnam, said just after My Lai. "Well, this just isn't so. American troops are as capable as any other of committing atrocities."[44]

My Lai removed inhibitions on talking about the nature of the Vietnam War. Ex-soldiers appeared on television to confess to having shot children. Others, in hearings conducted by the National Committee for a Citizens Commission of Inquiry on United States War Crimes in Vietnam, told of rape, the machine-gunning of women and children in fields, torture, and murder. Lieutenant-Colonel Anthony Herbert, the most-decorated American soldier of the Korean War, a battalion commander of the elite 173rd Airborne Brigade, claimed he had reported seeing a United States lieutenant allow a South Vietnamese soldier to slit a woman's throat while her child clung screaming to her leg. Colonel Herbert alleged that when he made his report, his superiors told him to mind his own business.[45]

It emerged that some incidents had actually been reported at the time, and had passed with little or no notice. John Shaw of *Time*, for example, had reported as early as 1965 that "the marines have begun to kill prisoners, embittered perhaps by a recent incident; they wounded two Vietcong in an ambush, took them to a field hospital, where navy doctors expended twelve hours and several hundred pounds of invaluable ice in saving them. Then the South Vietnamese army claimed the prisoners, took them up in a helicopter, and pushed them out the hatch."[46] A Japanese photographer, Akihiko Okamura, had published photographs of the water torture of Vietcong suspects in 1964.[47] And, unless it should appear that only the South Vietnamese soldiers were guilty of atrocities, in July 1967 *Newsweek*, complimenting the United States forces on their restraint in the use of terror, in contrast with the methods of the Vietcong, said that fewer than a dozen American atrocities had been reported and verified in the course of the war.

But, before My Lai, anyone seeking evidence of the nature of the Vietnam War need only have consulted official records. The writer Norman Poirier used the files of the judge-advocate-general of the navy, in Washington, to compile a story of how a squad of nine Marines gang-raped a young Vietnamese mother at Xuan Ngoc on the night of September 23, 1966, and gunned down her entire family—herself, her husband, her two children, and her sister. When the Marines returned in the morning to make the carnage look like an engagement with the Vietcong, they found that one of the children, a five-year-old girl, was still alive, and so one of the Marines stood over the child "and with his M14 rifle bashed its brains in." They were exposed by the recovery of the mother, who had been left for dead, were arrested and tried, and six of them were convicted. Poirier's account of the incident appeared in Esquire in August 1969—*three months before* the story of My Lai broke. Despite the fact that *Esquire* sent proofs to the major American newspapers, to promote the article, it created hardly a ripple of interest.

Daniel Lang, in his book *Casualties of War*,[48] which was based on court files, tells of a patrol of five United States soldiers, operating in the Central Highlands, who abducted a young Vietnamese girl. Four of them raped her, and then ripped her belly open and blew her head off. The fifth soldier reported the incident, and proceedings were initiated against the others, who, after some reluctance on the part of the army, were brought to trial, then retried, and sentenced to rather light terms of imprisonment. Lang's book was reviewed in *Newsweek* in the very issue that was devoted to the My Lai story. The reviewer wrote: "The brutal killing of a Vietnamese civilian...should not in itself, surprise us...after all, no one seriously informed about the war in Vietnam believes that U.S. body counts have not included a number of civilians all along."

Correspondents in Vietnam were well aware of this. As proof, there is the manner in which they were able to recall, after the My Lai story broke, incidents they themselves had witnessed, and I have spoken to some who agree that the killing of Vietnamese civilians was a well-known fact. They did not write this, because the killing of civilians was not unusual either on a small or on a large scale, and because their public, certainly in the United States (as Poirier's *Esquire* article showed), was not ready to listen. In August 1965, CBS showed a harrowing documentary on the nature of the war in Vietnam. It depicted United States Marines turning their flamethrowers on a village south of the Da Nang air base. Vietnamese children and elderly couples were shown pleading for their homes to be spared. In all, 150 homes were levelled in retaliation for a short burst of gunfire from the village. After the broadcast, CBS's switchboard was jammed with calls from viewers attacking the film as a piece of Communist propaganda abetting the enemy's cause, a viewer reaction that must have made CBS think twice about using films of a similar sort again.

Philip Jones Griffiths, the British photo-journalist, accompanied a unit of the Americal Division on a mission in Quang Ngai in September 1967. The Americans approached a fortified village called Red Mountain, not far from Mo Duc, and lost two men in a grenade exchange. Several armed Vietcong were killed, the village occupied, and about fifteen women and children rounded up and herded together. The Americans withdrew, and the captain called in an artillery strike. As Jones Griffiths remembers: "I said to the captain, 'Hey, what about those civilians? They'll be killed.' The captain looked straight at me and said, 'What civilians?'" If one asks Jones Griffiths why he did not write about this incident—he had photographed the women and children huddled together, just before they were killed by the artillery strike—he replies: "If I had gone back to Saigon and into one of the agencies and had said, 'I've got a story about Americans killing Vietnamese civilians,' they would have said, 'So what's new?' It was horrible, but certainly not exceptional, and it just wasn't news."[49]

Neil Sheehan of the *New York Times*, a fine political reporter and military analyst, defended the correspondents' attitude in his newspaper in 1971. "I had never read the laws governing the conduct of war, although I had watched the war for three years in Vietnam and had written about it for five…The Army Field Manual says that it is illegal to attack hospitals. We routinely bombed and shelled them. The destruction of Vietcong and North Vietnamese army hospitals in the South Vietnamese countryside was announced at the daily press briefings, the Five o'Clock Follies, by American military spokesmen in Saigon…Looking back, one realises that the war crimes issue was always present." Sheehan described the ravaging of five fishing hamlets on the coast of Quang Ngai by United States destroyers and bombers, which killed, he estimated, as many as 600 Vietnamese civilians. "Making peasants pay so dearly for the presence of guerrillas in their hamlets, regardless of whether they sympathised with the Vietcong, seemed unnecessarily brutal and politically counter-productive to me. When I wrote my story, however, it did not occur to me that I had discovered a possible war crime."[50]

Peter Arnett, a correspondent for the Associated Press, agrees with Sheehan and goes further—that even if he had known he was witnessing a war crime, he would not have described it as such, because that would have been making a judgement, and as a correspondent for the AP he dealt in facts, not judgements.* "I

---

* This was true of most of the American correspondents. They did not consider it their job to speculate on the morality of the war. It was in direct contrast to the attitude of the American correspondents in the Spanish Civil War, who had considered it their job to do exactly that.

accompanied Neil Sheehan on some of those military operations he wrote about; I watched hooches burning down; I saw the civilian dead. I did not write about war crimes either. We took pictures of those burning buildings, we told of the civilian dead and how they died, but we didn't make judgements because we were witnesses, and, like witnesses to robbery, accident, or murder, surely it was not for us to be judge and jury."[51]

So the My Lai massacre was revealed because it was written not by a war correspondent on the spot, but by a reporter back in the United States who was capable of being shocked by it, and because he wrote the story at a moment when, for a variety of reasons, the American public was prepared to read, believe, and accept it. Foremost among these reasons was the change in attitude in the United States brought about by the 1968 Tet offensive. Throughout 1967, the army in Vietnam and the Pentagon in Washington had led the public to believe that victory was just around the corner. Then, on January 31, 1968, the Vietcong and the North Vietnamese launched a major offensive throughout South Vietnam. A commando squad of Vietcong succeeded in getting briefly into the compound of the United States Embassy in Saigon, the former imperial city of Hué was occupied for twenty-five days, and nearly every town, city, and major military installation came under fire.

It is now clear that the attack on the United States Embassy was inflated beyond its military significance and that the Tet offensive as a whole was such a military disaster for the Vietcong that they never really recovered. But it was also a traumatic shock to the American public. The attack on the embassy was given extensive television coverage and became, for many Americans, the first battle of the war that was immediately understandable. It showed the Vietcong, supposedly on their last legs, attacking the heart of the American presence in South Vietnam. How was this possible? As Walter Cronkite, the CBS Evening News anchor man said when he read the news agency tapes in the CBS newsroom in New York, "What the hell is going on? I thought we were winning the war." Or, as the *Washington Daily News* demanded, WHERE WERE WE? WHERE ARE WE?

Coming, as it did, just before the first primaries in a presidential election year, the Tet offensive caught the administration at its weakest politically, and dealt a powerful blow to its sagging credibility. When Senator Eugene McCarthy, running on a peace platform, won the New Hampshire primary, President Johnson was faced with an extremely difficult situation. He resolved it by announcing, on March 31, that he would not run for a second term and that he was prepared "to move immediately toward peace through negotiations." Yet the new President, Richard Nixon, seemed just as determined to carry on the war, which had become the longest in the nation's history, and which, by late in 1969, had cost the United States more than 300,000 dead and wounded. A political and emotional climate was created in which more and more Americans were prepared to believe that the war had long since ceased to be a just cause. At this moment My Lai emerged. It provided the basis for an examination of America's motives, of the nature of the war, and of the national conscience, and a concrete moral reason for withdrawal from it. My Lai made it clear that the cost of continuing in Vietnam was too high. From then on, the question of getting out was one of timing and no longer one of principle.

Unfortunately, My Lai had two unexpected repercussions. From this moment on, the media, especially in the United States, decided that the war was all but over. The amount of space and time devoted to it began to decline. The number of correspondents accredited by MACV (Military Assistance Command, Vietnam) in Saigon provides some measure of this loss of interest. In 1968, at the height of the Tet offensive, there were 637 accredited correspondents; in 1969, 467; in 1970, 392; in 1971, 355; in 1972, 295. By mid-1974, only thirty-five correspondents remained, mostly American and Japanese.* All the correspondents I have spoken with who were in Vietnam during this period remarked that it became noticeably more difficult, from 1969 on, to get their stories used. ABC and NBC both told their Saigon staffs and free-lancers in that year that the story would now be the negotiations in Paris and that film footage from Vietnam should be angled to the withdrawal of the American forces.[52]

This suggests a serious misjudgement on the part of editors and television producers, for the period 1969–73 saw major escalations and changes in the war. Two other countries, Laos and Cambodia, became involved, there was a stepping up of bombing operations by the United States, in highly controversial circumstances, and there was the creation of some 3 million more refugees. Anthony Lewis of the *New York Times*, one of the few correspondents to draw

---

* The exception to the loss of interest appeared to be the *New York Times*. In the first half of 1972 it had eight men on the Vietnam story, more on a war story than at any time since the Second World War.

attention to this, complained, in April 1971, that "as Americans are told by their government that the war is winding down, the number of Vietnamese, Cambodians, and Laotians being killed and maimed and made homeless is at a record high level. In 1971, more civilians are being killed and wounded in the three countries and more made refugees than at any time in history. Most of those casualties are caused, and people made refugees, by American and Allied military activity."[53] So, at a time when the most damage of the war was being inflicted on Indo-China, the news coverage was at its worst, because editors and producers had decided that the ground war was virtually over and that, with the steady withdrawal of United States troops under way, public interest had declined. The second unfortunate result was that those editors and producers decided that there was no further interest in American atrocity stories. One example will illustrate both points.

In November 1971, Kevin Buckley, *Newsweek*'s bureau chief in Saigon, and Alec Shimkin, a *Newsweek* reporter, were working on the history of the war. Buckley, who was on his second spell in Vietnam, had long been interested in the level of civilian casualties and hoped one day to find documented evidence on which to base a story. He decided that while he and Shimkin were going through the files the bureau had accumulated over the years, they would look out for possible leads on this subject. In due course Shimkin came across an old MACV handout that set them after the story. It was a report on a campaign in late 1968 in which the United States forces claimed that 11,000 of the enemy had been killed in action and 700 weapons captured. The discrepancy between the number of enemy dead and the number of weapons captured seemed amazing. Had there really been only one gun for every fifteen Vietcong? Or had all those killed not been soldiers? Buckley and Shimkin made a few tentative enquiries and quickly realised that there must have been something seriously wrong with the operation. "MACV began volunteering lies about it and I realized that we were on to something," Buckley has recalled. "We dropped everything else and spent two and a half months on it."

What the *Newsweek* men had uncovered was the result of "Operation Speedy Express," part of an "accelerated pacification programme" that ran from December 1968 through May 1969 in the former Vietcong stronghold of Kien Hoa, in the Mekong Delta. During the operation, thousands of civilians had been killed by the United States Army's notorious Ninth Infantry Division. This division was reported by the Associated Press, in

December 1969, to pride itself "on killing a hundred Vietcong a day every day." The AP noted, however, that American civilians in the provinces often complained to newsmen that innocent Vietnamese civilians were sometimes included in the totals. Buckley and Shimkin examined the records of "Speedy Express," interviewed pacification officials, talked with participants in the fighting, and combed through hospital records. They travelled throughout Kien Hoa on foot, by jeep, in boats, and by raft, talking to the people— Shimkin spoke fluent Vietnamese. One American official they spoke to estimated that, of the 11,000 Vietnamese who had been killed, 5,000 would have been non-combatants. As his researches progressed, Buckley kept *Newsweek* informed. "We had all the material to make a big prize-winning investigation. No one had ever documented civilian casualties so thoroughly and harshly. I told New York it was not another My Lai. There were no GIs face-to-face with Vietnamese babies. But this was killing on a much larger scale. This was policy. This was the stuff the war had been made of."

Buckley sent in the story in January 1972, and was disappointed when the foreign editor, Edward Klein, wrote saying that he wanted to brood on the best way of using it. Buckley sent a barrage of cables asking for some indication of when the story would run, but received no answer. "I just couldn't understand it. I considered quitting, but then my tour of duty was over and I went on a long vacation." In New York, Buckley resumed his efforts to get the story into *Newsweek*. "I felt like the mad inventor in the patent office. Everyone kept saying, 'You're much too upset. It's not that important.' I said that if they were not going to use the story then I wanted to free-lance it. They said no, because it would look as if *Newsweek* had been too timid to run it. At last I got a reason out of the editor, Kermit Lansner. He told me that it would be a gratuitous attack on the administration at this point to do another story on civilian deaths after the press had given the army and Washington such a hard time over My Lai."

On June 19, 1972, nearly six months after Buckley had written the story, *Newsweek* reversed its decision and ran it, under the heading PACIFICATION'S DEADLY PRICE. Buckley says, "It was savagely cut, but it still made the point. There was a flurry of low-level Congressional interest and then it faded. The Pentagon reaction was totally deceitful, so I pressed *Newsweek* to run a second piece. I wanted to expose the Pentagon's defense and demolish a letter to the editor from Robert Komer, the deputy ambassador who had been in charge of pacification until November 1968. But *Newsweek* refused to carry a second article and I was allowed only a tiny rebuttal to Komer. Looking back, what I remember most vividly was that the editor seemed to view the story not only with indifference but with utter boredom"*[54]

---

* Two letters to *Newsweek* asking for its version of this affair were not answered.

# Chapter Seventeen

# War is Fun
# 1954–1975

I think that Vietnam was what we had instead of happy childhoods.

—United States war correspondent

---

A Gallup poll in mid-1967 revealed that half of all Americans had no idea what the war in Vietnam was about. Just after the Tet offensive in 1968, the chairman of the Appropriations Committee of the House of Representatives, without whose consent there would be no money for the war, genuinely seeking enlightenment, asked the Chief of Staff of the United States Army: "Who would you say is our enemy in this conflict?"[1]

Clearly, those charged with the responsibility of informing the United States public about Vietnam had not fulfilled their task. Given that the issues were complex and the facts unpalatable, this failure has never been satisfactorily explained. True, the whole story did come out in the end, but the feeling of the American reader that he was not getting a satisfactory running story of the war still concerns those correspondents who did their best to provide it. The most likely theory is that the combination of low understanding of the war at home and high drama in Vietnam created a challenge that few correspondents were able to meet. And when such correspondents were present, too often their efforts were frustrated by the attitude of their editors in the United States.

All sorts of correspondents, from all sorts of publications, went to Vietnam. There were specialist writers from technical journals, trainee reporters from college newspapers, counter-insurgency experts from military publishers, religious correspondents, famous authors, small-town editors, old hands from Korea, even older hands from the Second World War, and what Henry Kamm of the *New York Times* called "proto-journalists," men who had never written a professional word or taken a professional photograph in their lives until the war brought them to Saigon. They all wrote stories that were used and presumably read or took photographs that were bought and reproduced. Michael Herr, who went to Vietnam for *Esquire*, estimated that, at a time when there were between 600 and 700 accredited correspondents, "only fifty gave journalism a better name than it deserved, particularly in Vietnam."

Ambition, principally, had brought them all there. The war was the biggest story in the world at the time—"the longest-running front-page story in history," as a United Press man put it; "the best story going on anywhere in the world at the moment," said Peter Arnett—and there was no better place for a young reporter to put a gloss on a new career or an old reporter to revitalise a fading one. Herbert Matthews had made it sound better in the pre-Second World War days: "If you have not seen a battle, your education has been somewhat neglected—for after all, war has ever been one of the primary functions of mankind, and unless you see men fight you miss something fundamental."[2] But what it comes down to is that war provides rich material for a correspondent, and Vietnam was the richest ever. "You see these things, these terrible things," said Charles Mohr, "but in an odd way they're good stories."[3]

The mechanics of becoming accredited were straightforward. The correspondent applied to his nearest South Vietnamese embassy for an entry visa. It was usually granted.* In Saigon, the correspondent reported to the U.S. authorities with a letter from his newspaper requesting accreditation and accepting responsibility for him. If he wished to be accredited as a free-lance, he needed letters from two organisations saying that they were prepared to buy his dispatches. The correspondent was then issued an accreditation

---

* Apart from the case of Martha Gellhorn, the only correspondents I know personally who were refused visas were Philip Jones Griffiths, William Shaw-cross of the *Sunday Times*, whose refusal in 1972 was because his reporting during an earlier visit had been "negative," and John Philby, who was deported from Saigon in 1968, presumably because his father is Kim Philby of the KGB. Other correspondents were denied visas but told to reapply for them later, when whatever offences they had committed would have been forgotten.

card identifying him and stating: "*The bearer of this card should be accorded full co-operation and assistance…to assure the successful completion of his mission. Bearer is authorised rations and quarters on a reimbursable basis. Upon presentation of this card, bearer is entitled to air, water, and ground transportation under a priority of 3…*"

The correspondent signed an agreement to abide by a set of fifteen ground rules, dealing mainly with preserving military security, and was on his way. Some got a tailor to run up a safari jacket—Saigon tailors called it a "CBS jacket"—with matching trousers, which looked vaguely like a uniform, not, in most cases, out of any sense of commitment, but so as to be less conspicuous in a military situation. On his army fatigues he could sew his official identification, his name and organisation, thus: JOHN SHAW, TIME, or, to the disbelief of most GIs, in his particular case, ALAN WILLIAMS, QUEEN.

The MACV card would admit the correspondent to the daily briefing on the war's progress given at the Joint United States Public Affairs Office (JUSPAO), which had been created to handle press relations and psychological warfare. ("I never met anyone there," claimed one correspondent, "who seemed to realise that there was a difference.") If he was prepared to believe JUSPAO, a correspondent could cover the war simply by attending the briefings each day. Most correspondents considered them a waste of time, but one, Joe Fried of the *New York Daily News*, built up a reputation, during his nine years and eight months in Vietnam—"longer than anyone and without a vacation"—by his daily, persistent, and provocative questioning, sometimes driving the briefing officer into revealing an item of genuine news value.

For the correspondent who preferred to spend more time in the field, the problem was not in finding material, but in the risk of being overwhelmed by it. Murray Sayle wrote to me saying: "I arrived here as everyone else does, hoping to sum it all up in 1,000 crisp words. I wind up in the hotel on Friday nights trying to make some sense out of a great whirl of experience—the ghastly sights you see and your own feelings of fear and loneliness."

Sayle, then working for the *Sunday Times* of London, wrote an article on April 28, 1968, describing a day in his life in Vietnam. It is worth looking at as an example of the "whirl of experience" a correspondent could expect to face as he tried to follow the war. "I begin the day at sea approaching the mouth of the Perfume River aboard the American landing craft Universal No.70, bound for Hue with 190 tons of reinforcing sheet for runways. I am trying to get to Camp Evans, north of Hue, where it is unofficially reported that a big battle is developing—but it is impossible to fly direct from Da Nang."

Sayle leaves the boat and sets out to walk to Phu Bai, a big American base, seven and a half miles away. Crossing a floating bridge, he is overtaken by an American and two South Vietnamese soldiers escorting four barefoot Vietcong prisoners, three boys and a girl, all about seventeen years old. He is mistaken for part of the escort and finds himself in the interrogation room at the headquarters of the South Vietnamese First Infantry Division, where the proceedings open with the interrogating officer kicking one of the prisoners in the stomach "with his well-polished, heavy military boots."

At this point the American soldier realises that Sayle is a correspondent and asks him to leave. Sayle, feeling shaken, has a cup of coffee at the Cercle Sportif, or what is left of it, and then hitches a ride with a convoy of United States army trucks, "many of which are decorated with little rows of two, three, or four yellow figures wearing conical hats and sandals, each one neatly crossed out."

As he nears Phu Bai, there is a tremendous explosion, followed by leaping sheets of orange flame and billowing smoke—a helicopter has shed a rotor blade and crashed into the base ammunition dump. While he waits for a helicopter to take him to Evans, Sayle watches a Vietnamese engraving mottoes on the soldiers' cigarette lighters. "Favourites are 'Make war, not work' and 'I pass through the Valley of Death unafraid, for I am the meanest bastard in the valley.'" At Evans, Sayle joins the officers' chow line for dinner: deep-frozen shrimps, grilled steak, plum tart, and coffee. Then the colonel whose battalion is to make the first air assault in the morning outlines his plan to fourteen correspondents and photographers, who draw straws for the order in which they will go. Sayle draws the first wave, with a French news agency man and an Italian photographer. He fills two water bottles, collects a C ration, and finds an empty stretcher in the press tent, which turns out to be alongside a battery of two 175-millimetre guns firing two rounds of harassment and interdiction at nothing in particular every half-hour through the night. "Thinking about copy deadline, I suddenly remember the date—tomorrow is Anzac Day and the day after is the fourteenth anniversary of the Geneva agreements which ended the French war in Vietnam."

As well as trying to assess the significance of so varied a day, correspondents faced other major difficulties. Covering the war was highly dangerous, and Vietnam had no respect for reputations. Forty-five war correspondents were killed in Vietnam and eighteen listed as missing. Those killed included such experienced correspondents as Larry Burrows, Dickey Chapelle, Marguerite Higgins (who died in the United States of a tropical disease contracted in Vietnam), François Sully, and the author and historian Bernard Fall. They died in helicopter crashes, from stepping on land-mines, and, in one instance, directly at the hands of the Vietcong. This occurred in May 1968, when five correspondents driving in Cholon were attacked, and, although the one survivor said they had shouted "*Bao chi*" ("press"), they were machine-gunned. The next day, a United Press photographer called Charlie Eggleston took a weapon and announced that he was going out on a mission of revenge. He, too, was shot dead, but, as the story in Saigon went, not before he had first killed three Vietcong.

There was some argument among correspondents, after the Cholon incident, about the wisdom of carrying arms. The difficulty was that if even one correspondent continued to go armed, this entitled the Vietcong to assume—as perhaps they had in the Cholon case—that all the correspondents were armed, and to react accordingly. Nothing came of the discussions, and many correspondents continued to carry personal weapons, ranging from Sean Flynn's pearl-handled twenty-two-calibre pistol in a shoulder holster to Peter Arnett's Mauser machine pistol. Ward Just noted that most of these weapons were seldom fired, "save for one legendary American correspondent who lived in the field with the First Cavalry Division and left Vietnam with three notches in his belt." This was Charlie Black, a correspondent for the *Columbus Inquirer*, of Columbus, Georgia, home of the First Cavalry. Black has not denied the charge. "I'm not really a Wyatt Earp, but if some guy comes after me I answer back."[4]

Another daily difficulty was that not all military authorities welcomed correspondents or understood their function. In fact, some actively hated them. These ranged from officers who felt that correspondents were undermining the war effort—"My Marines are winning this war and you people are losing it for us in your papers"—to GIs who resented the correspondents' freedom to choose whether and when to risk their lives. "Those bastards," one rifleman said, watching a jeepload of correspondents drop Michael Herr and drive away. "I hope they die."[5] This visible enmity and the recurring accusation that they were doing a lousy job of reporting the war—"Why don't you guys tell it like it really is?"—caused considerable introspection among correspondents. What should be their attitude to the war, and how should they report it? Peter Arnett's method was to get out with the units doing the actual fighting.

From the time Arnett arrived in Vietnam in 1962, a tough twenty-seven-year-old New Zealander, until the war's end thirteen years later, he spent more time in the field than any other correspondent. "It's essential that a reporter see for himself those thousands of little battles at the lowest command levels to begin to comprehend what it is all about. With luck, with enough small definitions, he might be able to begin to generalise, but to stand off and take a long-range view has been proved erroneous time and again."[6] In the field, as elsewhere, Arnett determined to "observe with as much professional detachment as possible, to report a scene with accuracy and clarity." Above all, he never became *involved* in what he was reporting or photographing, and that made him, according to the author Marina Warner, "as hardboiled as a Chinese thousand-year-old egg."

Arnett has described his standing one hot noon outside the Saigon market and seeing a Buddhist monk squat on the pavement, squirt gasoline over himself from a rubber bottle, flick a cigarette lighter, and turn himself in a matter of minutes into a blackened corpse. "I could have prevented that immolation by rushing at him and kicking the gasoline away. As a human being I wanted to, as a reporter I couldn't."[7] So Arnett photographed the monk ablaze, beat off the Vietnamese secret police trying to grab his camera, raced back to the Associated Press office, and sent his photograph and story round the world.

Other correspondents, particularly photographers, tended to agree with this view of their rôle. (Television was in a class of its own here and must be dealt with as such.) Even Philip Jones Griffiths, whose portrayal of suffering Vietnamese civilians forms perhaps the best photographic testament of the war, has said, "Your job is to record it all for history. You can't not feel involved, but you have to steel yourself and do your job, take your photographs. That's what you're there for. It's no use crying. You can't focus with tears in your eyes. It's better to do the breaking down later in the darkroom."[8]

Clearly, this emotional detachment came more easily to some correspondents than to others. Clare Hollingworth of the *Daily Telegraph*, who had been reporting wars since 1939, was intrigued by the conflict in Vietnam. "The Americans were fighting a war with fantastic weaponry. I made it my business to know what weapons, planes, etc, were being used there. I love weapons and know a fair amount about them. I daresay I can take a machine-gun apart and put it together again, and as fast as any man. The tactical side appealed to me immensely. My emotions weren't really involved."[9] To remain as detached as this, it was necessary for a correspondent to keep aloof from debate on the origins of the war. As Julian Pettifer of the BBC said, "There is simply no point in arguing whether the war is right or wrong. You're always left with the fact that it is there and it's your job to cover it."[10]

But, while most correspondents saw their rôle in terms as clear and uncomplicated as this, others went through deep and some-times agonising examination of their motives and began to question whether it was possible to cover the war with an untroubled con-science. Usually, the first serious doubt appeared under pressure. Alec Shimkin of *Newsweek* was on Route 1, near the village of Trang Bang, in 1972, when the Vietnamese air force dropped napalm on their own side and burned two infants to death. Shimkin came back down the roadway towards a group of correspondents, who were hoping to get from him an eye-witness account of what had happened. But Shimkin was temporarily crazed with fury and grief, and he shouted, "Goddamn you! Leave me alone. Get the hell out," at the correspondents who approached him.[11] Whether the incident would have had any lasting effect on Shimkin must remain speculation, because he was reported soon afterwards as missing, presumed dead, at Quang Tri.

Marina Warner, reporting at the time for the *Spectator*, recalls the effect on her of her first encounter with civilian casualties. "I saw this old woman coming down the road with a child in her arms. The child's flesh was falling off. I said to myself, 'My God, I've seen this all before.' I had. On television. Somehow seeing it before on television took away some of the reality and I wasn't as shocked as I had expected to be. But later, when the horror sank in, I stood on the roadway exposing myself to fire when I didn't need to. And I stood there longer than I needed to. It was some sort of expiation. I had the feeling that if I could have been wounded it would have taken away the guilt I felt about the burnt child, the guilt I felt about Vietnam."[12]

Murray Sayle went out on the "body detail" that brought back the bodies of the four correspondents killed in the attack in Cholon in 1968. He wrote to me: "There's a strange calm about the dead, they don't feel any pain. You look at them and then look away and when you look back they look exactly the same. When you see people badly hit you feel very healthy and you think, when I get out of here without a scratch I will have beaten the system and nothing can ever be as bad as hearing the shooting and that second or two before you know if it is you or not. Then, when it's not you, you feel like an impostor, an intruder, crouching off to the side, notebook in hand. I sometimes feel I am engaging in some clinical investigation of my own motives at the expense of other people."

Those correspondents sufficiently frank to admit it agree that there are moments in war when the exhilaration compensates for all the horror, all the doubt. Some of them look for historical or psychological justification. Tim Page, who worked for *Life*, says, "War has always been glamorous. And I don't care who he is, if you put a gun into a man's hand, then he feels bigger."[13] Others simply accept it without question. "I can't explain it," says Peter Gill of the *Daily Telegraph*, "but there is something fantastically exhilarating about being terrified out of your wits." Chris Dobson of the *Daily Mail* agrees. "When I'm actually taking part in an action it's always as though I'm three martinis up. I'm in another, a higher, gear, and it's marvellous."[14] And Horst Faas, the Associated Press photographer, for whom war has become a way of life, says, in his urbane German accent, "Vot I like eez boom boom. Oh yes."[15]

This fascination for violence and death, along with the struggle the more sensitive correspondents had in trying to reconcile their hatred of war with their very real enjoyment of it, puzzled and annoyed some observers. "It is impossible to realize how much of Ernest Hemingway still lives in the hearts of men until you spend time with the professional war correspondents," wrote Nora Ephron in *New York* magazine. "Most of the Americans are stuck in the Hemingway bag and they tend to romanticize war, just as he did. Which is not surprising: unlike fighting in the war itself, unlike big-game hunting, working as a war correspondent is almost the only classic male endeavor left that provides physical danger and personal risk without public disapproval and the awful truth is that for correspondents, war is not hell. It is fun."

It would be hard to disagree with Nora Ephron's accusation when applied to most correspondents in most wars. But, just as the First World War marked a turning point in the history of war correspondents—never again could a war be reported so badly—so Vietnam stands out, for it was there that correspondents began seriously to question the ethics of their business. Photographers were particularly troubled, because their craft is by its nature more obviously voyeuristic and intrusive than that of a writer. So in Vietnam, while one found photographers who, like Horst Faas, enjoyed taking hard-news pictures of violent events, and for whom death and atrocity held no horror,* there were also men like Larry Burrows, who began to wonder what it was all about.

Burrows, a Londoner, who lived in Hong Kong and worked for *Life*, was described by the former *Picture Post* editor Tom Hopkinson as "the greatest war photographer there has ever been." When he first went to Vietnam, in 1962, he was able to rationalise his attitude: "It's an important time in history and if I can convey a little of what goes on, then it's a good reason to be here." But later he began to shield his readers from the horror of the war. "I was trying to take a shot of this guy who was dying in the helicopter. I never took his face. I don't like making it too real. I've wondered about that point quite a lot. I think if the pictures are too terrible, people quickly turn over the page to avoid looking. So I try to shoot them so that people will look and feel, not revulsion, but an understanding of war." The more Burrows thought about the soldier in the helicopter series—"Yankee Papa 13"—the more it appears to have worried him. "I was torn between being a photographer and the normal human feelings. It is not easy to photograph a pilot dying in a friend's arms and later to photograph the breakdown of the friend. I didn't know what to do. Was I simply capitalising on someone else's grief?" He felt the troops' resentment more keenly. "They look up from their dying friends and see me shooting pictures. They feel that I am capitalising on their misery and get very angry." Burrows was killed in a helicopter crash in February 1971, and so we will never know where this self-questioning would have led him. But we have an indication, from an encounter with Burrows described by *Esquire* writer Michael Herr.

Burrows and Herr were on a landing zone when a Chinook helicopter arrived. Burrows ran down and photographed the crew, the soldiers coming down an incline to get on board, three wounded being carefully lifted up, six corpses in closed body bags. Then he took one picture each of the helicopter rearing, settling, and

---

* On the walls of Faas' office in Saigon were all those photographs that the Associated Press considered too shocking to use. *Town* magazine, in December 1964, listed some of them—severed heads floating in a river, a face with gouged eyes, a hand hanging from a piece of string, a Vietcong suspect being tortured by a soldier who has a comic-strip balloon making him say, "That'll teach you to talk to the press."

departing. "When it was gone," Herr wrote, "he looked at me and he seemed to be in the most open distress. 'Sometimes one feels like such a bastard,' he said."[16]

Herr said that correspondents discussed the problem often, and in the end "there's no way around it; if you photographed a dead marine with a poncho over his face and got something for it, you were some kind of parasite. But what were you if you pulled the poncho back first to make a better shot, and did that in front of his friends?...What were you if you stood there watching it, making a note to remember it later in case you might want to use it?"

If a photographer puzzled over his professional ethics too long, he risked missing a picture. Harri Peccinotti spent weeks in Vietnam, for *Nova*, a London magazine, waiting for one particular photograph—a South Vietnamese woman loading her husband's body into a body bag and onto a helicopter taking the dead and wounded from a place where there had been a battle. Eventually, the circumstances were right photographically, even better than Peccinotti had hoped for: the woman had her child with her. But, at the moment he could have taken the picture, the helicopter crew asked for Peccinotti's help in getting the wounded on board. "I had to make a choice. I went to help the wounded and I never got the photograph."[17]

In 1967, Donald McCullin of the *Sunday Times* said he would like to do war photography every day of the week. "I used to be a war-a-year man, but now that's not enough. I need two a year now. When it gets to be three or four, then I'll start to be worried." McCullin admitted that he tended to romanticise war, but insisted that "photographically war can be very beautiful." In 1970 he was wounded and was taken from the front, with other casualties, in the back of a truck. "I knew the man next to me had died when his toes next to my face went lifeless and began to move with the jolting...it's incredible to see somebody not alive. I don't want to be maimed, but why them and not me?" McCullin recovered and went back to photographing in Vietnam. Now he became less reckless and much more calculating—"I know just what photograph justifies what risk"—and, although he still found danger exhilarating, he noticed that his detachment had gone. "Almost without realising it, I found myself getting involved with helping wounded and carrying stretchers and that sort of thing. And my photography started to suffer. It started to come second."[18]

The most intrusive medium in Vietnam was television, and, as the war went on, the hunger of editors for combat footage increased. "Before they were satisfied with a corpse," Richard Lindley, a British television reporter, said. "Then they had to have people dying in action."[19] Michael Herr described a truck carrying a dying ARVN soldier that stopped near a group of correspondents. The soldier, who was only nineteen or twenty, had been shot in the chest. A television cameraman leaned over the Vietnamese and began filming. The other correspondents watched. "He opened his eyes briefly a few times and looked back at us. The first time he tried to smile...then it left him. I'm sure he didn't even see us the last time he looked, but we all knew what it was that he had seen just before that."[20] The Vietnamese had seen the zoom lens of a sixteen-millimetre converted Auricon sound camera capturing his last moments of life on film that, if the flight connections worked and the editors back at the network liked it, would be shown in American living rooms within forty-eight hours.

This little item would not be exceptional. During the Tet offensive, a Vietnamese in a checked shirt appeared on television being walked—that is, dragged—between two soldiers. The soldiers took him over to a man holding a pistol, who held it to the head of the man in the checked shirt and blew his brains out. All of it was seen in full colour on television (and later in a memorable series of photographs taken by Eddie Adams of the AP).

Any viewer in the United States who watched regularly the television reporting from Vietnam—and it was from television that 60 per cent of Americans got most of their war news—would agree that he saw scenes of real-life violence, death, and horror on his screen that would have been unthinkable before Vietnam. The risk and intrusion that such filming involved could, perhaps, be justified if it could be shown that television had been particularly effective in revealing the true nature of the war and thus had been able to change people's attitudes to it. Is there any evidence to this effect?

The director of CBS News in Washington, William Small, wrote: "When television covered its 'first war' in Vietnam it showed a terrible truth of war in a manner new to mass audiences. A case can be made, and certainly should be examined, that this was cardinal to the disillusionment of Americans with this war, the cynicism of many young people towards America, and the destruction of Lyndon Johnson's tenure of office."[21] A *Washington Post* reporter, Don Oberdorfer, amply documents, in his book *Tet*, the number of commentators and editors (including those of Time Inc.) who had to re-examine their attitudes after extensive television—and press—

coverage brought home to them the bewildering contradictions of a seemingly unending war.

Television's power seems to have impressed British observers even more than American. The director-general of the Royal United Service Institution, Air Vice-Marshal S. W. B. Menaul, believes that television had "a lot to answer for [in] the collapse of American morale in relation to the Vietnam war." The then editor of the *Economist*, Alistair Burnet, wrote that the television reporting of Vietnam had made it very difficult for two American administrations to continue that war, "which was going on in American homes," irrespective of the merits or demerits of why the United States was actually involved in Vietnam. Robin Day, the BBC commentator, told a seminar of the Royal United Service Institution that the war on colour-television screens in American living rooms had made Americans far more anti-militarist and anti-war than anything else: "One wonders if in future a democracy which has uninhibited television coverage in every home will ever be able to fight a war, however just…The full brutality of the combat will be there in close up and colour, and blood looks very red on the colour television screen." And the Director of Defence Operations, Plans and Supplies at the Ministry of Defence, Brigadier F. G. Caldwell, said that the American experience in Vietnam meant that if Britain were to go to war again, "we would have to start saying to ourselves, are we going to let the television cameras loose on the battlefield?"[22]

All this seems very persuasive, and it would be difficult to believe that the sight, day after day, of American soldiers and Vietnamese civilians dying in a war that seemed to make no progress could not have had *some* effect on the viewer. Yet a survey conducted for *Newsweek* in 1967 suggested a remarkably different conclusion: that television had encouraged a majority of viewers to *support* the war. When faced with deciding whether television coverage had made them feel more like "backing up the boys in Vietnam" or like opposing the war, 64 per cent of viewers replied that they were moved to support the soldiers and only 26 per cent to oppose the war. A prominent American psychiatrist, Fredric Wertham, said, in the same year, that television had the effect of conditioning its audience to accept war, and a further *Newsweek* enquiry, in 1972, suggested that the public was developing a tolerance of horror in the newscasts from Vietnam— "The only way we can possibly tolerate it is by turning off a part of ourselves instead of the television set."

Edward Jay Epstein's survey of television producers and news editors, for his book *News from Nowhere*, showed that more than two-thirds of those he interviewed felt that television had had little effect in changing public opinion on Vietnam. An opinion commonly expressed was that people saw exactly what they wanted to in a news report and that television only served to reinforce existing views. The *New Yorker*'s television critic, Michael J. Arlen, reported, on several occasions, that viewers had a vague, unhappy feeling that they were not getting "the true picture" of Vietnam from the medium.[23] So if it was true that television did not radically change public opinion about the war, could it have been because of the quality of the coverage?

Television is a comparatively new medium. There were 10,000 sets in the United States in 1941; at the time of Korea there were 10 million, and at the peak of the Vietnam War 100 million. There was some television reporting in Korea, a lot of it daring—an American general had to order the BBC cameraman Cyril Page to get down off the front of a tank to which he had tied himself so as to get a grandstand view of the battle as the tank went into action. But, until Vietnam, no one knew what problems the prolonged day-by-day coverage of a war by television would produce. The first was surprising—a lack of reality. It had been believed that when battle scenes were brought into the living room the reality of war would at last be brought home to a civilian audience. But Arlen was quick to point out, in *The New Yorker*, that by the same process battle scenes are made less real, "diminished in part by the physical size of the television screen, which, for all the industry's advances, still shows one a picture of men three inches tall shooting at other men three inches tall."[24] Sandy Gall of ITN found shooting combat footage difficult and dangerous, and the end result very disappointing. "I think you lose one dimension on television's small screen and things look smaller than life; the sound of battle, for example, never coming across. I am always let down when I eventually see my footage and think, Is that all? The sense of danger never comes across on television and you, the correspondent, always look as though you had an easy time of it."[25]

For many Americans in Vietnam, there emerged a strange side to the war that became directly related to television—the fact that the war seemed so unreal that sometimes it became almost possible to believe that everything was taking place on some giant Hollywood set and all the participants were extras playing a remake of *Back to Bataan*. GIs—and even correspondents—brought up on Second World War movies shown on television, used to seeing

Errol Flynn sweeping to victory through the jungles of Burma or Brian Donlevy giving the Japanese hell in the Coral Sea, tended to relate their experiences in Vietnam to the Hollywood version of America at war.* Michael Herr, making a dash, with David Greenway of *Time*, from one position at Hué to another, caught himself saying to a Marine a line from a hundred Hollywood war films: "We're going to cut out now. Will you cover us?" One should not be surprised, therefore, to find that GIs sometimes behaved, in the presence of television cameras, as if they were making *Dispatch from Da Nang*. Herr describes soldiers running about during a fight because they knew there was a television crew nearby. "They were actually making war movies in their heads, doing little guts and glory Leatherneck tap dances under fire, getting their pimples shot off for the networks."[26]

So it is not difficult to understand how, when seen on a small screen, in the enveloping and cosy atmosphere of the household, sometime between the afternoon soap-box drama and the late-night war movie, the television version of the war in Vietnam could appear as just another drama, in which the hero is the correspondent and everything will come out all right at the end. Jack Laurence of CBS, an experienced war correspondent, who spent a lot of time in Vietnam, had this possibility brought home to him in Israel during the 1973 conflict. He was in a hotel lobby, and a couple who had just arrived from the United States recognised him and said, "We saw you on television and we knew everything was going to be all right because you were there."[27] There is not much a television correspondent can do about such a situation as that; it seems inherent in the nature of the medium. However, correspondents, or, more fairly, their editors, do have something to answer for in their selection of news in Vietnam.

Years of television news of the war have left viewers with a blur of images consisting mainly of helicopters landing in jungle clearings, soldiers charging into undergrowth, wounded being loaded onto helicopters, artillery and mortar fire, air strikes on distant targets, napalm canisters turning slowly in the sky, and a breathless correspondent poking a stick microphone under an army officer's nose and asking, "What's happening up there, Colonel?" (The only honest answer came, in 1972, from a captain on Highway 13. "I wish the hell I knew," he said.) The networks claimed that combat

---

* The arrival in 1965 of Flynn's son, Sean, as a correspondent tended to confirm this feeling.

footage was what the public wanted; that concentrating on combat prevented the film's being out of date if it was delayed in transmission; that it was difficult to shoot anything other than combat film when only three or four minutes were available in the average news program for events in Vietnam; and that the illusion of American progress created by combat footage shot from only one side was balanced by what the correspondent had to say.

This is simply not true. To begin with, combat footage fails to convey all aspects of combat. "A cameraman feels so inadequate, being able to record only a minute part of the misery, a minute part of the fighting," said Kurt Volkert, a CBS cameraman. "You have to decide what the most important action is. Is it the woman holding her crying baby? Is it the young girl cringing near her house because of the exploding grenades? Or is it the defiant looking Vietcong with blood on his face just after capture?"[28] When the cameraman's thirty minutes of combat footage are edited down to three minutes—not an unusual editing ratio—the result is a segment of action that bears about as much relation to the reality in Vietnam as a battle scene shot in Hollywood does. In fact, the Hollywood version would probably appear more realistic.

The American viewer who hoped to learn something serious about Vietnam was subjected, instead, to a television course in the techniques of war, and he was not sufficiently exposed either to what the war meant to the people over whose land it was being fought, or to the political complexities of the situation, or even to the considered personal views of reporters who had spent years covering the situation. Yet, even by the networks' own standards, the limited aspects of the war that the viewer was permitted to see could produce excellent television. One of the most dramatic pieces of film on the war was shot by a CBS team on Highway 13 late in April 1972. A South Vietnamese mine, intended to stop advancing enemy tanks, had caught a truck loaded with refugees. The film showed dead children, distressed babies, and a woman weeping over the body of her son. The reporter, Bob Simon, described what had happened and then, with perhaps the best sign-off line from Vietnam, said simply, "There's nothing left to say about this war, nothing at all." "Morley Safer's Vietnam," an hour-long report by the CBS correspondent in Saigon, was Safer's own explicit view, and was hailed by *The New Yorker*'s critic, Michael J. Arlen, as "one of the best pieces of journalism to come out of the Vietnam war in any medium." But film like this was rare.

Competition for combat footage was so intense that it not only forced American television teams to follow each other into what the BBC's correspondent Michael Clayton called "appallingly dangerous situations," but it also made editors reluctant to risk allowing a team the time and the freedom to make its own film of the war. Where were the television equivalents of Martha Gellhorn's series on Vietnamese orphanages and hospitals, or Philip Jones Griffiths' searing book on the nature of the war, *Vietnam Inc.*? True, television was handicapped by its mechanics–a three-man, or even a two-man, team loaded with camera, sound equipment, and film is less mobile and more dependent on military transport, and in a dangerous situation more vulnerable, than a journalist or a photographer. In its presentation, too, television is sometimes handicapped by its commercial associations. The Vietnamese cameraman Vo Suu filmed the brutal shooting of a Vietcong suspect by General Nguyen Ngoc Loan during the Tet offensive. NBC blacked out the screen for three seconds after the dead man hit the ground, so as to provide a buffer before the commercial that followed. (What television *really* wanted was action in which the men died cleanly and not too bloodily. "When they get a film which shows what a mortar does to a man, really shows the flesh torn and the blood flowing, they get squeamish," says Richard Lindley. "They want it to be just so. They want television to be cinema." )[29]

American television executives showed too little courage in their approach to Vietnam. They followed each other into paths the army had chosen for them. They saw the war as "an American war in Asia—and that's the only story the American audience is interested in," and they let other, equally important, aspects of Vietnam go uncovered.

All this said, attempts to film the war from the other side were even less successful. James Cameron, Romano Cagnoni, and Malcolm Aird went to North Vietnam in 1965. They went as an independent team—Cameron to report, Cagnoni to take photographs, and Aird to make a film—paying their own expenses. Although the North Vietnamese had given them visas, they were not freely welcomed. "We were treated with considerable suspicion," Aird said, "and it took not just days but weeks to break this down. Even then, we were not able to film all the things we naively supposed we would be able to film—stuff like bombs falling and American prisoners.* But in 1965 any film at all out of North Vietnam was news."

*A Canadian television team was allowed to film an American POW camp in 1970.

The film Cameron and Aird made, before the North Vietnamese suddenly and without explanation asked them to leave, presented a sympathetic view of the country. "It was interesting to see how quickly you are on the side you are working with," Aird said. "In North Vietnam the Americans to us were the enemy."[30]

The North Vietnamese themselves had no correspondents as we understand the word. They followed the progress of the war as best they could from party newspapers, government broadcasts, and large wall posters. The flavour of the news presentation in the North can best be had by extracts from wall posters appearing in Hanoi on March 21, 1975, as the North Vietnamese army pushed south towards Saigon: "The South attacks and rises. Very big victories. Nearly a million countrymen have risen to be their own masters. Complete liberation of five provinces." Then followed a list of casualties inflicted and equipment captured. The posters ended with "Long live the victory of the soldiers and people of the western region."

Western correspondents were allowed into the North only if the North Vietnamese government could see some advantage to itself from the visit. This is not to say that the North Vietnamese dictated what the correspondents wrote, but it does help to explain why Western correspondents who went to the North were looked upon with suspicion in their own countries. They had to be prepared for attacks on their reliability, their competence, and their professional ability. "The kindest thing anyone could say of me," says Cameron, "was that I was a misguided, gullible Commie tool."[31]

Harrison F. Salisbury of the *New York Times*, the first correspondent from a major United States newspaper to go to North Vietnam, writing from Hanoi in December 1966, said: "Whatever the explanation, one can see that United States planes are dropping an enormous weight of explosives on purely civilian targets." This forced the administration to concede that American pilots had accidentally struck civilian areas while attempting to bomb military targets, and made Salisbury a much-hated figure in Washington. Secretary of State Dean Rusk asked the *New York Times'* publisher how long Salisbury planned to stay in Hanoi. The Pentagon called him "Ho Chi Salisbury of the *Hanoi Times*." The *Washington Post* alleged that the casualty figures he gave after one raid that he reported were exactly the same as those in Communist propaganda pamphlets, and a *Post* article said that Salisbury was Ho Chi Minh's new weapon in the war. William Randolph Hearst, Jr., reminded his readers of the treasonable war-time broadcasts by

Lord Haw-Haw and Tokyo Rose. The columnist Joseph Alsop wrote: "Whether a United States reporter ought to go to an enemy capital to give the authority of his by-line to enemy propaganda figures is an interesting question." Some of his critics accused Salisbury of being politically naive, of not giving proper attribution of his sources, and, as in Cameron's case, of being duped by the Communists. The Pulitzer Prize jury recommended him for a prize by a vote of four to one, but the Pulitzer Advisory Board rejected the recommendation by six votes to five. Being a war correspondent on the enemy side was clearly not the easiest way to advance one's career.

Others who went to Hanoi later included Mary McCarthy, Anthony Lewis, Michael MacLear from the Canadian Broadcasting Corporation, and R. K. Karanjia from India, and Agence France Presse maintained a bureau there throughout the war. But to be a war correspondent with the Vietcong in South Vietnam was a much rarer occurrence.

Wilfred Burchett, the Australian who had sent the first story to the West from Hiroshima and who had reported the Korean peace talks from the North Korean side, began reporting the Vietnam War in 1963, free-lancing for the Japanese *Mainichi* group, the British Communist daily *Morning Star*, and the American *National Guardian*, and working from the Vietcong side. Burchett made no pretence about where his sympathies were—"The US puppet regime, no matter what new personalities the puppet masters may push to the top in the endless cycle of coup and counter-coup, is doomed." But his reports on Vietcong schools, arsenals, hospitals, the administrative structure, transport, and commissary made intriguing reading: "Hunting teams attached to every unit ensured that there was always something to go with the rice. The 'something' varied from elephant steaks—the Americans bombed and strafed them from the air as potential 'supply vehicles'—to jungle rats, with monkey, wild pig, porcupine, civets, and other wild creatures in between."[32]

Burchett travelled mainly on foot or by bicycle, occasionally on horseback or by motorised sampan. He was several times within a few miles of Saigon and appeared to have no trouble in traversing at night even the Saigon-controlled areas. But, although he wore the typical native black pyjamas and conical straw hat, his bulk, his colouring, and his features clearly distinguished him as non-Vietnamese, and the United States forces soon heard rumours of a "white man" working with the Vietcong. (Madeleine Riffaud of the

French Communist paper *L'Humanité* was travelling with Burchett at this stage, but, being slight and dark, she was able to pass as a Vietnamese.) Burchett has said that the American military authorities' reaction to his presence was to try to kill him. "My size and grey hair probably showed up on reconnaissance photographs, because four planes came over one morning, headed straight for our overnight camp, and bombed it, one after the other. Fortunately, the guards with us had dug shelters immediately on our arrival the previous night and the first blast almost blew us into the holes. The first string landed within two or three hundred yards, but the jungle absorbed most of the blast and the shrapnel." *[33]

Madeleine Riffaud was the only woman correspondent with the Vietcong, but there were many with the American forces, either on brief visits or on long-term assignments. Jillian Robertson, of the *London Sunday Express*, went on a bombing mission in South Vietnam in a B-57—"Before, I had just been a spectator of this war, now I was part of it."[34] Patricia Penn wrote in the *New Statesman* about amputees at a Quaker limb centre at Quang Ngai—"Ho Min, who's seven, lost his parents when he lost his leg. He sits crying alone in a corner, soaking his stump in a bucket of antiseptic. Now and then he lifts it out of the liquid, stares at it puzzled, and then— as if for an answer—looks at me"[35] Victoria Brittain, a resident correspondent for *The Times* of London, mixed straight reporting with articles on child victims—"Even a 'relatively good' orphanage is chaotic, filthy, stuffed with children so starved of adult contact that the moment you step inside the courtyard your whole lower body and legs are covered with small exploring hands."[36] Gloria Emerson of the *New York Times* wrote a fine series of articles on refugees, mentioning in one of them Richard Hughes, a former correspondent, who had abandoned journalism in Vietnam to run four orphanages.

Lest this concentration on personal experience and human-interest reporting give the wrong impression, it should be noted that there were also women writers who were interested in the political, cultural, and historical background of the war, Frances FitzGerald probably being the best known.

---

\* Burchett, who told the author that it is not his style to refuse a proffered hand, must nevertheless have remembered this incident when, after the banquet at Hangchow during President Nixon's visit to China in February 1972, Chou En-lai, with a mischievous light in his eye, introduced Nixon to Burchett. "Ah, yes," Nixon said, shaking hands. "You're an Australian correspondent. I've heard of you."

There were also women combat correspondents. Catherine Leroy, a French photographer in her early twenties, was captured at Hué and photographed the Vietcong troops in action before they released her. She had mixed feelings about the war: "I want people who see my pictures to hate war as I do. But although I am afraid, I have to be there when the killing starts."[37] Oriana Fallaci, an Italian correspondent, said she wanted to report a war because "I was a little girl in the Second World War and my father was a partisan. So I went to Vietnam because it was the war of our time." She interviewed General Vo Nguyen Giap, commander-in-chief of the North Vietnamese army, and, in the South, President Thieu—"He was very passionate, and he even cried. They were real tears. I really liked him."[38] Kate Webb, a New Zealander, worked for the United Press and saw more action than most men did. She was among the first correspondents into the compound of the United States Embassy after the Vietcong had occupied it during the Tet offensive in 1968. She described it later: "It was like a butcher shop in Eden, beautiful but ghastly. The green lawns and white ornamental fountains were strewn with bodies."

Kate Webb was captured by North Vietnamese troops in Cambodia in April 1971 and held for twenty-five days before being released—"I was asked, 'If you really are an objective reporter, as you say, you must want to stay with us, having spent so much time with the other side. Do you want to go back to your family or stay with us?' I thought of my own dictum—dead men don't write stories. Then I answered seriously, 'I'd like to stay with you a few weeks and then return home.'" She could describe in graphic terms what it was like being on patrol in Vietnam: "The first time I went out, there was a bit of a fire fight and I was so scared that I wet my pants. I hoped the GIs would think that it was sweat and that no one would notice. Then I saw that some of the GIs had wet pants, too, and it didn't matter any more."[39]

What Henry Kamm of the *New York Times* called proto-journalists were the non-professionals, who "come without real involvement, come with the vocation of being onlookers, of mixing with those, like the press, who have a safe share in the war." Some of these went on to become correspondents or photographers. (One of them, Tim Page, prefers the description "mercenary journalists.") Some correspondents have objected to being bracketed with them, on the grounds that they were not serious professionals, interested in reporting the war, but "thrill seekers," gun-carrying hippies, who smoked pot and used acid and sometimes heroin, and that, although they looked young and harmless, they were really old and deadly. "Tim Page was twenty-three when I first met him," wrote Michael Herr. "And I can remember wishing that I'd known him when he was still young."[40]

But the accreditation system in Vietnam made it possible for anyone calling himself a free-lance journalist to get an MACV card. All he needed were two letters from agencies or newspapers saying that they would be prepared to buy his material. The Associated Press, for one, would lend virtually anyone a camera, complete with film, light metre, and brief instructions on its use, promise to pay a minimum of $15 for any acceptable picture, and provide a letter to help the new man get his accreditation. A local or home-town newspaper would usually be prepared to provide the second letter. After that, the correspondent was on his own. Transport was free, he could live on C rations, and in the field he was not likely to be charged for accommodations. If he was prepared to take risks, he could find himself comparatively rich overnight.

Tim Page was twenty when he first arrived in Vietnam. At the end of a hippie trip across Asia, he found himself in the middle of a battle at Chu Lai. A series of his photographs appeared in *Life* on September 3, 1965, covering six pages, and for these *Life* paid him $6,000. Over the next eighteen months, mostly by taking photographs where other photographers were not prepared to go, Page made $28,000—not a lot by professional standards, but a lot of money for an orphan boy from a London suburb. Page, Eddie Adams, Sean Flynn, Steve Nerthup, John Steinbeck, Jr., and Simon Dring moved around together. Page and Flynn used to ride in and out of some combat areas on Honda motor-cycles. They had a flip, throwaway attitude to the war, but some of it was quite perceptive. "No one wants to admit it," Page says, "but there is a lot of sex appeal and a lot of fun in weapons. Where else but in Vietnam would a man get a chance to play with a supersonic jet, drive a tank, or shoot off a rocket, and even get highly paid for it?"[41]

Page was slightly wounded in the fighting at Chu Lai, and then more seriously during the Buddhist riots in 1966, receiving shrapnel in the head, chest, and arms. In 1967, a B-57 mistook a United States coast guard cutter, in which Page was travelling, for a Vietcong vessel, and in nine strafing and bombing runs it sank the ship, killed three of the crew, and wounded eight. Page received multiple wounds, and needed twelve operations and weeks in hospital to recover. In 1969, he got out of a helicopter near Cu Chi to help pick up two wounded. The sergeant with him stepped on a mine, which blew off the sergeant's legs and sent a two-inch piece of shrapnel through Page's forehead, above the right eye, and deep into the base of his brain. For some time he was close to death; he recovered sufficiently to be moved to a hospital in Japan, then to the Walter Reed Army Hospital, in Washington, D.C., and finally to the Institute of Rehabilitation Medicine, in New York. He was eighteen months recovering. *Time* and *Life* had bought most of his photographs, and they undertook to pay his hospital bills. They came to $136,000.

While he was still receiving treatment, he had a letter from a British publisher asking him to write a book to be called *Through with War*, which would "once and for all take the glamour out of war." Page remembers his bewilderment. "Jesus! Take the glamour out of war. How the hell can you do that? You can't take the glamour out of a tank burning or a helicopter blowing up. It's like trying to take the glamour out of sex. War is *good* for you."

The type of war that Page and others found glamorous—the ground war of attrition against the North Vietnamese and the Vietcong—began to wind down from 1969 on. The American public had been aware of the war in Vietnam in proportion to the number of American combat troops involved and the level of casualties they suffered. President Nixon's policy became, therefore, steadily to withdraw these troops, to pass the ground war over to the Vietnamese, to order the remaining GIs to fight as little as possible, and to switch the weight of the American attack to the air. Since the bombing campaign was not very evident to the American public, the war seemed to fade away. Correspondents attuned to battle reporting found fewer battles to report, editors and producers became less willing to devote space and time to a war that the administration assured them was as good as over, and those reporters who went digging for other stories about Vietnam found that the army had suddenly become extremely obstructive and had started "administering the news with an eye-dropper," as *Time* magazine's correspondent Jonathan Larsen wrote.

There were two main reasons for this. The military authorities did not want reported the sad state of the United States Army, and they wanted to encourage public apathy about the war by keeping as secret as possible the escalation of the bombing. They were not successful on the first count. The year 1971 saw a series of stories revealing the massive heroin problem among United States troops (about one in ten was addicted),[42] the "fragging," or blowing up by grenades, of unpopular officers (forty-five killed, 318 wounded in 1971), the staggering desertion rate, the number of combat refusals, and the growing tendency to regard an order simply as a basis for discussion. The *Washington Post* headed its series on the problem ARMY IN ANGUISH, and Colonel Robert Heinl, a military historian, wrote in the *Armed Forces Journal* that conditions in Vietnam among the American forces "have only been exceeded in this century by the French Army's Nivelle mutinies in 1917 and the collapse of the Tsarist armies in 1916 and 1917."[43] GIs were photographed carrying peace symbols, a picture appeared in *Newsweek* of a helicopter with a sign on the side saying "My God! How'd we get into this mess?"[44] and CBS News ran film of GIs smoking pot from a gun barrel.

There was less success in revealing the new emphasis in the war—the intensified bombing of North Vietnam, Laos, and Cambodia. There can be some excuse for the correspondents' failure here, because reporters and photographers were not allowed on air strikes and the official concealment operation was massive—*Newsweek* described it as "the most systematic military cover-up in the history of America's role in the Indo-Chinese war." A former United States Air Force major later revealed—and an embarrassed Pentagon later confirmed—that the United States, over a period of fourteen months in 1969–70, had conducted a clandestine bombing campaign against Cambodia, whose neutrality Washington then professed to respect. Scores of American pilots took part in the cover-up by making fictitious reports, and the Pentagon did its bit by falsifying statistics. What the military was so anxious to conceal was that the bombing of Indo-China was on a scale far greater than anything previously known. During the whole of the Second World War, less than 80,000 tons of bombs fell on Britain. In Indo-China, the United States dropped more than 4 million tons—fifty times as much. Or, put another way, the United States used explosives cumulatively equal to hundreds of the nuclear weapon used at Hiroshima.

The military successfully hid the real extent of this bombing campaign behind a screen of lies, evasions, and "newspeak." The Pentagon insisted that its air operations were announced daily by MACV in Saigon. To see how informative these announcements were, it is necessary to quote only one. On March 10, 1972, MACV's release 70–10 said: "Yesterday U.S. aircraft, including U.S. Air Force B-52s, continued air operations along the Ho Chi Minh trail in Laos. In addition, U.S. aircraft flew combat missions in support of Royal Laotian forces in Laos. Yesterday, U.S. aircraft, including U.S. Air Force B-52s, continued air operations against enemy forces and their lines of supply in Cambodia." How many aircraft? How many tons of bombs? What, exactly, was attacked? Were any of the targets (as revealed in classified American military documents quoted in *Air War in Indo-China*)[45] civilian villages that the air force was ordered to destroy—in the mind-boggling "newspeak" phrase—"so as to deprive the enemy of the population resource"? William Shawcross, writing in the *New Statesman*, quoted a Pentagon spokesman as saying, "We do not hit civilian targets. Correction. We do not target civilian targets." To explain how targets that were clearly civilian came to be hit, the spokesman produced explanations involving terms such as "collateral damage" and "circular error probability."

The correspondents did their best. At briefings in Saigon, they pressed for details of targets in North Vietnam. Had the civilian population been attacked? Had Hanoi airport been attacked? Were pilotless aircraft being used? Peter Hazelhurst of *The Times* reported a briefing in Saigon in December 1972 at which the spokesman refused to answer a single question. Frustrated American correspondents said angrily, "Aren't you ashamed of America? The North Vietnamese, the Russians, and the Chinese know what targets have been hit. It's happened. They all know, except the American public."[46] Their protests were useless. The surge in the air war in Indo-China remained poorly reported, and what was revealed passed with amazingly little outcry. Shawcross wrote: "One day Nixon and his [bombing] philosophy will be as despised as the Spanish inquisitors are today. But given the Americans' apparently total lack of interest in what their country is doing, now that they themselves are not dying doing it, that will be a long time yet."[47]

American reaction might well have been different if the same attention that had been paid to the ground conflict in Vietnam had been given to the air war, if the reader had been told graphically and at the time about the bombing of Indo-China. In the face of official obstruction—at one stage of the surge in the war, the military authorities imposed an embargo on the news and then an embargo on the embargo—how could this have been achieved?

There is reason to believe that much, if not all, of the major news about Vietnam could have come out at the time. Even the information eventually revealed in the Pentagon Papers was available or could have been deduced at the time, as I. F. Stone demonstrated, by diligently ploughing through government reports and transcripts of open hearings, and by reading between the lines. It must also have been possible to do this in connection with the bombing of Indo-China, as the experience of Tom Oliphant, a Washington correspondent for the *Boston Globe*, illustrates.

Oliphant discovered in 1972 that, although the total tonnage of bombs dropped on Indo-China each month was not announced, the figure was available on enquiry at the South-East Asia Section of the Public Information Office of the Defense Department. No national newspaper, no wire service, no network took advantage of this to present the figures every month and compare them with previous months' totals. So Oliphant began to do it himself. True, there was no breakdown of the figure for South Vietnam, North Vietnam, Laos, or Cambodia, and no other detail to make the stark figure more easily understandable. But it was a beginning, and if other correspondents had supported Oliphant by making similar enquiries, there is no telling what they might have been able to squeeze out of the Defense Department. Oliphant wrote in *Ramparts*, in November 1972: "The press can find a way to gather information which the MACV never mentions. If it does, and if the information starts to flow on a regular day-in-day-out basis, the great mass of Americans will draw the appropriate conclusions."

In the end, the Vietnam War was better reported than any of the other wars examined here. But this is not saying a lot. True, there was no censorship, and correspondents were free to move around at will. However, as journalist Murray Kempton has reminded us, with a million-dollar corps of correspondents in Vietnam the war in Cambodia was kept hidden for a year.

There have been many suggestions as to what went wrong. Drew Middleton, the military correspondent of the *New York Times*, blames the very fact that there were no censors. "On three trips to Vietnam," he said in a letter to the author, "I found generals and everyone else far more wary of talking to reporters precisely because there was no censorship. Their usual line with a difficult or sensitive question was 'You must ask the public relations people about that.' The latter, usually of low rank, clammed up, and the reporter and the public got less…Comparing the Second World War and Vietnam, I think there was a hell of a lot more original reporting in the first and not so much sitting around in bars— although there was plenty of drinking—and conning each other on stories."

David Halberstam wrote to me: "The problem was trying to

cover something every day as news when in fact the real key was that it was all derivative of the French Indo-China war, which is history. So you really should have had a third paragraph in each story which would have said, 'All of this is shit and none of this means anything because we are in the same footsteps as the French and we are prisoners of their experience.' But given the rules of newspaper reporting you can't really do that. Events have to be judged by themselves, as if the past did not really exist. This is not usually such a problem for a reporter, but to an incredible degree in Vietnam I think we were haunted and indeed imprisoned by the past."

Was it possible that, as Michael Herr wrote in *Esquire*, "conventional journalism could no more reveal this war than conventional firepower could win it"? "All it could do was view the most profound event of the American decade and turn it into a communications pudding, taking its most obvious, undeniable history and making it into a secret history." More than one correspondent felt that journalism was not the best medium for capturing the real war. Gavin Young, one of the best British reporters to cover the war, wrote: "Correspondents are bound to be haunted by the feeling that there is probably only one way to work the various elusive aspects of the war into one wholly satisfactory picture. Apart from the aid programmes, the military operations, the political ups and downs, how can one depict the human facets of such a complete tragedy? What of the thoughts and feelings of the Vietnamese? How has the war affected their lives and art, their outlook on foreigners, and different cultures? How if at all, have the Americans been changed by contact with the Vietnamese?"* Young concluded, "The Vietnamese War awaits its novelist."[48]

So in the reporting of Vietnam each day's news was swiftly consumed by the next day's. Too few correspondents looked back and tried to see what it added up to, too few probed beyond the official version of events to expose the lies and half-truths, too few tried to analyse what it all meant. There were language problems: few correspondents spoke French, much less Vietnamese. There were time problems: Kevin Buckley's investigation into "Operation Speedy Express" took two men two and a half months. And there were cultural problems: apart from Bernard Fall's and Frances FitzGerald's, there were no serious attempts to explain to Americans something about the people they were fighting. On the whole, writers for non-

---

*Young wrote this before Frances FitzGerald went into the question in *Fire in the Lake*.

daily publications came out better than most of their colleagues, because, free from the tyranny of pressing deadlines, they could look at the war in greater depth—reporters like Tom Buckley in the *New York Times Magazine*, Jonathan Schell of *The New Yorker*, and Sol Sanders of *U.S. News & World Report* are examples, apart from those already mentioned, that spring to mind.

It was a frustrating war for correspondents, with no neat, no simple, no easily drawn conclusions. Nicholas Tomalin of the *Sunday Times*, later killed in the Middle East, caught the frustration particularly well in an article he wrote, in March 1969, on the battle of Bien Hoa. Tomalin set out the circumstances of the battle in some detail: 500 Vietcong and North Vietnamese soldiers attacked the American air base at Bien Hoa in broad daylight, after infiltrating nearby villages. Following a fierce fight, the Americans repulsed them, inflicting heavy casualties. During the battle, the hamlet of Thai Hiep, built specifically for Roman Catholic refugees from Hanoi, and thus regarded as staunchly anti-Communist, was levelled by American air strikes because the enemy had made a stand there. "Except that it was fought in daylight, it was an archetype of virtually all the significant battles in Vietnam. The side that won Bien Hoa wins the war." But when Tomalin came to tell his readers who *had* won the battle, he found himself unable to decide. He quoted Radio Hanoi as claiming a victory because the battle had proved that even the "most secure" areas of Vietnam were still totally vulnerable and that Communist troops could be defeated only by blasting Vietnamese villages and civilians into oblivion. He quoted a United States army information officer who "after telling me what a famous victory Bien Hoa was…paused and said reflectively, 'I'm not sure why I'm giving you all this crap. I'm a VC supporter myself.' "[49] In the end, clearly dissatisfied that he could do no better, Tomalin reached a conclusion that eventually applied equally well to the 1973 cease-fire. No one had won.

Of the many correspondents involved in reporting Vietnam, few remained untouched by the experience. Of the principal characters in the My Lai story, Seymour Hersh won a Pulitzer Prize; Ronald Haeberle decided to go back to being a photographer, but found that when prospective employers learned that he was the man who had taken the massacre pictures, no one wanted to employ him. Other correspondents moved to other wars—there were noisy reunions in Bangladesh and later in Tel Aviv. Few believed that the cease-fire in Vietnam would last, and when the North Vietnamese attacked in April 1975, forcing the South Vietnamese army to retreat in confusion, many old Vietnam hands hurried back to the front. They were not as welcome as in earlier days. The South Vietnam army newspaper, *Tien Tuyen*, called them "the enemy within," and said that their reporting was playing a major part in the Communist successes. When Saigon finally fell, on April 30, and the war was at long last over, some correspondents found it hard to believe. Peter Arnett's comment summed up their feelings: "I never thought I'd live to see the day I'd watch a North Vietnamese platoon...in the square in front of the Rex Movie Theatre."

But in between the cease-fire and the North Vietnamese drive to victory, other correspondents had second thoughts about their job, and some became uncertain whether they wanted to continue. Jack Laurence of CBS had worrying nightmares. "One I always have is seeing myself jump out of a window. I was starting to worry about whether I could keep my head straight...Maybe people like Horst Faas have some kind of steel inside them that psychologically shuts out the horror and prevents them from being affected emotionally. I'm not saying everyone is unaffected by it. I don't know what other people's nightmares are. I only know mine."[50]

## *Chapter Eighteen*

# Britannia Rules the News
# 1975–1989

Harry: Ah well, Barry, the military knows best!

Barry: So it would seem.

Harry: You'll learn that as you go along, son, and you'll find that we
   journalists are dependent on them for everything; food,
   drink, fags, information—the lot.

Barry: In that case, why do they bother having us here at all, Harry?

Harry: Because Mr. and Mrs. Average-Punter-back-home will
   believe what *we* tell them, because we have journalistic
   integrity, and a degree of objectivity the military can *never*
   provide.

Barry: Yes, but *what* do we tell them??

Harry: Hang on. I'll ask the major.

—*IF...* a strip cartoon by Steve Bell in *The Guardian*, June 10, 1982.

---

In the years that followed the Vietnam war, correspondents had a
lean time. In Vietnam, the United States military had accepted
war correspondents, called on all ranks to give them full co-operation and assistance, fed them on a reimbursable basis, briefed them,
armed them when necessary, defended them, drank with them,
and, in general, treated them like members of the team. The military was not happy with what it got in return. No doubt some of the
reporting improved the image of some officers and there were
Ernie Pyle type correspondents who wrote nice things about the
GIs for their folks back home to clip and keep, but the stories that
are fixed in international memory about the U.S. military in Viet-

nam are the atrocity at My Lai, Tomalin's account of a day with General Hollingsworth ("The General Goes Zapping Charlie Cong"), Herr's stories about GIs and drugs, and Pilger's description of American servicemen "fragging" their officers. It would be difficult, therefore, to find an American military man who had served in Vietnam who would say, hand on heart, that the war correspondents did a great job and that they were a fine bunch of men.

During the fighting, correspondents learned to live with accusations that their reporting was helping the enemy, but the post-war conclusion went further. It was summed up by Robert Elegant, a long-serving Asia expert and a former Vietnam correspondent himself. He accused the correspondents not merely of contributing to the Communist victory but of being directly responsible for it: "For the first time in modern history the outcome of war was determined not on the battlefield but on the printed page and, above all, on the television screen…never before Vietnam had the collective policy of the media—no less stringent a term will serve—sought by graphic and unremitting distortion, the victory of the enemies of the correspondents' own side."[1]

Elegant was wrong. Most of the correspondents in Vietnam told the story as they saw it. Their problem was that the war became so complex that it was virtually impossible to understand it in all its ramifications and therefore impossible for the correspondents to convey those ramifications to their readers. They, like everyone else involved in the war, were overwhelmed by it. However, the importance of Elegant's accusations lay not in its validity but in the way it was received. Throughout the world governments took note of Elegant's conclusions, saw the danger of giving the media unfettered access to the war zone, and made contingency plans to control the flow of information if war should come. Suddenly, from Rhodesia to Afghanistan, correspondents found doors closed to them.

The swing began in Rhodesia. With the war in Vietnam over and Cambodia closed, the battle between the white rebel government led by Ian Smith and the black guerrilla nationalists for control of the one-time British colony became the war correspondents' next location and for a while the Meikles Hotel in Salisbury resembled Saigon's Continental Palace as the pressmen trooped in for their daily briefing. To the average reader it appeared that the correspondents were doing a reasonably good job. They filed stories nearly every day; these appeared authoritative, and they were from experienced correspondents with a wide spread of political opinion. True, in retrospect, few got the outcome of the war correct, but public memory is short and newspapers are reluctant to hold inquests. much less public inquests, into their coverage of controversial events.

In fact, the coverage of Rhodesia was deeply flawed from the beginning. The problem, stated briefly, was this: how could any war correspondent give a balanced account of a war where one side was Anglo-Saxon, entrenched in the cities, with access to the resources and the techniques of public relations, and where the other side consisted of people of a different race and culture, operating in the remote countryside, and who had neither the means nor—and this may be more important—the inclination to compete in terms of propaganda?

The answer is that no war correspondent could. The better ones soon became tired of regurgitating official hand-outs from the Smith regime in Salisbury and went home. But no newspaper wanted to admit that it had given up trying to present a balanced view of the war, so stories from Rhodesia continued to appear, particularly in British newspapers. Who was sending them? Few readers of the London *Daily Telegraph* realised that the paper's correspondent in Salisbury, Brian Henry, was the same person as the *Daily Mail*'s Peter Norman, who was in turn the same person as the *Guardian*'s Henry Miller. And that in real life all these correspondents were a Rhodesian journalist called Ian Mills, who, as it happened, was also the BBC's correspondent.[2]

The dangers in this practice of the "multiple correspondent" immediately became apparent. One is that Mills, a competent journalist, could have become too busy to do much else than take whatever official information he could get and send it off to his many outlets together with what comment he could obtain on the telephone. He would hardly have had time to investigate the truth or otherwise of what he was being told, especially if such an investigation could involve long absence from his base. Next, with similar stories appearing in a variety of newspapers under a variety of names, the reader could feel that each confirmed the accuracy of the other. He would then tend to place more weight on the story's facts than if he knew that all the stories were actually written by the one correspondent. Finally, Mills was—with his dependence on official sources—in no position to do some really hard reporting on the most controversial aspect of the struggle: the allegation that at least one of the atrocities attributed to the guerrillas was actually the work of the Rhodesian Army's dirty tricks squad, the Selous Scouts.

Christopher Mullin, a British journalist working as a freelance, set out one such allegation in the *New Statesman* of February 25, 1977, quoting as his source the Roman Catholic Commission for Justice and Peace. Mullin said that on June 12, 1975, eight men, who claimed that they were guerrillas, visited the Karima village on Mount Darwin and called a meeting. In front of the villagers the men beat the village headman and then left, taking him with them. As soon as they had left, Rhodesian security forces opened fire on the villagers from the direction in which the guerrillas had left. Twenty people, most of them women and children, died. The next day the headman reappeared apparently uninjured.

Mullin wrote that two days later the Rhodesian army issued a communiqué in which the incident was described as follows: "On the night of June 12, a security force was alerted by the sound of a man being clubbed in his kraal. On approaching the kraal to investigate the incident the patrol came under fire from a terrorist group. In the ensuing fight 20 persons were killed. The victim of the terrorist atrocity was a local headman who survived this vicious assault. He was rescued by the patrol and received medical attention. This is yet another example of innocent persons being forced at gunpoint to witness atrocities against their tribal leaders. There were no security force casualties."

Mullin pointed out several difficulties with this version of events. There was no fight, the only shots fired were by security forces, no guerrillas were either killed or captured, the only casualties were innocent villagers, and the headman appeared uninjured. Mullin concluded by quoting the Catholic Commission's verdict: "Those who survived the shooting at Karima believe that the terrorists were not terrorists at all, but were part of a trap set by the Rhodesian security forces."

Mullin's sceptical reporting was the exception. Most correspondents did not question the Rhodesian claim of a casualty ratio of up to twenty to one in their favour (was this feasible, or did innocent villagers become terrorists after they were killed?). No one wrote in any detail of the secret trials or the weekly hangings, and the Rhodesian government's version of the raids into Mozambique to hit guerrilla camps was largely accepted without question.

The difficulties in Rhodesia added to the growing disillusionment of the old school of war correspondents. Young war correspondents with little or no experience began to take their place and this together with the military's changed attitude, produced the first of several disasters.

In October 1975, five correspondents (three Australians and two British immigrants) all working for Australian television networks, all of them under thirty years of age—the youngest only twenty-one—arrived in Timor to cover the fighting between the Indonesian government forces, and the nationalist Fretilin guerrillas from Portuguese Timor in the eastern part of the island. Only two had had brief experience of war reporting. As the Australian weekly newspaper, the *National Times*, was later to report, "They went straight from chasing fire engines in Australia to irregular warfare in Timor."

The correspondents contacted the Fretilin leadership and said that they wanted to go up to the border between Indonesian and Portuguese Timor where there had been clashes. Fretilin was unhappy about this and made the correspondents sign an absolution of responsibility. Although they had difficulty in persuading a driver to take them to the border, they eventually found one. In a small village called Balibo they filmed a report of a Fretilin statement that it would not defend the village against an expected Indonesian attack.

On October 12 Fretilin withdrew all but a small number of guerrillas from the village, and, more important, took away all their vehicles. Despite this, the Australians stayed on. They painted on the wall of the house in which they were living a crude Australian flag and the word "Australia." In an interview filmed for transmission to Australia one of them said, "We're hoping this will afford us some protection." Incredible as it may seem, the only conclusion is that the correspondents planned to remain in a village they knew could be attacked by Indonesian troops, that they hoped to film the attack,that they were relying on the fact that they were Australians, and that they expected the attackers, many of whom could not have been literate in their own language, much less English, not only to recognise that fact but to respect it.

The Indonesians attacked Balibo at dawn on October 16. The main evidence of what happened came from Fretilin guerrillas who survived the attack and reached safety. They said that when firing began the Australians came out of their house and began filming. When the Indonesian troops entered the village the Australians ran back towards their house, but kept stopping, turning, and pointing their cameras. The Indonesians opened fire on them and one correspondent fell. The others then gestured towards the painted flag on the wall of their house, and shouted "Australians, Australians." The Fretilin survivors, who were by now hiding in the scrub on the edge of the village, said three more Australians were shot (or killed by mortar fire, according to another survivor) and the fifth gunned down as he ran through the back door of the house trying to get away.

The Australian government later investigated the incident but over the years failed to produce a satisfactory explanation of how the correspondents died, how much the Australian authorities knew of what was happening at the time, or what role the Indonesian military played in the men's deaths. Theories abounded. The Indonesians expected to find Portuguese troops fighting with Fretilin and in the heat of battle they did not wait to find out whether the five white men they encountered in Balibo were Portuguese soldiers or Australian correspondents. The Indonesians knew that the correspondents were there and had orders to kill them all so as to discourage further reporting from the area. The Indonesians came across the correspondents but did not understand what they were doing in a battle zone and killed them anyway because the concept of a correspondent as an observer whose neutrality is to be respected is a western one, and to have believed that this concept offered any protection in a remote guerrilla war was a fatal mistake. As an Australian doctor—who was with the correspondents before they went to the battle zone—said later, "All of us had a feeling of levity. We minimised the risks, believing in some way we were immune."

Twenty-four years later Balibo was again uppermost in the minds of Australian correspondents as history seemed to repeat itself. After a United Nations-supervised referendum in 1999, a majority of East Timorese voted for independence from Indonesia. Fighting immediately broke out between the pro-Indonesian militias, supported by the Indonesian army, and pro-independence groups.

There was always the possibility that the East Timor situation might blow up. But Australia had remained confident that it could rely on Indonesia to maintain order. After all, Australia had carefully cultivated its giànt northern neighbour and had gone to great lengths to win over its senior Indonesian army officers, inviting them to take part in joint operations, training some of them and getting to know and trust them.

When it became clear that far from maintaining order, Indonesia was encouraging the excesses of the militia in East Timor, Australia turned to the United States for help, calling on the "special relationship" it believed existed between the two countries. Washington said no. Instead a United Nations force, headed by 4,500 Australian troops, had to go in to restore order and prevent further massacres.

"Australia has discovered the unhappy truth," wrote Doug Bandow in the *Japan Times*. "The world is full of countries claiming to have special ties to America...Washington rightly believes that East Timor is largely Canberra's problem, which demonstrates that the alliance with America is much less than many Australians apparently believed...Washington's unwillingness to jump into the Indonesian imbroglio reflects a long overdue sense of realism...It's time Canberra and other US allies began assuming responsibility for their own security."

But for journalists, Balibo's significance in 1975 was that it marked what must have seemed like an open season for killing war correspondents. Two months later another Australian correspondent, Roger East, who had gone to East Timor to investigate the deaths of the other five was, according to an eyewitness, seized by Indonesian soldiers, bound, and then shot by firing squad. An American television correspondent, William Stewart, was shot dead by government troops in Nicaragua in 1979; Olivier Rebbot, a free-lance photographer working for *Newsweek* was killed in crossfire in Salvador in 1981, and two other photographers wounded there in a mine explosion. In one twelve-month period seven correspondents were killed in Central America alone.

What happened because of this casualty rate only increased the danger. Experienced war correspondents professionally assessed the risk and decided that it was too high. American newspapers, television and radio stations began to have problems finding correspondents willing to chance their lives, especially in Central America.[3] As a result the number of young and raw reporters and stringers in the American press corps there increased. This not only affected the quality of the coverage but made the risk of further casualties more likely.

But nowhere did the correspondent face such danger as in the Lebanon. With no clear division between the front line and everyday life, even crossing the street became risky. Christopher Morris, a BBC television reporter described what working in Beirut was like. "Not only is everyone armed," Morris said. "but they are armed with sophisticated weapons which they use unpredictably. [The Chinese waiter in his restaurant owned a rocket launcher.] Shells are falling all over the place and the air is alive with shrapnel. It's very easy to get killed—no difficulty whatsoever."

It was not surprising then, that Canadian television's Clark Todd was killed in 1983 and cameramen Dick Hill, of the BBC and Sebastian Rich, of Independent Television News, were wounded the following year. After four visits to the Lebanon in as many years, Rich made the mistake of thinking he was invulnerable. "I'd spent my life filming other people lying in gutters with their heads blown off," Rich said. "But looking through the camera, it always seemed somehow detached. You thought it could never happen to you."

Rich made a quick recovery from a shallow stomach wound but vowed never to return to the Lebanon—"they really don't care who they kill"—and admitted that his attitude to war reporting had changed. "I used to be naive enough to think I could influence other people's attitudes towards war but having watched my own family's reactions to television I realise that people only see it as something that goes on in the background. Viewers turn off their sets even though someone has actually risked his life to bring them those pictures."[4]

So danger and lack of access combined in the eighties to produce a poor quality of reporting from world trouble spots. Afghanistan was reported from across the border in Pakistan, from brief visits to Kabul, or from furtive interviews with guerrilla fighters who soon developed a reputation for being willing to tell the correspondent whatever he wanted to hear. In such circumstances many a correspondent became the tool of the intelligence agencies. Desperate for some sort of a story to justify the cost of getting to wherever he was, and anxious to maintain his reputation, he became easy prey for the CIA or the KGB line. The published casualty figures for Soviet forces in Afghanistan thus varied from a low of 1,200 to a high of 10,000. Yet it was difficult to find a Western correspondent who had seen for himself a single Russian body.

The nearest to a reliable source at one stage illustrates the convoluted manner in which facts have to emerge when a correspondent has no access. An Independent Television News correspondent, in the Soviet Union for the 1980 Olympic Games, did some pre-games human interest interviews. One of these was with a family which spoke of a neighbour's grief over the death of a son in Afghanistan, the first real evidence that the Russians had suffered any casualties at all. Philip Jacobson, a sceptical and seasoned correspondent, later wrote in the London *Sunday Times* of the death of two Russian soldiers and used photographs of the men and their letters from home, taken from their bodies by the guerrillas, as proof of their deaths. Jacobson decided that on the basis of his careful investigations outside Afghanistan that the Russian casualties were somewhere between 600 and 1,500 and that infectious hepatitis was probably causing more casualties than the guerrillas.[5]

Jacobson also gave an illuminating example of guerrilla propaganda. On July 16, 1981, the guerrilla spokesman released to correspondents based in Pakistan details of fierce fighting around the northern Afghanistan city of Mazar-I-Sharif, near the Russian border. The communiqué spoke of heavy Russian casualties, burned-out tanks, and successful guerrilla ambushes. Unfortunately for the guerrilla spokesmen, a British television team was in Afghanistan on a rare visit and happened to be filming in Mazar-I-Sharif at precisely the moment the fierce fighting was said to be taking place.

The television cameras recorded a scene of utmost tranquillity with long lines of Soviet trucks grinding towards the frontier totally unprotected by armour or helicopter gunships. It is little wonder, then, that the editor of the *Toronto Sun*, Peter Worthington, declared that Afghanistan was one of the worst reported wars of recent times. "The fighting there is the subject of rumour, unconfirmed reports, and widespread ignorance," he said, "and the media are the prime villains."[6]

By the time Worthington made these remarks many of the war correspondents mentioned in this book had seen the writing on the wall and had gone on to other careers. They had realised that in limited engagements or revolutionary situations like Afghanistan and Iran they would not have proper access, that if the United States ever embarked on another war like Vietnam it would have second thoughts about allowing correspondents the same freedom, and that in an all-out nuclear war there would not be any correspondents anyway. As well, some became disillusioned with the path the Western press seemed to be taking, the pressure from the head office for what one correspondent called "assertive, dogmatic journalism" that no longer left any room for Tennyson's "honest doubt," a chance for the reader to make up his own mind.

Then in the summer of 1982, Britain and Argentina went to war over the Falklands (or the Malvinas), an inhospitable group of islands in the South Atlantic. All over the world battle-hardened correspondents took their safari jackets out of mothballs and prepared to cover a good old-fashioned war in which they could re-live some of their former glory. They reckoned without the British Ministry of Defence (MoD) and the government of Argentina.

When it was all over, the press decided that everyone had

emerged well from the campaign except the MoD which was roundly attacked for the way it had handled the news. It had "failed miserably" to keep the nation informed; it had been "caught on the hop" by the speed of events; it had been "tardy and mean" with information. Though understandable, this criticism missed the point. It assumed that the British government and the press had the same aim—to give the public all the facts about the war as swiftly as possible—and that the only reason that this did not happen was as a result of the Ministry's bureaucratic blunders. In fact the MoD achieved *exactly* what its political masters wanted it to do, and its role in the Falklands campaign will go down in the history of journalism as a classic example of how to manage the media in wartime.

As we have seen, all studies of propaganda tell what a powerful weapon it is; that since armies fight as people think, it is essential to control that thought. This means some form of managing the news, and the only question is the degree to which the news should be managed openly and the degree to which it should be managed subtly. Argentina chose the open method, which at least has the benefit of honesty. In Argentina during the war the newspapers printed what they were told to print; disobedience was punished by closure.

But a democratic government cannot afford to be as crude as that. It never goes in for summary repression or direct control; it nullifies rather than conceals undesirable news; it controls emphasis rather than facts; it balances bad news with good; it lies directly only when it is certain that the lie will not be found out during the course of the war. This was the method Britain chose and there are lessons for journalism in how it achieved such an outstanding success.

The British MoD started with one major advantage: it and only it controlled access to the war zone. The very nature of the campaign—a seaborne task force sailing to invade a group of islands 8,000 miles from Britain and 400 miles from the nearest land mass —meant that correspondents could not get to the war unless the MoD took them. In return for access to the action the correspondent had to accept the MoD ground rules. These were crippling.

First, no correspondents other than British were allowed to accompany the task force; there was no room for impartial neutrals. Next, there is evidence that individual British correspondents were vetted. Donald McCullin, a brilliant and compassionate war correspondent with sixteen years of battle experience all over the world, was repeatedly turned down by the MoD when he applied to join

478

the press corps. The excuse was that there was insufficient accommodation on board any of the ships, although as McCullin pointed out, they managed to accommodate three million chocolate bars. His own guess at the real reason seems to be the right one: that his type of war photography threatened the image of the war which the military wanted to convey.[7]

The seventeen correspondents who were eventually accredited had to sign forms agreeing to accept censorship at source by the six MoD "public relations officers." There was no way around this because, as well as controlling access, the MoD also controlled the means of communication. And to give the correspondents an idea of their duties, they were all issued an MoD booklet telling them that they would be expected to "help in leading and steadying public opinion in times of national stress or crisis."[8]

The British media accepted this one-sided control from the MoD because there was no way out of it and because it was an improvement on its first plan, namely that there should be no correspondents with the task force at all and that the nation would be kept informed of the war by a once-daily "official communiqué", as in the Second World War.[9] The rest of the world looked at the alternatives and flinched. In the United States, ABC television was considering chartering a tramp steamer, offering space to other American television networks and newspapers, and then heading off into the battle zone. The *Washington Post* offered $5,000 for a berth but an early estimate of the cost was more than $100,000 a head.[10] The clinching factor in abandoning the idea was that the British threat to fire on any ship in the "total exclusion zone" which the MoD had declared around the islands, did not make any mention of exemption for American press boats.

With all the correspondents in the task force operating under MoD control, only two other sources of information remained: Argentina and the MoD briefings in London. The former was rightly suspect, but the latter at first looked promising, the MoD spokesman offering an assurance that, within the strictures of military security, he would be frank and truthful. In the event he proved a master of the delphic phrase and his promise to tell the truth did not include telling all the truth as soon as he knew it. "We have no reports of any major Argentine warships or auxiliaries having penetrated the maritime exclusion zone," he would say. And after a few seconds for closer word-by-word study, the press corps would be on its feet trying to pin him down. What did he mean by "reports"? Why "major" warships? Did that exclude small ones and if so, how small? Did "penetrated" mean from the mainland to the islands or from the islands to the mainland as well? And so on.[11]

The press corps was right to be suspicious because governments, even democratic ones, have a long record of lying in wartime when it suits them. As we have seen, the American government lied about the number of ships sunk at Pearl Harbor in 1941. The British government regularly inflated the number of German planes shot down during the Battle of Britain. Britain officially claimed that it was bombing only military targets in Germany and when German and some neutral correspondents wrote the truth, Britain dismissed it as propaganda. The U.S. Navy suppressed all mention of Japanese kamikaze attacks on American ships for six months, and the U.S. government told the press that the enormous explosion in New Mexico on 16 July 1945—the testing of the first atom bomb—was "an ammunition dump explosion."

It will be a long while before all the lies told about the Falklands emerge; some lies told about the Second World War came to light only thirty years later. But already we have been told that the MoD lied when it denied reports that the aircraft carrier *Invincible* had suffered a breakdown of one engine soon after leaving Portsmouth. It is now agreed that those reports were correct and that the MoD lied because it wished to keep the information secret in case it would help Argentina.[12] That this is a valid reason is irrelevant here; the point is that in wartime official promises to tell the truth are worthless.

More serious than the lies were suppression, and subtle control of emphasis. In the weeks immediately after the war, correspondents back from the front rushed into print with "the untold story," incidents that the MoD censors had refused to pass at the time. The intriguing thing about most of these stories was that the information they contained would have been of no value to Argentina whatsoever. What they did do was to paint too vivid a picture of the war, a picture of two groups of highly-trained men on two otherwise peaceful South Atlantic islands doing some very nasty things to each other. If you need to maintain popular support for a war, this is not the sort of thing you want the people back home—particularly the relatives of servicemen—to read.

This was also the reason why television film was deliberately delayed, in at least one incident—that of the attack on the landing craft *Sir Galahad*—until the war was over. Close-ups of men with their fried skin peeling away were not the images of war that the MoD wanted beamed into the nation's living rooms at peak viewing time. But in the euphoria of victory and with the emphasis now placed heavily on bravery, comradeship and sacrifice, the film no longer posed a danger to morale, and it went out to great acclaim, few bothering to ask where it had been in the intervening period.[13]

So the MoD was brilliant—censoring, suppressing, and delaying dangerous news, releasing bad news in dribs and drabs so as to nullify its impact, and projecting its own image as the only real source of accurate information about what was happening. But there is one worrying factor in this accusation: despite its skills, the MoD could not have achieved what it did without some compliance from the British media; if it was rape, then it was rape with contributory negligence.

Some newspapers contributed as a matter of policy. They supported the government all the way, even to the extent of attacking other newspapers or television programmes that expressed the slightest reservation about Britain's actions. This helped create a climate in which to dissent was little short of treason. In fact the BBC, criticised in the past as a bastion of British conservatism, an arm of government, part of the Foreign Office and so on, found itself this time accused of "damaging the country's war effort."

Other newspapers, irrespective of the line they took in their editorials, were prepared to accept as accurate and fair whatever their correspondents with the task force sent back. This is as it should be; if you are not prepared to print what your correspondent on the spot writes, then why bother to send him? But what no one had anticipated was that seasoned correspondents who had reported other people's wars with commendable objectivity found, when reporting their own country's war, that patriotism was a stronger driving force than professionalism. They praised the courage, determination, loyalty and leadership of the British troops and denigrated that of the Argentinians. In moments of defeat they offered their readers solace, and, in victory, jubilation. In short they became an integral part of the task force, propagandists for the British cause.

Max Hastings (who won an award for his reporting from the Falklands) in a front page story in the *Daily Express* headed WHY NONE OF US CAN BE NEUTRAL IN THIS WAR, wrote, "Most of us decided before landing that our role was simply to report as sympathetically as possible what the British forces are doing here today." In justification Hastings quoted his father, a noted war correspondent in the Second World War, "When one's nation is at war, reporting becomes an extension of the war effort."[14] Michael

Nicholson, of Independent Television News, had covered fourteen wars in his career as a television reporter. Asked on his return how this war differed from the others, he replied, "They were other people's wars. This was Britain's war. It was *my* war."[15]

This attitude is at least understandable. And in a war of national survival—which the Falklands was not—few would quarrel with it. What was alarming was the opinion expressed by a number of powerful journalists in Britain: not that the reporting of the Falklands was flawed, but that much of it should not have been reported at all. Paul Johnson, a former editor of the *New Statesman* and then a commentator on the press for *The Spectator*, wrote that he had been staggered by the details published about the task force. "The Ministry has had to steer a difficult path between giving away nothing of use to the enemy and satisfying the media's insatiable appetite and on the whole it has done well, erring if anything on the side of over-disclosure."[16] Milton Shulman, the theatre critic, said that Argentina had invaded the Falklands because its leaders had reason to believe that the British lacked the will to fight. This was because the space given to those who disagreed with Mrs Thatcher—"the defeatists and the cautious...the Left and the criers of woe"—had encouraged the junta in that belief, and any enquiry into the causes of the conflict would have to take this into account.[17]

It is now clear that in the wars of our time, Vietnam was an aberration. The freedom given to correspondents there to go anywhere, see everything, and write what they liked is not going to be given again. And the Falklands provided a model of how to make certain that government policy is not undermined by the way a war is reported. The rules turned out to be fairly simple: control access to the fighting; exclude neutral correspondents; censor your own; and muster support, both on the field and at home, in the name of patriotism, labelling any dissidents as traitors. After all, as Hastings senior said, objectivity could come back into fashion when the shooting was over.

## Chapter Nineteen

# The Deadly Video Game
# 1990–1991

"The Patriot's success [at killing Scud missiles] is known to everyone. It's one hundred per cent."

—General Norman Schwartzkopf, the American commander
during the Gulf War.

"A post war review of photographs cannot produce a single confirmed kill of a Scud missile."

—U.S. Armed Services Committee report, August 1993

There were ominous indications in the early 1990s that the way Britain had controlled the media during the war in the Falklands had so impressed the military establishment in that home of free speech, the United States, that no war Americans now fought would be free of censorship, management and manipulation.

True, there could not be a return to the days of the First World War when an officer on the staff of the British general, Sir Ian Hamilton, summed up the military view of war correspondents—a properly run country did not need them. "It simply tells the people what it thinks will conduce to winning the war. If truth is good for winning the war, it tells them the truth. If a lie is likely to win the war, it tells them a lie."

The citizen of the last decade of the twentieth century was more sophisticated than his forebears of 1915 and in the intervening years the military establishment had developed a tried and tested

483

programme for managing news in a democratic society so as to ensure that public opinion supported the government of the day in pursuing its war aims. The media was reluctant to be managed and fought against it. But this was a battle it could not win—even if it had summoned the will to do so. Firstly, in wartime the media remained as divided and competitive as in peacetime. And it had little or no memory. War correspondents have short working lives and there is no tradition or means for passing on their experiences.

The military, on the other hand, is an institution and goes on forever. Wars are studied, lessons are learnt, systems are devised, tested and polished. The British Ministry of Defence has a manual, updated after every war, which serves to guide the way it will handle its relationship with the media in wartime—as does the Pentagon and every other major military power. What newspaper or television company does anything simliar?

All the military manuals follow basic principles—appear open, transparent and eager to help; never go in for summary repression or direct control; nullify rather than conceal undesirable news; control emphasis rather than facts; balance bad news with good; and lie directly only when certain that the lie will not be found out during the course of the war.

Building on this base, the United States military, which believed that it might have won the war in Vietnam if the reporting had not sapped the public's will for the fight, had its new media strategy in place when it invaded the Caribbean island of Grenada in October 1983 "to protect innocent lives and to help in the restoration of democracy." Basically the plan was to confront the media head on, to tell journalists that unlike Vietnam, this was a war they would not be allowed to cover. So the invasion took place in total secrecy—even the White House spokesman was not told about it and then all journalists were excluded from the island for three days.

When a few correspondents tried to reach Grenada by speedboat, a US fighter plane fired at them and forced them to turn back. The new relationship between the military and the media was summed up in an exchange later between one of the correspondents in the speedboat and U.S. Vice-Admiral Joseph Metcalf. The correspondent asked, "Admiral, what would have happened if we hadn't turned around?" The Admiral replied, "We would have blown you right out of the water."[1]

So Grenada became the "uncovered invasion" and all the major features of the operation were distorted by Administration lies, misinformation, secrecy and journalistic bickering. "All the justifications provided by the Administration for the attack (dutifully reported in the press) were later deemed to have been spurious," concluded Richard Keeble of City University, London.[2] White House communications director David Gergen resigned after the invasion in protest at the lying by his superiors.

On December 20, 1989, 24,000 American troops took part in the largest U.S. military operation since Vietnam. This was the invasion of Panama, supposedly to arrest the Panamanian leader General Noriega, on drugs charges. Although a pool system for the media was supposed to operate, for the first two days the only on-the-spot reports of the invasion came from correspondents detained by the military in a warehouse. Another one hundred journalists who had accompanied the troops with the promise that some of them would at least be allowed into a pool, were then told that, unfortunately, there was no provision for the media and therefore no facilities. The correspondents turned round and meekly returned home.[3]

Keeble says that the heart of the Pentagon media strategy was the representation of the invasion as swift and clean. Patrick Sloyan, of *Newsday* agrees. He wrote that the muzzling of the press in Panama created "the illusion of bloodless battlefields." Yet the Spanish language press in Latin America gave casualty figures of 2,000 civilian deaths and 70,000 casualties. In retrospect, the importance of Panama can be seen as the final testing ground of a military media strategy that was to change forever the ways wars would be reported in the West and which was deployed in all its notoriety in the Gulf War.

Iraq invaded and occupied Kuwait on August 2, 1990. Iraq's President, Saddam Hussein, had been quarrelling with Kuwait for some time, accusing the Kuwaitis of flooding the international market with low-cost oil, thus costing Iraq billions of dollars in revenue just at a time when it needed increased oil revenues to recover from the Iran–Iraq war. He also said that the Kuwaitis were taking too much oil from the Rumalia oil field along the disputed border between the two countries and demanded compensation.

Hussein apparently believed that the United States, which had "tilted" towards Iraq during the Iran–Iraq war, would accept his action. In a long interview with the American ambassador, April Glaspie, just eight days before the invasion, Glaspie had told him, "I admire your extraordinary efforts to rebuild your country. I know you need funds. We understand that and our opinion is that you should have the opportunity to rebuild your country. But we have no opinion on Arab–Arab conflicts like your border disagreement with Kuwait."[4]

Hussein was mistaken. President Bush issued statements condemning Iraq's "naked aggression" and calling for the unconditional withdrawal of Iraqi troops. He noted that the United States received nearly half its energy requirements from the Middle East: "We remain committed to take whatever steps are necessary to defend our long-standing vital interests in the Gulf." Bush then announced economic sanctions against Iraq and the dispatch of American troops to Saudi Arabia in a "wholly defensive role." He compared Iraq's take-over of Kuwait with the Nazi blitzkrieg in Europe in the 1930s and Saddam Hussein with Adolf Hitler.

It was then as if the Hitler comparison was a signal to the media. Keeble writes that the governments of the United States and Britain continued to play a dual role, calling for diplomacy but warning of military retaliation. "But most of the press had no time for talk—they wanted war and right now. From 3 August Fleet Street was on a virtual war footing."

In the United States there was no questioning of the decision to send troops to the Gulf. News coverage concentrated on the build up of the military force and most prominent columnists and almost every newspaper editorial urged war. In their analysis of American coverage of the crisis, Abbas Malek and Lisa Leidig wrote: "The press behaved more like a propaganda arm of the government promoting the idea of the inevitability of war in the Persian Gulf."[5]

In Britain, Martin Woollacott of the *Guardian* defended his view that war was inevitable. "War *was* inevitable from September. Neither side could make the necessary concessions because the purposes of the two sides were too radically opposed. A Middle Eastern leader had taken unilateral action to challenge the West's authority. And the prestige gained had to be wiped out."

But sizable minorities in both the United States and Britain were against such a war and although the mainstream media largely ignored their protests, these had to be dampened down unless they gained strength. Hussein had to be demonised. He was painted as being ruthless, another Hitler, a fanatic, deranged, a psychopath, hated by his own people and despised in the Arab world. Further, from the moment his troops had arrived in Kuwait they had committed unspeakable atrocities.

The most important of all these atrocity stories—both in its impact on public opinion and in its political influence—was the

486

Kuwaiti babies story. Its origins go back to the First World War when British propaganda accused the Germans of tossing Belgian babies into the air and catching them on their bayonets. Dusted off and updated for the Gulf War, this version had Iraqi soldiers bursting into a modern Kuwaiti hospital, finding the premature babies ward and then tossing the babies out of incubators so that the incubators could be sent back to Iraq.

The story, improbable from the start, was first reported by the *Daily Telegraph* in London on September 5, 1990 and two days later by the *Los Angeles Times*, which attributed it to Reuters. But the story lacked the human element—it was an unverified report, there were no pictures for television and no interviews with mothers grieving over dead babies. That was soon rectified. An organisation calling itself Citizens for a Free Kuwait (financed by the Kuwaiti government in exile) had signed a $10 million contract with the giant American public relations company, Hill and Knowlton, to campaign for American military intervention to oust Iraq from Kuwait.

The Human Rights Caucus of the U.S. Congress was meeting in October and Hill and Knowlton arranged for a fifteen-year-old Kuwaiti girl to tell the babies story before the Congressmen. She did it brilliantly, choking with tears at the right moment, her voice breaking as she struggled to continue. The Congressional Committee knew her only as "Nayirah" and the television segment of her testimony showed anger and resolution on the faces of the congressmen listening to her. President Bush immediately picked up on the story and referred to it six times in the next five weeks as an example of the evil of Saddam Hussein's regime. Amnesty International lent its weight to the atrocity in its report of human rights violations published on December 19.

The *Sunday Times* of London helped keep the story alive by tracing a Dr. Ali Al-Huwail, a Kuwaiti said to be living at a secret address in the United Arab Emirates. The doctor played down the number of babies said to have been murdered—he could vouch for "only ninety-two deaths." The article also quoted a "Franco-Jordanian doctor" who said he was sceptical of the account. But the newspaper chose to illustrate the story with a drawing of evil-looking Iraqi soldiers ripping the babies off their incubators.

In the Senate debate on whether to approve military action to force Saddam Hussein out of Kuwait seven senators specifically mentioned the incubator babies atrocity and the final margin in favour of war was just five votes. John R. Macarthur in his study of propaganda in the war says that the incubator babies atrocity was a definitive moment in the campaign to prepare the American public for the need to go to war.

It was not until nearly two years later that the truth emerged. The story was a total invention, a fabrication and a myth, and "Nayirah," the teenage Kuwaiti girl, coached and rehearsed by Hill and Knowlton for her appearance before the Congressional Committee, was in fact the daughter of the Kuwaiti ambassador to the United States. By the time Macarthur revealed this, the war was won and over and it did not matter any more.[6]

The "incubator babies" ploy was not the end of Hill and Knowlton's involvement in propaganda for the Kuwaiti government. The company developed press kits that were sent to American reporters, members of Congress and federal officials. They also sent more than 20 video news releases to more than 700 television stations around the world. Many ran the releases as straight news without mentioning that they came from Hill and Knowlton, public relations consultant to the Kuwait government.

News of this did not emerge until much later. When it did, some members of Congress were outraged and one, Representative Jimmy Hayes, said it should be illegal for foreign governments to run "a war lobby" and try to "buy" U.S. public opinion. It took the Center for Public Integrity in Washington to reveal one of the reasons that the Kuwaiti government hired Hill and Knowlton—many of the company's executives had served in the Reagan and Bush administrations and one, Craig Fuller, the company's new president, had been vice-President Bush's chief of staff.

President Bush had given Saddam Hussein a deadline of January 15, 1991 to withdraw from Kuwait or face military action by an American-led alliance. In the meantime newspapers on both sides of the Atlantic carried the results of public opinion polls which seemed to suggest that the British and American people would be wholeheartedly behind such an action, about 54 per cent backing war, 34 per cent against, and the remainder expressing no opinion. But Keeble points out that the way the questions were framed offered respondents who wanted Iraq out of Kuwait only one way to accomplish that—war.

At least one British newspaper was not beyond distorting poll results to further its editorial policy. On October 22, the *Mirror*, whose proprietor Robert Maxwell was pro-Israel, carried a rare article on the U.S. peace movement in which American protesters called on President Bush to bring home American troops. But the paper went on to report that 86 per cent of British people believed that "our boys should launch a military strike against the Iraqi tyrant." Keeble points out that no poll at that time was producing such a result. "It was an invention. But it became an accepted truth."

Meanwhile, journalists were discovering how the alliance was planning to implement its media strategy. The first troops left the United States for Saudi Arabia on August 7. Not a single war correspondent went with them—the Pentagon had not activated the promised press pool and individual journalists who applied for a Saudi Arabian visa were refused. President Bush hinted that operational security was the reason. "I'm glad that...many forces could be moved with not too much advance warning [to Iraq] and with not too much risk to Saudi Arabia or to these troops." When the media chiefs complained about being left behind, Bush said, "There's plenty of reporters in Saudi Arabia right now." This was simply untrue—not a single U.S. journalist was in Saudi Arabia.[7]

The Defense Department eventually obtained Saudi visas for 17 members of the national media pool and they arrived in Saudi Arabia on August 13. They were closely monitored by Pentagon officials who let them know that if they asked hard questions they would be perceived as "anti-military" and treated as such. There was only one big story to write at that time—that there were not sufficient American troops in the area to withstand an attack if Iraq were to launch one. The Pentagon told the reporters that if they wanted to stay in Saudi Arabia then they should not report this information. They accepted this restriction and did not do so.

Meanwhile the Defense Department was providing special access for those sections of the media it knew it could trust. A television production company called Quantum Diversified, working on a video about the National Guard funded by "well-financed patriots" was given free air travel to Saudi Arabia, access to anyone they wanted to interview, and military escorts to ease their way. A Pentagon official explained later that it was happy to work with organisations that did not put the military in a bad light. "I mean it doesn't make sense to give someone help when they're going to make you look like a bunch of buffoons."[8]

Three weeks after President Bush announced that he was doubling the size of the U.S. force in the Gulf (430,000 in total) to prepare for a possible offensive action, the United Nations passed a resolution giving Iraq until January 15 to pull out of Kuwait. When this deadline passed with no move by Iraq, on January 16 U.S. and coalition aircraft began the initial air attacks on Iraq.

The Pentagon decreed that coverage of the war would be through the "pool system." A limited number of correspondents would be chosen for each pool, escorted by military officers to cover various stages of the action as chosen by the military, and then be expected to make their reports available to their colleagues who were not in a pool.

There was an outcry from media organisations. They said that the "power to define coverage" amounted to censorship more dangerous than "blue pencil editing." ABC correspondent Judd Rose said that his pool wanted to visit a Patriot anti-missile battery because it had been used against a Scud missile attack the previous night. Instead the military sent them to a garage where trucks were being prepared.

But such was the competition among correspondents for good pool slots and so much time did they spend fighting with each other that they were unable to mount an effective opposition to the system. Some journalists and smaller media organisations decided to file a legal case against the Pentagon alleging that the pool system violated their First Amendment Right to freedom of expression. No major media organisation joined the action, although invited to do so, because they feared that the Pentagon might retaliate and kick them out of its pools, or that if they lost it would set a dangerous precedent. In the event, the war ended before the courts could rule on the issue, but once again the military had succeeded in dividing the media, the more easily to rule it.

British media groups, especially TV ones, were also by now fighting bitterly among themselves, accusing each other of trying to squeeze out their opposition. Sky's head of news, John O'Loan, said Sky had been "carved up" because they were new to the broadcasting-government establishment and their presence was not welcome. "When the crunch came the Ministry of Defence saw ITN and the BBC as the most reliable...It was unfair, unjust and completely stupid."

In Britain, the Ministry of Defence announced that it, too, would be operating a pool system for reporting from the war zone. Newspaper editors were called to the MoD and issued with notes for their own guidance in case, despite the system in operation in the Gulf, anything untoward should creep through to London. An editor who attended the briefing told me, "The amazing thing is that we were not invited to the MoD to discuss the guidelines. They were handed to us and it was assumed automatically that we would accept them."

In fact the BBC and ITV told their correspondents to accept the advice of the MoD minders unless there were very strong reasons for not doing so. This met with the approval of *The Economist* which said that once the war started, it was right to "suspend the normal play of democratic argument" and urged correspondents to do the same. "The truth about the Gulf War…must await the end of the fighting."

As well as dividing the British media and putting them into the pool system where they had to agree to submit all items, written or recorded, to censors before transmission back to London, the MoD had another more subtle plan to get the correspondents "on side." They had to wear uniforms. Alex Thomson, who was there for Channel Four News, said: "Some loved it, others had reservations, some tried actively to slip out of them when appearing on camera. …The powers that be wanted the journalists to meld, blend, bond even, with those around them."[10] Martin Bell, of the BBC, agreed: "You got a sense that the first priority was to train us up and make us one of them…In return for what we wanted, which was access, we should behave, and be seen to be, like soldiers. I think it was a psychological thing for them, they wanted us to be on side and not something separate from them. I wear their uniform, I get to join them on their tank—it was as simple as that."[11]

But what about those correspondents who did not necessarily want to be on side? Who did not want to be in a pool, or could not get a place in a pool. Many stayed in their hotels in Saudi Arabia and attended the daily Allied briefing where skilled officers made announcements on matters they wanted the public to know and then fielded awkward questions on matters they preferred to keep secret. It was either that or pack up and go home.

There were a few who were determined to get out there and do some old-fashioned reporting. They had a tough time. The military deemed them "unilaterals" and did its best to discourage them. By mid-February, more than twenty journalists had been detained or threatened with detention by the military before being sent back to Dahahran. Some were roughly treated. Wesley Bocxe, a *Time* photographer, was blindfolded, searched, and held for more than 30 hours by a National Guard unit.

And when a CBS television crew led by Bob Simon, an experienced Middle East correspondent, was captured by an Iraqi patrol in late January, the U.S. military said, in effect, "See. That's what can happen when you go it alone." (The Iraqis released Simon and his crew unharmed at the end of the war.)

But the lone correspondent's worst enemy turned out to be his colleagues in the pools. Robert Fisk of *The Independent*, London, a very experienced Middle East expert, refused to join any pool and went off on his own looking for stories. During the battle of Khafji, Fisk came across a pool of correspondents with a formation of Marines. An NBC-TV reporter in the pool spotted Fisk and shouted at him, "Get out of here you arsehole. You'll prevent us from working. You're not allowed here. Get out. Go back to Dhahran." He then called over a Marine public affairs officer and told him about Fisk's presence. The Marine shouted, "You're not allowed to talk to U.S. Marines and they're not allowed to talk to you."[12]

Recalling the event later, Fisk wrote: "It was a disturbing moment. By travelling to Khafji, *The Independent* discovered that the Iraqis were fighting in the town long after allied military spokesmen had claimed that it had been liberated. For the NBC reporter, however, the privileges of the pool and the military rules attached to it were more important than the right of journalists to do their job."

The trouble was that whenever journalists or their employers complained that the pool system and military briefings at which high-ranking officers told the media as little as possible amounted to censorship, the reply was on the lines of "Yes. So what?" The military and the American and British governments realised from their polls that the public knew that the news from the Gulf was being censored—and almost eighty per cent thought that this was a good idea. In fact, nearly sixty per cent thought that the authorities should exert more control over the coverage of the war.[13]

Imagine the military's frustration then about famous television correspondents over whom they could exercise no control—Peter Arnett of CNN, John Simpson of the BBC, and Brent Sadler of ITN. They had reported the first stage of the war, the bombing campaign, from Baghdad, the enemy capital. It was their vivid film of night skies alight with explosions and the exhaust flames of missiles, on a soundtrack of explosions and anti-aircraft fire, interspersed with breathless commentary—"a Tomahawk missile just went past my hotel window and turned right at the end of the street"—that gripped Western viewers and at first contributed to the impression that the whole thing was a surreal video game.

All three correspondents were attacked for daring to report

from the Iraqi side. Arnett, who had won a Pulitzer Prize for his reporting of the Vietnam conflict, made it clear that he was allowed to see only what his Iraqi "minders" wanted him to and that his reports were censored. Nevertheless he was was accused of endangering the lives of American servicemen.

On February 4, 1991, 21 members of the House of Representatives signed a letter to CNN saying Arnett's reports gave "the demented dictator a propaganda mouthpiece to over one hundred nations. The risk this presents—inciting fanatics and endagering our service personnel—lends great urgency to suggestions that CNN review its current policies on airing the voice of Baghdad."

Senator Alan Simpson accused Arnett of being a "sympathizer" with Iraq, and said his Vietnam reporting had been biased and his Vietnamese brother-in-law had worked with the Viet Cong. This brought outraged protests from Arnett's colleagues and Simpson partially apologised saying he should not have repeated rumours about Arnett's family and should not have called him a sympathiser—"dupe" or "tool" would have been more appropriate. On his return to the United States Arnett defended his role, saying that the media was partly to blame for the negative reaction because it had not educated the public about the function of a free press in wartime.

In Britain, the MoD seemed divided on whether reporting from the enemy capital was a good thing or not. Hugh Colver, in charge of the MoD's press office said some of his colleagues thought the correspondents were tools and should leave. Others felt that since this was a television war, if no British correspondents were in Baghdad, the Iraqis would film something themselves and send it out to a news-hungry world where it would be broadcast with no one to judge the context. And a third group found film of missiles soaring over Baghdad apparently to hit military targets with pinpoint accuracy not only good television but great for Allied morale.

This sophisticated and relaxed attitude changed, of course, when on February 13 two bombs dropped from a Stealth fighter-bomber on to a shelter in the Ameriyya district of Baghdad killed as many as 1,600 people, mostly women and children. Television film of the appalling carnage flashed around the world, although the BBC and ITN cut out the worst segments on the grounds of taste. The Allies replied that the shelter was a military bunker, a legitimate target, and if civilians had been killed it was because Saddam Hussein had put them there so that he could claim a propaganda victory if they were killed.

Reporters in Baghdad gave a different view. Jeremy Bowen of the BBC, interviewed live from London, refused to be drawn by the anchorman into agreeing that the shelter appeared to have a dual military purpose. Brent Sadler of ITN said, "Ameriyya is a middle-class residential area. I could see no military or strategic targets in the vicinity."

The bombing and the death toll caused immediate outrage in the British and American press—not because the Allies had incinerated hundreds of women and children but because of the way the Western media had reported it. Television should not have shown the carnage; it was unpatriotic to do so. The *Mail on Sunday* said that the coverage was "truly disgusting" and "deplorable." *Today* said that the correspondents were "a disgrace to their country." Conservative MPs called the BBC the "Baghdad Broadcasting Corporation." The *Express* said that weeping over inevitable and unavoidable enemy casualties would undermine support for the war. The *Los Angeles Times* said that the bombing of the shelter was a progaganda coup for Baghdad—"Iraq on Wednesday delivered the equivalent of a fuel air explosive through images of charred Iraqi women and children."

Eventually the Allied military commanders admitted that the bombing had been a mistake; U.S. intelligence had been at fault. But at the same time it was all Saddam Hussein's fault—he did put civilians into bunkers, and even though this time he had not, he was still to blame. Those who found this hard to swallow and tried to protest against the prosecution of the war in this manner were now subjected to blasts of abuse as bad as that formerly reserved for Saddam Hussein.

They were labelled: "friends of terrorists, ranters, nutty, hypocrites, animals, barbarians, mad, traitors, unhinged, appeasers and apologists for a dictator." Columnist Brian Hitchen, writing about an anti-war demonstration in London, said that the marchers were "the usual treacherous misfits trying to knife our boys in the back." The *Mirror* called peace demonstrators "misguided, twisted individuals always eager to comfort and support any country but their own. They are a danger to us all—the enemy within."

One reason for this almost hysterical reaction was that the reporting of the Ameriyya bombing threatened the most important element in the military's propaganda strategy—an attempt to change public perception of the nature of war itself, to convince everyone that new technology has removed a lot of war's horrors. From early on the military briefers were at pains to point out the "surgical" nature of air strikes on military targets: the cancer would be removed but the living flesh around it would be left untouched. "Smart" bombs dropped with "pinpoint accuracy" would take out only military installations; there would be little or no "collateral damage" (dead civilians). Iraq's military machine would be destroyed from the air so that any ground war would be over quickly (as indeed it was).

The picture that this painted was of a war almost without death, a sanitised version of what had gone on before. A new language was used to soften reality. Bombing military targets in the heart of cities was "denying the enemy an infrastructure." People were "soft targets." Saturation bombing was "laying down a carpet." The idea was to suggest that hardly any people were involved in modern warfare, only machines. This explained the emphasis at press briefings on the damage "our machines" had caused to "their machines" and the reluctance of briefing officers to discuss casualties—on either side. No more Vietnam-style "body counts."

The rationale was that the public no longer had the stomach for a war in which large numbers of civilians were going to be killed, especially by Western high-tech armaments. (As we shall see, by the time the century was running out, the American public, for one, also had no stomach for a war in which large numbers of American *servicemen* were going to be killed.)

The Ameriyya bombing did not dent the image of "surgical strikes" and the accuracy of "smart bombs" because the military argued that although it was a mistake to bomb the bunker when civilians were in it, it was still a precision strike—the smart bombs had gone straight down a ventilator shaft. It was not until the war was over that the truth about "smart bombs" emerged, along with the myth of the "clean," high-tech war.

General Merril McPeak of the United States Air Force said after the war that "smart bombs" accounted for just seven per cent of the bombs dropped on Iraq.[14] The rest were modern area impact munitions, like the cluster bomb, designed to devastate a wide area rather than confine their destruction to a precise target. Their use was largely kept from the media during the war. Even these bombs missed most of the time. The *Washington Post*, quoting a senior Pentagon source, said that of the 88,500 tons of bombs dropped on Iraq, no fewer than 70 per cent missed their target.

As for missiles, the correspondents fell for the public relations guff that the Pentagon military spokesmen spread about the Tomahawk missile. On January 25, 1991, Lt. General Thomas Kelly said that more than 200 Tomahawks had been fired successfully. Later the Pentagon claimed a 98 per cent launch success rate. No journalist thought to ask what this meant, exactly. They wished that they had when an article entitled "AWESTRUCK PRESS DOES TOMAHAWK PR" appeared in the *Bulletin of Atomic Scientists* in April that year.

The article explained that the term "launch success rate" had nothing to do with the Tomahawk's accuracy or its ability to hit its target. It simply meant that the missile had got out of its launcher without getting stuck or blowing up. The Tomahawk actually hit targets only slightly more than half the time.[15]

Never mind, at least another American weapon, the Patriot anti-missile missile was a roaring success. Every night on television in Britain and the United States viewers could see Saddam Hussein's ancient Scud missiles come lumbering across the sky heading for targets in Saudi Arabia and Israel. Then a small, faster missile would rise up from the ground, find the Scud and blow it to pieces before it could do any damage. Another success for the Patriot. The Patriot's fame began on January 18, 1991, when after being deployed to save Israel from the threat of a Scud bombardment, it achieved an historic knockout, the first defensive missile to destroy an incoming offensive missile.

President Bush told workers at the Patriot plant in the United States that the weapon had intercepted 41 out of 42 Iraqi missiles. The American commander, General Norman Schwarzkopf went further, telling correspondents, "The Patriot's success, of course, is known to everyone. It's one hundred per cent."[16] The *Sun* on February 28 described it as "the most famous weapon in the world."

Again it was not until after the war that the truth emerged. The "historic knockout" in Israel did not happen. Writing in the *International Herald Tribune* on September 25, 1992, Ben Sherwood revealed that there was no incoming Scud. A Patriot computer malfunction appeared to have caused the Patriot to fire itself at a cloud. An Israeli post-conflict examination of the success rate of the Patriots concluded that they had intercepted and destroyed one—or possibly none—of the Scuds. A U.S. Armed Services Committee report quoted in the *Guardian* of August 17, 1993 concluded, "A post war review of photographs cannot produce even a single confirmed kill of a Scud missile."[17]

It may even have been more dangerous for civilians when Patriots were used than when they were not, because they could come down in populated areas and explode themselves. Before Patriots were used 13 Scuds damaged 2,698 apartments and injured 115 people. With Patriots in use only 11 Scud attacks damaged 7,778 apartments, wounded 168 people and killed at least one.[18]

The truth about the Patriot and other high-tech weapons came out in testimony before the House Armed Services Committee. Former Defense Department official Pierre Sprey said, "The country has been poorly served by shamelessly doctored statistics and the hand-selected video clips of isolated successes that were pumped out to the media during the war in order to influence post-war budget decisions."[19]

Spellbound by the "Star Wars" nature of the conflict and lacking the knowledge to assess properly what the military were telling them, most correspondents—"pretty impressively ignorant about technology," according to one Defense Department scientist—unwittingly acted as unpaid publicists to help weapons manufacturers get government contracts.

What other myths did the war throw up? One of the most potent was the image of a dying crested cormorant choked, it was said, by a huge oil slick that the Iraqis had released from occupied Kuwait. The slick provided the allied leaders with a field day. Saddam Hussein, already "a lunatic" and a "barbarian," was now called "an environmental terrorist" by the British government, while President Bush implied yet again that he was unstable because he had released the oil for no military advantage. The story made headlines and news bulletins around the world, with pictures and film of the cormorant to illustrate most of them. It created an image of special appeal to environmentalists—who, until then, were among leading opponents of the war. But it was all untrue, a brilliant piece of propaganda.

The Iraqis had pumped some oil into the Gulf towards southeast Kuwait to frustrate possible amphibious landings. But the cormorant in the photograph was on the Saudi coast at least fifty miles away and the oil slick which was killing it had been caused not by the Iraqis but by the Americans who had bombed an Iraqi tanker. There was little to be gained by publishing a photograph of a cormorant dying from an oil spill caused by Americans and since there was an Iraqi spill anyway, why not blame the Iraqis?

On January 29, when the cormorant story had run its course and it did not matter any more, an announcement from Washington made small, downpage news. "The photographs of oiled seabirds widely published in the past three days since the weekend do not relate to the Sea Island (Iraqi) spill, it emerged yesterday.

497

General Tom Kelly, operations director for the U.S. Joint Chiefs of Staff, said the big slick had not yet reached the coast and the contamination seen came from an earlier raid on a Saudi refinery."

Even this was wrong because it still blamed the Iraqis and there had been no Iraqi raid on a Saudi refinery. It was to take nearly another month before an Associated Press story said a Saudi official had confirmed that the first crude oil to wash up on Saudi shores had resulted from an American attack and that Allied attacks were responsible for about a third of the oil pollution in Saudi waters.

The ground war which began on February 23, 1991 was an anticlimax. There was no enormous Iraqi army of one million strong battle-hardened troops to resist the armoured might of the Allies. There was no enormous Iraqi defence system with massive berms and a highly-sophisticated system of underground trenches. There was no "mother of all battles," no "largest ground offensive since the Second World War."

Instead there was what Richard Keeble has called "a series of massacres" and since they all happened so quickly to this day no one knows how many Iraqis were killed. Many Iraqi bodies were bulldozed dead and alive into mass graves, something not reported at the time. In fairness to the correspondents, since the ground war lasted only 100 hours, there was not much time to report anything. Benjamin Bradlee, former executive editor of the *Washington Post*, commented, "The trouble with this war was it was so fucking fast."

Many Iraqi soldiers were also burnt to ashes. Robert Fox of the *Telegraph* spent two days after the war travelling all along the front line. He wrote, "They were consumed in the most terrible way: there is so much fire, so much fissile capacity in these weapons now, I don't mean to be disgusting but they are just incinerated...A terrifying, novel aspect of this campaign is that not even the bones remain."[20]

Photographer Kenneth Jarecke was in an American pool travelling on the road towards Kuwait city when he came across an Iraqi army convoy that had been only partly incinerated. He looked around for one image that might convey the horror that lay all around and ended up focusing on the head of an Iraqi whose eyes had melted from their sockets, who nose was a stump, whose lips had been burnt off—just a blackened skull. It was a brilliant picture that captured the worst of war, but not a single newspaper in the United States would print it. In Britain it appeared in the *Observer* —but not on the front page—to roars of protest.

Television had film of the man and others like him but no station—except in Japan—showed any of it. ITN reporter Alex Thomson complained later: "The central truth here was a massacre. Large numbers of people, several hundred, had been horribly killed and the world had seen nothing of this during the entire course of the war to date. Seldom had the job of the correspondent looked so clear cut than it did on Mutla Ridge: show people, tell people. The whole point about the Gulf War was that it was censored to such a degree that the images went in precisely the opposite direction. They gave the casual sense that no one had died or been hurt. Mutla Ridge was a rare, golden opportunity to try to put that right …It was crucially important to report, to show at last that this war like any other was about killing people. Not only this, these people were manifestly not fighting, but fleeing in panic."[21]

How many Iraqis died? General Colin L. Powell, chairman of the U.S. Joint Chiefs of Staff, estimated 250,000. A Freedom of Information request to the Pentagon produced a figure of 100,000 killed and 300,000 wounded. As for Allied casualties, 353 died but only 46 were killed on active service and of these more than half were the result of "friendly fire." In short, while the massacres were going on, the greatest threat to allied soldiers were other allied soldiers. Of British deaths, nine were from friendly fire. After the war, they became the centre of an unsuccessful campaign by their relatives to force the American pilots who had bombed them to attend the coroner's inquiry.

War correspondents, like all good journalists, are closely attuned to their readers' mood. They knew during the Gulf War— and this is an unpalatable fact—that the average British reader, tabloid or serious paper, felt little sympathy or sense of identification with Islam or Arabs and considered them to be unstable, fanatical and dangerous. This was why it was so difficult to find reasoned historical articles about the war and its causes. Who bothered to explain how Britain virtually created Iraq, that Britain's idea after the First World War was to colonise it with Indian farmers and run it from Delhi as part of the Empire, that Britain rigged Iraq's elections and imposed a puppet king on them and that when they revolted, Britain bombed their villages and even considered the use of poison gas?

Iraq had found some measure of independence by 1932 but Britain intervened again in 1942 to overthrow the pro-German nationalist government. In short the British and the Iraqis had been at each other's throats on and off for seventy years. This was the history that threw up Saddam Hussein and without taking it into account what hope was there for understanding his motivations or the feelings of his people? It was the duty of the media to explain this but it failed.

The Gulf War marked an important turning point in the history of war correspondents. Not only was it a war in which the military succeeded in changing people's perceptions of what battle was really like, one in which the "surgical" precision of new high-tech weapons meant few if any civilian casualties, but one in which the way the war was communicated was as important as the conduct of the war itself. As historian James Combs concludes: "With their political and military power to command, coerce and co-opt the mass media, the national security elite can make the military event go according to script, omit bad scenes and discouraging words and bring about a military performance that is both spectacular and satisfying."[22] Or, as put more brutally by Barry Zorthian, chief Pentagon public affairs spokesman during the Vietnam War, to a National Press Club forum on March 19, 1991: "The Gulf War is over and the press lost."

## Chapter Twenty

# The Military's Final Victory
# March–June, 1999

"Kosovo…turned out to be the most secret campaign in living memory."
—British historian Alistair Horne.

"You have to plan your media strategy with as much attention as you plan your military strategy."
—Colonel P. J. Crowley, spokesman for the U.S. National Security Council.

———

The bombing campaign against Serbia which Nato waged between March and June 1999 may have been its first war since it was created in 1949—to defend the West against the Soviet Union—but it brought to it all the skills for managing the media and arousing public support that its member countries, particularly the United States and Britain, had polished during the Gulf War.

The Balkans had been in turmoil since the collapse of the Soviet Union in 1989 and Yugoslavia began to splinter into small independent states. Vicious civil wars broke out between Serb, Croat and Muslim groups, sometimes with atrocities and heavy loss of life. Western media called this fighting "ethnic cleansing", and painted it in black-and-white terms with simple "goodies and baddies." It appeared beyond the international community to do anything about it. When the Serbs began their final assault on the town of Srebrnica, in eastern Bosnia in July 1995, as many as 7,000 Muslim men were killed—even though the United Nations had declared it a safe area. When David Rohde, a reporter for the *Christian Science Monitor*, entered Serb territory and brought out the first evidence of this slaughter, many correspondents who had covered the Bosnian civil war were deeply affected and urged that nothing like this should be allowed to happen again.

Early in 1999 when western negotiators felt that they had failed to get the Serbian leader, Slobodan Milosevic, to stop the "ethnic cleansing" of Albanians in the Yugoslav province of Kosovo, to withdraw the army the Serbs had stationed there, and to allow Kosovar refugees who had fled to neighbouring states to return home, an alliance of Nato members decided that they would use force and bomb him into submission.

Once this decision had been made, a meticulously prepared system of propaganda and media control—especially in the United States and Britain—swung into action. Colonel P. J. Crowley, spokesman for the American National Security Council said, "You have to plan your media strategy with as much attention as you plan your military strategy."[1]

Wartime news breaks down into two main sections—news of the fighting and the justification for it. Governments want to control both but they devote most attention to justifying what they are doing. "To sell a war in a democracy when you're not attacked, you have to demonise the leader or show that there are humanitarian reasons for going in," said S. Robert Lichter, president of the Center for Media and Public Affairs in Washington. "George Bush demonised Saddam Hussein. We did something of the same with Milosevic."[2]

Ideally, both aims can be addressed at the same time. Governments can tell the public how the fighting is progressing and use the opportunity to remind everyone what the war is all about and what a monster the enemy is. This is what happened in the Kosovo war. Never before had so many sources been available to war correspondents.

In Brussels, where Nato had its headquarters, there was a daily briefing conducted by the Nato spokesman, a Briton, Dr. Jamie Shea, who had started at Nato as a career bureaucrat, a minute-taker, in 1983. His job was to relay what war historian Alistair Horne called "the predigested spin that had been chewed over at length by a committee of Nato ruminants."[3] Some war correspondents referred to him as "Nato's propagandist-in-chief" but Shea saw himself as an active participant in the battle and was proud of his role.[4] "Every time I see Serb TV, I know why we're doing this," he said.[5]

Shea was assisted by various Nato officers whose job it was to provide convincing technical detail to back up his more general briefings. Shea and the Nato officers were on a podium with high-tech equipment for displaying images to illustrate their points—maps, film from cockpit cameras, gun and bomb sights and target details. The journalists sat below the podium in rows of seats like in a classroom. And, again like in school, they had to attract the attention of the podium to ask a question. From a psychological viewpoint, there was no doubt about who was in control.

In London, the Chiefs of Staff met with their closest advisors at 8 A.M. every day in the bunker beneath the Ministry of Defence building. Half an hour later they joined the Defence Secretary George Robertson who chaired a meeting of officials from other departments, the director of defence intelligence and media relations staff. At these meetings decisions were taken about what Robertson and other ministers would tell reporters at briefings later in the day.

British army officers were meanwhile preparing their media programme should there be a land operation in Kosovo. Lieutenant-Colonel Nick Clissitt—who went into Kosovo with the army at the end of the war—was one of a new generation of what used to be army press officers but who now ran the army's "media operation." Being a press officer was once thought to be a backwater job but running a media operation was now considered "high profile" and attracted many of the brightest officers. All of them had been on courses with professional media training companies so that they could appear on television themselves and handle tough interviews. "We've learnt that perception is just as important as reality," said Clissitt, repeating the propagandists' mantra.[6]

Then there was a higher level of media management, one handled by Alastair Campbell, press officer and adviser to the British Prime Minister, Tony Blair. Campbell ran the government's presentation of the reasons for the war and what it wanted to achieve in Kosovo and was brought in to set up Nato's media operations centre when Nato was on the defensive after mistakenly bombing a refugee convoy at Djacovica. Campbell, whose philosophy is "It's presentation not just performance that matters," was frank about his aims: "It was vital to try to hold the public's interest *on our terms*." (author's emphasis.)[7]

In Washington, the White House press spokesman, Joe Lockhart, liaised with London to co-ordinate the alliance stance and there were media briefings at the Pentagon from spokesman Kenneth Bacon.

According to Dr. Peter Phillips of Project Censored at Sonoma University, California, the U.S. Government also used private public relations consultants to "spin and distort news stories". As well, it set up the International Public Information Group (IPI) to "squelch or limit uncomplimentary stories regarding U.S. activities and policies as reported in the foreign press." The IPI would also use "governmental resources to repress [unfavourable] foreign stories that may reach the American public."

In Britain the U.S. embassy offered British newspapers commentaries on the Kosovo war, some written by prominent people (Elie Wiesel, Nobel Peace Prize winner was one) free of charge. U.S. embassies in other main cities in Europe sent out similar articles to newspapers, emphasising that although the U.S. government owned the copyright to the articles, there was no need for the newspapers to tell their readers this. Needless to say, none of these articles opposed Nato's actions.[8]

Everything was in place for saturation coverage of a war that was—by the standards of other wars of the twentieth century—a fairly small affair. There were more war correspondents than ever before—eventually an astonishing 2,700 media people accompanied Nato forces when they entered Kosovo at the end of the bombing campaign. (In Vietnam at its peak there were about 500 war correspondents.) The revolution in communications technology—the satellite phone, "the star of the war"; instant television links from the front to the studio and between correspondents in the field; electronic transmission of still photographs, and the latest arrival at the front, the internet—should have provided the public with an unprecedented overview of the war. The ordinary, literate citizen would know more about the causes of the war, the aims of the participants and how it was being fought than any other war in history.

Instead, the public drowned in wave after wave of images that added up to nothing. "Kosovo...turned out to be the most secret campaign in living memory," wrote historian Alistair Horne when it was over.[9] "We were given lots of material but no information," said Sky correspondent Jake Lynch. Journalist Peter Dunn said it was "the first international conflict fought by press officers."[10] A disgruntled army officer said, "It's all being run by the press people. They are the real War Cabinet."[11] The *New York Times* complained that Nato briefings provided polemics and rumour but few facts. General Sir Michael Rose, former commander of the UN force in Bosnia, said that at Nato "rhetoric has taken over from reality."[12]

The media itself must shoulder a large share of the blame for

504

the poor way the war was covered. Many war correspondents realised this, as witness an article in the *Observer*, "FOR THE MEDIA, THE WAR GOES ON" by columnist Henry Porter. Porter wrote, "The war...has ended with the media feeling far from satisfied with its own behaviour. A distinctly rancorous dispute has broken out between those journalists who feel that the media rolled over to become Nato's gullible plaything, and those who allege that some of the reporters based in Belgrade were dangerously compromised in their relations with the Serbs." [13]

There were other divisions. To appreciate them we have to accept that this was a surreal war. Was it a war at all? There was no declaration of war, Blair did not consult Parliament before committing Britain to support Nato's action, and the aim was not even to defeat Serbia but only to "degrade" its armed forces to force it to stop the "ethnic cleansing" of the inhabitants of Kosovo. It was fought entirely from the air by means of a high-altitude bombing campaign, so no one—except the victims—really knew what was happening on the ground.

Britain had war correspondents stationed in Serbia's capital, Belgrade, throughout the war, and Serbian correspondents attended Nato briefings in Brussels. The Serbian Information Office in London remained open throughout the war and its spokesman appeared on British television. When three American airmen were taken prisoners-of-war by the Serbs, they handed them back. Not a single Nato soldier was killed in action and not many Serb ones, either. Instead, the casualty lists were filled with civilians (between 10,000 and 15,000) in keeping with the trend that has shifted the danger of dying in war from soldiers to civilians—at the beginning of the century, ninety per cent of casualties in war were soldiers; at the end of the century ninety per cent of casualties in war were civilians. [14]

Since they could not go to the actual battle ground, correspondents either gathered at Nato headquarters in Brussels or clustered along the borders of those countries surrounding Kosovo and tried to peer over. There they were interviewed on television by fellow correspondents in London. "What appears to be happening in Kosovo today, William?" "Well, it's very difficult to say, Rob, but the agencies are expecting a new batch of refugees later this afternoon and I'm told we should be able to learn something from them." According to veteran correspondent Robert Fisk, this surreal war was reported by largely two types of journalists—the sheep who blindly followed Nato's word on everything, and the "frothers." He defined "frothers" as those who had "convinced themselves of the justice of the war and the wickedness of the other side."[15]

Fisk, who was part of a third group of correspondents, those who chose to go to Belgrade and report the war from the Serb side, had himself experienced the ire of the frothers when he wrote a story identifying Nato markings on bomb fragments so as to "help" Nato determine who was responsible for the bombing of a refugee convoy. As reporters gathered for Nato's next briefing in Brussels, one of the frothers railed at Fisk saying that if he really wanted to help Nato he should travel around Kosovo and write about Serb atrocities.

Then there were the veterans like John Simpson of the BBC (in Belgrade) Christiane Amanpour of CNN (left Belgrade after Serb threats), Julian Manyon of ITN (Belgrade), Juan Carlos Gummucio of *El Pais*, (inside Kosovo), Maggie O'Kane of the *Guardian*, Janine di Giovanni of *The Times*, and Marie Colvin and Jon Swain of the *Sunday Times* (all over the place). The number of women in this short list of veterans reflected their increased numbers and influence in the ranks of war correspondents. Irene Slegt, a Dutch correspondent, said later what many women war correspondents were reluctant to put into words: "We are more courageous…You see men losing it quicker."

The accusation by some male war correspondents—also seldom put into words—that some women correspondents used their sexual allure to gain an advantage with the army—had unwitting support in an article by Julian Manyon. Manyon said he had shared a taxi in Kosovo with a woman war correspondent who said she had earlier broken off an affair with a French colonel serving in the Organisation for Security and Co-operation—"I was fond of the colonel but he was weak and had to go."[16]

And then there were the "war junky" correspondents, those for whom a quick race along the edge of death provided a thrill like nothing else in life. Take Anthony Lloyd of *The Times*. Before he became a war correspondent in Kosovo, Lloyd served in the Light Division where he recalled a fellow officer's words: "We want to know what killing is like." Lloyd added: "If you are a young man of combat age, frustrated by the tedium and meaninglessness of life in 20th century Europe, you may understand them. If not, you will probably think they come from a psychopath."

(But then what should we make of the views of Nato Supreme Allied Commander, General Wesley Clark on "the pure philosophy of the bayonet?" Or the young American pilot interviewed at the Nato base at Avieno in northern Italy before he went off to bomb Kosovo: "It's a lot of fun. I love my job…It's like playing a video game and riding a roller coaster at the same time.")[17]

Before he went to Kosovo, Lloyd wrote a book about his war correspondent experiences—*My War Gone By, I Miss It So*. "I was delighted with most of what the war offered me: chicks, kicks, cash and chaos; teenage punk dreams turned real and wreathed in gun smoke." And of his fellow war correspondents he writes: "…an affable clan of damaged children, a concentration of black sheep taking their chances in the casino of war…they could fight and fuck one another with the abandon of delinquents in care, but they also looked after one another, linked by altruistic camaraderie common to any pariah group. I fitted in just fine."[18]

All of them—sheep, frothers, veterans, war junkies—would, if they were honest, admit that they went to report the war burdened with certain preconceived ideas. They were not immune, for instance, to the propaganda sown by their governments as to what the war was all about. The war, said Tony Blair, was not just a military campaign. "It is a battle between Good and Evil; between civilisation and barbarity." Minister after minister appeared on television and radio to hammer the point that there had been years of talks with the Serb leader, Slobodan Milosevic and all the while the ethnic cleansing of the Kosovars continued. No decent community could stand by and do nothing. To stop this ethnic cleansing was a righteous cause.

Newspaper columnists picked up this grand theme. "There is a chance here to make the new world of the twenty-first century less dark and bloody than the world we are leaving behind," said Jonathan Freedland of the *Guardian* in a debate on 11 May. "This is a test for our generation, for time, for confidence in Europe and for the left. The test is before us—will we let it pass?"[19]

But war demands absolutes. If Nato's cause was righteous, just and honorable—if God was on Nato's side, as General Clark suggested—then the Serb cause must be evil, cowardly and dishonorable. There could be no glimmer of good on the Serb side, no innocent Serbs. Propaganda works best not with argument but images. The images that the British government called up to demonise the Serbs came from Britain's finest hour, the Second World War. The Serbs were Nazi thugs, intent on genocide. Milosevic was likened to Hitler. The words "Gestapo," "Auschwitz-style furnaces" and "Holocaust" were used.

When Tony Blair wrote a victory address for the *Sun* on June 4, he said, "The Kosovars will return to the scene of the nightmare they fled: to their burnt-out homes, to the corpses of their loved-ones. We will see for ourselves precisely what they fled: only now will we see the full horror of ethnic cleansing." Mark Lawson pointed out the following day that the carefully-floated ghost behind this prose was the liberation of the Nazi death camps in 1945.[20]

The propaganda worked. It usually does. It infected the normally level-headed Clare Short, International Development Secretary, who declared that in this instance even pacifists were fascists. "Blair's Babes Bay for Blood," wrote author Fay Weldon. "White feathers are back in fashion."[21] Robert Fisk wrote, "In just a few short sound bites we are now bestialising a whole people."

The simplest way to bestialise the enemy is the atrocity story. There are, of course, atrocities in every war and they are not the monopoly of one side, as witness what happened at My Lai in Vietnam. (By one of those strange coincidences which war produces, the official American apologist for My Lai was none other than General Wesley Clark.) The pressure on the media in Nato countries to publish atrocity stories from Kosovo was intense. Nato needed evidence of ethnic cleansing and Serbian atrocity to convince the alliance of the moral rectitude of its humanitarian war and each ghastly murder, rape, act of pillage or arson that could be attributed to the Serbs helped to demonise them. The trouble was that although many atrocity stories were true, others were not. They were Kosovar propaganda eagerly disseminated by alliance politicians.

Early in the war the British Foreign Secretary Robin Cook announced to the press that Serb forces in the village of Goden had brutally executed twenty Albanian schoolteachers in front of their pupils. According to some European papers the Serbs had in fact decapitated the schoolteachers. Atrocity stories are notoriously difficult to confirm because in most cases the eyewitnesses are also the victims and therefore often no longer around to testify. But Cook was convinced that this atrocity had taken place—until the Serbs pointed out that Goden had a population of 200, which, allowing for say 60 schoolchildren would have given it the highest pupil/teacher ratio in the world. The story was false.

One correspondent who took the trouble to check out an alleged Serbian atrocity story found that Cook then put his own spin on the reporter's facts. The Serb authorities escorted Julian Manyon to the

Kosovar village of Korisa the day after Nato had bombed it, killing some 80 Albanian refugees.

Nato's first response had been to suggest that the refugees had been killed by Serb artillery fire. Then Jamie Shea changed his tune and admitted that Nato had indeed attacked the village because it was a "legitimate military target." It housed a Yugoslav army command post. (Pentagon briefers even showed a video of a laser-guided weapon blasting the "army command post.") If any Albanians had been killed then it was because the Serbs had used them as "human shields." Shea urged Manyon and other western correspondents to "break free of their minders" when they reached Korisa and "do a thorough investigation."

Manyon, a respected journalist with long experience, did just that. "I picked my way through the pathetic wreckage of the refugee encampment, peering into and behind two smashed barns and a damaged car-repair shop but, regrettably, found not the slighest sign that a military command post had been there at the time of the attack." As for the "human shields," Albanian survivors told him that after weeks hiding in the hills, they had been told by Serb policemen to return to their village. They were placed at one end of the village under the guard of about five policemen pending, they were told, a decision as to where they should live. "We saw no evidence to suggest that they had been positioned to protect any particular military target. Sadly, it seems more likely that Nato simply mistook the mass of tractors for a Serb army concentration."

At his next press briefing, Mr. Cook picked up some of the detail from Manyon's report and that of other journalists. "It was the Serb forces that took the refugees off that hillside. It was the Serb forces that made them…assemble between those two courtyards." But then Mr. Cook added his own spin—"It was the Serb forces that concentrated them near the command post." The fact that the war correspondents at the scene had come to the opposite conclusion was not mentioned.[22]

The truth—as Nato itself admitted—was that Nato not only bombed civilian targets accidentally but that it also bombed them deliberately. In April, Kenneth Bacon, revealing the Nato bombing of electricity transformers in Belgrade, "a new class of targets", agreed the aim was to force the Serbs "to put pressure on their leadership to end this". In May, General Michael Short, in charge of targeting policy, told the *International Herald Tribune*, "I think no power to your refrigerator, no gas to your stove, you can't get to work because the bridge is down—the bridge on which you hold your rock concerts and on which you all stood with targets on your heads—that needs to disappear at three in the morning." In June, Wesley Clark admitted to the BBC's Mark Urban that Nato's planes were targeting "phase 3" (civilian) targets without the approval of Nato's decision-making body, the North Atlantic Council of Ambassadors in Brussels. But most journalists still accepted Nato's line that civilian casualties were "mistakes".

Perhaps the most emotionally-charged atrocity story, one that surfaces in every war, is rape. Rape has occurred in every war in history. In many societies it has been considered, along with loot, to be the warrior's reward for victory. According to historian Joanna Bourke in *An Intimate History of Killing*, American instructors taught recruits rape and mutilation techniques and the fact that Marines were allowed to rape women was "an inducement to encourage Marines to volunteer for Vietnam".

But since individual rape stories in wartime have become so common as to lose their impact, propagandists in recent wars in the Balkans had to strive for new levels of horror. The Bosnians accused the Serbs of using rape as a way of polluting their ethnic identity and quoted Bosnian women as saying that their assailants had told them that they were raping them to impregnate them with a Serbian baby.

In Kosovo, the Kosovo Liberation Army (KLA) accused the Serbs of using rape as an instrument of terror by setting up "rape farms" (whatever they may be) and "rape camps"—a new version of concentration camps—where Serb soldiers raped Kosovar women. Correspondents who reported these accusations coined a phrase of their own, "systematic rape", without properly explaining what they meant by the term. If they meant that Serb soldiers who raped Kosovar women did so on orders from Serbian Army high command, then they produced no evidence for this.

But British newspapers printed these stories as fact, not allegations. The *Star* of April 21 said, "Serbs have established a sex hotel so their troops can take turns to rape young girls in comfort." A story by Matt Frei in the *Sunday Telegraph* of 18 April was headed, "Hundreds, perhaps thousands of women trying to reach Kosovo have been raped by Serb soldiers. Matt Frei in Albania hears the harrowing story of one girl's ordeal—and the evidence that rape has become part of the systematic oppression of the Kosovars."

Frei was careful in his story to say that he had been able to speak only to one rape victim but had heard "scores of accounts of women being dragged from their vehicles and tractors by Serbian soldiers." But most of the accounts turn out to have been from other refugees. Frei's main source for the rape camps is revealed in his first paragraph as none other than the Foreign Secretary, Robin Cook, who "confirmed Nato's *suspicion* that the Serbs had set up at least two rape camps inside Kosovo." (author's emphasis)

Mr Cook had said, "Young women are being separated from the refugee columns and forced to undergo systematic rape in an army camp." But his evidence for this again came from other refugees. Some readers believed it all. The Prime Minister's wife, Cherie Blair said, "I'm just horrified about the rape camps and the thought of using rape as a weapon of war."[23]

The correspondents then descended on countries bordering Kosovo to find a rape victim. There is a notorious story from previous wars that the way to do this is to shout at refugees, "Is there anyone here who's been raped and speaks English?" Humanitarian workers were furious at this media invasion and complained that one woman, raped by Serbian soldiers and then forced to leave her country, was traumatised all over again by a journalist pestering her for her story.

So what was the truth? Audrey Gillan of the *Guardian*, one of the few sceptical, level-headed correspondents in the field, said that among the rape victims arriving in Macedonia, "nobody spoke of anything like the camps the British Foreign Secretary referred to." And she reported that Benedicte Giaever, the co-ordinator for the OSCE's field office in Skopje, told her that there had been rape, but not systematic and not on a grand scale.

A senior OSCE source told Gillan that he suspected the KLA had been persuading people to talk in bigger numbers, to crank up the horror so that Nato might be persuaded to send in ground troops faster. Robin Cook's rape camp was an attempt to get the British public behind the bombing.

At the beginning of the war Nato had promised a swift, conclusive campaign. The overwhelming weight of the Nato air attack would quickly bring the Serbs to their knees. When this did not happen the correspondents in Brussels grew restless, and when on April 14 Nato bombed a convoy of Kosovar refugees—the very people Nato wanted to save—the alliance media strategy fell apart. The refugees were travelling in a line of tractors on their way to Albania when near Djacovica bombs from an American plane fell out of the sky and killed many of them (the exact number was unclear).

Shea later admitted that the first he heard of this was when he received a telephone call from a journalist in Belgrade who tipped him off that the Serbian authorities were arranging a facility trip to the area for Western correspondents to show them something important. But before Nato could co-ordinate its response, CNN had gruesome pictures of bodies and parts of bodies of people who were obviously civilians alongside the burnt-out shells of what were obviously tractors.

A stream of conflicting stories then emerged from Nato. Interviewed on National Public Radio in the United States, General Clark agreed that civilians had been killed at Djacovica but they had been shelled by the Serbs. Ken Bacon at the Pentagon said no civilians had been killed at all—only a military target had been hit. Then Nato said that civilians had been killed because the Serbs had used them as a human shield. Mark Laity of the BBC later explained his attitude. "I took the view right from early on that there was a propaganda war here and my judgment was that the Serbs were quite capable of deliberately misleading. We believed—and subsequent events proved beyond doubt—that the Serbs were killing a lot of Albanians deliberately. So if they killed Albanians and could blame it on Nato as well, it's kind of a double whammy."[24]

The next day Nato produced a tape for the correspondents at the Brussels press briefing. On it a pilot explained the trouble he had taken in order to make sure that the target he was about to bomb was not a civilian one. Nato allowed the correspondents to assume that this was the pilot who had actually bombed the convoy. By next day they knew it was not: Nato had fooled them.

With Nato paralysed by confusion, Prime Minister Blair and President Clinton acted to avert a propaganda disaster. Again one of Shea's contacts tipped him off. "An old Nato friend who had since moved to the National Security Council in Washington rang to tell me that he had just listened into a conversation between Clinton and Blair. He said. 'Your life's about to change.'"[25]

The next day Alastair Campbell, Blair's press secretary and advisor, arrived in Brussels and proceeded to reorganise Nato's media arm. Two meeting rooms were requisitioned, twenty-five staff brought into from just about every Nato country, the latest communications technology installed and, working to Campbell's blueprint, the MOC, Media Operations Centre or "Media Manipulation Centre", as some correspondents called it, swung into action.

In the comparatively short history of media management in

wartime there can have been no system so skilfully designed to win the propaganda war. Nothing was left to chance. The reporting of every correspondent writing about Kosovo was monitored and if necessary instantly rebutted. Nato's line on every likely aspect of the war was developed, polished and rehearsed. (Shea made a brigadier general, about to appear on television, rehearse his statement twice.) There was even a section of the MOC which spent its time dreaming up pithy phrases for Shea to insert into his briefings with the hope that they would appeal to the headline writers and to television producers looking for a good sound bite.

The goal was to reverse the propaganda advantage that Belgrade had gained through Nato's bombing of the convoy at Djacovica and regain the moral high ground. As Shea put it: "The evil here is not our mistake. The evil here is Milosevic." So on Campbell's advice, from then on whenever Nato made a mistake it did not deny it but put the ultimate blame on Milosevic. The dubious reasoning went that if Milosevic had not forced Nato to resort to bombing to bring him to heel, then Nato bombers would not have made mistakes and civilians would not have been killed. By the same sort of logic, Ho Chi Minh was responsible for the American atrocity at My Lai.

It was this insistence that Nato was to blame for nothing and everything was the fault of the evil Milosevic that was behind the British government's attack on those correspondents reporting the war from Belgrade, especially on John Simpson, the BBC's foreign affairs editor. How could the star war correspondent of a British institution like the BBC even bear to be in the capital of a country at war with his own and where such a "monstrous evil" existed? Clare Short suggested that if Simpson and his like had been around in the Second World War they would have reported, "Mr. Hitler criticised the bombing from his bunker today."

But Simpson, on his thirtieth war, was well able to defend himself. He said he found the notion that a reporter had an implicit obligation to put patriotism above his duty to report the truth "sad and depressing." He added, "Journalism is about telling people more, not less. There was no point in staying in Belgrade if we couldn't work properly, but we were free to say what we wanted to say. I said what I bloody well wanted, and I find it ludicrous and offensive to suggest that I was this glove-puppet for Milosevic."[26]

By the third week the bombing campaign had created the worst refugee crisis since the Second World War as one million refugees fled Kosovo into neighbouring countries. The combination of ethnic cleansing by the Serbs and bombing by Nato had turned a local crisis into an international disaster.

Nato remained upbeat about the military success of the campaign. The Serbian army was hurting, its tanks and artillery were being steadily destroyed. Or were they? While the war was on, Nato said that it had destroyed more than a quarter of the Yugoslav army's 300 tanks in Kosovo and a third of its 500 heavy guns. When the war was over and Nato was able to assess on the ground the effects of the bombing, it changed this to 93 tanks, 153 armoured personnel carriers, 300 other vehicles and 400 guns.[27]

The Serbs admitted to 13 tanks. *Jane's Defence Weekly* said that there was no proof for either figure and the truth probably lay somewhere in between. But Paul Beaver of *Jane's* said that he had spent ten days in Kosovo immediately after the end of the war and had travelled all over the province by road and air. "I saw one tank that had been destroyed, one that had been damaged and two damaged tank transporters."[28] The human cost, according to Belgrade, was 600 soldiers and police killed and 2,600 civilians. Nato suffered no casualties.

General Clark explained the discrepancy between Nato's figures during the war and afterwards by pointing out that at briefings he had always used the word "struck", not "destroyed" when referring to hits on Serbian targets. Few correspondents were prepared to explain why they had accepted Nato claims so uncritically. Mark Laity of the BBC did. "I made the judgement that battle damage assessment was more accurate this time. I was wrong. I mean, I just got it wrong."[29]

There were also major differences over "collateral damage"—an important matter to resolve because it went to the heart of whether Nato deliberately switched to bombing civilian targets when its campaign to "degrade" the Yugoslav army in Kosovo failed. Nato's position was that it had flown 10,000 strike sorties and there had been only 20 instances of collateral damage, a praiseworthy result in a campaign of this size. Belgrade said that, on the contrary, Nato bombers had hit 33 hospitals and 340 schools and this could not have been entirely accidental.

An American military analyst, Professor Anthony Cordesman, said after the war that there had actually been hundreds of instances of collateral damage, some of them admittedly minor, but that "lying with numbers doesn't really help Nato."[30] Robert Fisk said that the nature of some of the bomb attacks demolished Nato's claims that they were accidental. Instead it appeared that Nato had deliberately targeted civilians. "The first indication we had that something was really wrong came when a Harrier jet attacked a bridge at Grdulice when a train was approaching. Clark was to say later that the train's appearance that afternoon was a 'freakish coincidence'—the arrival of a passenger train on a main line apparently being 'freakish' to a Nato general, though most of us have seen trains on bridges before. Nato said that the rockets had already been released when the pilot saw the train.

"The passengers told a different story. They said that the first rockets hit a road bridge above the train and the falling concrete cut the electric cables which gave the locomotive its power. This appears to be what we see on the bit of film Nato released at the time. But the passengers said that the plane then hovered over a field for a few seconds—it was, of course, a British-made Harrier—then fired a second rocket into the train.

"There were many other equally disturbing incidents. At Varvarin, for example, American jets hit the narrow road bridge at midday—too narrow for any tank—and then, just when rescuers had emerged to help the maimed, [including the local priest] the planes returned to bomb the rescuers.

"Was Nato unwilling to risk the life of a single western soldier to save the Kosovo Albanians from the mass graves, so desperate to end the war that it turned on the civilians in the hope that it would break Milosevic (a man who cared precious little for his own civilians, let alone any others)? I still find it difficult to shake off this horrible suspicion. Yes, the Serb monsters were were evil beyond imagination. I saw the ethnic cleansing as it took place. I visited those mass graves. But was this an excuse for Nato to destroy so many innocent lives?"[31]

Alex Thomson, chief correspondent of Channel 4 News also took Nato to task. "If Jamie Shea says, 'It is not Nato's policy to target civilians', and Nato then deliberately reduces make-up ladies and cleaners at Belgrade's TV station to pink mist, I think there's a problem…"[32]

There was a bigger problem about the bombing of the TV station than Thomson imagined. Nato's stated reason for attacking the TV station was that as Milosevic's principal propaganda outlet it had a long record of inciting ethnic violence. But consider this. Two days before the bombing, the CNN team in Belgrade received a tip from its headquarters in Atlanta that the station was a target. The team immediately removed all its equipment from the building.

The next day the Serbian information minister Aleksander

Vucic received by fax an invitation to appear on the CNN TV chat show "Larry King Live". He would be interviewed in the Belgrade studios down the line from the United States. He agreed and a time was fixed for him to report to the studios. Since he was to go on air at 2.30A.M., CNN asked him to arrive at the make-up room at 2 A.M. At six minutes past two, the first Nato missile slammed right into that very make-up room incinerating the make-up woman. Fortunately for him, Vucic was not there—he was running late—otherwise he too, would have been killed. Was all this a coincidence, as CNN claims? Or was it an assassination plot inspired by one of the many American special operations outfits?

There were other mysteries about the bombing campaign which should have demanded more attention from the media. The bombing of the Chinese embassy—a mistake, said Nato—made headlines. But readers would have had to have looked very hard to discover that Nato had also hit the residence of the ambassador from India, a country which had earlier declared that Nato's bombing campaign was against international law.

In its protest, the Indian government said, "This [attack] has happened despite the addresses of the Indian embassy having been provided to the US government on request of the latter soon after the bombing of the Chinese embassy in Belgrade."

The response from General Mike Jackson when ordered by General Clark to stop the Russians from occupying Pristina airport—"I'm not going to start the Third World War"—made headlines. But where were the headlines about a much more likely spark for a Third World War—the secret response of Russia's military establishment to Nato's bombing campaign?

Code-named "West-99", this was an enormous series of military exercises simulating Russia's reponse to a theoretical Nato invasion. And it involved Russian strategic bombers flying in the last days of June within striking distance of the United States.[33]

Brian Whitmore, of the *Moscow Times*, reported a rise of hatred for America in Russia. He said that prior to the bombing a large majority of Russians were favourably disposed toward the United States. "After the bombing began polls showed just 14 per cent of the population favourable and 72 per cent hostile."[34]

The ethnic cleansing of the Kosovars made the front pages of most of the newspapers and occupied many hours of television. When the war ended and the Serb army withdrew from Kosovo, the subsequent ethnic cleansing of the Kosovar Serbs was largely relegated to the inside pages and seldom mentioned on television.

The words "ethnic cleansing" were rarely used.

The *Guardian* carried a Reuters report from Pristina on August 12, quoting the UNHCR as saying that the capital's population had shrunk to under 2,000 from an estimated 40,000 a few months earlier. It said that the Serbs had been forced to flee by ethnic Albanian gangs employing tactics similar to those used by the Serbs earlier in the year. "Ethnic cleansing" was not mentioned, the headline was simply "Pristina's Serbs flee in thousands" and the story was buried on page 15.

Six days later the *Guardian* returned to the subject with a report from its own correspondent, Chris Bird, with details of the killing of Serbs, including an elderly woman murdered in her home, but again the words "ethnic cleansing" were not used. A Serb interviewed by Bird got it right: "We've been satanised in the West so no one is paying attention to what is happening here."

The *Guardian* redeemed itself that same day on its Comment page when it gave Jonathan Eyal, director of studies at the Royal United Services Institute in London, two columns to sum up the outcome of the war and used the headline: "Kosovo spews new refugees: Nato fought to stop ethnic cleansing. It is happening again." Eyal said that the murder of Serbs was a daily event and the province was now almost ethnically "pure." "It is a fact that the war which began as a crusade against ethnic cleansing is about to conclude with precisely that outcome." The BBC added on October 18 that 240,000 Serbs and others had been driven out of Kosovo.[35]

Why did the war end when it did? If you believe Nato or any of the alliance governments it ended because the bombing campaign had succeeded. The high-tech weapons performed largely as advertised and Milosevic and the Serb people no longer had the stomach to see their country being destroyed around them. If you believe some of the correspondents, the war ended because during peace talks on June 3 the Russians urged Milosevic to do a deal, threatening to cut gas supplies to Serbia.

It took the BBC's documentary division to reveal why Russia, which had steadfastly supported their fellow Slavs throughout the war, brought this pressure to bear on Serbia. The second BBC programme on Kosovo called "An Audit of War" broadcast on October 18 said, "Shortly after Serbia accepted the peace deal the International Monetary Fund provided Russia with nearly three billion pounds to pay off the interest on its foreign debts."[36]

This leaves us with the most intriguing question of all—what was the war really all about? The *Spectator* doubted if it was actually about the ethnic cleansing of the Kosovars. "In the three years leading up to 25 March 1999, between two and three thousand people had died in Yugoslavia's latest ethnic conflict," wrote Mark Steyn, the magazine's American correspondent. "Not a pretty sight. But let's say it was the upper number, 3,000. That still gives it a lower murder rate per capita than New Orleans or New York …Washington, Oakland, Houston, Las Vegas, Dallas.

"Sitting in Belgrade browsing through the homicide statistics Slobo must have thought that the Americans of all people would appreciate how some societies can tolerate a level of slaughter others might find excessive." But, said Steyn, Milosevic failed to understand a crucial distinction—if you kill people in drive-by shootings, liquor store hold-ups and child custody disputes, that was the sign of healthy mature democracy. But if you killed people because of an ongoing blood feud rooted in centuries of history, that was barbaric.[37]

Perhaps President Clinton gave the game away when early into the bombing campaign he tried to ease America's doubts. "Had we not acted," he said, "the Serb offensive would have been carried out with impunity." The bombing, therefore, was to punish the Serbs. Punishment is an established part of U.S. foreign policy. Gary Sick, who was then in charge of Gulf policy at the National Security Council, said after Iran took American hostages in Teheran in 1979, "There was a strong view…that Iran should be punished from all sides."

But what was Serbia being punished for? "For the humiliation we suffered at their hands in Bosnia," according to Robert Fisk.[38] "For daring to resist the project of establishing the West's hegemony" said the celebrated Russian dissident Alexander Zinoviev in *Le Monde*.

"Using humanitarian arguments as a mere pretext, and backed by an immense media machine, the Western powers are trying to force the creation of a single system of global governance to suit their own interests," Zinoviev said.

An immense media machine? Zinoviev said that the situation in the Balkans had been "totally falsified" by the Western mass media to an extent which Goebbels would never have dreamed possible. Nato's propaganda was even worse than old Soviet propaganda because there was no serious opposition to it.[39]

It is certainly true that for the most part the anti-war lobby in the West had trouble being heard. Columnist Jeremy Hardy writing in the *Guardian* said that the anti-war movement did what it could

518

but never really believed that an ashen-faced General Clark would tell Nato, "Oh my God, they're holding a benefit at the Hackney Empire."[40]

Although about a third of the British people were against the war, their meetings and demonstrations received little coverage as did protests abroad. "One hundred thousand people in the streets of Rome including 182 members of the Italian parliament," wrote John Pilger in the *Guardian*. "Thousands in Greece and Germany, protests taking place every night in colleges and town halls across Britain. Almost none of it is reported." [41]

"We were only mentioned when being abused by Blairite MPs and liberal columnists," said Hardy. Letters to the editors complained that citizens who were against the war had no means of dissenting through the democratic process. Those few MPs who opposed the bombing were not permitted to test the feeling of either the parliamentary Labour Party or Parliament through votes.

As Professor Vic Allen, of Keighley, West Yorkshire wrote, "Is it not gratuitous to condemn Milosevic for acting as a dictator when, in Britain, a cabal of politicians can implicate all of us in an unwarranted act of carnage without our consent."[42]

And, almost as if part of this "carnage without our consent," assertive dogmatic journalism with no room for Tennyson's "honest doubt," no chance for the readers or viewers to make up their own minds, brought about a situation where even to express the slightest reservation about the latest atrocity story, or to show the slightest disagreement with government policy in Kosovo, was regarded as little short of treason.

Nevertheless, when the war ended those who had supported it it called for those who had opposed it to apologise. "Here is mine," wrote Jeremy Hardy, speaking for many. "I am sorry that children have been blown apart in my name in order that Nato could assert its ascendancy. And I am sorry that we couldn't stop it, but I never thought we stood much chance. Those who have wagged flags for the most powerful war machine in history may feel reflected glory but I'd say they placed their bets quite safely...For the most part those of us who opposed the war were ignored, which is not surprising since we don't have an army."[43]

In the flush of victory few wanted to know the cost in either human or financial terms. The BBC documentary, "Audit of the War", estimated that the war had cost £31.6 billion and had turned Yugoslavia into the poorest country in Europe, one that if it receives no outside help will take at least 40 years to rebuild itself. Nato's bombing of the country's petro-chemical industries threatened to pollute the whole area. Water supplies for up to ten million people were at risk. A United Nations team recommended urgent humanitarian relief to prevent disaster. No one was prepared to estimate how long Nato's K-FOR (45,000 strong) would be deployed in Kosovo but a lengthy stay could cost £6 billion to £14 billion.

On the human front, only Julian Manyon made the point that the war had been the third major disaster for the Serbs this century. Fighting against Germany in the First World War resulted in the deaths of almost a million people, about a fifth of the population. In the Second World War the people of Belgrade demanded the repudiation of a pact with Hitler which would have allowed the Germans to use Yugoslavia as a staging area for their attack on Greece. "Without regard for the German subjugation of the rest of continental Europe, the crowds chanted 'Bolje rat nego pakt'—better war than pact—and 'Bolje grob nego rob'—better grave than slave." Hitler's answer was similar to Nato's—to bomb Belgrade, reducing much of the city to ruins—and then send in his armies. Manyon quoted the Serb historian Dusan Batakovic: "The idea of cost/benefit analysis is unknown to Serbs."[44]

Reporter Edward Stourton, interviewing General Dan Leaf, commander of the U.S. Air Force 31st Fighter Wing in the BBC documentary "How the War Was Spun" suggested that Nato, as well as doing follow-up studies in Kosovo on its accuracy when bombing military targets, could also trace those people who were in the refugee convoy which Nato bombed at Djacovica and find out what had really happened. Leaf showed little enthusiasm for the idea. "If Milosevic hasn't killed them all, perhaps…If we could find out who was in the convoy and I don't know if there has ever been a determination who these civilians were."[45]

But the BBC found and interviewed the surviving members of one Kosovar family, the Bajramis (an elderly woman, her two adult sons and her daughter-in-law) who had been in the convoy heading for the border with Albania. Sokol Bajrami, one of the sons, said there were no Serb police where his tractor was but "I can't say what was at the end of the convoy." He continued, "When the first two bombs fell, my wife fell from the powerful blast on to the ground. I lost my hand from the blast. I saw it flying off. Holding my arm I managed to stop the tractor and get into the field."

His sister-in-law Xheverja Bajrami said, "My husband called out to his brother then the bomb fell hitting my husband. The tractor was pushed aside and I saw my husband die." The mother, Rukhmani

Bajrami, added, "To see one son die and the other wounded —I can only say that I would rather die than see such days again."[46]

When the bombing ended and the war correspondents were at last able to enter Kosovo, high on their agenda was to find mass graves. There was no doubt that the Serbs had killed Kosovars during the war. But were there "mass" killings, "mass" executions, "mass" graves? And if so, were they part of a "systematic" campaign? Ben Ward, a researcher for Human Rights Watch, had been cautious during the war. "There doesn't appear to be anything to support allegations of mass killings. It is generally paramilitaries who are responsible. It doesn't seem organised. There appear to be individual acts of sadism rather than anything else. There seems not to be a policy or instruction, but that isn't to say that people have not been given the latitude to kill. However, I don't think at this stage we have anything that adds up to the systematic killing of civilians."[47]

Audrey Gillan had written during the war: "What we have here is a situation where Western journalists accept details without question. Almost every day, the world's media, jostling for stories in Macedonia, strain to find figures that may well not exist." Gillan became determined to find the evidence and she worked very hard to do so. She admitted to making a little girl cry "in order to try to prove to myself that there was truth in her story" that she had been wounded by the Serb bullet that killed her grandmother.

But in the end she failed. "Watching the television images and listening to the newscasters thunder about further reports of Serb massacres and of genocide, I feel uneasy about saying that they have very little to go on. Yet almost every journalist I spoke to privately in Macedonia felt the same way. The story being seen at home is different from the one that appeared to be happening on the ground." Gillan wrote the story as she saw it but it was not used in the *Guardian*. She published it instead in the *London Review of Books*.[48]

The thousands of media people searching for mass killings caused unhappy reflection among some correspondents. "The flood of atrocity stories has caused reporters based in the region to dub themselves 'mass graves correspondents'," wrote Chris Bird, Belgrade-based correspondent of the *Guardian*. "An ethnic Albanian man approached us in the street with a hint of the pornographer. 'Il y a un massacre pas loin d'ici,' he said in hushed French. When we looked unimpressed, he added urgently, 'Vingt cadavres sans têtes'."[49]

Dr. Mark Almond, a Balkans expert at Oxford University, had an explanation for this media obsession with massacres. He said

Nato's propaganda effort had a twofold motive. First, because it launched its air campaign without making proper provision to protect the very people it sought to liberate, it needed to cover its dereliction by pushing hard the line of injustice and atrocities.

"Next, self-righteous people very often feel that it's not a sin for them to tell untruths because it's in a good cause...I suspect that people within Nato say that 'because there are no pictures of what's really going on in Kosovo, we have to tell people.' And the temptation is to say, 'We know [the Serbs] are awful, we know they've been awful in the past, so they must be awful now, although we don't know exactly what they're doing, so let's reach into the drawer of atrocities from previous wars and find the worst we possibly can.'"[50]

The American government decided that 500,000 Kosovar Albanians missing, feared dead, was an impressive figure and this was the one issued by the State department on April 19. The U.S. defence secretary, William Cohen, reduced this on May 16 to 100,000. "We've now seen about one hundred thousand military-aged men missing," he told CBS News.[51] "They may have been murdered." The British government said on June 17 that the Serbs had killed 10,000 ethnic Albanians in Kosovo in more than 100 massacres and this is the figure Robin Cook insisted in November was still correct.

But before the western media lost interest, no one had been able to uncover evidence to justify even this greatly reduced estimate. A German doctor who had spent the war in a refugee camp in Macedonia told *Die Welt*: "It was very surprising that a large number of journalists either could not or would not perceive that the majority of people in refugee camps were men of military age. It was always represented as if there were no men in these camps at all. Even when the journalists were told this they refused to take account of it." [52]

On July 9, United Nations officials announced that they were investigating what could be a mass grave near the village of Ljubenic in the west of Kosovo that could contain 350 bodies. This figure appeared in newspapers around the world but when the true figure turned out to be five it was hard to find a newspaper that even mentioned it. Other sites were being examined. But the total remained well short of 10,000.

The *Mirror* had offered an explanation. On July 7, Don Mackay reported from the Trepca copper mine in Kosovo. Mackay interviewed a former mine worker, ethnic Albanian Hakif Isufi, who told him he had seen dozens of trucks pull into the mine on the night of June 4. He said he had seen Serb soldiers unloading heavy bundles from the trucks and soon afterwards he heard the noise of the mine furnaces being started. Although Hakif said he could not make out what the bundles were, Mackay had no hesitation in deciding for him: "What Hakif saw was one of the most despicable acts of Slobodan Milosevic's war—the mass dumping of executed corpses in a desperate bid to hide the evidence. War crimes investigators fear that up to 1,000 bodies were incinerated in the Auschwitz-style furnances of the mine with its sprawling maze of deep shafts and tunnels."

Although Hakif had not told Mackay that the bundles were bodies, althought there was no evidence that even if they were bodies they were then burned, and the 1,000 figure was no more than a "fear" of unnamed war crimes investigators, the *Mirror* published the story under the headline "1,000 CORPSES DESTROYED IN MINE FURNACES".[53] But after the war a long investigation of the mine conducted by the UN War Crimes Tribunal found no evidence that any such event had ever taken place.[54]

So what is the final count likely to be? The chief Spanish inspector Juan Lopez Palafox said that Nato had told his team of forensic scientists to be ready to perform more than 2,000 autopsies. "The result is very different," he said in late October. "We only found a hundred and eighty-seven cadavers and now we are going to return to Spain."[55]

With twenty forensic teams in Kosovo throughout the summer, the total number of bodies exhumed by early November was 2,108. But both US State Department officials and UN investigators warned that some of the dead in graves already examined were fighters of the Kosovo Liberation Army, or may have died ordinary deaths. "EARLY COUNT HINTS AT FEWER KOSOVO DEATHS" said the *New York Times* on November 11.

When John Laughland had first suggested in the *Spectator* on October 30, 1999 that there was no evidence of mass graves in Kosovo and that the number of Albanians killed by Serbs had been inflated by Nato propaganda, there was uproar. But Laughland stood by his story. He replied: "The pattern which is emerging is not so much of a systematic attack on the Albanian population as such—Nato's *casus belli*—but rather of a low-level civil war with casualties on both sides, a situation greatly aggravated by Nato's attacks. The fighting was of an utterly different scale from that in either Bosnia or Croatia." He then quoted from a German Foreign Ministry report which totally demolishes the reasons Nato gave for going to war. "An explicit political persecution of the Albanian population cannot be established even in Kosovo…The actions of the [Serb] security forces are not directed against Kosovo Albanians as an ethnically defined group but instead against military opponents and their real or supposed supporters."[56]

The fact is that many Kosovars simply lied about "massacres" they said they had witnessed. At the height of the conflict, the story of a teenage Kosovar, Rajmonda, was beamed around the world. After Serbs had killed her sister, Rajmonda told CBC-TV, she had started killing Serbs indiscriminately to exact her revenge. When the war was over, Rajmonda admitted it was all a lie. A friend of her family excused her. "If this small lie...made some kind of impact on what Western countries did in Kosovo, then it's worth it."[57]

Nato may even have inflated its so-called victory. During the war there had been much debate about the Rambouillet Accords, which set out Nato's demands on Yugoslavia if she was to avoid being attacked. What the Accords did and did not say, set two *Guardian* journalists at each other's throats. John Pilger said in his column that Nato had demanded that, "The economy of Kosovo shall function in accordance with free-market principles" and that another clause read, "Nato personnel shall enjoy, together with their vehicles, vessels, aircraft, and equipment, free and unrestricted passage and unimpeded access throughout the Federal Republic of Yugoslavia."[58]

Commenting on these clauses in the next day's *Guardian*, its diplomatic editor, Ian Black, said that the first clause would be "damning proof that Nato really is the military arm of unreconstructed international vampire capitalism. But that sentence does not exist." Of the second he wrote: "Is Pilger seriously suggesting that Nato planned to occupy all Yugoslavia and nobody noticed except him?"[59]

When Pilger wrote to the *Guardian* to complain about the attack on him, Black conceded that the Accords did indeed contain the reference to a free-market economy and that Pilger's quotation of the clause about unimpeded access for Nato throughout all Yugoslavia was accurate. But he continued to maintain that the document did not outline the military occupation of all Yugoslavia. Pressed by Kenny Coyle of *The Morning Star* Black refused to confirm or deny whether he had read the full text of the Accords.[60]

When the war ended, Pilger returned to the Accords and pointed out that in the peace agreement that ended the war, this condition about unimpeded access had disappeared, along with a call for a Kosovar plebiscite and separation of Kosovo from Yugoslavia.[61] Others agreed. "The main Serb objective in this war was to eliminate

The KLA and not lose Kosovo," wrote Lee Brimmicombe-Wood, of Godalming, Surrey, in a letter to the *Guardian* on June 9. "By this criteria, Serbia has wrung a victory, however Pyrrhic."

The lies, manipulation, news management, propaganda, spin, distortion, omission, slant and gullibility of the coverage of this war, so soon after the media debacle in the Gulf, has brought war correspondents to crisis point in their short history. Their role has never been more insecure. What are war correspondents for? What is expected of them? Who still believes them? There was a U.S. Congressional fact-finding mission to Yugoslavia on April 18–21 because some congressmen felt that they could not trust the media or the Administration to tell them what was really happening.

"Congress had until this mission been virtually totally reliant on the Administration's view of events and on the media, which had been greatly influenced by the only real source of information and opinion available—the Administration," the mission reported. "The enormous confusion which has taken place due to media manipulation on all sides has only contributed to the blood lust which—if it is the only basis for decision making—could lead to a much wider and longer war."[62]

The sad truth is that in the new millennium, government propaganda prepares its citizens for war so skilfully that it is likely that they do not want truthful, objective and balanced reporting that good war correspondents once did their best to provide.

Studies carried out after the Gulf War by Dr. David E. Morrison, of the University of Leeds, showed that although most people did not think that war correspondents should suspend impartiality in wartime, a substantial minority thought that the reporting should always emphasise the British side. And if there were a British mistake that caused the war to go badly, more than half those questioned for the study felt that this mistake should never be reported, or only after the war was over.

Further, in the Gulf War, where reporting was dominated by television as in no other war, most British—and, presumably, American—viewers were quite content with the reporting and considered it to be accurate and fair. If viewers had any complaint at all, it was that TV stations devoted too much time to the war ("squeezed it for everything it was worth") and that this disrupted their favourite programmes. There was little demand for television to show "the true face of battle," many viewers saying that images of bomb victims and battle casualties would be "too upsetting."[63]

## Chapter Twenty-one

# No More Heroes
# March–April, 2003

"This is a f——ing war, asshole. No more questions for you. Why don't you just go home."
>—Pentagon official to war correspondent at Coalition
>Central Command headquarters, Qatar

"Despite scouring two national newspapers every day, listening to the radio, surfing the web and watching the TV news, I have absolutely no clue how the war is going."
>—Letter to the editor, *The Guardian*, London

———

The United States considered Iraq to be unfinished business. Washington's failure—for whatever reason—to drive on to Baghdad in the last days of the Gulf War in 1991 and unseat Saddam Hussein, rankled and especially so with President George W. Bush and his neo-Conservative administration. Within days of the devastating terrorist attack on the World Trade Center on September 11, 2001, the more hawkish of Bush's advisers were pressing for an immediate response, an awe-inspiring display of American military might. Afghanistan was the logical first target since its Taliban government harboured the alleged instigator of the 9/11 attack, Osama bin Laden. But even as the bombing of Afghanistan got under way, the Pentagon was preparing for war on Iraq—to topple Saddam Hussein and impose a "regime change" on the country.

The argument went: Saddam Hussein is an evil dictator; he is rich, aggressive and repressive; he organised the invasion and annexation of a member state of the UN (Kuwait) and ruthlessly suppresses his own people; he is working hard to acquire weapons of mass destruction and when he does, he will be prepared to use them; he has ignored all efforts by the international community to restrain him; the only method he understands is force so we are therefore justified in a pre-emptive strike. (Although, when the war ended it appeared that Saddam Hussein had nothing that warranted pre-empting.) Further, a regime change in Iraq could mean the beginning of a new era in the Middle East. Other repressive regimes in the region would see what happened to Iraq and learn the lesson. The removal of Israel's main enemy in the region would help resolve the Israel-Palestine conflict.

Did Iraq's huge oil wealth not play a part in America's decision to invade? Some sectors of the Bush administration denied this. Others argued that Iraq's oil riches were definitely a factor and that Washington should admit this and defend it. Philip Bobbitt, holder of the Walker Centennial Chair in Law at the University of Texas, summed it up: "It is only when great powers can find an intersection between their own strategic interests—which include their economic interests and the material well-being of their peoples—and humanitarian and human rights concerns, that these states will act with any chance of success in addressing these concerns."[1]

The anti-war lobby had several explanations for the U.S. determination to invade. One held that the invasion of Iraq was an excuse to set up a base there in order to gain control of cheap Middle Eastern oil reserves. The United States had risen to number one in the world on cheap fossil fuel and if it were to maintain that position, it had to ensure a guaranteed supply of cheap fossil fuel for at least the rest of this century. Another was that to deter any nation from ever challenging the United States, America had from time to time to frighten the rest of the world with a display of unmatchable military might. Iraq was a convenient target for such a display.

Historians will argue over the causes of the war for years to come. Whatever the reasons were, on March 20, 2003, a "Coalition of the Willing" consisting mainly of the United States, Britain, Australia and Spain, went ahead with plans to invade Iraq— and so the war began.

The build-up to war had taken so long and the issues had been so extensively debated that the media was determined that this would be the most thoroughly reported war of modern times. Nearly one thousand media personnel—on the ground, in the air and at sea— would miss nothing. It would be the biggest news-gathering operation in the history of television. Money would be no object—CNN alone would have a budget of $35 million to enable it to beat its bitter rival Fox News in the ratings battle. British TV-news networks would extend their budgets by a combined £22 million. All the channels would show everything live, a real-time war, 24 hours a day. Expectations were high, especially because, since Afghanistan, the arrival on the scene of Arab TV networks like al-Jazeera introduced the dazzling possibility of being able to show both sides of a war at once— a historical first. However, it did not work out like that.

A radical American plan for managing wartime media perpetuated an illusion that the Iraq war was a triumph for modern media and its technology. In reality, it was an overwhelming victory for the military and its propagandists. The principal architect of the American media plan was Bryan Whitman, Deputy Assistant Secretary of Defence. Its essence can be summed up in four points: 1. Emphasize the dangers posed by the Iraqi regime; 2. Dismiss and discredit those who cast doubt on these dangers; 3. Do not get involved in appeals to logic but instead appeal to the public's hearts and minds, especially hearts; 4. Drive home the message to the public: "Trust us. We know more than we can tell you." Whitman convinced his Pentagon bosses that this plan could not only shape opinion in the United States but all over the western world. He was proved right.

A lot of thought went into how the media would be managed once the war began. There had to be at least an appearance of openness and truthfulness. Briefings by officers trained to deal with the media would be held at Central Command headquarters. These briefings would give journalists an overall view of the war's progress, "the big picture", where everything would be put into context. Yet while this would be easy to control, it would lack visual appeal. What the networks needed was compelling action footage and because of the 24-hour news cycle, they would need a lot of it. The idea of several hundred TV crews wandering around the battlefield looking for action was a military nightmare. The Pentagon could impose the "pool" system whereby it would escort a small number of war correspondents to the front and they would file "pooled reports" for the rest of the media. But the media so hated this in the first Gulf War that John R. MacArthur wrote in his account of censorship, *Second Front*: "It was difficult to find anyone who didn't ... count Desert Storm a devastating and immoral victory for military censorship and a crushing defeat for the press and the First Amendment."

In Afghanistan, the balance had moved even further in favour of the military because of the Coalition's reliance on air power (impossible for the media to cover) and special operations (off limits for the media) until even the few pools that were arranged were abandoned. In one instance, when US forces were hit by "friendly fire", journalists stationed in a nearby marine base were locked in a warehouse so that they could not report it. Later, journalists received a press release from public affairs officers, giving an account of what had occurred. The release had been compiled at Central Command in Tampa, Florida. Similarly, when American Special Forces raided the headquarters of Taliban leader Mullah Omar in the middle of the night, the only coverage they allowed was their own. The raid was a disaster, the official account a whitewash, and the whole charade exposed by Seymour Hersh in *New Yorker* magazine on November 12, 2002. It was reporting like this that inspired Whitman to suggest that the Pentagon's approach to the media needed reappraising.

Since the end of the Cold War, the United States had developed methods of warfare that reduced the number of American military casualties. Then, in 1999, NATO's first war—the 78-day bombing campaign against Yugoslavia—was won by air power alone, employing the highest proportion of precision weaponry ever used in an air operation and without *any* loss of life in combat operations on NATO's side—an event unprecedented in the history of warfare.[2] This success had an unexpected side effect—with few or no British and American casualties to report, the western media began to concentrate on enemy casualties, especially civilian. The military regarded this as a dangerous development because it could erode public support for a war.

Slowly, and then with a rush, reports began to appear of civilian casualties from American bombing in Afghanistan. "More than 300 people killed in one night," wrote Richard Lloyd Parry of the *Independent*. "In a family of 40 only a small boy and his grandmother survived." In the *Daily Mirror*, John Pilger wrote, "Out of sight of television cameras, at least 3,767 civilians were killed by US bombs between October 7 and December 10, an average of 62 innocent deaths a day, according to a study carried out at the University of New Hampshire in the US. This is now estimated to have passed 5,000 civilians deaths: almost double the number killed on September 11."[3]

So the Pentagon sought a media strategy that would turn attention back to the military's role in the war, especially the part played by ordinary American service men and women. This would require getting war correspondents "on side". But every system that the Pentagon had tried for managing the media in wartime before now had aroused the media's ire precisely because it felt it was being *managed*. What if, instead of managing the media, the Pentagon *incorporated* the media into the national war effort—enlisting its vast resources in the service of the country as it had done in the Second World War.

It was Whitman who came up with the idea of "embedding" where correspondents would be placed with military units in the field from where they would transmit "products" or information compiled at the Pentagon, foreign capitals and "in theatre", with the assistance of mobile press pools, combined information press centres (CIPCs) and sub-CIPCs. Public Affairs Officers (PAOs) from the Pentagon would scan all the media—print, electronic, domestic and international—all the while blending 24-hour news channels, nightly news shows and news-magazine formats with entertainment companies. This would provide comprehensive coverage of the war while giving the impression that the news was coming directly from amidst the troops in the field: "the best representatives to convey America's intentions and capabilities."[4]

It was a comprehensive and cleverly devised plan but one in which—although not many realised it until it was too late—the traditional war correspondent had been by-passed.

In practice, the Pentagon would offer media organisations, both American and foreign, the opportunity of placing a correspondent inside a specified military unit for the duration of the war. As Whitman himself described it, the ideal "embed" would receive basic training with his or her unit and then follow it from load-out to deployment through combat to "the march on whatever capital we happen to march on", to the return trip home and the victory parade. "This could take two weeks, two months, two years," he warned. And if reporters left a unit, there was no guarantee they could return or even join another unit—"embedding is for life". Embeds would have an honorary officer's rank and could wear uniform if they so chose. Their unit would provide them with accommodation, transport, food, lodging and protection. They could accompany troops into battle and write what they liked as long as it did not reveal information of value to the enemy.

This is remarkably similar to the arrangements the British army made for six war correspondents in the First World War (see Chapter 5). They were embedded with the British Expeditionary Force in France, given the honorary rank of captain, wore uniform, were assigned orderlies, chauffeurs and conducting officers, shown what the general staff felt they should see, then allowed to write about it and submit it to the censors who sent it to the War Office in London which then passed the despatches on to the various newspapers. At the end of the war all six correspondents were given Knighthoods for services rendered. The system worked brilliantly for the military but was a disaster for journalism—"There was no more discreditable period in the history of journalism than the four years of the Great War," wrote historian Arthur Ponsonby in 1928. The problem was set out by one of the correspondents, Sir Philip Gibbs, in 1923: "We identified ourselves absolutely with the Armies in the field ... We wiped out of our minds all thought of personal scoops and all temptation to write one word which would make the task of officers and men more difficult or dangerous. There was no need of censorship of our despatches. We were our own censors."[5]

Did the same thing happen in Iraq? No matter how determined embedded correspondents may have been to maintain their distance and objectivity, once the war had started, almost without exception, they soon lost all distinction between soldier and correspondent and began to use the pronoun "we" in their reports. "We are coming under fire ...we are advancing ... we can see." Clive Myrie of the BBC said an embedded correspondent could feel under pressure in a tight situation to help his unit out. "We were in a ditch under fire and this guy says, 'Make yourself useful.' This guy was throwing flares at me and I'm throwing them at a guy who's got to light them and who's sending them into the sky and I'm thinking what am I doing here?"[6]

I was able to find only two instances of embedded correspondents who reported critically on the behaviour of US troops they were embedded with and which went against the official account of what had occurred. On March 31, US soldiers opened fire on a civilian van, which had failed to stop at a checkpoint, and killed seven Iraqi women and children. US officials said that the driver of the car failed to stop after warning shots and that troops had fired at the passenger cabin as "a last resort". But William Branigin of the *Washington Post*, embedded with the Third Infantry, witnessed the shooting and reported that no warning shots were fired and that ten rather than seven people were killed.

Mark Franchetti, of the London *Sunday Times*, embedded with a US Marines brigade, wrote about how "shell-shocked young American soldiers had killed at least 12 civilians trying to flee from

Nassiriya. Franchetti did not spare his readers: "Down the road, a little girl no older than five and dressed in a pretty orange and gold dress, lay dead in a ditch next to the body of a man who may have been her father. Half his head was missing. Nearby, in a battered old Volga, peppered with ammunition holes, an Iraqi woman, perhaps the girl's mother, was dead, slumped in the back seat. A father, baby girl and boy lay in a shallow grave ... As I walked away, Lieutenant Matt Martin, whose third child, Isabella, was born while he was on board ship en route to the Gulf, appeared beside me. 'Did you see all that?' he asked, his eyes filled with tears. 'Did you see that little baby girl? I carried her body and buried it as best I could. It really gets to me to see children being killed like this. But we had no choice.'" Franchetti said Martin's distress was in contrast to the bitter satisfaction of some of his fellow marines as they surveyed the scene. 'The Iraqis are sick people,' said Corporal Ryan Dupre, 'and we are the chemotherapy.'[7] One wonders whether Branigin or Franchetti will be welcomed by the military as embeds in another war.

For the rest of the embeds, the considered conclusion of that old-fashioned correspondent, Sydney H. Schanberg (the former *New York Times* man whose reporting from Cambodia in the 1970s was featured in the film *The Killing Fields*) sums up their predicament: "Embedded means you're there," he said. "It also means you're stuck." CNN's star war correspondent Christiane Amanpour discovered this to be true when she complained to British army chiefs that unilateral correspondents were getting better footage than she was. They told her: "If you wish to go [with them] you can, but we won't re-embed you if you come back." Amanpour translated this as: "Play by the rules or f—— off."[8]

So, embedding turned out to be a triumph for the Pentagon as far as controlling correspondents was concerned. But Whitman wanted more from the system than just that. He envisaged it as capable of generating the sort of propaganda that would encourage a dubious American public to support the war. The way to produce this kind of propaganda, Whitman decided, was to make real war appear more like a Hollywood movie. He reached this conclusion after the amazing success of "Profiles from the Front Line", a prime-time television documentary series that followed the US forces in Afghanistan. The idea for the series had come from Jerry Bruckheimer, the producer who made *Black Hawk Down*—the feature film which transformed an American military disaster in Somalia into a movie triumph. Back in 2001, Bruckheimer and fellow producer Bertram van Munster, the man behind the reality television show "Cops", pitched to the Pentagon the idea of "Soldiers"—a reality television series that would document war through the eyes of American servicemen and women.

Van Munster said: "What these guys are doing out there, these men and women, is just extraordinary. If you're a cheerleader of our point of view—that we deserve peace and that we deal with human dignity—then these guys are really going out on a limb and risking their own lives." He then went on to identify the key concept behind embedding, "You can only get accepted by these people [soldiers] through chemistry. You have to have a bond with somebody. Only then will they let you in."[9] Defense Secretary Donald Rumsfeld himself gave the "Soldiers" project a green light: Hollywood and the Pentagon working in perfect symmetry. The series went to air just before the invasion of Iraq and its success was influential in deciding the American media strategy for the war.

In order for embedding to be a successful wartime media strategy, correspondents would need to bond with their unit —"get close up and personal", provide warm, human-interest stories about soldiers, go for maximum imagery but with little insight into the wider picture. The key was to ensure the right television footage and in case the embeds failed to get this, the Pentagon would use its own camera crews as back-up, editing the footage itself and then presenting it to broadcasters as a "ready-for-air" package. All this would be complemented by media briefings from Central Command where, in a multi-million-dollar press centre, military spokesmen would put everything into context and paint the broader picture. Consequently, the embedding part of the strategy worked so well that it will now, without question, be part of any future war.

The media briefings ran into trouble from the outset. The problem was that the war correspondents did not understand the role they were expected to play. They thought they were there to hold the military to account for what was being done in the public's name, to praise real triumphs but to expose mistakes, exaggeration, and false claims. In return, they expected the military spokesmen to brief them fully, truthfully and frankly and—while withholding information that could be of value to the enemy—give them an accurate and complete picture of the progress of the war.

The press centre had everything from a coffee bar to stacks of TV monitors so the 700 war correspondents could watch the war

534

unfold before their very eyes. Or they could sit in chairs, listen to the briefing officers at the daily conference, ask them questions and hope that they would answer them. They knew that the briefing officers were under the watchful eyes of Jim Wilkinson from the Pentagon and Simon Wren from 10 Downing Street. They knew that daily tactics for handling the media were worked out in long conference calls with the White House and 10 Downing Street, and that the briefers had a list of topics to be avoided at all costs (the "poo list") which included depleted uranium and the bombing of a Baghdad marketplace. Questions were rationed, follow-up questions were frowned upon and answers were often evasive. It was clear that, from the military's point-of-view, the system was very effective. A Canadian correspondent commented, "No matter how sceptical you remained at the end of the day, when you came to write your story, you still had to use their message track."

One whose scepticism finally got the better of him was New York magazine writer Michael Wolff. "I realised that every day you got to know less and less so that by the end of your stay you'd know absolutely nothing." So when Wolff's turn for a question came, he asked the briefing officer, General Vince Brooks, "Why are we here? Why should we stay? What's the value of what we're learning at this million-dollar press centre?" He soon had an answer. "Fox, with its extreme, love-it-or-leave approach to the war ... took me apart: I was clearly a potential traitor." Then, according to Wolff, right-wing commentator Rush Limbaugh disclosed Wolff's email address on his website, and in one day Wolff had received 3,000 hate emails. (Limbaugh's website manager denied posting the email address and pointed out that it appeared at the bottom of Wolff's columns.) Finally, Jim Wilkinson took Wolff aside and after a barbed exchange started by Wolff over why Wilkinson was wearing an army uniform when he was a civilian ("I'm in the reserves"), Wilkinson told Wolff, "This is a f——ing war, asshole. No more questions for you. Why don't you just go home?"[10]

Wolff realised that the press conferences were not for the benefit of the correspondents. How could they be? What correspondent worth his salt would be content repeating information to camera that had already been televised as told by some general? The correspondents were merely extras in a piece of theatre. The system was designed not to inform journalists but to play over their heads toward an international TV audience, which soon accorded the briefing officers the status of soap stars. The military did worry about correspondents boycotting the press conferences though, and every day removed any empty chairs from the briefing area. As Wolff said, "What if they gave a war and the media didn't come?" The play could not have taken place if the correspondents had packed up and gone home, but given the competitive nature of war reporting, there was never any danger of that.

The correspondents' main failure at Central Command was in not holding the Coalition accountable for the misinformation it was disseminating. Stories were floated, picked up, exaggerated, confirmed and then turned out to be wrong. Basra was secured— it fell seventeen days later. Um Quasa fell daily. Saddam Hussein had been killed; Tariq Assiz had defected—both stories were wrong. There was an uprising in Basra that never happened even though Central Command announced at a briefing that it had. Was this deliberate strategic disinformation? Paul Hunter of the Canadian Broadcasting Corporation offered one view: "If word comes out at Centcom that there's an uprising against Saddam's regime, [that is because] they [Centcom] can be thinking, planning and hoping that the information will be picked up and local people will build on that and an idea will become a reality even if it never existed in the first place."[11]

With the embedded correspondents performing exactly as the Pentagon and the Ministry of Defence hoped they would——and the generals' theatre at Central Command playing to worldwide TV audiences, that left for the Coalition only the problem of the "unilaterals", the name they bestowed on those intrepid Western correspondents determined to report the war independently, and the newly-arrived Arab TV networks. Since there would be little point in the unilaterals reporting alongside Coalition units, and thus competing with or duplicating the work of the embeds, it became apparent early on that most of the unilaterals planned to report from the Iraqi side.

This infuriated the Pentagon and the Ministry of Defence and they did their best to prevent it. The Pentagon wrote officially to al-Jazeera asking it to remove its correspondents from Baghdad, and Downing Street made the same request to the BBC. In the United States, a Pentagon spokesperson called all the American media bosses to a meeting in Washington to tell them how foolhardy and dangerous it was to have correspondents in the Iraqi capital. After the death of ITN reporter Terry Lloyd, and the probable deaths of two of his team (they remain missing) who had been operating as "unilaterals", the Coalition Commander, General Tommy Franks, went out of his way to reinforce the Pentagon message by pointing out that no embedded correspondent had been killed.

We now enter a delicate area. The Pentagon made it clear from the beginning of the war against Iraq that there would be no general censorship. What it failed to say was that war correspondents might well find themselves in a situation similar to that in Korea in 1950. One American correspondent described this style of media management as like the military telling them, "You can write what you like—but if we don't like it we'll shoot you."

The figures in Iraq tell a terrible story. Fifteen media people dead, with two missing—almost certainly dead. If you consider how short the campaign was, Iraq will undoubtedly become notorious as the most dangerous war for journalists ever.* This is bad enough. But it is a fact that the largest single group of them were unilaterals reporting from the Iraqi side who were killed by the American military. We know that the Americans do not target journalists. General Vince Brooks, deputy director of operations, said so. But some war correspondents did not believe him, such as the group of Spanish journalists who demonstrated outside the US embassy in Madrid shouting "murderers".[12]

I believe that the U.S. administration, in keeping with its new foreign policy, has an attitude to war correspondents that reflects the now somewhat infamous statement made by President Bush when declaring war on terrorists: "You're either with us or you're against us." Reporting from the enemy side was considered by Washington as "being against us" and anyone who did so risked being shot. If the correspondents did not like this, the Pentagon did not care. Welcome to new and highly dangerous world of the war correspondent in the twenty-first century.

The media should have seen it coming. In 2002 BBC correspondent William Reeve—who had just re-opened the Corporation's studio in Kabul—was giving a live, down-the-line TV interview for BBC World when he was suddenly blown out of his seat by an American smart missile. Then, four hours later and just a few blocks away, the office and residential compound of al-Jazeera was hit by two more American missiles. The BBC, al-

---

* To put these figures into perspective: when the BBC's "War Report" went into the front line to capture the sights and sound of battle during the final campaigns in Europe of the Second World War; out of a team of eighty-four, only two—Guy Byam and Kent Stevenson—were killed in the period from June 6, 1944 to V.E. Day, May 8, 1945.

Jazeeera, and the US Committee to Protect Journalists thought it prudent to find out from the Pentagon what had gone wrong and, if war came to Iraq, what steps they could take to protect their correspondents. The Pentagon, in the figure of Rear Admiral Craig Quigley, Deputy Assistant Defence Secretary for Public Affairs, was frank and unapologetic. Nothing had gone wrong. Quigley said that the Pentagon was indifferent to media activity in territory controlled by the enemy, and that the al-Jazeera compound in Kabul was considered a legitimate target because it had "repeatedly been the location of significant al-Qaeda activity".[13] Al-Jazeera said that this activity consisted of interviews with Taliban officials, something that it had hitherto thought to be normal journalism, and that it believed that its office was bombed in revenge for acting as a broadcast conduit for tapes from Osama bin Laden.

All three organisations concluded that the Pentagon was determined to deter Western correspondents from reporting any war from the "enemy" side, that they would view such journalism in Iraq as activity of "military significance", and might well bomb the area. Former BBC war correspondent Kate Adie, who had been making her own enquiries at the Pentagon, reached the same conclusion. The officer who briefed her went even further than Quigley. When Adie queried the consequences of such a potentially fatal policy, the officer replied, "Who cares ... They've been warned."[14]

Let us consider the example of what al-Jazeera was doing in Iraq and how the American military responded to it. From the beginning, al-Jazeera's coverage was controversial. It had its own film crews all over Iraq and it took videotapes from Iraqi TV. It had no qualms about showing horrific images of the dead and maimed of war. It broadcast footage of dead Coalition soldiers and the interrogation of frightened American prisoners of war. In news terms, this was so sensational that some Western TV networks picked up al-Jazeera's transmissions and rebroadcast them. It made the Coalition Commander, General Tommy Franks, look at best naive and at worst a liar. At a Central Command briefing he told the world's press that American bombers were using only precision weapons and were hitting only military targets. The very next day, al-Jazeera broadcast to an Arab audience estimated at fifty million, disturbing pictures of Iraqi women and children killed by Coalition bombs—thus fuelling anti-American sentiments.

Washington regarded al-Jazeera as an enemy propaganda station and tried to deter Western TV networks from rebroadcasting al-

Jazeera material. Nasdaq and the New York Stock Exchange barred the station and a concerted attack by mysterious hackers shut down its website. Al-Jazeera was well aware of Coalition hostility. "But what can they do to us?" the editor, Ibrahim Hilal, said. "Apart from bombing our offices in Baghdad—and we've had guarantees that they won't."[15] But that is exactly what the Americans did do.

On April 8, as Coalition forces closed in on Baghdad, a US plane bombed al-Jazeera's offices in the city, killing Tarek Ayyoub, one of its cameramen. Ibrahim Hilal said al-Jazeera had got the message: "Americans want war done without any witnesses." That same day, two other war correspondents were killed by Americans at locations that were known to the Pentagon as housing media. Reuters cameraman Taras Protsyuk was killed when an American tank fired a shell at the Reuters suite on the 15th floor of the Palestine Hotel. José Couso, a cameraman for the Spanish TV channel Telecino, was wounded in the same attack and later died in hospital. American forces also opened fire on the offices of Abu Dhabi TV, whose identity is spelled out in large blue letters on the roof.

When news of the attack first came, the American command said nothing—until it emerged that the French TV channel, France 3, had filmed the tank aiming and firing. Then the Coalition put out a series of contradictory accounts. Colonel David Perkins, Commander of the 3rd Infantry Division's 2nd Brigade, said Iraqis in front of the hotel were firing rocket-propelled grenades at the tank. Then the Division's Commander, General Bouford Blount, issued a statement saying that the tank had come under sniper fire from the hotel's roof and had fired at the source of the shooting which had then stopped.

Correspondents in the Palestine Hotel insisted that there had been no grenades and no sniper fire. Sky's correspondent David Chater said he had not heard a single shot. The BBC's Rageh Omaar said that none of the other journalists in the hotel heard any sniper fire. But the most telling evidence that the tank fired without provocation was that France 3's cameraman had started filming some minutes before the tank opened fire and his camera's sound track records no shots whatsoever. Severine Cazes, of Reporters Without Borders, said, "We want proof that this was not a deliberate attack on journalists."

The facts of the case were then obscured by an official Spanish government statement about the death of José Couso. The Defence Minister, Frederico Trillo, announced that the Coalition had actually declared the Palestine Hotel a military objective 48 hours before it was attacked and that the correspondents should have left.[16] This was news to the correspondents who all denied knowledge of any warning. "Journalists", a watchdog group that defends press freedoms, joined Reporters Without Borders in demanding an investigation and in a letter to the US Defence Secretary, Donald Rumsfeld, said it believed that the attacks on correspondents violated the Geneva Convention. The family of José Couso agreed and announced in May 2003 that it planned to bring war-crimes charges against three American servicemen. It asked a Madrid court to issue international arrest warrants for Sergeant Shawn Gibson, said to have been in charge of the tank that fired the shot at the Palestine Hotel, his immediate superior, Captain Philip Wolford, and their commanding officer, Lieutenant Colonel Philip de Camp.[17] International lawyers were not hopeful that the Couso family's case would get very far, especially since, at the time of writing there has been be no official explanation beyond the Pentagon's statement that the Americans had fired "in an inherent act of self-defence" and no apology.[18]

There has, however, been a defence of the tank crew from an American correspondent embedded with them. Jules Crittenden of the *Boston Herald* wrote that Gibson saw what he believed to be an Iraqi forward observer post, someone with binoculars and a telephone, in a tall building across the Tigris. Wolford gave him permission to fire. Crittenden agrees that the crucial question is: did Gibson or, more importantly, Wolford know that this was the Palestine Hotel, packed with correspondents?

Of Gibson, Crittenden says he shared a tent with him in the Kuwaiti desert, "where I knew him to be quiet and thoughtful, with compassion for the Iraqis he had killed in the first Gulf War. He was a devout man who kept a bible on his cot and read it often." Crittenden quotes Gibson on the Palestine shooting as saying, "I have prayed on it." As for Wolford, Crittenden says that investigators for the Committee to Protect Journalists (CPJ) were unable to show that Wolford knew about the hotel—a negative and hardly robust defence. Crittenden concludes: "It is indisputable that the Pentagon should have ensured that units in Baghdad were aware of sensitive sites. By failing to do so, they failed their own soldiers and placed our journalistic colleagues in jeopardy. But a lawsuit by the Cuoso (sic) family targeting the soldiers involved and the CPJ's second-guessing aspersions are not helpful."[19]

To sum up: The Pentagon made it clear that it did not not want correspondents to report from enemy territory. It repeatedly asked media organisations in the United States and Britain to withdraw their people from Baghdad. It warned them how dangerous it could be if they decided to remain. Before the war, the Pentagon admitted it was indifferent to media activity in territory controlled by the enemy and would not allow the presence of journalists to inhibit it from attacking areas of military significance. The BBC, the CPJ and al-Jazeera all came to the conclusion that journalists might well be at increased risk as a result of this attitude.

Since intent is so hard to prove, it would be a big jump from the facts gathered here to accuse the Pentagon of specifically targeting journalists working in enemy territory. But I certainly believe that the Pentagon would have considered the deaths among correspondents who did report from enemy territory to have the advantage of deterring others. No one would have ordered attacks on journalists as such. Rather, there would have been an understanding that if journalists reporting from enemy territory got in the way of a military operation, or if a broadcaster was deemed to be channelling propaganda helpful to the enemy cause, and the Pentagon decided it was necessary to, say, bomb the area where those correspondents were known to be located, then it would do so. The circumstantial evidence certainly suggests that in this sense, independent war correspondents may now be acknowledged as enemy targets.

Was Terry Lloyd of ITN, and his team of unilaterals, a target? The sole survivor from the four-man team, cameraman Daniel Demoustier, certainly thinks so. The team had heard that Basra had fallen (it had not) and started to drive toward it. They ran into Iraqi fire, so turned around and went back in the direction of Kuwait. "We came under fire again," Demoustier, who was driving, recalls. "The firing came from American tanks. I ducked down under the steering wheel. The windscreen disappeared. I looked to my right. Terry had gone."[20]

Even though all correspondents laboured under the same Pentagon-inspired restrictions, the reporting of the war was very different on the two sides of the Atlantic. For the Americans, the war was essentially a military story and a sanitized one at that. With five out of ten Americans believing that most of the terrorists who carried out the attack on 9/11 were Iraqis, the American media decided that its readers and viewers were not interested in the plight of Iraqi victims of the war.[21] The *New York Times* said it aimed to capture the true nature of the war but avoided "the gratuitous use of images simply for shock value". Steve Capus, executive editor of NBC's "Nightly News" complained, "You watch some Arab coverage and you get the sense that there is a blood bath at the hand of the US military. That is not my take on it."

The biggest radio group in the United States, Clear Channel, used its stations to organise pro-war rallies. McVay Media, one of America's largest communications consulting companies, advised its radio clients to play "patriotic music that makes you cry, salute and get cold chills" and under no circumstances cover war protests because they will "hurt your bottom line".[22] The *San Francisco Chronicle* sacked a reporter, Henry Norr (57), after he was one of 1,300 people arrested at an anti-war protest.[23] Chris Hedges, a foreign correspondent on the *New York Times* and a Pulitzer Prize winner, was booed from the stage at a ceremony at Rockford College in Illinois on May 20 as he tried to deliver an anti-war protest speech. His microphone was unplugged, graduate students and audience members turned their backs on him in silent protest and others rushed up the aisle, shouting to drown him out.[24] The Director General of the BBC, Greg Dyke, said he was shocked while in the United States by how unquestioning the broadcast news media was during the war. He said American TV news stations "wrapped themselves in the American flag and substituted patriotism for impartiality."[25]

War correspondents should have seen this coming after what had occurred in Afghanistan. All five major US television networks acceded to a request from National Security Adviser Condoleeza Rice to censor statements from Osama bin Laden and al-Jazeera TV; bookseller Barnes and Noble began cancelling readings of books critical of President Bush; and the *New York Times* ran a report on an anti-war rally under the headline: "Peace Protesters in Washington Urge Peace With Terrorists". Website columnist Joel Lee described the reporting from Afghanistan as "Parochialism of fantastic proportions, ten-second soundbites at the expense of context and substance, all-terror-all-the-time (as one friend of mine put it) ... a shameful and uncritical acceptance of Pentagon handouts instead of substantial critical coverage of the ground situation in Afghanistan."[26]

The main problem with the coverage of the Iraq war was that there was so much of it, more than any brain could absorb. Anyone so inclined could have spent 24-hours-a-day immersed in war news. There were more live pictures from the battlefield than for any previous war. Split screens, feeds from every front, crosses to Washington, then to Coalition headquarters in Qatar, then to

Downing Street, then back to a real-time firefight near Basra, some pretty pictures of missiles leaving a warship somewhere in the Gulf (but not of their arrival in a marketplace in Baghdad), interview after interview (often one journalist interviewing another), back to the expert in the studio, then back to breaking news which is breaking yet again about a town that has finally fallen. And throughout it all, echoing out of the all-pervasive mist of war came a tone of barely-suppressed hysteria. It took a confused *Guardian* reader to sum it up: "Despite scouring two national newspapers every day, listening to the radio, surfing the web and watching the TV news, I have absolutely no clue how the war is going."[27]

It was recognition that more was not necessarily better that provoked British news executives into an unseemly competition to prove who had contributed the best journalism. The demands of 24-hour coverage meant that the BBC's man in Baghdad, Rageh Omaar, was on British screens so often that he soon developed the status of a pop star. The popular press referred to him as "the Scud stud", *Viz* magazine called him the "best-loved, bullet-dodging, dreamboat war correspondent" and by the end of the war T-shirts with his portrait were on sale in Britain.[28] So, when one newspaper had a headline reading, "Rageh Omaar wins it for BBC in Baghdad", David Mannion, editor of ITV News, rushed into print to plug the achievements of ITV correspondents John Irvine, Neil Connery and Julian Manyon. He proudly proclaimed: "Expert observers ... believe that the ITV News coverage of Baghdad was the finest, boldest and most comprehensive in the world." A few days later, Richard Sambrook, the BBC's Director of News, quoted a survey showing that "the BBC—uniquely out of the broadcasters analysed—was even-handed in its reporting of the US military action and in reporting of casualties." This was one battle of the war that rumbled on long after the fighting was over.

In an information war heavy with symbolism, the reporting of two particular events ensured that everyone will remember them even when the war itself fades into history. These were the toppling of the statue of Saddam Hussein and the saving of Private Jessica. Yet both stories were manipulated by propagandists, and war correspondents must accept some responsibility for colluding in that manipulation.

The destruction of the statue of Saddam Hussein, as seen on television and on the front pages of newspapers around the world, began with cheering Iraqis attaching a rope to the statue's neck and hauling on it. When it refused to budge, American marines brought in an M-80 recovery tank with a long boom and chains. This approach worked. The statue hesitated, bent at the knees and toppled into the dust. In symbolic terms, this marked the end of Saddam Hussein and the Coalition's victory.

But let us analyse what occurred and why. Although there were lots of other statues of the President, the toppling of this one conveniently took place just opposite the Palestine Hotel in Fardus Square, Baghdad, where, as has been noted, most members of the international media were still staying. Without the media's presence, the event would have meant nothing. Long-distance shots showed that the Iraqis who helped topple the statue and later celebrated its fall numbered no more than 100 (early BBC reports suggested even fewer, and some commentators joked that the correspondents outnumbered the celebrating Iraqis). US tanks and marines cordoned off the square but they allowed these Iraqis through. So who were they?

At least some of them were members of the Free Iraqi Forces, headed by Iraqi National Congress founder, Ahmed Chalabi—the Pentagon's favourite to head a new Iraqi government. One of Chalabi's lieutenants, photographed as the Pentagon flew him and his boss into the southern Iraq city of Nassiriyah, is the same man shown on film dancing on Saddam's statue. So what exactly happened? Was it as portrayed—a spontaneous outpouring of joy by ordinary Iraqis delighted at being liberated and determined to show their contempt for their former leader? (As reported, for example, in the *New York Times* in a dispatch from John F. Burns on 20 April, 2003). Or was it a pre-planned event in the theatre of propaganda, the most-staged photo opportunity since the raising of the flag at Iwo Jima in the Second World War? Excited TV presenters told their viewers they were witnessing history. But whose version of history?[29]

Private Jessica Lynch became an icon of the war, and the story of her capture by the Iraqis and her rescue by US Special Forces was one of the great patriotic moments of the conflict. Private Lynch, a 19-year-old army clerk from Palestine, West Virginia and a member of the US Army's 507th Ordnance Maintenance Corps, was captured on 26 March, 2003 when her company took a wrong turn just outside Nassiriya and was ambushed. Nine of her fellow soldiers were killed and Private Lynch was taken to the local hospital, which at the time was swarming with Iraqi soldiers. Eight days later, a US Special Forces team stormed the hospital, rescued Lynch from her bed and whisked her away by helicopter. The whole dramatic event was captured on video by a Pentagon team using night-vision cameras.

At Coalition headquarters in Qatar, the war correspondents corps was summoned from their beds in the early hours to hear the good news. President Bush and Donald Rumsfeld had already been briefed. Now it was the correspondents' turn. They were given five-minute-long videotapes of the rescue—green, grainy shots of crouching Navy Seals and Army Rangers, guns at the ready, taking over the hospital and carrying Private Jessica to safety on a stretcher. According to the Pentagon, Jessica had stab and bullet wounds and had been slapped about in her hospital bed during interrogation. She had been rescued thanks to a courageous Iraqi lawyer, Mohammed Odeh al-Rehaief, who had told the US Special Forces where she was being held. This was the story that, first the American public then the rest of the world, learnt that morning.

The response was extraordinary. President Bush announced that he was "full of joy for Jessica Lynch". Her rescue was hailed as a testament to a core American value—they took care of their own people. General Brooks said in his briefing to the international media, "Some brave souls put their lives on the line to make this happen, loyal to a creed…they'll never leave a fallen comrade." Private Jessica Lynch became the first hero of the second Iraq war, complete with "America Loves Jessica" fridge magnets, T-shirts, mugs, country songs, an NBC made-for-TV movie and a sign outside her town saying, "Home of Jessica Lynch, ex-POW". The Iraqi lawyer who revealed Jessica's whereabouts, was flown to America, granted asylum, and signed a $500,000 deal for a book, *Rescue in Nassiriya*, which will be published in October, 2003.

There is only one problem—it did not happen like that. Jessica Lynch *was* captured and she *was* in the hospital in Nassiriya and she *was* taken from there by US Special Forces. But the rest was all a fiction, an audacious piece of Pentagon news management that probably would not have been revealed if it had not been for a courageous BBC documentary called "War Spin".[30]

In the documentary, Iraqi doctors in the modern, well-equipped Nassiriya Hospital say they provided the best treatment they could for an enemy soldier in the midst of war. "I examined her. I saw she had a broken arm, a broken thigh and a dislocated ankle," said Dr Harith al-Houssona, who looked after her. "There was no [sign of] shooting, no bullet inside her body, no stab wound—only road traffic accident. We gave her three bottles of blood, two of them taken from the medical staff because there was not enough at this time." Lynch was assigned the only specialist bed in the hospital and one of only two nurses on the floor, Khalida Shinah, who recalled, "I was like a mother to her and she was like a daughter to me."

Two days before the American Special Forces team hit the hospital, Dr. al-Houssona said he had decided that Private Jessica was well enough to be moved, so he put her in a hospital ambulance and told the driver to take her to the nearest American checkpoint. The driver quickly returned, complaining that as he had approached the checkpoint, the Americans opened fire on his vehicle. That same day, the Iraqi soldiers who had been in the hospital packed up and left. Did the Americans know this? According to Hassam Hamoud, a waiter at a local restaurant, they did. He saw the American advance party land in town and its Arabic interpreter approached him and asked where the hospital was. "He asked: 'Are there any Fedayeen over there?' and I said, 'No'." All the same, the next night the Special Forces team, with cameras rolling, broke down doors and to the sound of loud explosions, lots of gung-ho shouting, ducking and dodging, stormed into the hospital and rescued Private Lynch.

None of the details provided to the BBC by the doctors and nurses at the Nassiriya hospital made it to the Pentagon video or to any subsequent explanations or clarifications by the US authorities. Could the Pentagon story be true and the Iraqi version propaganda? The Pentagon's response when confronted by the BBC, and the reaction of Simon Wren, Downing Street's media man in Doha, suggest not. The BBC presenter John Kampfner asked Bryan Whitman, architect of the Pentagon's media strategy for the war, if he would release the full video tape of the rescue rather than the edited version. Whitman said no, he would not. Nor would he comment on the injuries Private Lynch had sustained. When Kampfner pressed him, Whitman smiled and said, "I understand that there is some conflicting information out there and in due time the full story will be told, I'm sure." Jessica herself could have resolved all the conflicting information in a single interview but the Pentagon would not allow it. It explained that she had no memory of the incident and probably never would.

After the war, Simon Wren described the Pentagon's treatment of the Lynch case as embarrassing, "hugely overblown" and symptomatic of a bigger problem in the different styles of British and American news management. He agreed that there was conjecture about the case but pointed out that, either way, it was not the main news of the day. "This was just one soldier, this was an add-on, human interest stuff. It completely overshadowed other events, things that were actually going on on the battlefield. It overshadowed the fact that the Americans found the bodies of her colleagues."[31] Wren missed the point here—the Pentagon media people knew exactly what they were doing and at that time had little interest in the main military news of the day. They knew that the eventual outcome of the war was not in doubt. Their aim in the meantime was to sell the war to the American public, and the Private Jessica story did exactly that.

So where does the war correspondent go from here? The United States—and Britain will undoubtedly follow—now has a policy for managing the media in wartime that it knows will both work and gather wide public support. As noted, this method of media management has an underlying principle in keeping with President Bush's demand that: "Either you are with us, or against us." In future, all media organisations wishing to report a war will be offered a stark ultimatum: you can either embed a correspondent with an American or British unit and follow the rules we will set out for you, or; you can make independent arrangements to cover the war from the American or Coalition side but, in so doing, apart from allowing you to attend our briefings—providing you accept our rules for the running of them—do not expect any help from us at the frontline. However, if you decide to cover the war from the enemy side and you get in our way, then we may well fire on you.

Alarmingly, within weeks of the end of the war, media bosses on both sides of the Atlantic had virtually accepted that this would be the way future wars would be reported. Richard Sambrook, Director of News at the BBC, said: "The embeds are undoubtedly the future. If they are the only form of conflict coverage possible then it would be very one-sided and you wouldn't get the full picture of what was happening. That would worry me journalistically, yes."[32]

War correspondents could protest about the new system by refusing to cover a war at all. However, such a stance would only prove self-defeating, as the Pentagon has made it clear that it would have its own reporting units ready to take over the role of the correspondent, if need be. It was as if it said to the media, "if you refuse to report the war, we'll do it ourselves. And what's more, with the help of Hollywood, we'll do it better. And when we've done it, we'll hand the finished product to your bosses and let's just see whether they use it or not." Daniel Demoustier, the cameraman who was nearly killed in the American attack on the ITN team, saw this coming. Protesting at apparent ready acceptance that embedding correspondents was the future, he issued a challenge to these rule-makers: "Let the army do it. Put a colonel there, give a soldier a camera and he [the colonel] can say what's happening."[33]

It appears that the Pentagon's policy will work. Fear for the lives of correspondents who want to be independent will deter their organisations from allowing them to be so. As well, insurers will either refuse to underwrite the risk to correspondents' lives or demand prohibitively high premiums. Public concern? The Pentagon is not the slightest bit worried about public unease over Coalition attacks on journalists because it is convinced that the public, especially the American public, would support its view and its actions, and if not, then they know how to employ the kind of media strategies that successfully drum up public support

Given the increased danger; greater degree of manipulation and control by government; and the new emphasis on seeing the war through the eyes of soldiers, the age of the war correspondent as hero appears to be over. Whether war correspondents would wish to continue as propagandists and myth-makers, plying their craft subservient to those who wage wars, is a decision they will need to make for themselves.

# Selected Bibliography

Adams, E. D. *Great Britain and the American Civil War*. London: Longmans, Green, 1925.

Andrews, J. Cutler. *The North Reports the Civil War*. Pittsburgh: University of Pittsburgh Press, 1955.

——.*The South Reports the Civil War*. Princeton: Princeton University Press, 1970.

Angell, Norman. *The Public Mind*. London: Noel Douglas, 1926.

Arlen, Michael J. *The Living Room War*. New York: Viking, 1966.

Arnold-Forster, M. *The World at War*. London: Collins, 1974.

Aronson, James. *The Press and the Cold War*. Indianapolis: Bobbs-Merrill, 1970.

Atkins, J. B. *The Life Of Sir William Howard Russell*, vols. 1-2. London: John Murray, 1911.

Baker, Carlos. *Ernest Hemingway*. London: Collins, 1969.

Baldwin, Hanson W. *Great Mistakes of the War*. London: Alvin Redman, Ltd., 1950.

Barnett, Corelli. *The Desert Generals*. London: William Kimber, 1960.

Beach Thomas, William. *A Traveller in News*. London: Chapman and Hall, 1925.

Bechhofer, C. E. *In Denikin's Russia*. London: Collins, 1921.

Bentley, N., ed. *Russell's Despatches from the Crimean War*. London: Andre Deutsch, 1966.

Bolin, Luis. *Spain, the Vital Years*. London: Cassell, 1967.

Brophy, John, and Partridge, Eric. *The Long Trail*. London: André Deutsch, 1965.

Brown, D., and Bruner, W. R., eds. *How I Got That Story*. New York: Dutton, 1967.

——. *I Can Tell It Now*. New York: Dutton, 1964.

Bullard, F. Lauriston. *Famous War Correspondents*. Bath: Sir Isaac Pitman and Sons, 1914.

Burchett, Wilfred. *Passport*. Australia: Nelson, 1969.

Calder, Angus. *The People's War*. London: Jonathan Cape, 1969.

Calder, Ritchie. *The Lesson of London*. London: Secker and Watburg, 1941.

Cassidy, Henry C. *Moscow Dateline*, 1941–1943. London: Cassell, 1943.

Chesnut, Mary Boykin. *A Diary from Dixie*. Boston: Houghton Mifflin, 1949.

Churchill, Winston S. *My Early Life*. London: T. Butterworth, 1930.

Clark, Alan. *Barbarossa*. London: Hutchinson, 1965.

Collier, Richard. *The Sands of Dunkirk*. London: Collins, 1961.

Cooper, Bryan. *The Ironclads of Cambrai*. London: Souvenir Press, 1967.

Cruttwell, Charles R. M. F. *History of the Great War, 1914–1918* Oxford: Oxford University Press, 1936.

Cutforth, Rene. *Korean Reporter*. London: Allan Wingate, 1952.

D'Abernon, Edgar Vincent. *The Eighteenth Decisive Battle of the World*. London: Hodder and Stoughton, 1931.

Daniell, Raymond. *Civilians Must Fight*. New York: Doubleday, 1941.

Davis, Burke. *To Appomattox*. New York: Holt, Rinehart and Winston, 1959.

Davis, Richard Harding. *A Year from a Correspondent's Notebook*. New York: Harper, 1898.

Divine, A. D. *Dunkirk*. London: Faber and Faber, 1945.

Eaton, Clement. *The Growth of Southern Civilisation*. New York: Harper and Row, 1961.

Elson, R. T. *Time Inc*. New York: Atheneum, 1968.

Farrar-Hockley, A. H. *The Somme*. London: B. T. Batsford, 1964.

Fisher, J., ed. *Eyewitness*. London: Cassell, 1960.

Fitzgibbon, Constantine. *The Blitz*. London: Wingate, 1957.

Forbes, Archibald. *Memories and Studies of War and Peace*. London: Cassell, 1896.

Fredborg, Arvid. *Behind the Steel Wall*. London: Harrap, 1944.

Fuller, J. F. C. *Decisive Battles of the Western World*. London: Eyre and Spottiswoode, 1954.

Furneaux, R. *News of War*. London: Parrish, 1964.

Gallagher, O. D. *Retreat in the East*. London: Harrap, 1942.

Gardner, Brian. *Mafeking: A Victorian Legend*. London: Cassell, 1966.

Gernsheim, Helmut and Alison. *Roger Fenton*. London: Secker and Warburg, 1954.

Gibbs, Philip. *Adventures in Journalism*. London: Heinemann, 1923.

——. *The Battles of the Somme*. London: Heinemann, 1917.

——. *Realities of War*. London: Heinemann, 1920.

Gramling, O. *AP: The Story of the News*. Ann Arbor: University Microfilms, 1968.

Greer, H. *A Scattering of Dust*. London: Hutchinson, 1962.

Gunther, John. *The Riddle of MacArthur's Japan, Korea and the Far East*. London: Hamish Hamilton, 1951.

Halberstam, David. *The Making of a Quagmire*. London: Bodley Head, 1965.

Halliday, E. M. *The Ignorant Armies*. London: Weidenfeld and Nicolson, 1961.

Hersey, John. *Hiroshima*. New York: Knopf, 1946.

Hersh, Seymour. *My Lai 4*. New York: Random House, 1970.

Hibbert, Christopher. *The Destruction of Lord Raglan*. London: Longmans, 1961.

Hicks, J. D., Mowry, G. E., and Burke,

R. E. *A Short History of American Democracy*. Boston: Houghton Mifflin, 1966.

Higgins, Marguerite. *War in Korea*. New York: Doubleday, 1951.

*The History of The Times*. 5 vols. London: The Times, 1935–1952.

Hohenberg, John. *Foreign Correspondence*. New York: Columbia University Press, 1967.

Huberman, Edward and Elizabeth, eds. *War: An Anthology*. New York: Washington Square Press, 1969.

Irving, David. *The Destruction of Dresden*. London: Kimber, 1963.

Johnston, George. *My Brother Jack*. London: Collins, 1964.

Jullian, Marcel. *The Battle of Britain*. London: Jonathan Cape, 1967.

Kato, Masuo. *The Lost War*. New York: Knopf, 1946.

Koop, Theodore F. *Weapon of Silence*. Chicago: University of Chicago Press, 1946.

Kruger, Rayne. *Goodbye Dolly Gray*. London: Cassell, 1959.

Lampe, David. *Pyke, the Unknown Genius*. London: Evans Bros., 1959.

Lasswell, H. D. *Propaganda Technique in the World War*. London: Kegan Paul, 1927.

Liddell, Robert Scotland. *On the Russian Front*. London: Simkin Marshall, 1916.

Lytton, Neville. *The Press and the General Staff*. London: Collins, 1921.

Marchant, Hilde. *Women and Children Last*. London: Gollancz, 1941.

Matthews, Herbert. *The Education of a Correspondent*. New York: Harcourt Brace, 1946.

——. *Eyewitness in Abyssinia*. London: Secker and Warburg, 1937.

——. *A World in Revolution*. New York: Scribners, 1971.

Matthews, Joseph J. *Reporting the Wars*. Minneapolis: University of Minnesota Press, 1957.

McKee, Alexander. *The Race for the Rhine Bridges*. London: Souvenir Press, 1971.

Middleton, Drew. *The Sky Suspended*. London: Secker and Warburg, 1960.

Miller, Webb. *I Found No Peace*. New York: Simon and Schuster, 1936.

Monks, Noel. *Eyewitness*. London: Frederick Muller, 1956.

Montague, C. E. *Disenchantment*. London: Chatto and Windus, 1922.

Moorehead, Alan. *Gallipoli*. London: Hamish Hamilton, 1956.

Morris, J. A. *Deadline Every Minute*. New York: Doubleday, 1957.

Morrison, Ian. *Malayan Postscript*. London: Faber and Faber, 1943.

——. *This War Against Japan*. London: Faber and Faber, 1943.

Murrow, Edward R. *In Search of Light*. New York: Knopf, 1967.

——. *This is London*. London: Cassell, 1941.

Neuberg, A. *Armed Insurrection*. London: N. L. B., 1970.

Oberdorfer, D. *Tet*. New York: Doubleday, 1971.

Ogden, R., ed. *The Life and Letters of Edwin Lawrence Godkin*. New York: Macmillan, 1907.

Orwell, George. *Homage to Catalonia*. London: Secker and Warburg, 1938.

Panichas, G. A., ed. *Promise of Greatness, 1914–18*. London: Cassell, 1968.

Percival, A. E. *The War in Malaya*. London: Longmans, 1949.

Peterson, H. C. *Propaganda for War*. Norman: University of Oklahoma Press, 1939.

Pethybridge, R., ed. *Witnesses to the Russian Revolution*. London: George Allen and Unwin, 1964.

Pitt, Barrie. *1918, the Last Act*. London: Cassell, 1962.

Ponsonby, Arthur. *Falsehood in Wartime*. *London*: George Allen and Unwin, 1928.

Price, Morgan Philips. *My Three Revolutions*. London: George Allen and Unwin, 1969.

Pullen, John J. *The Twentieth Maine*. London: Eyre and Spottiswoode, 1959.

Ralph, Julian. *War's Brighter Side*. London: Pearson, 1901.

Ransome, Arthur. *Six Weeks in Russia in 1919*. Glasgow: Socialist Labour Press, 1919.

Read, J. M. *Atrocity Propaganda, 1914–1919*. New Haven: Yale University Press, 1941.

Reed, John. *Ten Days That Shook the World*. London: Lawrence and Wishart, 1961.

Regler, G. *Owl of Minerva*. London: Rupert Hart-Davis, 1959.

Reynolds, Quentin. *Only the Stars Are Neutral*. London: Cassell, 1942.

Roberts, Brian. *The Churchills in Africa*. London: Hamish Hamilton, 1970.

Robertson, Terence. *Dieppe: The Shame and the Glory*. London: Hutchinson, 1963.

Russell, William Howard. *The British Expedition to the Crimea*. London: George Routledge and Sons, 1877.

——. *My Civil War Diary*. Edited by Fletcher Pratt. London: Hamish Hamilton, 1954.

——. *My Diary North and South*, vols. 1–2. London: Bradbury and Evans, 1863.

St. John, Robert. *From the Land of Silent People*. London: Harrap, 1942.

Shaw, Bernard. *What I Really Wrote About the War*. London: Constable, 1931.

Snow, Edgar. *Battle for Asia*. New York: Random House, 1941.

Snyder, L., ed. *Masterpieces of War Reporting*. New York: Messner, 1962.

Snyder, L., and Morris, R., eds. *A Treasury of Great Reporting*. New York: Simon and Schuster, 1949.

Soutar, Andrew. *With Ironside in North Russia*. London: Hutchinson, 1940.

Speer, Albert. *Inside the Third Reich*. London: Weidenfeld and Nicolson, 1970.

Squires, James Duane. *British Propaganda at Home and in the United States from 1914 to 1917*. Cambridge, Mass.: Harvard University Press, 1935.

Steer, G. *Tree of Gernika*. London: Hodder and Stoughton, 1938.

Stone, I. F. *The Hidden History of the Korean War*. New York: Monthly Review Press, 1969.

Storey, Graham. *Reuters Century 1851-1951*. London: Parrish, 1951.

Swettenham, John A. *Allied Intervention in Russia*. London: George Allen and Unwin, 1967.

Talese, Gay. *The Kingdom and the Power*. New York: World Publishing Co., 1969.

Terraine, John. *Impacts of War, 1914 and 1918*. London: Hutchinson, 1970.

Thomas, Hugh. *The Spanish Civil War*. London: Eyre and Spottiswoode, 1961.

Thompson, G. P. *Blue Pencil Admiral*. London: Sampson, Low, Marston, 1947.

Thompson, Reginald. *Cry Korea*. London: Macdonald, 1951.

Toland, John. *The Last 100 Days*. London: Arthur Barker, 1965.

Tolischus, Otto D. *Tokio Record*. London: Hamish Hamilton, 1943.

Warren, Robert Penn. *The Legacy of the Civil War*. New York: Random House, 1961.

Waugh, Evelyn. *Scoop*. London: Chapman and Hall, 1938.

Wells, H. G. *War and the Future*. London: Cassell, 1917.

Werth, Alexander. *Russia at War*. London: Barrie and Rockliff, 1964.

White, W., ed. *Hemingway By-line*. London: Collins, 1968.

Wood, Evelyn. *The Crimea*. London: Chapman and Hall, 1895.

# Notes on Sources

**Chapter One**
**"The Miserable Parent of a**
**Luckless Tribe"**

1. *The History of The Times*, vol.2, p. 169.
2. *The History of The Times*, vol. 2, p. 168.
3. *Strand Magazine*, vol.4, p. 571.
4. J. B. Atkins, *The Life of Sir William Howard Russell* (London: John Murray, 1911), pp. 28-42.
5. *The Times* archives.
6. R. Ogden, ed., *The Life and Letters of Edwin Lawrence Godkin* (New York: Macmillan, 1907), p. 23.
7. Ogden, p. 66.
8. Ogden, pp. 100-01.
9. Atkins, p. 156.
10. Atkins, p. 160.
11. F. Lauriston Bullard, *Famous War Correspondents* (Bath: Sir Isaac Pitman and Sons, 1914), p. 47.
12. Ogden, p. 99.
13. *The History of The Times*, vol. 2; p. 166.
14. William Howard Russell, *The Great War with Russia* (London: George Routledge and Sons, 1895), p. 136.
15. Bullard, p. 44.
16. *The Times* archives.
17. *The Times* archives.
18. C. Woodham-Smith, *Florence Nightingale* (London: Collins, 1951; Fontana edition, 1964), pp. 98-99; *The History of The Times*, vol.2, p. 186.
19. *The History of The Times*, vol. 2, p. 177.
20. *Strand Magazine*, vol.4, p. 573.
21. Helmut and Alison Gernsheim, *Roger Fenton* (London: Secker and Warburg, 1954), p. 87.
22. U.K. Public Record Office, W.O. 28/131.
23. *The Times* archives.
24. Ogden, pp. 102-03.

**Chapter Two**
**The First Challenge**

1. *New York Times*, September 25, 1901.
2. *Journalism Quarterly*, vol. 6, no. 1, p. 1.
3. R. Ogden, ed., *The Life and Letters of Edwin Lawrence Godkin* (New York: Macmillan, 1907), p. 205.
4. "Army Correspondence," *Nation*, July 27, 1865.
5. J. Cutler Andrews, *The North Reports the Civil War* (Pittsburgh: University of Pittsburgh Press, 1955), p. 640.
6. William Young in *New York Herald*, April 11, 1864.
7. *New York Times*, November 7, 1861.
8. O. Gramling, *AP: The Story of the News* (New York: Associated Press, 1940), p. 49.
9. Ogden, pp. 204-05.
10. *Chicago Daily Journal*, April 22, 1924.
11. Stedman papers, Columbia University Library, New York, N.Y.
12. Andrews, p. 49.
13. Andrews, p. 71.
14. *Journalism Quarterly*, p. 4.
15. Andrews, p. 167.
16. Andrews, p. 682.
17. *Cincinnati Daily Times*, November 10,1863.
18. Andrews, p.699.
19. R. S. Thorndike, *The Sherman Letters* (New York: n.p., 1894), p. 189.
20. J. D. Hicks, O. E. Mowry, and R. E. Burke, *A Short History of American Democracy* (Boston: Houghton Mifflin, 1966), p. 377.
21. *New York Times*, July 15-16, 1863.
22. John J. Pullen, *The Twentieth Maine* (London: Eyre and Spottiswoode, 1959), pp. 154-57.
23. Mary Boykin Chesnut, *A Diary from Dixie* (Boston: Houghton Mifflin, 1949), p. 400.

24. *New York Times*, April 16, 1864.
25. *Mobile Daily Advertiser and Register*, October 24, 1862.
26. Burke Davis, *To Appomattox* (New York: Popular Library, 1959), p. 343.
27. *Cincinnati Daily Times*, April 10, 1862.
28. *New York Times*, July 6, 1863.
29. *Savannah Republican*, December 4, 1864.
30. *Historical Outlook*, May 1928, p. 204.
31. *Historical Outlook*, p. 207.
32. E. D. Adams, *Great Britain and the American Civil War* (London: Longmans, Green, 1925), p. 154.
33. Adams, p. 178.
34. *The History of The Times*, vol. 2, pp. 360-66.
35. *The History of The Times*, vol.2, p. 373.
36. T*he History of The Times*, vol. 2, pp. 375 ff.
37. J. Bigelow, *Retrospections of an Active Life* (New York: Baker and Taylor, 1910), p. 362.
38. C. Mackay, *Through the Long Day* (London: n. p., 1887), p. 215.
39. *The History of The Times*, vol.2, p. 378.
40. Adams, p. 189.
41. *The Times*, August 4,1864.
42. *The Times*, November 4, 1862.
43. *The History of The Times*, vol. 2, p. 380.
44. *The Times*, January 5, 1865.
45. *The History of The Times*, vol. 2, p. 388.
46. *The History of The Times*, vol.2, p. 389.
47. G. A. Sala, *My Diary in America in the Midst of War* (London: Tinsley Brothers, 1865), p. 280.

## Chapter Three
## The Golden Age

1. *The History of The Times*, vol. 2, p. 434.
2. F. Lauriston Bullard, *Famous War Correspondents* (Bath: Sir Isaac Pitman and Sons, 1914), p. 247.
3. D. Barker, *G. K. Chesterton* (London: Constable, 1973), p. 150.
4. *The Times* archives.
5. Bismarck to van Roon, July 26, 1870.
6. Archibald Forbes, *Memories and Studies of War and Peace* (London: Cassell, 1896), p. 7.
7. Bullard, pp. 13-14.
8. Bullard, p. 16.
9. *Daily News*, December 1870-January 1871.
10. *Daily News*, May 26, 1871.
11. *Daily News*, July 28-August 26, 1876.
12. Bullard, p. 106.
13. Forbes, pp. 41-42.
14. *Daily Mail*, April 29, 1898.
15. Richard Harding Davis, *A Year from a Correspondent's Notebook* (New York: Harper, 1898), p. 113.
16. L. Snyder and R. Morris, eds., *A Treasury of Great Reporting* (New York: Simon and Schuster, 1962), p. 236.
17. R. W. Stallman and E. R. Hagemann, eds., *The War Dispatches of Stephen Crane* (London: Peter Owen, 1964), p. 8.
18. *New York Journal*, May 11, 1897.
19. Stallman and Hagemann, pp. 196-99.
20. *New York World*, December 12, 1894.
21. Snyder and Morris, p. 247.
22. Norman Angell, *The Public Mind* (London: Noel Douglas; 1926), pp. 76-77.
23. Luigi Barzini, *Avventure in Oriente* (Milan: Mondadori, 1959), pp. 28-30.
24. R. Furneaux, *News of War* (London: Parrish, 1964), p. 197.

## Chapter Four
## Quite Another Game

1. Dispatch to *Morning Post*, January 22, 1900.
2. Rayne Kruger, *Goodbye Dolly Gray*

(London: Cassell, 1959), p. 78.

3. Kruger, p. 451.

4. Brian Gardner, *Mafeking: A Victorian Legend* (London: Cassell, 1966; Sphere edition, 1968), p. 179.

5. Winston S. Churchill, *My Early Life* (London: T. Butterworth, 1930), p. 266.

6. *Pearson's Illustrated War News*, December 30, 1899.

7. Brian Roberts, *The Churchills in Africa* (London: Hamish Hamilton, 1970), p. 279.

8. *The Times*, February 23, 1944.

9. E. E. Reynolds, *Baden-Powell* (Oxford: Oxford UniversityPress, 1942), p. 100.

10. J. Neilly, *Besieged with Baden-Powell* (London: Pearson, 1900), pp. 227-30.

11. Kruger, p. 145.

12. R. Furneaux, *News of War* (London: Parrish, 1964), p. 197.

13. Neilly, p. 91.

14. Kruger, p. 461.

15. Julian Ralph, *War's Brighter Side* (New York: Appleton, 1901), p. 4.

16. Kruger, p. 436.

17. Kruger, p. 95.

18. U.K. Public Record Office, W.O. 32/8061.

19. Norman Angell, *The Public Mind* (London: Noel Douglas, 1926), p. 75.

20. Furneaux, p. 206.

21. F. Lauriston Bullard, *Famous War Correspondents* (Bath: Sir Isaac Pitman and Sons, 1914), p. 317.

22. Bullard, p. 225.

23. Kruger, p. 201.

24. Ralph, pp. 284-86.

25. *American Historical Review*, January 1901, p. 299.

## Chapter Five
## The Last War

1. Both quoted in "1914-1918: What Was It Like," *Sunday Times Magazine*, February 26, 1964.

2. *The Collected Poems of Siegfried Sassoon 1908-1956* (London: Faber and Faber, 1961), p. 75.

3. Philip Gibbs, *Realities of War* (London: Heinemann, 1920), p. 403.

4. J. M. Read, *Atrocity Propaganda, 1914-1919* (New Haven: Yale University Press, 1941), p. 211.

5. Read, pp. 206-07.

6. *Morning Post*, June 22, 1915.

7. For Reuters' rôle in both world wars, see Graham Storey, *Reuters' Century, 1851-1951* (London: Parrish, 1951).

8. H. D. Lasswell, *Propaganda Technique in the World War* (London: Kegan Paul, 1927), p. 192.

9. Lasswell, p. 22; Joseph J. Matthews, *Reporting the Wars* (Minneapolis: University of Minnesota Press, 1957), pp. 165-66.

10. *The War Dispatches of Sir Philip Gibbs* (Isle of Man: Gibbs and Phillips, 1964), p. 4.

11. *The History of The Times*, vol. 4, p. 221.

12. Philip Gibbs, *Adventures in Journalism* (London: Heinemann, 1923), p. 179.

13. *Corriere della Sera*, August 25, 1914.

14. T*he History of The Times*, vol. 4, pp. 222-26; Wickham Steed to editor of *Daily Telegraph*, November 10, 1934, and Hamilton Fyfe to editor of *The Times*, April 4, 1935, in *The Times* archives.

15. *The History of The Times*, vol. 4, p. 232.

16. *The History of The Times*, vol.4, p. 233.

17. Gibbs, *War Dispatches*, pp. 64-65.

18. Lasswell, p. 136

19. William Beach Thomas, *A Traveller in News* (London: Chapman and Hall, 1925), p. 122.

20. Arthur Ponsonby, *Falsehood in Wartime* (London: George Allen and Unwin, 1928), p. 134.

21. Gibbs, *Adventures*, p. 231.

22. *The History of The Times*, vol. 4, p. 218.

23. G. A. Panichas, ed., *Promise of Greatness*, 1914–18 (London: Cassell, 1968), p. 170.

24. C. E. Montague, *Disenchantment* (London: Chatto and Windus, 1922), pp. 97–98.

25. *Sunday Times Magazine*, March 22, 1964.

26. Philip Gibbs, *The Battles of the Somme* (London: Heinemann, 1917), p. 17.

27. Beach Thomas, p. 109.

28. General Hamilton to Committee of Imperial Defence, quoted in *Sydney Morning Herald*, January 25, 1969.

29. Interview with A. W. Bazley, assistant to C. E. W. Bean, Australian official war correspondent.

30. *Sydney Morning Herald*, November 20, 1968.

31. *Evening Standard*, October 23, 1969.

32. Gibbs, *Adventures*, p. 249.

33. H. G. Wells, *War and the Future* (London: Cassell, 1917), p. 189.

34. *Sunday Chronicle*, February 29, 1920.

35. *The Times*, November 4, 1925; see also Ponsonby, pp. 103–13.

36. Ponsonby, p. 90.

37. Ponsonby, p. 78.

38. J. F. C. Fuller, *Decisive Battles of the Western World* (London: Palladin, 1970), p. 347.

39. Charles R. M. F. Cruttwell, *History of the Great War, 1914–1918* (Oxford: Oxford University Press, 1936), p. 412.

40. Gibbs, *Realities*, p. 27.

41. *Sunday Chronicle*, February 29, 1920.

42. A. H. Farrar-Hockley, *The Somme* (London: B. T. Batsford, 1964; Pan edition, 1966), p. 37.

43. Farrar-Hockley, p. 253.

44. Gibbs, *Adventures*, p. 243.

45. *The History of The Times*, vol.4, p. 345.

46. *The History of The Times*, vol. 4, p. 228.

47. *Historical Studies*, University of Melbourne, October 1969.

48. Gibbs, *Realities*, p. 411.

49. G. Seldes, *The Truth Behind the News 1918-28* (London: Faber and Gwyer, 1929), pp. 11-23.

**Chapter Six**
**Enter America**

1. *News Chronicle*, August 23, 1914.

2. Irvin S. Cobb, *The Red Glutton: With the German Army at the Front* (London: Hodder and Stoughton, 1915), p. 234.

3. J. A. Morris, *Deadline Every Minute* (New York: Doubleday, 1957), p. 65.

4. United Press file, London, September 8, 1915.

5. Morris, p. 67.

6. Morris, p. 68.

7. Morris, p. 70.

8. Gay Talese, *The Kingdom and thePower* (New York: New American Library, 1969), pp. 167-68.

9. Arthur Ponsonby, *Falsehood in Wartime* (London: George Allen and Unwin, 1928), p. 130.

10. See H. C. Peterson, *Propaganda for War* (Norman: University of Oklahoma Press, 1939).

11. Peterson, p. 27.

12. F. Palmer, *With My Own Eyes* (Indianapolis: Bobbs-Merrill, 1934), p. 315.

13. Peterson, p. 231.

14. H. D. Lasswell, *Propaganda Technique in the World War* (London: Kegan Paul, 1927), p. 95.

15. T. E. Lawrence to Mrs. Bernard Shaw, March 19, 1924, letter in British Museum.

16. J. F. C. Fuller, *Decisive Battles of the Western World* (London: Palladin, 1970), p. 392.

17. *Foreign Affairs*, January 1932, pp. 316-23.

18. B. Hershey, "Sons o' Guns of August," *Dateline*, Overseas Press Club of America, 1966, pp. 44-45.

19. *Chicago Tribune*, February 26, 1917.

20. "The War Between Hard Covers," *Dateline*, Overseas Press Club of America, 1968, p. 95.

21. O. R. Pilat, *Pegler, Angry Man of the Press* (Westport: Greenwood Press, 1973), p. 77.

22. Heywood Broun, *The AEF—with General Pershing and the American Forces* (New York: Appleton, 1918), p. 92.

23. S. L. A. Marshall, "Weaponry," *Dateline*, Overseas Press Club of America, 1968, pp. 100–01.

24. See *Collected Edition of Heywood Broun* (New York: Harcourt Brace, 1941); Palmer, *With My Own Eyes*.

25. Pilat, p. 80.

26. *The Story of the New York Times* (New York: Simon and Schuster, 1951), pp. 216–18.

27. Morris, pp. 91–92.

28. Philip Gibbs, *The Pageant of the Years* (London: Heinemann, 1946), p. 241.

29. B. Hershey, *How I Got That Story* (New York: Dutton, 1967), pp. 21–27.

## Chapter Seven
## The Remedy for Bolshevism Is Bullets

1. Walter Lippmann and C. Merz, "A Test of the News," *New Republic*, August 4, 1920, p. 10.

2. Lippmann and Merz, p. 42.

3. Interview with Robert Liddell, honorary colonel in the 165th.

4. Interview with Liddell.

5. *The History of The Times*, vol. 4, p. 243.

6. *The History of The Times*, vol. 4, p. 243.

7. *The History of The Times*, vol. 4, p. 244.

8. *The History of The Times*, vol. 4, p. 244.

9. *The History of The Times*, vol. 4, p. 244.

10. *The History of The Times*, vol. 4, p. 245.

11. Interview with Morgan Philips Price.

12. *Manchester Guardian*, March 16 and 21, 1917.

13. R. Pethybridge, ed., *Witnesses to the Russian Revolution* (London: George Allen and Unwin, 1964), p. 129.

14. *The History of The Times*, vol. 4, pp. 247–48.

15. John Reed, *Ten Days That Shook the World* (London: Communist Party of Great Britain, 1926; Penguin edition, 1966), p. 129.

16. Reed, p. 133.

17. Graham Storey, *Reuters: The Story of a Century of Newsgathering* (New York: Crown, 1951), pp. 165–66.

18. *Manchester Guardian*, November 20, 1917.

19. *Daily News*, November 16, 1917.

20. Reed, p. 74.

21. Interview with Price.

22. *The History of The Times*, Vol 4, p. 344.

23. *The History of The Times*, Vol.4, p. 258.

24. *The Times*, August 31, 1917.

25. *New York Times*, February 26, 1918.

26. Interview with Price.

27. *The History of The Times*, Vol.4, pp. 265–68.

28. Interview with Price.

29. Interview with Price.

30. Morgan Philips Price, *My Three Revolutions* (London: George Allen and Unwin, 1969), pp. 116, 127, 132.

31. *Observer*, February 10, 1918.

32. Interview with Price.

33. Interview with Price.

34. E. M. Halliday, *The Ignorant Armies* (London: Weidenfeld and Nicolson, 1961), p. 14.

35. *New York Times*, December 17, 1918.

36. Harold Williams to *New York Times*, June 8, 1919.

37. C. E. Bechhofer, *In Denikin's Russia* (London: Collins, 1921), pp. 12–38.

38. *The Times* archives.
39. *The History of The Times*, vol.4, p. 467.
40. Carl W. Ackerman cable to *New York Times*, November 26, 1918.
41. John A. Swettenham, *Allied Intervention in Russia* (London: George Allen and Unwin, 1967), p. 247.
42. B. Horrocks, *A Full Life* (London: Collins, 1960), pp. 37-57.
43. *The Times* archives.
44. Halliday, pp. 55, 79, 96, 103, 183; Swettenham, pp. 66, 205, 225.
45. Halliday, p. 182.
46. Andrew Soutar, *With Ironside in North Russia* (London: Lawrence and Wishart, 1961), p. 222.
47. Soutar, p. 107.
48. Soutar, p. 152.
49. War Office to General Ironside, April 1919, quoted in W. E. Ironside, *Archangel, 1918-19* (London: Constable, 1953), p. 124.
50. Private papers of Morgan Philips Price.
51. Halliday, p. 201.
52. Quoted in Halliday, p. 196.
53. J. F. C. Fuller, *Decisive Battles of the Western World* (London: Paladin, 1970), p. 400.
54. *The Times* archives.

**Chapter Eight**
**The Real Scoop**

1. Ralph Deakin to George Steer, May 21, 1935, *The Times* archives.
2. Evelyn Waugh, *Waugh in Abyssinia* (London: Longmans, Green, 1937), pp. 48-49, 50-52.
3. Deakin to Steer, November 29, 1935, *The Times* archives.
4. Interview with O. D. Gallagher.
5. Steer to Deakin, July 23, 1935, *The Times* archives.
6. Interview with Gallagher.
7. Interview with Gallagher.
8. Webb Miller, *I Found No Peace* (London: Harmondsworth, 1940), p. 235.
9. Herbert Matthews, *Eyewitness in Abyssinia* (London: Secker and Warburg, 1937), p. 36.
10. Matthews, p. 72.
11. Waugh, p. 124.
12. Noel Monks, *Eyewitness* (London: Frederick Muller, 1956), p. 46.
13. *Time*, January 27, 1936.
14. Deakin to Steer, November 29, 1935, *The Times* archives.
15. Steer to Deakin, October 18, 1935, *The Times* archives.
16. O. Gramling, *AP: The Story of the News* (New York: Associated Press, 1940), p. 414.
17. Christopher Sykes, "Evelyn" (manuscript).
18. Monks, pp. 49-53.
19. *Time*, January 27, 1936, and November 18, 1935.
20. *Corriere della Sera*, November 19, 1935.
21. Matthews, pp. 169-71.
22. Herbert Matthews, *The Education of a Correspondent* (New York: Harcourt Brace, 1946), p. 28.
23. Matthews, *Education*, p. 8.
24. Interview with Christopher Holme.
25. Interview with Herbert Matthews.
26. Quoted in Matthews, *Education*, p. 58.
27. Interview with Matthews.
28. *Time*, April 20, 1936.
29. Steer to Deakin, April 4, 1936, *The Times* archives.
30. Interview with Gallagher.

**Chapter Nine**
**Commitment in Spain**

1. George Orwell, *Homage to Catalonia* (London: Secker and Warburg, 1953; Penguin edition, 1966), p. 240.
2. Herbert Matthews, *The Education of a Correspondent* (New York: Harcourt Brace, 1946), pp. 67-68.
3. Interview with Martha Gellhorn.
4. Letter from Drew Middleton to author, November 1, 1972.
5. Herbert Matthews, *A World in Revolution* (New York: Scribners, 1971), p. 6.

6. Hugh Thomas, *The Spanish Civil War* (London: Eyre and Spottiswoode, 1961; Pelican edition, 1968), p. 307.

7. Quoted in Gay Talese, *The Kingdom and the Power* (New York: World Publishing Co., 1969), p. 54.

8. Matthews, *Education*, p. 69.

9. *News Chronicle*, May 23-28, 1937.

10. Arthur Koestler, *The Invisible Writing* (London: Hutchinson, 1969), p. 407.

11. C. Cockburn, *I Claude* (London Penguin, 1967), p. 193.

12. Patricia Cockburn, *The Years of the Week* (London: MacDonald, 1968; Penguin edition, 1971), p. 215.

13. Cockburn, *The Years*, p. 231.

14. Thomas, p. 231.

15. Interview with Gellhorn; see also *Ken*, September 22, 1938.

16. E. Knoblaugh, *Correspondent in Spain* (London: Sheed and Ward, 1937), pp. 86-87.

17. Matthews, *World in Revolution*, pp. 25-28.

18. Interview with Herbert Matthews.

19. Matthews, *World in Revolution*, p. 19.

20. *Chicago Tribune*, August 30, 1936.

21. C. Gerahty, *The Road to Madrid* (London: Hutchinson, 1937), p. 98.

22. G. Steer, *Tree of Gernika* (London: Hodder and Stoughton, 1938), p. 159.

23. Steer, p. 243, and interview with James Holburn.

24. *The Times* archives.

25. Interview with Christopher Holme.

26. H. Southworth, "Gernika! Gernika!" (manuscript).

27. Deakin to Stirling, October 20, 1936, and Deakin to de Caux, June 13, 1937, *The Times* archives.

28. *The History of The Times*, vol.4, p. 907.

29. Letters between *The Times* and Rowe and Maw, solicitors, of London, April 4, 1939-July 11, 1939, *The Times* archives.

30. Thomas, p. 539.

31. Letter from Hugh Thomas to author, June 20, 1973.

32. Letter from Herbert Southworth to the author, July 16, 1973.

33. Letter from John Hersey to the author, June 14, 1974.

34. Letter from Ted Allan to the author, October 4, 1974.

35. Interview with O. D. Gallagher.

36. See *Fotografia Italiana*, June 1972, pp. 21-62.

37. Carlos Baker, *Ernest Hemingway* (London: Collins, 1969), p. 377.

38. Baker, p. 395.

39. G. Regler, *Owl of Minerva* (London: Rupert Hart-Davis, 1959), p. 293.

40. Baker, p. 401.

41. Baker, p. 402.

42. J. Gurney, *Crusade in Spain* (London: Faber and Faber, 1974), pp. 126-28.

43. Interview with Gellhorn.

44. Matthews, *World in Revolution*, p. 17.

45. *New Statesman*, May 1, 1937.

46. J. Meyers, *A Reader's Guide to George Orwell* (London: Thames and Hudson, 1975).

47. Orwell, p. 220.

## Chapter Ten
## "Their Finest Hour"

1. Angus Calder, *The People's War* (London: Jonathan Cape, 1969), p. 58.

2. Calder, p. 267.

3. *Fortune*, November 1939, p. 91.

4. G. P. Thompson, *Blue Pencil Admiral* (London: Sampson, Low, Marston, 1947), p. 42.

5. *Fortune*, p. 90.

6. Arvid Fredborg, *Behind the Steel Wall* (London: Harrap, 1944), pp. 9-31.

7. *"Der Propagandatruppe Glanz und Elend,"* *Die Welt*, May 2, 1970.

8. Interview with Albert Cusian.

9. *The Times*, October 24, 1939.

10. Letter to author, August 7, 1968.

11. Interview with O. D. Gallagher.

12. Letter from Kim Philby to author,

February 18, 1974.

13. L. Snyder, ed., *Masterpieces of War Reporting* (New York: Messner, 1962), p. 203.

14. "The Press VI: The Story of the War Reporters," unidentified publication, London, August 1940, p. 19.

15. "The Press VI", p. 23.

16. "*Der Propaganda truppe.*"

17. Letter from Drew Middleton to the author, March 10, 1975.

18. Joseph J. Matthews, *Reporting the Wars* (Minneapolis: University of Minnesota Press, 1957), p. 182.

19. *Sunday Times*, February 4, 1940.

20. "*Der Propagandatruppe.*"

21. "*Der Propagandatruppe.*"

22. *Chicago Daily News*, April 25, 1940; *Baltimore Evening Sun*, April 16, 1940.

23. CBS broadcast, April 22, 1940.

24. *New Statesman and Nation*, April 20, 1940.

25. Snyder, p. 47.

26. Snyder, p. 66.

27. *Life*, July 8, 1940.

28. CBS broadcast, June 21, 1940.

29. Noel Monks, *Eyewitness* (London: Frederick Muller, 1956), pp. 125-29.

30. *Sunday Dispatch*, June 2, 1940.

31. *New York Times*, June 1, 1940.

32. CBS broadcast, June 2, 1940.

33. *Daily Sketch*, June 7, 1940.

34. Richard Collier, *The Sands of Dunkirk* (London: Collins, 1961); interview with Collier.

35. *Green Howards Gazette*, November 1962.

36. *Observer*, June 6, 1965.

37. P. Auphan, *U.S. Naval Institute Proceedings*, June 1956.

38. Quoted in Calder, p. 140.

39. D. Brown and W. R. Bruner, eds., *I Can Tell It Now* (New York: Dutton, 1964), p. 28.

40. B. Collier, *A Short History of the Second World War* (London: Collins, 1967), pp. 155-56.

41. B. Page, "Winston Churchill and the War of Dreams" (manuscript).

42. Marcel Jullian, *The Battle of Britain* (London: Jonathan Cape, 1967; Panther edition, 1969), pp. 89, 112, 113,155.

43. Jullian, pp. 198, 218, 219.

44. Interview with Gallagher.

45. Interview with Barry Cornwell.

46. P. Addison, "The Fears That Flawed the Finest Hour," *Sunday Times Magazine*, May 21, 1972.

47. C. Bekker, *Angriffshohe 4,000* (Oldenburg: Stalling, 1964); quoted in Jullian, p. 141.

48. Jullian, p.142.

49. Calder, pp. 229-30, 168.

50. Raymond Daniell, *Civilians Must Fight* (New York: Doubleday, 1941), p. 307.

51. Calder, p. 568.

52. Calder, pp. 176, 178.

53. D. Smith, "The Battle of the Merseyside," *Liverpool Daily Post*, March 29, 1971.

54. Calder, p. 204.

55. *The Times*, November 8, 1940.

56. Snyder, p. 95.

57. Calder, p. 232.

58. CBS broadcast, May 5, 1941.

59. CBS broadcast, October 1, 1940.

60. Letter from Drew Middleton to author, November 1, 1972.

61. *Esquire*, April 1970.

## Chapter Eleven
## The Struggle for Mother Russia

1. Arvid Fredborg, *Behind the Steel Wall* (London: Harrap, 1944), pp. 32-33.

2. *History of the Great Patriotic War* (Moscow: Central Committee of the CPSU, 1960-1963), vol. I, pp. 434-35.

3. Alexander Werth, *Russia at War* (London: Barrie and Rockliff, 1964), p. 179.

4. *The Times*, November 21, 1941.

5. Article by Ehrenburg in *News Chronicle*, November 7, 1942.

6. Henry C. Cassidy, *Moscow Dateline, 1941-1943* (London: Cassell, 1943), p. 44.

7. Quentin Reynolds, *Only the Stars Are Neutral* (London: Cassell, 1942), pp. 97-99; Cassidy, pp. 74-75.

8. R. T. Elson, *Time Inc.* (New York: Atheneum, 1968), p. 475.

9. Cassidy, p. 65.

10. Reynolds, p. 185.

11. Werth, p. 184.

12. *Sunday Chronicle*, October 19, 1941.

13. Reynolds, p. 200.

14. Interview with Ewan Butler.

15. Ministry of Information to Ralph Deakin, March 30, 1942, *The Times* archives.

16. *The Times* to Ralph Parker, March 17, 1943, *The Times* archives.

17. Interview with Ed Stevens.

18. For tank figures, see J. F. C. Fuller, *Decisive Battles of the Western World* (London: Palladin, 1970), p. 464, and Alan Clark, *Barbarossa* (London: Hutchinson, 1965); for lack of winter clothing, see Clark.

19. R.Ogorkiewicz, "Tanks and the Soviet Army," *The Times*, December 14, 1970.

20. Alan Clark, "The Germans Start to Remember Napoleon," *Evening Standard*, October 24, 1964.

21. General Heinz Guderian quoted in Werth, p. 258.

22. *Völkischer Beobachter*, June 29, 1941.

23. Fredborg, p. 61.

24. Fredborg, p. 63.

25. Fredborg, p. 75.

26. *Daily Sketch*, October 8, 1943.

27. *New York Times Book Review*, May 10, 1962.

28. *News Chronicle*, November 7, 1942.

29. *Sunday Times*, September 28, 1941.

30. Interview with Stevens.

31. *Red Star*, end of December 1942; quoted in Werth, pp. 535-36.

32. All diary entries quoted are from Clark, *Barbarossa*.

33. *Daily Dispatch*, January 18, 1943.

34. *Daily Sketch*, September 7, 1942.

35. *The Times*, February 4, 1943.

36. Werth, pp. 547-48.

37. Werth, pp. 562-63.

38. Werth, pp. 682-83.

39. "Turning Point: The Battle at Kursk," Associated Television, London, April 30, 1972.

40. Fletcher Pratt, "How the Censors Rigged the News," *Harper's Magazine*, February 1946, p. 98.

41. Quoted in Gay Talese, *The Kingdom and the Power* (New York: World Publishing Co., 1969), p. 436.

42. Werth, p. 666.

43. R. Luckett, "A Million Russians Fight for Hitler," *Sunday Times Magazine*, May 21, 1972.

44. Werth, p. 666.

45. Interview with PK officer Graf Clemens Podewils.

46. *Daily Herald*, October 9, 1961.

47. *The Times*, May 11, 1973.

## Chapter Twelve
## Remember Pearl Harbor

1. Edgar Snow, *Battle for Asia* (New York: Random House, 1941), p. 45.

2. Interview with O. D. Gallagher.

3. *Corriere della Sera*, December 18, 1937.

4. D. Brown and W. R. Bruner, eds., *I Can Tell It Now* (New York: Dutton, 1964), p. 43.

5. J. A. Morris, *Deadline Every Minute* (New York: Doubleday, 1957), p. 242.

6. *The Times*, December 16, 1941.

7. *The Times*, December 17, 1941.

8. *The Reports of General MacArthur* (Washington: U.S. Government Printing Office, 1966), p. 4.

9. Theodore F. Koop, *Weapon of Silence* (Chicago: University of Chicago Press, 1946), p. 148.

10. Koop, p. 144; for organisation of OWI, see *Public Opinion Quarterly*, spring 1943.

11. Koop, p. 250.

12. *Harper's Magazine*, p. 98.

13. Koop, p. 270.

14. John Steinbeck, *Once There Was a*

*War* (London: Heinemann, 1959; Corgi edition, 1961), pp. 11-15.

15. Barbara Tuchman, *Sand Against the Wind* (London: Macmillan, 1971), p. 334.

16. Tuchman, p. 361.

17. Tuchman, p. 251.

18. Tuchman, p. 354.

19. *New York Times*, October 6, 1944.

20. Fletcher Pratt, "How the Censors Rigged the News," *Harper's Magazine*, February 1946, p. 98.

21. *Reports of MacArthur*, p. 39.

22. Hanson W. Baldwin, *Great Mistakes of the War* (London: Alvin Redman, Ltd., 1950), p. 68.

23. *Daily Express*, August 5, 1945.

24. *The Times*, March 27, 1942.

25. Noel Monks, *Eyewitness* (London: Frederick Muller, 1956), p. 154.

26. *Reports of MacArthur*, p. 38.

27. Interview with a former Australian serviceman; name withheld at his request.

28. Monks, pp. 164-65.

29. See G. Long, *MacArthur as a Military Commander* (London: Batsford, 1969).

30. Monks, p. 173.

31. *Chicago Tribune*, June 17, 1942.

32. Interrogation files, G-2 Historical Section, U.S. Army GHQ, FEC; see also *Reports of MacArthur*, p. 38.

33. *Chicago Tribune* archives.

34. *Public Opinion Quarterly*, spring 1943, p. 121.

35. Morris, p. 251.

36. *Yomiuri*, December 10, 1941.

37. Interview with Gallagher.

38. O. D. Gallagher, *Retreat in the East* (London: Harrap, 1942), p. 71.

39. J. Leasor, "Singapore, the End of the Line," *Sunday Times Magazine*, April 30, 1967.

40. Gallagher, p. 72.

41. Ian Morrison, *This War Against Japan* (London: Faber and Faber, 1943), p. 126.

42. Morrison, p. 189.

43. Interview with Gallagher.

44. Associated Press dispatch, February 11, 1942.

45. Tuchman, p. 280.

46. Tuchman, p. 300.

47. *History in the Writing* (New York: Time Inc., 1945).

48. *The Decisive Battles*. The War Against Japan, vol. 3 (London: HMSO, 1962).

49. *The Times*, June 30, 1943.

50. *Newspaper World*, February 20, 1943.

51. Masuo Kato, *The Lost War* (New York: Knopf, 1946), pp. 87-140.

52. Interview on Thames Television, April 10, 1974.

53. Interview with Torao Saito.

54. Letter from Allan Clifton, formerly of Australian Army Intelligence, to author, December 21, 1973.

55. *Sunday Times*, August 2, 1970.

56. A. E. Percival, *The War in Malaya* (London: Longmans, 1949), p. 325.

57. *Atlantic Monthly*, October 1943, pp. 47-48.

58. *Newsweek*, July 20, 1942.

59. Fletcher Pratt, *Harper's Magazine*, pp. 99-100.

60. *Melbourne Herald*, September 29, 1943.

61. Fletcher Pratt, *Harper's Magazine*, pp. 104-05.

62. United Press dispatch, October 25, 1944.

63. Koop, p. 245.

64. *Baltimore Sun*, May 28, 1945.

65. R. C. Mikesh, *Japan's World War II Balloon Bomb Attacks on North America* (Washington: U.S. Government Printing Office, 1973).

66. Steinbeck, p. 15.

67. Quoted in John Hohenberg, *Foreign Correspondence* (New York: Columbia University Press, 1967), p. 364.

68. *The Surrender of Japan*. The War Against Japan, vol. 5 (London: HMSO, 1969).

69. Koop, p. 268.

70. Hohenberg, p. 376.

71. Radio Tokyo beamed to the United States, recorded by the Associated Press.

72. Domei bulletin, Okayama, August 6, 1945; quoted in Masuo Kato, *The Lost War* (New York: Knopf, 1946), p. 219.

73. Interview with Wilfred Burchett.

74. L. Snyder and R. Morris, eds., *A Treasury of Great Reporting* (New York: Simon and Schuster, 1949), p. 705.

## Chapter Thirteen
## Never Again

1. Alan Moorehead, *A Late Education* (London: Hamish Hamilton, 1970), pp. 123, 131.

2. *The Times*, July 2, 1943.

3. Interview with Ronald Monson.

4. L. Snyder, ed., *Masterpieces of War Reporting* (New York: Messner, 1962), p. 211.

5. Robert St. John, *From the Land of Silent People* (London: Harrap, 1942).

6. John Hohenberg, *Foreign Correspondence* (New York: Columbia University Press, 1967), p. 355.

7. Interview with Richard Hughes.

8. Letter from Drew Middleton to author, November 1, 1972.

9. *Public Opinion Quarterly*, spring 1943, p. 133.

10. Moorehead, p. 60.

11. *Manchester Guardian*, May 11, 1943.

12. *New York World-Telegram*, April 17, 1941.

13. Corelli Barnett, *The Desert Generals* (London: William Kimber, 1960; Pan edition, 1962), p. 101.

14. D. Flower and J. Reeves, *The War 1939–45*, vol.1 (London: Cassell, 1960; Panther edition, 1967), p. 405.

15. Barnett, p. 197.

16. Flower and Reeves, p. 350.

17. Angus Calder, *The People's War* (London: Jonathan Cape, 1969), p. 286.

18. M. Arnold-Forster, *The World at War* (London: Collins, 1974), p. 277; D. Watt, "Britain and America Heavily Defeated," *Sunday Times Magazine*, June 4, 1972.

19. "How the Dambusters' Courage Was Wasted," *Sunday Times Magazine*, May 28, 1972.

20. R. Crossman, "The Wartime Tactics That Led to Watergate," *The Times*, May 16, 1973.

21. *New York Times*, January 18, 1943.

22. CBS broadcast, December 3, 1943.

23. *The Strategic Air Offensive Against Germany, 1939–45* (London: HMSO, 1961), vol.2, pt. 4, p. 195.

24. G. P. Thompson, *Blue Pencil Admiral* (London: Sampson, Low, Marston, 1947), p. 179.

25. John Toland, *The Last 100 Days* (London: Arthur Barker, 1965; Mayflower edition, 1968), p. 157.

26. *Daily Telegraph*, February 15, 1945.

27. *Observer Magazine*, February 15, 1970.

28. David Irving, *The Destruction of Dresden* (London: Kimber, 1963), pp. 216-19.

29. Quoted in *Daily Telegraph*, March 5, 1945.

30. Reuters, April 25, 1944.

31. B. Oldfield, *Never a Shot in Anger* (New York: Duell, Sloan and Pearce, 1956), pp. 117, 139.

32. Oldfield, p.189.

33. Letter from Drew Middleton to author, November 1, 1972.

34. Interview with Cyril Ray.

35. Interview with Evelyn Irons.

36. Interview with Ronald Monson.

37. U.K. Public Record Office, CAB 98/22/3830.

38. Public Record Office, CAB 98/22/3830 Annex 14: "The Public Relations Aspect."

39. Terence Robertson, *Dieppe: The Shame and the Glory* (London: Hutchinson, 1963), p. 156.

40. Canadian Press cable, August 19, 1942.

41. Interview with Ross Munro.

42. Interview with Munro.

43. Noel Monks, *Eyewitness* (London: Frederick Muller, 1956), p. 195; AP dispatch from Algiers, November 23, 1943.

44. Monks, pp. 196–97; AP dispatch from Algiers, November 23, 1943.

45. Theodore F. Koop, *Weapon of Silence* (Chicago: University of Chicago Press, 1946), p. 261.

46. *The Times*, November 24, 1943.

47. *Deutsche Allgemeine Zeitung*, February 19, 1944.

48. *Daily Telegraph*, March 16, 1944.

49. D. Brown and W. R. Bruner, eds., *I Can Tell It Now* (New York: Dutton, 1964), pp. 84–85.

50. *New Yorker*, August 19, 1944.

51. Interview with Reginald Thompson.

52. BBC, September 19 and 27, 1944.

53. Interview with Cyril Ray.

54. Oldfield, p. 172.

55. *Baltimore Evening Sun*, December 21, 1944.

56. *Observer Magazine*, December 21, 1969.

57. Alexander McKee, *The Race for the Rhine Bridges* (London: Souvenir Press, 1971), p. 205.

58. Oldfield, p. 186.

59. Interview with Evelyn Irons.

60. *New York World Telegram*, May 3–5, 1943.

61. Lindsey Nelson, "Sorry to Tell You Sir," *Dateline*, Overseas Press Club of America, 1965, p. 105.

62. Albert Speer, *Inside the Third Reich* (London: Weidenfeld and Nicolson, 1970), p. 411.

63. Fletcher Pratt, "How the Censors Rigged the News," *Harper's Magazine*, February 1946, p. 98.

64. Information bulletin, USSR Embassy, Washington, November 1943.

65. Marguerite Higgins, *News Is a Singular Thing* (New York: Doubleday, 1955), p. 95.

66. Interview with Ronald Monson.

67. *News Chronicle*, May 2, 1945.

68. *New York Times*, April 8, 1945.

69. Toland, p. 410.

70. CBS broadcast, April 15, 1945.

71. *The Times*, February 23, 1944.

72. *Daily Telegraph*, February 17, 1944.

73. Boyd Lewis, "V-E Day: Just the Beginning," *Bulletin*, Overseas Press Club of America, May 1, 1965, p. 4.

74. Fletcher Pratt, *Harper's*, p. 103.

75. Oldfield, p. 250.

76. Toland, p. 646.

77. AP dispatch in *New York Times*, May 8, 1945.

78. Snyder, p. 471.

79. L. Snyder and R. Morris, eds., *A Treasury of Great Reporting* (New York: Simon and Schuster, 1949), p. 693.

80. Interview with Charles Lynch; see also *More*, November 1974.

## Chapter Fourteen
## Korea, the United Nations' War

1. Marguerite Higgins, *The Report of a Woman Combat Correspondent* (New York: Doubleday, 1951), pp. 40–42.

2. Higgins, p. 84.

3. Higgins, pp. 96–97.

4. Interview with George Johnston.

5. Reginald Thompson, *Cry Korea* (London: Macdonald, 1951), p. 39.

6. *The Times* archives.

7. Thompson, p. 36.

8. *Picture Post*, October 7, 1950.

9. Thompson, p. 36.

10. Interview with Rene Cutforth.

11. *Yorkshire Post*, December 18, 1950.

12. *Daily Worker*, November 29, 1950.

13. Letter from Alan Dower to author, January 4, 1974.

14. *Reynolds News*, November 5, 1950.

15. Interviews with Tom Hopkinson and James Cameron.

16. Interview with Rene Cutforth.

17. Edward R. Murrow, *In Search of Light* (New York: Knopf, 1967), p. 166.

18. Interview with Reginald Thompson.

19. Interview with Thompson.

20. Higgins, p. 101.

21. Thompson, p. 44.

22. Thompson, p. 228.

23. *Evening Standard*, July 20, 1950.

24. Television interview with Irv Kupcinet, December 22, 1960.

25. Television interview with ABC and NET, September 18, 1966.

26. Interview with Cutforth.

27. U.S. Senate sub-committee report, quoted in *Daily Mail*, November 20, 1957; *Sunday Express*, December 30, 1956; see also E. Kinkead, *Why They Collaborated* (London: Longmans, 1960).

28. C. Cunningham, former senior psychologist, POW Intelligence, in a letter to *The Times*, November 25, 1971.

29. *San Francisco Chronicle*, August 11, 1953.

30. *Observer*, August 23, 1953.

31. James Aronson, *The Press and the Cold War* (Indianapolis: Bobbs-Merrill, 1970), p. 113.

32. Aronson, p. 123.

**Chapter Fifteen**
**Algeria is French**

1. *New York Times*, May 12, 1945.

2. *Reynolds News*, May 13, 1945.

3. *Christian Science Monitor*, May 13, 1945.

4. *Pakistan Horizon*, March 1955.

5. Ansel E. Talbert, *New York Herald Tribune*, February 7, 1954.

6. *Scotsman*, August 21, 1954.

7. *Le Monde*, May 8, 1954.

8. *New York Herald Tribune*, November 11, 1954.

9. *Le Figaro*, November 11, 1954.

10. *L'Express*, December 30, 1955.

11. *The Times*, June 18, 1960.

12. *The Times*, December 30–31, 1955; *News Chronicle*, January 2, 1956.

13. *L'Humanité*, August 23, 1955.

14. Quoted in *L'Humanité*, August 26, 1955.

15. *Le Monde*, August 30, 1955.

16. *Combat*, August 31, 1955.

17. *Le Figaro*, August 26, 1955.

18. *Scotsman*, December 22, 1961.

19. Jean-Paul Sartre, *The Question* (London: John Calder, 1958), p. 11.

20. *Témoignage Chrétien*, April 10, 1959.

21. *Témoignage Chrétien*, December 21, 1959.

22. *Combat*, July 14, 1957.

23. *Johannesburg Star*, September 25, 1956.

24. *Listener*, November 18, 1954.

25. *London Evening Standard*, January 23, 1958.

26. *Daily Express*, July 14, '957.

27. *New York Times*, June 5, 1957.

28. H. Greer, *A Scattering of Dust* (London: Hutchinson, 1962), p. 200.

29. Greer, p. 38.

30. Greer, pp. 120–21.

31. Greer, p. 146.

32. Greer, pp. 147–48.

33. D. Brown and W. R. Bruner, eds., *How I Got That Story* (New York: Dutton, 1967), p. 303.

34. *Observer*, January 26, 1958.

35. *London Sunday Times*, May 17, 1959.

36. *L'Express*, June 4, '955.

37. Interview with John Wallis.

38. *The Times*, January 24, 1962.

39. P. Henissart, *Wolves in the City* (London: Paladin, 1973), p. 226.

40. Henissart, p. 279.

41. Henissart, p. 252.

42. *France Soir*, November 29, 1961.

43. *New York Times*, June 10, 1957.

**Chapter Sixteen**
**Vietnam**

1. *Newsweek*, June 29, 1960; *Time*, November 21, 1960.

2. *Times Talk*, April 1962.

3. John Mecklin, *Mission in Torment* (New York: Doubleday, 1965), p. xii.

4. Interview with John Shaw.

5. James Aronson, *The Press and the Cold War* (Indianapolis: Bobbs-Merrill, 1970), p. 182.

6. *Daily Telegraph*, March 10, 1962.

7. *Daily Mail*, February 16, 1963.

8. *The Times*, January 21, 1963.

9. David Halberstam, *The Making of a Quagmire* (London: Bodley Head, 1965), p. 268.

10. Aronson, p. 216.

11. Nora Ephron, "The War Followers," *New York Magazine*, November 12, 1973.

12. *New York Times Magazine*, October 9, 1966.

13. Hearings of U.S. Senate Committee on Foreign Relations, August 17, 1966.

14. *New Statesman*, September 23, 1966.

15. Aronson, p. 233.

16. Don Oberdorfer, *Tet* (New York: Doubleday, 1971; Avon edition, 1972), p. 381.

17. Interview with John Pilger.

18. Interview with Brian Moynahan.

19. *London Sunday Times*, November 26, 1967.

20. *Christian Science Monitor*, May 29-June 30, 1970.

21. *Sunday Times*, October 19 and October 10, 1971; *The Times*, July 12, 1971.

22. J. Lucas, *Dateline Vietnam* (New York: Award Books, 1967), p. 15.

23. F. Harvey, *Air War Vietnam* (New York: Bantam, 1967), p. 115.

24. Harvey, p. 184.

25. *Washington Post*, February 23, 1966.

26. Interview with John Shaw.

27. Harvey, p. 104.

28. P. Jones Griffiths, *Vietnam Inc.* (New York: Macmillan, 1971), p. 60.

29. Jones Griffiths, p. 62.

30. *Sunday Times Magazine*, June 25, 1972.

31. *Sunday Times*, June 5, 1966.

32. Major Anthony J. Asterita, APO San Francisco, "Humor in Uniform," *Reader's Digest*, April 1970.

33. *Sunday Times Magazine*, June 25, 1972.

34. Interview with Nicholas Tomalin.

35. *Guardian*, September 1966.

36. Interview with Martha Gellhorn.

37. Interview with Philip Jones Griffiths.

38. *Time*, December 5, 1969.

39. AP general manager Wes Gallagher, quoted in *Time*, December 5, 1969.

40. J. Eszterhas, "The Selling of the My Lai Massacre," *Evergreen Review*, October 1971.

41. Eszterhas.

42. *Life*, December 15, 1967.

43. *Time*, December 5, 1969.

44. Robert Rheault quoted in UPI feature "GIs Forget Enemy Is Human," *The News*, Mexico City, April 11, 1970.

45. Anthony Herbert in television interview, London, July 1, 1971.

46. *Time*, August 6, 1965.

47. *Daily Telegraph Magazine*, September 25, 1964.

48. Daniel Lang, *Casualties of War* (New York: McGraw-Hill, 1969).

49. Interview with Jones Griffiths.

50. *Sunday Telegraph*, April 4, 1971.

51. Address at Pennsylvania Press Conference, May 15, 1971.

52. J. Epstein, *News From Nowhere* (New York: Random House, 1973), pp. 17, 250.

53. *New York Times* news service, April 2, 1971.

54. Letter from Kevin Buckley to author, March 7, 1974; interview with Buckley.

## Chapter Seventeen
## War Is Fun

1. Don Oberdorfer, *Tet* (New York: Doubleday, 1971; Avon edition, 1972), p. 100.

2. Herbert Matthews, *The Education of a Correspondent* (New York: Harcourt Brace, 1946), p. 44.

3. Nora Ephron, "The War Followers," 26. *New York Magazine*, November 12, 1973.

4. Interview with Charlie Black.

5. *Esquire*, April 1970.

6. Quoted in H. Mulligan, "Three Years of Reporting in Vietnam," an

AP feature on Arnett circulated to editors, 1965.

7. Address at Pennsylvania Press Conference, May 15, 1971.
8. Interview with Philip Jones Griffiths.
9. *Daily Telegraph Magazine*, May 31, 1968.
10. *Daily Telegraph Magazine*, May 31, 1968.
11. *Spectator*, July 1, 1972.
12. Interview with Marina Warner.
13. Interview with Tim Page.
14. Quoted in J. Bradshaw, "The Trouble-shooters," *London Daily Telegraph Magazine*, May 31, 1968.
15. *Spectator*, July 1, 1972.
16. *Newsweek*, February 22, 1971; *Radio Times*, October 2, 1969; *Sunday Times*, February 14, 1971; *Esquire*, April 1970.
17. Interview with Harri Peccinotti.
18. Interview with Donald McCullin.
19. *Spectator*, July I, 1972.
20. *Esquire*, April 1970.
21. J. Epstein, *News from Nowhere* (New York: Random House, 1973), p. 9.
22. Royal United Service Institution seminar, London, October 13, 1970; Alistair Burnet quotation from *UK Press Gazette*, December 21, 1970.
23. See Michael J. Arlen, *The Living Room War* (New York: Viking, 1966).
24. Arlen, p. 8.
25. *Daily Telegraph Magazine*, May 31, 1968.
26. *Esquire*, April 1970.
27. Ephron, "The War Followers."
28. Kurt Volkert, "Combat Cameraman—Vietnam," in *Dateline* (New York: Overseas Press Club, 1968).
29. *Spectator*, July 1, 1972.
30. Interview with Malcolm Aird.
31. Interview with James Cameron.
32. Wilfred Burchett, *Passport* (Australia: Nelson, 1969), p. 257.
33. Interview with Wilfred Burchett
34. *Sunday Express*, February 13, 1966.
35. *New Statesman*, May 29, 1970.
36. *The Times*, June 5, 1972.

37. *Observer Magazine*, September 3, 1967.
38. *Newsweek*, January 22, 1973; *U.K. Press Gazette*, February 12, 1973.
39. Interview with Kate Webb.
40. *Esquire*, April 1970.
41. Interview with Tim Page.
42. Report to U.S. House of Representatives Committee on Foreign Affairs, May 25, 1971.
43. *The Times*, October 18, 1971.
44. *Newsweek*, February 22, 1971.
45. R. Littauer and Cornell University faculty and student groups, *Air War in Indo-China* (Boston: Beacon Press, 1971).
46. *The Times*, December 21, 1972.
47. *New Statesman*, December 29, 1972.
48. *Encounter*, December 1966.
49. *Sunday Times*, March 2, 1969.
50. Ephron. "The War Followers."

## Chapter Eighteen
## Britannia Rules the News
1. Robert Elegant, "How to Lose a War: Reflections of a Foreign Correspondent" in *Encounter*, August 1981.
2. *New Statesman*, February 25, 1977.
3. *UK Press Gazette*, May 25, 1981.
4. *Sunday Times*, February 12, 1984.
5. *Sunday Times*, July 26, 1981.
6. *UK Press Gazette*, June 23, 1981.
7. *The Times*, June 17, 1982 and in interview with McCullin.
8. Interview with MoD press officer.
9. *Listener*, May 6, 1982.
10. *UK Press Gazette*, May 24, 1982.
11. *Listener*, May 6, 1982.
12. *The Times*, July 3, 1982.
13. ITN News, June 24, 1982.
14. *Daily Express*, June 8, 1982.
15. ITN News, 24 June, 1982.
16. *Spectator*, June 5,1982.
17. *Standard*, June 25, 1982.

## Chapter Nineteen
## The Deadly Video Game
1. General Norman H. Schwartzkopf, *It Doesn't Take a Hero*

(London/New York: Bantam, 1992), p. 258

2. Richard Keeble, *Secret State, Silent Press* (London: John Libby, 1997), p. 42.

3. Keeble, p. 54.

4. Micah L. Sifry and Christopher Cerf (eds.), *The Gulf War Reader* (New York: Random House, 1991), p. 130.

5. Abbas Malek and Lisa Leidig, *US Press Coverage of the Gulf War* (London: Media Development, 1991), p. 15.

6. Keeble, p. 143.

7. Jacqueline Sharkey, *Under Fire* (Washington: the Center for Public Integrity, 1992), p. 108.

8. Sharkey, p. 113-14.

9. Alex Thomson, *Smokescreen* (Tunbridge Wells: Laburnham, 1992), p. 8-9.

10. Thomson, p. 11.

11. Thomson, p. 12.

12. Robert Fisk, *Out of the Pool* (Mother Jones, May-June 1991) p. 58.

13. Sharkey, p. 140.

14. Thomson, p. 104.

15. Keeble, p. 149.

16. Keeble, p. 148.

17. Keeble, p. 148.

18. Mark Miller, *Patriotic Blindness and Anti-Truth Weapons* (London: 'Index on Censorship' No.10, 1991), pp. 32-34.

19. Sharkey, p. 151.

20. Keeble, p. 154.

21. Thomson, p. 259-60.

22. Keeble, p. 8

**Chapter Twenty**
**The Military's Final Victory**

1. Kosovo: How the War was Spun, BBC 2, October 16, 1999.

2. *New York Times*, June 21, 1999, Business p. 16.

3. *Spectator*, July 3, 1999, p. 13.

4. *Sunday Telegraph*, April 18, 1999, Review p. 3.

5. BBC 2, October 16, 1999.

6. *The Independent*, June 29, 1999, Review p. 12.

7. BBC 2, October 16, 1999.

8. *Observer*, May 2, 1999, p. 31.

9. *Spectator*, July 3, 1999, p. 13.

10. Peter Dunn, *All Aboard the Atrocity Bus* London: The Journalist's Handbook, Carrick Media, 1999), p. 4.

11. Dunn, p. 8.

12. *Sunday Times*, April 18, 1999, p. 17.

13. *Observer*, July 4, 1999, p. 16.

14. UNDP, *Human Development Report* ( New York: Oxford University Press), p. 47.

15. *Observer*, July 4, 1999, p. 16.

16. *Spectator*, May 22, 1999, p. 17.

17. BBC 2, October 16, 1999.

18. *Spectator*, July 24, 1999, p. 30-31.

19. *LM* magazine, No. 121, p. 25.

20. *Guardian*, June 5, 1999, p. 22.

21. *Observer*, May 2, 1999, p. 31.

22. *Spectator*, May 22, 1999, pp. 16-17.

23. The Journalist's Handbook, p. 5.

24. BBC 2, October 16, 1999.

25. BBC 2, October 16, 1999.

26. *Guardian*, June 21, 1999, Media pp. 2-3.

27. *Guardian*, June 30, 1999, p. 15.

28. Kosovo: An Audit of War, BBC 2, October 18, 1999.

29. BBC 2, October 16, 1999.

30. BBC 2, October 18, 1999.

31. *Independent*, September 17, 1999, Review p. 1.

32. *Guardian*, July 12, 1999, Media pp 4-5.

33. *The Kosovo Fallout*, http://www.transitions-online.org./july99/packjul9.html

34. *Kosovo Fallout*

35. BBC 2, October 18, 1999.

36. BBC 2, October 18, 1999.

37. *Spectator*, May 1, 1999, p. 11.

38. *Independent*, June 21, 1999, Review p. 5.

39. *The Week*, June 12, 1999, p. 12.

40. *Guardian*, June 12, 1999, Comment.
41. *Guardian*, May 18, 1999, p. 21.
42. *Guardian*, June 11, 1999, p. 21.
43. *Guardian*, June 12, 1999, Comment.
44. *Spectator*, May 29, 1999, p. 16.
45. BBC 2, October 16, 1999.
46. BBC 2, October 16, 1999.
47. Audrey Gillan, *The London Review of Books*, Vol. 21, No. 11, May 27, 1999.
48. Gillian, *London Review of Books*.
49. *Guardian*, June 21, 1999, p. 18.
50. *Sydney Morning Herald*, April 24, 1999, p. 22.
51. *New York Times*, November 11, 1999, p. A6.
52. John Laughland, *The Spectator*, October 30, 1999, p. 24.
53. *Mirror*, July 7, 1999.
54. *New York Times*, November 11, 1999, p. A6.
55. *Spectator*, October 30, 1999, p. 24.
56. *Spectator*, November 20, 1999, p. 22.
57. *Spectator*, October 30, 1999, p. 25.
58. Interim Agreement for Peace and Self-Government in Kosovo (Ramboullet Accords), Chapter 4: Economic Issues, article 1, paragraph 1, February 23, 1999 and Appendix B: Status of Multi-National Military Implementation Force, paragraphs 6–11.
59. *Guardian*, May 19, 1999, Comment.
60. *Morning Star*, May 20, 1999.
61. *New Statesman*, September 6, 1999.
62. Report of the International Strategic Studies Association, Washingon, April 1999.
63. David E. Morrison, *Television and the Gulf War* (London: John Libby, 1992), pp. 6, 27.

## Chapter Twenty-one
## No More Heroes

1. *Guardian*, June 7, 2003, "What's in it for US?"
2. Daya Kishan Thussu, Goldsmiths College, University of London, *Managing the Media in an Era of Round-the-Clock News*.
3. *The Mirror*, July 2, 2002, "The Rogue State".
4. Alternet, February 20, 2003, *Pentagon's Recipe for Propaganda*.
5. Philip Gibbs, *Adventures in Journalism*, Heinemann, 1923, p231.
6. BBC 2, May 18, 2003, *War Spin*.
7. *Sunday Times*, 30 March, 2003, "US Marines Turn Fire on Civilians at the Bridge of Death".
8. *Guardian*, June 2, 2003, "Media Monkey's Diary".
9. *Guardian*, May 15, 2003, "The Truth About Jessica".
10. *Guardian*, April 14, 2003, "I Was Only Asking".
11. BBC 2, May 18, 2003, "War Spin".
12. *Guardian*, April 11, 2003, "Anzar Faces the Anger of the Press Pack".
13. *Guardian*, April 8, 2002, "Don't Get in Our Way".
14. RTE 1, March 9, 2003, "The Sunday Show".
15. BBC 2, June 1, 2003, "Al-Jazeera Exclusive".
16. *Guardian*, April 11, 2003, "Anzar Faces the Anger of the Press Pack".
17. *Guardian*, May 30, 2003, "US Soldiers Face War Crimes Charge".
18. Sky News, May 20, 2003.
19. *Boston Herald*, June 2, 2003, "Death of Journalists was an Accident of War".
20. BB2 2, May 18, 2003, "War Spin".
21. Princeton Survey Research Associates for Knight Ridder, January 1–8, 2003.
22. American Newsreel, April 7, 2003, "Patriotism Pays".
23. Reuters, April 23, 2003
24. Coldtype.net, May 30, 2003.
25. *Guardian*, April 25, 2003."Dyke strikes out at US media". *Daily Mail*, May 15, 2003, "Hardcastle".
26. Zena.secureforum.com.
27. *Guardian Letters*, April 9, 2003, "Media in the Front Line".

28. BBC 1, May 27, 2003, "Breakfast".
29. www.informationclearinghouse. info/article2842htm#top
30. BBC 2, May 18, 2003, "War Spin".
31. *Guardian*, May 15, 2003, "The Truth About Jessica".
32. BBC 2, May 18, 2003, "War Spin".
33. BBC 2, May 18, 2003, "War Spin".

# Index